THE WORLDS OF MEDIEVAL EUROPE

THE WORLDS OF
MEDIEVAL EUROPE

Second Edition

Clifford R. Backman
BOSTON UNIVERSITY

New York   Oxford
OXFORD UNIVERSITY PRESS
2009

OXFORD
UNIVERSITY PRESS

Oxford University Press, Inc., publishes works that further
Oxford University's objective of excellence
in research, scholarship, and education.

Oxford   New York
Auckland   Cape Town   Dar es Salaam   Hong Kong   Karachi
Kuala Lumpur   Madrid   Melbourne   Mexico City   Nairobi
New Delhi   Shanghai   Taipei   Toronto

With offices in
Argentina   Austria   Brazil   Chile   Czech Republic   France   Greece
Guatemala   Hungary   Italy   Japan   Poland   Portugal   Singapore
South Korea   Switzerland   Thailand   Turkey   Ukraine   Vietnam

Published by Oxford University Press, Inc.
198 Madison Avenue, New York, New York 10016

http://www.oup.com

Oxford is a registered trademark of Oxford University Press

Library of Congress Cataloging-in-Publication Data

Backman, Clifford R.
    The worlds of medieval Europe / Clifford R. Backman. —2nd ed.
        p.   cm.
    Includes bibliographical references and index.
    ISBN 978-0-19-533527-9
    1. Europe—History—476-1492.   2. Civilization, Medieval.   3.   Feudalism—Europe.
4. Monarchy—Europe.   5. Kings and rulers, Medieval.   6.   Mediterranean Region—Civilization.
7. Byzantine Empire—Civilization—1081-1453.   8. Middle Ages.   I. Title.
    D131.B33   2008
    940.1—dc22

                                                                                    2007028378

9 8 7 6 5

Printed in the United States of America on acid-free paper

**This book is for Scott Austin Backman,
who knows all the things that matter most.**

❧

"Counseille me, Kynde," quod I, *"What craft be best to lerne?"*

"Lerne to love," quod Kynde, *"and leef alle othere."*

[William Langland, *PIERS PLOWMAN* 20.206–207]

Contents

ACKNOWLEDGMENTS

The time I have spent working on this book has been challenging, humbling, and exhilarating, and I have learned to depend more than ever on the kindness of friends. For all their help, patience, and sustaining love, I thank David and Heather Sundahl, Daniel and Martha Stid, Lisa Lovett and Julie Reuben, Bruce Schulman and Alice Killian, "Grandma Perc" Thornberg, Bill Wallace, Jim and Laura Wooster, Cheryl and Paul Minor, Bill and Alice King, and Andrea Suess Taylor. Many colleagues helped out with information, recommendations, and encouragement; I thank especially Paul Freedman and Caroline Walker Bynum, who showed great kindness at a particularly difficult time. Nancy Lane, former history editor at Oxford University Press, first persuaded me to write this book, and Gioia Stevens, Linda Jarkesy, and Peter Coveney helped guide me through to the end. Linda especially proved helpful during the challenging task of revising the manuscript, and Peter was an ideal harbor pilot steering the ship into port. I am grateful to the numerous readers, both faculty-specialists and students, who commented on the initial prospectus and the subsequent drafts of the manuscript; I have heeded most of their advice and am solely responsible for all that remains incorrect, misplaced, or misleading. My wife Nelina gave her usual scrupulous attention to my writing style, striving as ever to stamp out the worst of my idiosyncrasies. More than a few of them remain in evidence here despite her best efforts. I am aware of my many faults as a writer, but I happen to remain rather fond of some of them. Our six-year-old son Scott sat on my lap and helped me print out the final copy of the manuscript while waiting patiently for his turn to use the computer; if there are any errant S-C-O-T-Ts buried in the text, the reader will know whom to blame.

Eliza McClennen drew the maps that appear throughout the book and has my thanks for her good cheer and speedy pen. Working with her again after too long a hiatus was one of the many pleasures I had in writing the book. Several of my students at Boston University—especially Letta Christianson, Andrew Donnelly, Ali Glass, and Chris Halfond—helped select the maps and photo illustrations and suggested source quotations that they had found most enlightening in the classroom. They will all have been graduated by the time this book appears in print. I shall miss seeing them around the office.

Each chapter has a *Suggested Reading* list appended to it. I have tried to make the lists as up to date as possible and to avoid repetition between them. Each list recommends pertinent "Texts" (primary sources, usually historical or literary, that were written in the period that each chapter discusses and that illustrate many of its chief themes), "Source Anthologies" (collections of primary materials, usually in abbreviated form and organized around a central topic), and "Studies" (works of recent scholarship on ideas, events, or people mentioned in the chapter). The lists make no claim to be comprehensive; I hope they are merely a useful beginning to further research. I have tried to limit the lists only to books that are still in print, hence many well-known classics of medieval scholarship are omitted. In the case of reprints, I have given the publication dates of the most recent editions.

On the matter of dates, I should say that I have chosen to run counter to the growing trend among historians to use the Common Era. I endorse the use of the Common Era in general, since it has the attraction of religious non-partisanship in a religiously heterogeneous society, but at least one aspect of the present book is the formation of the older tradition itself: how and why western Europe developed the sort of society that chose the birth of Jesus as its chronometrical focal point. Thus I use the traditional B.C. (Before Christ) and A.D. (Anno Domini) designations. My aim throughout, however, is not to endorse a bias but to supply the context that gave birth to it.

Passages from the Hebrew Bible are quoted from *Tanakh: The Holy Scriptures According to the Traditional Hebrew Text* (Jewish Publication Society, 1985); passages from the New Testament are quoted from *The New Jerusalem Bible* (revised edition, 1985); and passages from the Qur'an are quoted from *The Holy Qur'an: English Translation of the Meanings, with Commentary* (King Fahd Holy Qur'an Printing Complex, 1410 A.H.). I have borrowed one translation, in Chapter 15, from *Women's Lives in Medieval Europe: A Sourcebook*, edited by Emilie Amt (1993). All other translations in this book are my own.

INTRODUCTION

Why the Middle Ages Matter

Anyone who has ever laughed her way through *Monty Python and the Holy Grail*, felt her soul stir when standing in one of Europe's great cathedrals, grown excited when reading about the chivalric exploits of mail-clad knights, or thrilled to the sound of Gregorian chant knows that the Middle Ages are fun. There is no harm in admitting it. Signs of the pleasure we take in medieval life abound in our culture, from the mock sword fights of our childhood to the prominence of medieval settings in our popular literature and movies, from the crowds that flock annually to costumed medieval fairs to the groups of college students who enroll in classes on Chaucer and Dante. Part of our enjoyment derives from the perceived strangeness of medieval life. Until we become more familiar with them, medieval people strike us as rather odd: We marvel at their actions or laugh at their absurdities because they seem more unlike us than any other of our ancestors do. After all, as is well known, people in medieval Europe believed in miracles and witches. They long thought the surest way to determine whether or not a man was guilty of a crime was to tie him up and throw him into a lake that been blessed by a priest.[1] They were convinced that daily bathing was harmful to one's health; that magical incantations could transform common metals into gold; that a reliable method of contraception was for the woman, during intercourse, to wear a necklace of strung weasel-testicles; that one could rid oneself of toothache by spitting into the opened mouth of a frog; and that the appearance of comets usually signified some kind of heavenly favor or disfavor for whatever was happening in the realm at the time.

But the Middle Ages have a real significance far greater than their entertainment value, and so long as we merely revel in the fun of their uniqueness we will never fully understand our medieval ancestors or learn what they have to teach us. The starting assumption of this book, therefore, is that the Middle Ages really do matter and that studying them is important. The simplest reason for this assertion is that despite initial appearances the medieval world and the modern world have many things in common, and by understanding the origins of contemporary phenomena we gain if not a truer than at least a more sophisticated appreciation of them.

---

1. If the "pure" water "accepted" the man—that is, if he drowned—he was proved innocent.

How is this so? We can trace a surprising number of modern ideas, technologies, institutions, and cultural practices back to the medieval centuries—by which we mean the period roughly from 400 to 1400. Parliamentary government, banks, algebra, mechanical clocks, trials by jury, female playwrights, polyphonic music, universities, paper mills, citizen armies, distilled liquor, medical dissection, the novel, law schools, eyeglasses, the modern calendar, insurance companies, navigational maps, bookstores, the mafia, and even an early version of the game of baseball all appeared for the first time in western history in the Middle Ages. Modern ideas about the nature of citizenship and the authority of the State, about law and romance, about the need to control the manufacture and distribution of weaponry, also first materialized in these centuries. Even something as modern, if not postmodern, as the literary theory of deconstruction has roots in the medieval philosophers' debates over Realism and Nominalism, although those roots stretch back even further to the time of Plato.

Recognizing the medieval/modern connection illumines and enriches our understanding of the world around us. Why the tradition of college campuses having their own autonomous police forces? Because universities, when they came into existence at the very end of the twelfth century, were designed as self-governing institutions legally independent of the urban communities that housed them. This tradition is also the origin of the famous "town/gown" tensions that have always characterized urban universities: Students on boisterous weekend exploits might damage urban property, but they stood outside the jurisdiction of the urban police. Why do priests raise the offering of the Mass above their heads when they celebrate Communion? Because the medieval Church taught that the faithful had only to see the bread and wine, not partake of them, in order to receive the spiritual benefit of the Mass. How did the popular custom of decorating baskets of eggs and awaiting pleasant bunnies at Easter begin? Peasants on medieval manors owed a special tax to their lords every Easter Sunday, which, lacking money, they paid with what they had available.[2] Why do we purchase tourist trinkets when we travel—such as Eiffel Tower key chains to prove we've been to Paris, or beer steins to commemorate our trips to Munich? Because medieval pilgrims often undertook their voyages as an imposed penance for their sins and had to provide proof of their successful journeys in order to receive pardon; bringing back a trademark local ware was the easiest way of proving that one had in fact reached one's assigned destination. Knowing such things adds a rich texture to our lives that we should not deprive ourselves of.

While these points are significant by themselves, medieval history has an even larger importance for modern students. Medieval civilization was an alloy, the product of the amalgamation of three distinct cultures: classical Rome, Latin Christianity, and early Germanic society. It was a civilization that, for all its ethnic, social,

---

2. That's right: The Easter bunny was eaten by the nobles.

and political plurality, regarded itself as an organic whole. The medieval world-view regarded life as an essential unity—that is, it believed that there existed a super-arching unifying structure, divinely and naturally ordained, that held together and gave meaning to the obvious pluralism and diversity of everyday existence. This unifying vision is the most distinctive characteristic of the medieval mentality. Whether in terms of its intellectual and artistic life, with their emphases on the systematizing of knowledge and the integration of motifs, genres, and styles into larger constructs; or in terms of its political and social life, with their emphases on state-building and the interdependence of each segment of society in prescribed roles; or in terms of its ethnic, sexual, and religious relations, with their attempts to regulate the roles of each group and the rules of their interaction—the principal thrust of medieval civilization was to connect what was disparate and to find stability in the multifarious unity that resulted. John of Salisbury, an important political theorist of the twelfth century, provided an illustration of this belief in organic wholeness when he likened a political state to the human body:

> Those who guide religious life [in any given commonwealth] should be respected and honored as the body's soul. . . . The role of the body's head is played by the prince, who is subject only to God and to those who represent Him on earth and carry out His sacred office, just as in a human body the head is both animated and governed by the soul. The place of the heart is filled by the central court, from which all actions, whether good or bad, originate. Judges and local administrators represent the eyes, ears, and tongue; and their civil servants and military men correspond to the hands. . . . Tax officials and accountants correspond to the stomach and the intestines. . . . Peasants identify with the body's feet, since they work upon the soil . . . and propel the weight of the entire body forward.

Such a mentality categorized individuals and established legal and social hierarchies, but the essential cast of this mind was to unite, not to atomize, the distinct elements of society. It assigned a role for every individual but always integrated those individuals into the larger social body.

This concern to find and define a collective cultural identity greater than individual traits of ethnicity, social class, political tradition, and gender is the medieval world's most lasting legacy; and in light of our contemporary concerns about social diversity and cultural pluralism, the medieval struggle to establish a meaningful, ordered sense of heterogeneity-within-unity takes on a particular relevance, not as a prescription for how to resolve contemporary issues about individual or group identity but as an illuminating example of how questions that confront us were dealt with in the past. Just as in any other aspect of our public and private lives, it helps to know that other people have confronted similar problems, and we can learn valuable lessons from their successes and failures.

This book will emphasize the ways in which medieval people sought to recognize heterogeneity and difference while seeking to create a meaningful unity out of it, and this emphasis sets us apart from more traditional ways of writing medieval history. With regard to politics, we will pay less attention to the specific details of individual rulers than do other books, and will emphasize instead how the varying political traditions of medieval Europe (generally rural-monarchical in northern Europe, and urban-communal in the Mediterranean lands) emerged as responses evolving from different local needs yet aiming at the same goal of creating a stable ordering of Christian society. We will discuss how techniques of food production in rural areas, or the regulated ethnic demography of urban centers (that is, allowing Jews to live in this quarter of the city, Muslims in that quarter, Venetians over here, Barcelonans over there, etc.) exemplified efforts to modulate social organization and identity. We will examine phenomena such as scholasticism and cathedral building as models of how thinkers, architects, and artists sought to meld vast all-encompassing superstructures of diverse ideas, styles, and techniques into harmonious wholes. And on the darker side, we will consider how the medieval mania for identifying lepers, heretics, Jews, homosexuals, witches, criminals, and other general "evil-doers" characterized both a desire to stamp them out at times, and, at other times, to define their proper (if decidedly inferior) place in the hustle and bustle of everyday life.

Medieval Europe emerged slowly from the rubble of the fallen Roman Empire and struggled through several centuries of warfare, poverty, and disease before achieving a tentative, fragile stability under the Carolingian rulers of the eighth and ninth centuries. After the Carolingians, a second period of disarray descended, until at some point in the eleventh century Europe quite literally rebuilt itself—physically, politically, spiritually, economically, and socially—and entered a period of impressive expansion, wealth, stability, and intellectual and artistic revival. Many of those gains were lost, as we shall see, in the calamities of the fourteenth century; but by that point the foundations were securely laid for Europe to move into the Renaissance with both the technological and economic means, and the ideological convictions, that would prepare Europe to dominate the globe. The long centuries of the Middle Ages saw western Europe transform itself from a sparsely populated, impoverished, technologically primitive, socially chaotic, and often barbaric place to the world's wealthiest, best educated, most technologically developed, and most powerful civilization to date. As we shall see, much of that transformation depended precisely on the ways in which the many worlds of the Middle Ages tried to fashion the connections and conflicts of everyday life into a unified vision of human existence.

THE WORLDS OF
MEDIEVAL EUROPE

PART ONE

THE EARLY
MIDDLE AGES

∽

The Third through
Ninth Centuries

CHAPTER 1

THE ROMAN WORLD
AT ITS HEIGHT

The Roman Empire of the first and second centuries A.D. comprised the largest, wealthiest, most diverse, and most stable society of the ancient world. No other ancient empire—not the Assyrian, not the Persian, not the Athenian—had succeeded on such a scale at holding together in harmony so many peoples, faiths, and traditions. Historians commonly describe these two centuries as the period of the *Pax Romana* ("the Roman Peace"), an age when a strong central government engineered and maintained the social stability that allowed people to prosper. The sheer vastness of the empire was astonishing: It stretched over three thousand miles from west to east, from the Strait of Gibraltar to the sources of the Tigris and Euphrates rivers, and reached northward to Hadrian's Wall, a fortification built in A.D. 122 to protect Roman Britain from the Picts of Scotland, and southward to the upper edge of the Sahara. Within this vast territory lived as many as fifty to sixty million people.

The prosperity of those centuries came at a high cost. Rome's rise to power was the result of military might, after all, and long centuries of warfare had preceded "the Roman peace." In the Punic Wars of the third century B.C. Rome defeated Carthage, its main rival for control of the western and central Mediterranean, then turned its eyes eastward and subdued the weakened Greek states left over from the collapse of Alexander the Great's empire. But soon after it had conquered the known world, the Roman state went to war against itself: Civil wars raged for well over a century as various factions struggled not only to control the new superstate but to reshape it according to opposing principles. Some factions favored preserving the decentralized administrative practices of the early Republic, while others, such as the faction led by Julius Caesar, championed a strong centralized authority; some favored a rigid aristocratic authoritarianism, while others promoted a more radically democratic society. These long wars ended in a bizarre compromise. The empire of the Pax Romana period was a thoroughly centralized state that delegated most of its day-to-day authority to local officials; and it was a decidedly hierarchical society, almost obsessive in its concern to define every individual's social and legal classification; and yet it remained a remarkably fluid world in which a family could rise from slavery to aristocratic status in as few as three generations.

Two factors did the most to shape the Roman world and foster its remarkable vitality and stability: the Mediterranean Sea and the Roman army.

THE GEOGRAPHY OF EMPIRE

The Roman world, like the medieval world that succeeded it, was centered on the Mediterranean. The sea provided food, of course, but more importantly it provided an efficient and ready means of transport and communication. When the Romans referred to the Mediterranean as *mare nostrum* ("our sea") they were not being merely possessive but were in fact recognizing that the sea was the essential physical infrastructure that held together the entire empire. As a general rule in human history, seas do not divide people; they unite them. This is especially true of the Mediterranean. Since the Strait of Gibraltar—its opening to the Atlantic Ocean— measures only eight miles across, the Mediterranean has very little tide-variation and is naturally protected from all but the worst of Atlantic storms. With the sea's smooth waters and temperate climate, sailors from the earliest centuries found it easy to traverse the Mediterranean even in primitive vessels. Moreover, since early navigation relied more on using coastal landmarks than on steering by the stars, the sea's natural division into two basins and its abundance of islands and peninsulas enabled traders to reach faraway ports without ever losing sight of land. These geographical features meant that in Roman times, and even many centuries before Rome, peoples from regions as far apart as southern Spain and northern Egypt could be, and were, in regular if not continuous contact with one another.

In fact, they had to be. The Mediterranean basin is surrounded by mountains along its northern and eastern shores and by deserts along its southern expanse. This relative shortage of hinterland, coupled with the basin's characteristic long summer droughts, meant that most Mediterranean coastal societies had difficulty producing locally all of the foodstuffs and material goods necessary to life, and hence they had to trade with one another in order to survive. The physical characteristics of the sea made such contact possible. One should therefore think of the various cultures of the Mediterranean world as component parts of a single, large sea-based civilization linked by similar agricultural techniques (the need for terracing the arid hinterlands and the use of sophisticated irrigation networks, for example), similar diet (with olive oil, wine, hard grains, and fish predominating), and similar social organization (the norm was independent coastal cities dominated by trade, and therefore by traders and tradesmen, rather than by large-scale landowners). Thus when the Romans referred to "our sea" they meant not just the body of water controlled by the Roman administration, but the body of water that itself controlled the lives of the empire's inhabitants.

Roman adminstration of its vast empire would in fact have been impossible without the sea. No matter what an emperor may have thought of himself and his authority, his real power extended no further than his ability to enforce his will, and the qualities of the Mediterranean were such that the emperor's power reached very far indeed. Well-equipped ships fanning out from Rome could scatter throughout the entire sea in two weeks. In ideal sailing weather, for example, a ship could reach Barcelona in only four days; a fleet setting out for Alexandria could drop anchor there in little more than a week. This fact allowed Roman law, and the military muscle needed to enforce it, to be put into direct and effective practice. The news of local rebellions reached Rome quickly, and Roman forces were just as quickly dispatched to the trouble spots before the rebellions had a chance to grow. No land-based empire could hope to possess the political, commercial, and cultural cohesiveness offered by the Mediterranean.

And in fact, it was when Rome began to extend its dominion away from the sea basin that its first difficulties arose. Rome's eastward expansion into the Tigris-Euphrates river valley brought the empire into contact, and instantly into conflict, with the Parthian Empire, but it was the northern reach of the empire into western and central Europe that proved the greatest threat to Roman order. A series of mountain ranges had always protected the Mediterranean world from the less advanced nations of the European continent. The Pyrenees mountains offered a strong border protecting Roman Spain from the Celts of Gaul (modern-day France), while the Alps and Balkan mountains had always shielded the Mediterranean from the numerous Germanic and Slavic peoples. But in the first century B.C. a Celtic group known as the Helvetii were driven from their homelands beyond the Rhine and Danube, and settled first in the area that today makes up Switzerland before migrating further westward across the territory of central France. This mass movement threatened the Roman province of southern Gaul, and in order to defend it Julius Caesar began his campaigns to push the Roman frontier northward. These campaigns began Rome's larger involvement in continental Europe, and the subsequent need to find a strategically defensible frontier ultimately pushed her borders all the way to the Danube and Rhine rivers and to northern England.

Continental Europe was a decidedly different place from the world of the Mediterranean. Comprised chiefly of a vast wooded plain, beginning in southern France and reaching northward to England and Scandinavia and eastward through Germany, Poland, and Russia, it was a world of immense, if still largely untapped, natural resources. Dense hardwood forest covered most of the land, offering abundant material for building. The land itself, once cleared, was heavy and wet. This made it more difficult to work than Mediterranean soil—heavier plows and stronger draught animals were needed, for example, and more collective labor—but it could produce two crops a year. Cereal production dominated here, unlike the viticulture (grape and olive vineyards) of the south. Given the density of the forest, the numerous rivers of the north served as the main conduits of commerce and contact. Continental Europe therefore could support a large population, but the conditions of the land meant that settlements were widely scattered and isolated from each other. In Roman times, less than ten percent of this land was inhabited. People tended to cluster around clearings they had carved out of the forest and to carry out the whole of their lives there, working the soil. Goods could be traded up

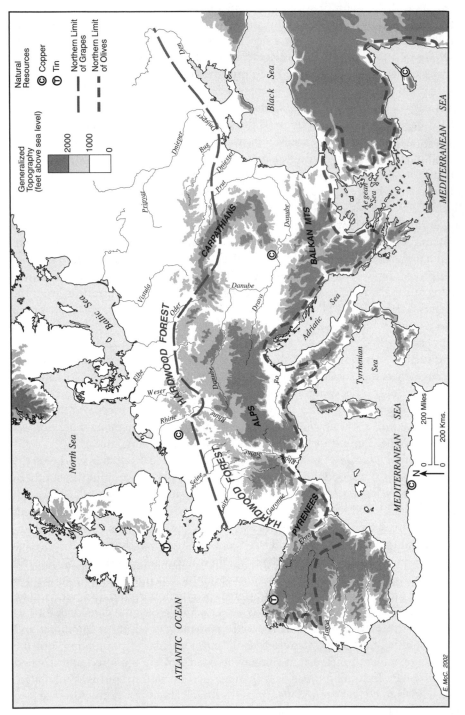

The topography of Europe

and down the river valleys but not over the land itself. Northern groups thus had considerably less contact with one another than Mediterranean peoples did, and they developed clannish and conservative cultures that were resistant to change and suspicious of outsiders. That is why the immigration of a large number of new-comers, such as the Helvetii, could set off such widespread unrest. Continental life in the ancient world therefore remained more disparate and static, and also more fragile, than Mediterranean life, and these features made it more difficult to administer. Unlike the urban scene that characterized the south and supported Roman administration, the rural and sedentary north was brought into the Roman world, and was maintained in it, only by military occupation.

THE ROLE OF THE MILITARY

The army was the second chief structure on which the Roman Empire was built and it differed significantly from the other military forces of the ancient world. Semiprivatized in the period of the Republic, it came to possess an extraordinary degree of organization and professionalization under the emperors. Soldiers fought for the glory of the Roman state, but also for regular wages and a portion of whatever booty they could haul away from whomever they conquered. After subduing a region, the army confiscated whatever money was at hand, carried away whatever portable property they desired, divided up the choicest bits of real estate they fancied, and sold into slavery the prisoners of war they had captured. War was a highly profitable business. Because of the natural wealth inherent in continental Europe, inland Egypt, and the Near East (the three main sites of Roman aggression—the first taken largely by Caesar and Claudius, the second by Augustus, and the third by Trajan and Hadrian) the army's success in pushing the Roman frontier forward brought in enormous amounts of money that, until the later decades of the second century, more than compensated for the cost of the warfare itself.

The army as a rule did not permanently occupy the lands it had conquered. To do so might have prolonged local resentments; but permanent occupation was also unnecessary, given the ease of transporting soldiers across the sea. A more commonsense approach called for conquering a region, redrawing the local administrative practices along Roman lines (although usually keeping the local elites in power), then withdrawing the troops at the first available moment. They could always return quickly enough, if events warranted it. For this reason, a permanent military presence is a remarkably reliable indicator of where the trouble spots were. Continental Europe, as it happened, had the largest and most permanent network of garrisons. Resistance to Roman power had been strong, but the main threat to stability came from the difficulty of administering so vast an expanse of land. The sedentary rural populace did not experience the daily interaction with other cultures that the south did, and this meant that they were more resistant to "Romanization." And since troops could not deploy with the same ease that they could in the south, the only alternative was permanent settlement. The greatest concentration of troops existed along the furthest borders of the empire; but a network of smaller military camps stood behind them, stretching from the Atlantic opening of the Loire to the mouth of the Danube at the Black Sea.

The army's significance rested upon more than its record of battlefield victories, for the army was the single most important instrument for "Romanizing" the conquered peoples and turning them into peaceful elements of a stable society. The army accomplished this transformation by charting a new direction in social engineering. Earlier empires, such as the Athenians of the fifth century B.C., had steadfastly maintained a separation of the conquerors and the conquered, and ruled over their realms with very little interaction with their subjects. Roman practice was different. They enlisted soldiers from all ethnic groups throughout their empire— Italians, Egyptians, Celts, Dacians, Hibernians, Libyans, and more—and used them to help bring Roman culture to the provinces. Soldiers learned to speak Latin, to know and obey Roman law, to practice Roman religion. Soldiers served for twenty years, during which time they were stationed in province after province (but almost never in their native territory), and after retirement were encouraged to marry local women. They received handsome severance payments of cash and/or land. This practice produced two important results. First, the empire had a steady stream of volunteer recruits attracted by the opportunity to make money, see the world, receive an education, earn an honored place in society, and retire at an early age with land to farm and money to fund the operation. (The empire at its height boasted of a military force, including auxiliaries, of three hundred thousand men.) Second, army service had the intended effect of eroding an individual soldier's sense of identification with his native ethnic group and of inculcating his self-definition as a "Roman"—that is, as a member of a society and civilization that was larger than mere ethnicity. To be a citizen of the empire implied something more than a mere legal classification; it meant that one belonged to and represented an ideal of social organization, a vision of human unity and cohesion. Roman civilization, in other words, resulted from the intentional blending of cultures and races, and whereas Roman religion, administration, architecture and urban design, literature, and art all contributed to "Romanization," the army played the first and most important role in that process.

ROMAN SOCIETY

But while Roman society in the first and second centuries A.D. was stable, it was hardly static. Sharp distinctions of social and legal class existed, but since one's class was determined more by one's wealth than one's ancestry, individuals could frequently pass from one stratum to another. A sense of public spirit was required as well, since Roman tradition expected the rich to put their personal wealth to public use—either to build or maintain roads, repair aqueducts, feed and house troops, or aid the poor. The essential social distinction lay between the *honestiores* ("the better people") and the *humiliores* ("the lesser people"), yet important gradations existed within each group. The honestiores enjoyed significant legal protections, such as the right to lighter penalties if they were convicted of a crime, and immunity from torture. The humiliores, by contrast, fared far worse, even if they held Roman citizenship. A "lesser person" convicted of a capital crime such as murder or treason had to face a brutal death by being torn apart by wild beasts or by crucifixion, which killed by slowly constricting the circulatory system.

Four main groups made up the honestiores: senators, equestrians, the *curiales*, and all army veterans. Out of a total population of fifty to sixty million at the empire's zenith, roughly one thousand men, and their immediate families, qualified for the senatorial order; this class derived its name from the fact that they alone had the right to serve in the Roman Senate. Considerably larger was the class of the equestrians, which numbered perhaps fifty thousand. In earlier times the equestrian order had comprised those who had served in the Roman cavalry, although by the first two centuries A.D. merchants, financiers, and large property-holders predominated. Custom demanded that an individual had to come from a family that had been free-born for at least two generations before being admitted to this order—an indication of the flexibility of Roman class consciousness. Just below the equestrians stood the rank of curiales. This was the largest of the privileged classes, numbering in the hundreds of thousands, and by the third century they were the most significant. Curiales served as unsalaried magistrates who conducted the day-to-day administration of the cities and towns. A unique characteristic of the curiales is that in this order alone a woman who held the social rank could also hold the political authority that might accompany it. Army veterans were also numerous, but since they tended to retire after their service to rural estates, they generally played larger roles in local political and social affairs while exercising little collective influence over high imperial matters.

The humiliores consisted of everyone else in the empire except for slaves, whom the law regarded as property. The overwhelming majority of these "lesser people" worked on the land either as free farmers, tenants, or hired hands on a great estate. Skilled and unskilled laborers, craftspeople, merchants, and clerks made up the free commoners in the cities. As for the slaves, the females were usually reserved for domestic service—in part to keep them available for sexual exploitation by their masters—but the males were especially vital throughout the urban and rural economies, working in homes, shops, fields, quarries, and mines. Slaves of Greek origin frequently worked as tutors to children.

The economy grew as the empire grew. Naturally, the sheer internal peace and order of the empire encouraged economic growth, but we can identify a few specific causes of the general prosperity of these years. One obvious influence was the army. Unlike today's military forces, ancient armies had few stockpiles of equipment, transport vehicles, blankets, or food. These supplies had to be procured, and therefore produced, wherever the soldiers traveled. The twenty-five legions of the Roman army needed vast stores of food, clothing, and ironwork every day and thus represented itinerant mass markets that constantly spurred local production. It took

the hides of fifty thousand cattle, for example, to make the tents for a single le-
gion. Moreover, legions on the march often built new fortified camps as they
progressed—complete with central command buildings, guard posts, and wooden
walled perimeters—that formed the nuclei of permanent settlements once the army
moved on. These settlements frequently became centers of exchange for local farmers and manufacturers, and occasionally grew into full-fledged cities.[1] As these local economies became more sophisticated, regional trade increased. The agricultural
abundance of northern Europe was carted south and soon rivaled the traditional
grain-producing centers of Sicily and Egypt. Techniques of Mediterranean olive-
and grape-viticulture traveled northward. Spices and silks came from the eastern
provinces, and animal products dominated the exports of inland Spain.

The family formed the basic unit of society and economic production. In Roman times the word *familia* meant "household" rather than "family" in the modern
sense, and it included wives, sons, daughters, concubines, attendants, servants, and
slaves. The Roman family thus was a larger, more inclusive institution than we are
accustomed to, but hardly more benevolent for it. Characteristically for the ancient
world, society was rigidly patriarchal. Fathers possessed a legal authority known as
patria potestas ("paternal power") that gave them, quite literally, control of the very
lives and deaths of all the members of their families. If circumstances warranted it,
a Roman father had the right to put to death any member of his family at any time.
Acts this grave were usually limited to exposing unwanted babies soon after
birth—whether to avoid having an extra mouth to feed during economic hard
times, for example, or to get rid of a physically defective child—but in theory a father could legitimately kill anyone under his authority, free or unfree, male or female, young or old. The law also recognized the father as the sole possessor of a
family's property. Anything acquired by anyone in the family belonged, in theory,
to the father alone. But it remains unclear how often these theoretical powers were
actually put to use.

Wives represented a partial exception to paternal power. Older Roman tradition held that a daughter remained under her father's authority until her marriage,
after which she fell under the power of her husband (unless in their marriage contract the husband specifically relinquished this right). However, by the Pax Romana
period most Roman marriages were "free"—meaning that the husband never succeeded entirely to the father's power. Thus a grown woman, whether married or
not, could live a relatively independent life after the death of her father. She could
own property, run a business, save her own money. Women ran their households,
oversaw the comings and goings of the servants, and tended to the education of the
children. Since Roman women tended to marry while still in their early teens (the
average age at which men married was 27 or 28), they had generally not received
more than an elementary education, and so their primary duty was to their chil-

---

1. Laon, in northern France, is an example.

dren's moral, not intellectual, education. The extent to which women succeeded in instilling in their children a sense of virtue, piety, and loyalty to the familia determined the degree of respect accorded to them. Unmarried women had relatively few options available to them. Roman society recognized only a handful of "occupations" suitable for single women: as priestesses of all-women religious cults, midwives, concubines (officially recognized mistresses), or prostitutes. Some found work as laundresses, others as laborers in brick-making factories. A few references even exist to female gladiators. But most often unmarried non-aristocratic women found refuge in joining the familia of a male relation.

ROMAN GOVERNMENT

The Romans had a particular genius for government. The political institutions of the Republican period had proved sufficiently effective and flexible to create a vast domain and to inaugurate the process of Romanization. Those institutions then transmuted, albeit violently, during the civil wars of the late Republic into an imperial system that was at once more centralized and more localized than earlier practices. Hard headed pragmatism, not lofty idealism, directed imperial governance. The Romans took pride in their achievements; they recognized that their cultural attainments in poetry, the arts, literature, and philosophy fell somewhat short of Greek glories, and that their knowledge of the sciences paled next to that of the Persians, but they felt sure that they surpassed all previous societies in knowing how to rule people. Bearing witness to this conviction, and propagandizing the new empire's historical mission, the poet Virgil wrote:

> *Others shall cast their bronze to breathe*
> *With softer features, I well know, and shall draw*
> *Living lines from the marble, and shall plead*
> *Better causes, and with pen shall better trace the paths*
> *Of the heavens and proclaim the stars in their rising;*
> *But it shall be your charge, O Roman, to rule*
> *The nations in your empire. This shall be your art:*
> *To lay down the law of peace, to show mercy*
> *To the conquered, and to beat the haughty down.*

Virgil wrote those lines especially in honor of the first Roman emperor, Augustus, who ruled from 27 B.C. to 14 A.D. Augustus had emerged from the civil wars as the sole victor and quickly set about to reform the Roman constitution. He established a form of governance known as the *Principate*, according to which the emperor possessed absolute control of both the civil and the military branches of government; the Senate was reduced to a mere cipher. Augustus and his immediate successors Tiberius (A.D. 14–37), Caligula (37–41), Claudius (41–54), and Nero (54–68)—carefully maintained the popular fiction that the Senate still formed the seat of power, but in reality they ran the government as a dictatorship. They purged the Senate of political rivals and recruited talented individuals from throughout Italy, regardless of their social class, to fill the purged seats. They appointed all provincial governors and, once these officials' loyalty and efficiency had been proven, gave them more local autonomy than governors had held previously. They imposed inheritance taxes on the empire's wealthiest citizens and used the revenues generated to fund the rapidly growing imperial army. Government became more streamlined and effective, and the prosperity unleashed by the Pax Romana made most people willing to put up with the loss of their political freedom under the new regime.

Maintaining the pretense of republican government often proved difficult. Caligula and Nero were both mentally unstable and indulged themselves in outrageous behavior—much of it grossly violent—that shocked the stolid morals of the senators and undermined public faith in the imperial office. Nero's death by suicide put an end to this so-called Julio-Claudian dynasty and triggered a struggle for succession. But no clear system for imperial succession had been agreed upon: The Senate insisted on its traditional right to elect the next ruler, but the army demanded that it had the sole right to choose since it was the backbone of the empire itself. For the next three centuries conflict arose between these two bodies virtually every time the imperial office became vacant, with the army usually winning. Indeed, a series of able, disciplined, and conscientious generals held the emperorship from Nero's death to the end of the Pax Romana period. Vespasian (69–79), although he was a modest man of middle-class background, encouraged the development of the imperial cult, whereby the emperor was worshiped as a living god, as a means of consolidating control over the provinces. His sons Titus (79–81) and Domitian (81–96) further centralized imperial administration while extending Roman citizenship and bringing large numbers of provincials into the Senate. They also began construction on the Roman Colosseum.

The empire's highest point was reached in the so-called Age of the Five Good Emperors. Nerva, a senatorial appointee, ruled only two years (96–98) but established a precedent for the next hundred years by formally adopting the most capable general and statesman he could find and establishing him as his heir to the throne. Upon Nerva's death, therefore, imperial power passed peacefully to Trajan (98–117), Hadrian (117–138), Antonius Pius (138–161), and Marcus Aurelius (161–180). During these years the empire flourished as never before. Trajan's conquests of Armenia, Assyria, Dacia (modern-day Romania), and Mesopotamia brought the empire to its greatest geographic expanse and made vast mineral resources, especially the extensive Dacian gold mines, available for exploitation. Hadrian secured the frontiers by increasing the soldiery and building fortifications like the wall named after him in northern England. The quiet and peaceful reign of Antonius Pius culminated in the celebrations that marked the nine hundreth anniversary of the founding of the capital city (traditionally ascribed to the year 753 B.C.). And the good fortune continued under Marcus Aurelius, who was able to enjoy the stability of the times long enough to earn a reputation as an accomplished

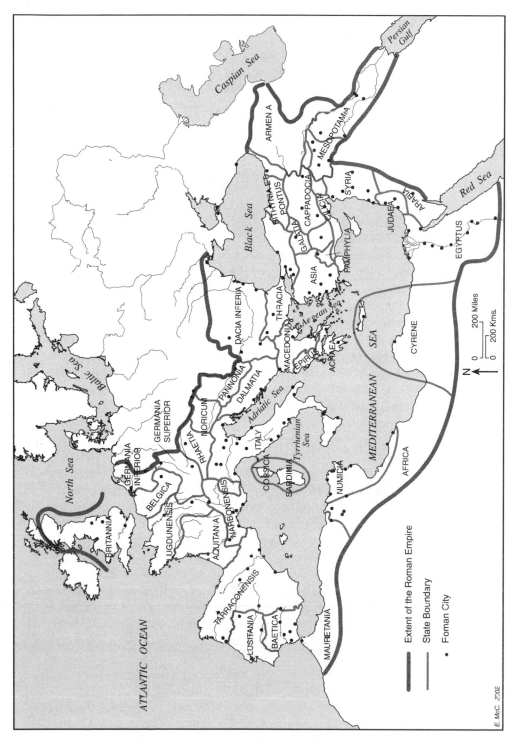

The Roman Empire at its greatest expanse

ATLANTIC OCEAN

North Sea

Baltic Sea

BRITANNIA

GERMANIA INFERIOR

BELGICA

LUGDUNENSIS

AQUITANIA

NARBONENSIS

GERMANIA SUPERIOR

RHAETIA

NORICUM

PANNONIA

DALMATIA

Adriatic Sea

ITALY

CORSICA

SARDINIA

Tyrrhenian Sea

TARRACONENSIS

LUSITANIA

BAETICA

MAURETANIA

NUMIDIA

AFRICA

MEDITERRANEAN SEA

Black Sea

DACIA INFERIA

THRACIA

MACEDONIA

EPIRUS

ACHAEA

Aegean Sea

ASIA

BITHYNIA ET PONTUS

GALATIA

CAPPADOCIA

PAMPHYLIA

CILICIA

SYRIA

CYRENE

Caspian Sea

ARMENIA

MESOPOTAMIA

JUDAEA

ARABIA

EGYPTUS

Red Sea

Persian Gulf

N

0   200 Miles

0   200 Kms.

— Extent of the Roman Empire

— State Boundary

• Roman City

E. McC. 2002

13

Stoic philosopher. While we may question Edward Gibbon's judgment that "Their united reigns are possibly the only period of history in which the happiness of a great people was the sole object of government," the age of the good emperors indeed marked the high point of Roman life.

As far as they could, the emperors tried to unify and regularize the administrative life of the empire while allowing local customs to continue. Roman citizenship was gradually extended to larger and larger portions of the population until by A.D. 212 virtually every person living in the empire who was not a slave became a citizen. Cities received charters that gave them broad jurisdictional authority. Responsibility for municipal government fell increasingly upon the local curiales, the propertied urban elites who epitomized the civic-mindedness of the Roman spirit. They presided over the city and town councils, collected taxes, and organized the construction and maintenance of public works. They received no salary for these services. Instead, Roman custom allowed them to collect more tax revenue each year than the central administration demanded, and they pocketed the surplus. Such a system clearly invited some abuse, but the empire at its height experienced surprisingly little egregious corruption and heard surprisingly little complaint from the masses. While the rewards for urban administration could obviously be very considerable, in prestige as well as in wealth, the curiales also assumed responsibility for paying certain public expenses and making up budget deficits out of their own pockets. In less prosperous regions of the empire the property qualification for curial status was low, and the curiales in such places were often hard put to meet these expenses. The fact that they continued to serve in office attests to the depth of the public spirit of the empire at its zenith.

THE CHALLENGES OF THE THIRD CENTURY

At the end of the second century, the empire began to confront a number of serious challenges. Agricultural and industrial production declined, inflation ran rampant, the imperial coinage was debased, the autocratic nature of the military government became aggressively overt, disease and poverty carried off hundreds of thousands of people, civil wars erupted between claimants for the imperial throne, and the confidence and public-spiritedness of earlier years gave way to fear, flight, and depression. Matters only grew worse throughout the third century, when civil strife became so bad that in the forty-five years from 239 to 284 no fewer than twenty-six emperors ruled, only one of whom died a natural death, the rest falling victim to battlefield defeat, assassination, formal execution, or forced suicide. Dio Cassius, writing in the third century, described the Roman world around him as "a golden kingdom turned into a realm of iron and rust." Cyprian, the Christian bishop of Carthage and an early martyr, more than once announced his belief that the world was coming to an end. What had happened to the Pax Romana?

No single answer exists. Rome's decline resulted from a combination of internal weaknesses and external pressures. Many of these problems were of long standing, but for various reasons they came to a head in the third century. The geographic expansion of the empire under Trajan and Hadrian had created as many long-term problems as it had generated short-term gains. The conquest of Mesopotamia, for example, indirectly triggered a revolution in the Parthian Empire that brought a new regime—the Sassanids—to power, who struck back against the Romans and drove them from the southern half of the rich Tigris-Euphrates river valley. Determined not to lose face or control of the trade routes that connected the empire with India, the Romans conscripted more and more soldiers and settled into a protracted conflict that undermined eastern commerce. No booty came from this war, and the escalating cost of the conflict sent imperial officials scrambling to raise funds. The low point came when the emperor Valerian personally took command of a campaign in Syria, only to end up as a Sassanid prisoner-of-war. He died in captivity in 260.

More troublesome still were the various, and extremely numerous, Germanic groups who lived beyond the empire's Rhine-Danube border in northern Europe. These early Germans were hardy nomads who spent their lives hunting and fighting in the forests and plains beyond the Roman frontier; contact between them and Rome went back at least to the second century B.C., and during the age of the Pax Romana a fragile peace characterized their relations. Occasional raiding expeditions moved back and forth across the Rhine-Danube border, but with one or two exceptions no full-scale conflicts broke out. By the third century A.D., however, conditions had changed dramatically. The Germanic population had grown to such an extent that the various tribes began to fight bitterly between themselves for control of nomadic routes and patches of cultivated land. These clashes often led to vendettas between clans that propelled the violence into generation after generation. In order to survive, the Germans had to find more land for themselves; but expansion to the east was impossible, since new nomadic groups emerging from the Eurasian steppe increasingly competed for the same land. The only alternative was to move westward and southward into Roman territory.

By far the most aggressive of the Germans was a group known as the Goths, who crossed the lower Danube and moved into Dacia, the site of the extensive gold and mineral deposits conquered by Trajan in the early second century. In order to defend Dacia and to counterattack the Sassanids, the empire transferred several legions from the Rhine region, which allowed other Germanic groups like the Alemanni (the word means "all men" and suggests a confederation of several tribes rather than a single ethnic group) and the Franks to cross the border there and move into northern and central Gaul. In order to slow the flood of in-comers, Rome began to conscript Germanic soldiers as *federati*—that is, as semi-Romanized recruits who represented the first line of defense against the onslaught.

Indeed, the federati characterize much of what was happening within the Roman army at that time. The army no longer served as an instrument of Romanization. Instead, it sought recruits on the local scene, whether it was northern Gaul or northern Mesopotamia, and tried to entice them into immediate service on the spot with promises of higher wages than they could hope for in any other occupation. It became an army of mercenaries rather than an implement of social organization. Discipline broke down, and with it went the sense of identifying with an ideal larger than personal or tribal well-being. Consequently, the soldiery recognized their importance to whomever was on the throne, and began to insist upon ever higher salaries and more frequent donatives (gifts from the state). Political power became overtly military in nature: Whoever could command the loyalty of the greatest number of troops was likely to attain the imperial office. To hold onto his throne, for example, Caracalla (211–217) not only increased the size of the army dramatically but he also raised the soldiers' salaries by nearly fifty percent. This raise set off a virtual bargaining war between generals aspiring to imperial glory, and explains the high turnover of the imperial office throughout the third century.

Military setbacks, combined with the harsh new taxes needed to pay for mercenaries, an outbreak of plague, and a series of earthquakes in the 250s and 260s, dealt a severe blow to the Roman economy. Actions like Caracalla's set off a crushing wave of inflation that continued throughout the century. Merchants and financiers found it unwise, if not impossible, to invest over the long term or in new manufactures, and matters worsened when several short-lived emperors attempted to cover their military expenditures by debasing the coinage. As civil warfare, Germanic invasion, economic hardship, and plague carried off more and more people, the tax base gradually eroded, which made the curiales, who had embodied the public-spiritedness of Rome in its heyday, flee their obligations and their cities, thus depriving society of its leaders precisely at the time when it needed them most. Cities, roads, and water systems fell into disrepair since there was less and less money to pay for their upkeep and, as the century continued, fewer people to do the labor and direct the projects. Free farmers unable to earn their living became indentured farmers, called *coloni*, to owners of larger estates. Piracy returned to the Mediterranean, and international trade slowed accordingly. As times worsened, people who owned gold and silver tended to hoard it, thus reducing the amount of precious metal in circulation; this hoarding had the unintended consequence of forcing the revolving-door emperors to issue increasingly debased coinage, which of course only exacerbated the problem of runaway inflation.

In the words of a prominent figure in Carthage, this third century was an age in which "food was scarce, skilled labor in decline, and all the mines tapped out." And he was writing even before the wave of plagues and earthquakes hit in the 260s.

REFORM, RECOVERY, PERSECUTION, AND FAVOR

Periods of chaos often inspire societies to creative reforms. Crises, if they are severe enough, can shake people out of set patterns of behavior and belief and can instill a willingness, even an eagerness, to try new approaches to old problems. So it was with the Roman Empire, which responded to its challenges, once the civil wars ended, by drastically reshaping its administrative practices, its military structure, and its system of tax collection. These reforms hardly made the Roman world prosper again, but they did succeed in restoring a degree of order that enabled the empire to survive for another century and a half. The key figures in this transformation were the emperors Diocletian (284–305) and Constantine (306–337).

Diocletian managed to defeat or intimidate his rivals long enough to seize the throne in 284, and to avoid assassins long enough to inaugurate widespread reforms. A career military man from the Balkan province of Illyria, he had an undistinguished family background and very little education. He possessed a quick mind, however, and a strong will. Above all, Diocletian thought in purely practical terms; being free of philosophical and theoretical interests, and being personally removed from Roman cultural traditions, he confronted the imperial crises with a clear-headed willingness to consider any available option. To him, whatever worked was right and needed no further justification.

What worked, in Diocletian's eyes, was a radical decentralization of the imperial administration. No single individual could possibly manage the defense and administration of so vast a territory, and so he divided the empire into four semi-autonomous prefectures and placed a sort of mini-emperor in charge of each. Each of the two senior rulers held the title of Augustus, and the two junior rulers were referred to as Caesars. Everyone regarded Diocletian himself as the senior Augustus theoretically in control of the entire empire, but in reality each member of the *tetrarchy* ("rule of four") governed independently. Upon the death of an Augustus, his corresponding Caesar succeeded to the higher office and appointed his own lesser associate from among the most capable soldiers and administrators under his command. No pretense of senatorial election remained, and no longer did the dictatorship hide behind a democratic mask; this was to be an administration of autocratic meritocracy. Within each prefecture, the mini-emperors ruled by straightforward decree. The Senate played no governmental role whatsoever, and Diocletian further undermined the power of the order by eliminating the legal and social distinctions between the Senators and the equestrians and by moving individuals brought up through the military ranks into the highest levels of the aristocracy.

Diocletian confronted the empire's military crisis principally by devising a new strategic position based on the idea of defense rather than conquest. He replaced the mobile legions—which were essentially an offensive force—with a network of permanently settled frontier forces. The soldiers, composed increasingly of recruited federati, fanned out along the borders in smaller groups and farmed the land directly. This created, in effect, an entire perimeter defense. The fact that these soldiers supported themselves on the land helped to reduce the direct cost of maintaining so large an army.

Nevertheless, the government needed significant increases in tax revenue. With the economy in a state of near collapse, Diocletian took quick action. He put an end to the debasement of the currency by altering the rural tax system so that it did not use money at all. Taxes in the countryside were henceforth assessed and paid in kind rather than in coin: Officials now collected grain, meat, wine, cloth, livestock, eggs, and leatherwork from the people. Such goods retained their value regardless of fluctuations in the economy and provided a temporary reprieve from the falling currency. In the cities, a combination of new head- and property-taxes were levied, but again a non-currency alternative was made available: One could pay one's taxes by performing labor on public works projects. The hyperinflation in the economy presented another problem. Diocletian's solution was to set fixed limits to wages and prices; those who violated the edict were sentenced to death. And in order to make tax collection easier, the government restricted people's movement and freedom. Tenant farmers no longer could move away from their farms but were tied to the land; their children were required to work the same land in their turn. In the cities, workers in various occupations were forbidden to seek other types of work. The children of tradesmen had to follow in the same trade, in the same shop, and produce the same goods as their fathers. These measures made it possible for the government to budget: Knowing exactly how many people worked at various occupations in every region of the empire, they therefore knew exactly how much tax revenue they could count on year after year.

Diocletian's last major action hardly deserves to be called a reform, but it certainly marked a significant change in Roman practice. Seeking a popular scapegoat for the empire's ills, Diocletian seized upon the small sect of Christianity (whose origins and rise we will examine in the next chapter) and subjected it to brutal persecution. Earlier rulers—such as Nero, in the first century, or Decius and Valerian, in the third—had launched sporadic attacks against the Christians, but none of these approached the systematic nature of Diocletian's move. Traditionally, Roman society tolerated non-Roman religions and indeed usually sought to incorporate them into the Roman pantheon; those religions that resisted assimilation were allowed their freedom, provided that their followers made a token bow to the official pagan cult once a year. But the early Christians refused to compromise, which left them exposed to periodic oppression. Diocletian began his so-called Great Persecution in order to keep Christianity from spreading within the army, but it soon turned into a general purge of society that resulted in tens of thousands of people being arrested and executed—most popularly by being mauled by wild beasts before large cheering crowds.

A new civil war broke out when Diocletian retired in 305, and the war dashed his hopes for a smooth succession. After seven years of fighting, Constantine, the son of one of Diocletian's "Caesars," emerged as sole ruler. He carried on with most of Diocletian's administrative reforms, streamlining and centralizing the workings of the government and ruling more and more by decree. Indeed, the office of emperor took on elevated proportions. His official title changed from the traditional *princeps* ("leader") to *dominus et deus* ("lord and god"). Few people were allowed into his presence. Those given such a rare privilege had to prostrate themselves, face down, on the floor at his feet and kiss the hem of his robe. (Apart from satisfying imperial megalomania, this practice also made it easier for Diocletian and Constantine to avoid assas-

*Bust of Diocletian, reformer of the empire,
initiator of the Great Persecution of Christians.
Source: Erich Lessing / Art Resource, NY*

sination.) Constantine built on a majestic scale: Palaces, arches, public baths, and stadiums rose all around, each filled with statuary and decorated to exalt the glory of the emperor. His largest work by far was the construction of a new capital city, named Constantinople after himself, on the site of the ancient Bosporus city of Byzantium.[2] The location was significant in that it reflected a growing awareness that only the eastern half of the empire seemed likely to survive. The western half

2. It is today's city of Istanbul, on the promontory separating the Aegean and Black seas.

Head of Constantine. This is a remnant from a massive statue,
one of many that he erected in the empire. The eyes appear over-large because
they were intended to be viewed at a great height. Source: Erich
Lessing / Art Resource, NY

faced far greater military and economic problems, and being considerably less ur-
banized than the east it lacked many of the resources necessary to address those
problems. Constantine and his successors certainly did not give up entirely on the
west, but they proved increasingly unwilling to devote much energy or capital to
prop up the state there. In its new geographic centering and its increasingly Greek-
and Persian-influenced culture and court ceremony, the empire from the early fourth
century onward evolved into a new kind of society, still professing to be Roman but
in reality already well on its way to being the eastward-looking Byzantine state of
the medieval period.

Constantine altered Diocletian's reforms in one fundamental way. In 312, just prior to the battle that won him the imperial throne, Constantine converted to Christianity. According to his biographer and friend Eusebius, Constantine received a vision on the night before the battle promising him victory if he converted, and on the following morning he saw the heavens open and a brilliant Cross hanging in the sky, together with the words "With the help of This, you will be victorious." Whatever actually happened that night, Constantine renounced traditional paganism and declared his loyalty to the Christian God. Having won the throne, he put an end to the persecution of Christianity and extended the traditional policy of religious toleration to include Christianity explicitly. With its new protected status, the Christian faith began its ascendancy in the western world.

SUGGESTED READING

Texts

Ammianus Marcellinus. *History*.

Dio Cassius. *History*.

Josephus. *Antiquities*.

———. *The Jewish War*.

Marcus Aurelius. *Meditations*.

Plutarch. *Parallel Lives*.

Suetonius. *The Twelve Caesars*.

Tacitus. *The Annals*.

———. *The Histories*.

Source Anthologies

Beard, Mary, John North, and Simon Price. *Religions of Rome*, 2 vols. (1998).

Kaegi, Walter Emil, Jr., and Peter White. *Rome: Late Republic and Principate* (1986).

Kraemer, Ross E., *Maenads, Martyrs, Matrons, Monastics: A Sourcebook on Women's Religions in the Greco-Roman World* (1988).

Lefkowitz, Mary R., and Maureen B. Fant. *Women's Life in Greece and Rome: A Source Book in Translation*, 2nd ed. (1992).

Lewis, Naphtali, and Meyer Reinhold. *Roman Civilization: Selected Readings*, 3rd ed. (1990).

Shelton, Jo-Ann. *As the Romans Did: A Sourcebook in Roman Social History* (1997).

Studies

Balsdon, J.P.V.D. *Romans and Aliens* (1979).

Cameron, Averil. *The Mediterranean World in Late Antiquity, A.D. 395–600* (1993).

Campbell, J.B. *The Emperor and the Roman Army: 31 B.C.–A.D. 235* (1984).

Dixon, Suzanne. *The Roman Family* (1992).

Evans, John K. *War, Women, and Children in Ancient Rome* (1991).

Gardner, Jane F. *Women in Roman Law and Society* (1986).

Garnsey, Peter, and Richard Saller. *The Roman Empire: Economy, Society, and Culture* (1987).

Greene, Kevin. *The Archaeology of the Roman Economy* (1986).

Hallett, Judith P. *Fathers and Daughters in Roman Society and the Elite Family* (1984).

Horden, Peregrine, and Nicholas Purcell. *The Mediterranean World: Man and Environment* (1987).

Jones, A.H.M. *The Later Roman Empire*, 2nd ed. (1986).

Lintott, Andrew. *Imperium Romanum: Politics and Administration* (1984).

MacMullen, Ramsay. *Constantine* (1969).

———. *Corruption and the Decline of Rome* (1988).

Millar, Fergus. *The Emperor in the Roman World, 31 B.C.–A.D. 337* (1992).

Rawson, Elizabeth. *Intellectual Life in the Late Roman Republic* (1985).

Treggiari, Susan. *Roman Marriage: "Iusti coniuges" from the Time of Cicero to the Time of Ulpian* (1991).

West, D.A., and A.J. Woodman. *Poetry and Politics in the Age of Augustus* (1984).

Whittaker, C.R. *Frontiers of the Roman Empire: A Social and Economic Study* (1994).

Williams, Stephen. *Diocletian and the Roman Recovery* (1997).

Wolfram, Herwig. *The Roman Empire and Its Germanic Peoples* (1997).

Zanker, Paul. *The Power of Images in the Age of Augustus* (1988).

CHAPTER 2

THE RISE OF CHRISTIANITY

Explaining the rise of Christianity is no easy matter. The broad outlines of its rise seem clear enough, but the specific mechanisms by which the faith spread, the specific groups who were attracted to it and the reasons for their attraction, the specific impact of the new faith on society, even the specific content of the faith itself at any given moment remain elusive even after two thousand years of investigation. These issues also remain highly contentious, since few people confront the historical problem of Christianity with absolute objectivity. But the importance of the problem can hardly be exaggerated: Christianity has fundamentally influenced every aspect of Western civilization, from its religious beliefs to its artistic development, from its conception of time and history to its sexual morality, from its understanding of law and political authority to its music. It has guided and comforted millions of people, but it has also been used to justify the persecution and killing of millions of others. Understanding the rise of Christianity therefore is central to understanding Western history, and this is especially true for the medieval period, when the Christian faith dominated society to a degree unmatched in any other era.

The New Testament is our principal source for tracing the story of Jesus and his first followers, and therein lies much of the problem. The writers of the four Gospels—Matthew, Mark, Luke, and John—were not interested in writing comprehensive, fact-filled biographies of Jesus; they aimed instead to produce interpretive sketches that would elucidate certain aspects of his teaching and the meaning of parts of his ministry. They share a generally consistent chronology, but each Gospel contains much material that is unique to itself, depending on the audience it was intended for. Matthew, for example, wrote his Gospel specifically for an audience of Jews and consequently emphasized those episodes in Christ's life and those parts of his teaching that demonstrated how Jesus fulfilled the scriptural revelation of the Hebrew Law and prophets. Luke, by contrast, wrote for a Gentile audience and stressed the twin themes of Christ's mercy and forgiveness, and his particular interest in bringing salvation to the poor and lowly. Matthew's Jesus and Luke's Jesus are certainly compatible, but their personalities do clash at times: Whereas the Jesus of Luke's Gospel shows a particular tenderness and mercy toward women, for example, women hardly figure at all in Matthew's version of Jesus' life, and in fact he appears there to be indifferent to women, including his own mother. Moreover, the Gospels frequently contradict one another on particular facts—even very important ones. Matthew, Mark, and Luke, for example, all insist that the Last Supper took place on Passover and Jesus' trial and crucifixion on the following day; but this chronology presents us with an apparently insuperable challenge, for to many scholars it is all but unimaginable that the Jews in Jerusalem would have interrupted their most holy religious observance in order to conduct a trial. The Gospel of John, on the other hand, tells us that the trial and crucifixion took place sometime "before the festival of Passover," but omits from the narrative any mention of a special meal.[1] John also goes quite out of his way ("This is the evidence of one who saw it—true evidence, and he knows that what he says is true—and he gives it so that you may believe as well") to insist that the Romans never broke Jesus' legs while he hung on the cross (a technique used to quicken the victim's death), when in fact no one we know of ever claimed that they had done so. Quirks and contradictions like this hardly negate the Gospels' value as historical sources, but they do complicate matters considerably.

The remaining books of the New Testament consist of the Acts of the Apostles (written, according to tradition, by Luke), which tells of the actions taken by Jesus' followers in the years immediately after his death; the letters of Paul—an early persecutor of the Christians who, after a dramatic conversion, became one of their greatest leaders—to several of the earliest Christian communities in the eastern Mediterranean; several other brief letters attributed to the apostles James, Peter, John, and Jude; and the highly symbolic poetic vision of Christ's return on Judgment Day called the Apocalypse or the Book of Revelations, which purports to record a mystical experience granted to the apostle John. None of these writings is contemporary with Jesus himself. They were written between thirty and sixty years after his death. Several other non-canonical texts survive, such as the so-called Gnostic Gospels discovered in 1945 at Nag Hammadi in Upper Egypt and the Dead Sea Scrolls found in 1947 at Qumran. But apart from these, little survives to tell us about the expansion of Christian belief in the Pax Romana period. Archeology provides a few clues, and so do some incidental remarks in writers like Tacitus and Josephus. Occasional letters and other writings by Christian leaders like St. Irenaeus and apologists like Tertullian and Origen provide evidence of the development of Christian doctrine but say little about the faith's growth within Roman society. Not until Constantine's conversion in 312 does substantial information begin to survive to tell us about the gradual Christianization of the West.

This revolution was arguably the slowest in Western history. From our modern vantage point, the ultimate success of Christianity might seem an historical inevitability, but in fact the spread of the new faith was extraordinarily slow and uncertain. Its progress was continually hampered by persecution, internal division,

---

1. Compare the versions in Matthew ch. 26, Mark ch. 14, Luke ch. 22, and John ch. 13.

intellectual skepticism, the resilient attraction of paganism, the rival appeal of Judaism, and the proliferation of heresy. Even after three hundred years of fervent preaching, prayer, writing, acts of charity, and the reported performance of countless miracles, Christians made up no more than 5 percent of the Roman population by the time of Constantine's conversion, and probably even less than that; some scholars have suggested a figure as low as less than 1 percent. Not until many centuries later was the western world fully Christianized. We need to consider this slow Christian revolution in two contexts: that of the Jewish world out of which it came and that of the pagan world into which it blossomed.

BEFORE CHRIST

The idea of a *messiah*—that is, a divinely appointed savior who would deliver the Jews from oppression and lead them into a glorious new age of freedom and fulfillment—has roots in Judaism that reach back as far as Moses. Usually emerging in times of political turmoil, the belief in a heaven-sent rescuer recurred thoughout Jewish history, and with each new occurrence the role of the messiah took on larger proportions. Moses was prophesied to lead the Jews to a promised land where they might live freely; the prophecies of Nathan, some eight hundred years later, foretold the arrival of the messianic King David and promised that under his rule the Jews would attain "fame as great as the fame of the greatest on the earth." Many of the Psalms proclaimed that the messiah's sovereignty would be worldwide. Whatever the extent of his authority, though, the messiah's mission was clearly viewed as an *earthly* mission, one designed to win for the Jews security and prosperity in this life, rather than spiritual rewards in a life hereafter.

The nature of belief in the messiah changed somewhat over the course of the last two centuries before Jesus' birth, until it became explicitly apocalyptic. Persecution of the Jews by the Seleucids ended with the Maccabaean revolt in 142 B.C., but the Jews enjoyed only a brief period of freedom because Roman armies conquered Judaea in 63 B.C. and added the region to the empire. Frustration at this subjugation naturally led many Jews to question why the righteous continued to suffer—and an increasingly popular answer, encouraged by a variety of eastern religious influences, was that the world was ruled by the forces of evil. Evil ensnared God's people, and their suffering resulted not just from external persecution but from intrinsic internal flaws—in other words, from *sin*. New emphasis was placed on sinfulness as the fundamental human condition and the cause of Jewish suffering. This shift naturally led to a changed role for the anticipated messiah: He, when he came, would save the Jews not just from political oppression but from the state of sin itself. For some Jews, the messiah, in other words, would not merely reform the world—he would end it and release his people from the bonds of mortality. Such ideas were not unique to Judaism at this time. The whole region of the eastern Mediterranean in the last two centuries before Jesus, and in the first century after him, was ablaze with religious speculation and innovation, and many new so-called mystery religions arose at this time that offered their followers just this type of an apocalyptic vision of salvation.

Within Judaea itself, several religious and political factions rivalled one another. The *Sadducees*, a small group composed chiefly of wealthy landowners and the hereditary priest-caste, were the most forthright in dismissing all apocalyptic belief as a perversion of traditional Judaism, and were the most outspoken supporters of the Roman-controlled puppet-kings. Aligned with them but more middle-class in origin were the *Pharisees*, who likewise championed strict adherence to Jewish Law and ritual, although they differed from the Sadducees by placing greater emphasis on the oral law passed on by the rabbis than on the ceremonies of the Temple cult.[2] These were by far the most traditional parties, and their passive conservatism earned them considerable scorn by the writers of the Gospels. (The Talmud has some harsh things to say about them as well.) A group known as the *Zealots* advocated direct political and violent action to overthrow the Roman state, but seem not to have held any particular spiritual platform. The *Essenes*, by contrast, promoted an intensely personal spiritual reform that focused on the ideas of repentence, meditation, and ultimate union with the divine. This was the group that best characterized the rising apocalyptic ideas of the age.

Jesus' teachings as recorded in the Gospels have more in common with the Essenes than with any other Jewish faction. Little is known of Jesus' early life, but at age thirty he began to travel throughout Judaea preaching the imminent approach of the "kingdom of God," and he enjoined his followers to prepare for that kingdom by repenting their sins and extending charity and forgiveness to all:

> *Blessed are the merciful—*
> *they shall have mercy shown them.*
> *Blessed are the pure in heart—*
> *they shall see God.*
> *Blessed are the peacemakers—*
> *they shall be recognized as children of God.*
> *Blessed are those who are persecuted in the cause of uprightness—*
> *the kingdom of Heaven is theirs.* [Matthew 5:7–10]

The approach of God's kingdom necessitated a complete surrendering of oneself to God—exemplified in the increasingly popular practice of baptism—and a rejection of this world. Jesus professed respect for traditional Jewish ritual but accused groups like the Pharisees and Sadducees of empty religious formalism, a mere "going through the motions" instead of the total giving up of oneself to the Lord that Jesus demanded:

---

2. Some of the Pharisees also accepted the radical notion of an afterlife and the bodily resurrection of the pious, although this was a minority view. The most prominent figure among the Pharisees was the great Babylonian scholar Hillel (ca. 30 B.C.–A.D. 10) whose commentaries on the Law formed the core of what later developed into the *Talmud*, the chief legal text of medieval Jews.

> But when the Pharisees heard that [Jesus] had silenced the Sadducees they got together and, to put him to the test, one of them put a further question [to him], "Master, which is the greatest commandment of the Law?" Jesus said to him, " 'You must love the Lord your God with all your heart, with all your soul, and with all your mind.' This is the greatest and the first commandment. The second resembles it: 'You must love your neighbour as yourself.' On these two commandments hang the whole Law, and the Prophets too." [Matthew 22:34–40]

Jesus' emphasis on "loving your neighbor" implied more than a desire to have everyone get along together; it aimed to tear down the ethnic, class, and gender distinctions that characterized his time. He eschewed the practices of the Temple elders and directed his message at groups who were marginalized from mainstream Jewish life: Galileans and Samaritans (both regarded as inferior rustics), prostitutes and adulteresses, and the laboring poor made up his first followers. Unlike other charismatic figures of the time, Jesus welcomed women into his following and did not require them to abide in the shadows; nor did he limit his ministry to Jews, but reached out to Gentiles (all non-Jews) as well. In arguing that everyone is equal in God's sight and is therefore equally deserving of love and kindness, Jesus seemed to deny the particularity of the Jewish covenant with God, which understandably provoked the ire of the Jewish leaders in Jerusalem. Those leaders also took offense at Jesus' irregular observance of Jewish ritual, his assertion of his power to forgive sins, which they viewed as an usurpation of God's unique authority, and his followers' proclamation that he was in fact the messiah. Ultimately, according to the Gospel writers, the Temple elders tried him for blasphemy and handed him over to the Roman officials for punishment. The Romans, for their part, were just as anxious to get rid of the troublemaker as the Jews were. Jesus' claim of the title "King of the Jews" had the whiff of treason in it and justified the sentence of crucifixion that he received.

After Jesus' execution his body was placed in a tomb, at the entrance to which a large boulder was placed and a Roman sentry stationed in order to prevent any one from interfering with the burial. Three days later, however, his followers—who were in hiding, since the Romans were still on the lookout for them—claimed to have seen him alive, risen from the dead. More than that, they later said that he came to them in their hiding place and spent forty days with them, giving them encouragement and urging them to preach his message throughout the world, after which he miraculously ascended into heaven. Whatever one may believe about the story of the resurrection, it is clear that *something* extraordinary happened to his followers to transform them from a small group of cowering outcasts who literally feared for their lives, to a suddenly emboldened corps of witnesses who marched into public and loudly proclaimed his message, being willing to face persecution and death for his sake. What that something was, however, we cannot objectively say.

THE GROWTH OF THE NEW RELIGION

From its Jewish origins, Christianity spread out into the polytheistic pagan world. The Romans maintained an official cult—the familiar deities of Mount Olympus, plus the worship of the emperor as the chief priest of the Olympians and as a minor deity himself—but in general they tolerated the religions of all the peoples in the empire, so long as followers were willing to recognize the official cult on certain significant public holidays. For most of the inhabitants of the empire, this practice presented no problem. Polytheistic religions generally accommodate one another rather easily: If one believes that there are a multiplicity of gods, each presiding over various places, practices, or natural phenomena, the idea of adding new gods to the list whenever one encounters a new place, practice, or phenomenon requires no great mental effort and poses no fundamental challenge to the gods already worshiped. The Roman state religion was itself the product of accommodation, a grafting of the Greek gods and goddesses (Zeus, Hera, Aphrodite, Hephaestus, Ares, and the rest) onto the older and more intimate Roman tradition of worshiping household deities and local nature-gods. The deities of the Greek pantheon acquired Roman identities—thus Zeus became known as Jupiter, Hera as Juno, Aphrodite as Venus, Hephaestus as Vulcan, Ares as Mars, and so on—and a few new traits, but otherwise they underwent no profound changes. The priests who led public worship of the state gods were not, as in Christianity, a separate celibate caste, but were instead drawn from the families of honestiores who held the civil magistracies. Like the government officers, priests served finite terms and were motivated as much by a sense of civil service as by piety. Priesthood in the state cult was a stage in one's public career, not a spiritual calling.

The nature of priesthood does not mean that the Romans did not take their religion seriously. To them, divine figures and forces governed every aspect of life, and one ignored them at one's peril. This animism characterizes the more intimate aspect of their religion. Every Roman familia, they believed, had its own protective domestic spirits, called *Lares*, who watched over its prosperity and controlled its fate. Propitiating these deities with prayers and rituals was an everyday concern that generally followed precise and rigorous formulas—any stumbling over the words or fumbling with the rites rendered the ceremonies useless and they would have to be repeated. Similarly, Roman animism held that powerful nature spirits inhabited the surrounding streams, trees, groves, springs, and fields; wherever there was life, they assumed a spirit to be, and consequently they sought to ensure the fertility of their fields, the flowering of their trees, and the abundance of their waters by offering prayers and sacrifices to the spirits within. Once again, strict observance of custom was the rule; failure to do so vitiated the value of one's offerings and threatened the basic supports of life. It is important to bear in mind that the Romans found their religion comforting rather than constricting and terrifying; much of its emotional appeal lay precisely in the deep satisfaction of performing meaningful rites well. Traditional paganism offered an explanation for both the negative and the positive workings of the world. Nothing happened without a reason.

But the civil wars at the close of the Republican period challenged this status quo. The spectacle of consuls, senators, and generals contending savagely with one another, of armies sweeping through the Mediterranean, of Parthian and Germanic hordes pressing upon the borders, of rebellions in Judaea, of slave revolts and their bloody aftermaths, and of economic decay made it hard for many people to continue believing that human life followed a predictable or understandable course. Either the gods had abandoned them, many felt, or they had turned against them. To fill the growing spiritual void, many people in the first century B.C. and the first century A.D. began to seek fulfillment and rescue in new varieties of paganism. These new cults were not altogether incompatible with the state religion, and hence were generally not subject to persecution, but they differed from the official cult and traditional animism in several fundamental ways.

These new cults are known as the *mystery religions*. The name derives from the fact that they rested on a belief in a number of sacred and eternal mysteries that initiates could approach via a new kind of sacramental priesthood. These new priests possessed spiritual power, not just ritual responsibilities, and having been granted unique access to the eternal mysteries by the gods, they alone could pass on the means to an otherworldly salvation. Hence the central nature of these new cults differed radically from traditional religions in that they focused less on explaining the events and actions of mortal life on earth, and more on preparing a way for humans to enter the real life that exists outside the bonds of earthly existence. They offered consolation, love, and eternal rewards rather than a mechanical view of the workings of the world, and they inspired love in their faithful rather than awe. One such cult, for example, centered on the worship of Isis—the Egyptian "Goddess of Ten Thousand Names"—along with her husband Osiris and their son Horus. In this cult the deities did not merely govern the world: They loved the humans who lived in it and desired their happiness. Isis exhorted her followers to chastity outside of marriage, fidelity within it, and kindness and charity to all. Her cult was open to all, but we know that it appealed particularly to the women of the central and eastern Mediterranean. The liturgies conducted by the priests of Isis commemorated a miraculous and salvific event: the finding of Osiris in the underworld by the mourning Isis after his death. The return of these gods from the place of the dead represented the resurrection from death they promised to all of their followers who lead upright lives. Another popular new cult worshiped the Persian god Mithras. Representing the powers of Light and Truth, Mithras also loved his devotees and promised them eternal salvation, a promise he could keep since he himself had been resurrected three days after his own death. His followers (a group open only to men) believed that Mithras' power derived from his capturing and killing of a sacred bull whose body and blood represented the source of life. Consequently, the mysterious initiation at the center of Mithraic ritual was bull-sacrifice. Initiates were baptized in the blood, and the regular worship ceremonies involved a sacramental meal in which believers received some aspect of the godhead's blessing and promise. Baptism and obedience to the moral teachings of the god entitled followers to salvation.

Christianity was one of these mystery religions, and it is easy to see the elements it shared with them. It offered solace from the sufferings of life and the promise of eternal joy. It was led by a sacramental priesthood that initiated believers into the faith via baptism and strengthened them in their faith with a holy meal of bread and wine, which Christians, commemorating the Last Supper episode of the first three Gospels, understood to be the body and blood of the resurrected Christ. Christianity emphasized the love that God has for all people, and it exhorted believers to moral reform based on the ideals of love and charity. The point of this is not to say that Christianity cynically borrowed or stole its central ideas from other faiths and therefore represents a man-made patchwork religion, but rather to show that belief in Jesus' divinity and his priesthood arose in a social and spiritual atmosphere that was amenable to such beliefs. Christianity, in other words, fitted into the eastern Mediterranean scene much like a key fits into a lock. And it was this fit that made it possible for the faith to start its slow rise.

Many factors contributed to that rise. First was the zealous preaching, organizing, and, according to Scripture, the miracle-working of the *apostles* (the word derives from the Greek term for "messenger"). These men—and the New Testament records that Jesus granted this special status only to certain of his male followers— were the recognized leaders of the tiny Christian community, and they possessed a unique authority that Jesus gave to them when he first appeared after his resurrection:

> In the evening of that same day, the first day of the week, the doors were closed in the room where the disciples were, for fear of the Jews. Jesus came and stood among them. He said to them, "Peace be with you." . . . The disciples were filled with joy at seeing the Lord, and he said to them again, "Peace be with you. As the Father sent me, so am I sending you." After saying this he breathed on them and said, "Receive the Holy Spirit. If you forgive anyone's sins, they are forgiven; if you retain anyone's sins, they are retained." [John 20:19–23]

By granting them the power to forgive sins or condemn them, Jesus singled these figures out as a special caste—a priesthood in the mold of the other mystery religions. The miraculous power given to them was then shown in the Acts of the Apostles, which narrates those individuals' sudden ability to perform miraculous healings, speak in tongues, cast out demons, and raise the dead. Commanded by Jesus to preach and baptize in his name, the apostles, under the leadership of Peter, began to organize the first Christian community in Jerusalem. At first, they preached only to other Jews and continued to follow Jewish Law and traditions. Under the influence of an extraordinary new convert, though, the early church began to aim at a wider audience.

This new convert was Paul of Tarsus. Paul was a Hellenized Jew from southern Anatolia, a Roman citizen, and prior to his conversion a dedicated Pharisee

with the name of Saul. He had spent several years harassing, beating, and impris-
oning Christians as rebels against Jewish tradition; in fact, he probably took part
in the stoning to death of Stephen, the first Christian martyr. But around the year
A.D. 36 he experienced a dramatic conversion while traveling to Damascus armed
with arrest warrants for the Christians residing there. All of a sudden, as he described it:

> I saw a light from heaven shining more brilliantly than the sun round me and
> my fellow-travellers. We all fell to the ground, and I heard a voice saying to me
> in Hebrew, "Saul, Saul, why are you persecuting me?" Then I said, "Who
> are you, Lord?" And the Lord answered, "I am Jesus, whom you are persecut-
> ing." [Acts 26:13–15]

The experience changed his life—as signified by the new name he adopted—and
it also changed Christianity itself. Until this point the apostles had aimed their
message only at the Jews of Palestine and Syria, and they still regarded themselves as Jewish. Their preaching emphasized the events of Jesus' life and his eth-
ical teachings. Converts continued to obey Jewish dietary restrictions, to undergo
circumcision, and to observe the Sabbath. But Paul sought to universalize the
Christian message. His preaching and writings stressed the significance of Jesus'
death and resurrection, not his life. While continuing to embrace the Jewish moral
tradition, he taught that Jesus, not the Jewish Law, was the only path to salvation.
Paul's Jesus possessed the apocalyptic character of the divine rescuers found in
other mystery religions of the age: More than any other early Christian, Paul insisted that Jesus *was* God, not just a heavenly chosen or divinely inspired messianic figure, and that his victory over death rescued all people, whether Jewish or
not, from sinfulness. This had to be so, since sinfulness was innate in all human
nature.

Given his universalist outlook, Paul considerably expanded the Christian campaign to preach and convert. He crisscrossed through Palestine, Asia Minor, Greece,
and Italy, establishing Christian communities wherever he went while elucidating
his ideas on everything from predestination to sexuality in a series of remarkable
letters that provided the basis for the New Testament. By the time of his death in
A.D. 67 (tradition has it that he died in Rome during Nero's persecution, along with
the apostle Peter), dozens of Christian communities existed in the eastern Mediterranean. No other figure in early Christian history did so much to increase the size of
the church, to develop its doctrine, or to establish a clear distinction between Christianity and its Jewish origins. The implications of Paul's activities, as we shall see,
were enormous.

As Paul broadened the scope of Christian appeal, other forces were besetting
Judaism. The Jewish revolt against Rome in A.D. 70 resulted in the destruction of the
Temple in Jerusalem and the decimation of the Jewish community there. Most of the
remaining Palestinian Jews rallied to the conservatism of the Pharisees, and thereby
underscored their differences with the growing number of Christians. Many others,

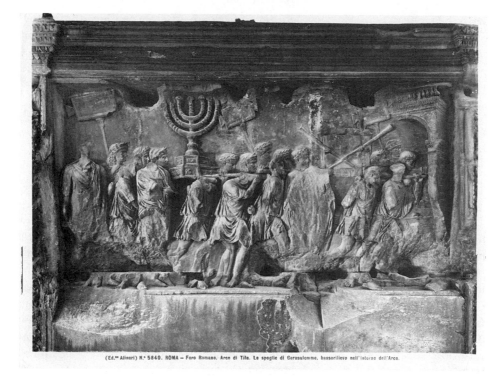

(Ed.ⁿⁱ Alinari) N.° 5840. ROMA — Foro Romano. Arco di Tito. Le spoglie di Gerusalemme, bassorilievo nell'interno dell'Arco.

This shows the victorious Romans carting off the goods from the Temple
at Jerusalem, which they destroyed after quelling the Jewish Revolt.
This marks the beginning of the Jewish diaspora and catalyzed the development
of rabbinic Judaism. Source: Alinari / Art Resource, NY

though, converted to Christianity until the problem of conversion became so bad
that in A.D. 85 the synagogue liturgy placed a formal anathema on Christian preachers. The next wave of Jewish rebellions throughout the Mediterranean in 115 and
the second revolt in Judaea in 132–135 further stigmatized the Jews as troublemakers
in the Pax Romana, and increased Christians' desire to disassociate themselves from
their religious ancestors. This desire accounts for much of the occasionally harsh
anti-Jewish sentiment expressed in the New Testament. Most historians of anti-
Semitism, in fact, trace the roots of that phenomenon precisely to this development
in early Christianity—the desire to define itself in terms of being explicitly *not Jewish*. Anti-Semitic prejudice dates back even farther into the past, of course, but there
is no doubt that the effort by the Christians and Jews of the first two centuries A.D.
to disassociate themselves from each other established a painful tradition of distrust
and hostility between the two faiths that would carry on throughout the entire medieval period, and beyond.

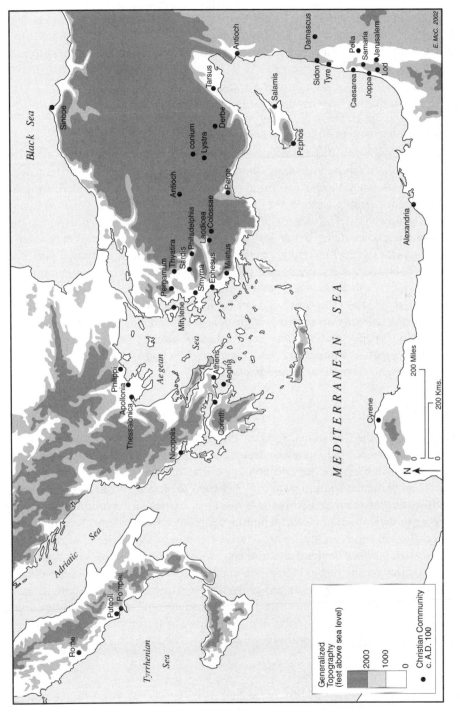

The spread of Christianity

Much of Christianity's appeal lay in its egalitarianism. Since most early Christians believed that Jesus' Second Coming was imminent, they felt no need to bother with political and social distinctions, and taught the essential dignity and worthiness before God of all believers regardless of their social status, ethnic background, or sex. As Paul put it:

> For all of you are the children of God, through faith, in Christ Jesus, since every one of you that has been baptised has been clothed in Christ. There can be neither Jew nor Greek, there can be neither slave nor freeman, there can be neither male nor female—for all of you are one in Christ Jesus. [Galatians 3:26–28]

But an egalitarian spirit did not necessarily mean that everyone would play equal roles in the church's day-to-day life. The existence of a separate sacramental priesthood alone was enough to put an end to that idea. Women were excluded from the priesthood, for example, since it was assumed that Jesus intended such exclusion when he bestowed the Holy Spirit only on that first group of men mentioned before. Women, who made up the majority of early Christians, did serve in other important capacities as the faith slowly grew. Each Christian community was presided over by a *bishop* (Greek *episkopos*, and Latin *episcopus*—from which comes the English word *episcopal*) who was regarded as a direct spiritual successor to the original apostles. Assisting the bishop was a corps of priests and deacons. Priests, as sacramental figures, led worship services, while deacons administered the communities' charities and tended to the churches' material possessions.[3] The tight organizational structure of these communities made it possible for them to wage effective campaigns of preaching, conversion, and baptism.

THE PROBLEM OF PERSECUTION

But as the zeal of the Christians won converts, it also secured for them the hostility of the Roman state. Christians sorely tested the empire's general policy of religious tolerance. The problem had little to do with Christian beliefs about Jesus' divinity; rather, it was the stubborn refusal of the Christians to recognize that any other gods existed—including the living emperor himself—or to make the symbolic gesture of sacrificing to the state cult on official holidays. Christians held themselves aloof, denounced the state gods as idols, and refused to serve in the imperial army. To the Romans, such a stance undermined the very spirit that the empire was based on: recognition that one belonged to a larger, organic social fabric, and the centrality of civic-mindedness to the creation and protection of that fabric. The Christians' tendency to practice their rituals in private—usually in individual homes or workplaces—also contrasted with the public nature of pagan practices and added to an atmosphere of suspicion about what the new believers were up to. Rumors

---

3. Women frequently served as deacons in the early Church; see St. Paul's commendation of "Phoebe, a deacon of the church at Cenchreae, so that you may welcome her in the Lord . . . for she has been a benefactor of many and of myself as well." [Romans 16:1–2]

flew about that the secretive Christians indulged in sexual orgies, practiced cannibalism and ritual torture, and engaged in incest. The fact that many Christian communities held property in common raised fears that they might seek to abolish private property and the social and legal distinctions it established in the Roman world.

So it was that the Romans began to persecute them. The first great purge took place in A.D. 64 in Rome itself, in the aftermath of a great fire that destroyed nearly three-fourths of the city. A Christian community had only recently been established in the city, and they made an easy scapegoat for the tragedy. As Tacitus described it:

> Nero laid the blame on a group known to the people as "Christians" and who are hated for the abominable things they do, and he inflicted the most extraordinary tortures on them. . . . An immense number of them were arrested and convicted, less so for having set fire to the city than for their general hatred of mankind. Every imaginable mockery attended their deaths. Some were covered with animal hides and were torn apart by wild dogs [in the amphitheater]; others were crucified; still others were covered with pitch and set ablaze, and were used as living torches at [Nero's] night-time games.

Nero's suppression of the Christians continued until his own death in 68. No formal campaigns against them occurred throughout the second century—the high point of the Pax Romana—although numerous popular attacks took place, to which imperial officials usually turned a blind eye. The emperor Septimius Severus began the anti-Christian campaign anew in 193 when he issued edicts to all the provincial governors to imprison and execute the Christians in their territories and to destroy their churches and writings. The short-lived emperor Maximin enacted similar measures; Decius, who ruled from 249 to 251, attempted to stamp out the faith by torturing Christians until they apostatized, rather than kill them outright. But the bloodiest and most comprehensive persecution took place in the reign of Diocletian (284–305) in which tens of thousands were beaten, branded, decapitated, drowned, hanged, crucified, and fed to beasts in Roman amphitheaters.

The result of these actions, though, was the opposite of what the Romans had intended. Large numbers of Christians did renounce their views under duress, but many more accepted martyrdom willingly. They viewed their deaths, after all, as merely the start of newer and better lives in which they would be reunited with Christ. We see an example of this in the prison memoir written by Vibia Perpetua (also known as St. Perpetua) as she awaited execution in Carthage in 203. This memoir is the earliest surviving account written by a Christian woman, and it provided a model for the genre of *saints' lives* that proved so enduringly popular in the Middle Ages.

> A few days later word went around that we [i.e., the Christians imprisoned with her] were going to be put on trial, so my father, who was worn out with exhaustion, came from the city to see us again, hoping to persuade me to renounce my faith [and sacrifice to the emperor]. . . . I was sorry for him because he alone, out of all my family, could not rejoice at my martyrdom. I comforted

him and said, "Whatever happens at my trial is according to God's will. He, not we, has control of our lives." But he went away very sad indeed. A day or two later we were just beginning our dinner when we were suddenly summoned to trial. We came to the forum . . . where a very large crowd soon gathered. We appeared before the tribunal. My companions were questioned first, and they confessed [to being Christians and refusing to sacrifice to the emperor]. Then it was my turn. My father suddenly appeared again, carrying my [infant] son in his arms. He drew me aside and said, "Have mercy on your child! Perform the emperor's sacrifice!" And Hilarian, the judge, likewise appealed to me . . . saying, "Will you not take pity on your father's great age, or on your son's great youth?" . . . I simply answered, "I am a Christian." . . . Then Hilarian passed judgment on us all and sentenced us to be thrown to the beasts. Cheerfully we returned to our prison cell.

The more the Romans persecuted such people, the stronger grew their commitment. No doubt many who witnessed such behavior were puzzled at the Christians' willingness to die and thought it ridiculous. But to others it appeared as a kind of rare bravery and made them wonder if there was something to the faith after all. People certainly did not flock to the new religion in large numbers, but those who did accept Christianity did so with a resolve that made the movement impossible to stamp out. As Justin Martyr (d. 165)—whose name tells his story— coolly warned the soldiers about to execute him: "You can kill us, but you can't hurt us."

THE PROBLEM OF HERESY

In some ways, heresy posed a greater threat than persecution did. The word derives from the Greek term *hairesis*, meaning "choice," and it refers to the choices that Christian believers had to make between contending and occasionally contradictory ideas put forth by their bishops on matters of doctrine. It happened like this. While the basic ideas of Christianity—love of God, love for one another, Jesus as messiah—were easy enough to absorb, other aspects of the faith required some kind of explanation before they could be embraced. For example, Jesus exhorted his apostles to baptize people "in the name of the Father, the Son, and the Holy Spirit" while asserting at the same time that he himself shared in God's divinity [John 14:9–11]; and in creating the sacramental priesthood after his resurrection, he bestowed the Holy Spirit upon them through his own breath, thereby implying that he was the Spirit as well. So are there three gods? How can one god be three things at the same time? Or how could Jesus himself have been entirely divine and entirely human at the same time? As Christianity spread throughout the eastern Mediterranean, among an educated urban populace, people demanded some sort of rational explanation of these mysteries that could satisfy their minds as much as the basic appeal of the faith satisfied their hearts. In other words, the religion needed to develop a *theology*—that is, a system of rational thought that elucidates religious mysteries.

But how and by whom is a theology authorized? Responsibility for doctrine lay with the bishops, but what if the bishops disagreed with one another? Communication between the early Christian communities was sporadic to say the least, and left each group in the position of having to resolve its own difficulties as they arose. Fracturing of the Christian message was inevitable under the circumstances, and no universally recognized mechanism existed for clearing up the confusion. Christian ideas and practices differed quite widely from community to community. The situation had become so confusing by the third century that it is more accurate to think not of *Christianity* at all, but rather of many little *christianities*. Relations between these contending visions of the faith were very strained and occasionally violent. The neo-pagan emperor Julian (d. 363) even declared that wild beasts were kinder to one another than were Christians who disagreed over theological issues. While Julian's comment needs to be taken with a grain of salt, one can see what he meant by looking at the conflict over one of those disputes—a bitter disagreement among North African Christians over the efficacy of sacraments performed by so-called unworthy priests. Many Christians had apostasized during the Roman persecutions, denouncing Christ, surrendering biblical books to be burnt and other Christians to be imprisoned, and proclaiming allegiance to the state gods. Such failures had generated harsh feelings among the betrayed, but afterward most communities had tried to recognize that frightened and tortured individuals deserve forgiveness. Traitors who later wished to be restored to the faith, so long as they repented their actions and recommitted themselves to Christ, had generally been welcomed back into their communities. But what about priests or bishops who had surrendered? If they wished to return, could they? And were they still priests, with the power to perform the sacraments? Many Christians took a very hard-line stance with these figures, and argued that when a priest openly repudiated Christ he lost absolutely and forever that spiritual authority conferred upon him by his ordination. If such a priest baptized another individual, for example, then that individual was not actually baptized; after all a priest cannot pass on to someone else, they maintained, the divine grace that he himself no longer possesses. From there it was a short route to the general conclusion that the moral worthiness of a priest determines the efficacy of the sacraments he performs. This rigorous stance came to be known as *Donatism*—named for Donatus (d. 355), a North African bishop who had led the cause. Conflicts between Donatist and non-Donatist Christians were constant and bitter. The Donatists regarded themselves as the church of the martyrs, those who had faced persecution and never faltered; the others, to them, were contemptible weaklings. To those weaklings, the Donatists were haughty and stiff-necked belligerents who did not understand the first thing about mercy and forgiveness. Each denounced the other, they hurled anathemas at and pronounced excommunications upon each other, and they frequently came to blows. The strife continued for four centuries, until Muslim armies conquered the region and wiped out or subsumed both communities.

By far the most widespread heresy, though, was *Arianism*—named after its founder Arius, an Alexandrian priest and theologian. Trying to understand the knotty problem of the Trinity (that is, the Christian belief that God is comprised of three separate "Persons"—the Father, the Son, and the Holy Spirit), Arius concluded that just as human sons do not exist until their fathers beget them, so too did Jesus not exist until his earthly birth and that, therefore, it is incorrect to believe that he shares fully in the divinity of God the Father. Jesus was not God, Arius taught, but neither was he an ordinary human; Arians believed that Jesus occupied a halfway position between God and man. While Arianism thus demoted Jesus, in one sense, it nevertheless had the advantage, to many, of being rationally satisfying; consequently its version of Christianity gained many followers in the east, including a number of influential bishops. And as we shall see in the next chapter, Arianism competed with Nicene Christianity for two centuries as the dominant version of Christianity in western Europe, after it was adopted by many of the Germanic nations who poured into the collapsed western half of the Roman Empire in the fourth and fifth centuries.

CONSTANTINE AND THEODOSIUS: AN IMPERIAL CHURCH

The conversion of Constantine put Christianity on a new path. It is worthwhile to review what we said about his conversion in the previous chapter. Believing he had done all he could to reform the empire, Diocletian resigned from the imperial office in 305 and forced his coemperor Maximian to do the same. He assumed that the resignations would allow the peaceful transition of power that he had arranged for in his constitutional reforms, but he was immediately proved wrong. At least a half-dozen rivals instantly challenged one another for the throne and began to marshal their respective armies. After six years of civil war only two contenders remained: Constantine and Maxentius. Their armies met at the Milvian Bridge outside of Rome in 312. According to a biography of Constantine by his friend Eusebius of Caesarea, Constantine, who was already familiar with Christianity through the conversion of several family members but who still observed the pagan gods and rituals, had a miraculous vision the day before the battle started.

> A most extraordinary sign suddenly appeared to him out of the heavens—a thing that would be hard to believe, were it not for the fact that Constantine himself attested to it. . . . Around noon, when the sun was just starting its descent, he suddenly saw before his eyes a vision, a Cross made up of light, situated just above the sun and bearing an inscription that said "Use this, and conquer." . . . He thought about the meaning of this until night came. Then Christ Himself, the Lord, appeared to Constantine in a dream and extended to him the same sign that he had seen in the daytime sky, and commanded him to make a likeness of it and to use it as a shield in battle.

The following morning Constantine ordered the Christian symbol to be drawn on his soldiers' shields. His army won the battle, and Constantine converted to Christianity (although he was not baptized, as was common then, until just before his death many years later). He then marched into Rome and assumed the throne. His reign lasted from 312 to 337.

Whether or not this conversion occurred precisely as Eusebius described it, it seems clear that Constantine's conversion was genuine. Given the fact that Christians by 312 still made up only a tiny percentage of the population, it is hard to see what strategic value there was in such a move, even if that percentage was increasingly made up of members of the aristocracy. The senatorial class, the civil service, and above all the army were still overwhelmingly, if not intractably, pagan, and it makes little sense to think that Constantine would have risked alienating these people for the sake of a much-maligned new religion that he was not sincerely devoted to. Some have suggested that the tight organizational structure of the church might have been the attraction—an antidote to the decaying municipal institutions around the Mediterranean—but Christian bishops and deacons knew little about running courts of law, maintaining roads and aqueducts, or regulating marketplaces. Constantine's faith may well have evolved over the remaining years of his life, but it seems certain that, whatever happened at the Milvian Bridge, he made a genuine commitment to Christianity in 312.

As soon as he was in control of the government, Constantine issued the *Edict of Milan* (313), which rescinded the persecution of Christians and granted the faith, its followers, and its priests equal status with the recognized pagan cults.[4] This recognition obviously put an end to the killing of Christians and allowed them to emerge from hiding, but Constantine was determined to do more. He gave bishops civil authority over the Christian communities in each Roman city. He exempted Christian churches from taxation, relieved all clergy of the obligation to perform military service, paid reparations to Christian communities for the damages caused by the persecutions, and opened the imperial treasury to build hundreds of new churches, to provide them with books and vestments, to educate Christian priests, and to organize missionary campaigns throughout the empire. In order to house the large Christian communities in Rome and to encourage pilgrimages, Constantine built the great basilicas of St. John Lateran and St. Peter's at Rome, plus the Church of the Nativity at Bethlehem and the Church of the Resurrection (later known as the Holy Sepulchre) at Jerusalem. What all of this meant for Christianity was not just a new lease on life but an extraordinarily rapid growth. By the time of Constantine's death

---

4. The key passage in the *Edict* runs as follows: "Out of the conviction that freedom of worship should never be denied to anyone, and that everyone should be granted the right to adhere to the religion that best suits his desires, and to do so to the degree that he wishes . . . we grant to Christians and to all the people [of the empire] unlimited right to follow the religious devotions they desire; and we grant this in the hope that whatever Divinity there might be in heaven will be favorably disposed and inclined towards us and all those under our authority."

in 337, Christians made up as much as 50 percent of the urban population in western Anatolia, in Dalmatia and Illyria, in Roman Syria and upper Mesopotamia, and along stretches of North Africa. No figure since Paul of Tarsus had done so much for the expansion of the religion. At the same time, though, Constantine continued to treat pagans respectfully and even allowed them to continue worshiping him as a pagan god.

Partially in order to disassociate imperial power even further from paganism, Constantine moved the capital of the empire from Rome (the symbolic home of classical paganism) to Byzantium. There on the long spit of land between the Black Sea and the Mediterranean he built his massive new capital city, which quickly came to be known as Constantinople (modern-day Istanbul). His reasons were not purely or even primarily religious. It had become clear throughout the trials of the third century that the western half of the empire was considerably weaker than the eastern half. It lacked the urban development, the commercial wealth, and the educational sophistication of the east, and it faced more fully the threat of Germanic invasion. In making this move, Constantine was hardly surrendering the west to the advancing Germans, but he made it clear where his priorities lay. From this new city he began to work in earnest to Christianize his realm, and immediately found himself embroiled in the problem of heresy—which up to this point had been kept partially under control by the persecutions that had kept all Christians, of whatever sort, in hiding. The Edict of Milan, however, rapidly brought to light the full extent of doctrinal division between Christians. Freed to speak openly and with assumed imperial support, all the different "christianities" emerged in full force and threatened to undermine the whole Christianization process.

Constantine tried to put an end to this conflict by convening a council of all Christian bishops at Nicaea (323–325). Approximately two hundred bishops or legates attended, mostly drawn from the east. Although the council intended to address all the differences among Christians, Arianism was clearly at the head of the agenda. After much debate—much of it very angry—the council approved a definitive statement of what Christian belief was: the Nicene Creed. The language was slightly revised at a subsequent council in 381, but the essentials were established at Nicaea. The creed ran:

> We believe in one God, the Father, the Almighty,
>   maker of heaven and earth, and of all that is, seen and unseen.
> We believe in one Lord, Jesus Christ, the only Son of God,
>   eternally begotten of the Father, God from God, Light from Light,
>   true God from true God, begotten—not made—
>   one in Being with the Father.
>   Through him all things were made.
>   For us men and for our salvation he came down from heaven;
>   by the power of the Holy Spirit he was born of the Virgin Mary,
>   and became man.

For our sake he was crucified under Pontius Pilate; he suffered, died, and was
     buried.
On the third day he rose again in accordance with the Scriptures;
he ascended into heaven and is seated at the right hand of the Father.
He will come again in glory to judge the living and the dead, and his kingdom
     will have no end.
We believe in the Holy Spirit, the Lord, the giver of life,
     who proceeds from the Father and the Son.
With the Father and the Son he is worshiped and glorified.
He has spoken through the prophets.
We believe in one holy catholic and apostolic Church.
     We acknowledge one baptism for the forgiveness of sins.
     We look for the resurrection of the dead and the life of the world to come.
     Amen.

The structure and content of the creed tells us much about the differences that existed between Christians. The first section dispenses with God the Father in a single sentence—little disagreement there. But the second section, on Christ, explodes with detail. Virtually each line represents a response to or judgment on a particular heresy (the passage from "eternally begotten of the Father" to "one in Being with the Father" represents the formal rejection of Arianism). Some early communities had believed that Jesus existed as a man even before his earthly birth; this idea too was done away with. Others had doubted or rejected the belief in Jesus' ascension, others in his return, still others in the eternality of his heavenly kingdom. The Holy Spirit presented difficulties too. What was its relationship to the other members of the Trinity? Did it emanate from the Father or from the Son, or both? Is it to be accorded the same veneration? If it too is co-eternal with the Father and the Son, why is it not mentioned in the Old Testament? The creed took a position on all these issues. The last section, on the Church itself, informs us of one of the most pressing controversies in religious practice for early Christians—is more than one baptism required? Many early Christians had practised infant baptism, with a second baptism following upon entry to adulthood. Other communities preached the non- or partial-resurrection of the dead (i.e., that only Christians' souls, not their bodies, would be raised up), but the creed took a stance on that as well. The text is therefore as much a register of Christian differences as it is a proclamation of Christian unity and is therefore one of our key pieces of evidence about the early history of the faith.

Most of the representatives of the defeated "christianities" recognized the authority of the council and added their names to the creed and other council proclamations, but many others—most notably Arius—did not and were determined to continue preaching their own understanding of the faith. As it happened, their condemned status in the east led them to seek new converts and supporters in the west, precisely at the same time the government in Constantinople was starting to turn its back on the western empire. This gave the Arians an important head start in evangelizing to the advancing Germans.

Constantine made Christianity first a tolerated religion, then a favored one, but he did not make it the official religion of the empire. That was the work of the emperor Theodosius (378–395). Between Constantine and Theodosius a brief effort had been made by the emperor Julian—Constantine's nephew—to breathe new life into paganism (361–363), but the Christians had advanced too far to be stopped. Julian's immediate successors began a new offensive by actually starting to take away official recognition from paganism and rescinding the privileges of pagan priests. Pagan disestablishment became complete when Theodosius came to the throne. He began by ordering the removal of the statue of the winged Roman goddess of Victory, along with the altar dedicated to her, from the Senate chamber in Rome. He had Christian teachings incorporated in civil legislation. Finally, in 391, Theodosius made Christianity the official religion of the empire, removing the last vestiges of tolerance for paganism. He closed all pagan temples, confiscated their holdings, and had the buildings reconstituted as Christian churches. Pagans were not forced to convert to Christianity, although certain pagan practices, such as divination, were condemned as high treason.

The implications of this change for Christianity were obviously enormous. The faith continued to grow at an extraordinarily rapid speed and began to take on, for the first time in its history, a large-scale and fairly cohesive institutional structure, at least in the east. But these gains came at a considerable price, for the "imperialization" of Christianity in the fourth century established a precedent that reverberated throughout the Middle Ages: that of secular control of the Church. The authority of the Council of Nicaea owed more to the fact that it was Constantine's council than it did to any other factor. Constantine himself knew this, and one of his reasons for calling the council in the first place was in order to establish his authority over the fledgling Church. Both during and after the council he referred to himself as a bishop—and in fact in later Orthodox liturgies he came to be known as the "Peer of the Apostles" or the "Thirteenth Apostle." According to contemporary accounts it was Constantine's own specific wording concerning the Arian controversy that worked its way into the Nicene Creed.[5] Later, once Theodosius made Christianity the official religion of the empire and Christian teachings had been interwoven with civil law, not only were pagans laying themselves open to charges of high treason but so were all Christian heretics. To break the law of the Church was, in no very indirect way, to break the emperor's law. In asserting imperial control of the Church, the emperors were not being merely power-hungry and megalomaniacal but were in fact following Roman tradition. Since the time of Augustus the emperor had been the chief priest, the *pontifex maximus*, of the state cult, invested with full religious authority and himself revered as

---

5. If true, this is highly ironic since Constantine himself had strong pro-Arian tendencies.

a deity. To men like Constantine and Theodosius, all that had changed was the religion over which they held sway.

Christianity's rise as an imperial cult also had significant consequences for Jews. From the fourth century onward, traditional Roman toleration of Judaism was withdrawn in favor of ever-increasing legal restrictions of Jewish activities, whether religious or secular. Decrees forbidding Jews to hold public office went hand-in-hand with decrees requiring Jewish communities to assume, collectively, the financial responsibilities of the municipal curiales who fled their positions. Laws were issued forbidding or severely restricting the decoration of synagogues or the rebuilding of older structures. The Jewish patriarch of Jerusalem was stripped of his right to be addressed as "Your Excellency." Converts to Judaism suffered the confiscation of all their goods and relinquished the right to draft wills. Imperial law identified Christian marriage to a Jew as a form of adultery, subject to its penalties. Few of these new laws arose from any political or constitutional necessity; instead, they all reflect the hardening attitudes that accompanied—for many people, at least—the imperialization of the Christian faith.

RESPONSES TO IMPERIALIZATION

Not all Christians, and especially not all Christian clergy, were comfortable with the growing state control of the Church in the fourth and fifth centuries, and this discontent set the stage for a number of dramatic confrontations between political and ecclesiastical authorities. These confrontations had important implications because they foreshadowed, and for some people established a kind of legal precedent for, the violent Church-State clashes of the eleventh and twelfth centuries. Since Christian bishops were regarded as the direct heirs of the spiritual authority of the original twelve apostles, they were not inclined to accept imperial control lightly; this was especially so in the western half of the empire, where the influence of the Constantinople-based emperors was on the wane. As early as Theodosius' establishment of Christianity as the official state religion, strong voices rose up to limit the emperor's power and to assert that the State was in fact subject to the authority of the Church, at least in matters of faith. But that assertion was not the Church's only concern. Just as critical, especially for common believers far away from the centers of power, was the uneasy relationship between Christian faith and classical culture itself. Just as Christians of the first and second centuries struggled to disassociate themselves from the Jewish tradition they had emerged from, so too in the third through fifth centuries did Christians attempt to come to grips with their classical pagan heritage. Was it a waste of time for Christian believers to read the poetry of Homer or Horace? Could anything of true spiritual value be gained from Plato's philosophy or Cicero's essays, or had Christian revelation superseded and nullified the insights to be found there? As the Christian apologist Tertullian (d. 225) once asked, "What does Athens have to do with Jerusalem?"

A fifteenth-century painting of the four Latin Doctors.
From left to right they are
St. Ambrose, St. Jerome, St. Augustine,
and Pope (and St.) Gregory I. Source: Scala / Art Resource, NY

While many figures were important in the effort to establish the Church's political and social autonomy and to define its relationship with classical culture, the
leading roles were played by four men known as the *Four Latin Doctors*: St. Ambrose of Milan (d. 397), St. Jerome (d. 420), St. Augustine (d. 430), and St. Gregory
(d. 604). We will discuss Gregory in the next chapter, but need to examine the first
three now.

St. Ambrose (340–397) was the bishop of Milan, which by the fourth century had
superceded Rome itself as the dominant city on the Italian peninsula. He was a gifted
orator who combined a flair for philosophical scholarship with a keen sensitivity to
political realities on the street. He owed his prominence to his reputation for sanctity and charity, but his success in office owed as much to his sharp political acumen. Seizing the opportunity of there being a pro-Christian boy as Roman emperor
in 384, for example, Ambrose quickly wrote to the youth, Valentinian II, and
warned him against even thinking of reversing the restrictions recently placed on
pagan cults by his predecessors. "Those so-called gods are nothing but demons," he

wrote; and if Valentinian were to do anything whatsoever to rescind the restrictions, Ambrose would bar him forever from the Milan church. Two years later, in response to a request from Valentinian's mother that Ambrose turn over a relatively minor church building in Milan for the use of the local Arians (there were many influential Arians still in the imperial court whom the mother was trying to appease), Ambrose flatly refused her and gathered his parishoners into a ring around the church where they taunted the imperial guards who came to take possession of it. When the soldiers refused to take the church by force, Valentinian and his mother relented; stung by the defeat, Valentinian reportedly complained to his soldiers, "If Ambrose gave the word, you'd hand me over in chains to him." The most dramatic event of Ambrose's career was his confrontation with the emperor Theodosius. Theodosius was a sincere Christian, but was also a ruthless figure determined to tighten his authority over the crumbling empire. When a local rebellion broke out in Thessalonica, in Greece, Theodosius quelled it and ordered a massacre of the city's population, to serve as an example for others. Ambrose was outraged and went so far as to excommunicate the very man who had made Christianity the official religion of the empire, and forced him to submit to public penance:

> You have a tremendous zeal for the Christian faith . . . but you also have an exceedingly violent temper. . . . What happened in . . . Thessalonica is without precedent; while I could not prevent its happening, I did repeatedly denounce it at court as an atrocity . . . and now I can neither explain nor excuse it . . . I advise you, urge you, beg you, admonish you—you who were once an example of such great piety, renowned for your clemency—to repent. I grieve that you do not mourn the deaths of so many innocents. . . . If you dare to enter my church, I will not perform the Mass. . . . You may make your offering [to Christ] only after you have received [my] permission.

Ambrose's stature and commanding personality ultimately forced even the emperor, quite literally, to his knees, and established beyond doubt that the state had to submit to the church in matters of morals. This episode would be recalled many times over in the clashes of the eleventh and twelfth centuries. It is significant, though, that no doctrinal or theological issue was at stake; if one had been, Theodosius' response to Ambrose's challenge might very well have been different.

St. Jerome (340–420), by contrast, played little role in politics. Born of wealthy Christian parents in the Balkan province of Dalmatia, he received a superb education in classical literature in Rome and may have been preparing for a career in government. But he had too subtle a mind and too explosive a temper to succeed in civil service. Moreover, his youthful thirst for sexual adventure was just as strong as his love of learning, and, after spending his days pouring over the poetry of Virgil and the speeches of Cicero, he devoted his nights to pleasure. Wracked with remorse after each experience, he began to probe the causes of his weakness for temptation and the reasons for his overwhelming guilt, and he gradually turned to the Bible. He eventually lived with a priest named Chromatius who had turned his household into a sort of monastic community, and Jerome found that the ascetic life—rigorous self-discipline, simple living, regimented labor, and above all long hours of study and meditation—fitted his spiritual needs well. Determining that life in Rome corrupted the spirit, he set out for the east intending to make the pilgrimage to Jerusalem. His health broke down around Antioch, however, and he took refuge with another ascetic priest named Evagrius. There, surrounded by books, Jerome threw himself back into his studies but was terrified by a dream in which Christ appeared to him and accused him of being more devoted to Cicero than to him. Consequently, Jerome decided to renounce classical culture and devote himself entirely to Christ.

Jerome's anguish over how to reconcile his love of God with his love of classical literature was not unique. Christians across Europe struggled to disentangle their faith from the culture that had helped to create it. The fact that Roman culture appeared to be in rapid decline made it easy for many Christians to reject it wholesale. Like Jerome, they decided that all the major characteristics of Roman life—its emphasis on urban life and trade, its materialism, its promotion of public service as an ideal, its stress on the centrality of the familia—were dangerous shams. As a consequence, Christians fled the cities in large numbers, to live in exile. Many lived alone as hermits in the wilderness; many others established monastic communities in remote settings far away from the fleshpots of the cities. When Jerome left Antioch to live alone in the Syrian desert, he found it a rather crowded place. Hermits wandered through the countryside, living in caves, in trees, in the open air. Some practiced self-flagellation; some dragged heavy weights that they had chained to their bodies. One well-known figure, St. Simeon Stylites, lived atop a sixty-foot pillar for nearly thirty years immersed in prayer and eating only whatever food his fanatical followers raised to him by a pulley.[6]

What drove people to this bizarre behavior was a desire for a living martyrdom. After all, the great martyrs of the persecutions were the folk-heroes of Christianity—the men and women who had faced death for their love of Christ. But how could one express the same degree of love, show the same self-denying bravery, when Christianity was not only no longer persecuted but was in fact privileged by the state? The answer, Christians felt, was to seek a kind of death-in-life by intentionally denying themselves shelter, pleasure, food, safety. They courted danger and loneliness and wanted to find the most difficult way possible to worship God.

Jerome spent several years in the desert developing his spiritual discipline. To help pass the time—and to take his mind off the sexual fantasies that continued to plague him—he began to study Hebrew with another hermit, a convert from Judaism. Within a few years Jerome had mastered the language. Finally tiring of life in the desert, he returned to Antioch, then moved to Constantinople just at the time Theodosius came to the throne. There Jerome began a prolific literary career, pub-

---

6.   The desert ascetics will be discussed more fully in Chapter 4.

lishing translations, histories, and exegetical treatises, and quickly earned renown. He returned to Rome in the 380s and became an adviser to the pope, Damasus, who assigned Jerome the task that dominated the rest of his life: a new translation of the Bible into Latin. A Latin version of the Bible (the so-called *Vetus Latina*, or "Old Latin") was already widely used, but it had been based on the Greek version of the Scriptures known as the *Septuagint*. Damasus originally wanted Jerome to sort out the various corruptions that had crept into the Vetus Latina via inept copyists, but it soon became apparent that only a fresh translation based on the original Hebrew text for the Old Testament would do. Jerome was the only person for the job, and he devoted the next twenty years to producing his new Latin Bible, which came to be known in the Middle Ages as the *Vulgate*.

Jerome's work was hardly welcomed by most Christians—in fact many sharply criticized him for it, for it seemed to them that he was reforging the link between Christianity and Judaism just when most Christians had managed to break it. True to his temperament, Jerome dismissed his critics as "a pack of howling dogs" and kept on laboring in his study in the new monastery he founded in Bethlehem. His stature as a Biblical scholar and the stylistic magnificence of his translation eventually won out, and his Vulgate became the authoritative version of the Bible for all of western Europe. Jerome also wrote a series of highly influential introductions to most of the books of Scripture, compiled several encyclopedias, penned a series of biographies of Christian ascetics, and produced theological works on a variety of topics—in all of which he relied on classical models of literary expression. The man who once had fled Rome as the seat of all moral evil came to view the Roman legacy, in his old age, with veneration.[7] Unable to shake off his love for the classics, he came to the resolution that Greek and Roman literature and philosophy can indeed be of use to a Christian, provided that they are used in the service of Christianity rather than enjoyed for their own sake. That resolution established an important legacy for the rest of the Middle Ages.

St. Augustine of Hippo (354–430) was a pupil of Ambrose, a friend of Jerome, and without a doubt the outstanding genius of the medieval Church. He wrote on every topic from Christology to the nature of time, from the philosophy of history to the structure of language systems, from the calculation of the Day of Judgment to the physiology of mourning. With his famous *Confessions*, which he wrote shortly after becoming the bishop of Hippo (an important North African port city), he virtually invented the genre of autobiography. His life's work forms the intellectual foundation for nearly all later medieval philosophy and theology.

Augustine began, like Jerome, as a devotee of classical literature. Raised from birth as a Christian, he wore his religion lightly in his early years and by his teens had sloughed it off altogether. As a student in cosmopolitan Carthage, he was something of a literary pedant and remained blissfully ignorant of philosophy and science. Also

---

7. When Rome was sacked by the Visigoths, in 410, Jerome lamented: "The light of the world has been extinguished; it is as though the whole world has perished in the ruins of this one city."

like Jerome, he indulged in nighttime bouts of drinking and womanizing. He did not share Jerome's sense of guilt and self-defilement over those adventures, though, perhaps because he soon devoted himself to a single woman who remained his mistress for the next fifteen years. Instead, Augustine came to feel that he was simply *missing something*: There had to be more to life than reciting poetry, drinking wine, and tumbling around in bed (pleasant though these be). The first important change came when he read Cicero's *Hortensius,* a passionate exhortation for people not merely to experience life but to seek wisdom and understanding about it. As Cicero wrote, "If the souls we possess are in fact eternal and divine, then we must conclude that the more we let them engage in what comes naturally to them—that is, contemplation and the search for knowledge—and the less we keep them trapped in vices and follies, the easier it will be for them to rise up to their home in heaven." Here was pagan wisdom that complemented Augustine's dormant Christianity.

His mind caught fire, and as his restless intellect grew so did his spiritual yearnings. But he found himself unable to reconcile the God of the Old Testament with the God of the New. After a brief flirtation with the Manichaeans (another mystery cult, one that posited the existence of two gods—one good, one evil—who are eternally pitted against one another, human beings providing the battleground), he moved to Milan to take a post as a professor of rhetoric and there came under the influence of St. Ambrose. Augustine's reawakening to Christianity coincided with romantic tragedy, for his family had arranged a marriage for him to a Milanese heiress with good social connections, and they forced Augustine to dismiss the mistress who had been loyal to him all those years and who had borne him a son ("This was a blow that broke my heart and made it bleed—for I did love her dearly."). He put off the unwanted marriage and immersed himself in philosophy and the reading of Scripture. After three years of study he committed himself to Catholicism and was baptized by Ambrose. By this time he had already begun to sketch the outlines of a comprehensive Christian philosophical system based on the then-current doctrines of the Neo-Platonists.

Plato, of course, had insisted that fundamental reality lies in the abstract ideas or concepts that gave shape to the mere physical reality of earthly life. (Thus, for example, it is the abstract yet real concept of "Justice" that really matters, from the eternal and philosophical view of things, not the individual actions and practices that make up what we call "justice" in day-to-day life.) The Neo-Platonists followed that line of thought by arguing that the natural world around us is nothing more than the dimmest possible reflection of divine reality. Philosophical enlightenment was thus a process of ascent, the rising up of consciousness from the muck and mess of the material world to comprehend the organizing principles that govern it. It isn't the house that matters, in other words, but the blueprint for its design.

Augustine built his Christian philosophy on this foundation, but with an important difference. While he agreed that the material world was inferior to the spiritual, and therefore ought not to be the central concern of our lives, it was nevertheless the beautiful creation of a loving God. Augustine's writings overflow with sensitive evocations of the glories of earthly life that often seem at odds with the stern moralism of his theology. He delights in describing the gentle movements of a baby when nursing, the sense of swooning created by artful music, the pleasures of gardening, the hypnotic effect of various types of light ("Light, the Queen of All Colors: it pervades everything I see throughout the day; the constantly changing pattern of its rays entices me. . . . Its grip on me is so tight that if I am suddenly deprived of it, to have it back is all I can think of."). There is no point in denying the splendors of creation, but that is precisely the point, Augustine says, where we should *start* thinking—not, as in his earlier years, stop. Whatever his topic, Augustine constantly uses metaphors drawn from the material world to explicate his ideas:

> *To enjoy* a thing means to embrace it with love for its own sake; but *to use* a thing means to put it to work in order to obtain something else that is loved . . . Imagine that we are a pair of travellers who are unable to live happily except in our own home; we are miserable in our wandering and want nothing more than to put an end to it and return to our native land. We need various types of land and sea-transport to help us reach home. But now imagine that the homeward journey itself delights us—the amenities of the trip, the movement of our vehicles. We begin to enjoy those things which we are using. If this were to happen, we would not wish to end our journey quite so quickly and we would be trapped in a perverse pleasure that alienates us from the very home that is the source of our happiness. That is what mortal life is like; we are wanderers separated from God, and if we desire to return to our homeland [i.e., to God] we ought to *use* this world we live in, but not *enjoy* it.

For Augustine the journey home to God is the central point of life. The Fall of Man in the Garden of Eden left a permanent stain of sin upon us, however, one that was not removed until God Himself took human form in the person of Jesus and made our salvation possible. By living unselfishly and piously we can hope to make it home, but there is no guarantee of our success. To Augustine, nobody "deserves" salvation—that is, no one can claim to be worthy of spending eternity in God's presence—and consequently only those who have received divine grace will receive that greatest of gifts. Thus, to Augustine, humans have free will to choose good or evil, but God too is free to bestow His grace wherever He wishes. Our duty is to do our best, live rightly, and hope things will turn out—but we can never be sure of our salvation.

Augustine's greatest work was the massive treatise called *The City of God*. Written over the course of thirteen years, it provided a Christian philosophy of history—a way of interpreting the story of human life—that offered a radical new vision. The predominant classical notion of history regarded it as essentially circular: Life progressed in an endless series of cycles that pointed to no particular end and served no particular purpose. Although a few pagan cults had a conception of an afterlife, most of these were amoralized shadowy worlds to which all people went regardless of their beliefs or actions on earth; the pagan gods thus had no "divine plan," and the main thrust of their religions was to enforce proper behavior in this life without regard to any theoretical "next" life. Augustine opposed this view with a linear model of history that begins with God's unique act of creation, moves through God's renewal of the world with the Incarnation of Christ, and culminates in Christ's Second Coming and the end of the world. History is a story with a beginning, a middle, and an end. In this way, human life is ennobled with a purpose. We have been placed here for a reason, which is to manifest the glory of God and to work toward our salvation. Augustine's scheme thereby places an intrinsic value on the experiences of every human individual. What matters in history, therefore, is not the fate of kingdoms and empires, economic systems, and social structures, but rather the spiritual and moral development of every individual human from the highest emperor to the lowest slave.

But while history progresses to a specific, story-ending Day of Judgment, Augustine warns, we must not waste our energies in trying to determine when that day will arrive. From the time of Jesus' crucifixion, many Christians had taken literally his teaching that the kingdom of God was fast approaching, and they effectively exiled themselves from society in order to prepare for the coming apocalypse. Such expectations survived throughout the Middle Ages (and are still with us), but Augustine argued forcefully that to speculate about the end of the world was futile and hubristic—that none of us can figure out God's plan, and none of us ought to try. Augustine's position became the law of the medieval Church.

His inspiration for *The City of God* was an event that many in fact took as a sign of the approaching end: the sacking of Rome in 410 by the Visigoths. This event stunned the entire western world and many pagans blamed the calamity on the Christians. As Christianity had grown, the empire had weakened, as pagan critics saw it, and the Visigothic nightmare was simply the inevitable consequence of Theodosius's rash establishment of the upstart religion as the official state cult. What began as a defense of the faith against that charge slowly turned, in the composing of it, into a grand theory of history and eschatology that dominated the western mind for well over a thousand years.

The works of Ambrose, Jerome, and Augustine mark an important point—the point where Christian thought finally managed to fuse with and proceed beyond the classical culture that had spawned it. With these three men Christianity entered its intellectual maturity, and it stood ready to withstand the challenge that came with the collapse of the western half of the empire and the flood of Germanic immigrants in the fifth century. In that challenge, the fourth of the great Doctors of the Church—St. Gregory the Great—would benefit from the work of his predecessors.

Suggested Reading

Texts

Eusebius of Caesarea. *The History of the Church.*
Josephus. *The Jewish War.*
St. Augustine. *The City of God.*

————. *Confessions.*
The Dead Sea Scrolls.
The Gnostic Gospels.
The Nag Hammadi Library.
The New Jerusalem Bible.

Source Anthologies

Barrett, C.K. *The New Testament Background: Writings from Ancient Greece and the Roman Empire That Illuminate Christian Origins* (1993).

Ehrman, Bart D. *The New Testament and Other Early Christian Writings: A Reader* (1997).

————. *After the New Testament: A Reader in Early Christianity* (1998).

Elliott, J.K. *The Apocryphal Jesus: Legends of the Early Church* (1996).

Hillgarth, J.N. *Christianity and Paganism, 350–750: The Conversion of Western Europe* (1986).

MacMullen, Ramsay, and E.N. Lane. *Paganism and Christianity, 100–425 CE: A Sourcebook* (1992).

Morrison, Karl F. *The Church in the Roman Empire* (1986).

Nichelsburg, George, and Michael Stone. *Faith and Piety in Early Judaism: Texts and Documents* (1991).

Peters, Edward. *Heresy and Authority in Medieval Europe: Documents in Translation* (1980).

Vermes, Geza. *The Complete Dead Sea Scrolls in English* (1995).

Studies

Brown, Peter. *Augustine of Hippo: A Biography* (1969).

————. *Authority and the Sacred: Aspects of the Christianization of the Roman World* (1996).

————. *The Body and Society: Men, Women, and Sexual Renunciation in Early Christianity* (1988).

Burkert, Walter. *Ancient Mystery Cults* (1987).

Clark, Gillian. *Women in Late Antiquity: Pagan and Christian Lifestyles* (1993).

Fox, Robin Lane. *Pagans and Christians* (1986).

Fredriksen, Paula. *From Jesus to Christ: The Origins of the New Testament Images of Jesus* (1988).

————. *Jesus of Nazareth, King of the Jews: A Jewish Life and the Emergence of Christianity* (1999).

Herrin, Judith. *The Formation of Christendom* (1987).

Irving, J. *The Midrashic Process: Tradition and Interpretation in Rabbinic Judaism* (1995).

Jones, A.H.M. *Constantine and the Conversion of Europe* (1962).

Kelly, J.N.D. *Jerome: His Life, Writings, and Controversies* (1975).

Kraemer, Ross, and Mary Rose D'Angelo, ed. *Women and Christian Origins* (1999).

MacMullen, Ramsay. *Christianizing the Roman Empire, A.D. 100–400* (1984).

————. *Paganism in the Roman Empire* (1981).

McNamara, Jo Ann. *A New Song: Celibate Women in the First Three Christian Centuries* (1983).

Meeks, Wayne A. *The First Urban Christians: The Social World of the Apostle Paul* (1983).

Pagels, Elaine. *Beyond Belief: The Secret Gospel of Thomas* (2003).

————. *The Gnostic Gospels* (1979).

Rokeah, David. *Jews, Pagans, and Christians in Conflict* (1982).

Rousseau, Philip. *Ascetics, Authority, and the Church in the Age of Jerome and Cassian* (1978).

———. *Basil of Caesarea* (1994).

Salisbury, J.E. *Church Fathers, Independent Virgins* (1992).

———. *Perpetua's Passion: The Death and Memory of a Young Roman Woman* (1997).

Segal, Alan F. *Rebecca's Children: Judaism and Christianity in the Roman World* (1986).

———. *Paul the Convert: The Apostolate and Apostasy of Saul the Pharisee* (1990).

Stark, Rodney. *The Rise of Christianity: A Sociologist Reconsiders History* (1996).

CHAPTER 3

EARLY GERMANIC SOCIETY

Of the three elements that went into forming medieval civilization, the Germanic element is the most difficult to pinpoint. There are two reasons for this. First, the Germanic peoples who flooded western Europe in the fourth, fifth, and sixth centuries were a highly heterogeneous group who resist easy generalization. In fact, they were not all even German: Many groups traced their lineage to the Celts, the Slavs, and the Altaic and Iranian "Scythians"—a catchall term used by classical writers for anyone from the east whose true origins they did not know. Alans, Alemanni, Angles, Avars, Burgundians, Franks, Gepids, Heruli, Huns, Jutes, Lombards, Ostrogoths, Rugians, Saxons, Suevi, Thuringians, Vandals, and Visigoths (have I forgotten any?) all poured into western Europe from their homelands—some from the Baltic, some from the Balkans, others from the Eurasian steppe—and altered the entire demographic and social structures they found there. Not that that was their intent. Most of the new immigrants wanted to preserve Roman life, or at least the better aspects of it, and to assimilate into it. While to many Roman eyes these newcomers were indistinguishable from each other, the differences that existed between the groups were significant and had important consequences for the type of Europe that emerged in the Middle Ages. Second, so many things in the ancient world had already changed, or had started to, by the time the Germans came, that it is extremely difficult to know which changes to attribute to the Germans' influence. The Roman decline began long before the Germanic threat along the Rhine-Danube frontier became serious; Christianity secured its first foothold long before the first German heard the Word preached. The influx of the Germans certainly affected both the fall of Rome and the rise of Christianity and speeded them toward what they were to become, but it remains impossible to gauge the precise nature of the Germans' contribution.

Once again we are hampered by our sources. The early Germans were preliterate and left no records of their own; thus we must look at them through the eyes of the usually hostile pagans and Christians they were in competition with. Fortunately, a fairly substantial archeological record remains, one that helps to offset some of the biases of our written sources, but since the Germans did not build in stone, the surviving evidence is fragmentary and hard to interpret. One can tell only so much from pieces of jewelry, bits of crockery, and leather helmets with sword-gashes in them—although those last items certainly tell us one thing for sure. Most of the detailed written evidence about the Germans dates from the fourth century onward, after they had already been significantly Romanized and Christianized. Hence, sifting through this material is tricky but essential if we are to have any picture at all of their origins. The picture that emerges is of a vibrant and complex society—group of societies, to be more precise—that showed an impressive ability to adapt to changing times.

GERMANIC LIFE

The early Germans had a notably fluid social structure. Based in principle on the clan, or extended family, their populations tended to group around military chieftains who could assure a certain degree of safety from attack and booty from raids upon others. Several clans might make up a larger unit called the tribe, a designation that did not necessarily indicate a shared ethnicity. The word *tribe*, from the Latin *tribus*, had a pejorative sense for the Romans and meant something akin to the modern English word *horde*. The clans that made up a tribe usually shared the same language, or had closely related dialects, and followed complementary customary codes. But these were ad hoc arrangements; tribes formed and disbanded with more than enough regularity to keep the Romans confused and frustrated. A similar fluidity existed within each clan, and loyalty to the individual chieftains waxed and waned with each group's military and material fortunes. Today's hero could be tomorrow's villain, depending on his success at defending the clan and providing for it. In the course of the fourth and fifth centuries, these clans and tribes slowly coalesced, under Roman influence, into still larger units: In making peace treaties or in allowing for Germanic immigration, the Romans preferred to deal with larger "nations" *en bloc*, and so helped to create artificial kingdoms out of the hodgepodge of clans and tribes. The ablest of the tribal warlords assumed a new status—that of *dux* (or "leader")—that in time evolved into a primitive sort of kingship. These newly created kingdoms then fabricated legendary ancestries for themselves to make it look as though their roots went back far into the past. Thus to refer to a group such as the Visigoths or the Alans is in one sense to refer to an historical fiction.[1]

Prior to the third century most of the Germanic peoples—some of whose archeological remains near Jutland and along the southern and eastern Baltic coasts can be traced back to 1200 B.C.—were agriculturalists with a high degree of social organization. They tended to live in nucleated villages of modest size, seldom involving more than a couple of hundred people. A nucleated village was one in which the inhabitants lived in a central cluster of houses (mere hamlets, really), from which the crop fields radiated out, with meadows and pastures lying just beyond. Such a structure usually required a certain degree of collective labor and sharing of tools, characteristics which suggest that early Germanic society had a degree of institu-

---

1.   This process of "people-making" and the creation of legendary histories is called *ethnogenesis*.

tional and social development that historians have been slow to credit them with. Wheat and barley dominated their earliest farms, but other cereals like oats and rye were also grown. Their diet focused on cereals, meats, dairy products, fish, and beer; viticulture was unknown to them, as, therefore, were olive oil and wine. There are signs that their populations swelled significantly starting in the first century B.C. and continuing until the third century A.D. Increased need for food and the desire to avoid Asiatic nomads like the Alans and Huns began to force many thousands of these Germans toward the Roman border. Thus by the time the Romans became familiar with Germanic culture in any detail, they encountered Germans displaced from their agricultural way of life and living largely as pastoralists, hunters, and warriors. This false impression of Germanic culture, canonized by Tacitus in his *Germania*, lingered for many centuries.

Nonetheless, warfare and violence certainly characterized the life of these tribes by the time the Romans encountered them, but these attributes were due more to the harsh conditions they lived in than to any genetically-ingrained bellicosity. Conditions were harsh for them because the new territory they inhabited beyond the Rhine-Danube frontier was comprised of heavy soil that was also densely forested ("their land bristles with thick forests and putrid swamps," wrote Tacitus); clearing, draining, and tilling that land required a degree of social organization and technological development that the Germans simply did not possess. Their original homelands had lighter, sandier soils that required lighter, simpler plows; it took a long time for the displaced Germans to adapt to the requirements of densely forested, heavy-clay Europe. As a consequence, crop yields remained low and famine continuously threatened. When food ran out, the Germans attributed it to the ill-favor of the local deities and so abandoned their temporary villages to search for new settlements. The panic-driven nature of this wandering accounts for much of the inter-tribal warfare of the Germans: Competition for scarce resources often led to violent clashes.

In these struggles it was the responsibility of the clan leaders—the warrior chieftains—to defend the group. They fought chiefly with iron-tipped spears, bows and arrows, and short knives. Only the elite possessed swords, since iron was expensive. The Germans' most important innovation was their reliance on cavalry, as opposed to the Roman reliance on infantry; German horsemen used a stirrup that allowed them far more stability in the saddle than had been possible before. The Visigothic victory over the Romans at the battle of Adrianople (378) signaled the supremacy of this way of fighting and anticipated the development of the mounted medieval knight, although it would be a mistake to trace a direct line of descent from Visigothic horsemen to medieval knights. Many stages of development, some of them indirect and unexpected, lay between. What the early Germans may have lacked in discipline, they made up for in zeal. Tacitus described their fighting this way:

> When battle is joined it is considered a disgrace for their chieftain to be surpassed in boldness or for his followers not to live up to his prowess. Moreover,

it is a lifelong reproach and shame to survive your fallen chief and come back alive from the field. To protect and defend the chief and to dedicate one's own feats of arms to his renown is the very height of their loyalty. The chief fights for victory, but his followers fight for him. If it should happen that their homeland is lulled into long periods of peace and quiet, many of its high-born youths will voluntarily set out in search of tribes that are waging some war—for their race is unaccustomed to peace, and they earn names for themselves more readily in times of troubles; also, one cannot maintain a large following except by war and violence.

War for the Germans was thus a means of social engineering. Among a people that lacked rigid social hierarchies, one could advance oneself within the clan or tribe by feats of arms, or perhaps create a new such group under one's direct rule. It was a brutal sort of meritocracy, but it meant in the long run that the Germanic groups were led by men with talents for ferocity and ambition precisely at the point, in the fourth century, when the western Roman Empire was dissolving amid the disputes of squabbling courtiers who were not up to the task of holding it together.

A fragment of a poem called the *Hildebrandslied* ("The Song of Hildebrand") illustrates the culture of violence among the warriors. This fragment of only sixty-eight lines is the oldest surviving example of Germanic epic poetry; it was preserved accidentally in the binding of another manuscript prepared in the monastery of Fulda around the year 800. The epic tells of the adventures of Hildebrand, a popular legendary figure for several of the Germanic tribes, who leaves his family behind and sets off with his band of warriors to drive away the invading Huns. At the point where the fragment begins, Hildebrand has returned after many years and is confronted by his long-abandoned son Hadubrand, who mistakes his father for a Hun chieftain. Hildebrand, for his part, also fails to recognize his son, and before they begin to battle he asks his young foe to identify himself:

> *. . . He began by asking,*
> *In very few words, who his father might be*
> *From among all the heroes of the people:*
> *"Oh, what ancestry have you, young warrior?*
> *Name but one [clan-member] and I will know the others,*
> *For in this kingdom all the clans are known to me."*
> *Then Hildebrand's son, Hadubrand, answered:*
> *"The tale I heard long ago*
> *From the elders and wisemen of old—*
> *That my father was called Hildebrand. My own name is Hadubrand.*
> *Long ago he journeyed to the east, fleeing the wrath of Otaker,*
> *Together with Dietrich and his many warriors . . .*
> *He was the greatest of Dietrich's warriors*
> *And always fought at the the head of the army. . . .*

Hildebrand then offers Hadubrand a ring to prove that he is in fact his long-lost father, but Hadubrand suspects a trick and is determined to slay the intruder. Before they come to blows, Hildebrand stops to lament:

> *"Now Sorrow—the supreme lord, our woeful destiny—is fulfilled!*
> *Through sixty summers and sixty winters I have traveled,*
> *Battling always in the forward-most line, and yet*
> *I did not meet my death in any place.*
> *But now either my own son will cut me down with his sword,*
> *Bringing me down to death with his blow, or else I must kill him!*
> *. . . Only the most repulsive coward out of all the peoples of the east*
> *Would refuse you battle now." . . .*
> *Then they spring at each other with their spears*
> *Showering fierce blows; their shields protect them.*
> *They clash again, their swords swinging violently.*
> *Their shields break under the blows*
> *Until the linden wood [that the shields were made of] grows light,*
> *Having been ground away by their weapons. . . .*

The fragment ends here, but we know from later references that Hildebrand kills his son. What is striking here is the glorification of violence itself, regardless of the reasons for it. To Hadubrand, and presumably to the poem's audience, Hildebrand's abandonment of his family is not to be condemned but praised because Hildebrand in his exile at least earned a reputation for fierceness. Upon his return, Hildebrand refuses to let anything like mere fatherly sentiment get in the way of another opportunity to kill a foe and win renown. In the *Hildebrandslied*, violence is lifted above moral concerns and is simply accepted as a fact of life and the chief means for the hope of glory.

Much of the violence of Germanic life was turned inward. Feuds and vendettas were common and often engulfed whole clans in generations of bloodletting. Once again, the hardscrabble nature of life explains this trait. To kill a man was quite literally to threaten the existence of his entire family, since without his labor food-acquisition was thrown into doubt and without his fighting skill the survival of the clan was put at risk. Most clans and tribes regarded individual murder as warfare upon the whole family, and consequently the victim's relations responded in kind by declaring war upon the murderer's family. But this sort of in-fighting obviously throws the entire society into chaos if left unchecked. Over time, the Germans developed a system of compensatory payments—called *wergeld* ("man-money," literally)—that took the place of the blood feud. These payments varied depending upon the sex and social status of the victim and his or her age. Military chieftains and aristocratic women of child-bearing age were the most valued, aged slaves the least. An elaborate scale of payments took shape that eventually accounted not only for murder but for injury—so much was owed for the loss of an eye, so much for a stabbing in the stomach, so much for the cutting off of a limb, and so on; everything was assigned a monetary value, right down to the price for the fifth toe on the left foot. The wergeld system differed from tribe to tribe in its specifics but was characteristic of them all.

Wergeld was not as primitive as it sounds; our modern personal-injury insurance policies are based on exactly the same idea. The Germanic groups possessed intricate systems of customary law that they had built up over the course of many centuries, and what may at first strike us as their primitive nature is rather a reflection of their practical orientation and development. Unlike the classical legal tradition, which from the time of Plato onward began by defining abstract notions like *justice, commonwealth,* and *authority* before moving into the concrete details of specific situations, Germanic law was constructed from the ground up, without an ideological blueprint. The Germans pieced together their ways of regulating behavior in a step-by-step fashion, taking each situation as it arose and coming to some sort of group consensus about it. Once a conflict had been resolved, it served as a precedent for resolving future situations that fit the same circumstances. The fact that few conflicts share all circumstances in their entirety explains the baroque proliferation of statutes regarding everything from assault to adultery, from the theft of pigs to the plundering of corpses. These customary codes—which were passed down orally for generations, and began to be written down in the fifth, sixth, and seventh centuries—therefore resemble nothing so much as our modern system of torts.

These laws tell us much about the treatment and status of women. Tacitus asserts that chastity before marriage and faithful monogamy within it were the norm for all the tribes and that all German men regarded their wives with due honor, but he romanticizes the degree of equality and mutual respect that women enjoyed. In fact, Germanic custom regarded women as legal minors regardless of their age, under the permanent guardianship of their fathers and husbands. The sole exception to this rule were the Visigoths, who settled in Spain in the sixth century; they allowed a single woman to be a free adult after the age of twenty. For the others, though, Germanic practice of male "protective ownership" of women (known by the Latin term *mundium,* meaning something along the lines of "uprightness" or "integrity") was similar to the Roman custom of patria potestas—and it was precisely similarities such as this which eased the amalgamation of Roman and Germanic cultures in the early Middle Ages. To the Salian Franks, for example, who settled in northern France in the fifth and sixth centuries, a woman who married without her guardian's consent permanently forfeited all her property; moreover, any one of her family members had the right to kill her for the offense. Among the Burgundians, who in the fifth century gradually settled in eastern France and parts of what is today Switzerland, any woman who left her husband for any reason faced being drowned in a swamp.

Strict divisions of labor characterized German life, with women responsible for all the agricultural work (plows and oxen-yokes were common marriage gifts presented by men to their brides), for pottery-making, and for whatever simple textile-weaving was done. Men, on the other hand, did the fighting and the hunting, plus the blacksmith-work that both activities depended on. A girl was considered of marriageable age as soon as she began to menstruate and was able to produce children, usually around the age of fourteen or fifteen. Women and girls dressed quite well-covered—as much a result of the cold climate in which they lived as of social mores—but Germanic custom also made every attempt to protect women from male lechery and to protect men from women's supposed power to incite lecherous behavior. To judge from the surviving texts, in fact, the early Germans were quite obsessed with sex: The variations in sexual relations, protection against sexual crimes, the regulation of sexual enticements—all dominate Germanic law codes. The Alemanni, who moved into what later became Swabia, heavily fined any female whose clothing exposed her above the knee and any man who loosened or fondled a woman's hair. The Salian Franks levied a fine on anyone who, without cause, touched an unmarried adult female anywhere at all.[2] A Burgundian fiancée who sampled someone else's wares before her wedding was to be punished with beatings and whippings "until her blood flows." Concubinage, a legally sanctioned form of living together without being married, remained common and so did prostitution, though it was heavily regulated. The movement of so many contending tribes and clans into the west created an atmosphere of continual danger. So present was the fear of sexual violence, writes Paul the Deacon, an eighth-century chronicler, that certain Lombard women

> used to put the flesh of raw chickens under the band that held up their breasts; this, once the heat spoiled and putrified it, gave off a horribly foul odor. Thus when the Avars [another invading tribe] tried to violate them they found that they could not bear the stench; and thinking that the smell was natural to these women, they ran away, cursing loudly that all Lombard women stink.

Accusations of malodorousness plagued most of the tribes. Sidonius Apollinaris, a fifth-century Roman aristocrat, famously commented: "Happy is the nose that cannot smell a barbarian."

Germanic religion was polytheistic, based on the belief in a multitude of nature gods and spirits. Such spirits were thought to exist everywhere—in rivers, sacred groves, mountains—and to be the causes of natural phenomena. Major deities like Wotan (or Odin) and Tor (or Thor) represented the forces of the Sun and Thunder, respectively, and figured in the stories that made up Germanic mythology. But the Germans came into contact with Christianity fairly early on, in its heretical Arian form. Many of the Arian leaders, as we have seen, abandoned the empire in the east after their condemnation at the Council of Nicaea. The Arian missionary Ulfilas (d. 383) traveled north from Nicaea beyond the Danube and converted the rulers of several tribes of the Goths. He also translated the Bible into the Gothic tongue, for which he created an alphabet.[3]

---

2. For the curious: a finger cost you fifteen *solidi*, an elbow thirty, and a breast forty-five.
3. A fragment of this Bible still exists: The *Codex Argenteus*, a sixth-century copy, preserves most of the four gospels. It is in the university library in Uppsala, Sweden.

Thus many of the Germans who moved into the faltering Roman Empire were Arians. It is difficult to say how seriously the commoners took their new faith, since their conversions often resulted from the blunt command of their chieftain-kings instead of genuine personal inquiry. But they certainly took seriously the legacy of Arian resentment against the Nicene Christians, whom they of course regarded as heretics. The conflicts that arose in the fourth and fifth centuries therefore had a religious element to them, even if the religions themselves were present only in name.

MIGRATIONS AND INVASIONS

Contact between the Germanic peoples and the Roman world existed long before the empire's crisis in the third century. The first known use of the Latin term *Germani*, referring to rebellious slaves captured beyond the Rhine, dates to the first century B.C., but contact with the Germanic world even predated that. Prior to Caesar's conquest of Gaul, most Romans had simply never bothered to distinguish between the Germans and the Celts, instead lumping them together under the term *barbarians*. While there were innumerable confrontations along the Rhine-Danube border over the centuries, Roman contact with the Germans for the most part benefited both societies. The Germans learned Roman concepts of statehood and statecraft, agricultural techniques, and eventually knowledge both of Latin and writing; the Romans used Germanic immigration to settle the land and stabilize the frontier. The border between their two worlds was in fact an extremely porous one, with families, clan groups, warrior bands, traders, travelers, and emissaries constantly moving back and forth. Roman civilization, after all, had been built on the idea of absorbing and accommodating different peoples; what mattered was to integrate new immigrants in an orderly fashion. Germanic immigrants underwent Romanization and served in the army as *federati* (allied troops). By the fourth century, Romanized Germans actually made up the bulk of the imperial army in western Europe.

But by the late fourth century, the Roman crisis was full-blown and it became impossible to control Germanic migration. Several factors caused the Germans to push westward in increased numbers. First was the general problem of overpopulation. As their numbers grew over the centuries, the Germanic groups found themselves in stiffer competition for the land and resources available in their corner of the Eurasian continent. The Roman territories, despite the problems they were experiencing, were considerably wealthier, the land itself more fertile, and the general climate more tolerable than what was available north of the Danube and east of the Rhine. Added to the economic lure of the empire was the desire to flee the blood feuds that increasingly characterized Germanic life. As the struggle for survival intensified, conflicts between clans and tribes became more frequent, and drove many to seek a more peaceful life within the Roman world. A third fac-

*A second-century stone image of a Germanic swordsman
battling a Roman legionnaire. Source: Erich Lessing / Art Resource NY*

tor was the approach of the Huns, a fiercely aggressive group of warrior-nomads from central Asia. As the Huns defeated nation after nation, they spread terror throughout the Germanic lands. Recognizing that they were powerless before these new invaders, the Germans sought refuge with the Romans. Thus what had long been a stable process of more or less orderly migration and acculturation turned into a full-scale invasion of terrified, starving, and desperate—and therefore aggressive—Germanic groups into the empire. Modern Germans refer to this period of their history as the *Völkerwanderung,* or the "Wanderings of the Peoples." The word carries too benign a sense to fit the life-or-death quality of the migrations, but it is important to recognize that this was in fact the transplantation of migrants eager to adopt, and adapt themselves to, the Roman world rather than an effort to conquer and destroy it.

Matters reached critical stage in 376 when the Huns arrived at the easternmost reaches of Europe, the territory that today roughly corresponds with the country of Romania. There they crushed the Ostrogoths and sent them fleeing into the Balkans. The Visigoths, who were the Huns' next target, pleaded with the emperor in Constantinople for permission to settle within the imperial province of Moesia, which lay just south of the Danube. The emperor Valens (r. 364–378)—an Arian Christian, he sympathized with the Visigoths, who had some time before converted to Arianism—granted them refuge on the usual condition that they serve as federati and defend that section of the border. Valens failed to provide the arms and materiel he had promised, however, and left the Visigoths exposed to continued attack from the Huns and scorn from the local population for their failure to defend them. There is evidence too of rampant corruption among local imperial officials, who cheated the Visigoths of promised goods and assistance. The Visigoths responded by renouncing their alliance with the empire and going on a rampage. They plundered the province of Thrace and began to march on Constantinople itself. Valens, at the head of the imperial army, met them in battle near Adrianople in 378. The Visigoths defeated the Romans and killed Valens, then went on to pillage much of Greece.

Theodosius (r. 379–395)—the man who declared Christianity the official religion of the empire—restored some order to the region by skillful diplomacy, but the harm had been done. From his time on, hordes of panicked and pillaging Germans crashed through Roman defenses almost at will. Later emperors survived the onslaught in two ways. First, they relied increasingly on the power of German generals familiar with the fighting strategies and tactics of the invaders. This practice enabled them to dispel all but the largest of the attacks, but it came at a high price. Within just a few years the generals themselves were in real command, often using the emperor as a mere puppet to be set up or pulled down at will. Second, the emperors focused their energies on defending and preserving the eastern half of the empire only, and opened up the west to the newcomers. One reason they were able to get away with this was because the western half was "ruled"—albeit in name only—by a mentally unstable youngster named Honorius (r. 395–423). Honorius is remembered chiefly for ordering the murder of his most capable general, a Vandal soldier named Stilicho, in 408. Stilicho's death (and Honorius' survival) left Italy virtually defenseless just at the time when the Visigoths became restless again, under the leadership of an ambitious warrior-king named Alaric, and moved westward. With no one to oppose them, Alaric and the Visigoths seized control of Italy and in 410 sacked Rome itself. The news of this event stunned the world. From his monastery in Bethlehem, St. Jerome wrote, "The most terrible news has arrived from the west. Rome is taken, and the lives of her citizens have had to be ransomed. . . . My voice fails me and sobs choke my speech. The city that conquered the whole world has itself been conquered!" The catastrophe inspired St. Augustine to begin writing *The City of God*. But the significance of Rome's fall was chiefly symbolic. Alaric himself died shortly thereafter, and the Visigoths

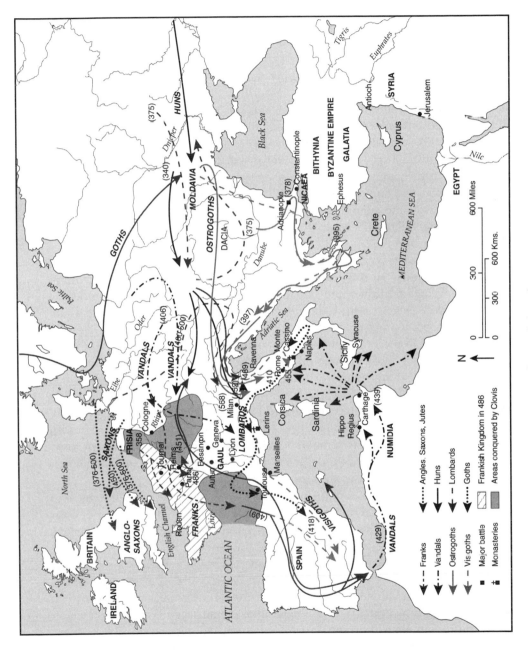

Germanic invasions

abandoned Italy and eventually established themselves in southern France and Spain.

Throughout the rest of the fifth century, countless other Germanic tribes swept through the west. They were usually in small groups, but occasionally organized themselves in larger confederations or "kingdoms." We do not know exact numbers, of course, but historians generally agree that several hundred thousand Germans entered western Europe at this time. The Alans and Suevi plundered their way diagonally through France, from the northeast to the southwest, before ultimately settling in northern and western Spain. The Vandals followed at their heels and in 429 crossed the Strait of Gibraltar and took control of the western portion of North Africa. (St. Augustine died while they were besieging his city of Hippo.) The Burgundians trekked from their homeland in what is today northern Poland to eastern France; there they were stopped by an army of Huns who slaughtered them in such numbers that popular legends recalling the tragedy began to form and later worked their way into epics like the *Nibelungenlied*. Groups of Franks moved into northern and central France, while large numbers of Angles, Jutes, and later Saxons crossed into England.

These movements convulsed western Europe and disrupted agriculture, trade, and civic life. But the Germans' aim was never to destroy Roman society. The confederation of clans and tribes into "kingdoms" was itself a means to accommodate themselves to the needs of the tottering empire. Kings and kingdoms were established not as autonomous splinterings of the empire but as imperially recognized federati, allies of Rome. Nevertheless, Roman life disintegrated. The cities of western Europe fell into decay through pillage, neglect, and abandonment. In order to preserve the state, administrators in the west raised taxes to exorbitant levels, which prompted city-dwellers—or at least the wealthier ones—to flee the cities altogether and take up residence in country estates, where they survived by bribing officials, generals, and warlords to turn blind eyes to their retreat. The government in turn placed all its demands on the common populace, who found the burden so intolerable that many frankly welcomed the arrival of Germanic kings who offered far easier terms in return for popular support.

One group, though, was never welcomed anywhere: the Asiatic Huns who from 433 to 453 were ruled by the savage warlord Attila. From their base in what is today Hungary, Attila's soldiers terrorized Europe. Aiming first at the wealthier east, they slaughtered people throughout the Balkans and advanced to Constantinople itself; but when they proved unable to break through the fortifications there, they turned their eyes westward. Attila's army was not entirely Hunnish. Like the Roman army it confronted, it was made up of an array of volunteers and conscripts from all the peoples it had faced. They tore through central Europe quickly, burning and pillaging everything in sight. In 451 near Châlons in northeastern France, however, a coalition of Roman soldiers and Germanic armies defeated Attila, whose successes had always resulted from quick

The use of cavalry by the early Germans became increasingly common and increasingly effective. This bas-relief, however, depicts a Roman soldier, on foot, lopping off the head of a German horseman. Source: Erich Lessing / Art Resource NY

raids instead of pitched battles. Defeated in Gaul, Attila turned toward Italy where he once again plundered with abandon. In Aquileia he so terrorized the populace that they fled into the swamps at the head of the Adriatic and lived on muddy outcroppings beyond the shore's reach; these fetid settlements eventually developed into the great merchant city of Venice. Attila flattened Milan and Pavia next, but disease began to weaken his forces soon thereafter. As they moved toward Rome, they were met by an embassy of local officials led by the bishop of Rome, Pope Leo I (440–461). The pope persuaded Attila to withdraw— probably by promising food, medicine, and supplies to the suffering Hunnish soldiers, although popular legend had it that Leo frightened Attila by summoning the miraculous appearance of Saints Peter and Paul with swords drawn and stern looks on their faces. We have no way of knowing for sure what really happened, but Attila did agree to return to Hungary, where he died shortly thereafter—following an overly energetic wedding night, according to another popular legend, with his young Germanic bride.

Attila's empire broke up quickly after his death and the Huns never again threatened the west, but their brief appearance in Europe had three important consequences. First, as one of the prime motivating forces for the flight of the Germanic groups into the empire, the Huns indirectly served as a catalyst of Roman decline. Second, their defeat at the hands of the largely German imperial army and the temporarily united Germanic "kings" boosted the newcomers' morale and helped to legitimize those leaders and justify their new "royal" status. Lastly, the negotiated settlement outside Rome greatly enhanced the prestige of the pope in secular affairs. Only two decades after the withdrawal of the Huns, the Roman Empire in the west formally ceased to exist. In 476 Odoacer, another in a long string of German generals who dominated Italy, deposed the last of the puppet emperors in the west—a boy named Romulus Augustulus—and ruled in his own name. Like other German kings, he sought some sort of legal recognition of his new title from either the emperor in Byzantium, the pope in Rome, or both. But by 476, almost exactly one hundred years after the start of the Völkerwanderung, the motley mass of Germanic clans and tribes had begun to develop into meaningful "nations" of people, tens of thousands strong, under the leadership of single individuals—henceforth called *kings*—whose status had been achieved by force but who actively sought legal and religious legitimation from both the secular authority in Constantinople and the ecclesiastical authority of the bishop of Rome.

Europe's First Kingdoms

The Ostrogoths

The three most significant of the so-called *Germanic successor states* were the kingdoms of the Ostrogoths in Italy, the Franks in Gaul or northern France, and the Visigoths in Spain. The Ostrogoths, an offshoot of the older Gothic group smashed by the Huns in 375, had united in the early fifth century and from their position on the middle Danube began to press once again on the Eastern empire. In 489 their talented and ambitious king Theodoric accepted an invitation from the emperor in Constantinople to lead his people into Italy, overthrow Odoacer, and restore Italy to the empire. This emperor, Zeno, probably had no real interest in regaining Italy; all he wanted was to get rid of the Ostrogoths as quickly as possible. Theodoric leapt at the chance, though, and led his army down the peninsula. After four years of fighting, he finally forced Odoacer to agree to share Italy, then murdered him with his own hands at a banquet arranged to celebrate the supposed settlement. From 493 to 526 Theodoric ruled Italy with a firm though surprisingly tolerant hand, and he helped restore a substantial degree of prosperity. He also encouraged a revival of classical learning at his royal court in Ravenna that had enormous consequences for medieval cultural development.

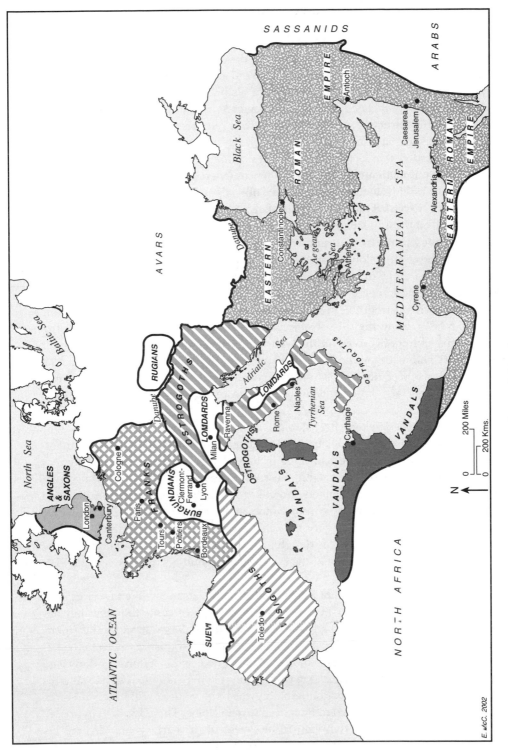

Germanic kingdoms

SASSANIDS

ARABS

Black Sea

EASTERN ROMAN EMPIRE

Antioch

Caesarea
Jerusalem

Alexandria

Cyrene

MEDITERRANEAN SEA

EASTERN ROMAN EMPIRE

Constantinople

Aegean Sea

Athens

AVARS

Danube

RUGIANS

OSTROGOTHS

LOMBARDS

Danube

Milan

Ravenna

Adriatic Sea

LOMBARDS

Rome

Naples

Carthage

Tyrrhenian Sea

OSTROGOTHS

VANDALS

VANDALS

VANDALS

North Sea

Baltic Sea

ANGLES & SAXONS

London

Canterbury

Cologne

FRANKS

Paris

BURGUNDIANS

Clermont-Ferrand

Lyon

Tours

Poitiers

Bordeaux

ATLANTIC OCEAN

SUEVI

Toledo

VISIGOTHS

NORTH AFRICA

N

0   200 Miles
0   200 Kms.

E. w/cC. 2002

Theodoric had spent several years as a diplomatic hostage in Constantinople when he was young, and it was there that he developed his admiration for Roman culture. It is doubtful that he ever learned to read and write, but he enjoyed hearing poetry read and was generous in support of historians and philosophers. He also understood the significance of cities and began to rebuild much of Italy's dilapidated urban infrastructure, with scores of new or refurbished hospitals, aqueducts, road networks, ports, administrative offices, and town squares to his credit. Agriculture rebounded, thanks to the army's stabilization of the countryside. Patterning his policies on Roman models, Theodoric encouraged inclusiveness and toleration in all aspects of life. He appointed Roman officials to the highest levels of his administration. He settled his people on the land according to an old Roman principle that recognized the indigenous population as the "hosts" and his Gothic newcomers as the "guests," rather than simply displacing the conquered by the conquerors. He aimed above all at long-term stability, which he felt could be achieved only through the peaceful working and living together of the Romans and Germans. Significantly, Theodoric never claimed to be the king of Italy: His royal status pertained only to his Ostrogothic subjects, and he ruled the Roman populace according to Roman laws, using the title of *patricius* ("patrician"). Although he himself, like most of his Ostrogoths, was an avowed Arian, he refused to suppress Catholic Christianity and made public funds available to both churches for the construction of new houses of worship. He also encouraged, and paid for, the work of both Arian and Catholic scholars. But despite his best efforts, relations between the two groups remained strained.

Theodoric hoped to keep Italy stable by promoting stability across Europe. One way to accomplish this was to help the new kings across western Europe restore order to their realms just as he had done in Italy. A carefully considered system of marriage alliances linked him with the ruling families of the other "successor states"; these marriages legitimated and enhanced the prestige of those rulers and provided Theodoric with reliable information about events across the continent. He himself took a Frankish princess for his wife; he married his sister to the king of the Vandals in North Africa; both his daughters married other kings—one the king of the Visigoths, the other the king of the Burgundians—and his niece was wedded to the king of the Thuringians.

Theodoric's kingdom did not survive his death in 526; in fact the first cracks began to emerge as early as 518. In that year a new emperor came to power in Constantinople, named Justin, who initiated a new round of persecutions of the Arians in the east. Theodoric took this as a signal that it was time to turn away from the tolerant policies of his middle years, and he began to take action against Catholicism. He urged the pope, John I, to travel to Constantinople to persuade Justin to stop his attacks on the Arians, and even though John was largely successful in this mission, Theodoric nonetheless arrested him on his return to Rome. The pope died in prison, and Theodoric reverted to the open ruthlessness of his early years, driving his Catholic subjects into exile or prison and ordering all Catholic churches to be handed over to the Arians. This alteration of his course led many of the king's counsellors to complain, and Theodoric began to suspect plots against him everywhere and to purge his government of supposed spies and traitors. The last years of his reign provide a sad spectacle of constant suspicion and violence. Compounding difficulties, Theodoric left behind only a daughter, named Amalasuntha, who was quickly assassinated. Rulership of Italy passed again from one rival to another, all of whose inability to maintain relations with Constantinople as Theodoric himself had done deprived Italy of the trade that had fed its brief economic recovery. The significance of this failure was tremendous, since it symbolized, among other things, the growing separation between western Europe and the Byzantine Empire.

The Ostrogothic era ended in 568 when the peninsula was overwhelmed by a new Germanic group, the Lombards. As latecomers to the west, the Lombards had had little contact with Roman culture, but they had already converted to Arian Christianity. Led by their elected king Alboin, the Lombards had little difficulty in destroying the feuding Ostrogothic generals who in any case had already been crushed by the brief reconquest of southern and central Italy by Byzantine soldiers sent out by their new emperor Justinian.[4] But Alboin died unexpectedly in 572—his wife had him assassinated after he had forced her, as a macabre joke, to drink wine from a cup made of her father's hollowed-out skull—after which the Lombards' tribal leaders simply refused to elect another king. Instead, they divided themselves into approximately thirty separate principalities, the most important of them being Milan in the north, Spoleto in the center, and Benevento in the south. Italy would not be a united country again until 1870.

The Franks

Meanwhile a powerful new force emerged in northern Gaul: the kingdom of the Merovingian Franks. Like most of the newcomers, the Franks were a heterogenous alliance of dialect-groups later linked by legendary origin. From their homeland on the eastern shores of the North Sea, they migrated southward along the coastline in the third and fourth centuries, settling first in the region of what is today Holland and Belgium, but then drifting inland to northern Gaul.[5] They served the Romans as federati for a time, but broke away from the western empire shortly before its collapse in 476 and began to carve out settlements for themselves while uniting under a series of warrior-kings for protection. One of the first of these was the half-legendary Merovech, for whom the dynasty is named. In 481 an intelligent but brutal fifteen-year-old named Clovis succeeded to the throne of one of the main Frankish divisions, near Tournai, and began to consolidate his control over surrounding groups. He made war on other Franks, on the Burgundians, the

---

4. See the discussion in Chapter 5, to follow.
5. There is evidence that some of them went on pillaging raids as far away as northeastern Spain.

Alemanni, and whenever necessary upon the Gallo-Roman aristocrats who occasionally rose up against him. His army fought well, and Clovis also knew how to take advantage of his own reputation for savagery by frightening people into submission without having to lift a sword against them. He kept a keen eye on potential rivals. Since the idea of monarchical authority residing within a single family was fast developing, he saw those rivals inevitably among his own relations—and so he took every opportunity that presented itself to kill them off. The following anecdote, told by Gregory of Tours in his *History of the Franks*, provides a chilling glimpse into Clovis' character:

> The king at Cambrai at that time was Ragnachar, a man so lost to lechery that he could not even leave the women of his own family alone. He had a counselor named Farro who defiled himself with the same filthy habit. It was said of this man that whenever Ragnachar had anything—whether food, gift, or anything else—placed before him, he would proclaim "It's good enough for me and Farro!" This put all the the Franks in their retinue in a great rage. And so Clovis bribed Ragnachar's bodyguards with arm-bands and sword-belts that looked like gold but were really just cleverly gilded bronze, and with these he hoped to turn Ragnachar's men against him. Clovis then sent his army against Ragnachar; and when Ragnachar dispatched spies to bring back information on the invaders and asked them upon their return, how strong the attackers were, they replied: "They're good enough for you and Farro!" Clovis himself finally arrived and arranged his soldiers for battle. Ragnachar watched as his army was crushed and tried to sneak away, but his own soldiers captured him, tied his hands behind his back, and brought him—together with Ragnachar's brother, Ricchar—before Clovis.
>
> "Why have you disgraced our Frankish people by allowing yourself to be tied up?" asked Clovis. "It would have been better for you if you had died in battle." And with that, he lifted his axe and split Ragnachar's skull. Then he turned to his brother Ricchar and said, "And as for you, if you had stood by your brother's side he would not have been bound in this way." And he struck Ricchar with another blow of his axe and killed him. When these two were dead, the bodyguards who had betrayed them discovered that the golden gifts they had received from Clovis were fake. It is said that when they complained of this to Clovis he answered, "That is all the gold a man should expect when he willingly lures his own ruler to death," adding that they should be grateful for escaping with their lives instead of being tortured to death for having betrayed their masters. . . .
>
> Now both of these kings, Ragnachar and Ricchar, were relatives of Clovis; so was their brother Rignomer, whom Clovis had put to death at Le Mans. Then, having killed all three, Clovis took over their kingdoms and their treasuries. He carried out the killing of many other kings and blood-relations in the same way—of anyone, really, whom he suspected of plotting against his realm—and in so doing he gradually extended his control over the whole of Gaul. One day he summoned an assembly of all his subjects, at which he is reported to have remarked about all the relatives he had destroyed, "How sad it is for me to live as a stranger among strangers, without any of my family here to help me when disaster happens!" But he said this not out of any genuine grief for their deaths,

but only because he hoped somehow to flush out another relative whom he could kill.

But Clovis did more than murder, and his Franks farmed as much as they fought. In fact, they owed much of their success to their ability to appeal to, and accommodate themselves to, the Gallo-Roman aristocracy. Clovis treated the Gallo-Romans, in fact, with surprising leniency; most of his Franks were settled onto farms in the relatively depopulated northern zones, a practice that left the older aristocratic landholders secure further south. In essence, they offered Clovis their support in return for his leaving them alone, and the result was a considerably expanded kingdom.

Clovis also allied himself with the Catholic Church in Gaul, most of whose bishops came from the Gallo-Roman aristocracy. Clovis' wife, Clotilde, was Catholic and presumably exerted some sort of influence over him, but as usual Clovis was probably guided more by political opportunism than by any sincere interest in Christianity. Alliance with the Church meant alliance with the Gallo-Roman nobles in the short term and it led ultimately to papal recognition of his kingship, which Clovis probably foresaw. Nevertheless, he did eventually convert around the year 500 A.D. The story given by Gregory of Tours has it that Clovis, experiencing his first battlefield defeat at the hands of the Alemanni, called out to Christ, offering to convert in return for victory on the field; Gregory tells us that Christ came immediately to Clovis' aid, scattered the Alemanni, and led the Franks to a glorious rout.

> Then King Clovis asked to be the first one baptized by the bishop [Remigius of Reims, who was in attendance]. He stepped up to the baptismal font like a new Constantine, seeking to wash away the scabs of his old leprosy and be cleansed in that flowing water, to free himself of the ugly stains he had borne for so long.

According to legend, Constantine had suffered from leprosy and was miraculously cured by his baptismal waters. Gregory invokes the legend here to suggest that Clovis' ruthlessness and savagery were likewise washed away, but also to posit, however improbable the comparison, that Clovis represents for the Church in the west what Constantine represented for it in the east—namely, the divinely chosen secular leader whose power could be utilized in the service of the faith.

Clovis ordered the baptism of the three thousand soldiers who had fought with him that day, and subsequently of all his Frankish subjects. But no instruction in the faith accompanied any of these baptisms, and so even though the Franks were vaguely familiar with Christianity through their contact with the Christian Gallo-Romans, the most that we can say happened with the Franks is that they added Christ to the pantheon of pagan gods they continued to worship. Paganism flourished in Gaul, in both its Roman and Germanic forms, for centuries after the formal conversion of the Franks around the year 500, as it did in the realms of all the other Germanic kingdoms. In fact, paganism, the worship of sacred groves, and the practice of magic and divination characterized popular religious life in many parts of northern Europe until well into the eleventh century, especially in rural areas.[6]

Buoyed by the legitimacy bestowed upon Clovis' rule by his alliance with the Church, the Franks expanded aggressively. Their first campaigns after their conversion aimed eastward, back into the Germanic homelands east of the Rhine. After virtually annihilating the Alemanni, they fought against the Saxons, whom they quickly persuaded to flee across the North Sea into England. Reestablishing their control of the Rhine river valley proved significant, because it meant that of all the Germanic groups now dominant in the former western empire only the Franks had direct and continuous contact with the Germanic homelands. This contact had two principal effects: It meant that the Franks were in the best position to replenish their numbers with other migrants of Germanic stock, and also that Frankish society remained the most intensely Germanic of all the early medieval kingdoms, with the least amount of assimilation between their Frankish and Roman heritages. Once they had solidified this link with the Germanic homeland, the Franks swept southward in the hope of reaching the Mediterranean. They were frustrated in this hope by Theodoric and his Ostrogoths, who moved quickly to occupy the region of Provence. Theoderic also pieced together a temporary alliance with the Visigoths who lived in Spain and in Septimania (a small coastal region between Provence and the Pyrenees); these combined forces managed to turn back the Frankish tide and keep them a distinctly northern European kingdom. But this was only the first salvo. From Clovis onward, virtually all the Frankish kings for the next seven hundred and fifty years had their sights set on extending their dominions to the Mediterranean shoreline—until Louis IX finally succeeded in the middle of the thirteenth century.

As with Theodoric and his Ostrogothic realm, Clovis' vast kingdom also did not long survive its founder. By long-standing tradition, the Franks customarily divided a dead man's belongings among all his sons. Since the Frankish kingdom was itself Clovis's personal possession (he certainly regarded it that way, to say the least), tradition called for dividing the realm between his heirs. Thus what was Europe's largest and most powerful kingdom turned instantly, after Clovis died in 511, into four smaller realms. Each of those, subsequently, was subdivided upon the death of its ruler—and the process continued until the original kingdom devolved into a mass of petty princedoms.

The Visigoths

The Visigoths, who had been forced to withdraw from Italy shortly after they sacked Rome in 410, settled in southern France in 418 and established their capital at Toulouse. They were interested in Spain, but the peninsula at that time was en-

---

6. The Latin word *paganus*, from which we derive our "pagan," originally meant "country-dweller."

gulfed in warfare between the remaining Hispano-Roman forces and the attacking Germanic groups known as the Suevi and the Vandals (from whom we derive the word *vandalism*—which gives one a sense of what they were like). The advance of the Vandals into North Africa, however, made Visigothic migration into Spain possible, while the southward expansion of the Franks under Clovis (especially after his defeat of the Visigoths at Vouillé in 507) made it necessary. Certain inroads had already been achieved by that time, though. The Visigoths had defeated the Suevi in 456 and driven them into the furthest northwest reaches of the Spanish peninsula, and had followed up that victory by extending their own control southward to the Strait of Gibraltar by 584. Despite these victories, however, the Visigoths' kingdom remained weak. Their survival depended in large measure on their alliance with Theodoric's Ostrogoths, and in fact it may be best to regard early Visigothic Spain, in the political/military sense at least, as an Ostrogothic dependency; one of the kings of Visigothic Spain, Theudis (r. 531–548), was actually an Ostrogothic general sent over from Italy.

Relations between the Visigoths and the Hispano-Romans were strained, of course. The Visigoths were nominally Arian Christians, while the Hispano-Romans were for the most part Catholic. The Spanish territories also had a significant Jewish population—perhaps the largest in western Europe at that time—which complicated the social scene in the cities because neither of the Christian groups knew how to deal with the Jews, while each of them also tried to court their support at various times. The Visigoths numbered only two to three hundred thousand people, whereas the indigenous population of Spain may have been as high as seven million. Because of their relatively small numbers the Visigoths did not attempt to lord it over their subjects or force their own ways on them. In fact, the majority of the Visigoths remained on the French side of the Pyrenees until several decades into the sixth century, and those who did live in the Spanish territories resided in concentrated military garrisons. By making little attempt actually to settle the countryside, the Visigoths maintained the generally peaceful atmosphere but did little to promote acculturation. A ban on intermarriage also kept them and their subjects apart from each other until the late sixth century. At that time the Visigoths moved their capital to Toledo, in the very heart of Spain, bringing most of their population with them in an effort to foster a greater sense of shared destiny. This was a strategic necessity. Warfare among the petty principalities in the wake of the breakup of Clovis' Frankish kingdom and Theodoric's Ostrogothic one, coupled with the arrival in Italy of the highly aggressive Lombards, left the Visigoths sorely exposed; their best hope for survival was in finding a modus vivendi with the Hispano-Romans.

Recared, king of the Visigoths from 586 to 601, eased this process considerably by converting from Arianism to Catholicism one year after gaining the throne. A church council held at Toledo in 589 formally enacted this conversion for the kingdom as a whole. Numerous revolts broke out among Visigothic warlords and Arian bishops almost immediately, but these crumbled relatively quickly in the absence of significant popular support. The need to acculturate to the majority population was self-evident. Once religious unity had been imposed, Recared set to work to further the unification of the realm. Since the Visigoths lacked any well-developed political institutions, he promoted unification by working closely with the Catholic Church within Spain. The king appointed bishops, convoked ecclesiastical councils, and sanctioned all conciliar decrees, whereas the bishops actively endorsed and propagandized the kingship and protected the king's person against the nobility. Such protection was necessary, since the nobles frequently suffered from what Gregory of Tours called the *morbus gothicus* ("the Gothic disease")—namely, a striking propensity to assassinate their own kings.

Constantly surrounded by high ecclesiastics and acting through them, the Visigothic kings made it appear that their government was in fact a theocracy. That definition misinterprets the nature of Visigothic rule, though. If anything, the churchmen in Spain focused on limiting the power of all central government. The most comprehensive Visigothic law code, the *Liber Judiciorum* ("The Book of Judgments") promulgated in 654, exercised the first explicit limitations on royal power in Europe's history:

> The monarchy and the people of the kingdom are to be subject to the same reverence for the laws. . . .

> Gifts presented to the king are not to be regarded as his personal property but as being held in custody for the people and the realm. . . .

> This law will endure forever, unchanged, and no one shall be allowed to ascend to the royal throne until he has sworn to obey it in all its particulars. . . .

It is difficult to imagine Clovis or Theodoric attaching their seals to such a code. Provincial and local government under the Visigoths remained little changed from Roman times with the exception that civil and military authority, which the Romans had traditionally tried to keep separate, were formally joined.

The desire for religious unification of the kingdom led to the enactment of wide-ranging and severe anti-Jewish legislation. From Recared's conversion until the conquest of Spain by the Muslims in 711, a campaign to suppress Judaism continued without relief. Jews could not marry Christians, own Christian slaves, or hold any public office which had jurisdiction over Christian subjects. In 613 a royal decree ordered all Jews to accept baptism or be expelled from the country. Circumcision was forbidden and Jewish holidays condemned. It is unclear whether enforcement of the laws was as rigorous as the legal rhetoric would make one expect; many Jews did submit to baptism, but the majority did not and simply took their ritual life underground. The height of the oppression came in 694 when a new law compelled the Jews either to convert or be forced into slavery, with all their property being confiscated. Given their experience under the Visigoths, it hardly comes as a surprise that, in 711, the bulk of Spain's Jews welcomed the Muslim armies as liberators.

GERMANIC CHRISTIANITY AND THE FOURTH "DOCTOR OF THE CHURCH"

What did the Germans believe and when did they believe it? That is not an easy question to answer. We can often pinpoint the precise date of the conversion of whole kingdoms, but doing so misleads us into thinking that Christianity had advanced further than it actually had done. As mentioned above, Clovis' acceptance of baptism around the year 500 and his command that all his soldiers and subjects convert as well hardly means that Catholic Christianity was a meaningful presence in any of their lives. But conversion by command was the model for Christian expansion in the west. Unlike the early growth of the faith in the east—where it began as an urban phenomenon among the laboring and merchant classes and gradually worked its way up the social scale, culminating in Constantine's conversion—Christianity in the west spread chiefly from the top of society down to the masses. As the king believed, so did his people; or at least they had better pretend to do so, if they wanted to avoid the royal wrath. Christianity, whether in its Arian or Catholic forms, rested lightly on most Germans for several hundred years after their "official" conversions. They worshiped Christ but they also continued to worship their traditional Germanic deities, plus whatever Roman gods happened to impress them. Pragmatism, not principle, guided their religious lives: They venerated whatever divine power produced results. Belief in a pagan rain god might wane during a long drought, but a crop-saving downpour that happened to occur after a ritual appeal would reaffirm the god's status immediately. Faith in Christ might be fervent, but if lightning happened to strike a Christian church, then veneration of Thor or Jupiter could return quickly. Recared's Arianism was by all accounts sincere, but it proved to be no match for the practical need to accommodate his Hispano-Roman subjects.

The scarcity of priests complicated matters. Since most of the population lived on isolated farms scattered throughout the forest, few believers saw a priest, heard a sermon, received the sacraments, or had any religious instruction more than once or twice a year; many would-be devout believers had to wait years between priestly visits. Meaningful Christianity had a difficult time sinking roots in this situation. Whatever religious instruction there was tended to fall to the women, who introduced their faith to their children. Christianity had always depended for its success on its appeal to women, and females probably made up the majority of believers from the very start. Missionary efforts in the west usually aimed first at the female members of the aristocratic and royal families, and priests working among the masses also found their highest degree of success among women. But without any sustained and reliable priestly presence, Christianity all too easily fell away entirely in the countryside or became amalgamated into the continuing paganism. Pagan folklore thus blended with Christian teachings, and pagan heroes were turned into Christian saints. Sites of pagan worship often provided the foundation of Christian churches, with the pagan idols remaining. Indeed the same building was frequently used by both pagans and Christians.

Confronting this problem head on, Pope Gregory I (r. 590–604), one of only two popes in history known as "the Great," urged his missionaries to take advantage of the situation and wean the people gradually from their older ways.[7] In a famous letter to the priests he had sent to convert the Anglo-Saxons in England, in 601, he wrote:

> I have decided that the peoples' temples to their false gods should not be destroyed, not on any account. The idols within them should be destroyed, but the temples themselves you should simply purify with holy water; moreover, you should set up [Christian] altars in them and place sacred relics in them. If the temples are solidly built, they should be purified from demon-worship and re-dedicated to the service of the true God. This way, I hope, the people, seeing that we have not destroyed their holy sites, may abandon their erring ways: by continuing to congregate regularly in their accustomed site, therefore, they might come to know and adore the true God. Since they now have the tradition of regularly sacrificing numbers of oxen to their false gods, let some other ritual be substituted in its place—a Day of Dedication, perhaps, or a feast of the holy martyrs whose relics are enshrined there.... They should no longer sacrifice their oxen to devils, but they certainly may kill them for food, to the praise of God, and thank the Giver of all gifts for the bounty they are thus enjoying. In this way, if we allow the people some worldly pleasures they will more readily come to desire the joys of the spirit. For indeed, it is not possible to erase all errors from stubborn human minds at a single stroke, and if anyone wishes to reach the top of a mountain he must advance step by step instead of in a single leap.

Gregory's approach had important implications. He recognized that conversion, if it is to be sincere, is not the matter of an instant; spectacular tales of dramatic battlefield conversions like Constantine's or Clovis' are, he recognized, narrative devices used to spice up history books, whereas true conversion is a slower and more gradual process. What Gregory wanted was a genuine and meaningful commitment to Christ by all the Germans, even if this meant advancing only in tiny increments. Therefore he advocated a tolerant stance that let the people approach Christ at their own speed.

Gregory was the fourth of the Latin "Doctors of the Church," after Saints Ambrose, Jerome, and Augustine, and while he may not have equalled his predecessors in scholarly sophistication, he far surpassed them in his sympathetic understanding of people's instincts, desires, and capabilities. He was born into a Roman family of considerable wealth and high social status, but entered a monastery shortly after his father died in 575, using part of his inheritance to finance the new institution. The next four years, he later wrote, were the happiest years of his life. But in 579 he was sent to Constantinople as the papal ambassador, a high-profile position that brought him considerable attention. He remained there for about eight years, gaining experience and observing at first hand the full extent of imperial control of the

---

7.   The other is Pope Leo I (r. 440–461), who turned back Attila the Hun's army.

eastern Church. Upon his election to the papacy, he determined to keep the western Church free of Byzantine control. More than anyone else, Gregory deserves credit for the authentic conversion of the Germans. He initiated the first organized campaigns to proselytize, with handpicked and specially trained missionaries. He remained in constant contact with these missionaries, coordinating their efforts and advising them on specific issues. The letters he wrote to his missionaries show him to have been highly sensitive to the needs of the Germans being preached to. Gregory understood that with the advent of the Germans, an entirely new Europe was coming into being, a change so large that the Church, if was to survive, had to respond with compassion and understanding instead of harsh commands. His missionary to the Anglo-Saxons, St. Augustine of Canterbury (not to be confused with St. Augustine of Hippo), for example, found that although the Anglo-Saxons were predominantly pagan, there were a few Christian communities among them—and yet these differed sharply from one another in terms of their rituals, prayers, and ideas. Augustine wrote to Gregory asking for advice about how to confront the situation. The pope replied:

> My dear brother, you are familiar, of course, with the practices of the Roman Church, in which you were brought up. But if you encounter other customs, whether they derive from Rome or Gaul or anywhere else, that strike you as being more acceptable to God, then I would like you to choose carefully from among them; use whatever you have gainfully learned from *all* of the churches as you teach the church in England, where the people are still new to the faith. Things should not be loved on account of the places they come from. Places should be loved for the good things that emanate from them. Therefore choose from all of the churches whatever you find that is pious, faithful, and right. And after you have tied these things together like flowers into a bouquet, so to speak, then let the people of England accustom their minds to them.

Augustine also noted that ancient Anglo-Saxon custom required a ceremonial purification of a woman's body after she had given birth and that they had asked him how this ritual accorded with Christian teaching. Specifically, they wanted to know how many days after giving birth must a woman wait before being allowed to reenter a church. Gregory answered:

> You know the rule as given in the Old Testament: thirty-three days if the baby is male, sixty-six days if the baby is female. But this needs to be understood as just an allegory, for the truth of the matter is that a woman would be doing nothing wrong at all if she were to enter a church and give thanks to God even in the very hour of her delivery.

Gregory's respect for German customs and conditions is also evident in the *Roman Ordinal* that he compiled.[8] He drew intentionally on all the Germanic churches, and included prayers and rites as had developed under the Franks, the Burgundians, the Visigoths, the Ostrogoths, and the Lombards. The purpose of this inclusiveness

---

8. An ordinal is a liturgical handbook that contains the daily services for an entire ecclesiastical year.

was not only to provide a sort of ritual touchstone, to allow a degree of liturgical diversity among the churches, but to promote unity by defining those regional differences as variations on a single, universally accepted, liturgy.

The Anglo-Saxons were not the only group to embrace Christianity thanks to Gregory's efforts. He also paved the way for the Arian Lombards to accept Catholicism by carefully cultivating a friendship with Theodolinda, the queen of two successive Lombard kings. Word of the conversion of Recared, the Visigothic king, to Catholicism reached Gregory just as he came to the papal throne; he spent the next fourteen years nurturing closer ties with the royal court and doing all that he could to bring the bulk of the people into the Church. He continued the struggle against the Donatists and Arians in Vandal-dominated North Africa as well, though with less success. For all these efforts, not to mention his prolific and immensely influential theological writings, Gregory is rightly regarded as the first pope to command universal respect. His authority rested more on the uniqueness of his personality than on his official position—that is, people revered him as the leader of the Catholic Church more because he was Gregory than because he was the pope—but his extraordinary success certainly paved the way for what the papacy would become. The essence of the man can be seen in the title he used for himself in his correspondence: *servus servorum Dei*, the "servant of the servants of God."

SUGGESTED READING

Texts

Bede. *Ecclesiastical History of the English People.*
———. *Lives of the Abbots.*
Gregory I, Pope. *The Dialogues.*
———. *Forty Homilies on the Gospels.*
———. *Moralia.*
———. *Pastoral Care.*
Gregory of Tours. *The Glory of the Martyrs.*
———. *History of the Franks.*
Isidore of Seville. *Etymologies.*
Paul the Deacon. *History of the Lombards.*
Tacitus. *Germania.*
The Burgundian Code.
The Lombard Laws.

Source Anthologies

Hillgarth, J[ocelyn]. N. *Paganism and Christianity: The Conversion of Western Europe, 300–750* (1986).
Murray, Alexander Callander. *From Roman to Merovingian Gaul: A Reader* (2000).

Studies

Bachrach, Bernard S. *Armies and Politics in the Early Medieval West* (1993).

Barnwell, P. S. *Emperor, Prefects and Kings: The Roman West 395–565* (1993).

Collins, Roger. *Early Medieval Spain: Unity in Diversity, 400–1000* (1983).

Fletcher, Richard. *The Barbarian Conversion: From Paganism to Christianity* (1998).

Geary, Patrick. *Before France and Germany: The Creation and Transformation of the Merovingian World* (1988).

———. *The Myth of Nations: The Medieval Origins of Europe* (2002).

Goffart, Walter. *Barbarians and Romans, A.D. 418–584: The Techniques of Accommodation* (1980).

Heather, Peter. *Goths and Romans A.D. 332–489* (1991).

Innes, Matthew. *State and Society in the Early Middle Ages: The Middle Rhine Valley, 400–1000* (2000).

James, Edward. *The Franks* (1988).

———. *The Origins of France: From Clovis to the Capetians, 500–1000* (1982).

Mayr-Harting, Henry. *The Coming of Christianity to Anglo-Saxon England* (1972).

Riché, Pierre. *Education and Culture in the Barbarian West: Sixth through Eighth Century* (1976).

Russell, James C. *The Germanization of Early Medieval Christianity* (1994).

Thompson, E. A. *The Early Germans* (1965).

———. *The Goths in Spain* (1969).

———. *Romans and Barbarians: The Decline of the Western Empire* (1982).

Todd, Malcolm. *The Early Germans* (1992).

Van Dam, Raymond. *Leadership and Community in Late Antique Gaul* (1985).

Wallace-Hadrill, J. M. *The Barbarian West, 400–1000* (1952).

———. *Early Germanic Kingship in England and on the Continent* (1971).

———. *The Frankish Church* (1983).

Wells, Peter S. *The Barbarians Speak: How the Conquered Peoples Shaped Roman Europe* (1999).

Wolfram, Herwig. *History of the Goths* (1988).

———. *The Roman Empire and Its Germanic Peoples* (1997).

Wood, Ian. *The Missionary Life: Saints and the Evangelisation of Europe, 400–1050* (2000).

CHAPTER 4

CLOISTER AND CULTURE

By the end of the fourth century the age of Christian persecution and martyrdom had ended, and while this was certainly a good thing it also ushered in an entirely new and unexpected set of problems. How, in an era when Christianity was not only the favored religion but was in some places downright fashionable, could one evince the same heroic devotion, the same selfless piety and steadfastness, as those believers who had literally given their lives to Christ? The lure of Christianity, after all, entailed the promise of a transformative experience: One's life became radically and permanently changed through belief in Jesus. And yet in a world in which Christianity was slowly becoming commonplace—and especially after the emperor Theodosius' decision to make it the official religion of the empire—how was genuine, transformative commitment to be distinguished from mere conformity with the established faith? This problem confronted the more well-to-do and educated sectors of Mediterranean society in the fourth and fifth centuries particularly—as shown, for example, in the personal struggles of figures like St. Jerome and St. Augustine of Hippo—as Christianity absorbed and adapted itself to classical culture. Well-to-do Christians became increasingly indistinguishable from non-Christians in terms of their daily lifestyles, their aesthetic values, their education, and their intellectual interests. For many caught in this conundrum, the conviction arose that the surest expression of an authentic Christian commitment lay in the adoption of an ascetic lifestyle: that is, through the intentional and public renunciation of the wealth and status into which they had been born, in favor of a life of solitary prayer, self-discipline, chastity, and study.

It was hardly a new idea. Ascetic rigor had been a common feature of Judaism at least since the Maccabean period, two centuries before Christ, and the pagan classical world had a well-developed notion of the philosophical life, one devoted to contemplation of life's meaning rather than to involvement in its mundane realities, as an ideal of human existence. As the eastern Mediterranean world became fully—and, as many feared, complacently—Christianized, the appeal of the ascetic life became irresistible.

THE RISE OF MONASTICISM IN THE EAST

The question, of course, was precisely how to lead such a life. Two options existed, either to live in isolation as a hermit or to join a specially constituted spiritual community. First, like St. Jerome, one could lead an utterly solitary life in the desert or wilderness, either huddling in a cave or tent, or facing the elements in a makeshift shack or ruined building. Such solitary figures—revered in the Middle Ages as the "Desert Fathers"—spent their lives in constant prayer, fighting off the ever-present temptation to return to the world. The earliest known figure in this movement was St. Anthony (d. 356), the son of a well-established farmer along the upper Nile, in Egypt. Born into the faith, he experienced intensely all the ambivalence of well-to-do Christians of his time. One day shortly after the death of his parents and his inheritance of the family's riches, according to a contemporary biography by St. Anthansius:

> [h]e was turning these things [i.e., his new wealth and status] over in his mind when he entered the local church, where it happened that the Gospel lesson was being read aloud; that's when Anthony heard the Lord's command to the rich man: "If you wish to be perfect, go and sell what you own and give the money to the poor, and you will have treasure in heaven; then come, follow me." [Matthew 19:21] As if by divine guidance, then, the memory of all the saints came to him, and it seemed to Anthony that the passage had been read for his benefit alone.

Taking the lesson to heart, Anthony immediately stepped out, sold his estate, and gave away all his money except for an endowment that he set aside for his unmarried sister. He then pledged himself to a hermit's life, living on the desert's edge, praying continually, surviving by begging and offering his manual labor for hire, and committing long passages of the Bible to memory.[1] He lived in caves and desolate cemeteries until finally, around 285, he took up residence in an abandoned military outpost, where he spent the next twenty years.

As those years passed, Anthony developed a reputation for holiness, and, against his will, he began to attract disciples—so many, in fact, that "the desert surrounding his encampment became choked with monks." This unwanted crowd made Anthony restless, and the start of Diocletian's Great Persecution gave him an excuse to leave. He journeyed to Alexandria and ministered to the Christians imprisoned there. It was a dangerous thing to do, but he managed to avoid arrest; when the persecution ended after Constantine's conversion, Anthony again sought solitude, this time on a mountain near the Red Sea. But by now his reputation as a holy man was greater than ever, and he never again experienced the peace of being alone with God. Disciples, doubters, the confused, and the merely curious came to him from miles around; his opinion was sought in settling local disputes; his words carried the force of prophecy and sometimes of law. In the end, he relented and established a permanent, though small and informal, monastic community. Bible-reading, prayer, and fasting were the centerpieces of the community's life. Anthony himself, despite years of living under the harshest

---

1. The word *hermit* derives from the Greek *eremia,* meaning "desert."

of circumstances and holding himself in the severest discipline—"He kept up his prayer-vigils to the point where he often continued all night long, without any sleep at all; he ate only once a day, after sunset, and sometimes only once every other day or once every four days; and his only food was bread, salt, and water"—lived to the astonishing age of 105. He died in early 356, having spent eighty-five years in self-exile.

Asceticism grew in popularity throughout the fourth century as more and more Christians found it difficult to reconcile themselves to their privileged status. Few equalled St. Anthony in rigor,[2] and it became increasingly common for those seeking a new type of Christian commitment to choose the second option—namely, to live together in a permanent spiritual community. The word *monastery* derives from a Greek verb meaning "to live alone," but most monasteries were communal in nature. Their "aloneness" consisted of their physical separation from mainstream society, but even more significantly aloneness was defined by the vows taken by monks when entering the community, in which they renounced the world, their social status, their wealth, and all their concerns for the world outside. Inside the monastery, a communal spirit and style predominated, one not quite egalitarian but something akin to it. Many of these monasteries were quite large: The community at Nitria, in lower Egypt, for example, had as many as five thousand monks. Literally thousands of monasteries sprang up across Egypt, Palestine, Syria, and Asia Minor in the fourth century, and as they multiplied and grew, it became evident that some type of formal organization was necessary. Five thousand people, no matter how holy and well-intentioned, cannot live together without some commonly agreed-upon system of rules. So it was that these communities created for themselves disciplinary codes—eventually called *Regulae*, or "Rules"— that organized their daily lives. Often a new community simply adopted a code already used somewhere else, helping to establish a sort of network of like-minded monasteries. Many of these Rules survive, and they provide valuable insight into the mentalities and daily realities of early monks. Through them we can also chart the evolution of the monastic movement as it spread northward and westward into medieval Europe.

One of the earliest was the *Rule of St. Pachomius*. For Pachomius (290–345), a native of Tabennisi in upper Egypt, the Bible formed the core of monastic life; indeed, there is little evidence that he ever read anything else. He came from a non-illustrious family and had served in the imperial army for a time. Originally a pagan, he converted after being befriended by a group of Christians while he was briefly imprisoned. He had only a rudimentary education and placed no great store in ideas. The Bible was all that he needed, and consequently he made it the focus of

---

2.   Although many tried: A fellow named Macarius of Alexandria, for example, once tried to stand upright in prayer, nonstop, throughout the entire forty-day season of Lent, while eating nothing but cabbage leaves.

his Rule. He required that anyone seeking to enter his monastery had first to show his qualifications by reciting from memory at least twenty Psalms and at least two of St. Paul's Epistles. (One was allowed to use two of the shorter ones.) If granted admission, the monk made his vows, put on his robe and cowl, and took up residence in one of the dormitories into which the overall monastery was divided. These dormitories were based on trade and craft: Those who had been cloth weavers in the outside world were housed together, as were blacksmiths, butchers, carpenters, scribes, and so on. The purpose behind this organization was to ensure the self-sufficiency of the entire community which, having renounced the world, would produce for itself all the material goods it needed for sustenance. Each dormitory had a senior monk in charge who was responsible for maintaining discipline and administering each monk's daily labor; the dormitory heads reported to the chief monk who held authority over the entire monastery; each monastery's chief monk answered, initially, to Pachomius himself and afterward to Pachomius' successors as leaders of the entire Pachomian network. The movement's survival was bolstered by close ties between the Pachomian monasteries and the Patriarch of Alexandria.

Since monastic life under the *Rule of St. Pachomius* focused exclusively on physical work, communal prayer, and Bible-reading—but not any other type of reading—Pachomian monasticism left no intellectual legacy of any significance. Monks received no education, studied nothing other than the Scriptures, engaged in no scientific work, and wrote no books of their own. They acquired well-deserved reputations for discipline and piety, but not for intellectual or cultural attainment. The movement therefore had relatively little direct influence outside its native Egypt—with one important exception. St. Pachomius was the first monastic leader to establish an organized, canonical network of *double monasteries* (although this term was not coined until the sixth century) in which male and female monks were linked. The sexes lived apart, either in discreetly separated cloisters within the monastery or in individual monasteries that shared a common administration. Female monks largely conducted their own spiritual lives—since there was no emphasis on the sacraments, there was no need for priests to be in charge—and devoted themselves to prayer and the Scriptures. The male monks entered the female convents regularly to tend to the women's material needs; conversely, the nuns were involved in food preparation for the men. But joint meals were expressly forbidden, and all interaction between the sexes was carefully regulated. Double monasteries became increasingly common throughout the east, until a church council in 787 forbade the establishment of any new such houses. But by then the idea had spread, and in the sixth, seventh, and eighth centuries double monasteries along the Pachomian model—although not using the Pachomian Rule itself—appeared in numerous sites in Spain, France, England, and Ireland.

The next great monastic Rule was that of St. Basil of Caesarea (329–379). Basil stands in sharp contrast to Pachomius. He was a Greek aristocrat of high birth, great wealth, and cultural refinement. He received his education in Constantinople and Athens, where he excelled in rhetoric. Given his background and skills, an administrative career in the imperial capital beckoned; but his family had instilled a profound commitment to Christianity in Basil (his grandmother, both his parents, his sister, and his two younger brothers are all saints); this commitment led to his decision in 358 to relinquish professional ambition and enter the church. He toured Syria, Palestine, and Egypt in order to examine the varieties of monastic life and was strongly tempted to take up a solitary ascetic life. But in the end he opted for the clerical life and was ordained a priest; he never forgot his monkish yearnings, however, and until his death in 379 he satisfied them with regular retreats. In 370 he was elected bishop of Caesarea, in which role he played an important part in several ecumenical councils, devoting himself especially to the effort to reconcile the various christianities while defending the Christian orthodoxy established at the Council of Nicaea.

Basil was a prolific writer—nearly four hundred of his letters survive—and his published works show the full range of his interests. Apart from his Rule, his most famous works are his "Address to Young Men on the Reading of the Works of the Gentiles," which examines the controversy over the appropriateness of classical literature for Christian readers, and his treatise *On the Hexaemeron* (also called *The Six Days of Creation*), which deals with the creation of the universe and shows a detailed familiarity with Greek astronomy and physics. His knowledge of philosophy was extensive, too, and his theological works are clearly influenced by the Neo-Platonic thought of figures like Plotinus. But it is his monastic Rule, whose actual title is the *Asceticon*, that matters most. It consists of a long series of questions and answers, and it gives the impression of being quite literally Basil's responses to specific questions posed to him by a monastic community already in existence, or else just coming to be. This impression is amplified by the fact that Basil shortly thereafter published a revised edition that shored up certain shortcomings in the initial version.[3]

Despite his own hermetic inclinations, Basil championed a monastic life that was considerably more communal in nature than the isolated rigorism of Pachomius. The monastic calling, he maintained, was a calling both to spiritual brotherhood and to service in the world. To those ends, Basil recommended that monasteries be placed within cities and villages, not on remote mountains or in blasted wildernesses; that monasteries be limited in size (thirty to forty members was the ideal) so that a true sense of community could develop; that monks worship together daily and that they worship regularly with the local lay populace in public churches attached to the monastery; and that monks should operate schools

---

3. For example, in the first edition Basil assumes without discussion that monks will always be celibate, whereas in the second edition he specifies at some length that all monks must take permanent vows of chastity. One can imagine the reasons for the change.

and hospitals for their townsfolk. To promote this last point, continuous study should be a hallmark of the monks' lives, and this study should consist of more than the Scriptures: grammar, music, and mathematics all have a place in monastic life, Basil argued. He also stated explicitly that monasteries should be under the absolute authority of their local bishops. Basil's aim, clearly, was to create a spiritual community that was truly a community rather than a collection of single ascetics inhabiting a common site—and a community, moreover, that was in service to the larger Christian society outside the monastery's walls.

Since his concern was to incorporate monasticism into the liturgical Church, Basil never founded a distinct Order. Yet his vision of monastic life proved an enduringly popular one, and Basilian-style monasteries quickly proliferated throughout the east from the fourth through the sixth centuries. During the sixth century, when the Byzantine Empire reconquered much of its old territory in the central and western Mediterranean (see the discussion in the next chapter), Basilian monasticism spread with it and significantly influenced the evolution of monastic life there. It remains the most characteristic form of monastic life in the Greek Orthodox Church today.

THE RISE OF MONASTICISM IN THE WEST

Monasticism first appeared in the west in the late fourth century. The earliest establishments that we know of in Mediterranean Europe resulted from the travels of various figures from the east, such as St. Athanasius (d. 371) who founded several houses in central and northern Italy. From here, trained missionaries brought the monastic ideal to Spain, North Africa, and southern and central France. St. Martin of Tours (d. 397) is perhaps the best-known early proponent of that ideal in the west. Converting at the age of eighteen, in the early years of a long military career, Martin spent several years after his discharge doing missionary work among the Arian Ostrogoths but soon decided to become a monk. He lived briefly in a few Italian monastic houses but then set off to establish a new community at Ligugé, just south of Poitiers; this appears to have been the first monastery ever established in France. In 371 Martin was elected bishop of Tours, and for the rest of his life he struggled to balance his monastic calling with his clerical responsibilities. He founded other monasteries, created a network of parish churches, counseled emperors, and appealed above all for an end to the violence engulfing western Europe.

But Martin's significance lay more in his biography than in his life: The *Life of St. Martin* written by Sulpicius Severus in the early fifth century became the model for all medieval *hagiography*, (literally, a "sacred writing,"[4] but used most commonly;

---

4. St. Athanasius also wrote a *Life of St. Martin* which was available in the west in a Latin translation by the end of the fourth century. Sulpicius Severus utilized some of its material for his own *Life*.

to mean the "biography of a saint"; these were not biographies in the modern sense, however, but rather idealized portraits written as edifying tales of Christian virtue.) The writing of "saints' lives" became one of the enduring passions of western medieval monks, and the reading of them both shaped and drove the cult of the saints that lay at the heart of popular religion in the Middle Ages. The *Life of St. Martin* portrays him as a western equivalent of St. Anthony, an ascetic who seeks communion with God through a kind of living martyrdom, but whose wide reputation for sanctity continually brings him back into the world. Like Anthony, Martin receives his initiation into the monastic life from a wise elder—in Martin's case, a man known as Hilary of Poitiers—and spends his early years of solitude combating various forms of temptation. Finally, Martin attains a state of grace that enables him to overcome his temptations. But the arrival of a constant stream of would-be disciples disrupt the saint's reverie, but in the end prove to be yet another vehicle by which the man of God serves the divine purpose; in the end, the saint dies a peaceful death, surrounded by his praying, weeping brethren, and his soul is taken into heaven.

This basic pattern repeated itself thousands of times over the next six to eight centuries of hagiographical writing. Most significantly, however, the *Life of St. Martin* placed special stress on a unique new element: It emphasized the miraculous power of the saint. Martin, according to the text, did more than live a pious life—he performed miracles. In a typical example, Martin and several of his monks traveled through the countryside preaching and pulling down pagan shrines.

> St. Martin once demolished an ancient pagan temple somewhere, and when he was about to cut down a pine tree that was near to it, the temple priest and some others began to riot. They had watched patiently while their temple was destroyed—since that had been ordered by the king—but they would on no account suffer their tree to be felled. Martin calmly reminded them that there was nothing religious about a tree and that they ought to follow the Lord whom he himself was serving. He added too that cutting down the tree was necessary, since it was dedicated to a demon.
>
> But then one of the men, who was bolder than the rest, said to him, "If you have such confidence in this God you claim to follow, let *us* cut down the tree so that it falls straight on you—and see if you survive! If your God is with you, as you say, you'll escape [being crushed]."
>
> Martin, confiding calmly in the Lord, promised the men that it would be done. The whole crowd agreed to the deal, thinking it would be worth sacrificing the tree in order to vanquish the enemy of their sacred woods.
>
> Now this pine tree inclined to one side, so it was obvious where it would fall. Martin was bound to the spot where everyone knew the tree would land, and then the men began to chop away at the tree with terrific excitement and abandon. A crowd of watchers gathered from afar. Little by little the tree began to teeter and threatened to crush Martin. The monks, at a distance, grew pale with terror as the danger came ever closer; indeed, all faith and hope left them, so certain were they of Martin's imminent death.
>
> But Martin waited bravely, having full confidence in the Lord, and when the

pine tree began to crash to the earth and collapse upon him, he raised his hand, made the sign of the Cross, and called out to God. And then, just as if a sudden whirlwind rose in its path, you might say, the tree split into two halves [each falling on either side of Martin]. The people standing about suddenly threw themselves on the ground, and as the din filled the sky, they all marveled at this miracle. The monks cried out in joy, and the name of Christ was proclaimed by everyone at once. Martin, well satisfied, decided to leave that region that very day.

Surviving being crushed was hardly the extent of Martin's miracles. He went on to cure the mortally ill, drive out demons, restore sight to the blind, and even, in his most spectacular miracle, raise a slave from the dead. Gregory of Tours, author of the *History of the Franks*, also wrote a miracle-filled book, *On the Virtues of the Blessed Bishop Martin*, that narrated scores of miraculous deeds performed at the site of Martin's tomb. Martin's miracles were later illustrated in the wall paintings and carvings that decorated a church built in his honor at Tours in the late fifth century. The inscription above the entry of the church prepared the worshipers for what they were about to behold, while making a curious backhanded slap at the *Life of St. Martin* itself.

> After you have bowed low to the ground, with your face pressed into the dirt and your tears streaming from your eyes onto the trodden soil, then lift your head and, with awestruck glance, behold the miracles that surround you and devote yourself to the cult of Martin, the best of all patrons. No book can tell so well the magnificent achievements recorded here in stone. The earth itself is not large enough to contain all of Martin's glory: God's Heavenly Court has absorbed it, and the stars in the sky have inscribed it in shining jewels. If you would seek Martin's help, look for him beyond the stars, in Heaven, and inquire of the host of angels in that eternal realm. There you will find him joined to the Lord as he follows eternally in the footsteps of the Eternal King. If you are doubtful, behold the miracles you see portrayed here, miracles through which the True Redeemer gives honor to the worthiness of His servant. As you look upon these things (may they always be remembered!) and you repeat to others what you are about to see, you will become the newest member of a company of witnesses numbering in the thousands. With God's help, Martin brings to new life all the miracles told in the Holy Scriptures: he brings a blessing and a cure to all—the blind, the crippled, the poor, those possessed by demons, the heart-broken, the sick, the weak, the downtrodden, prisoners, the afflicted, and the needy—and each of his cures is a miracle worthy of an Apostle. Whoever enters this church weeping, leaves it rejoicing, with all his troubles vanished. Martin is the cure for all sadness. Seek his help! No knock on his door is in vain! Truly, his generosity and goodness extend throughout the entire world.

The medieval belief in miracles is difficult for modern readers to understand. It had obvious origins in the miracle stories told in the New Testament, such as Christ's raising of Lazarus from the dead or Peter's curing the lame; but it had roots as well in the Germanic and classical pagan traditions. The belief starts from the assumption that divine power is, by its very definition, capable of being at work in this world. Everything from earthquakes to eclipses, from outbreaks of disease to victories in battle, can be interpreted as signs of heavenly approval or disapproval. Throughout history, societies have commonly believed that certain individuals, whether through initiation in mystical rites or through random divine selection, have gained access to this power and become its transmitters. As an anthropological type, the miracle-working Christian saint has much in common with Muslim Sufis, transcendental Buddhist masters, and east African animist holy men with their *barakah* (ability to cast spells). Belief in their power derives from a simple observation that life is, in fact, miraculous. Miracles do not contradict reason; instead, they complement it by explaining all those things that reason cannot yet comprehend. But did the readers of the *Life of St. Martin* and its progeny believe the specific literal assertion that Martin split a tree in half with a wave of his hand? We cannot say for sure, but it is clear they believed that it *could* be true, that God's power *could* do such a thing. As the main production sites of medieval saints' lives, monasteries were the institutions chiefly responsible for shaping and promoting the belief in saintly miracles in the early Middle Ages.

But while the dominant strain of medieval monasticism came from the Mediterranean world, an important variation emerged independently in the north that had significant influence on medieval life. The variation arose spontaneously, without any visible influence from or knowledge of the movement in the south. It appeared primarily among the Celtic people of what is today northwestern France and the British Isles, and was, if anything, even more popular than its southern counterpart. For the Celts, monasticism offered an escape from rural misery and clan warfare. This was especially the case in Ireland, where the famous missionary St. Patrick discovered to his surprise that the young men and women he converted to Christianity positively insisted on forming separate communities in isolation from the rest of society. Given the fact that the overwhelming bulk of St. Patrick's success was with the younger elements of the Irish population, the quick rise of separatist Christian communities there may have had an element of youth rebellion in it. Rebellion certainly played a part in the case of St. Brigid (d. 528) who became one of Ireland's patron saints. She was the daughter of a prominent landowner and his slave-mistress, and although her father recognized his paternity he nevertheless dismissed Brigid and sent her away to be raised by a foster mother. By the time she was in her teens, however, Brigid had become an accomplished seamstress and housekeeper, had become literate, and was a beauty—thus a valuable item on the marriage-market. When her long-absent father suddenly reappeared on the scene and tried to force her into a financially desirable marriage, she refused on the spot and vowed her perpetual virginity. Her father fumed and threatened, but Brigid stood firm and soon after took the veil and founded her own convent at Kildare. Ireland by the year 600 had well over a hundred thriving monasteries and abbeys and was easily the most fully monasticized region in Europe.[5]

Monasticism also quickly took root in Wales and England, albeit a bit later than in Ireland. Establishments at places like Liancarven and Ynys Pyr, in Wales, and at Iona and Lindisfarne, in northeastern England, earned reputations as models of discipline and pious living. The latter two also contributed to a cultural revival known as the *Northumbrian Renaissance*, which we will discuss in the next chapter.

Early monasticism was an eclectic phenomenon in western Europe. Personalities, rather than programs, drove the movement. Gradually the southern and northern strains of monastic life made contact, and one result was the proliferation of Rules. Few of these were composed whole; most new establishments patched together Rules for themselves by borrowing snippets from other Rules. Thus we find passages of the *Rule of St. Pachomius* and the *Rule of St. Basil* appearing in monasteries in Spain, the Netherlands, and central France. Penitential decrees from the Irish and British houses are scattered in Rules as far away as Bavaria. In northern France alone, around the year 600, we know of at least twenty of these hybrid Rules. But as this hybridization occurred, so too did something else—the development of a self-awareness of monasteries as the sole outposts of authentic Christianity. Commitment to Christ that was anything less than total, medieval monks and nuns came to believe, was no commitment at all. Here is how one monastic writer, St. John Cassian, described the evolution of this view:

> The monastic lifestyle had its origins in apostolic times and in the preaching of the Apostles, for the mass of believers in Jerusalem were exactly as they are described in the book of *Acts*: "The whole group of believers was united, heart and soul; no one claimed for his own use anything that he had, as everything they owned was held in common; they sold their goods and possessions and shared out the proceeds among themselves according to what each needed." And again: "None of their members was ever in want, as all those who owned land or houses would sell them, and bring the money from them, to present it to the Apostles; it was then distributed to any members who might be in need."
>
> The entire Church, in other words, was then of a character that now can only be found—and even so, only with some difficulty—in our monasteries. When the Apostles' time ended, though, the fervor of most Christians began to abate, especially the fervor of those who had come to Christianity from foreign nations. Of these people the Apostles, out of consideration for the newness of their faith and for their still-ingrained pagan ways, had demanded only that they should abstain from idol-worship, fornication, unclean food, and violence; but the exception made for these nations on account of the comparative weakness of their new-found faith soon began to undermine the purity of the Church as it had existed in Jerusalem. . . . But those few who still maintained

---

5. Some scholars have suggested that Brigid is a semi-legendary figure or even a Christianized version of an Irish pagan goddess. The jury is still out on these issues, yet the element of youthful rebellion against the strictures of clan life emphasized here would be true in any case.

*Early images of Christ in the west emphasized his power more than his mercy.
This Christ Pantokrator (the "all-powerful") fresco comes from the monastery of San
Clemente de Tahull, in Catalonia. It was painted in the late eighth century, when the
region formed part of the Spanish March—the borderland separating the Carolingian
realm from that of Muslim Spain. Source: Erich Lessing / Art Resource, NY*

the fervor of apostolic times and remembered that earlier state of perfection
abandoned their cities and broke off relations with those who believed that a
carefree and luxurious life was a birthright and acceptable in the eyes of the
Church of God. These few began to live in the countryside or wilderness, isolated and alone, and there they began to put into practice those things that they
understood the Apostles to have decreed for all Christians everywhere. This
whole system of monastic life, in other words, grew out of the faith of those
disciples who cut themselves off from the world's spreading evil.

*A sixth-century Byzantine fresco from Ravenna. Christ appears dressed
as a Roman soldier; the shoulder-clasp identifies him as an officer. He is carrying
a Cross in a manner of a sword while trampling a lion and a serpent.*
Source: Erich Lessing / Art Resource, NY

This may sound like spiritual snobbishness (which it is, and therefore it is all the more rewarding to point out that Cassian got his biblical verses mixed up [cf. Acts 2:44–45 and 2:33–35]), but it illustrates two important medieval facts.

First was the popular assumption of early medieval society that in all probability only professed monks and nuns would be saved on Judgment Day. The great bulk of sinning non-Christians would be cast into eternal torment—everyone expected that; but for all run-of-the-mill Christians—those peasant farmers, housewives, merchants, craftsmen, millers, sailors, midwives, and maids who had tried to lead good Christian lives but who did not take monastic vows—there was no guarantee of salvation at all.

One might hope for mercy on that terrible day, but the odds were slim. This view often strikes modern readers as a conundrum, since modern Christianity typically stresses Jesus' loving kindness. But early medieval thought and preaching emphasized the difficulty of getting into Heaven, not the promise of salvation to all; and early medieval art depicted Christ as a stern judge, a king with a bad temper, rather than a loving and gentle spirit. This characterization derives chiefly from the pagan traditions that Christianity had supplanted. To the Germans divinity was something to be feared, not loved; appeased, not appealed to. The Germanic gods wreaked havoc on earth: Thunder, earthquake, famine, and disease were their signature activities—not blessings and rewards. To the pagan Romans, too, the power of the gods inspired awe rather than adoration. Jupiter was the "Thunder Wielder," Apollo brought disease as often as healing, and Hera spent at least as much time trying to destroy her enemies as she did protecting women in childbirth. As these societies coalesced from the third to the eighth centuries, they attributed to Christ some of the characteristics of divine power that lay imbedded in their traditional cultures. One consequence of this assumption of a monastic monopoly on salvation was the widespread trend of individuals taking monastic vows in old age, as death was approaching. For every youthful St. Martin or St. Brigid, there was a handful of elderly men and women seeking to fulfill their Christian life as it entered its last chapter.

Second, the development of western monasticism had clear implications for emerging ideas about social class. The call to monastic life entailed not just an embrace of a life of prayer, chastity, poverty, work, and study; it also involved, and generally required, a renunciation of wealth and status. But those who have no wealth to renounce can hardly point to their embrace of poverty as proof of their spiritual virtue. The monastic life thus evolved into the exclusive domain of the well-to-do. A practical consideration played a role here: When one entered a medieval monastery one renounced one's wealth in favor of other family members or of the poor, but one also pledged part of one's wealth to the monastery itself. Such pledges provided an endowment, a way to help the community meet the increased expense of having another mouth to feed, another body to shelter, another mind to educate. For the most part, only those individuals who had some form of wealth to donate to the monastery could enter. These endowments occasionally took the form of money or precious items, but since the early medieval economy was so primitive, the most common form of payment was land. This land became the permanent property of the community, and it generated the food and revenue that guaranteed the community's self-sufficiency. As monasticism grew in popularity, the relative wealth of these institutions grew apace and widened the economic and social rift that separated the monastic world from the secular world.

CULTURAL LIFE IN THE WEST: CASSIODORUS, BOETHIUS, AND ST. BENEDICT

These early monasteries provided, if not the sole, then at least the most numerous and important sites of intellectual and cultural life in western Europe. Regardless of the particular Rule each followed, nearly all western monasteries and convents demanded of their members a life of study as well as prayer, and since study requires books, monasteries became centers of book production—copying, chiefly. Most of what survives of the classical and early Christian legacy we owe to the industry of these monk-scribes; but they also produced a fair amount of original intellectual work, and their ideas had a lasting influence on the next thousand years of medieval life. Three figures stand out in the sixth century: Cassiodorus, a leading statesman in Theodoric's Ostrogothic kingdom; Boethius, a philosopher and government official who wrote *The Consolation of Philosophy*—arguably the most-read book of the entire Middle Ages after the Bible; and St. Benedict of Nursia, founder of the greatest monastery of the Middle Ages and author of the most widespread monastic Rule in the west.

Cassiodorus (485–580) spent his early years in public service and rose to the position of "Master of Offices" under Theodoric—something akin to being the king's prime minister. Cassiodorus devoted himself especially to reconciling the Romans with their Germanic conquerors, a job he was well suited for, given his own descent from a prominent Roman family. But at the midpoint of his long life he withdrew from the world and established a monastery at Vivarium, in his native southern Italy, and took up the contemplative, scholarly life. He himself never took monastic vows, however, and was content to serve as the patron and headmaster of his new community.

Paralleling his earlier political concerns, Cassiodorus devoted his scholarly career to reconciling the Roman and Germanic cultural traditions. He wrote a lengthy, though now lost, *History of the Goths*, and he followed it with an even more ambitious world history that placed the Roman-Germanic-Christian synthesis in a universal perspective. He compiled an anthology of important Byzantine chronicles and oversaw their translation into Latin. Translation, in fact, remained a lifelong passion of his. Painfully aware of the intellectual decline of the west and the rapid disappearance of the knowledge of Greek, Cassiodorus set to translating as many early Christian texts—chiefly sermons and exegetical writings—from that language as he could find. Even more pressing, though, was the decline in literacy overall. In 537 Cassiodorus compiled another anthology, called the *Miscellany*, in which he collected many of the letters he had written while serving as "Master of Offices." He intended these to aid other writers by providing models of correspondence.

Specifically for his monks Cassiodorus wrote commentaries on the Psalms, the Gospels, the Acts of the Apostles, and on Paul's Letter to the Romans. His most influential work overall was the *Institutes*, in which he sought to create an entire curriculum of study for all monks. The chief emphasis here was on preparing the monks for the proper and complete understanding of the Scriptures—for only after achieving this goal, Cassiodorus argued, could one fully appreciate the teachings of the Church. He based his curriculum on a model developed earlier by a scholar named Martianus Capellanus. It stressed the primacy of the seven "liberal arts": grammar, rhetoric, and dialectic (which Cassiodorus grouped together under the rubric of the *trivium*), followed by geometry, astronomy, music, and mathematics (grouped as the *quadrivium*). Specifically, the trivium gave one the language-ability needed to read, speak, and think in Latin, while the quadrivium introduced the skills needed for the literal, symbolic, and allegorical interpretations of Holy Writ.

Why would one need to know astronomy and mathematics in order to understand the Bible? First and foremost, in order to date biblical events, and therefore their commemoration, accurately. The Romans used a solar calendar and numbered the years from the touchstone-date of the legendary founding of the city (753 B.C., by our system of reckoning), but the Jews used a lunar calendar that numbered the years from their traditional date of the creation of the world (3761 B.C., to us). These numerical differences, coupled with the difficult calculation of astronomical events such as comets and solar or lunar eclipses, made establishing a clear chronology of biblical events exceedingly complicated. The fact that biblical history reaches back in time far earlier than the Romans only exacerbated the problem, because then one had to contend with the numerous chronometrical systems of the Greeks and Egyptians as well. Moving forward in time only introduced more calendrical complications, since a number of Christian scholars from the early third century on tried to introduce a new set of figures. One such writer, Hippolytus of Rome, created a dating system (known as A.M.I, or "Annus Mundi I—"*annus mundi* being Latin for "the year of the world") that was loosely based on the Hebrew tradition but which pushed the creation of the world even farther back in time, so that Christ's Incarnation occurred in what Hippolytus reckoned to be the year 5500. About one hundred years later Eusebius of Caesarea adjusted the system by about three hundred years (A.M.II) so that the Incarnation occurred in year 5228. Both systems remained in use among Christians for several centuries.[6] The difficulties created by all this confusion are obvious, and they made knowledge of both mathematics and astronomy key to interpreting Scripture. How else to know when to celebrate Easter—traditionally the first Sunday after the first full moon after the spring equinox?

Music, too, had an essential role to play. Under the influence of the *Rule of St. Basil*, the singing of psalms became a centerpiece of monastic worship. By the end of the sixth century, in fact, most western monasteries sang the entire Psalter every week. Far from being the silent, gloomy enclosures of our imaginations, medieval monasteries were filled with music, and the choirmaster—or cantor—was second only to the abbot in terms of his importance to the community.

It was another figure, though, who did most to popularize the trivium and quadrivium. Anicius Manlius Torquatus Severinus Boethius—Boethius, for short—was the greatest philosopher of the early Middle Ages. Born in Rome in 480, he studied in the philosophical academies in Athens and Alexandria as a young man. He also served as a high official in the Ostrogothic court, until he fell from grace

---

6. As we will see later, the A.D. (now C.E.) system of dating did not become widespread in the west until the eighth century. Therefore to the Christians living in Merovingian France, for example, the conversion of Clovis that we date to the year A.D. 500 took place in what they regarded as either A.M.I 6000 or A.M.II 5728. To those who followed the A.M.I system, Clovis' conversion presumably had symbolic significance since it marked the start of a new millennium.

amid rumors of his supposed involvement in a plot against the king. After a harsh imprisonment, during which he wrote his most influential book, he was tortured and executed in 524.

As a scholar, Boethius had two great goals: to translate the complete works of Aristotle and Plato into Latin, and to create a philosophical super-system that harmonized both writers' work and established it in a specifically Christian context. He failed on both accounts, but the significance of his efforts set the course for much of medieval Europe's intellectual life. He managed to produce full translations, along with commentaries, of Aristotle's *Topics*, *Prior Analytics*, *Posterior Analytics*, *Sophistical Fallacies*, *On Interpretation*, and the *Categories*; he also Latinized Porphyry's *Isagoge*, or "Introduction to Aristotle," as a beginner's guide for students. It is uncertain whether he ever got around to translating Plato: A Latin translation of Plato's *Timaeus* was made in Boethius' time, but scholars are divided on whether Boethius himself prepared it. Nevertheless, for the next six hundred years, virtually all that western Europe knew of Greek philosophy, especially logic, came from Boethius.

He had a remarkably capacious and all-embracing mind. "The Aristotelian and Platonic philosophies harmonize with one another in every way," he wrote; "they do not contradict each other at all, as so many people believe. I will prove it." Unfortunately, he did not live to see the task through, but we do know the broad outlines of his thought. Throughout the dozen or so original works he produced along with his translations, Boethius continually stressed both the multifaceted nature of existence and the implicit harmony of the universe—and therefore of all its knowledge. Since God is the creator of all being and the source of all knowledge, this transcendent unity in life cannot be otherwise. Ideas or qualities that appear to be disjointed, arbitrary, or unrelated, Boethius argues, are simply separate facets of a single truth. An individual human life, for example, is comprised of the multiplicity of distinct forms that give it shape. For example, the existence of a variety of distinct, and at times contradictory, roles in the life of an individual woman—roles as daughter, sister, wife, friend, mother, student, shopkeeper, widow, midwife, grandmother, or nun—does not mean that that woman does not exist. If anything, the reality of her existence is established and proven by the multiplicity of her roles. More than any other single thinker, Boethius is the architect of the medieval worldview of "diversity within unity."

The way to understand the world, then, is to break it into its constituent parts. Boethius focused his efforts on differentiating and categorizing the philosophical and liberal arts. He divided philosophy into two main branches—practical and theoretical—and then further subdivided each of those into three parts. Practical philosophy, he argued, was comprised of ethics (the study of morals), politics (the study of justice and the ways of seeking it), and economics (the study of human relations, particularly in regard to the family). Theoretical philosophy he broke down into natural philosophy (the study of matter), mathematics (the study of the forms taken by matter), and theology (the study of forms in the abstract). The truths produced by each of these disciplines, he asserted, would complement one another and ultimately result in a unified understanding of human existence. His passion for drawing distinctions and then for recombining what he had differentiated made him a natural enthusiast for the trivium and quadrivium suggested by Cassiodorus, and in fact it was his strong advocacy of that program that assured its success in western monastic life, even though he himself never became a monk.

At least not in any official sense. Boethius' last years were spent in a harsh solitary confinement that would have been a dream come true for someone like St. Anthony, and there Boethius wrote his most famous and influential work, *The Consolation of Philosophy*. Second only to the Bible, the *Consolation* is by far the greatest "best seller" of the Middle Ages: From the sixth through the thirteenth centuries, most of the educated men and women of Europe, and virtually all cloistered religious, were familiar with it. King Alfred the Great of England personally translated it into Anglo-Saxon in the ninth century, and in the fourteenth Geoffrey Chaucer rendered it into Middle English. In the sixteenth century, England's queen Elizabeth I also translated it. The book tells of Boethius' gradual enlightenment about the final realities of human fate, the instability of life, and the inscrutability of God's ways. His guide on this spiritual journey is a personified Lady Philosophy, and the book proceeds as a dialogue between them, interspersed with highly skillful poetic interludes.

The most powerful image used in the *Consolation* is that of Fortune's Wheel: It represents the world's changeability, the apparently random anarchy that can suddenly reduce even the most secure and stable of lives to misery. Throughout the book, Boethius looks at Fortune as the enemy, the foe who has not only brought him to prison but who symbolically represents the greatest challenge to his treasured view of the intrinsic coherence and stability of creation.

> *O God who created the laws for all things,*
> *Look down upon this earth's misery!*
> *Is Man so insignificant a part of all*
> *As to deserve the upsets of Fortune?*
> *O Lord, You who hold the crashing waves in check*
> *And who rule the stars in Your might,*
> *Bring stability back to the lands of this earth!*

With Philosophy's guidance, however, Boethius slowly comes to a Job-like understanding of human suffering. Rather than lamenting the unpredictablity of Fortune as the destroyer of coherent meaning in life, he learns to view it as a mechanism of God's purpose—and whereas no mind can comprehend God's intent, Boethius concludes, our faith in God's goodness assures us that Fortune's role is not one of random chaos but is rather an essential part of God's plan, as much under His guidance as anything else. But Boethius cannot leave the matter at that, for it raises the issue of predestination. He solves the problem with the ingenious (and original, for its time) argument that the question of God's foreknowledge of our actions is irrelevant; since God exists outside of time, His knowledge of things cannot be differentiated as past, present, or future. We are still possessed of free will and are responsible for our actions—and to that extent, coherence still exists. The book ends with the assurance that "no hope placed in God is in vain, and no prayers are without their effect—as long as they are made in the right spirit. So avoid vice and cultivate virtue; lift up your thoughts to the right kind of hope, and offer your prayers on high with a humble spirit. There is a great expectation made of you, if you will but be honest with yourself—an expectation to be good, for you live in the sight of a Judge who sees all things."

The single most influential figure in medieval monasticism, though, was St. Benedict of Nursia (480–547). Thanks to Pope Gregory the Great, who wrote an enormously popular *Life of St. Benedict*, we know a good deal about him.[7] Born into an aristocratic family from central Italy and filled with romantic images of the great imperial capital, Benedict traveled to Rome as a young man in order to study literature. When he arrived there, though, he recoiled from the licentiousness and materialism he found. It was not so much the immorality of life he saw there that disturbed him—after all, he knew history well enough to know that far worse things had gone on in Rome in the past—as it was life's a-morality: the nonchalant sensuality and moral laziness of the place. Benedict understood that conscious self-discipline provided the best defense against the kind of weakness that made men surrender themselves to easy pleasure.

He retired to a cave near Subiaco (a highly symbolic choice, since the cave stood near the villa where the emperor Nero had indulged in some of his worst excesses) and spent three years in solitary meditation. Temptation was soon hot on his heels. As Gregory memorably tells it:

> This holy man soon experienced more temptations of the flesh than he had ever known before, for the Spirit of Evil kept flashing before his mind's eye the image of a woman he had once seen. So feverishly did Temptation inflame Benedict's mind with the image of this woman that he nearly lost control of himself, out of passion. He became so overwhelmed with lust that he was just about to give up his solitude, when God, in His mercy, suddenly looked upon him and restored his sense. Benedict then saw several thickets of gorse and thorn bushes growing nearby, pulled off his clothes, and threw himself headlong and naked into the stinging and prickling nettles. He rolled himself back and forth over them for a long time, and when he came out at last his whole body was covered with wounds; but it was through these wounds of the flesh that he drained from his body the wounds to his spirit, by turning his lust into pain. He ached painfully on the outside, but he had managed to put out the forbidden fire within.

Just as vexing, though hardly so dramatic, was the arrival of disciples. But Benedict soon decided that communal life had its advantages—not least among them less painful ways of keeping one's mind off lustful fantasies. He helped his followers

---

7. The *Life of St. Benedict* is part of a much longer book by Gregory called *The Dialogues*, but was often reproduced as a stand-alone text by monastic scribes.

build a primitive monastery along Egyptian models, with monks living separately in individual cells that were grouped together in a loose community. But he gradually came to favor a more truly communal form of monastic life, and left Subiaco sometime in the 520s to found a new establishment at Monte Cassino, a hilltop sanctuary that had previously been the site of a prominent pagan shrine.

Monte Cassino was to become the greatest monastery of the Middle Ages. From its humble start, a single oratory that Benedict dedicated to St. Martin of Tours, it grew into one of the largest monasteries and most important intellectual centers in Europe. Destroyed by the Lombards in 581, it was restored in the eighth century and Charlemagne himself visited it in 787. It flourished as a center of manuscript production and book illumination, developing its own distinctive script known as *Beneventan minuscule*, and over the centuries it built up an extraordinarily rich library of classical and Christian texts. It also created an enormous archive of other sorts of material—letters, land grants, charters, commercial contracts, and so on—that comprised one of the largest collections of medieval material in Europe.[8]

From the start, Benedict intended Monte Cassino to be different. The Rule that he wrote for it—the *Rule of St. Benedict*, or simply the "Benedictine Rule"— emphasized the monastery's intellectual mission.

> And therefore we intend to establish a school in service to the Lord, and it is our hope that in founding it we are creating nothing overly severe and arduous. If a certain strictness appears to result from [the ensuing] regulations, [be aware that] they are intended only for the correction of vices and the maintenance of charity; so do not be faint-hearted and flee from the way to salvation. The path to salvation cannot be anything other than narrow. But as we progress in our faith and in our spiritual life our hearts swell until we tread the path of God's Commandments with a feeling of ineffable love. In this way, by never taking leave of His school and by preserving His teachings within this monastery until our very deaths, we may by degrees share in Christ's suffering and thereby earn a share in His heavenly kingdom.

Despite Benedict's warnings, however, his Rule proved to be not very austere at all. He allowed his monks and nuns sufficient food (two or three dishes and a cup of wine, per meal), ample sleep, warm clothes, and a balanced regimen of prayer, study, and manual labor. Such moderation had a wide appeal, and by the end of the ninth century virtually every monastery in Latin Europe followed the Benedictine Rule.

The monks' days were ordered around seven daily prayer services called *offices*. The monks rose from their beds around 2:00 A.M. and met for a one-hour service called *matins*. Each monk then spent an hour in private meditation, then they recongregated for a brief communal prayer called *lauds*. Breakfast followed, during which no conversation was permitted (the monks communicated by sign

---

8.   The great bulk of this treasure, though, and the entire abbey itself, was destroyed in February 1944 by Allied bombers who attacked Nazi soldiers who were using the monastery as a command-post. The Italian government later rebuilt the abbey, and in 1964 Pope Paul VI reconsecrated it in a solemn ceremony and proclaimed St. Benedict the patron saint of all Europe.

language). Then another quick thanksgiving—*prime*—after which the monks put in roughly four hours of either study or physical labor, depending on the season. A brief break followed, during which the monks had some light refreshment, followed by another thanksgiving (*terce*, or *sext*); they then returned to study or labor for a few more hours. *Nones*, yet another brief service, preceded the main meal of the day (which took place roughly at noon during the summer, and at 3:00 P.M. in the winter). The second major service of the day, called *vespers*, followed; and after this the monks enjoyed a period of quiet reading. A last thanksgiving prayer, *compline*, ended the day, and the monks generally retired to their beds by 7:00 P.M.

The emphasis on manual labor aimed to inspire humility—a necessary aim since most monks came from prominent, if not aristocratic, families, in which physical work was regarded as undignified. But it was the stress on study that had the largest consequences for medieval Europe. The houses quickly incorporated the curriculum of the trivium and quadrivium into their observance and thus helped regularize European education. Benedictine houses monopolized book production until the twelfth century, and during that period virtually every scholar in Europe either was a Benedictine or had been educated by them.

Two last characteristics of Benedictine monasticism stood out. First the Rule, while it allowed for moderation, nevertheless emphasized obedience and discipline under the authority of the abbot. Benedict judiciously employed a military vocabulary when describing his monastic ideal and stressed the need for order and regulation. Thus when he described his "school in service to the Lord" in the passage quoted above, he used the Latin word *schola*, a term that originally was used to identify an elite unit in the Roman army. Benedictine monks prided themselves on their discipline and came to be known as *milites Christi* or "soldiers of Christ." Second, the Rule came to serve as a prototype for later legal constitutions: It identified an executive authority—the abbot—who was required not only to follow the regulations set down by the Rule but who was also required, when confronted with issues having a significant impact on the entire community, to consult with the entire congregation before taking action. The notion of limited sovereignty—that is, of executive figures who, to an extent, enact the will of self-governing communities rather than simply impose their absolute will upon them—was novel to the west, and the Benedictine monastery provided a constitutional model for many of the new cities that emerged in the eleventh and twelfth centuries.

Suggested Reading

Texts

St. Athanasius. *Letter to Marcellinus.*
———. *The Life of St. Anthony.*
———. *The Life of St. Martin.*

St. Benedict. *The Benedictine Rule.*

Boethius. *The Consolation of Philosophy.*

Cassiodorus. *Institutes.*

———. *Miscellany.*

Gregory I, Pope. *Life of St. Benedict.*

Gregory of Tours. *The Glory of the Martyrs.*

———. *History of the Franks.*

Sulpicius Severus. *The Life of Saint Martin.*

Source Anthologies

Bettenson, Henry. *Documents of the Christian Church* (1967).

Hillgarth, J[ocelyn] H. *Christianity and Paganism. 350–750: The Conversion of Western Europe* (1986).

Morrison, Karl F. *The Church in the Roman Empire* (1986).

Noble, Thomas F. X., and Thomas Head. *Soldiers of Christ: Saints and Saints' Lives from Late Antiquity and the Early Middle Ages* (1995).

Peters, Edward. *Monks, Bishops, and Pagans: Christian Culture in Gaul and Italy, 500–700* (1975).

Peterson, Joan M. *Handmaids of the Lord: Contemporary Descriptions of Feminine Asceticism in the First Six Christian Centuries* (1996).

Waddell, Helen. *The Desert Fathers* (1936).

White, Caroline. *Early Christian Lives* (1998).

Studies

Brown, Peter. *The Body and Society: Men, Women, and Sexual Renunciation in Early Christianity* (1990).

———. *The Cult of the Saints* (1981).

———. *Society and the Holy in Late Antiquity* (1982).

Burton-Christie, Douglas. *The Word in the Desert: Scripture and the Quest for Holiness in Early Christian Monasticism* (1993).

Elm, Susanna. *Virgins of God: The Making of Asceticism in Late Antiquity* (1994).

Gibson, Margaret. *Boethius: His Life, Thought, and Influence* (1981).

Johnson, Penelope D. *Equal in Monastic Profession: Religious Women in Medieval France* (1991).

Lawrence, C. H. *Medieval Monasticism: Forms of Religious Life in Western Europe in the Middle Ages* (2001).

LeClercq, Jean, O.S.B. *The Love of Learning and the Desire for God: A Study of Monastic Culture* (1982).

Murray, Alexander Callander. *After Rome's Fall: Narrators and Sources of Early Medieval History* (1999).

O'Donnell, James J. *Cassiodorus* (1979).

Rousseau, Philip. *Ascetics, Authority, and the Church in the Age of Jerome and Cassian* (1978).

———. *Pachomius: The Making of a Community in Fourth-Century Egypt* (1986).

Stancliffe, Clare. *St. Martin and His Hagiographer: History and Miracle in Sulpicius Severus* (1983).

Van Dam, Raymond. *Saints and Their Miracles in Late Antique Gaul* (1993).

White, L. Michael. *Building God's House in the Roman World: Architectural Adaptation among Pagans, Jews, and Christians* (1990).

CHAPTER 5

THE EMERGENCE OF THE MEDIEVAL WORLDS

The changes that took place from the third through the sixth centuries were dramatic, but even so they did not quite manage to destroy the lingering sense of European or Mediterranean unity. Germanic kings still looked to Byzantium for legitimization of their monarchies. The rulers in Constantinople still evinced some interest in retaining influence, if not actual control, over western affairs. Mediterranean traders still plied the trunk routes, though in smaller numbers than before. The leaders of western and eastern Christianity, for all their differences, still recognized a fundamental communion of their religious beliefs and observances. Writers like Augustine, Boethius, and Cassiodorus still assumed a basic level of continuity, however tenuous, between the Greco-Roman tradition and the classical-Germanic-Christian amalgamation that was slowly taking shape.

In the seventh and eighth centuries, however, a number of new developments shattered whatever remained of that unity. Some developments were political in nature, some economic, and some religious. They resulted in a divided western world, a composite civilization made up of Latin Europe, Byzantium, and the vast Islamic empire. These three worlds viewed each other with considerable suspicion and hostility for several centuries, until the crusade movement broke the deadlock and inaugurated a new phase in their relations. For Latin Europe especially these years are known as the *Dark Ages*, a pejorative term that we would do well to discard but for the fact that these years are indeed "dark" in the sense that we cannot see precisely what took place. Our sources are too few and scattered to permit more than a glimpse of events. That glimpse certainly suggests that this was an era of some chaos, but it was a creative chaos, one in which the blending of the Roman, Christian, and Germanic traditions was completed. A recognizable and distinctly medieval civilization was coming into being—a new world characterized as much by its distrust of the Byzantine east and fear of the Islamic south as it was by its three-part inheritance—and it had its first clear manifestation in the Carolingian world that began in the early eighth century.

CONTINUITY AND CHANGE IN NORTHERN EUROPE

On a political level, the seventh and eighth centuries in northern Europe were marked by unremitting warfare. Most wars were intense local contests rather than large-scale conflagrations, with small bands of petty lords and their followers vying with each other for control of individual patches of land. A chief cause of this warfare was the Germanic custom, found especially among the Franks, of dividing a dead man's estate between all his legitimate sons. Since the only significant source of wealth in these centuries was land, all farms and estates, and the regions or districts they were in, were continually divided and redivided as they passed through successive generations. As estates grew smaller and life grew precarious, people resorted to violence in order to increase the lands they controlled. Petty lords by the tens of thousands battled each other constantly, in the hope of carving out a larger dominion for themselves. But such success, when it occurred, was usually short-lived since the restored estates or districts were redivided once again among the successful petty lord's heirs.

Much the same thing happened at the upper level of society, since the kingdom itself was regarded as the king's own possession. Clovis had created a large and powerful kingdom for himself, but when he died in 511 it was parceled out between his four sons. The eldest, Theuderic, later had two sons; the second, Chlodomer, had three sons; the third, Childebert, had two daughters, so his inheritance passed to the fourth brother, Lothar, who made up for Childebert by having seven sons. In only two generations, in other words, a single kingdom had devolved into twelve separate principalities—and this was only the start of the process. Given the constant division and redivision, not to mention the temperament of this family, wars, murders, plots, and palace-overthrows became commonplace. Occasionally a singularly bloody-minded individual like Chilperic (d. 584; one of Lothar's seven sons) managed to build a relatively large realm for himself by killing off his rivals and seizing whatever lands appeared vulnerable, but as soon as he died that realm was again split up between *his* sons, and the whole process repeated itself. The ensuing confusion effectively destroyed whatever regional trade existed, ruined whole towns and villages, and reduced the rural populace to famine. It is against this background that we must read Gregory of Tours' *History of the Franks*, our principal source for this period, which begins with a famous lament and apology:

> A great number of things keep happening—some good, some bad. The people of the various petty princedoms keep quarreling with each other in the fiercest way imaginable, while our rulers' tempers keep bursting into violence. Our churches are assailed by heretics, then re-taken in force by our Catholics; and whereas Christian faith burns hot in the hearts of many, it is no more than lukewarm in those of others. Church buildings are pillaged by the faithless as soon as they are gifted by the faithful. But no one has yet emerged who is a sufficiently skilled writer that he can record these events in a straightforward way, whether in prose or in verse. Throughout the towns of Gaul, in fact, the knowledge of

writing has declined to such an extent that it has virtually disappeared altogether. . . . [And so] I have undertaken this present work in an effort to preserve
the memory of the dead and bring them to the attention of those to come. But
my style lacks all polish, and I have had to devote too much of my attention to
the clashes between the good and the wicked.

Gregory's pages bristle with wars, assassinations, torturings, conspiracies, riots,
famines, and plagues. Like a witness to a car-wreck who cannot take his eyes off the
carnage in front of him, he focuses almost obsessively on the cruelties of the age:

This Rauching [a petty prince] was extraordinarily vain—a man filled to bursting with pride, arrogance, and impertinence. He treated his servants as though
he denied that they were human beings at all. . . . For example, whenever a servant stood before him, as was usual, with a lighted candle while Rauching ate
his meals, Rauching would force the poor fellow to bare his legs and hold the
lit candle between his knees until it burned down to a stub. Rauching would
then demand that a new candle be lit, again and again, until the servant's legs
were entirely scorched. If the servant cried out or tried to run, a drawn sword
quickly stopped him, and Rauching would convulse with laughter as he
watched the man weep.

Gregory tells literally hundreds of such stories and paints so relentlessly awful a
portrait of his age that we are hardly surprised, at the book's climax, when he tells
us that life had become so unbearable for everyone that many thousands of people began to believe that the end of the world was approaching. Apocalyptic
tremors came from all the corners of Gaul, he tells us. The most significant of
these episodes was the appearance in the 590s of a "false Christ" from Bourges, in
central Gaul. This man was apparently a local woodsman who had been attacked
by a swarm of bees—bee-imagery is a common trope of apocalyptic anecdotes—
and was driven insane by the poisonous stings. Believing himself to be Christ, he
traveled throughout central Gaul accompanied by a woman friend whom he now
believed to be the Virgin Mary, and preached the imminent approach of Ar-
mageddon. Rumors of his miraculous healing powers spread through the countryside, and he soon attracted numerous hangers-on, "not only the uneducated,"
Gregory assures us, "but ordained priests as well." As the number of his followers
grew, the false Christ ordered them to attack the merchants and landlords they encountered and to distribute the booty among the local poor; he thereby earned
himself a reputation as a kind of early Robin Hood. He was finally caught and
killed by an overzealous soldier from the court of the bishop of Le Puy (whom the
false Christ had apparently targeted as his next victim) and his followers were
dispersed.

It is difficult to know what to make of such stories, and scholars still debate
them vigorously. Did the false Christ episode actually occur? Probably, at least in its
bare outlines. But did people genuinely believe this fellow to be Christ returned to
Earth, and the world to be coming to its end, or did they just join enthusiastically in a
mad adventure that clearly had elements of social rebellion in it? Were conditions in
early medieval Gaul really so bad as Gregory portrays them, or was he intentionally

exaggerating the miseries around him in order to remind his readers of the fragility of life and the need to put right one's relationship with God?

There is in fact some evidence that life in the early medieval north was not quite so relentlessly terrible as Gregory insists. The familia (in the Roman sense) had become the normative social unit for the Germans too, and the Germanic law codes, which began to be written down precisely at this time, paid scrupulous attention to the rights of all familia members. The concerns of freemen predominate in these codes. Free status meant that one had the right to bear arms, to give evidence in legal disputes, and to express one's opinion in local community actions. In other words, the focus on the rights of freemen suggests a growing awareness of a communal identity larger than the familia and larger than the local tribe. Regardless of where one lived in the north, one had, or was developing, something akin to a legal right to be regarded as a member of a distinct people and tradition. The concept of the *personality of the law* meant that if one was a free Burgundian, one had the right to be judged by Burgundian law even if one was living in a Frankish land, for example, or if one was a Visigoth, to be judged by Visigothic law even if one lived among the Saxons. This may seem like a small advance, but the recognition that anyone had any rights at all undermines the dreary picture of unchecked brutality Gregory of Tours paints for us.

Moreover, as efforts to secure these rights increased so did the institution of slavery decrease. Slaves had been ubiquitous in ancient times, and slavery was a common fate of defeated soldiers between the third and sixth centuries, but in the seventh and eighth centuries a number of changes in servile status took root in the north. The Franks recognized a legal classification known in Latin as the *litus* (literally, "the blemished one"), denoting someone who lacked a freeman's status but who was not regarded as the outright property of someone else. Such a person could not be bought or sold, as a slave could, nor be forced to marry (or not to marry) according to his master's wishes; at the same time, a litus was not free. He was, if anything, "mortgaged" to the land on which he worked and he owed his labor to the land itself, though not to the landlord. Among the Lombards, an *aldius* was in much the same position between free and unfree, yet not outright chattel. Another way to think of this change, subtle though it may seem, is the difference between ownership and dependence. A person who is literally owned by another person possesses no rights whatsoever and is in fact (or at least in law—which can be a very different thing) an object, a piece of property that may be bought, sold, beaten, abused, or discarded as the owner wishes. But a dependent at least enjoys recognition of his or her human-ness and has a right to hope for the kind of fundamentally decent treatment that any Christian might expect from another Christian. The law codes of the seventh and eighth centuries are notable for their effort to secure at least this basic decency in the treatment of the unfree.

While women were still regarded as distinctly inferior to men, during this period they began to receive somewhat gentler treatment. The spread of Christianity no doubt contributed to this gentling but so too did a basic demographic reality: namely, a pronounced shortage of women. In times of famine or disease—frequent enough in these years—families continued to resort to infanticide as a means of protecting the food supply or of saving an infant from senseless suffering, and since parents tended to single out females for killing (the stronger males were needed to help work the land), there was over time a disparity between the numbers of grown men and women. Women also had considerably shorter life expectancies than men, attributable chiefly to the dangers of childbirth. And the growing popularity of convent life meant that even fewer women were available as potential marriage partners, at least among the upper orders of German society. As the "value" of women therefore increased, according to a crude formula of supply and demand, the law codes adapted by assuring them certain protections. In marriage, for instance, the groom paid a dowry to the bride, not the other way around; this practice provided the wife with a modicum of insurance in case her husband died before she did and gave her a piece of property that she controlled directly and in her own name. He also presented her with a *Morgengab*, or "morning gift," after their wedding night as compensation for her lost virginity. These dowries and gifts were often sizable and left many women in positions of considerable relative wealth.

Convents, as mentioned, grew increasingly popular. Female monastic houses had existed for centuries, but usually in partnership with a male monastery and with the male abbot in charge of the female house (exceptions existed in the female double-monasteries discussed in the last chapter). But starting in the sixth century, free-standing convents began to dot the landscape and attract numerous followers. Some of these houses were quite large; the house at Laon had over three hundred nuns in residence. The increase in female monastic vocation was probably related to a fifth-century church ruling that women could no longer be ordained as deaconesses. Denied this clerical status, devout women turned to the one vocation still available to them. The first Rule devised specifically for independent nun-communities was written in the early sixth century by Caesarius of Arles. He urged a one-year apprenticeship period for all newcomers before they took lifelong vows, a sharing in all the house's domestic work, and absolute obedience to the mother abbess. Clothing and food were to be kept simple. Caesarius also specified that all nuns were to learn how to read and were to spend the first two hours of every day in quiet study. Caesarius' Rule proved to be a popular one and was adopted by many convents across northern Europe.

One convent that adopted it was the abbey established at Poitiers by St. Radegund (d. 587). A Thuringian princess, Radegund was abducted by the Frankish king Lothar (Clovis' fourth son) when she was only six and was forced to marry him a dozen years later. Disgusted by his violence and lechery, she left him after a few years and established the abbey of Sainte-Croix at Poitiers with her own money. She earned a reputation for piety and charity, and her abbey began to receive novices from throughout Gaul. Many newcomers came from the high Frankish aristocracy and even from the royal family itself, which meant that Sainte-Croix developed considerable political influence. For example, Chilperic shut up his daughter Basina at Sainte-Croix in order that she might pursue a religious life but decided to remove her a few years later when he thought he might form an alliance with the Visigothic king Recared, to whom he offered Basina as a wife. Radegund, perhaps remembering her own experience as an unwilling bride, refused to hand the nun over. Chilperic threatened to attack the abbey, but Radegund stood firm and thereby blocked an alliance that would have significantly altered the political balance in western Europe. Radegund was also an influential patron of literature—especially in her close friendship with the poet Venantius Fortunatus, perhaps the most talented writer of the age—and wrote some capable verse of her own. Some of her correspondence with the Byzantine emperor Justin II and his wife Sophia also survives.

A pact signed in 613 settled a particularly bitter war between Clovis' descendants that had important implications for subsequent political and social development. (The war ended with its chief protagonist, the Frankish queen Brunhilde, having her limbs tied to four horses who were driven in opposite directions until she was torn apart.) Exasperated by the entire line of Clovis—arguably the most dysfunctional family in European history—the Frankish nobles insisted that political authority devolve from the monarchy and be invested in the landed elites. Kings thereafter became increasingly irrelevant, and political power and social privilege came to reside in those who possessed the land. Lordship began to replace kinship as the essential element of early medieval authority, but this transition would require several more centuries to reach maturity.

Another part of northern Europe that experienced widespread change at this time was England. In the fifth and sixth centuries a steady stream of Germanic invaders and immigrants had poured into Celtic England: Angles and Saxons (from the regions of today's southern Denmark and northern Germany, respectively) predominated, but they were joined by numbers of Jutes, Frisians, and Swabians as well. Unlike most of the other Germans, the Angles and Saxons had had virtually no previous contact with the Roman or Christian worlds, an insularity that had two important consequences. First, the Angles and Saxons had not organized into larger "kingdoms" the way others had done. When they came to England, they arrived in very numerous but small bands often no larger than individual clans, which meant that the political organization of the invaders would be a long time coming. Second, they had no desire to assimilate with the indigenous Celts, as the Franks had sought to assimilate with the Gallo-Romans or the Visigoths had with the Hispano-Romans. The Angles and Saxons, who quickly began to interbreed (thereby becoming *Anglo-Saxons*), regarded the Celts as filthy barbarians who needed to be driven from the land. Making up in superior numbers for what they lacked in organization, the Anglo-Saxons forced the Celts from the green plains of England (which took its name from the newcomers: *Angle-land*) up into the highlands of Wales and Scotland, or all the way to Ireland. Anglo-Saxon success was near-total, the only significant Celtic victory against them being a battle at Badon Hill around the year 500 when the Celts were led, according to an obscure ninth-century source called the

A page from the Anglo-Saxon Chronicle, one of the most important secular texts to survive from Germanic Britain. This is an eleventh-century copy of the Chronicle (which is actually a compendium of several narratives). The page shown tells of one of King Alfred's victories over the Danes in 871.Source: HIP / Art Resource, NY

Historia Brittonum ("History of the Britons"), by a warrior-lord named Arthur. This was the origin of the folk-legends that eventually grew into the well-known cycle of Arthurian stories.

Anglo-Saxon England was almost entirely rural. This had to be, since the still-pagan Anglo-Saxons regarded cities as evil sites inhabited by demon-spirits. They settled instead in small farming villages throughout the countryside, clearing the land, draining swamps, and defending themselves against Celtic raids by organizing into local militias called *fyrds*. Having virtually no trade with continental Europe, no known state organization, no Christian Church, and a reputation as a superstitious violent wasteland, Anglo-Saxon England was widely regarded by the rest of western Europe as the end of the world—the last, poorest, and most backward frontier of civilization. Mediterranean writers referred to it as the "Isle of the Dead." But they were wrong. The Anglo-Saxons ultimately organized themselves into seven distinct kingdoms—East Anglia, Essex, Kent, Murcia, Northumbria, Sussex, and Wessex—and developed a unique power-sharing system under the guidance of a *bretwalda*. The bretwalda was a sort of over-king, the recognized leader of the seven monarchies; he settled disputes between the lesser kings and organized joint military ventures in times of crisis. The office circulated in a set pattern from kingdom to kingdom.

The most important of the bretwaldas was King Ethelbert of Kent (d. 616). He was married to a Frankish princess, Bertha, a devout Catholic. When St. Augustine of Canterbury[1] came to England in 597 at Pope Gregory I's behest, Ethelbert allowed him to preach, granted him and his colleagues a place to live, and bestowed ample provisions on them. Ethelbert insisted, however, that he himself would never give up his old pagan beliefs. The combined efforts of Augustine and Bertha proved too much for him, though, and Ethelbert soon became England's first Christian king. Aided by the royal court, Christianity spread quickly. Pope Gregory corresponded regularly with Ethelbert, instructing him in the duties of Christian kingship and encouraging him in his holy work. Ethelbert was also the first English king to write down his laws. The fact that he wrote them in Old English instead of Latin was practical (Latin was a thoroughly unknown language among the Anglo-Saxons at that time), but it also reflects England's unique development: Alone among the kingdoms of the early Middle Ages, England emerged from the interaction of the Germanic and Christian traditions, without the third element of the classical heritage.

Signs of the assimilation of Christianity and Anglo-Saxon culture can be seen in the survival of the names of pagan deities within the Christian calendar: Days dedicated to the honor of the gods Tiw, Woden, and Thor survive as our "Tuesday," "Wednesday," and "Thursday," while the most important day in the Christian calendar—Easter—derives its name from the pagan goddess Eostre. Within a century most of England's warrior elites had become more or less fully Christianized, although conversion of the rural masses took much longer. The last stronghold of paganism was the Isle of Wight, which formally adopted Christianity in 686.

But Christianity had existed in England prior to the arrival of the Anglo-Saxons. Early missionaries like St. Ninian and St. Patrick had converted many Celts in the early fourth and late fifth centuries. When the Anglo-Saxons drove the Celts into the highlands, Celtic Christianity went into exile as well. Cut off from the rest of the Christian world, it developed in isolation. It was a strongly rural and monastic version of Christianity, and it embraced a rigorous penitential discipline that

---

1. Not to be confused with St. Augustine of Hippo, one of the four "Doctors of the Church."

A manuscript painting from the twelfth-century Life *of St. Edmund,
showing the arrival of various Germanic groups (Angles, Jutes,
and Saxons) in England.*
Source: The Pierpont Morgan Library / Art Resource, NY

may seem shocking today. Anyone found guilty of engaging in pre- or extramarital
sex, for example, had to perform penance (that is, to live on bread and water) for up
to three years, according to the *Penitential* of St. Columbanus. Whippings and banishment from the community also figured large in the penitential codes, but restric-
tion of the diet remained the most common form of punishment for misbehavior.
By the sixth and seventh centuries, Celtic Christianity had attained a high degree of
scholarly and artistic sophistication, and Celtic monastic schools—especially those
in Ireland—were probably the best in Europe at that time. Their most famous ac-

complishments were their magnificent illuminated manuscripts; the best-known of these today are the *Lindisfarne Gospels* and the *Book of Kells*, which date to the eighth and early ninth centuries, respectively.

When the Anglo-Saxons adopted Roman Catholicism, the two versions of Christianity came head to head. Celtic Christianity differed from the Roman form in a number of ways, the most important being the rural and monastic character of the Celtic faith as opposed to the episcopal form of the Roman. The two churches also followed different calendars, the Celtic church using a lunar formula, the Roman church a solar formula. A council was convened at Whitby, in Northumbria, in 663 to settle the dispute.[2] At this so-called Synod of Whitby, the Roman Christians carried the day, and everyone present was called upon to declare obedience to the pope. Celtic Christianity survived in the highlands for nearly two hundred more years, but it gradually gave way to the Roman form. The Celtic influence can be seen in the ascetic discipline and intellectual rigor that characterized English monasticism.

CONTINUITY AND CHANGE IN THE MEDITERRANEAN

The collapse of Roman rule in the fifth century set in motion a wave of political instability in the Mediterranean which we have already discussed in part. In the west, Visigothic Spain, Vandal North Africa, and Ostrogothic Italy eventually emerged as the dominant states; but more significant was the power and influence of the surviving eastern half of the Roman Empire centered on the city of Constantinople—the Byzantine Empire. The Byzantine world was vast: It wrapped, like a reversed letter "C," around the eastern shores of the Mediterranean, incorporating all the territory that today makes up the countries of Albania, Bosnia, Serbia, Macedonia, Greece, Bulgaria, Turkey, Syria, Lebanon, Israel, Egypt, and Libya. Its predominant public and official culture was both Greek and Christian, but the empire comprised a wide array of ethnic, linguistic, social, and religious groups. Despite its size and complexity, however, the Byzantine world was relatively easy to govern at first. Centered on the Asia Minor land mass, the empire had a strong and diverse economic base that enabled it to withstand its frequent invaders, while the easy communications provided by the sea and the empire's sophisticated administrative machinery provided a consistent degree of civic order. Unlike the west, it was an urban society with much higher levels of population density, literacy, and *per capita* wealth. Asia Minor and the Balkan regions were the main centers of grain production and animal husbandry, while fish, timber, and mineral ores came from the Black Sea territories; Greece contributed mostly wines and olive oil. Islands like Cyprus and Rhodes served as staging posts and sites of specialized industries like

---

2. The king of Northumbria, named Oswy, was a Celtic Christian, but his wife Eanfled was a Roman Christian. Tiring of celebrating Easter on different days each year (and arguing about the difference), they decided to sponsor a debate between leaders of each church to settle the matter.

silk weaving. The manufacturing of raw goods into consumer products—textiles, metalwork, ceramics, handicrafts, tools, and luxury items—took place in the cities, which were also the centers of administration, education, and finance.

The most important of those cities, after Constantinople itself, were Alexandria, Antioch, Caesarea, Damascus, Jerusalem, and Thessalonica. Merchants, scholars, and diplomats from these cities traveled throughout the Mediterranean, up the Nile River, and down the Red Sea. The Byzantine *solidus*, a gold coin stamped with the image of the emperor, became the international currency standard.[3] Hundreds of primary schools, urban academies, aristocratic salons, and private tutors passed on the intellectual and artistic tradition of classical Greece and Greek Christianity. Byzantine scholars remained devoted to the works of the ancients, so much so that most of their intellectual output consisted of commentaries on writers like Homer, Plato, Aristotle, Thucydides, Galen, and Euclid instead of original creations of their own. They compiled scores of dictionaries, grammars, encyclopedias, and catalogs to aid the reader of the classics. When they did attempt original works, they continued to follow classical models. For example, an early Byzantine historian like Menander the Protector, who composed a lengthy history of the years from 558 to 582, followed the ancient Greek tradition of writing detailed, analytical histories of specific events as Herodotus and Thucydides had done; these differed from the larger-scale universal narratives of the west. Unlike the ancients, however, early Byzantine scholars made little contribution to science.

In all the major cities, but especially in Constantinople, the populace was divided into powerful factions that were based not so much on economics or classes as they were volitional loyalties; indeed these factions—the most notorious of which were the "Greens" and "Blues" in Constantinople—bear close resemblance to the passionate (often violently so) loyalties between rival soccer teams in modern European cities. These groups did not represent particular political programs, nor did they consist of discrete ethnicities, yet their influence on events was significant: At public entertainments like chariot races or animal fights, these factions staged mass rallies that frequently bubbled over into stadium violence, and whenever any local ruler was alleged to favor a particular group its rivals quickly took to the streets. At least once, in the sixth century, team-violence nearly brought down the empire in a riot known as the Nike Rebellion.

When the last western emperor Romulus Augustulus was deposed in 476, his eastern colleague Zeno (r. 474–491) claimed to rule the entire restored empire. His claim was fanciful, though, since he was hard put just to hold on to power in Constantinople, but Zeno and his successors kept an eye on what was happening with the Ostrogoths, Visigoths, Vandals, and Franks, and they used to their advantage the western kings' tradition of turning to Constantinople for legitimization. Recall that Theodoric the Great's actual title was not "King of Italy" but *patricius*—that is, provincial governor for the eastern emperor. Even the fearsome

---

3. Archeologists have found evidence of *solidi* circulating all the way from Ireland to China.

Clovis, who might have settled for papal recognition as "King of the Franks," was thankful to receive appointment as *consul* from the Byzantine ruler Anastasius I (491–518).[4]

The two most important early Byzantine rulers were Justinian (r. 527–565) and Heraclius (r. 610–641); both were enormously ambitious men and grand failures. Justinian was the more complex personality. His parents were assimilated peasant Goths from the Balkans, and from his birth in 493 he was brought up to admire classical culture. He received a good education and was in fact more comfortable speaking Latin than Greek. He trained for a legal career, had a keen eye for talent, and was deeply interested in art, especially architecture. While still a young man he became an aide to his uncle Justin, a military adventurer with high connections. Justin's years of service to Anastasius I resulted in his being appointed successor to the throne; by that time, however, Justin was so old and decrepit that his nephew actually ran the empire for him. This apprenticeship served Justinian well, for once he was himself proclaimed emperor, after Justin's death in 527, he already understood the machinery of government, and specifically the ways in which that machinery had to be reformed if the empire was to survive.

His reforms were the most far-reaching since those of Diocletian in the third century. He professionalized the provincial administration, placed his officials on fixed salaries, and reinstated the statutes requiring sons to follow their fathers' professions if those fathers held positions of public trust. At the same time he centralized more authorities and prerogatives to the throne. Modeling himself after Constantine, Justinian enunciated a political doctrine known as *Caesaropapism*, which held that the emperor not only controlled the political state but the state religion also. This idea had been initially formulated by Constantine's biographer, Eusebius, who argued that Constantine had been chosen by God Himself as both protector and leader of His Church; he even referred to Constantine as the Thirteenth Apostle. All the Byzantine rulers after Constantine believed that they ruled by divine right, but Justinian gave this belief its fullest expression. He did not claim to possess any spiritual authority, yet he presided over Church councils and ratified their decrees. He appointed the Patriarch of Constantinople, redefined heresy as a crime against the state, and undertook the construction of the greatest church in eastern Christendom, the Church of Hagia Sophia ("Holy Wisdom") in Constantinople.

Hagia Sophia was in fact the culmination of a vast building program. Much of the capital city had been destroyed in a mass riot in 532 known as the Nike Rebellion.[5] The revolt began as a fight between Greens and the Blues, fans of the two most popular chariot-racing teams in the Hippodrome. Stirred up by nobles who

---

4. After getting the appointment, Clovis dressed in a toga and gave himself an imperial triumph through the city of Tours.
5. *Nike* is the Greek word for "Victory" and was reportedly the street chant of the rioters.

had spread a number of false rumors about Justinian's loyalties, the fans, who numbered perhaps fifty thousand, filled the stadium with violence, wrecked much of the building, and took to the streets. The ruin they caused was enormous. They destroyed most of the city center and killed thousands of innocent bystanders. It took several days for imperial soldiers to put an end to the carnage, but Justinian ultimately prevailed. Determined to make an example, Justinian tracked down as many of the rebels (and the nobles who had incited them) as he could; one chronicler reports that the emperor had thirty thousand people executed for treason. Then, having stunned the empire to silence with his harshness, Justinian set quietly to work to rebuild the city. A descriptive catalog of his building projects, commissioned toward the end of his career, credits Justinian with erecting several hundred separate buildings. Apart from the great church, Justinian rebuilt the palace complex and the hospitals, strengthened the city's fortifications, redesigned the major avenues and arcades to allow for easier movement and more attractive open space, and constructed a comprehensive system of underground reservoirs and sewers that gave Constantinople the most reliable water and waste system of any city in Europe until the nineteenth century. Hagia Sophia, though, was his masterpiece.[6] Composed chiefly of a vast central space formed by four great arches, the church was topped with a massive dome that rested on a row of arched windows that let in streams of light and made it appear that the dome was floating on air. A witness to the church's first public opening described it this way:

> When the interior of the church came into view and the sun lit up the marvels of the sanctuary, all sorrows left our hearts. As the rose-colored light of the new day streamed in, driving away the dawn's dark shadows and leaping from arch to arch, all the princes and commoners in the crowd broke out in one voice and sang songs of praise and thanksgiving. In that sacred court it seemed to them that the almighty arches of the church were set in Heaven. . . . Anytime anyone goes into that church to pray, he immediately realizes that it was the hand of God, not of man, that made it; and his mind is so lifted up to God that he is convinced that God is not far away—for surely God must love to dwell here in this sacred space He has willed into existence.

Arguably the most important of his reforms, however, was Justinian's ordering of the first comprehensive codification of Roman law, a text known as the *Corpus iuris civilis* ("Corpus of Civil Law"). It was a mammoth undertaking. Roman law had been built up incrementally, with each ruler issuing new mandates or edicts to meet situations as they arose; but that legal system was already a thousand years old by the time Justinian came to the throne and it had never been organized. Justinian set a team of legal scholars to work sifting, arranging, dating, and classifying these laws into a useful compendium. It is in three parts. The first part, called the *Codex Justinianus*, gathered together every imperial edict from the preceding four

---

6. Credit should go to the architects Justinian hired for the job: Isidore of Miletus and Anthemius of Tralles. Both geometricians by training, Hagia Sophia was their first attempt at architecture.

*The interior of Hagia Sophia (the "Church of Holy Wisdom") built
by the emperor Justinian. After the Ottoman Turks took
Constantinople in 1453 they rededicated it as a mosque.
Source: Vanni / Art Resource, NY*

centuries (laws later issued by Justinian himself and his successors were henceforth
appended to this volume and were called *Novellae*, or "New Items"). Since these
were the very centuries that saw the development of imperial autocracy, the *Codex
Justinianus* served as a kind of handbook to emphasize and justify the absolute authority of the emperor. The second part, the *Digest*, contained all the precedent-
setting legal judgments issued by Roman jurists in criminal and civil cases:
Organized into fifty books, the *Digest* covered every aspect of life from taxation to

inheritance, from slave-practice to property rights, from marriage to a city's right of eminent domain. It provided, in other words, a complete operational guide for governing civil society. The third and final part of the *Corpus*, called the *Institutes*, was an abridgment of the first two parts and was used as a textbook for the study of law in the schools.

While the *Corpus iuris civilis* is hardly a fun book to read, its significance can hardly be overstated; indeed, the *Corpus* may be the single most influential secular text in western history. It contributed in no small way to the survival of Byzantine life for nine hundred years after Justinian by guiding and modulating the urban and commercial scene upon which Byzantine life depended. It provided the means for the development of jurisprudence itself by offering a comprehensive view of law as a rational system of social organization rather than a messy congeries of accumulated individual pronouncements. The legalistic bent of the Western mind is inconceivable without the *Corpus*, as is much of modern statecraft itself. In western Europe the *Corpus* provided the model for the development of the Catholic Church's system of canon law. The rediscovery of the text in the eleventh century helped to trigger the cultural and intellectual flowering of the twelfth-century renaissance, and as the *Corpus* began to be implemented by the emerging feudal states of that time it became the dominant influence on western secular law-codes as well. And moving beyond the Middle Ages, the emphasis of the *Codex Justinianus* on political autocracy provided a rational basis and historical justification for the political absolutism of the seventeenth and eighteenth centuries. In the United States the system of precedent-setting torts can likewise be traced back directly to Justinian's achievement. The *Corpus iuris civilis* and Hagia Sophia are Justinian's two greatest monuments.

Justinian is also remembered for two stupendous failures: his attempt to reconquer the western Mediterranean, and his scandalous marriage. The two are linked, to a degree. Shortly before coming to the throne, Justinian, then forty, met a twenty-year-old actress named Theodora, the daughter of the bear-keeper at the Hippodrome and reputedly the most notorious prostitute in Constantinople.[7] Justinian fell passionately in love with her—in Procopius' words, he became her sex-slave—and despite the adamant opposition of his family he married her. By any measure, she was a formidable personality. Haughty, quick to anger, and ambitious, she also possessed keen intelligence and acted as her husband's closest advisor. Theodora was, in fact, the coruler with Justinian: She shared authority over all imperial officials and received foreign embassies in her own right; she also made them grovel on the ground before her.

---

7.   Most of what we know of Theodora comes from a wildly pornographic piece of political slander by Procopius of Caesarea, whom Justinian had appointed as his official biographer. Procopius dutifully published an authorized and praise-filled *History of Justinian*, and the catalog of building projects mentioned before; but he also published, anonymously, the *Secret History*, which is a masterpiece of character assassination. His portrayal of Theodora in particular is vulgar and cruel in the extreme and can hardly be believed. Nevertheless, he is correct about her low origins.

Both Justinian and Theodora were hungry for glory, and they determined to achieve it by reconquering the western Mediterranean provinces. Byzantine claims over the west had never been relinquished but the opportunity to act on them had never arisen until Justinian's time. In 531 the Byzantine government signed a so-called "eternal peace" with its traditional rival, the Persian Empire to its east. Just in case the eternal peace failed to live up to its name (which it soon did), Justinian built a chain of well-equipped fortresses throughout Syria. With his position supposedly thus assured, he loosed his forces on the central and western Mediterranean. They were led by his brilliant general Belisarius. The campaign began well, with a lightning strike against the Vandals that restored all of North Africa to Byzantine control. In 536 Belisarius landed in Sicily, which was then controlled by the Ostrogoths. He wrested the island from them and after four more years of fighting managed to take both Rome and Ravenna, the two traditional capitals of the western empire. But just as Justinian's dream seemed close at hand, the Persian ruler Chrosroes I broke the eternal peace, crashed through the Syrian defenses, and sacked the city of Antioch. Now forced to fight a two-front war, Justinian soon exhausted his treasury and was forced to give up the fight. In the west, the Greeks were regarded as hostile foreign tyrants, and in order to hold on to what they had reconquered they were forced to resort to harsh, and occasionally brutal, tactics that only added to the atmosphere of fear and resentment. Meanwhile, the advance of the Persians in the east and the arrival of new invading groups of Avars, Bulgars, and Slavs from the Asian steppe in the Balkans left the Byzantine realm in considerable danger. Shortly after Justinian's death, the Greeks were forced to withdraw. By 578 they had abandoned Spain, North Africa, and coastal France altogether and held only a few small enclaves in northern Italy. Southern Italy, however, with its close proximity to Greece, remained tentatively in their hands. Justinian's successors Maurice (r. 582–602) and Phocas (r. 602–610) managed to stabilize the Balkan frontier by paying huge sums of tribute to the Avars, Bulgars, and Slavs but lost nearly all the rest of the empire to the Persians who quickly overran Syria, Palestine, Egypt, and Asia Minor itself.

This was the situation when Heraclius (r. 610–641) came to the throne. With half the empire in foreign hands, the treasury depleted, public morale low, and a civil administration that under his predecessors had become notoriously bloated and corrupt, Heraclius resolved on yet another reform of the state, one that culminated in an extensive militarization of Byzantine society. The eastern empire had traditionally relied on a professional military: Soldiers signed on for a certain number of years of service and were paid a salary by the state. They supplemented their salary with booty, when booty was to be had, and received a pension after twenty-five years of service. By 610, however, the soldiers' pay had been frequently delayed or cut off altogether, depending on the state of the imperial coffers. Understandably, this circumstance weakened the soldiers' resolve to fight and forced the emperors to turn to unreliable foreign mercenaries willing to fight for a share of the unreliable spoils. It was this situation that had enabled the Avars, Bulgars, and Slavs to overrun the Balkans so easily, and had allowed the Persians to advance so far into the empire's eastern provinces.

Heraclius began by reorganizing the army into a new system of *themes*.[8] These themes had existed earlier as military units, but Heraclius began to identify individual themes with specific regions of the empire, and allowed the commanders of each theme to take over the civil administration of its corresponding district. In other words, he replaced the corrupt civil administration with the army itself. Direct pay to the soldiers was cut but was supplemented by the allotment of farmlands within each theme. This revision reduced the direct cost to the treasury, increased military morale (since the soldiers now had a reliable source of income), improved military effectiveness (since the soldiers had a vested interest in defending the land), and restored popular support for the imperial throne by removing the hated corps of bureaucrats who had overrun government in the years since Justinian's death.

Heraclius' reform stopped the hemorrhage of funds from the treasury but did little to replenish them. He raised taxes as high as he could without risking revolt, confiscated all that he could of the personal wealth of the displaced civil administrators, and relied occasionally on forced loans (especially from the empire's Jewish population); but by far his greatest new source of wealth was the eastern Church. The Patriarch of Constantinople, Sergius, who saw the empire's struggle to survive as a religious war, placed at Heraclius' disposal all the ecclesiastical and monastic treasure he commanded. This action—the State taking over the wealth of the Church in defense of the Christian faith—established an important precedent whose ramifications extended throughout the rest of the Middle Ages.

In the meantime, Byzantium's enemies pressed on all sides. Most significantly, Chosroes II unleashed a new campaign into the Holy Land. In 612 his forces smashed westward, took Antioch, then turned south and conquered Damascus in 613 and Jerusalem in 614. Religious antagonism played a role. Many of the region's Jews, tired of their minority status and smarting from Heraclius' forced loans, had supported the Persians' advance. A month after the Persian seizure of the city, Jerusalem's Christians rose up in revolt and took to the streets, smashing shops and assaulting as many of the Persian invaders and their Jewish collaborators as they could find. The Persian army responded with unprecedented violence: For three days they pillaged Jerusalem ruthlessly, razing churches and slaughtering the Christians. According to some witnesses, Jews from the surrounding countryside rushed to the city in order to share in the revenge-taking. When the carnage ended, hardly a single Christian was alive and hardly a single Christian church remained standing—including the Church of the Holy Sepulchre, which stood over the site of Jesus' grave and contained what was believed to be a fragment of the Cross on which he had hung. A later chronicler, Theophanes, summed up the scene with a few terse words:

> In this year the Persians conquered all of Jordan and Palestine, including the Holy City, and with the help of the Jews they killed a multitude of Christians—

---

8. The Greek word *theme* meant "regiment" or "division."

some say as many as ninety thousand of them. The Jews [from the country-side], for their part, bought many of the surviving Christians, whom the Persians were leading away as slaves, and put them to death too. The Persians captured and led away not only the Patriarch of Jerusalem, Zachariah, and many prisoners, but also the most precious and life-giving Cross.

Eyewitnesses estimated the number of slave-prisoners taken by the Persians between thirty-five and sixty-six thousand. Such figures are always suspect, but clearly the destruction of the city was a catastrophe. News of the slaughter horrified Christians throughout Byzantium and western Europe, and from this time onward a new element entered many medieval Christians' attitudes toward the east, an element of religious revenge-seeking that would culminate centuries later in the crusade movement.

Heraclius himself possessed many of the qualities of a crusader. He combined genuine piety with military activism and an apocalyptic sense of mission; he had little doubt that he was engaged in a life-or-death struggle for the survival of the Christian world, or at least the Greek-speaking portion of it, and that his foes were in fact the enemies of God. How else could one interpret the Persians' action? Chrosroes II, in a mocking letter he sent to Constantinople, hammered the point home:

> I, Chrosroes the son of the great Hormisdas, the Most Noble of all the Gods, the King and Sovereign-Master over all the Earth, to Heraclius, my vile and brainless slave.
>
> Refusing to submit yourself to my rule, you persist in calling yourself lord and sovereign. You pilfer and spend *my* treasure; you deceive *my* servants. You annoy me ceaselessly with your little gangs of brigands. Have I not brought you Greeks to your knees? You claim to trust in your God—but then why has your God not saved Caesarea, Jerusalem, and Alexandria from my wrath? . . . Could I not also destroy Constantinople itself, if I wished it?

Thus, when Heraclius was finally ready to launch his counterattack in 622, he deliberately chose targets of symbolic as well as strategic value. He sailed his forces out of Constantinople and all the way around Asia Minor to reach the Bay of Issus—the spot of Alexander the Great's first triumphant face-to-face battle with the ancient Persian ruler Darius nearly one thousand years earlier. Heraclius' first string of victories climaxed in his capture of Ganzak and Thebarmes (in what is today Azerbaijan), which were important spiritual centers of the Persians' Zoroastrian religion. After several more years of hard campaigning, Heraclius defeated the Persian army and regained most of the territory that had been lost to them. Chrosroes himself fell from power in a palace coup.

The chief significance of Heraclius' reign lies in his militarization of society—a change that provided, to an extent, a precedent for what would become the feudalism of western Europe—and in the intensification of religious antagonism between the Christian, Jewish, and eastern faiths. The emerging states of the west, as we have seen, looked to Byzantium for ideas and political justification; Heraclius' theme system, while it differed in important ways from the feudal practices of the west, influenced their development. Still, the religious legacy of Heraclius' reign may have had even greater influence over what was to follow. Hitherto, most of Christianity's factional strife had been internal, centered on competing understandings of the Christian mysteries. But relations across religious lines had received a hard blow in the seventh century. Chrosroes' successor on the Persian throne offered the Christians an olive branch—the restoration of all Byzantine territories, all Byzantine captives, and the surviving remnant of the True Cross—but that did little to dispel popular hostilities.

New violence could occur at any time, and in fact it was not long in coming. But an important change had taken place. In 622, at the very time when Heraclius launched his counterstrike against Persia, a charismatic spiritual leader in Mecca, in the Arabian peninsula, traveled with his tiny band of followers to the city of Madinah. This journey became commemorated as the *Hijrah* (literally, a "journey"; symbolically, an "Exodus") and it marked the formal beginning of a new religion and a new religious empire: Islam, under its leader Muhammad, the Prophet.

THE RISE OF ISLAM

Muhammad was born in the western Arabian city of Mecca, around 570. A merchant by trade, his family belonged to the Qur'aysh tribe that had traditionally served in priestly functions and was associated with the chief pagan temple, the Ka'aba. In 594 he married his employer, a well-to-do widow named Khadija and began to manage her affairs. From early life Muhammad had displayed a somewhat nervous and inward-turned temperament that, as he matured, developed into a keen spiritual instinct. But he was not sure where to target his spiritual energies; under the influence of Judaism and Christianity, the traditional paganism of the Arabs was giving way slowly to an as yet ill-defined monotheism, while contact with Persian Zoroastrianism (a sophisticated fire-based religion that viewed human life in the context of an apocalyptic contest between Ahura Mazda, the god of goodness, and Ahriman, the spirit of evil) added an urgent new tone of divine struggle to traditional Arab views of human fate. One of Muhammad's first biographers, Ibn Ishaq (d. 768), tells an anecdote about the tormented Muhammad crying out: "O God! I would so gladly worship You the way You want to be worshiped—but I don't know how!" Muhammad's long trading expeditions along the caravan routes to markets as far away as Syria suited his penchant for meditation and deepened his contact with other religious ideas. After years of spiritual searching, he was finally rewarded. One spring night, probably in the year 610, he experienced the first of what would become a torrent of mystical visions:

> In the year when Muhammad was called to be the Prophet, during the month of Ramadan, he went to Mount Hira with his family in order to devote himself to a private religious vigil.
>
> "One night," he reported, "the angel Gabriel came to me, carrying a strip of embroidered cloth, and said, 'Recite!'

" 'I cannot recite,' I answered. Then Gabriel choked me with the strip of cloth until I thought I would die. Then he released me, and said again, 'Recite!' "

The Prophet hesitated, and two times more the angel repeated his violent attack. Finally Muhammad asked, "What shall I recite?" And the angel replied:

Proclaim! (or Read!): In the name of Thy Lord and Cherisher,
Who created—created man, out of a leech-like clot:
Proclaim!: And thy Lord is most bountiful,—
He Who taught (the use of) the pen—
Taught man that which he knew not.
Nay, but man doth transgress all bounds,
In that he looketh upon himself as self-sufficient.
Verily, to thy Lord is the return (of all). [Qur'an 96.1–8]

"I awoke from my sleep," said Muhammad, "and it was as though this message had been written on my heart. I exited the cave, and while I stood on the mountainside I heard a voice calling: 'O Muhammad! You are Allah's Messenger, and I—I am Gabriel!' I looked up and saw the angel Gabriel in the form of a man, sitting cross-legged on the edge of heaven. I stood still and watched him; he moved neither forwards nor backwards—and yet whenever I turned my gaze away from him, I still saw him there on the horizon, no matter which way I turned."

These revelations continued throughout the rest of Muhammad's life and their substance forms the very core of Islamic faith. Muhammad's task, as given to him by Gabriel, was *to recite*—that is, to proclaim to his followers the contents of a divine text to which he was granted unique access. For Muslims this text is the Qur'an.[9] It is God's complete and final revelation of His commands and teachings, the last and most perfect in a series of holy books consisting of the Hebrew Bible and the Christian New Testament. Muhammad stands as the ultimate and supreme Prophet, the Messenger through whom God has made known to all men and women everything that is required for their right living on earth and their salvation in the world to come.

God, known to Muslims by the name of *Allah,* commanded Muhammad to proclaim an uncompromising monotheism: There is but one God, and God is One (and not—the Qur'an repeatedly emphasizes—as Christians believe, Three). He created the world out of His boundless love and compassion, and demands of us recognition of His sovereignty, our surrender (*islâm*) to His will, and our just treatment of one another. Islam has no priesthood; it requires no intermediaries between Allah and His creation, and although His presence is everywhere, He Himself, unlike the Arab pagan deities He supplanted, does not inhere in anything. The Qur'an describes Allah as being "nearer to man than his jugular vein" and always ready to come to his aid. These attributes clearly owe something to the

---

9. The word *qur'an* means a "reading" or a "recitation." It is sometimes transliterated as *Koran.*

Jewish and Christian traditions, with which Muhammad was familiar.[10] But the Muslim God owes something to pagan Arabia as well. Pre-Islamic Arabs believed that blind, inexorable fate controlled the destiny of mankind and that all that individual men and women could hope for was to propitiate the gods by prayer and sacrifice; otherwise, one was quite helpless. The all-powerful, all-present, all-knowing, but merciful and compassionate Allah offered an appealing alternative to the inscrutable pagan deities.

The central confession of Islam—"There is no God but Allah, and Muhammad is His Prophet"—is the first of the so-called Five Pillars of the Faith. The other four consist of: prayer five times a day at specified hours; the giving of alms through a special welfare tax called the *zakât*; ritual fasting during certain periods of the year, especially during the holy month of Ramadan; and pilgrimage to the holy city of Mecca, a journey known as the *hajj*. From the Qur'an and this central core developed the entire body of Islamic doctrine. The *hadith*—the non-Qur'anic teachings of Muhammad—formed the second major source of doctrine.

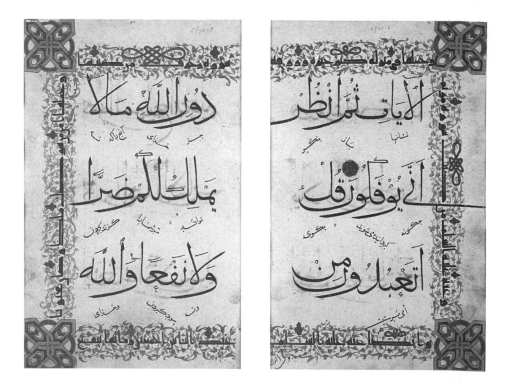

___

10. God even shares the same name in all three faiths: The Hebrew *Elohim*, the Aramaic *Elah* of Christ's time, and the Arabic *Allah* all derive from the same Semitic root.

Muhammad's success came slowly at first. He converted his wife and a few other family members but ran into resistance when he began to preach publicly. The Jews and Christians of Mecca disappointed him by refusing to embrace his revelation for he had believed it was his special mission to bring those people back to the Word of the God of Abraham, from which he claimed they had strayed. Then the elders of Muhammad's own Qur'aysh tribe began to oppose him. They found Muhammad's claim of a divinely ordained messengership odd, and Islam's condemnation of idolatry threatened the lucrative pilgrimage of pagans to the holy shrine of the *Ka'aba* (a huge black stone temple in Mecca that formed a kind of Arab pantheon, in which all gods were worshiped—it even included Christian icons). Finally in 622, worn out by resistance and saddened by the recent death of Khadija, Muhammad and his small band of faithful left Mecca and headed for the northern oasis city of Madinah.

This journey, honored by Muslims ever since as the *Hijrah* ("departure"), marks the beginning of the Muslim calendar and the symbolic start of the Islamic empire. The atmosphere in Madinah proved far more conducive to Muhammad's teachings, and adherents began to increase in number dramatically. Apart from the powerful simplicity of the Islamic message and the charismatic nature of the

---

Opposite page (Source: © British Museum / Art Resource, NY): Two pages from a Qur'an in kufic script. The text shown is a passage from verses 75–77 in the fifth surah ("chapter") discussing Christ and the Virgin Mary. The two verses are as follows (the Arabic words shown on these two pages appear in italics):

Christ, the son of Mary,
Was no more than
A messenger; many were
The messengers that passed away
Before him. His mother
Was a woman of truth.
They had both to eat
Their [daily] food.
See how Allah doth make
His signs clear to them [i.e., the Christians];
Yet see in what ways
They are deluded
Away from the truth!
Say "Will ye worship
Besides Allah something
Which hath no power either
To harm or benefit you?
But Allah—He it is
That heareth and knoweth
All things.

Prophet's personality, what attracted them was the compelling notion of the *ummah*—Islam as a religious community that transcends all other bonds of ethnicity, tribal loyalty, and social class. Prior to the coming of the Prophet, the Arab world was in a state of political collapse and tribal strife that later Arabs referred to as the "Age of Barbarism" (*al-jâhilîyah*). The warfare between Byzantium and the Persian Empire had triggered a serious economic decline in the northern part of the Arabian peninsula by severing its caravan routes to Syria, and the collapse of the Yemenite Himyarî kingdom in the south had removed the last stabilizing force over tribal rivalries there. To those caught in the middle, the concept of *ummah* offered an appealing alternative, a religious brotherhood, a vision of an egalitarian society larger than tribal faction and rigid social caste. Inspired by his continuing epiphanies, Muhammad issued the regulations that shaped Islamic life. He placed special emphasis on the significance of the nuclear family as the basic unit of society,[11] on the need to assist the poor, widows, and orphans, and on providing justice for all the members of the *ummah*.

Within a short time Muhammad was in control of Madinah, and therefore in control of the trade routes that linked it with Mecca to the south. This situation soon resulted in war with the Meccans, and by 630 the Prophet had captured the city which had sent him into exile eight years earlier. Now in control of the center of the peninsula, Muhammad plotted a grander campaign for dominion over the whole of Arabia and beyond. Islam was to be brought not only to the Arabs but to all peoples everywhere. The conversion of the nomadic Bedouins of the northern peninsula placed a powerful new military force at his command, and he directed them against the Christians and Jews of the region. He ordered the expulsion of all Christians and Jews who refused to convert to Islam, and the execution of those who resisted both conversion and expulsion. Thousands were killed. By the time of Muhammad's death in 632, Muslims controlled more than half of Arabia, including the entire Red Sea coast, and pressed aggressively on the Holy Land, with Byzantium and Persia within their sights.

Muhammad's death set off a succession crisis that was at once spiritual and political. During the Prophet's lifetime no distinction between his religious and civil authority ever appeared; the *ummah* was a sacred community, both a church and a state, and Islamic law did not separate—and in fact deemed it heretical to separate—the doctrines of faith from the rules governing daily life. Neither had Muhammad indicated a chosen successor. The majority of the faithful, acting on the Islamic egalitarian spirit—the "consensus of the community"—elected as the caliph (from the Arabic *khalifâh*, or "successor") Abu Bakr, the father of Muhammad's favorite wife A'yshah.[12] But a number of faithful rallied behind Alî, the husband of Muhammad's daughter Fatima, and championed him not as the elected successor

---

11. The family was understood in a different way than in the West. Qur'anic law permits a Muslim man to have as many as four wives at a time. Most Muslims, then as now, however, have practiced monogamy.
12. The Prophet ultimately took four wives following the death of Khadija.

to but as the inheriting descendant of the Prophet. This dynastic split marks the origin of the two principal divisions in the Islamic world: *Sunni* Muslims (the followers of Abu Bakr, and their successors) maintained that Islamic leadership is to be freely chosen from the tribe of the Qur'aysh by the entire community, whereas *Shi'ite* Muslims asserted that only the direct physical descendants of Muhammad and Alî possess legitimate authority.

For the time being, the Sunnis carried the day. Abu Bakr, even more than Muhammad himself, was devoted to the idea of military conquest, and during his short reign (r. 632–634) he completed the conquest of the Arabian peninsula. His successor, Umar (r. 634–644) took aim at the Byzantines (who were at that time engaged, under Heraclius, in their first counterstrike against the Persians) and seized both Syria and Egypt. The symbolic climax of these campaigns was the conquest of Jerusalem in 639. Given Islam's evolutionary relationship to Judaism and Christianity it was inevitable that Muslims' attention would eventually turn to the Holy City, and indeed *sûrah* (or "chapter") 17 of the Qur'an records Muhammad's own mystical "night journey," in which his spirit was transported from Mecca to Jerusalem, and from there (at the site of the Dome of the Rock) on a tour through the seven heavens. Jerusalem thereby became the third most holy city to all Muslims and an important pilgrimage site. Umar also scored victories against the Persians, whom Heraclius had already defeated and demoralized, and under the next caliph, Uthman (r. 644–656), the Persian realm was brought entirely under Islamic control. The Muslim world now spread from the Nile river to India.

The conquest of Jerusalem had immense symbolic and spiritual significance, but of even greater practical significance was the conquest of Egypt. Since ancient times Egypt had been the most important grain-producing region in the western world. The wealth earned through this trade now poured into Muslim coffers and enabled them to hire more soldiers, build more mosques, expand the civil administration, and fortify the cities of their empire. Moreover, the seizure of Alexandria, the cosmopolitan city at the head of the Nile delta, placed two extraordinary new tools in Muslim hands: ships and books. Alexandria, at the time of the Muslim victory, had approximately two-thirds of the Byzantine imperial fleet in its harbor. By acquiring these ships, the Arabs virtually paralyzed the Byzantines while securing for themselves the means of rapid expansion throughout the Mediterranean. For a desert people without a maritime tradition, the Arabs took to the sea with impressive quickness, and soon Muslim navies were attacking Crete, Rhodes, Cyprus, and Sicily. Command of the sea also made it easier to maintain communications and commercial links with the furthest reaches of the Muslim world, as Arab armies continued westward across North Africa. It took less than a single generation after the conquest of Egypt to add the entire northern coast of Africa to the empire. By 711 the Muslim armies had even crossed the Straits of Gibraltar and taken nearly all of Visigothic Spain.

Books comprised Egypt's second, and arguably most significant contribution to Islam, for it was there (as well as in cities like Jerusalem, Antioch, Tripoli, and

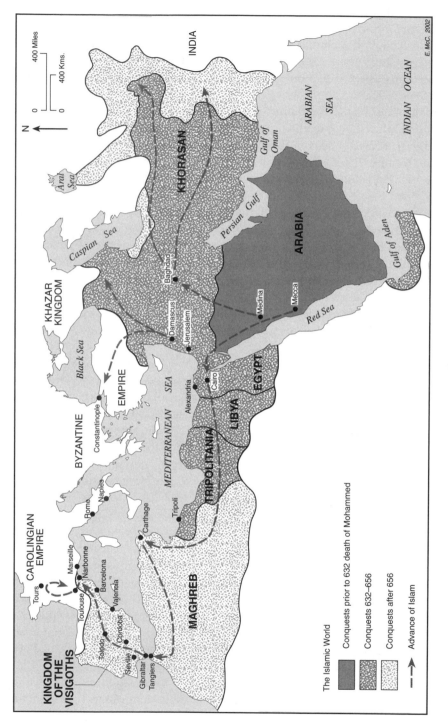

The Islamic Empire

INDIA

400 Miles

400 Kms.

N

Aral Sea

KHORASAN

ARABIAN SEA

INDIAN OCEAN

Gulf of Oman

Caspian Sea

Persian Gulf

ARABIA

Gulf of Aden

KHAZAR KINGDOM

Baghdad

Mecca
Medina

Red Sea

Black Sea

Damascus
Jerusalem

BYZANTINE EMPIRE

Constantinople

Cairo
Alexandria

EGYPT

LIBYA

MEDITERRANEAN SEA

TRIPOLITANIA

CAROLINGIAN EMPIRE

Rome
Naples

Tripoli

Tours

Marseille
Narbonne
Barcelona
Toulouse
Valencia
Cordoba
Toledo
Seville
Gibraltar
Tangiers

Carthage

MAGHREB

KINGDOM OF THE VISIGOTHS

The Islamic World

Conquests prior to 632 death of Mohammed

Conquests 632–656

Conquests after 656

Advance of Islam

E. McC. 2002

Baghdad) that the Arabs encountered and absorbed the legacy of western classical culture. Alexandria had once been the home of the greatest library in the western world. Established in Hellenistic days, it had been the central depository of the entire Greek literary, philosophical, and scientific traditions, and estimates of its collection of books have ranged from four hundred thousand to nearly one million. The overwhelming bulk of this learning had disappeared long before the Muslims' arrival, but enough survived in scattered collections to broaden and deepen the embryonic intellectual culture of Islam in powerful and exciting ways. Arab culture, like the caravan routes that fed it, had traditionally looked eastward to Persia and India. But the coincidence of Islam's hostile encounter with Persian Zoroastrianism—which the Muslims condemned as pagan idolatry, and whose libraries they gleefully burned to the ground—and its discovery of the western intellectual and cultural tradition meant that the Muslim world shifted much of its orientation. Western mathematics, medicine, philosophy (so long as it did not undermine Islamic doctrine), astronomy, and geography were all absorbed into Islamic culture, and for several centuries the Muslim world was in fact the chief preserver and continuator of the classical tradition, far more accomplished in these areas than Latin Europe.

The Umayyad dynasty—the series of caliphs from 661 to 750—ruled this empire from a new capital, Damascus. This site offered numerous strategic advantages, especially for pursuing the goal of conquering Constantinople. Time and again Arab forces tried to bring the city to its knees, but failed. Meanwhile, westward expansion halted, too. After conquering most of the Iberian peninsula in 711, the Muslims moved across the Pyrenees and into Frankish Gaul but were repulsed (as we will discuss more fully in the next chapter) in 732 by an upstart Frankish noble named Charles Martel. The Muslims retreated behind the Pyrenees and focused their energies on consolidating their control of Spain and furthering the Islamization of the populace. Nevertheless by the middle of the eighth century, an Islamic empire of immense size had been created, and justifiably or not, the peoples of medieval Europe and the shrunken Byzantine state felt themselves surrounded, dwarfed, and continually threatened by it.

A TRIPARTITE WORLD

Three distinct societies now comprised the medieval world: the Latin west, the Byzantine east, and the Islamic caliphate. But the points of contact between them, and the social and cultural traits they shared, are important to bear in mind. The shattering of Mediterranean unity was a reality, but for the time being a reality more in perception than in actual life; that is, people living in the eighth century certainly felt that western life had been irrevocably sundered and that three worlds now existed where there had previously been only one. But the reality was more complex.

For one thing, most of the Islamic world was Islamic in name only; a thin overgrid of devout Arab Muslims ruled a diverse populace of non-Muslim Persians,

Jews, Armenians, Copts, Syrians, Greeks, Berbers, Vandals, Mauretanians, Hispano-Romans, and Visigoths. Those rulers worked hard to promote Islam among their subjects, but most other aspects of daily life continued unchanged. Since the Arabs themselves tended to disdain agriculture, the bulk of the rural populace remained on the land, farming their traditional crops in traditional ways, while life in the cities continued to be dominated by local manufactures, market-squares, shopkeeping, schools, and urban administration. Islamic culture itself had developed little by the mid-eighth century; with most of their energies directed at conquest, Muslim leaders had not yet succeeded in bringing to life a full-fledged, distinctively Islamic intellectual or cultural tradition. Indeed, it was only in the eighth century that the Qur'an itself was finally written down and codified and that the Prophet's *hadith* were compiled. The only cultural practice that was becoming universalized in the Muslim world was the veiling of women.[13] By the eighth century, in other words, Islam was a faith and a state but not yet a distinct culture.

The Byzantine world, for all its tribulations, had changed chiefly in size. Reduced to less than half its pre-Justinianic area by the Arab advance, it underwent some significant transformation but less than one might expect. The most obvious change was Heraclius' promotion of the theme system. By the middle of the eighth century the Byzantine army numbered approximately eighty thousand men—down from the one hundred and fifty thousand of Justinian's time—and from their new "thematic" posts they took over civil administration. The army and the state, in other words, merged until the empire became quite literally a military state in a way that it had never been before. With so much of the government's business now devolved to the local level, the central administration in Constantinople shrank to no more than five or six hundred individuals, less than a quarter of its sixth-century high point. But while the empire was much reduced in size, it was a leaner, tighter, more cohesive and effective state than before.

At the same time it was inevitably a poorer one. Syria, Egypt, and North Africa had been the most profitable parts of the empire and these now lay in Arab hands. Moreover, several outbreaks of plague in the seventh and eighth centuries reduced much of the urban population. This resulted in an increased concentration of town-dwellers into smaller and more heavily fortified urban areas—a municipal reconfiguration that paralleled the streamlining of the government. Trade between inland towns declined rather sharply, but trade by sea between coastal cities continued. Surprisingly, the Byzantine coastal cities maintained commercial relations with the port cities of the Islamic caliphate even as their empires clashed; mutual economic interest prevailed over political and religious rivalry.

As for the Latin west, the seventh and eighth centuries were less a period of retrenchment than they were a struggle to create any kind of stable ordering at all. The

---

13. This had originally been a Persian, not an Arab, custom and was an emblem of aristocracy (the Persians' subject peoples having no right to look upon Persian women), but under Islamic influence it evolved into the practice of segregating men and women in order to preserve chastity.

arrival of the Lombards in Italy disrupted whatever normalization of life had occurred under the Ostrogoths. The equilibrium slowly introduced to Spain by the
Visigoths' conversion from Arianism ended abruptly with the Muslim conquest of
711. The Franks' apparently endless ability for internal strife consistently undermined what was arguably western Europe's most potent force for stability. From east
of the Rhine and north of the Danube, the ongoing predations of pagan Saxons and
Slavs frustrated attempts to establish a durable way of life. And the British isles,
which were perhaps the most ordered and steady territories in the west at the time,
lay at too far a remove from the rest of European life to have a lasting influence.

Nevertheless, while the age was chaotic, it was a creative chaos. Germanic and
Christian traditions began to coalesce into a distinct new order, and under the influence of the monastic movement the incorporation of classical culture into that order continued steadily. An entirely new culture was here in its embryonic phase,
and with it came a new sense of identity, one that found its first explicit expression
in the rise of the Carolingian empire.

SUGGESTED READING

Texts

Bede. *A History of the English Church and People.*

Comnena, Anna. *The Alexiad.*

Constantine Prophyrogenitus. *De administrando imperii.*

Gregory of Tours. *History of the Franks.*

Ibn Ishaq. *Life of the Prophet.*

Paul the Deacon. *History of the Lombards.*

Procopius. *The Secret History.*

Psellus, Michael. *Fourteen Byzantine Rulers.*

The Qur'an.

Source Anthologies

Barker, E. *Social and Political Thought in Byzantium from Justinian to the Last Palaeologus.*

Lewis, Bernard. *Islam: From the Prophet Muhammad to the Capture of Constantinople*, 2 vols.
(1976).

McNamara, Jo Ann, and John E. Halborg. *Sainted Women of the Dark Ages* (1992).

McNeill, William H., and Marilyn Robinson Waldman. *The Islamic World* (1983).

Peters, F[rancis]. E. *Judaism, Christianity, and Islam: The Classical Texts and Their Interpretation*,
3 vols. (1990).

Studies

Abun-Nasr, Jamil M. *A History of the Maghrib in the Islamic Period* (1987).

Ahmed, Leila. *Women and Gender in Islam: Historical Roots of a Modern Debate* (1992).

Al-Azmeh, Aziz. *Arabic Thought and Islamic Societies* (1986).

Bulliett, Richard W. *Islam: The View from the Edge* (1993).

Collins, Roger. *Early Medieval Spain: Unity in Diversity, 400–1000* (1995).

Davies, Wendy, and Paul Fouracre. *The Settlement of Disputes in Early Medieval Europe* (1992).

Dockray-Miller, Mary. *Motherhood and Mothering in Anglo-Saxon England* (2000).

Evans, J. A. S. *The Age of Justinian: The Circumstances of Imperial Power* (1996).

Fletcher, Richard A. *Moorish Spain* (1993).

Geary, Patrick. *Before France and Germany: The Creation and Transformation of the Merovingian Kingdom* (1987).

———. *The Myth of Nations: The Medieval Origins of Europe* (2002).

Haldon, J.F. *Byzantium in the Seventh Century: The Transformation of a Culture* (1990).

Herrin, Judith. *The Formation of Christendom* (1989).

Hourani, Albert. *A History of the Arab Peoples* (1991).

Humphreys, R. Stephen. *Islamic History: A Framework for Inquiry* (1991).

Hussey, Joan M. *The Orthodox Church in the Byzantine Empire* (1990).

James, Edward. *The Franks* (1988).

Kelly, Christopher. *Ruling The Later Roman Empire* (2004)

Kennedy, Hugh. *The Prophet and the Age of the Caliphates: The Islamic Near East from the Sixth to the Eleventh Centuries* (1986).

MacLeod, Roy. *The Library at Alexandria: Rediscovering the Cradle of Western Culture* (2000).

Moorhead, John. *Justinian* (1994).

Mottahedeh, Roy P. *Loyalty and Leadership in an Early Islamic Society* (2001).

Murray, Alexander Callander. *After Rome's Fall: Narrators and Sources of Early Medieval History* (1999).

Obolensky, Dmitri. *The Byzantine Commonwealth: Eastern Europe, 500–1453* (1982).

———. *Byzantium and the Slavs* (1994).

Peters, F[rancis]. E. *Children of Abraham: Judaism, Christianity, Islam* (1982).

———. *Muhammad and the Origins of Islam* (1994).

Richards, Jeffrey. *The Popes and the Papacy in the Early Middle Ages, 476–752* (1979).

Stowasser, Barbara. *Women in the Qur'an: Traditions and Commentaries* (1994).

Treadgold, Warren. *A History of the Byzantine State and Society* (1997).

Wemple, Suzanne F. *Women in Frankish Society: Marriage and the Cloister, 500–900* (1981).

Wood, Ian N. The Merovingian Kingdoms, 450–751 (1994).

CHAPTER 6

The Carolingian Era

In the eighth century a new aristocratic family rose to power in the Frankish territories and dramatically altered the development of western Europe. Thoroughly
Germanic in their character and culture, this family, known as the Carolingians,
helped effect the synthesis of Germanic and Christian culture and made important
inroads in bringing the classical legacy of the Mediterranean south into their northern realm. At the height of their power—under the ruler Charlemagne, or Charles the
Great (r. 768–814)—Carolingian authority stretched from the Atlantic coastline to the
upper reaches of the Elbe river and the middle reaches of the Danube, and from the
North Sea to the Adriatic. In fact the Carolingian Empire at its zenith virtually re-
created, with the exceptions of Britain and the Iberian peninsula, the western half of
the old Roman Empire itself, a fact that did not go unnoticed. The people of Charlemagne's time thought of themselves as living in a newly constituted Roman world,
and this self-redefinition received symbolic affirmation by the pope himself when,
on Christmas Day in the year 800, Leo III crowned Charlemagne emperor.

Carolingian Europe differed sharply from its Byzantine and Islamic neighbors.
It was overwhelmingly rural, and compared to the Byzantine and Islamic worlds, it
was technologically and culturally backward. Maps here can be misleading: With
the exception of its Italian sites, such as Rome, Ravenna, and Milan, and to a lesser
extent its commercial center at Barcelona in the Spanish March, the Carolingian Empire had no cities. Settlements such as Cologne, Mainz, Utrecht, or Tours were little
more than ambitious villages; even Paris itself, in Charlemagne's time, was no
larger than seven and one-half acres.[1] The Carolingians' subjects were scattered
rather evenly throughout the realm on smallish, individual farms. Large estates,
apart from those belonging to monasteries, were few. Farming methods remained
primitive and crop yields low. With little surplus available, little trade existed.
Moreover, the Carolingian world faced northward, no matter how hungrily the Carolingian rulers eyed the comparative wealth of the Mediterranean south. Nearly
all the main rivers in the Carolingian Empire flowed northward, into the North Sea
or the Baltic. One, the Loire, flowed westward into the Atlantic Ocean; and one, the
Danube, ran eastward into the Black Sea. But only the Rhône, in what is today

---

1. An area only one-tenth that of the university campus on which I am writing.

southeastern France, emptied into the Mediterranean. Since rivers comprised the most important means of transport in continental Europe, their direction meant that most nonlocal Carolingian commerce moved northward, and contacts with Anglo-Saxon England or the Scandinavian kingdoms were of greater significance than relations with Byzantium or the Islamic territories. Similarly, Carolingian contacts with eastern Europe remained tenuous. The peoples of the upper Balkans and of *Bohemia*, an imprecise geographical term at this time roughly designating Europe east of the Elbe, became Carolingian tributaries and made symbolic obeisance to Charlemagne's court, but their economic and cultural contacts with the west remained minimal; indeed, most of eastern Europe remained oriented to the east and south throughout most of the Middle Ages.

The greatest achievement of the Carolingian era was the formation of a cohesive western cultural identity. United under this family and linked together by the Carolingians' ardent promotion of Catholicism, the peoples of Europe began to think of themselves as *Europeans*—members of a distinct civilization larger than their composite ethnicities, a civilization that embraced and fused the classical, Christian, and Germanic traditions. They did not use the term Europeans to describe themselves, to be sure (although they did start to refer to the unified Latin world in general as "Europe"); instead, they identified themselves as members of a commonwealth known as *Christendom*. This collective identity, this dawning awareness that all the peoples of Europe were inextricably linked by their mutual relationship to the synthesized classical-Christian-Germanic tradition, both echoed and revivified the sense of cultural unity that ancient Rome had left behind. While the Carolingian era did not last very long, its formation of that collective identity was crucial; and its success, for all its limitations, proved great enough for that identity to survive even the collapse of the Carolingian Empire in the tenth century.

THE "DO-NOTHING" KINGS AND THE RISE OF THE CAROLINGIANS

Frankish kingship had never been very strong. Even under the most successful of the Merovingians like Clovis (d. 511) or Dagobert (d. 639), royal power was more a matter of effective brutality than political acumen. A variety of factors contributed to royal weakness. First, the physical underdevelopment of the realm made sound administration difficult: Without a network of cities from which to govern, and without adequate communications between them, royal administration had to be itinerant. Merovingian rulers traveled constantly, conquering lands, putting down rebellions, enforcing laws, forging links with local warrior elites, and raising funds wherever possible. But in the early Middle Ages a region whose king was not immediately present was a region without a king, and consequently farmers, merchants, monks, and warlords ignored royal decrees regularly. Second, given this state of affairs, the Frankish kings had to rely on the Germanic custom of gift-giving in order to secure their followers' loyalty; but since the primitive economy produced little actual money, the only thing the kings had to give away was the land itself. During the seventh and eighth centuries, the Merovingian kings repeatedly impoverished themselves by giving away extensive stretches of their territory to local warlords who did not hesitate to rebel if such gifts were not forthcoming. Third, the inheritance custom of dividing a man's possessions more or less equally among his legitimate heirs proved continually destabilizing. The division of a relatively peaceable realm into three, four, five, or more petty states, depending on the number of heirs, consistently exposed the Frankish territories to internal strife and made stable society impossible. It is hardly surprising, therefore, that the later Merovingians came to be dismissed contemptuously as the *Do-Nothing Kings*.

As royal authority degenerated, power passed to the scores of aristocratic warrior families who had received the land gifts. Chief among these, and certainly the most talented and ambitious, were the Carolingians. We do not know their origins, although they clearly descended from the Frankish warrior caste; moreover, they boasted of two Christian saints in their family tree: a woman, St. Gertrude of Nivelles (d. 659), and a man, St. Arnulf, who had been bishop of Metz in the early seventh century. At least by the middle of the seventh century, the Carolingians had secured their hereditary position as the *Mayors of the Palace* for Austrasia, one of the administrative provinces of the Merovingian kingdom, corresponding roughly to the Alsace-Lorraine region of today. The mayoralty put them in a position to control patronage; on behalf of the king they parceled out lands, cash awards, and government positions, and in so doing acquired a substantial body of followers who were loyal to them rather than to the do-nothing kings in whose name they acted. By 687, Pepin of Heristal, then the patriarch of the Carolingian clan, found himself sufficiently strong to undertake the conquest of Neustria, the neighboring administrative province, which made him the *de facto* ruler of all northern France. The Merovingian ruler in whose name Pepin governed was now little more than a puppet-king.

The Carolingians had a further advantage apart from talent and ambition: They had luck. For several consecutive generations, each leader of the clan had only one legitimate heir, which meant that their consolidated holdings never dissolved into the mass of splinter princedoms that the Merovingian royal realm had become. Their luck nearly ended with Pepin of Heristal, though, since he left two young sons behind him. But Pepin had also fathered a bastard son who, at Pepin's death, was already grown to manhood. His name was Charles Martel (Charles "the Hammer"—which suggests the essence of his personality). Charles took control of the government in 714, quickly disposed of his two half brothers, and seized control of the state, which he ran until his own death in 741.

Charles Martel combined ruthlessness and keen political instinct. He strengthened his hand considerably by forging closer relations with the Church. This may seem surprising in a man who had arranged the deaths of his two closest family members, but Charles Martel was sincerely devoted to the cause of Christianizing Europe. The cause needed help, frankly. By the eighth century, Christians—by which we mean people for whom the faith was a living reality and to whom the

Christian God was the only god, not just another in a pantheon of deities—still made up less than half the continental population. Moreover, those Christians were in continuous danger of relapse owing to the shortage of priests. (In the early Middle Ages, especially, individuals drawn to the religious life tended to opt for a monastic, rather than a priestly, vocation. Most professed Christians in Carolingian times were lucky if they saw a priest once a year.) Charles hoped to advance the Christianization of the Franks, but especially to encourage the conversion of the Frisians, a still pagan people living in what is today the Netherlands, and of the pagan Saxons living east of the Rhine river. Political calculations may have loomed larger in Charles' mind than religious convictions, since the Frisians and the Saxons represented the most immediate military threat to the growing Carolingian territories; but whatever his motivation, he dedicated himself to the religious cause with genuine enthusiasm.

Since the Frankish church was a shambles at the time, Charles seized instead on the missionary energies coming from the British Isles. Led by a series of ambitious Northumbrian monks, British missionaries had been at work among the pagan Germans since the seventh century. By Charles Martel's time, the most important figure in these efforts was an English Benedictine named Boniface (later canonized as St. Boniface [d. 754]; his original Anglo-Saxon name was Wynfrid). Boniface came from southern England and received his education in the monasteries of Exeter and Nursling. In 716, at the age of forty-one, he dedicated himself to converting the Germans and went all the way to Rome to receive an official commission in that ministry. He also eagerly accepted the material and organizational support offered him by Charles Martel. Backed by the pope and the Carolingian strongman, Boniface devoted the next forty years to bringing Christianity to the Saxons through a tireless campaign of preaching and teaching. He made thousands of converts, established dioceses, monasteries, and convents everywhere he went, and in appointing the men and women to head these new institutions he laid the groundwork of the entire German church. He himself became archbishop of Mainz by papal appointment in 732, and his stature established Mainz as the symbolic center of German Christianity, a status it retained throughout the rest of the Middle Ages.

Boniface tried to maintain his intellectual interests under what were obviously difficult conditions. Many of his letters survive in which he writes repeatedly to friends back in England, begging for books. Apart from the books of the Bible and the leading commentaries on them, he craved most especially the historical works of Bede and the pastoral writings of Gregory the Great. These books, repeatedly copied, formed the core of dozens of small monastic libraries that helped those houses to become important centers of learning during the *Carolingian Renaissance* of the ninth century. The most important of these was the great monastery at Fulda, in central Germany. Although Boniface himself produced no original works of lasting influence, his role in bringing the best of English evangelism and monastic scholarship to continental Europe was crucial. It also set an important precedent: Under Charles Martel's successors, and especially under his grandson Charlemagne, scholars and scribes from England formed the core of the intellectual revival and ec-clesiastical reform that lay at the heart of Carolingian interests.

But while he appreciated the support he received from the Carolingian court, Boniface did not hesitate to condemn its errors and abuses. In fact, he never was one to pull his punches if he thought a punch was in order. He once denounced the archbishop of Canterbury for permitting drunkenness in his church and for not tak-ing proper care of the young women in his diocese; having recently returned from a trip south to confer with the pope, Boniface wrote to the archbishop that he was shocked to find "there are entire cities in Lombardy and southern Gaul where there isn't a single prostitute who isn't from England! This is a scandal that disgraces your entire church!" Such a figure was not likely to condone Carolingian failings in the religious sphere. And failings there were, in plenty. The Frankish church had de-generated as badly as the do-nothing monarchy itself. Religious practice was irreg-ular, corruption abounded, and heresies sprang up anew. The most significant of these centered on a curious figure named Aldebert, who believed himself to be an angel and who carried with him a letter that he claimed to have received from Christ Himself. Aldebert traveled throughout Gaul, casting spells and curses "in the name of the angel Uriel, the angel Raguel, the angel Tubuel, the angel Michael, the angel Adinus, the angel Tubuas, the angel Saboac, and the angel Simiel!" His fol-lowers became so numerous that he began to consecrate churches to himself—to which he donated his fingernail clippings as "holy relics." Boniface struggled for the better part of a decade against such problems. He held a series of synods to con-demn particular abuses and tried to remodel the structure of the Frankish church. Of particular concern for the aged missionary was a recent new development in Charles Martel's treatment of ecclesiastical lands.

In an apparent contradiction of his campaign to foster Christian, or at least monastic, expansion, Charles had initiated in the 730s a risky new policy that in the end proved highly successful: Understanding that his power depended on his abil-ity to reward his supporters and recognizing also that the people of continental Eu-rope were feeling increasingly threatened by an aggressive Islamic world to the south and increasingly isolated from the Byzantines, he began to confiscate the lands of his own churches and parcel them out to win warriors loyal to him. Those lands were extensive, and seizing them gave Charles ample new wealth with which to attract soldiers to his cause. He justified himself by pleading that drastic circum-stances require drastic measures. If incompetents and evildoers have taken over the Frankish church, surely it cannot be wrong to deny them the means that keep them in power? Moreover, the Islamic threat to the south demanded quick action. A Mus-lim army (which was rather more of an expeditionary force than a full-blown in-vading army) had attacked Gaul in 732 and made straight for the city of Tours, the greatest pilgrimage site within the Frankish territories. Leading his much enlarged army, Charles defeated the Muslims in a battle on the plain midway between Tours and Poitiers, and immediately laid claim to be regarded as the hero of Christendom. His later victory over the Saxons of Westphalia in 738 added to his reputation and seemed to justify his landgrab even more. Boniface, for his part, rejoiced in the victories for the time-being and resigned himself to the Carolingians' unorthodox methods.

THE CAROLINGIAN MONARCHY

Charles Martel died in 741, having greatly expanded and centralized the Frankish lands. He left two sons, but one opted for the monastic life at Monte Cassino, so power passed smoothly to the second son, Pepin the Short (r. 741–768). Pepin was an impatient man who quickly grew tired of being the power behind the throne. He sent an embassy to the pope to ask a straightforward question: Is it right that he who bears none of the responsibilities of a king should possess the title of king, while he who bears all the responsibilities should not possess it? The Carolingians, he argued, as de facto rulers of the Franks and as the chief, if not the sole, effective defenders of Christianity in a barbaric world, simply *deserved* the throne. The pope at that time, named Zacharias (r. 741–752), was careful to stress that kingship was not, as a matter of principle, something that automatically "belonged" to whoever happened to exercise power, but he recognized that the Merovingians, by abandoning themselves to lechery and luxury, had lost God's favor. Thus, just as the ancient prophet Samuel had stripped Saul of his kingship over the Hebrews in Biblical times and bestowed it upon David, so now did Zacharias declare the last Merovingian king (a hapless fellow named Childeric) deposed.

> Therefore the aforesaid pope ordered the king [Childeric] and all the Frankish people to recognize Pepin, who was exercising all the powers of a king, as king, and to place him on the throne. This was carried out in the city of Soissons by the holy archbishop Boniface, who anointed Pepin and proclaimed him king. Childeric, the false ruler, had his head shaven and was sent to a monastery.

Pepin repaid the pope by marching his army into Italy and defeating the Lombards, who were then attacking the Church. Figuring that conquered Italy was now also his to dispose of as he saw fit, Pepin bestowed the central portion of the peninsula (roughly the middle third) on the papacy as an autonomous state. Henceforth, the pope stood as the spiritual leader of all Catholic Christians but also as the direct political ruler of an Italian principality known as the *Papal State*. But there was a problem. Some of the lands bestowed by Pepin had previously belonged to the Byzantines, who viewed Pepin's donation as a flagrant usurpation of imperial rights.

An enterprising scribe in the papal court responded to the Byzantine complaint by producing the most famous forgery in Western history. It is called the *Donation of Constantine*, and it was based on a popular legend that the emperor Constantine, when he moved the imperial capital to Constantinople, granted to the pope juridical dominion over the entire western half of the Roman Empire.[2] The *Donation's*

---

2. According to the legend, Constantine had contracted a severe case of leprosy that was miraculously cured by the intercession of Pope Sylvester I (314–335) and decided to reward the pontiff with half the empire.

forger did not invent the legend; he merely documented it. But the forgery implicitly sought to undermine the authority of Pepin's genuine donation as well: After all, if papal dominion over the west predated the rise of the Carolingians, then papal power could never be held to be subservient to Carolingian authority. The crucial clause ran as follows:

> To serve as a complement of my own empire and to insure that the supreme pontifical authority may never suffer dishonor—and that it may, in fact, be adorned with an authority more glorious than that of any earthly empire—I [Constantine] grant to the before-mentioned holy pontiff . . . the imperial Lateran palace, the city of Rome, the provinces, districts, and cities of Italy, and all the territories of the West. I hereby hand them over by imperial grant to his authority and to that of all his successors as pope. I have determined to establish this by a solemn, holy, and legally binding decree, and I grant it on a perpetual and lawful basis to the Holy Roman Church.

This "donation" formed the basis of papal political claims for the next five hundred years. The fact that it was a forged document troubled few people (the forgery was exposed at the end of the tenth century, but had been suspected from the start). To the early medieval mind, the genuineness of a document lay in its contents, not its form. If what a document said was true, in other words, it did not matter if the document itself was counterfeit. To create a false document was perfectly acceptable, so long as it was done to promote a legitimate claim.

Carolingian relations with the papacy grew even closer under Pepin's son and successor, Charles—eventually known as Charlemagne, or "Charles the Great" (r. 768–814).[3] To an extent, the Carolingian rulers and the popes legitimated each other's authority, and the resulting alliance helped to develop the idea of a superarching western Christian state. Charlemagne, after busy decades of conquest and reform, came to be viewed as the leader of a new society, Christendom. An important consequence of this new alliance and identity, though, was the effective estrangement of the western Christian world from the eastern.

Everything about Charlemagne was outsized. At nearly six-foot-four he towered above his contemporaries (archeological and forensic evidence shows that people in the Middle Ages were, on average, about six inches shorter than today); he ate vast quantities of food and drank wine to match; he was passionately devoted to swimming, hunting, and womanizing. A contemporary court scholar, Einhard, has left a vivid portrait of the man. Patterning his *Life of Charles* after the imperial biographies of the Roman writer Suetonius, Einhard emphasizes Charlemagne's enormous energy and drive.

> The top of his head was round and he had large, vibrant eyes. His nose was a trifle long, his hair very fair, and his countenance always cheerful and animated . . . He always enjoyed excellent health, except in the last four years

---

3. Charlemagne had a younger brother named Carloman, with whom he initially shared the realm; Carloman died in 771, only three years after Pepin, and the kingdom passed entirely to Charlemagne.

prior to his death when he fell victim to frequent fevers. In his last days he limped a bit on one side, but even then he paid more attention to his own inclinations than to the advice of his royal physicians, whom he despised because they wanted him to give up eating roasts, which he loved, in favor of boiled meat. As was common among the Franks, he exercised regularly on horseback and in the hunt . . . He loved the spray of natural hot springs and often swam—an activity he was so good at that no one could beat him—and that is why he built his palace at Aachen [the site of a hot spring] and lived there in his latter years. He used to invite his sons into his bath as well, along with his noblemen and friends, and sometimes even a corps of his royal escorts and bodyguards, so that more than a hundred people often bathed with him.

But Charlemagne was more than an energetic sensualist. He possessed a powerful sense of mission and saw it as his personal responsibility to complete the Christianization of Europe. A profound seriousness of purpose attended all that he did, and this seriousness, combined with his lifelong struggle with insomnia, kept him hard at work.

He habitually awoke and rose from his bed four or five times a night. He would hold audience with his retinue even while getting dressed or putting on his boots; if the palace chancellor told him of any legal matter for which his judgment was needed, he had the parties brought before him then and there. He would hear the case and render his decision just as though he was sitting on the bench of justice. And this was not the only type of business he would carry out at these hours, for he regularly performed any one of his daily duties, whether it was a matter for his personal attention or something that he could allocate to his officials.

Einhard also praises Charlemagne's intellect and dedication to learning, despite some personal handicaps:

He had the gift of easy and fluid speech and could express anything he wanted to say with extraordinary clarity. But he was not satisfied with the mastery of just his native tongue, and so he made a point of studying foreign ones as well; he became so adept at Latin that he could speak it as easily as his native tongue, and he understood much more Greek than he could actually speak. His eloquence was so great, in fact, that he could very well have taught the subject. And he energetically promoted the liberal arts, and praised and honored those who taught them. He studied grammar with Peter the Deacon, of Pisa, who was then a very old man. Another deacon, a Saxon from Britain named Albinus and surnamed Alcuin, was the greatest scholar of his time and tutored the king in many subjects. King Charles spent many long hours with him studying rhetoric, dialectic, and astronomy; he also learned mathematics and examined the movement of the heavenly bodies with particular attention. He tried to write too and had the habit of keeping tablets and blank pages under his pillow in bed, so that in his quiet hours he could get his hand used to forming the letters—but since he did not begin his efforts as a young man, but instead rather late in life, they met with little success.

Two unshakeable beliefs inspired all of Charlemagne's actions: belief in the Christian God and in his own duty to reunite all the territories of the former western Roman Empire. From 768, when he became the Frankish king, to his death in 814, he waged war on all of God's, and his, enemies: the Bretons, the Lombards, the Saxons, the Danes, the Frisians, the Slavs, the Avars, the Spanish Muslims. After consolidating his power on the throne, he began a series of campaigns against the Saxons. He attacked the Lombards of Italy when they again began to stir up trouble and vanquished them in 774. He incorporated their lands into his realm and began to use the title "Charles, king of the Franks and of the Lombards." It was roughly at this point that Charlemagne conceived the notion of systematically unifying the Christian west. This grand scheme meant more than mere conquest; a coherent campaign of political, social, religious, and intellectual reform had to accompany it.

He began by trying to subjugate the Saxons. In three years he reduced their rulers to obedience, and at the Diet of Paderborn in 777 they swore allegiance to him and underwent mass baptism. He then launched a premature assault on Muslim Spain in 778 and made it as far as Zaragoza before he was turned back; nevertheless, the territory he managed to conquer remained free. It became known as the Spanish March (the word *march* means "frontier") and ultimately developed into the county of Barcelona. On the return trek through the Pyrenees, a company of Basque renegades ambushed Charlemagne's rearguard and killed Count Roland, a Breton noble in Charlemagne's service. In later generations this improbable figure became the subject of popular legend and was canonized as the hero of an epic poem, *The Song of Roland*. The poem, however, turns Roland's death into a Christian tragedy by transforming his attackers into hordes of Spanish Muslims, who fall in spectacular numbers from Roland's mighty blows before he himself finally collapses on the battlefield.

After his Spanish misadventure, Charlemagne devoted the rest of his campaign to expanding his power to the north and the east. The Saxons rebelled again—perhaps having been encouraged by the Franks' setbacks in Spain—and reverted back to paganism. Charlemagne responded with a grimly determined savagery that shocked even his most ardent supporters, most notably his tutor Alcuin. On a single day in 782, for example, he ordered the beheading of forty-five hundred Saxon prisoners, and then went to Easter Mass. It took twenty more years of fighting to subdue the Saxons entirely, and another hundred years after that to complete their Christianization. In the meantime Charlemagne's forces pressed eastward into Bavaria, deposed the local ruler (who was Charlemagne's cousin) and annexed the whole territory, setting it up as a defensive East March province analogous to the "Spanish March" south of the Pyrenees; over the centuries this East March (*Ostmark*, in German) developed into the state of Austria. From the East March capital at Regensburg, Charlemagne launched attacks against the pagan Avars in what is today Hungary, and against the Slavs in the upper reaches of the Balkans. These campaigns proved highly profitable, for both groups had long survived on substantial tribute payments from beleaguered Byzantium and were rich in gold, silver, precious stones, spices, and eastern luxury fabrics. According to

A fitting image of Charlemagne, who spent much of his life on horseback, conquering and reconquering most of continental Europe. This bronze statue comes from the cathedral at Metz and was cast during the breakup of his empire by his many descendants. Source: Bridgeman-Giraudon / Art Resource, NY

one source, it took no fewer than sixty oxen to cart Charlemagne's eastern booty back to northern France.

This enormous expansion of his domain made Charlemagne the master of virtually all of western Europe. Of the regions once under Roman control, only Muslim Spain, Anglo-Saxon England, and southern Italy lay beyond his reach, but even they treated him with a certain deference. The symbolic climax of this reunification came on Christmas Day in the year 800, when Pope Leo III (r. 795–816) crowned Charlemagne emperor. According to Einhard, Charlemagne was incensed by the pope's action and insisted that he would not have gone to Mass that day, even though it was Christmas, if he had known what Leo was planning to do. But this scenario seems unlikely. Leo had been in direct contact with Charlemagne's court for at least six months prior to the coronation, and Charlemagne himself had been in Rome, manipulating events, at least since early November. The ruler who quite literally never slept was far too watchful and controlling a man to permit an undesired surprise coronation.

Most likely Charlemagne's chagrin, if it existed, had to do with the nature of the ceremony. In receiving the crown from Leo, Charlemagne feared legitimizing the notion that the imperial power was somehow subject to the papacy. Since Charlemagne's father had received the royal crown by papal grant, a papal conferment of the imperial crown could establish a dangerous precedent that undercut, if only in a symbolic way, Carolingian authority. And symbolism counted for a good deal in the early Middle Ages. When a person assumed a political office, after all, he did not simply "receive" his symbols of authority (whether a crown, a robe, a sword, or whatever) from someone else; instead, he fell to his knees before that individual, in front of a large crowd, and amid prayers of thanksgiving and praise vowed perpetual loyalty and due service for what was about to be given him. In a world largely without written contracts, such actions played an important role in establishing social and political relations. This scenario is almost certainly not what happened in Charlemagne's case, but it is probable that something in his coronation ceremony displeased him.

A second level of symbolism probably figured into the coronation as well. By Charlemagne's time the *anno Domini* system of dating was still relatively new in the west; Bede had begun to popularize it only in 725, with the publication of the final version of his treatise *On the Reckoning of Time*. Most educated people by the year 800 used the new system, but the great bulk of the populace—if they knew what year it was anyway (which may be doubtful)—probably still thought in terms of the old *annus mundi* system; and according to that system the year 800 was actually the year 6000. It is hard to know what, if anything, people thought about this. As we can see in our own time, millennial turns can provoke a variety of popular responses ranging from apocalyptic anxiety to bemused boredom. To many of those who were aware of the year 6000, Charlemagne's restoration of the western empire probably at least symbolized an important turning point in history, an attempt to capitalize on a calendrical quirk to signal the start of a bright new chapter in the evolution of Christendom. Like a modern politician who coordinates speeches and ribbon-cutting ceremonies to coincide with significant anniversaries, Charlemagne very likely chose this year for his coronation precisely for its symbolic, era-making value.

Whatever people thought about that day, Charlemagne certainly threw himself immediately into the exercise of his new power. He spent a few more months in Rome in order to bring some of the more flagrant Lombard outlaws to justice, and then returned to his new capital city at Aachen (Aix-la-Chapelle, in modern

The Carolingian Empire

Interior of the Palatine Chapel at Charlemagne's imperial capital at Aachen.
Source: Foto Marburg / Art Resource, NY

France), which he had ordered built in copy of Byzantine imperial buildings he had seen at Ravenna. This was not a coincidental or even essentially an aesthetic choice. The creation of the Carolingian dominion and the Franco-Papal alliance that authenticated it represented a fundamental turning point in European history, a declaration not only of independence from the Byzantine Empire (itself the care-taker of the cradle of western civilization in the eastern Mediterranean) but of equality with and succession to it. Western relations with Byzantium had been strained ever since Constantine moved the capital eastward in the fourth century. The Byzantines regarded the Latin westerners, for the most part, as backward and ill-educated poor cousins—members of the Christian family, to be sure, but hardly the sort of relatives to boast about. After Justinian's reconquests in the sixth century, Byzantine influence on the papal court remained strong, and the emerging Germanic kingdoms, as we have seen, continued to look to Constantinople for legitimation of their power.

Charlemagne's assumption of the imperial title, however, changed all that. From this point on, the west declared itself equal to the Greek east and free from its control; all subsequent medieval emperors defined their political legitimacy and sought to define their political policies by their relationship to the great Carolingian ruler and his successors rather than by their relationship with the Greeks. In medieval terms this was a *translatio imperii*, or "transferring of the empire." The Byzantines were hardly pleased by this claim but for the moment there was little they could do about it. Only in 812, after twelve years of diplomatic efforts, did the emperor in Constantinople, Michael I, finally recognize Charlemagne's title. Significantly, however, he agreed to allow Charlemagne only the title of "emperor," not "emperor of the Romans"; and Constantinople always remained reluctant to grant even this vaguer title to any of Charlemagne's successors.

CAROLINGIAN ADMINISTRATION

Governing an empire as vast as Charlemagne's posed unique problems. Unlike the western Roman Empire that it claimed to have recreated, Charlemagne's world was a land-based society in which travel was difficult and communication poor. Centered in the Frankish heartlands, it was overwhelmingly a rural, northward-oriented, peasant-dominated Germanic world. Despite his imperial title, Charlemagne's real power extended no further than his ability to enforce his authority. His court, therefore, remained itinerant. It traveled incessantly, holding assemblies, passing laws, adjudicating local disputes, collecting taxes, and trying above all to assert the unity of "Christendom" under Carolingian leadership. This need to be constantly on the move undermined efforts to create a stable government, for without a permanent, settled court Charlemagne's officials found it impossible to establish a systematic means of storing records, organizing the bureaucracy, or creating a treasury. Further problems plagued their efforts: the absence of a money economy, of a professional civil service, of a standing army or navy, or of a comprehensive (or, for that matter, even a primitive) network of roads and bridges.

The Carolingian court consisted chiefly of the emperor's own family and the clergy attached to their personal service. The principal magistrates were the *count palatine* (a sort of "first among equals" and overseer of the other Carolingian counts), the *seneschal* (the steward in charge of running the ruler's personal estates), and the *chamberlain* (or "Master of the Royal Household," the closest thing the court had to an imperial treasurer). This group held a great assembly once or twice every year, and sometimes more often than that, depending on immediate needs. These assemblies resolved whatever disputes were brought before them, whether legal, political, military, economic, or religious. In Charlemagne's world all these elements blended into one. The fundamental mission of the Carolingians can be best summarized by the word *campaign*; they were on a divinely appointed campaign to use whatever tools were available to complete the unification and Christianization of the Western world. A typical summons to one of these assemblies ran as follows.

> In the name of the Father, and of the Son, and of the Holy Spirit. Charles, the most serene, august, heavenly crowned, and magnificent emperor of peace, and also, by God's mercy, the King of the Franks and the Lombards, to Abbot Fulrad.
>
> You are hereby informed that I have decided to convene my General Assembly this year in eastern Saxony, on the river Bode, at the place called Stassfurt. I therefore command you to come to this place on the fifteenth day before the kalends of July—that is, seven days before the Feast of St. John the Baptist—with all your men suitably armed and at the ready, so that you will be prepared to leave from that place in any direction I choose. In other words, come with arms, gear, and all the food and clothing you will need for war. Let every horseman bring a shield, lance, sword, knife, bow, and supply of arrows. Let your carriage-train bring tools of every kind: axes, planes, augers, lumber, shovels, spades, and anything else needed by an army. Bring also enough food to last three months beyond the date of the assembly, and arms and clothing to last six.
>
> I command, more generally, that you should see to it that you travel peaceably to the aforesaid place, and that as your journey takes you through any of the lands of my realm you should presume to take nothing but fodder for your animals, wood, and water. Let the servants belonging to each of your loyal men march alongside the carts and horsemen, and let their masters be always with them until they reach the aforesaid place, lest a lord's absence may be the cause of his servants' evil-doing.
>
> Send your tribute—which you are to present to me at the assembly by the middle of May—to the appointed place, where I shall already be. If it should happen that your travels go so well that you can present this tribute to me in person, I shall be greatly pleased. Do not disappoint me now or in the future, if you hope to remain in my favor.

And this summons was for an empire largely at peace. The east Saxon campaign referred to here had both military and religious aims: to put down yet another Saxon rebellion, but more especially to evangelize the people living in the marshy regions around Stassfurt. All the materials that Abbot Fulrad had to bring with him were needed to build churches and monasteries as much as to undermine rebel fortifications.

Carolingian administration blended civil, military, and ecclesiastical authority into one; it was, in other words, a theocracy, and Charlemagne himself possessed (or wished to be thought to possess) a priestly aura. His laws, known as *capitularies*, dealt with ecclesiastical and even doctrinal matters as much as they did with taxation, diplomacy, criminal statutes, and educational reform. The crucial point is that Charlemagne did not think of himself as possessing both political authority and religious authority, for these, to him, were not separate things. There was only Authority, and he alone had it.

For practical purposes he divided his empire into administrative units called *counties* and placed his most loyal followers, whether lay or religious, in charge of them. These *counts* formed the backbone of his government. They possessed no legislative power of their own; their job was to defend the land and to enforce Charlemagne's laws and local customs. But delegating authority to local rulers posed potential problems. Under the do-nothing Merovingian rulers, the petty lords had succeeded in appropriating royal lands and prerogatives for themselves and had become virtually autonomous rulers in their own right. Charlemagne put an end to this brazen conduct. His conquests alone had removed from the scene many of the most obstreperous counts, and those who survived he reduced to obedience. He also made a point of assigning counts to counties in which they had no personal connections, and he expressly forbade counties to be passed on, like family legacies, to the children of any count. He sought to create a governing elite that was based on merit and on personal loyalty to the ruler himself—a corps of privileged individuals, but not an entrenched privileged class. Charlemagne kept an eye out for talented individuals wherever he went, regardless of their background, and he regularly awarded counties to newfound talents who impressed him and were willing to swear obedience and loyalty.

Even so, he checked up on his counts by creating a separate corps of itinerant court officials known as *missi dominici* ("traveling lords," or "emissaries"). These figures moved in regular circuits throughout the empire as Charlemagne's personal representatives. When one of these missi entered a county, he inspected local records and held open courts at which the inhabitants of the region gave evidence of the count's activities and his success or failure in carrying out Carolingian justice. The missi corrected abuses, announced new imperial decrees, and sent reports back to the imperial court about the counts' actions. It was a primitive system of government, but it provided the first modicum of European-wide justice and stability that the west had known since the third century. Necessity forced the emperor to allow his local representatives a degree of autonomy after a while. Imperial administration was never a monochromatic monolith, but a pragmatic balance of centralized aims and localized needs. Still, those who strayed too far from royal desires were quickly suppressed.

The ecclesiastical mission of the Carolingians forms one of their most important legacies. Beginning with Charles Martel in the early eighth century, the Carolingians interfered directly with the life of the western Church and instituted widespread reforms. These began with the evangelizing efforts of St. Boniface in central and eastern Europe, which Charles Martel had encouraged. Scores of new monasteries were established and formally endowed by the court, which made sure, however, to retain ultimate control over the ecclesiastical appointments made to them. The court helped to standardize the liturgy, to inaugurate a primitive system of parish churches, and to educate and train a new generation of clergy. Numerous capitularies dealt with ecclesiastical and doctrinal issues, the most important of these being the dispute over the use of *icons*, or religious images, in Christian worship.

This dispute, like Christianity itself, originated in the eastern Mediterranean. Icons had first appeared in Christian worship in Egypt and spread outward from there; whether statuary, painting, or mosaic, these images played an important role in propagating the faith. People who could not read the Bible could still learn the story of Jesus' Passion, for example, by following a pictorial narrative of it. Icons also provided a target for one's concentration in prayer; focusing on an image of the Virgin Mary, for example, when praying for Her intercession, helped to intensify the spiritual experience. But two problems complicated matters. First of all, the Bible itself condemned the practice: "You shall not make yourself a carved image or any likeness of anything in heaven above or on earth beneath or in the waters under the earth" [Exodus 20:4]. Over the centuries, many Christians had taken this commandment literally and had opposed any attempt to portray Christ and his saints in art. A second concern centered on the people using the images. Would uneducated new converts understand the difference between praying *before* a statue and praying *to* it? Since so much of the world was imperfectly Christianized, did it make sense to encourage a practice that might cause people to slip back into the pagan mode of worshiping images and idols?

Disagreement between *iconodules* (those favoring the use of icons) and *iconoclasts* (those opposed to them) reached its climax, and turned violent, in the eighth century. A group of bishops in Asia Minor persuaded the Byzantine emperor Leo I to issue a decree prohibiting the use of religious images in 730, and began a fierce campaign of stripping Christian churches and monasteries of their artwork—smashing statues, tearing down mosaics, and setting paintings ablaze. For the rest of Leo's reign, and throughout that of his son and successor Constantine V (r. 741–765),[4] the eastern church waged all-out war on icons and their supporters.

The dispute carried over to the western church as well. The use of icons in the west was not as widespread as in the east, but they still played an important role. Pope Gregory the Great had established a basic policy in the late sixth century, when orchestrating the conversion of the Germanic tribes: "To adore a picture is wrong, but to *learn* via a picture about what *is* to be adored is praiseworthy." To papal eyes, Leo's and Constantine's actions represented unsound theology and an unpardonable intrusion of the state in religious affairs. A papal synod at Rome in 731 consequently denounced iconoclasm and excommunicated the Patriarch of Constantinople, who had authorized Leo's initial decree. Relations with Byzantium quickly deteriorated, and the western Church was left without its traditional imperial protector. This highlights why the papacy turned so eagerly to the fast-rising Carolingians and why it placed so much emphasis on St. Boniface's missionary work among the Frisians and Saxons. Charles Martel, Pepin the Short, and Charlemagne may have treated the Frankish churches with a heavy hand, but they represented the best hope of stabilizing, renewing, and strengthening Catholic life.

---

4. Constantine V is unhappily best remembered for his nickname *Koprónimos*: "Constantine the Shithead."

Carolingian efforts to create a unified Christian state in the west, one independent of Byzantium, marked a kind of coming-of-age for the papacy, which successive popes tried to take advantage of by emphasizing their role in the creation and legitimization of Carolingian power.

The problem, though, was that the Carolingian rulers themselves felt differently. Charles Martel had plundered his churches mercilessly and without a thought for clerical complaints. Pepin had actually claimed the Frankish kingship even before Pope Stephen had officially offered it, and he viewed the papal action as little more than a formality, something akin to having a document notarized. As for Charlemagne, he made no secret of his own attitude toward the Holy See; the sole function of the pope, he wrote in a letter, is to serve as an example of pious Christian life: He is to be humble, meek, loving, generous, and devout. But he has no authority whatsoever. The empire itself *was* Christendom, and Charlemagne alone ruled it; the Church was merely an institution within Christendom, a tool or implement to be used as the emperor saw fit.

So even though Charlemagne agreed with the papal position about the use of religious images, it had to be made clear that icons were acceptable because Charlemagne, not the pope, said so. Consequently, he summoned scholars from all over Europe to a council at Frankfurt, where they reviewed all the arguments for and against religious imagery, and concluded with a definitive statement legitimizing their use. This was the so-called *Libri Carolini* (or "Charles's Book," appropriately). It advances a fascinating, if somewhat quirky, argument: that images themselves are unworthy of veneration for the simple reason that they are the products of human, not divine, hands. God's truth can be known only through the Holy Scriptures. But the very fact that images are not divine frees them from strictures on what they may or may not represent; human artistic expression, like human will, is entirely free.

The dispute over icons was not the only doctrinal issue to come before the court: It even issued edicts about the nature of the Holy Trinity. From at least the fourth century, Latin and Greek Christians had opposing ideas about the three-in-one nature of God. The Arian heresy was largely responsible for this; since the confrontation with Arianism necessitated further refinements of the basic orthodox position established at the Council of Nicaea. The Greeks had developed the position that the Trinity is indeed a union of three inseparable Persons but that these Persons act, and interact, in a particular way. The Holy Spirit, they maintained (and still do), originates in God the Father and proceeds thence to Christ the Son, from Whom it then emanates into the world. The Persons' relationship, in a word, is sequential. In the west, by contrast, a more closely integrated understanding of the Three became the norm. Latin Christians described the Holy Spirit as emanating equally and concurrently from the Father and from the Son.[5] St. Augustine fa-

---

5. In Latin, the word *filioque* is how one says "and from the Son." This disagreement is therefore known as the *filioque controversy*.

mously described this relationship as one of the Lover, the Beloved, and the Love that exists between them and holds them together. A Church council held at Toledo in 589 made the Augustinian position official, and to this day the Catholic creed asserts that the Holy Spirit "proceeds from the Father and from the Son."

This may all sound like bizarre theological hair-splitting, but the dispute had considerable ramifications. In order to combat Arianism, which by the sixth century had spread throughout the west, the Church had to place particular emphasis on the identification of Christ with the Father; it became a sort of spiritual battle cry, a proud point for self-definition in a Church struggling for survival. The choice of Toledo, in central Spain, for the council that formalized the Church's position was significant, too: It represented a declaration of victory over the Arian Visigoths, who had converted to the Catholic view after the conversion of their king Recared. Moreover, by convening the council so far westward, the Church virtually guaranteed that no Greek clergy would be present. The *filioque* edict, in other words, represented another symbolic declaration of independence from Byzantium.

The Carolingians also used the issue as a way of asserting themselves vis-à-vis Constantinople. To explain this, we need to return briefly to political events. In 797 the Byzantine empress Irene had led a palace coup against her unpopular and ineffectual son, Constantine VI. She ordered him blinded and left to die (which he obligingly did), and then took over the government. Irene was the first woman ever to rule the Roman or Byzantine empires in her own right, and her position on the throne was precarious.[6] Spotting his chance, Charlemagne in 802 sent an embassy to Constantinople offering Irene his hand in marriage. This wedding, if it had ever happened, would have led, for a while at least, to the legal reunion of the Byzantine and Frankish empires and would have encouraged the reunion of the Catholic and Orthodox churches. Restoring the entire western world under a single state and a single church—both, presumably, under his personal control—represented the culmination of Charlemagne's ideological vision and personal ambition. Irene replied that she was willing to consider the union.

But that prospect horrified the Byzantines. Even before Charlemagne's emissaries had left Constantinople, several leading Greek officials seized Irene and led her under armed guard to a convent, where they cut off her hair and forced her to take holy orders. She accepted her fate with good grace, perhaps viewing the life of a nun as a way of doing penance for her cruelty to her son. She stayed in the abbey and died there three years later, in 805. On hearing of the coup, a furious Charlemagne severed all ties with Byzantium. Apart from the political fallout of these events—the most surprising one being a brief alliance between Charlemagne and the Abbasid caliph Harun al-Rashid, in Baghdad, to fight against the Byzantines—

---

6. Incidentally, it was the unprecedented issue of having a woman on the imperial throne—a woman, moreover, who insisted that her subjects refer to her as *emperor* rather than *empress*—that Pope Leo had used to justify his bestowal of the imperial crown on Charlemagne in 800; the throne, he argued, had been vacant since 797.

these events also provided the context for Charlemagne's summoning a Church council at Aachen in 809, at which the western doctrine regarding *filioque* received the imperial stamp. Denied the eastern throne, he felt a need to delegitimate the eastern church. Trying as ever to put the best face on things, Pope Leo "affirmed" Charlemagne's action.

The iconoclast and *filioque* controversies, and Carolingian interference in them, illustrate well the theocratic vision that dominated Charlemagne's world. No aspect of life fell outside the bounds of the emperor's authority, and nothing less than the unification of the Christian world under Carolingian control could satisfy his vaulting ambition. After his symbolic dismissal of Byzantium in 809, Charlemagne became more realistic and moderate in his position, and his son and successor Louis the Pious (r. 814–841) never advanced any claims over the east. By the time of Charlemagne's death in 814, both the Latin State and the Latin Church had effectively proclaimed their total independence from Constantinople. Preserving that independence, however, would require a dramatic improvement in the west's educational and cultural levels, and both those goals depended on the development of the western economy.

CAROLINGIAN SOCIETY

A distinctively "Carolingian" society never existed. At best, the empire, for all its military might and ideological vainglory, was made up of probably fewer than twenty thousand men—counts, warriors, traveling lords, bishops, abbots, and monks—and a handful of notable abbesses. Beneath that thin overgrid lay a scattered mass of millions of peasants and artisans representing scores, if not hundreds, of different ethnicities and cultural traditions. Despite the Carolingian passion for regularization, most of these people continued to follow much the same ways of life that they had done before Pepin of Heristal and his descendants ever appeared on the scene, though with two changes: Over the course of the eighth and early ninth centuries they experienced a bit more peace and a great deal more pressure to accept Catholic Christianity. But beyond that life went on more or less unchanged.

Probably the only trait they all shared was poverty. Agriculture formed the base of the economy and employed the vast majority of the population, but it remained primitive. Most people used slow-moving oxen as the draft animals for their plows, which meant that they were able to cultivate relatively few acres, and they knew little about crop rotation, fertilization, or grain storage. As a result, crop yields remained low and the danger of famine never stood far off.

Peasants worked for the most part on individual family farms that they rented from the great lords of the manors that the Carolingians had distributed to their followers. Most of these farms were small; few families had more than twenty-five acres. Sometimes people lived together on larger farms made up of two or three families, on up to seventy-five acres, but farms any larger were rare. Carolingian capitularies recognized three different types of peasants. A *colonus* (fem. *colona*) was a legally free individual who held, but did not own, land and had relatively few obligations to the manorial lord other than paying rent. A *lidus* (fem. *lida*) was "half-free," meaning that he or she had fewer legal rights and generally owed higher rents and more services to the lord. The third class of peasants consisted of slaves, both male and female, who had no legal rights whatsoever and were little more than chattel.

A fair number of inventories survive from manors in the Frankish heartlands, and these give us an idea of what life was like for most commoners. These inventories itemize the names of the peasants on each estate, their children, the size of their individual farms, and the amount of rent and types of services they owed. The manor at Neuillay-les-Bois, in central France, was representative. It had a total of one hundred and thirty acres under plow; a grassland meadow of about a dozen acres; and a forest that measured approximately twenty-five square miles, which the lord (and the lord alone) used for hunting game and that the peasants used to provide forage for their pigs. Sixteen peasant families, comprising thirty-five adults and forty-two children, lived at Neuillay in the early ninth century and divided the one hundred and thirty acres between them, an average of fewer than ten acres per family. The Neuillay inventory lists each family's obligations to the lord; if we total their obligations up, these families owed their lord every year, in addition to one-quarter to one-third of their grain crops:

> five shillings and four pennies,
>
> twelve sheep,
>
> forty-eight chickens,
>
> one hundred and sixty eggs,
>
> six hundred planks of lumber,
>
> six hundred wood shingles,
>
> fifty-four hoops and staves [for making barrels],
>
> seventy-two torches,
>
> the meat from one-half an ox,
>
> four and one-half cartings [i.e., service to transport goods to market on the lord's behalf].

It is worth noting that not a single colonus, or free male, lived at Neuillay. They were presumably less desirable as tenants, since the lord's control over them was restricted by law. Only six women of colona status were present, two of whom were married to "half-free" men, and four of whom were married to slaves. Since children took on the legal category of their fathers rather than their mothers, and since marriages on the manor were subject to the lord's approval, there was clearly a downward pressure at Neuillay driving the peasants into legal slavery.

Nevertheless, a certain degree of fluidity existed. Men of colonus status did not appear frequently on manorial inventories because they did not necessarily live on manors; many of them owned farms independently. They had acquired these, for the most part, in the redistribution of lands confiscated from the Church by Charles Martel, Pepin the Short, and Charlemagne. As the empire grew, it quickly became obvious that the Frankish aristocracy alone could not supply enough soldiers to maintain it, and so the Carolingian leaders began to award non-manorial farms to Frankish freemen who would serve as infantry.[7] Whether by virtue of their own rent-free labor on the land or by their military service to the king, many of these peasants became relatively prosperous, and with wealth came the possibility of social advancement. In Charlemagne's time a surprising number of great ecclesiastical lords and high court officials came from peasant stock. Archbishop Ebbo of Reims, for example, was the son of a colonus, as was the court poet and scholar Walafrid Strabo, who became the private tutor to Charlemagne's own grandson.

Most Carolingian peasants, whether free or unfree, settled on farms near the numerous rivers and streams that flowed northward and westward. The soil in these river valleys tended to be wet and heavy with clay.[8] As a consequence, farmers tended to plow long furrows—since it was difficult to get the draft-oxen to turn—and this habit gave Frankish farmfields their characteristic rectangular shape, as opposed to the square fields favored by the Romans and Celts before them. Two crops were drawn annually from each field, with plantings in spring and fall, and harvests in late summer and late winter. The winter harvest (usually of a hardy grain like wheat; rye did not become common until the eleventh century) was considerably smaller than the summer harvest (barley, oats, and spelt), and it allowed at least some of the land to rest for a growing season each year. But local variations in climate, soil quality, and access to markets meant that Carolingian rural society had to be fluid; hence, wide differences in farm life existed. Three main styles (if we can call them that) of peasant housing existed. The most common was the sunken hut, a dwelling excavated below ground or cut into a hillside, on top of which sat a slanted thatch roof. Digging the floors below ground level or cutting the homes' foundations into a hillside helped to warm them in winter and cool them in summer but made the hovels very dark and dreary. The fact that farm animals were often brought into the dwellings—sometimes to provide warmth, sometimes to protect them from inclement weather—added to the rancid atmosphere. A second type of hut, single rooms elevated on moorings, was used primarily as a granary. These were far fewer in number, however, since they relied heavily on the use of lumber, a material far beyond what most peasants could afford. Nevertheless, some elevated huts have been located that were apparently used as dwellings. The most well-to-do freemen lived in *byre houses*, simple rectangular buildings measuring between twelve and twenty feet in width and from thirty to sixty feet in depth. These normally had only a single doorway, with an opening in their roofs to let in additional light (not to mention rain and snow) and to allow smoke from the internal

---

7. The Germanic word *frank* meant "free."
8. Archeological evidence shows that the water table along the Atlantic, North, and Baltic seacoasts was exceptionally high during the Carolingian period. No explanation for this exists.

hearth fire to escape. Most byre houses were divided into two areas, one for the families' living and working space, the other for storage or animal-housing. They had wooden frames and clay walls.

Rural life may have been relatively peaceful under the Carolingians, but it was hardly prosperous. Crop yields seldom rose above a two-to-one ratio—that is, one bushel of grain planted resulted in two bushels of grain harvested. Since at least one of the harvested bushels had to be used for the next planting, there remained little left for consumption. One indication of the harshness of peasant life is the fact that a common trope in Carolingian saints' lives presented the mere absence of famine in a given area as proof of a local saint's miracle-working. Even in the most fertile regions, farms needed to be at least fifteen to twenty acres in size in order to accommodate a single family with reasonable comfort; most individual Carolingian farms, however, were barely that size. Diet consisted primarily of grains—as bread, gruel, or beer—and vegetables and cheese (which could not be transported to market without spoilage). Meat and fish were eaten in small quantities, generally in stews.

Peasants made up the majority of the lower clergy; in fact, the law considered all members of the lower clergy to be peasants, regardless of their birth. Most local clergy acquired their posts by appointment from the estates' lords, who owned and controlled the churches on their land, and on the whole the clergy were a sorry lot. Illiteracy abounded, making it difficult to maintain any semblance of meaningful Christian life—how can you preach the Good News if you can't read it?—and morals were often loose. Priesthood in fact was scorned and derided as the lowliest of professions, such that better-educated freemen tried to avoid it for fear of being associated with slaves and scoundrels. Many peasants in fact were dragged into the priesthood against their will, for a peasant did not have the right to refuse his lord's appointment. Why would a lord want an illiterate and morally corruptible peasant as his local priest? Since they retained their legal status as the lord's peasants even after ordination, rural priests frequently owed him the ecclesiastical taxes raised by the churches to which they had been appointed. All peasants on an estate paid a *tithe*—that is, ten percent of their annual produce—to their local church. This ten percent, plus the twenty-five percent already paid to the lord in rent, went straight into the master's purse. Bishops and popes denounced this state of affairs, citing canon law that asserted that all the priests in any given diocese came under the authority and protection of the local bishop; but the lords by and large simply ignored them.

It is little wonder then that religious life for most commoners was a muddle. As relative newcomers to Christianity, unable to read the Scriptures themselves and under the spiritual guidance of uneducated and unwilling lackey-priests, Charlemagne's subjects were often Christian only in name. For those whose faith had some depth, popular worship focused less on the sacramental life of the Church and more on the veneration of local saints, ascetic discipline, and popular customs like singing hymns and praying as a family or in small groups. Individuals who lived devout lives became the objects of popular cults even during their lifetime and had far-reaching influence over society, as people came from long distances to behold them, hear their words, and seek their prophecies. Here too, a person of low birth could attain significant social standing and become venerated as a saint. A good example was a young Saxon woman of common stock named Liutberga, who was born during Charlemagne's reign and died during that of his son Louis (r. 814–841).

St. Liutberga was a servant in a convent near Windenhausen, in Saxony. A noblewoman who visited the convent was struck by the girl's sharp mind and sweet temper, and took her under her wing. Liutberga accompanied the noble lady until her death, and then stayed on at the manor of the noblewoman's son, where she quickly acquired a reputation for sanctity. Liutberga was lucky enough to learn how to read:

> [Apart from performing her duties as a servant] she was tireless in singing divine praises, psalms, hymns, and canticles; indeed she had the heart of an Apostle and offered the Lord all the devotion of her mind as a sacrifice. . . . She studied the Scriptures assiduously, meditating on them every day, and soon knew them so well that she could not have understood them better even if she had not suffered from the innate stupidity of her sex. . . . [Whenever she ventured into public] she wrangled with the men in the square about the allurements of this world and the enticements of the flesh, which lead men to lechery and peevishness.

In her middle age Liutberga requested her lord's permission to leave his manor and live out her years as a recluse. A wilderness hideaway was prepared for her, and she was shut in. But news of her sanctity continued to spread, and, like other recluses before her, she was soon deluged with rustic petitioners. She became something of a moral guardian for the nearby populace, one who even had recourse to the supernatural:

> A freeman named Hruodart, one of Bilihild's underlings, habitually pursued a certain young woman every time she came out of her house, in order to have sex with her. It happened one day, towards evening, that this woman was rushing to meet her lover at a place near Liutberga's remote hermitage. Liutberga, seeing her, cried out: "My dear daughter! Don't shy away from finishing the work that you see I have begun here [i.e., total devotion to God]. Labor of this sort will reward you; for one reaps everything that one sows, when it comes to good works. For everything that we do that is good, is of good benefit." [Liutberga] brought the woman some candles and lamps, since the time was right for them. But the girl was in a passion to join her lover, who was hiding nearby. . . . But then, all of a sudden, an evil spirit rose up. Its shape was hideous, with flames of sulphur pouring from its nose and mouth, its eyes crackling with fire, its black body extending immense claws. It positioned itself over the man, pressing its knees upon his chest; with gaping jaws it consumed his face and with its huge claws it ripped at his inner organs, like an eagle going after its prey. It tore away at his guts until the man's miserable soul departed from his body.

And it took no time at all before Liutberga was credited with the gift of prophecy.

> God rewarded her with the gift of prophecy and she was able to describe many
> events that would take place in the future. . . . As she herself foretold, she
> stayed in her isolated confinement for thirty years, and everything that she
> prophesied came true. . . . Even abbots and bishops took recourse to her and
> commended themselves to her prayers—either in person or through messen-
> gers; moreover, they kept her in their own prayers, giving thanks to the Lord
> for her with every other breath.

In the towns of the empire things were a bit better, but except for those places
that had a bishop in residence, probably not much better. Carolingian cities were
more administrative centers and temporary fortresses than municipalities based on
manufacture and trade, and consequently their populations remained quite low.
Little inter-city trade existed, since the roads linking cities, when there were roads,
ran through forests that harbored robbers, rebels, and runaways. Many surviving
texts describe the lawlessness of the wilderness. The lack of trade meant that a
money economy never really developed; and with land as the only source of
wealth, the only way for most people to advance economically was, for the aristocracy, to seize land from others, which meant endemic warfare, or, for the commoners, to try to bring more acres under the plow, which further atomized the
population as family farms continued to eat up the rough countryside.

Carolingian society, in short, was chaotic and fluid. It is little wonder, then, that
Charlemagne and his officials remained constantly on the move in the effort to
maintain order. The itinerant courtiers kept sharp eyes out for people of talent, and
it remained possible for even the lowest-born person to reach a position of power
and prestige through service to the State or Church.

THE CAROLINGIAN CULTURAL RENEWAL

Historians traditionally refer to the court-directed educational and artistic reforms
from roughly 790 to 870 as the *Carolingian Renaissance*. We probably shouldn't,
though, for compared to the great cultural and intellectual achievements of the
twelfth and fifteenth centuries, the Carolingian "renaissance" was a pretty modest
affair. No more than a few thousand people participated in it, and most of those
were involved in preserving the achievements of earlier ages rather than undertaking original thought or creative action. Copyists far outnumbered authors; painters, sculptors, and architects spent more time replicating Roman or Byzantine
models than in fashioning new expressions of their own. Their activity deserves respect, however. Without the copyists' labors, a great deal of classical Latin literature would have disappeared—and a world without Virgil, Cicero, Tacitus,
Suetonius, or Seneca (the most popular Roman authors in the Middle Ages) would
be a poorer place indeed. Keeping alive Roman styles of architecture and design
also helped to safeguard at least some of the classical tradition of mathematics and
basic science.

*An example of the superb skill of the painters and illuminators
who created the glories of the Carolingian Renaissance. This manuscript painting
of the four evangelists (Matthew, Mark, Luke, John) is preserved in the treasury
of the Palatine Chapel. Source: D.Y. / Art Resource, NY*

Still, the Carolingian renewal was more than just a salvage operation. Stan-
dardizing the liturgy, correcting literary and ecclesiastical texts, reforming orthography, and creating a sound system of weights and measures all constituted
genuine accomplishments. Poets like Theodulf of Orléans (d. 802), Sedulius Scotus (d. 858), and Walafrid Strabo (d. 849) wrote much supple and enduring verse;
scholars like the philosopher John Scotus Eriugena (d. 877) and the canon lawyer
known as "Pseudo-Isidore" made striking contributions to logic and ecclesiol-

ogy.[9] New musical styles, painting techniques, and literary genres emerged. Scriptoria flourished, the first European libraries were established, silk weaving made its first appearance in the west, and a surprisingly comprehensive network of monastic schools began to dot the European landscape. Considering the odds against them, on the whole, the artists and scholars of the Carolingian age did an admirable job.

Whatever this renaissance was or was not, it is clear that it began with Charlemagne, who viewed educational reform as a central aspect of his vision for Christendom. In the 780s he urged one his prominent abbots:

> In consultation with my faithful advisors I have decided that it is desirable that all the bishoprics and monasteries that Christ has entrusted me to govern . . . should devote themselves to the study and teaching of literature . . . for just as observance of a Rule disciplines a cleric's actions, so too will strict attention to study and teaching discipline and rectify his expressions. . . . In recent years I have received letters from various monasteries, describing their exertions on my behalf in holy and pious prayers, only to discover that while their sentiments were sound, their speech was extremely vulgar. . . . I have in fact begun to fear that these monks' illiteracy could result in a serious misinterpretation of Holy Scripture; and we all know that, as dangerous as misspoken words are, even more dangerous are misunderstandings of God's Word. Therefore I exhort you not only not to neglect literature but to strive to master it, with a sense of humble devotion that will be pleasing to God; for only then will you be able to ascertain, easily and properly, the secret mysteries of the Scriptures. . . . Let the men chosen for this work be those with both the will and the ability to learn and the desire to teach what they learn to others, and may this activity be pursued with a zeal equal to that of my own in prescribing it.

And in 789 Charlemagne issued a general decree to all his subjects:

> Let every single episcopal see and every single monastery provide instruction in the singing of psalms, musical notation, [Gregorian] chant, the computation of the years and seasons, and grammar. Moreover, let all the appropriate texts be carefully corrected.

The primary goal, in other words, was to reform the Church, to educate those illiterate peasant priests and half-taught monks who served the empire's churches, and the ultimate end was not "literature" (by which Charlemagne meant "letters" or "learning" in the broadest sense) for its own sake but specifically in order to further the Christianization of the world.

The man chosen to lead this campaign was an Englishman named Alcuin (ca. 730–804). He came from York, and he was a product of the vigorous Northumbrian monastic tradition that had produced earlier scholar-monks like Bede and St. Boniface.

---

9. We do not know "Pseudo-Isidore"'s real identity; in the Middle Ages his works were attributed to St. Isidore of Seville.

A portrait of St. Mark in the "Ebbo Gospel"
which was created during the reign of Louis the Pious.
Source: Art Resource, NY

Apart from overseeing the activities of all the court scholars, Alcuin devoted himself particularly to the enormous task of producing a new, corrected edition of St. Jerome's Vulgate Bible. Thousands of scribal errors had crept into the text over the centuries. Alcuin gathered and collated as many manuscripts as possible, from all over Europe, and combed over the texts word by word. His mastery of Latin enabled him to eradicate obvious errors; and in the process he not only produced a wholly new and accurate Bible, but he also introduced an entirely new way of writing. He created a new alphabet, called the *Caroline minuscule*, that was far more legible than earlier scripts (it is essentially his alphabet—that is, the letter shapes, both upper and lower case—that you are now reading); and in a second innovation, he introduced word spacing.

INROMANTIMESSENTENCESWEREWRITTENLIKETHISALLINCAPITALS
ANDWITHOUTSPACESBETWEENTHEWORDS.

The Romans' aim had been, in part, to save space on expensive writing surfaces, but, believe it or not, it may have aided the Roman style of reading as well. In ancient times reading was an oral activity: One pronounced the words as one read them. If you look again at the collapsed sentence above, you will find it is much easier to read aloud than silently. Alcuin recognized that medieval scribes—who were supposed to observe silence at all times, except when reciting the holy offices or when addressed by their abbot—found Roman script too confusing, and that this was one of the causes of the multitude of scribal errors. Alcuin's new writing system not only made it easier to produce reliable texts, but it also resulted in a new way of reading that became increasingly a silent, private pleasure rather than an oral, communal one.

Charlemagne, and his son Louis after him, recruited scholars from all across Europe. Einhard, Charlemagne's biographer, came from the eastern reaches of the Frankish territories. Paul the Deacon, a Lombard, produced a lively *History of the Lombards* that is one of our principal sources for the early history of that group. Two other Lombards, Peter of Pisa and Paulinus of Aquileia, were influential in consolidating and improving the grammars that became the standard for teaching monks their Latin. Paulinus also wrote a number of important treatises attacking the ideas of the last heresy known to have beset early medieval Europe—adoptionism (which maintained that the human figure of Christ, as opposed to the eternal Christ who has always existed with God in Heaven, was the "Son of God" only in the sense that He was a man "adopted" by the Lord). Adoptionism emerged in Spain, where it probably resulted from the influence of Islamic ideas about Christ—namely, that He was a holy man inspired with divine prophetic gifts, but was entirely and solely human in nature. Spain was also the birthplace of Theodulf, a Visigoth who later rose to become bishop of Orléans and then the abbot of Fleury. Theodulf, who was also no mean poet, was the principal author of the *Libri Carolini*—Charlemagne's response to the iconoclastic controversy. Sedulius Scotus came to the Frankish courts in the 840s from Ireland and wrote large quantities of accomplished verse and an irritating treatise called *On Christian Rulers*, which advocated such Carolingian orthodoxies as:

> *The king's most royal honor and most brilliant diadem consist*
> *Of his pious fear of God's Heavenly Throne and Love, for just*
> *As snow-white lilies lend grace to a field in flower, and roses*
> *Blush in scarlet, so does a just ruler produce a garland of virtues*
> *And bring forth the most blessed of fruits from the sublimity of his resolve.*

Another Irishman, John Scotus Eriugena, was the most astonishing intellect of them all, even though he is seldom read today. He came to the court during the reign of

Charlemagne's grandson, Charles the Bald, and somehow managed to learn Greek. His best-known work in the Middle Ages was a translation into Latin of a work called *On the Celestial Hierarchies* by Pseudo-Dionysius.[10] This was a Neo-Platonic work that attempted to describe the structural divisions of Heaven—a kind of celestial architecture—in which the author made fine distinctions between Seraphim, Cherubim, and Thrones (the higher Angels of Love); the Dominations, Powers, and Virtues (divine bureaucrats who watch out over the other angels); and Principalities, Archangels, and regular Angels (God's messengers and occasional soldiers). It all sounds very fanciful—but it illustrates an important conceptual understanding, the belief that the cosmos is *structured*, that a blueprint exists for its design, and that human beings, by exercising their rational faculties, can discern and comprehend the organization and purpose of the universe. John Scotus' most interesting original work was the *Periphyseon* ("On the Divisions of Nature") in which he elaborates his structural thesis about nature and the heavens. The world is an organic unity, in John Scotus' thought, and can only be properly understood *as a system*. His language is often difficult, which is one reason why he is so seldom read today, but he was one of the first philosophers in western history to posit a comprehensive system of natural laws. His philosophy emblematizes the whole Carolingian world view, and his influence on later medieval writers was considerable.

The point here is not to rattle off names but to highlight a significant trend. The Carolingian renewal centralized much of Europe's intellectual and cultural life by drawing grammarians, poets, artists, historians, and scholars into the Frankish heartlands. Most of whatever original cultural activity took place happened in the imperial court—whether Aachen itself or the peripatetic retinue that always followed the emperor—and throughout the rest of the empire relatively little was accomplished apart from copying and reproduction. The results of this centralization were impressive—since artists and intellectuals usually thrive in each other's presence—but centralization also meant the relative intellectual impoverishment of the non-Frankish territories. In the generations that followed Charlemagne, Louis, and Charles the Bald, western intellectual life and artistic activity hit a dismal low point. Older books continued to be copied (and it is worth mentioning that over eight thousand manuscripts survive from Carolingian scriptoria), but precious few new books were written. Apart from the composition of saints' lives, which continued to flourish as a literary genre, the only significant intellectual accomplishments of the late ninth and tenth centuries were the compilation of encyclopedias, like that of Rabanus Maurus (d. 856), which collected and preserved the ideas of others but advanced few of their own.

The other main strength of Carolingian art was in architecture. Apart from the

---

10.   Another unknown author who has been identified, at various times, as Dionysius the Areopagite—an Athenian philosopher whom St. Paul claimed to have converted to Christianity—and as St. Denis, the first Christian bishop of Paris. Both attributions are false, but we still do not know who Pseudo-Dionysius was.

*This tenth-century ceremonial cross, produced in Cologne, is a fine example
of medieval metalwork, ivory carving, and jewelry making. It is also
a crystal-clear example of Carolingian ideology, for it displays an image of the
emperor, not of Christ, at the center of the Cross. The emperor as savior of mankind.
This is a late Carolingian piece, made long after Charlemagne's death; but
somewhere he must be looking down at it rather fondly.
Source: Erich Lessing / Art Resource, NY*

imperial capital at Aachen and a handful of new monastic foundations, few Carolingian buildings stand today since wood was still the primary building material, but the stone structures that survive give clear evidence of the imperial ideology behind the Renaissance. The Palatine Chapel at Aachen, completed in 805, directly imitates the style of the old Roman imperial church of San Vitale at Ravenna. For nearly two hundred years it was the largest stone building north of the Alps.

A three-tiered octagon, it derives its heavy, almost stolid, grandeur from proportions drawn (according to legend) from the twenty-first chapter of the book of Revelations—the chapter describing the New Jerusalem. Imperial imagery was everywhere: The pulpit is decorated with fragments of Roman pottery and glass; the altar panel presents an image of the Passion of Christ in perfect Roman classical style; the main altarpiece—known as Lothar's Cross—has a portrait of the emperor Augustus at its center. The image is frankly blasphemous, since it invites an identification of the emperor with the Savior. But such was the view of the ruler that the entire Carolingian ideology was based upon.[11]

Still, the Carolingian renewal deserves respect. It brought a degree of cohesiveness to Christian life that was badly needed, and it also gave it a sense of purpose— a philosophic vision of how to order the world—that had repercussions through many centuries. The great intellectual revival and cultural blossoming of the twelfth and thirteenth centuries owed much to the often dreary labors of these Carolingian scribes.

Suggested Reading

Texts

Anonymous. *The Royal Frankish Annals*.

Anonymous. *The Song of Roland*.

Dhuoda. *Handbook for William*.

Einhard. *Life of Charlemagne*.

John Scotus Eriugena. *On the Divisions of Nature*.

Nithard. *Histories*.

Notker the Stammerer. *Life of King Charles*.

Paul the Deacon. *History of the Lombards*.

Pseudo-Dionysius. *On the Celestial Hierarchies*.

Source Anthologies

Davis-Weyer, Caecilia. *Early Medieval Art, 300–1150: Sources and Documents* (1986).

Dutton, Paul Edward. *Carolingian Civilization: A Reader* (1993).

———. *Charlemagne's Courtier: The Complete Einhard* (1998).

Godman, Peter. *Poetry of the Carolingian Renaissance* (1985).

Pullan, B. *Sources for the History of Medieval Europe from the Mid-Eighth to the Mid-Thirteenth Century* (1966).

---

11. In 1165 the emperor Frederick Barbarossa pushed the identification even further. He transferred Charlemagne's body to Aachen in a solid gold casket, and placed a reliquary on the altar which contained three relics: the loincloth of Christ, the Blessed Virgin's cloak, and a splinter of Charlemagne's skull.

Scholz, B. W., and B. Rogers. *Carolingian Chronicles: Royal Frankish Annals and Nithard's Histories* (1970).

Studies

Bachrach, Bernard S. *Early Carolingian Warfare: Prelude to Empire* (2000).

Barnwell, Peter. *Kings, Courtiers, and Imperium: The Barbarian West, 565–725* (1997).

Barraclough, Geoffrey. *Eastern and Western Europe in the Middle Ages* (1970).

Blumenthal, Uta-Renate. *Carolingian Essays* (1983).

Bullough, Donald. *The Age of Charlemagne* (1973).

———. *Carolingian Renewal: Sources and Heritage* (1991).

Collins, Roger. *Charlemagne* (1998).

———. *Early Medieval Spain: Unity in Diversity, 400–1000* (1983).

Duby, Georges. *The Early Growth of the European Economy: Warriors and Peasants from the Seventh to the Twelfth Century* (1974).

———. *Rural Economy and Country Life in the Medieval West* (1990).

Fichtenau, Heinrich. *The Carolingian Empire: The Age of Charlemagne* (1978).

———. *Living in the Tenth Century: Studies in Mentalities and Social Orders* (1991).

Fouracre, Paul. *The Age of Charles Martel* (2000).

Freedman, Paul. *The Origins of Peasant Servitude in Medieval Catalonia* (1991).

———. *Images of the Medieval Peasant* (1999).

Génicot, Léopold. *Rural Communities in the Medieval West* (1990).

Herlihy, David. *Medieval Households* (1985).

Koziol, Geoffrey. *Begging Pardon and Favor: Ritual and Political Order in Early Medieval France* (1992).

Lozovsky, Natalia. *The Earth Is Our Book: Geographical Knowledge in the Latin West, ca. 400–1000* (2000).

McKitterick, Rosamund. *Carolingian Culture: Emulation and Innovation* (1994).

———. *The Carolingians and the Written Word* (1989).

———. *The Frankish Kingdoms under the Carolingians, 751–987* (1983).

Nelson, Janet L. *Charles the Bald* (1992).

Reuter, Timothy. *Germany in the Early Middle Ages, 800–1056* (1991).

Riché, Pierre. *The Carolingians: A Family Who Forged Europe* (1993).

PART TWO

THE CENTRAL
MIDDLE AGES

The Tenth through
Twelfth Centuries

CHAPTER 7

THE TIME OF TROUBLES

The Carolingian world collapsed spectacularly. A combination of internal weaknesses and external pressures did the damage, and the sight was remarkable enough to make several writers at the time wonder whether the world itself was coming to an end—and they got at least a few people to believe them. (They were wrong, thankfully.) The dramatic downfall serves as a caution against overrating the Carolingian accomplishment in the first place, but it is clear nevertheless that the troubles that befell Europe in the tenth and early eleventh centuries were extraordinary in their degree and kind. In the words of one historian, Europe in the tenth century was "under siege." Enough of the old world survived from the collapse to maintain a sense of order and tradition, but the Europe that emerged from the wreckage was a radically re-created and reformed place. How did all this happen?

This troublesome century (interpreted broadly as the period from roughly 870 to just after the turn of the millennium) brought to an end the experimental period of western Europe's amalgamation of the Christian, Classical, and Germanic cultures. The precise challenges that this century threw at Europe, however, were altogether of a different sort than those that had ended the ancient world, and they took place within a much-changed context, characterized most notably by a world that was already, however imperfectly, Christianized. The interplay of new hardship and the residual strength of embryonic Christian identity meant that this "time of troubles" had more in common with the medieval world that emerged out of it than it did with the earlier cultural amalgam from which it sprang. Latin Europe in the 900s was a vastly different place from the Europe of the 700s, one that looked to a brighter future even as some of its inhabitants grimly prepared themselves for The End.

TROUBLE FROM WITHIN

In part, Carolingian luck simply ran out. For several generations in a row they had produced a single heir who held their lands together and continued the twin causes of unifying and Christianizing the west. But after the middle of the ninth century, an abundance of heirs appeared on the scene, and the empire was gradually carved up among them. Charlemagne's son Louis the Pious (r. 814–840) had received the empire intact, but he had few of his father's gifts for commanding loyalty and obedience. His reign marked the pinnacle of the Carolingian cultural renewal, the

groundwork having been laid during his father's time, but on the political and economic level his years on the throne were, if not a flat-out disaster, at least a miserable
muddle. The fault was not entirely his own. Charlemagne was a tough act to follow,
and Louis has always suffered from the inevitable comparison between them. He
was an earnest, intelligent, and cultivated ruler—a much better educated and more
"cultured" man than his father—but he never commanded the type of respect and
fear that his father had inspired and depended upon. He was rather straitlaced on
the moral level (hence his nickname), and he banished from the court all the dancing
girls and professional mistresses who had kept his father busy on sleepless nights;
he also took particular interest in the monastic reforms led by his advisor and friend
St. Benedict of Aniane (d. 822), a mirthless ascetic from Spain. With Louis' support,
Benedict produced an expanded and much more detailed edition of the *Benedictine
Rule*, to improve monastic discipline, and he enjoyed the unique privilege—granted
to him by Louis—of possessing complete jurisdiction over any monastery in Europe
that he decided to visit. Though well-intentioned, Louis' grant earned him the enmity of the very abbots and monks on whom his government depended.

One of the problems confronting the court was the fact that the empire had
stopped expanding. Military conquest played an important role in legitimating
early medieval rulers, and Louis' relative lack of a track record in that area undermined his authority in many of his contemporaries' eyes. More directly, though, the
absence of new conquests meant the absence of new lands to hand out to the warriors on whose support Carolingian rule had always depended. Ideals ran high in
the eighth and ninth centuries, but the fact remains that political support and social
unity still had to be bought, even by so inspiring a leader as Charlemagne. Unable
to buy his men's loyalty, Louis proved unable to command it. He had enough acumen to recognize that the Germanic custom of dividing inheritances boded ill for
the empire, and so he tried to institute the idea of *primogeniture*—that is, the handing over of an entire patrimony to the first-born son—only to find that resistance to
this idea was so hostile (none of the second- and third-born sons much liked the
idea, understandably) that he was reduced to performing a public penance in 822
"for all the ill things that he and his father had done." From that point on, few
things went right for him. His own sons, eager to insure their shares of the empire,
repeatedly rebelled against him, and once, in 832, virtually imprisoned their father
while their armies tore up the countryside. The following year the Frankish bishops
who had benefited from Louis' support of ecclesiastical reform threw in their lot
with the royal rebels and deposed Louis as unfit for office. A second public plea for
forgiveness put him back in power, nominally at least, but his last years on the
throne were wholly ineffectual. Filial infighting and self-serving belligerence
among the warrior caste quickly shattered the paper-thin social and political unity
created by Louis' forebears.[1]

---

1. Louis' penance resulted from more "ill things" than primogeniture alone; ecclesiastical and economic
policies played roles too.

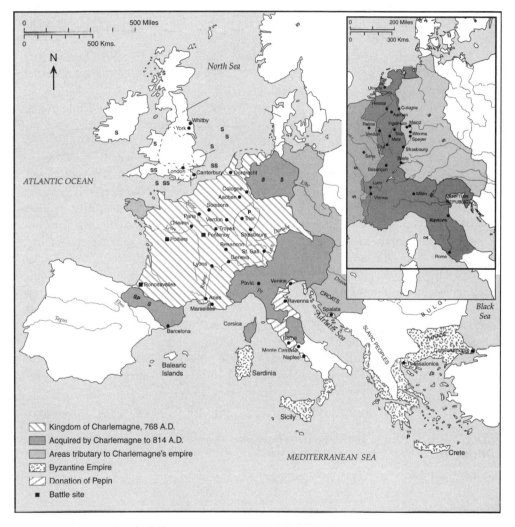

Carolingian partition

Matters only worsened after his death. Louis' three surviving sons—Lothair (r. 840–855), Louis the German (r. 840–876), and Charles the Bald (r. 840–877; he was half-brother to the first two)—fought incessantly, and each found more than enough warlords and clerics to support them. In 842 Louis and Charles decided to join forces against Lothair, and their armies sealed the bargain when Louis' men took a vow known as the *Oath of Strasbourg*. A court chronicler named Nithard happened to write down the specific words of the oath and thereby preserved the earliest known example of a proto-French language.[2]

Lothair surrendered before this joint attack, and in 843 the Treaty of Verdun formally divided the Carolingian empire into three independent kingdoms. Europe would never again be politically united.

The disintegration gained speed with every generation of multiple heirs. Lothair's death in 855 triggered the redivision of his kingdom—a narrow strip dividing what is today France and Germany, plus the Italian territories—into three smaller states, one to each of his sons: Louis II, Charles, and Lothair II (the Carolingians were never very original when it came to names).[3] Lothair II's early death tempted uncles Louis and Charles (the German one and the Bald one) to split the leftovers between them; but their own deaths, in 876 and 877 respectively, opened the door to yet another partitioning. From this point on, the dynastic narrative becomes hopelessly dreary. Something of the fate of Europe in these years, in fact, can be seen in the nicknames that historians have given to the later Carolingians: Charles the Bald was followed by Louis the Stammerer (r. 877–879), who was himself succeeded, ultimately, by Charles the Simple (r. 898–922).[4] Louis the German gave way in 876 to Charles the Fat (r. 876–887), who was followed by his second cousin Louis the Blind (r. 887–928), whose main political rival was his cousin three times removed, Louis the Child (r. 899–911). Along the way there was even a guy named Bozo, who actually was a rather capable fellow. Redivision followed upon redivision, until all semblance of unity was lost and constant struggles over bound-

---

2.   The simple fact that the soldiers, who came from the upper strata of society, could not speak Latin tells us much about the modesty of the Carolingian cultural achievement. It is hardly a moving text but it has a certain linguistic interest:

> *Pro Deo amur et pro christian poblo et nostro commun salvament, d'ist di in avant, in quant Deus savir et podir me dunat, si salvarat eo cist meon fradre Karlo et in aiudha et in cadhuna cosa, si cum om per dreit son fradra salvar dift.*

> For the love of God, the Christian people, and our common well-being, I will, from this day forward, give to my kinsman Charles all the aid he needs in every situation so far as God gives me the ability to understand and act, just as one ought, out of a sense of what is right, to give aid to one's own brother.

3.   There was a serious intent behind the repetition of names, actually: It aimed to introduce an aura of sacrality by constantly harkening back to family forebears.

4.   An intervening figure existed: Louis III (no nickname). He seemed to be a ruler of genuine promise, but he died in an unfortunate accident. Returning from a battle against the Vikings, he saw a young woman on a country lane who appealed to him. He chased after her on his horse. She ducked under a stone archway. He didn't.

aries became commonplace. In the words of the anonymous author of the *Annals of Xanten*, "the contests between our rulers in these lands—not to mention the depredations of the pagans—is too grim a tale to record."

So bad did these internecine struggles become that a Church council convened at Trosle, at which the gathered bishops bemoaned the ruin of all Christian society:

> Our cities are depopulated, our monasteries wrecked and put to the torch, our countryside left uninhabited. . . . Indeed, just as the first humans lived without law or the fear of God and according only to their dumb instincts, so too now does everyone do whatever seems good in his eyes only, despising all human and divine laws and ignoring even the commands of the Church. The strong oppress the weak, and the world is wracked with violence against the poor and the plunder of ecclesiastical lands. . . . Men everywhere devour each other like the fishes of the sea.

It is important to bear in mind the consequences of this devolution. The incitement to warfare and bullying that it produced is obvious; but of arguably even greater impact was the economic and social legacy of this type of political rot. The carving of a half-dozen separate states out of a single empire means the introduction of a half-dozen currencies, a half-dozen systems of law, a half-dozen standards for weights and measures. When three states turned into nine, and then into nineteen, and then into ninety, the complications created for the normal conduct of everyday life became enormous. Transporting goods to market became pointless when, in making that journey, a merchant had to cross eleven borders and pay an import duty to every local strongman: By the time the merchant reached whatever market he might have had, the cost to be reclaimed for the goods was so large that no purchaser would think the transaction worthwhile, even assuming that the purchaser had any money in the first place. Trade therefore all but disappeared, and life for most people returned to the subsistence level. Whatever "cities" existed at the time consequently entered a period of contraction and retrenchment. The political breakup of the Carolingian state, in other words, led to a virtual strangulation of the European economy; goods were produced and consumed on site, and trade diminished to the point of invisibility. The problem was recognized. Attempts were made at various times to stabilize coinages; to guarantee the safe passage of merchants; to rebuild roads, bridges, and lighthouses; even to construct canals linking some northern rivers. But trade networks had been weak enough even during the good years. Little could be done to keep them alive during the long decline.

Small wonder, then, that people began longing for the good old days and dreading the ones that were to come. A curious imaginative text survives from the late ninth century, from Mainz, in which the anonymous writer fabricates a prophetic dream of Charlemagne's:

> One night, after he had gone to bed and fallen asleep, [Charlemagne] had a dream-vision in which he saw a man approaching him, carrying a drawn sword. Frightened, he asked the man who he was and where he came from, and he heard this reply: "Take this sword, for it is a gift to you from God. Read

what is written upon it and memorize it, for what is written there will come to pass at the appointed time." [Charlemagne] took the sword into his hands and turned it over, inspecting it, and saw four words inscribed upon it. First, near the handle was the word *RAHT*. Next came *RADIOLEBA*. Following that was *NASG*. And finally, near the point, was the word *ENTI*.

[Charlemagne] then woke up and had a candle and writing materials brought to him, and when these came he immediately wrote down the words exactly as he had seen them in his dream.

The story then relates that when he turned to his court scholars for an interpretation the following morning they were all baffled, which prompted the emperor to do some analysis of his own:

"The sword, as God's Own gift to me, can only represent my authority, since that too was given to me by Him and it was by strength of arms, violently employed, that I managed to subject my enemies to my authority. Now those enemies are quiet, unlike in my ancestors' times, and wealth abounds. That must be what the first word, *RAHT* means. *RADIOLEBA*, the second word, must signify a loss of wealth and the rebellion of those subjugated peoples sometime after my death and during the reigns of my sons. *RADIOLEBA*, in other words, foretells that utter collapse will quickly follow me. But once my sons have died and the next generation—that is, *their* sons—starts to rule, then *NASG* will exist. Out of greed for money that generation will demand higher taxes and oppress all travelers and holy pilgrims. They will amass their treasures by flagrant crimes, sowing discord and shame. Amid florid justifications for their actions, or without any explanations whatsoever, they will seize even those ecclesiastical lands that I and my ancestors have given to God's Own priests and monks, and they will disperse them as rewards for their loyal followers—that is what *NASG* means. As for *ENTI*, the word appearing at the sword's far tip, it has one of two possible meanings: either the end of our dynasty (such that some new family will rule over the Franks) or the end of the world itself."

It was a fictional text, an imaginative fantasy using nonsense words, but it accurately described what had happened to Europe since 814, and as prophecy, it continued to be true through the next three generations.

TROUBLE FROM THE NORTH

On top of all this internal discord, a new wave of invasions beset Europe. Attackers came from three directions—the north, the east, and the south—and their impact was considerable. The northern Vikings got the most attention, both then and now, although that may not be deserved. But they certainly came in large numbers, and their ferocity terrified Europe. "From the fury of the Northmen, O Lord, please save us!" was a familiar prayer of the age, one that even entered the liturgy in England.

Their large numbers are easily explained. The early Scandinavians—that is, the people who today make up Sweden, Norway, and Denmark—practised polygamy (or at least their aristocratic/warrior castes did), and this, over time, led to a serious problem of overpopulation and land-shortage. Given Scandinavia's cold climate,

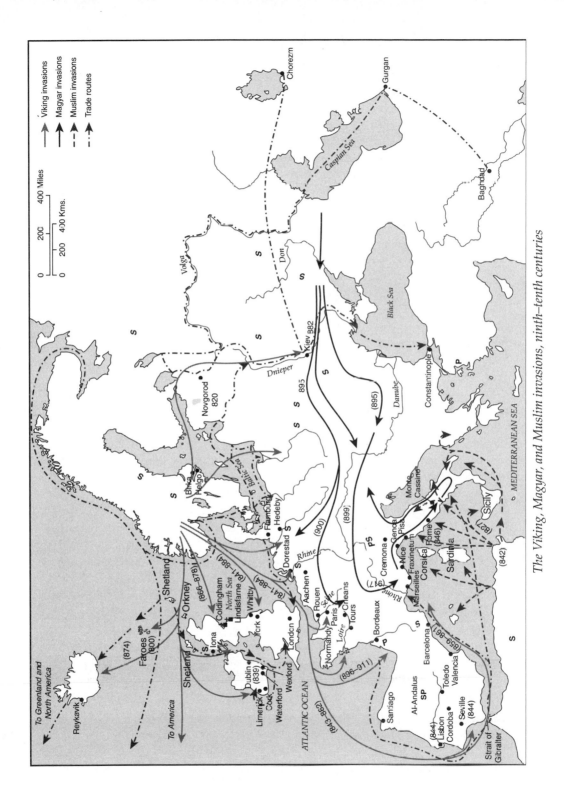

The Viking, Magyar, and Muslim invasions, ninth–tenth centuries

Legend:
- Viking invasions
- Magyar invasions
- Muslim invasions
- Trade routes

Scale:
0   200   400 Miles
0   200   400 Kms.

Map labels:
Reykjavik
To Greenland and North America
Faroes (800)
(874)
To America
Shetland
Orkney
Iona
Dublin (839)
Limerick
Cork
Waterford
Wexford
York
London
Lindisfarne
Coldingham
Whitby
Aachen
Rouen
Normandy
Paris
Seine
Orleans
Tours
Loire
Bordeaux
Santiago
Al-Andalus SP
Toledo
Cordoba
Valencia
Seville (844)
Lisbon (844)
Strait of Gibralter
Barcelona (859–86?)
ATLANTIC OCEAN
Dorestad
Rhine
Hamburg
Hedeby
Birka Helgo
Baltic Sea
North Sea
Novgorod 820
Kiev 882
Dnieper
Don
Volga
Chorezm
Caspian Sea
Gurgan
Baghdad
Black Sea
Constantinople
Danube
Rhone
Cremona
Nice
Genoa
Pisa
Monte Cassino
Rome
Fraxinetum (846)
Marseilles
Corsica (917)
Sardinia
Sicily (827)
MEDITERRANEAN SEA

Dates on routes:
(866–878)
(841–884)
(841–884)
(843–862)
(896–911)
(895)
(895)
(899)
(900)
(842)

173

often harsh terrain, and short growing season, there was little arable land available that could support habitation. Abundant seafood and animal meat helped to compensate for the relative lack of agricultural produce, but the rapid growth of the overall population in the seventh and eighth centuries led to dissension among the various clans and their heirs. Early Scandinavian society was atomized, but in contrast to the Carolingian world to its south this fragmentation was more the result of geography than culture. The mountainous fjords and crags of Norway created a natural division among the peoples inhabiting the land, and the relatively poor quality of the soil in flat Sweden (poor, that is, given the limits of their agricultural technology) meant that collective village farming was impossible. Instead, individual farmsteads were spread out over the prairie of southern Sweden, and borders were jealously guarded. In Denmark rather a different situation existed. There it was simply the lack of land that mattered. Caught on a spit—sometimes hilly but mostly flat and monotonous—between the Carolingians to the south and their more numerous Baltic rivals to the north, the Danes were perhaps the first to seek wealth and plunder overseas. As early as the 770s they had started to prey upon England, and in 793 they demolished the great monastery at Lindisfarne, the chief center and glory of the Northumbrian cultural revival.[5] The following year they plundered Jarrow, the monastery of Bede.

Geography also played an important role in determining the nature of the Vikings' campaigns. Of the three Scandinavian groups, the Danes may have had the least amount of naval experience and focused chiefly on the nearby British Isles. By following the northern European coastline they found it relatively easy to cross the English Channel and to attack Britain's eastern shores, wreaking havoc wherever they went. The Norwegians, by contrast, who had considerably more maritime experience, circumnavigated England and attacked Scotland, the Hebrides, Wales, and Ireland, before moving further south and besetting continental Europe. They struck at France and Spain, and then some of them, at least, moved through the Straits of Gibraltar to harass southern France, northern Africa, and parts of northwestern Italy. Having established outposts on several Mediterranean islands, the Norwegians lived for many years by piracy. The Swedes, on the other hand, focused their energies exclusively on the east. Crossing the Baltic along the traditional trunk routes, Swedish fleets easily made their way up the Daugava, Velikaya, and Dnieper rivers to sack the Slavic capital of Kiev and take command of all the region, uniting it into a powerful kingdom. (Thus the first "King of Russia," named Rurik, was actually a Swedish Viking.) By 818 some Swedes had raided as far south as the northern coast of Asia Minor; not long thereafter the emperor in Constantinople decided to make a virtue out of necessity and appointed some Swedes as his personal bodyguards. Thus was born the so-called *Varangian Guard*.

---

5.   This act inspired Alcuin of York to commiserate from Aachen with his Northumbrian king: "There has never before been seen in England an atrocity comparable to that which we have now suffered from these pagans. Their very voyage itself [i.e., from Denmark to England] was never heretofore thought possible. Now even St. Cuthbert's church, a site more sacred than any in all of England, stands dripping with blood, stripped of its wealth, and left helpless to further plundering from these pagans."

The ferocity of the Vikings is quite another matter to explain. They attacked in small numbers, on the whole, under the command of individual clan leaders and warrior princelings, and with the exception of the Swedes in western Russia they generally raided and withdrew rather than invaded and settled. No doubt their appearance accounted for some of the terror they inspired. The Vikings were considerably taller than the continental Europeans, had bright blonde or blazing red hair, spoke incomprehensible languages, carried broad battle-axes that they swung furiously and with considerably more force than the Europeans could muster with their broadswords. But by far the most frightening aspect of the Viking attacks was their unpredictability. A full-scale land invasion, after all, is something that one hears about as it gradually approaches. But Vikings ships had the ability to travel up-river since they drew so little water: A fully loaded Viking warship could sail in as little as four feet of water. This made it possible to strike with lightning speed far inland, without warning, and then disappear just as quickly. Viking fleets attacked Paris itself in 834, during the reign of Louis the Pious, and they even sacked the Muslim capital of Seville, in the middle of Spain, about a decade later. Such attacks continued with dreadful regularity throughout the tenth century.

Just as significant to the creation of the Vikings' fierce reputation was their choice of targets. Churches and monasteries predominated, since they were virtually alone in possessing actual money or valuable items like precious stones, spices, or luxury textiles. A typical account comes from the *Annals of Saint-Vaast*, a monastery near Corbie in northern France:

> Sometime after Fulk, a most worthy man, succeeded Hincmar as bishop of Rheims [in 882], the Northmen set fire to the monastery and church of St. Quentin, and shortly thereafter they put the torch to the church dedicated to the Holy Mother of God in the city of Arras. King Carloman [another late mini-Carolingian] chased after them but was unable to accomplish anything, for all his trouble . . . In the next spring the Northmen departed from Condé in search of coastlands to raid. Throughout the whole of the next summer they drove the people of Flanders from their lands and violently laid waste everything they saw, with sword and fire. That autumn Carloman hoped to defend his kingdom at last by stationing his army at the villa of Miannay, which lies opposite to Lavier in the region of Vithnau. The Northmen arrived at Lavier in October with full contingents of well-equipped cavalry and infantry; some of their ships also sailed up the Somme from the coast. Together, these forced Carloman and his entire army to flee to the other side of the river Oise. The Northmen then proceeded to winter at Amiens. From there they ravaged the whole land as far as the river Seine and around the river Oise, without facing any opposition whatsoever, and they burned to the ground all the monasteries and churches dedicated to Christ.

It is hard to know precisely what to make of all these tales of violence. Were the Vikings really as savage as these texts suggest? Were they driven by lust for money and land, or was there an element of religious hatred involved? The latter is not

An example of pre-Viking headwear. Dating to the seventh century,
this helmet probably is not much different from those worn by the Vikings
who beset Europe from the eighth century on.
Source: Werner Forman / Art Resource, NY

impossible, since we know that missionaries had attempted to bring Christianity to Scandinavia as early as Charlemagne's time, and possibly even earlier. Were they simply trying to find entry, from overpopulated Scandinavia, into underpopulated Europe? Do these passages merely reflect the hyperbole of churchmen aghast at what has befallen their churches? Do they reflect the real attitudes and fears of the common people? These are important questions because there are many indications that the commoners viewed the infighting of Europe's warriors as a far greater problem than the predations of the Northmen.

The truth probably consists of all these points of view, and we will never know the whole story. The scant nature of the surviving evidence assures that. After all, nearly every published scrap of writing that survives from the period 870 to 1030—not counting monastic duplicates—could be piled atop a single large dining table. No doubt the Vikings' ferocity appeared so great in part because Europe itself was so defenseless. The disintegration of Carolingian Europe made it impossible to raise an effective army against most Viking attacks, and hence whatever resistance there was generally existed only at the local level; even then, it was only a defensive resistance. Ironically, this situation enabled many local warlords to increase their power: As peasants scurried to them for protection, the warlords gradually took over all the roles that formerly could have been theirs only by a grant from the royal court. These warlords, in other words, often became autonomous mini-kings. Three things, however, altered the nature and size of the Viking threat somewhere near the middle of the ninth century.

First of all, their raids began to turn into invasions. As the text quoted above suggests, the Vikings started to spend winters on the North Atlantic islands and the Continent itself rather than hasten back north with their booty; this is a clear sign of their growing overpopulation problem. But many of these larger-scale attacks resulted from political rebellion. Sometime around 860, a man named Harald Finehair managed to subdue most of Norway and set himself up as her first king; this act triggered a mass migration of Vikings opposed to the notion of monarchy but unable to unite in opposition to Harald. Permanent Viking settlements cropped up soon thereafter in various parts of Ireland. A few years later, coastal settlements of Vikings were established on the eastern English coast. Several large Viking clans sailed to Iceland, where they carved up the land among themselves and, between bloody clan-struggles, managed to establish the western world's first parliament, called the *Althing*; it has convened every year without exception since 911. Tales of these Vikings are told in a highly stylized way in the Icelandic sagas.

The second change to the Viking threat was the remarkable defense against them waged by a new English king, Alfred the Great (r. 871–899). He was the only early medieval ruler who can bear comparison with Charlemagne.[6] When Alfred came to the throne in 871, the Danes had overridden all of England except for Alfred's realm of Wessex. He led several successful counterattacks against them, but the Vikings retaliated with a surprise invasion of Wessex late in 877 and drove Alfred into hiding on a remote inland swamp. He spent the winter rallying his forces, and the following spring, in a ferocious battle at Edington, he defeated the Vikings and forced them into a compromise agreement that divided England between them: Alfred retained free possession of southern and western England, while all the rest became the *Danelaw*—an independent Danish realm to which Alfred agreed

---

6. Among Alfred's marvelous traits, according to his official biographer Asser, was his exceptionally quick mind: Asser boasted that he had personally witnessed Alfred learn to read and speak Latin in a single day. The clever fellow simply memorized, phonetically, four passages from the Vulgate and repeated them aloud over and over until he somehow, miraculously, just "got it." All medievalists should be so lucky.

to pay annual tribute. Guthram, the new ruler of the Danelaw, agreed to accept Christianity. England remained thus divided until the middle of the tenth century, when Alfred's great-grandson Edgar (959–975) completed the reconquest of the Danelaw and reunited England.

The third change resulted from Alfred's limited success. Just as numerous Viking clans had refused to accept Harald Finehair's rulership in Norway, so too did many object to the new, quasi-monarchical Danelaw. They turned their attention instead to northwestern France, which became the new focus of Viking interests. The leader of the most powerful of these clans, named Rollo, struck repeatedly at the local Frankish ruler, Charles the Simple, and in 911 received from Charles recognition as duke of Normandy, in return for converting to Christianity and putting an end to his attacks. He moved swiftly to consolidate his power over the other clans in Normandy. The alliance between the West Frankish kings and the dukes of Normandy would prove to be a difficult one, but for the time being the Viking advance had been halted and the Northmen slowly began to assimilate with the peoples of western Europe.

TROUBLE FROM THE EAST

A different sort of trouble came from the east. There a new group of peoples called the *Magyars*, the ancestors of today's Hungarians, emerged from the Asiatic steppe. As with earlier invaders from the east, the Magyars were a motley group of various peoples united by a common language, and they turned their sights first on Byzantium. Not for long, though. The Byzantines, following a time-tested strategy, urged the new invaders further westward, but not before forging a temporary alliance with them in 896 against the Bulgars, a Slavic nation on Byzantium's northern border that had long been causing trouble for the Greeks. Together the Byzantines and Magyars smashed the Bulgars and sold most of their captured soldiers into slavery. The Magyars might well have stayed where they were, in the eastern Balkans [what is today the country of Bulgaria], except that the Bulgars who had escaped annihilation formed an alliance with yet another Asiatic-steppe nation called the Pechenegs, in order to drive the Magyars out. The alliance succeeded, and the Magyars moved further to the west and settled in what is today the nation of Hungary.[7]

They arrived in Hungary sometime around 899, and from that base they laid waste to much of northern Italy to such a degree, in fact, that formal liturgies in Lombardy began to include the prayer "Protect us, O Lord, from the arrows of the Hungarians!" The Germanic lands formed the Magyars' next target, and they plundered nearly as far as the old Carolingian capital of Aachen. Relying as they did on cavalry maneuvers, the Magyars generally avoided whatever fortified towns existed in eastern and central Europe, and focused their attacks instead on rural villages, where

---

7. The name *Hungary* derives from the name of one of the tribal groups that made up the Magyar migration—the *Onogurs*. It is just a coincidence that this territory was also the European base of the *Huns* in the fourth century.

they found it easy to capture prisoners to sell into slavery, to hoard foodstuffs and other goods, and to make a general nuisance of themselves by tearing up roads and destroying bridges. Although they too, like the Vikings, were not Christian, the Magyars did not single out Christian churches and monasteries for assault, or at least not in any particular manner. By the time of their invasions, Carolingian decay was already fairly well advanced, and the Magyars' initial focus on Italy held out the promise of considerable booty that could be gained at relatively small cost.

Their numbers, however, were not sufficient to maintain an ongoing land invasion, and they gradually settled on the fertile and sparsely populated Hungarian plains and took up lives of farming and pasturage. Enough of their nomadic warrior spirit survived, however, to keep some of them in the saddle, and raids into the eastern Frankish and Saxon lands continued for another generation. Finally, in 955, a Saxon duke known as Otto the Great (r. 936–973), who had been lucky enough to discover a massive silver lode in his homeland in the Harz mountains and who could therefore afford to hire all the soldiers he wanted, crushed the Magyar army in an awful battle at Lechfeld, and the Magyar threat to Europe effectively ended.

Other groups still troubled Latin and Greek Christendom, though. The Slavs, first mentioned by the sixth-century historian Jordanes, were a populous group of farmers and herdsmen living north of the Danube river and along the upper reaches of the Black Sea. A military alliance with the Avars gave them the strength to encroach upon Byzantine territory. Bands of Slavic adventurers reached the Aegean Sea by 600; by 700 they had overrun the entire Balkan region. The Slavs did not displace the indigenous populations of Serbs, Croats, and Macedonians, but their language quickly established itself as a common tongue between all these peoples (much like Latin provided a linguistic link between the Germanic peoples of the west). Conversion to Christianity soon followed, thanks to the efforts of two remarkable brothers—Constantine the Philosopher (d. 869) and Methodius (d. 885)—who created an alphabet for the Slavic language, standardized its grammar, translated the Scriptures and various liturgies into the language, and essentially founded the Slavic Orthodox Church. From this base, Christianity spread northward and eastward to the Bulgars and the Rus' (the progenitors of the Russians, with their capital at Kiev).

Conversion and literacy did not bring peace, though. The Slavic principalities formed a wedge between the Latin and Greek worlds, both of which resented their loss of control over the region. Charlemagne had established a tributary lordship over most of the Slavs, but the Carolingian breakup ended that. Byzantine rulers from Heraclius (d. 641) to Basil II (r. 976–1025) fought to reassert control over the region too, a ferocious cycle of campaigns, rebellions, and counterstrikes that left a legacy of the Slavs' deep resentment against both east and west.[8]

---

8. After suppressing a rebellion at Kleidion (a mountain pass in the Belasita mountains, near the Struma river) in 1014, Basil II reportedly ordered the blinding of 14,000 Bulgarian captives, allowing one man out of every 100 to retain one eye. For a career of such activities, Basil is remembered by the nickname *boulgaróktonos* ("the Bulgar-Slayer").

The loss of the Balkans accelerated an important change in Byzantine life that had begun with the Muslim seizures of Egypt, Palestine, and Syria—namely, a stark decline in urban life. While farming had always been the occupation of most of the empire's inhabitants, Byzantium's distinctive life and cultural strength had always centered on its cities. Trade and manufacturing fueled their economies; schools, libraries, theaters, and baths were their defining cultural hallmarks. But by the end of the tenth century nearly one-half of the empire's cities had fallen into Slavic and Arab hands, and those that remained underwent substantial retrenchment and reinvention.[9] Retreating behind heavy fortifications, cities like Corinth, Ephesus, Pergamum, Sardis, and Thessaloniki remained Byzantine but changed from economic and cultural emporia into civil and ecclesiastical administrative centers. Populations declined, since the stripped-down economies of the towns could support fewer numbers than before. Some sites, like Pergamum, seemed little more than frontier-camps or branch-outposts of the central government and the Orthodox hierarchy. Just as with the militarization of the countryside under the *theme* system, urban retrenchment resulted in an extension of state power; lacking the independent spirit that came with their former economic and cultural vibrancy, these towns and the rural areas they served came directly under the administration in Constantinople. As early as the eighth century the central government began to legislate directly the minutiae of town, village, and rural life. Legal texts like the *Farmers' Law* regulated details as minor as the following: "If a tree standing on one farmer's field overshadows a neighbor's field, the neighbor may trim its branches provided that his own field is a [vegetable] garden, but if it is not such a garden, he may not trim the branches."[10]

This was not an atmosphere in which intellectual life could thrive, and indeed the period from the seventh to the tenth centuries witnessed a stripping-down of Byzantine culture. Philosophy, science, and poetry became less creative; original works in these areas gave way to catalogs, lexicons, grammars, bibliographies, and commentaries on classical texts. Encyclopedias proliferated, but these were mostly uninventive, if highly detailed, bureaucratic manuals on matters of agriculture, court ceremony, guild activities, military tactics, and tax collection. Active intellectual life had left the urban classes and become the domain of Orthodox churchmen whose primary interests were doctrinal and exegetical. Saints' lives and devotional works were the norm here, and even in these genres more effort went into compil-

---

9. Changes in place names tell the story. In the Balkans, Adrianople was renamed *Edirne*, Beroe became *Stara Zagora*, Naissus changed into *Niš*, Philippopolis was rechristened *Plovdiv*, and Sardica became *Sofia*. Few toponyms changed among the cities lost to the Arabs for the simple reason that most of those cities predated the Byzantines and had well-established names of their own. The arrival of the Turks in the eleventh century, however, triggered another wave of name changes: Amida (*Diyarbakir*), Attaleia (*Antalya*), Melitene (*Malatya*), Nicaea (*Iznik*), Sebastea (*Sewas*), and Trebizond (*Trabzon*) are examples. The culmination of this process, of course, was Constantinople's renaming as *Istanbul* in the fifteenth century.
10. The *Farmers' Law* is of uncertain provenance. Some scholars date it as early as the seventh century, but most would prefer a later date. Texts of the law, however, multiplied dramatically in the tenth century, suggesting a sharp increase in its application.

ing and copying old texts than in creating new ones.[11] This intellectual ennui made Byzantine cities in the ninth and tenth centuries dull places and left them ill-equipped to handle genuine controversies like iconoclasm.

We have mentioned iconoclasm before, when the issue arose in the Carolingian realms. Its roots went back as far as the fourth century, when an early bishop, Eusebius of Caesarea (d. 340) argued against depicting Christ's image in art. Various arguments came and went over the centuries, both condemning and defending the use of religious icons in Christian worship, but the controversy was a comparatively minor one until the eighth and ninth centuries, when the astonishing rise of the Islamic empire led some Byzantine officials to wonder whether the use of icons—one of the criticisms of Christianity most repeatedly leveled by the Muslims, who regarded the practice as idolatrous—might explain the utter collapse of the Byzantine armies against the Arabs. Beginning with the emperor Leo III (r. 717–741), the rulers in Constantinople began a violent campaign to rid the empire of religious imagery. Icons were destroyed by the tens of thousands all across the shrunken empire—everything from small statuettes and necklace-crucifixes, to manuscript illuminations, wall paintings, mosaics, and large masonry decorations adorning churches and monasteries. It was, theological matters apart, an utter catastrophe for Christian art history; only the icon smashing of the early Protestant Reformers compares to it, in terms of destruction. The first wave of iconoclasm had passed by 787, followed by a period of unsteady truce between the factions on either side of the issue, but a second phase of image smashing occurred from 815 to 841, when the controversy finally ended with a general acceptance of the use of religious art.

The factions involved in the fight had complex motives. Military leaders clearly found the people's use of icons a convenient scapegoat for the army's failures against Islam; local civic officials used the war against art as an excuse to pillage the monasteries and churches in their districts. Religious figures who opposed icons quite possibly did so in order to control the saints' cults that comprised so large a portion of popular religious devotion, and to redirect religious life into mainstream parish and sacramental life. As cities became administrative shells, in other words, it was in the interest of the civil and religious authorities in those cities to suppress activities that were perceived to undermine the structures of administrative life in those cities.

The ninth and tenth centuries, in sum, brought dramatic, extensive changes to life in eastern Europe and the eastern Mediterranean that made for a troubled and troubling time.

---

11. A few original thinkers existed. Leo the Mathematician (d. 870), the metropolitan of Thessaloniki, was sufficiently renowned as an engineer to be invited to Baghdad by the Abbasid caliph al-Ma'mum; and Photius (d. 894), who was twice the patriarch of Constantinople (and twice driven from office by political enemies) wrote a revealing work called *Bibliotheca* ("The Library") which outlined his lifetime's reading, summarizing the contents, ideas, stylistic fine-points, and his personal reactions to the books he read in his adulthood. Scholars today use the *Bibliotheca* as a guide to literary and scientific works that no longer exist. Others use it—as presumably some used it in the Middle Ages—as a study-cheat.

TROUBLE FROM THE SOUTH

The least significant of the three new invasions, in terms of lives taken and damage done, but perhaps the most important in its long-term consequences, was the resurgence of hostility coming from the Islamic world. As the Carolingian world dissolved, Muslim armies went once again on the offensive. Fighting between Christian Europe and the Muslim south had never ceased altogether during the Carolingian period, but for a few generations both societies had focused more on internal development than on waging war with one another. Two factors triggered the new attacks: the obvious weakening of Europe's defenses, and the strengthening of the Abbasid dynasty after it seized the caliphate from the Umayyads in 750.

The era of the Abbasid dynasty (750–1258), and especially the first half of it, is regarded as Islam's Golden Age, the period when Islamic political and military might was at its peak, when artistic and intellectual achievements shone with the greatest glory, and when the fabled wealth of the enormous empire was the envy of the world. As with all golden ages, a romantic aura hangs over this period that is not quite deserved or that is at least overdone, but there is no denying the splendid achievements of Islamic civilization at this time, especially considering its rather modest origins. Nothing in western Europe could compare with the size, wealth, and beauty of Cordoba, Alexandria, Damascus, or Baghdad, or with the intellectual and artistic vitality that existed there. This flowering resulted from a handful of factors: the consolidation of Islamic belief, law, and social organization through the definitive compilation of the Prophet's Qur'anic revelations and *hadith*, which had hitherto been passed on orally; the assimilation of the Greek scientific and (to a much lesser extent) philosophical traditions; the general internal peace enjoyed by the empire; and especially the reorientation of the Islamic world to the Asiatic east, where commercial and cultural links with India and China offered riches and wonders far greater than anything available in the west.

The Abbasids came to power after a revolt that began in what is today Iran. From the rebels' point of view, the Umayyads had failed in their *jihad*, the struggle to obey Allah's will and Islamize the world. The stalling out of the campaign to crush the Byzantines, after Heraclius' successful defensive efforts in the first half of the eighth century, was widely interpreted as evidence of Allah's displeasure with the Umayyads and justified the rebellion; yet other, subtler motives existed as well. The Persians, who resided in Iran, regarded themselves as the cultural superiors of the comparatively rustic Arabs—although, as devout Muslims, they accepted the unique stature of the Arab Prophet and of Allah's revelation in the Arabic language. But unlike the Arabs, the Persians could point to a rich cultural legacy that went back more than a thousand years: Persian science, mathematics, poetry, architecture, astronomy, and music were among the glories of the ancient world. Once the Persians adopted Islam, a strong tension existed between the two cultures. The early Arabs, as the recipients of Allah's revelation and the soldiers on whose martial strength the empire had been created, tended to regard themselves as the sole possessors of authority within Islam; the Persians, on the other hand, embraced the faith but resented the often heavy-handed way in which they were treated by their new Arab rulers. And hence the revolt in 750.

The new Abbasid rulers were themselves Arab, but they popularly championed the notion that all the peoples of the Islamic world were equal in Allah's eyes—or at least so they claimed. The first Abbasid rulers, Abu al-Abbas (known by the nickname *al-Saffah*, or "the Butcher") and Abu Jafar (who took the name *Al-Mansur*, "the Conqueror"), awarded the majority of court positions to family members and agents, and executed any provincial administrators, military commanders, and government officials whom they deemed too wealthy, powerful, or popular. Paranoia about his political and physical security led Al-Mansur to build himself a new, heavily fortified palace in Baghdad (its official name was *Madinah al-Salaam*, or "City of Peace") on the west bank of the Tigris river at the point where it comes closest to the Euphrates. This was to become the magnificent capital of the empire and the economic and cultural hub of the Islamic world. Baghdad's population numbered in the hundreds of thousands, and its splendid palaces, lush gardens, and bustling streets became the setting for most of the tales of the *Arabian Nights* (also known as the *One Thousand and One Nights*) that were compiled in the first half of the tenth century.

But while the new dynasts protected their hold on the government, they greatly liberalized the cultural and social atmosphere so that Persian traditions of science, art, and philosophy entered the mainstream of Islamic life. This rich new element, coupled with the Greek legacy absorbed by the Arabs and the Arabs' own lengthy tradition of poetry and oral history, resulted in a wondrous proliferation of art and thought. The courts of the caliph, not to mention those of the Abbasids' administrative underlings and of prominent urban magnates, became strongly Orientalized. From the rather staid and pietistic nature of life in Umayyad Damascus, Islamic civilization after 750 began to explore and delight in the brilliant and sensual (but not sensuous) life of Persian culture.[12] The results were exhilarating even to the point of being gaudy. One Abbasid chronicler in the eleventh century proudly described the splendor of the caliphal court: An embassy from the provinces or from foreign lands could marvel at the sight of ornate reception halls, meticulous gardens, innumerable palace servants, eunuchs (mostly to serve the female members of the caliphal family), attendants, and an exhibition of elephants draped in brocaded silk. In a chamber known as the "Room of the Tree," a special sight awaited visitors.

> Here there is an artificial tree rising out of a large circular pool that is filled with crystal-clear water. This tree has eighteen branches, each of which spreads out into many smaller shoots. On each of these there is a cluster of large and small sculpted birds made of gold and silver. Most of the branches themselves are

---

12. Of course, there were exceptions. One extremely popular poet named Bashshar ibn Burd sang the glories of sexual love so wonderfully that the caliph al-Mahdi (775–785), the successor to al-Mansur, ordered him executed in 783 on the charge of threatening public morals. To the best of my knowledge, Bashshar's erotic works have never been translated into English.

made of silver, but there are quite a few made of gold as well, and these stretch out in a profusion of multi-colored leaves. Whenever the wind blows through the windows, the leaves sway gently and the gold and silver birds tinkle and rattle.

And on one occasion, a lucky poet whose verses happened to please the caliph Harun al-Rashid (r. 786–809) received in return for a single poem a gift of five thousand gold coins, a silk robe, ten Greek slave girls, and a thoroughbred horse.

Intellectual life also flourished, as texts and ideas poured in from the Arab homelands and the Greco-Roman Mediterranean, and from the Iranian Persians and the Hindus of India as well. History, poetry, jurisprudence, philosophy, astronomy, mathematics, medicine were all studied eagerly, and foreign works were quickly translated into Arabic. The enormous wealth generated by the new eastern orientation of the empire made possible a degree of patronage that produced an intellectual and cultural extravaganza. One of the first great Muslim scientists to incorporate the knowledge of both east and west was al-Kindi (d. ca. 850) who not only made important advances in optics and pharmacology but began the effort to reconcile Aristotelian philosophy with the revealed truth of the Qur'an. His contemporary al-Khwarizmi (d. 850) was the leading mathematician of his age who introduced decimal arithmetic, the concept of zero, the use of the abacus, and the origins of algebra, all of which he derived from mathematical texts from Persia and India. In medicine al-Razi (d. 925) wrote a definitive treatise on the nature and treatment of smallpox and measles, compiled an enormous medical encyclopedia for use in hospitals that remained the standard in the Islamic world until the sixteenth century, and composed a *Book of Secrets* that served as the basic chemistry textbook for the rest of the Middle Ages. The intellectual blossoming of Islam was based on its openness to ideas from its surrounding and component cultures.

On the social and political level, however, a different story unfolded. Many in the imperial palace deplored the ethnic egalitarianism of the Abbasids and the growing (so it seemed) lack of respect for social distinctions. "O Lord," cried one offended aristocrat, "the sons of whores have multiplied so much—please guide me to another land where I need not deal with bastards!" Groups which had eagerly accepted the Islamic faith balked at the apparently implied idea that they had to subject themselves to governance by haughty, militaristic Arabs, and they sought ways to justify their resentment in Islamic teaching about the "consensus of the community." Making matters worse, the Abbasids, in order to defend their dynasty, which had resulted from a violent revolt rather than election by the Islamic *ummah*, or community, cloaked themselves in a theocratic aura, emphasizing their divine right to rule as descendants of the Prophet, utilizing religious imagery and peppering their decrees with quotations from the Qur'an, and relying more and more on the office of the *qadi* (a religious judge who settled disputes in accordance with Islamic law) instead of the usual provincial and municipal governors. Not everyone was pleased by this "easternization" of the empire. The strongest objec-

One of the many mosques built by the Abbasids after they relocated
the capital of the caliphate to Baghdad.
Source: Werner Forman / Art Resource, NY

tions came from Muslim Spain and Muslim North Africa, which deeply resented the easternizing and theocratizing of Abbasid rule, and consequently declared their separation from the empire and established themselves as independent caliphates.

The creation of satellite Muslim states had a direct influence on the political fortunes of medieval Europe, for just as the Carolingian world was dissolving, a handful of new disparate Islamic realms formed—none of which was, for the time being, economically viable or politically stable. Spain, Morocco, and Tunisia were the first to break away, followed by Egypt and Syria. These rump states began to prey upon the collapsing Carolingian world, seeking new booty or trading posts, and in the process they reopened the trading connections that had previously defined Mediterranean life. Sicily was their main target, since it occupied so strategic a position at the center of the sea and also offered an abundant agricultural output, but the

Balearic islands of Majorca and Minorca and to a lesser extent Sardinia and Corsica also attracted attention. Once the Aghlabids of Tunisia had taken Sicily, in the mid-ninth century, they used it as a base for launching raids on the rest of Mediterranean Europe. They seized Bari, in southern Italy, in 840, and in 846 they sacked Rome itself. Only two years later they laid waste to Marseilles, France's chief Mediterranean port. Given their reduced numbers and the subsequent rivalries between the splinter states, they raided rather than conquered, but a handful of permanent outposts endured. From these places they raided as far inland as southern Germany, and, in their most spectacular adventure, destroyed St. Benedict's own monastery at Monte Cassino in 881. Meanwhile, the fundamentalist and militaristic Almoravids of northern Africa stormed over Spain, determined to stamp out what they regarded as the effete and compromising culture of the Cordoban caliphate.

The point is that few of these splinter states could, for the time being, entirely support themselves. Some religious antagonism existed between them. The Shi'ite Muslims who came to power in Egypt, known as the Fatimids, for example, had little sympathy for the Sunni Zirids of neighboring Tunisia, and they in turn were happy to do without the Aghlabids of today's Algeria or the chiefly Berber Idrisids of Morocco, not to mention the mainly Arabic Umayyad holdouts who retained control over Spain. Without sufficiently sustaining commercial contacts among themselves, each Muslim state had to turn instead to ties with Christian Europe, which led in turn to new Muslim raids: These were less of an invasive nature than they were an attempt to secure trading zones and areas of influence. While a good deal of violence marked this realignment—especially in its invitation to piracy—the end result was a considerably enhanced European-African and European-Near Eastern trade. The creation of the Islamic empire, in the first place, had created a kind of "Iron Curtain" across the the Mediterranean, interrupting trade and artificially cutting coastal societies off from one another. The breakup of that empire opened the door to renewed contact and a sparking of economic vitality.

But that does not mean that in the short term at least the renewed Muslim attacks were any less destructive. The attack on Rome in 846, for example, left thousands of dead in the streets and reduced hundreds of churches to ashes. The Arab seizure of Sicily, in particular, resulted in tens of thousands of Latin and Greek Christians dead, homeless, or exiled, and thereby created a particularly sensitive focal point for ethnic and religious antagonism. Muslim incursions into northern Italy and southern France left heaps of Christian dead behind them and they carted off many of the valuables found in Christian churches and monasteries. In their attacks, the Muslim armies—whether from Spain, Morocco, Tunisia, or Egypt—were aided by mercenaries and slaves brought north from sub-Saharan Africa, marking the introduction of Black Africans into European history. The largest Black populations lived in Fatimid Egypt and Umayyad Spain. The Spanish ruler al-Mansur (not to be confused with the Abbasid caliph of the same name) relied especially on these slave-soldiers in his campaigns in the 980s, when he sacked the city of Barcelona and the pilgrimage center of Santiago de Compostela.

Tensions between Sunni and Shi'ite Muslims had grown steadily over the years, and by the tenth century frequently boiled over into violence. Shi'ism, which had begun with the disputed succession to the caliphate, had evolved into a complex faith with its own liturgical practices, legal traditions, community organization, and social norms. Its most distinctive elements, though, were its dedication to a number of charismatic and spiritually infallible figures known as *imams*, and the practice of *takiyya*—religious concealment.[13] Rival traditions within Shi'ism disagreed on how many *imams* had arisen over the centuries, but all shared a belief that the last *imam* had gone into hiding, leaving the Shi'a bereft of their leadership, to keep the faith alive until the day when the hidden *imam* would return to earth in messianic form (called the *Mahdi*) to bring about the day of judgment. *Takiyya* permitted a believer to engage in activities contrary to his faith, in order to blend into a community and pass undetected: to drink wine, for example, to marry a non-Muslim, or even to deny one's faith. The idea was that to abjure what was most precious to one, in order to keep it from being suppressed by others, was the truest expression of love. (Shi'ite teachings include the following saying of Ali, the first *imam*: "The person among you who is most honored by Allah is the one who is most fearfully concealed. . . . Concealment is our *jihad*.") By such means, Shi'ism spread widely through the whole Islamic world. It was the majority sect only in certain parts of the empire—most notably in the area of today's Iran and southern Iraq, and in Fatimid Egypt—but was present everywhere.

The Muslim states that attacked Latin Europe in the ninth and tenth centuries also exerted considerable effort in uncovering and persecuting their Shi'ite minorities, even while continuing to suppress the last vestiges of North African Christianity.[14] Intrigues by warlords and by local reformist sects created a pervasive atmosphere of suspicion and hostility, which sometimes caused persecuted groups to lead the strikes upon Europe—in order to get away from their Muslim oppressors. These states were generally more tolerant of their large Jewish populations, though. North African Jews played vital roles in the Muslim cities as merchants, officials, and professionals. Most spoke Arabic as their common tongue, although they retained Hebrew for religious observances, and Jewish science and philosophy owed much to Muslim scholars.

THE END OF THE WORLD?

A number of post-Carolingian historians, amateur theologians, and general alarmists like Adso of Montier-en-Der, Raoul Glaber, and Adhemar of Chabannes

---

13. In Sunni Islam an *imam* is the clerical figure who leads the recitation of prayers in a mosque—an honored position but not one of unique spiritual authority. *Takiyya* also was accepted by Sunnis, but usually only in cases of physical endangerment. Another distinguishing feature of Shi'ite Islam was its practice of *mut'a* ("temporary marriage") which allowed a Shi'i to take a bride for a few as three days; so long as the man was not cruel to the woman and paid her the agreed-upon sum for her sexual services, no dishonor was accorded to either party.

14. With the exception of Egypt, Christian churches virtually disappeared from North Africa by 1100. Efforts to destroy them occurred occasionally in Egypt, as under the rule of al-Hakim.

feared that these calamities signaled the approaching End of the World. A crowd of apocalyptic prophets appeared in Catholic Europe in the tenth century, all claiming wide followings and reporting widespread signs of the imminent End. Apart from the obvious political and military troubles, they pointed to signs in the natural world—famines, comets, freak frosts, sudden river swellings, or the reported birth of albino cattle (it sounds strange, but that is one of the signs they expected to anticipate Judgment Day)—as evidence that human history was in fact approaching its long-predicted final chapter. To some of these prophets the fact that the ominous sounding year 1000 came ever nearer added urgency to their calamitous convictions; once that date had passed, most of them simply recalculated the arrival of doom in 1033 (that is, one thousand years after the presumed date of Christ's death, as opposed to his birth). When that date also failed to yield apocalypse, all sorts of recalculations took place: Perhaps the End would come in 1070 (the millennial anniversary of the Romans' destruction of the Temple in Jerusalem) or in 1096 (one thousand years after St. John's vision recorded in the *Book of Revelations*)? It is easy to laugh at this sort of paranoid calculus, but it is important to recognize, even if only as a telling narrative sideline, that quite a few intelligent faithful, and possibly more than that, believed that the disintegration of Christendom in the tenth century portended the world's end. Historians disagree vigorously about the extent to which such fears and expectations existed, but the fact of their existence is indisputable.

Whether the atmosphere of the late ninth to early eleventh centuries deserves to be called apocalyptic, the era did represent an important turning point. Many contemporaries noted it. The ninth-century Frankish noblewoman Dhuoda observed, in the spiritual manual that she wrote for her son, that "the troubles and wretchedness of this world grow worse by the day," and that

> my tremendous fear and sorrow about what the future may bring scatters my thoughts in every direction, to the point that I don't even have any confidence whether or not I deserve to be saved, at the world's end. Why is this? Because I have sinned in both word and deed . . . In trying to serve my lord and master, your father Bernard, in his duties in the [Spanish] March, and to make myself not entirely useless—so that he would not abandon me, as so many men do to their wives—I have gone deeply into debt. Needing the money, I borrowed from both Christians and Jews. I have paid them back as best I could, and will continue to do so as long as I can. But if any debts remain after my death, I beg you to seek out those creditors and return their money to them out of your own resources, if any remain.

She closed her testimonial with an exhortation for her son to carve these painful words on her tombstone:

> *Behold here, O Reader, the little verses of my epitaph.*
> *Fashioned out of the earth itself, here lies the earthly body of Dhuoda.*
>   Glorious King, receive her.
> *The earth now around her has retaken*

The lowly dust of which she was made.
> Gracious King, grant her favor.

The dark soil of this grave, moist with her tears,
Is all that remains of her.
> May You, Heavenly King, pardon her sins.

Whoever you are, man or woman, young or old,
As you tramp back and forth before this space, I beg you to repeat these words:
> *"O God, Most Holy, cast off her chains."*

Enclosed now in the tomb of bitter death
She has ended her life in dust.
> O God, O King, forgive her sins.

All of you, now, say in prayer,
Lest the serpent Satan snatches off her soul:
> *"Most merciful God, grant her peace."*

Let no one pass this place without reading these words,
I beg you all to pray, with the words aloud:
> *"Sweet God, give Dhuoda peace."*

And may You grant, Kind Father, that she may bask in the light
Of your saints eternally, and receive Your "Amen"
After her passing.

This is not great poetry, and Dhuoda's book is not very impressive as an intellectual work, but it is deeply moving and clearly speaks to a sensation that one kind of world was ending and that another was beginning.

Dhuoda's fears, debts, and anxieties were not unique. When Duke William of Aquitaine, in southwestern France, established an independent monastery at Cluny in 910, he did so in the spirit that "I ought to give some small portion of the earthly wealth I have received, for the good of my soul . . . And therefore may everyone who lives in the unity of the Christian faith and who expectantly awaits Christ's merciful forgiveness, and who shall continue to do so until the end of the world, know that, out of my love of God and my Savior Jesus Christ, I deliver over to the holy apostles Peter and Paul all those possessions I hold at Cluny." The German abbess and playwright with the tongue-twisting name of Hrostvitha von Gandersheim (935–973) wrote a half-dozen moralistic yet surprisingly engaging plays for the nuns under her care, in which she offered such insights as:

> From this deed [the main character's execution by soldiers on account of her re-
> fusal to have sex with a Roman general] there comes a supreme joy for me, and
> a supreme sorrow for you. The cruelty of your evil leads to your eternal
> damnation in Hell—whereas I shall receive the reward of martyrdom and the
> crown of virginity! I am about to enter the heavenly bridal chamber of the Eter-
> nal King, to Whom be all honor and glory forever.

While melodramatic, such attitudes held meaning. The people of medieval Europe, whether or not they believed silly prophecies about the world's end, felt keenly that

an important turning point had been reached, a moment when the call of Christianity became proactive and demanded explicit, overt, and determined action instead
of the forebearance and timidity of earlier centuries. As early as 989, at an evangelical revival known as the *Peace of God* at Charroux, the Frankish bishops under the
leadership of the archbishop of Bordeaux declared

> an anathema upon all who violate churches! . . . an anathema upon all who
> steal from the poor! . . . an anathema upon anyone who harms a clergyman!

Liturgical cursing of this sort defined the age, at least within the Carolingian heart-
land. Churches started to lash out at their enemies with the only weapon they had:
spiritual condemnation. At the abbey of Saint-Martial in western France, for example, in 1016 the monks anathematized the warlords who had long been preying on
the monastery in these memorable words:

> May the curse of every one of God's saints fall upon them! May the Lord's an-
> gels and archangels curse them! May the patriarchs and prophets curse them!
> May all the apostles, martyrs, confessors and holy virgins curse them—
> especially Saint-Martial—to whom they are doing so much evil! . . . May they
> be cursed in the cities and in the fields, in their homes and out of doors, when
> standing and when sitting, when lying down or standing up, while sleeping or
> while awake, while eating and while drinking! May they be cursed in castles
> and in villages, in forests and in waters! May their wives, children, and com-
> rades be cursed! . . . May the Lord deliver their bodies over as fodder for the
> birds in the sky and the beasts upon the land! May the Lord strike them from
> the soles of their feet to the top of their heads! . . .

And as late as the 1060s, just as the Church was lifting itself out of the ashes, so
prominent a figure as St. Peter Damian (d. 1072) could thunder:

> If anyone should hope to attain the pinnacle of [Christian] perfection, let him
> lock himself up behind the walls of a monastery; let him devote himself to spir-
> itual restfulness; let him be as terrified of being about in the world as he would
> be of drowning himself in a pool of blood. For truly, this world is more and
> more poisoned every day with the filth of so many crimes that any mind
> geared to holier things is befouled by the mere thought of them.

We need to read such passages with a skeptical eye (Peter Damian, for example,
thundered about everything, all the time), but the frequency of such attitudes in the
tenth and early eleventh centuries reflects an important change in the European
mood and mentality. An age of aggression and action was in the making.

There was yet one more cause of Christian despair and anger: the corruption of
the Church itself. Precisely at a time when the people of Christendom felt the
strongest need for spiritual guidance and solace, the Catholic Church was in no
state to offer either. That wasn't the Church's fault—at least not entirely. For the
most part, the Church in the tenth century did not "become corrupt" so much as it
"was corrupted" by greedy warlords, petty princes inheriting ever-smaller pieces of
patrimonies, and urban magnates feeling the pinch of economic hard times. Taking
their lead from the early Carolingians themselves, these rulers began simply to

plunder the churches' buildings, treasuries, and estates, and to commandeer their offices. The tenth-century Church quite simply fell victim to a "hostile takeover," a modern term that is remarkably apt.

There were lots of ways to plunder a church or monastery. One could attack it with one's soldiers and ransack the place—as many did. But while that could produce a sudden windfall of profits, it did not secure a steady income. Therefore a different sort of pillaging became popular. Local barons asserted that the churches and monasteries within their territories were in fact their personal property, to dispose of as they saw fit, and consequently many took over these sites by forcing the local bishops, priests, and abbots out, and installing their own agents instead. This practice rewarded the agents and secured their continued loyalty, and it remunerated the barons themselves since they generally took a share of the churches' annual revenues. To be fair, at least some of these installees took their ecclesiastical responsibilities seriously, or tried to; but most of them received their new posts because of their cold-blooded willingness to wrench every last penny out of the peasants who worked the land. If they carried out any priestly duties at all, they did so poorly and without any real interest. They were hardly the sort of figures to whom the suffering masses would turn for spiritual guidance.

Another form of pillage was simply to sell a church office to the highest bidder, a practice known as *simony*.[15] Simony ran rampant in the tenth and eleventh centuries, until the Church was literally flooded with people who had taken on offices as investments instead of spiritual callings. Once again, some simoniacs (that is, people who purchased their priesthoods, episcopacies, or abbacies) had sincere motives and wanted to do their new jobs well; but the overwhelming majority simply desired the powers of the offices, their accoutrements, their social position, and their wealth. Many people who purchased episcopacies never set foot in their dioceses. Many simoniac priests never gave a single sermon, delivered a single sacrament, or even cracked open a Bible. From these figures too, the faithful masses stayed away in droves.

The problem simony represented was not just that the practice looked bad; it represented a spiritual crisis of the first order. To Catholics, the priesthood that Christ created when he appeared to the apostles after his resurrection was a group that possessed spiritual power, aspects of God's own grace. These priests in turn passed on that grace to the faithful through the Church's sacraments—which Catholics believed (and still do) were absolutely essential to salvation. But did a priest who purchased his priesthood from the local warlord truly possess that grace? If not—and the story of Simon Magus suggests a negative verdict—were any of the sacraments he performed valid? Could one pass on to others something that one did not oneself possess? A faithful peasant couple, wanting to have their newborn child

---

15. The name derives from the character of Simon Magus, who offered to buy the miraculous healing powers shown by the apostles after Pentecost (see Acts, ch. 8).

baptized, had every reason to be terrified: What if their priest was not really a priest? Must their child be condemned to eternal damnation (since only those who have been baptized can be saved) because of this other person's fault? Compounding matters, one could never be sure who was a "legitimate" cleric and who was not. What if those peasants' priest was a pious, devout soul who entered the priesthood out of a genuine conviction and desire to serve Christ, and who had successfully completed all the required training for the office—but the bishop who had ordained him was a simoniac (and the priest did not know it)? In that case, was he still really a priest? What if that bishop was himself pious and devout but he had been ordained bishop by a simoniac archbishop? The spiritual problem was urgent and keenly felt. If one took the view that no one in the Church, at any level, who was a simoniac could legitimately pass on grace, then by the middle of the eleventh century, it is possible that as many as two-thirds of the priests in medieval Europe were not really priests, and therefore all the faithful they ministered to (if they ministered to them at all) had no hope of salvation.[16]

The problem reached as high as the Holy See itself. Throughout the tenth and eleventh centuries, a large group of urban aristocratic families in Rome treated the papacy as a political plaything, seizing the office, buying it, and selling it almost at whim. The papacy after all was a choice political plum, one that controlled considerable wealth—the tithes paid by Europe's churches and monasteries, plus the revenues of the papal estates—but in carrying out their schemes most of the magnates looked only to advance their family interests. Few cared about what was happening outside the Roman walls. Like many of the corrupt and lax figures occupying the priesthoods, episcopacies, and abbacies in Europe, many of these popes were married or had coteries of mistresses with whom they lived openly. The low point in papal history came in the middle of the tenth century, when Rome came under the political domination of a woman named Theodora (the widow of the preceding papal tyrant) and her daughter Marozia. Many scurrilous stories about these two circulated at the time, and still do today; between the two of them, Theodora and Marozia are reputed to have been either the wives, mistresses, and/or murderesses of a half-dozen popes, while also, in some reports, they administered the largest whorehouse in Rome. If even a tenth of the stories told about them are true, they were an interesting pair indeed. Their control of the city passed to Marozia's son, who became Pope John XII (r. 955–963). John was an ignorant, spoiled, and spiteful man with gross sensual appetites; probably even the emperor Nero would have blushed had he witnessed John in action.

As we shall see in the next three chapters, the Church's loss of moral authority in the tenth century, at the time of Europe's greatest need, had important ramifications for the way that Europe recovered from the crisis and began to rebuild itself— politically, economically, socially, and spiritually—in the eleventh century.

---

16.   The theological problem of clerical fitness was an old one, dating back at least to the fourth-century debate over Donatism, but at stake in the tenth century were popular fears and (mis)understandings, not ecclesiastical doctrine.

SUGGESTED READING

Texts

Anonymous. *The Anglo-Saxon Chronicle.*

———. *The Arabian Nights (One Thousand and One Nights).*

Asser. *The Life of Alfred.*

Damian, St. Peter. *Letters.*

Dhuoda. *Handbook for William.*

Flodoard. *Chronicle.*

Hrotsvitha of Gandersheim. *Plays.*

Ibn al-Haytham. *The Book of Discussions.*

Ordericus Vitalis. *The Ecclesiastical History.*

Raoul Glaber. *The Histories.*

Saxo Grammaticus. *The History.*

Abbot Suger of St. Denis. *The Deeds of Louis the Fat.*

Source Anthology

Dutton, Paul Edward. *Carolingian Society: A Reader* (1997).

Head, Thomas. *Medieval Hagiography: An Anthology* (1999).

Pullan, Bruce. *Sources for the History of Europe from the Mid-Eighth to the Mid-Thirteenth Century* (1966).

Page, R.I. *Chronicles of the Vikings: Records, Memorials, and Myths* (1995).

Studies

Bartlett, Robert. *The Making of Europe: Conquest, Colonization, and Cultural Change, 950–1350* (1994).

Bois, Guy. *The Transformation of the Year One Thousand: The Village of Lournand from Antiquity to Feudalism* (1992).

Duby, Georges. *The Early Growth of the European Economy: Warriors and Peasants from the Seventh to the Twelfth Century* (1974).

Dunbabin, Jean. *France in the Making: 843–1180* (1985).

Fichtenau, Heinrich. *Living in the Tenth Century: Studies in Mentalities and Social Orders* (1990).

Godman, Peter. *Poets and Emperors: Frankish Politics and Carolingian Poetry* (1986).

Godman, Peter, and Roger Collins. *Charlemagne's Heir. New Perspectives on the Reign of Louis the Pious, 814–840* (1990).

Head, Thomas. *Hagiography and the Cult of Saints: The Diocese of Orléans, 800–1200* (1995).

Holmes, Catherine. *Basil II and the Governance of Empire, 976–1025* (2006).

Jones, Gwyn. *A History of the Vikings* (1984).

Kennedy, Hugh. *The Prophet and the Age of the Caliphates* (1986).

Koziol, Geoffrey. *Begging Pardon and Favor: Ritual and Political Order in Early Medieval France* (1992).

Kreutz, Barbara M. *Before the Normans: Southern Italy in the Ninth and Tenth Centuries* (1991).

Landes, Richard. *Relics, Apocalypse, and the Deceits of History: Ademar of Chabannes, 989–1034* (1995).

Landes, Richard, and Thomas Head. *The Peace of God: Social Violence and Religious Response in France around the Year 1000* (1992).

Leyser, Karl. *Rule and Conflict in an Early Medieval Society: Ottonian Saxony* (1979).

Logan, F. Donald. *The Vikings in History* (1991).

Madelung, Wilfred, and Paul Walker. *The Advent of the Fatimids: A Contemporary Shi'i Witness Account of Politics in the Early Islamic World* (2000).

McKitterick, Rosamund. *The Frankish Kingdoms under the Carolingians: 751–987* (1983).

Nelson, Janet L. *Charles the Bald* (1993).

Poly, Jean-Pierre, and Eric Bournazel. *The Feudal Transformation, 900–1200* (1991).

Reuter, Timothy. *Germany in the Early Middle Ages: 800–1056* (1991).

Sawyer, Peter H. *Kings and Vikings: Scandinavia and Europe, AD 700–1000* (1982).

Wickham, Chris. *Early Medieval Italy: Central Power and Local Society, 400–1000* (1981).

CHAPTER 8

Revolutions on Land and Sea

Historians frequently abuse the term *revolution*, using it either to exaggerate the importance of whatever they're talking about at any given moment or to justify their interest in it in the first place. In fact, historians sometimes seem to have an actual love affair with the word, as a cursory glance through almost any armful of recent books would suggest: Thus we have "revolutionary artistic movements," "intellectual revolutions," "revolutions in literary studies," "revolutionary notions of statecraft," "technological revolutions," "revolutionized concepts of religious identity," "revolutions in ways of doing business," "revolutionary approaches to the theater," and even "democratic revolutions" (an obvious oxymoron). Usually what is being described is simply *change*, and change is the norm in human life. Nothing ever remains entirely static, and if every change is described as a revolution then the term loses its meaning. Revolution is not simply speeded-up change, either; for as one aspect of life accelerates, many others usually accelerate, too, just to keep pace. Revolution instead is the radical, permanent, and usually unpredictable alteration of the fundamental structures and assumptions governing and ordering any aspect of human life. True revolutions in history are relatively rare—which may be a blessing, and may be not.

To many medievalists, what happened in Europe over the course of the eleventh century certainly has all the appearance of a genuine revolution: They argue that by the year 1100 hardly any aspect of life—social structure, economic practice, political institutions and thought, religious observance and beliefs, architectural and artistic styles, philosophical assumptions and methods, cultural and racial prejudices and interrelations, sexual practices and mores, diet, dress, the measurement of time, or even the techniques of manufacturing alcohol—was what it had been in the year 1000. The break, it seemed, was total. French medievalists often refer to the eleventh century as that of *la grande mutation*, or "the great change," and they contend that it was precisely at this time and directly as a result of the great change that the first lineaments of the modern world emerged. Not all medievalists share this view; many—and perhaps even most—scholars, French and otherwise, argue for a greater degree of continuity and gradual evolutionary change over this century, and reject the idea of a fundamental and radical shift. The debate is a vigorous one that shows no sign of abating soon. It is in fact one of the most interesting debates currently astir among medievalists. Whether or not we accept the idea of *la grande mutation*, it is certainly clear that the eleventh century was one of unusually high drama.

Let us view this drama literally from the ground up, with the lowest and largest order of medieval society—the peasantry. In this chapter we will examine the changes in European demography (that is, the growth of the population in absolute numbers) and the changes that took place in the way those people were settled on the land, plus the changes in agriculture, social organization, and sex relations. Then we shall turn to developments in Mediterranean life: trade, navigational knowledge and expertise, inter-racial and inter-religious relations, and political organization. Chapter 9 will focus on the differing developmental paths followed by northern and southern Europe, and will shift emphasis to the rural aristocracies and urban elites. In Chapter 10 we will look at the great ecclesiastical reform movement—often named the *Gregorian Reform*, after the most controversial, though not necessarily the greatest, figure in that movement. But it is important to bear in mind that the events described in these three chapters happened more or less at the same time, and frequently had considerable influence on one another. The last two chapters of this part of the book will then examine the world of the twelfth century, an age of political solidity, intellectual efflorescence, economic vitality, and cultural confidence quite at odds with the despairing gloom of the "time of troubles" discussed on Chapter 7.

CHANGES ON THE LAND

Until the end of the eleventh century, if not even later, over ninety percent of the northern European population led agrarian lives. Most people worked the land itself, either farming, flock-keeping, or foresting; a far smaller number made their livings in agricultural manufacturing: blacksmithing, butchery, milling, coopering (barrel-making), and simple weaving. Fewer still worked as miners or quarrymen, as river ferrymen, tanners, or carters. But all remained tied, in one way or another, to the land. Estimates of the average overall European population in the eleventh century range from thirty to forty million, roughly two-thirds of whom lived in northern Europe—which means that throughout the entire century, somewhere between eighteen and twenty-four million people in the north knew only the agrarian lifestyle, and a poor one at that.

But conditions for medieval peasants improved considerably at this time and remained surprisingly favorable for the next three hundred years. The gradual subsiding of the foreign invasions played a significant role, simply in terms of putting an end to the carnage, but other factors counted at least as much. Ample scientific evidence—gained by techniques like tree-ring observation and pollen analysis— shows that the years from roughly 1050 to 1300 were ones of exceptionally clement weather: Average annual temperatures rose several degrees, rain fell plentifully, and winters remained relatively mild. These factors increased agricultural yields and raised European farm production to levels above mere subsistence for the first time, perhaps, since the fourth century. But that was not all. The physical dangers of the tenth century caused a change in the pattern of land settlement itself, at least in the Frankish territories that, together with England, are the best documented part of Europe for this era. In the face of political disintegration, Viking attack, and the recurring threat of Muslim and Magyar advance, the small farmers of the north began to abandon their more or less isolated family farms and congregated in small, concentrated communities. Surviving texts only hint at this mass movement but we find ample evidence of it in archeological records and in the place-names that emerged in the tenth and eleventh centuries. New communities in France, for example, some of which developed into feudal manors while others formed the nuclei of what later became full-fledged towns, tended to take place-names that ended with the suffix *-bourg* or *-ville*. New German settlements can be identified by the suffixes *-berg*, *-burg*, *-dorf*, or *-feld*. Frequently these suffixes were preceded by the name of the individual warlord/strongman around whose fortification the rustics clustered: thus France's *Joinville* ("John's village") or Germany's *Wolfsburg* ("Wolf's Stronghold"). This flight to safety by the farmers does not explain the entire rural revolution of the central Middle Ages, but it is one of the most important elements in it.

There was, farmers hoped, some safety in numbers; but they quickly found out that there certainly was an increased crop yield. By living collectively, they could share their labor, skills, and resources; moreover, in times of attack they could turn for protection to the local warlord and his soldiers. In other words, they gave up their autonomy in return for communal life and warrior-protection. In this way, the warlords acquired a kind of *de facto* jurisdiction: In return for permission to settle on the lord's manor and to work his land, the commoners agreed to submit to his legal authority. In this way, a true peasantry came into being. Congregations of peasants who placed themselves and their descendants under the protection of warlords became known as *serfs*—from the Latin *servus*, or "slave." But serfdom was not the same everywhere. As a contractual relationship, the specifics of each arrangement varied widely, depending on local conditions and needs. In the mountainous regions of Germany, for example, few great landlords existed because the land itself was naturally given to division; consequently, free ownership of small peasant farms remained widespread. In northern and central France, by contrast, where the terrain was flat and the land almost uniformly fertile, serfdom was ubiquitous and powerful lords were able to command manors of enormous size. The monastic manor of St. Germain-des-Prés just outside Paris, for example, consisted of so much farmland that it needed fifty-nine watermills to grind the grain produced by the manors' serfs. Moreover, the status of an individual serf had much to do with what a refugee peasant had to offer a lord in return for his protection. A farmer who was lucky enough to have some money, special skills, tools, or animals to offer could negotiate a more liberal sort of serfdom for himself and his family, with greater

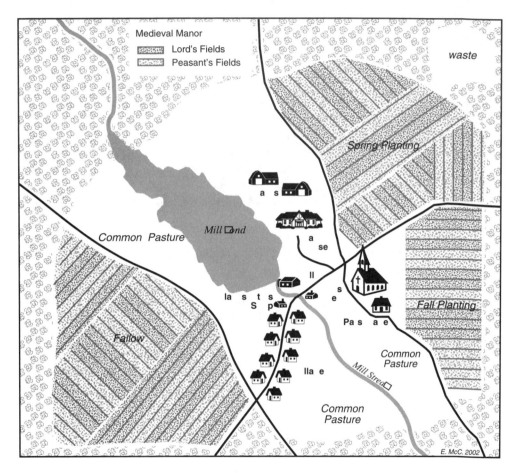

A medieval manor

privileges or lessened rents; a refugee-farmer with nothing to offer but the labor of his bare hands was in a much inferior position and could probably expect to win the lowest sort of manorial servitude.

The word *peasant* does not mean simply a poor farmer. The word itself derives from the Latin term *pagensis*, which in classical times denoted a "country rustic" or "agricultural laborer" but not a free farmer. In the early Middle Ages, the derivative term *paganus* designated a "pagan." Thus from the very start, to be a peasant carried with it a derogatory sense, an association with social inferiority. Strictly speaking, the free farmers of the Carolingian era (the male lidus and female lida) were not peasants because they possessed—in theory, at least—legal autonomy. But those free farmers declined in number over the ninth and tenth centuries as they either slid into debt-slavery or came under the power of a warlord holding sway over a primitive agricultural community. Those communities increasingly centered on the rural village. Villages of one sort or another had always existed, but by the eleventh century they came to dominate, if not define, northern European agricultural life. They ranged widely in size: Some villages contained no more than a few score individuals, while others held as many as two thousand. The land itself belonged to the local baron, who allowed the peasants to live and work on it in return for a share of the proceeds and subordination to his authority.

Differences in terrain and available resources made for some variation, but a basic general pattern existed. In the center of a typical village lay a small cluster of peasant cottages, huts, and workshops. The landlord usually also provided a public oven for baking bread, although peasants had to pay a fee to use it. In larger villages a tavern and a church dominated the central living area—and in some cases they were actually the same building, though not at the same time.[1] Surrounding the village center lay the crop fields—"open fields" in the sense that they were not divided by fences or hedges. Since there usually was only a single team of oxen per manor (it took eight oxen to make up a plow-team, far beyond what any single peasant could afford), plowing the fields had to be a cooperative process. Within each field individual plow-strips were assigned to each of the peasants. The physical realities of plowing determined northern Europe's system of rural measures. The plow-strips averaged two hundred and twenty yards in length, which was as far as the average team could pull a plow through the heavy soil without resting; this length became known in English as a *furlong* (a "furrow's length," literally). Moreover, an average of sixteen and one-half feet separated the strips, which was as tight a turning-radius as one could persuade eight oxen to make at the end of a furlong; turning the plow-team required some force, and hence the width measurement became known, appropriately, as a *rod*. In a full day's hard labor, a team could plow four of these strips in one day, and this area—a rectangle four rods in width and one furlong in length—made up an *acre* (from the Latin *ager*, meaning a "field").

---

1. Nowadays we convert unused churches into condominiums; in the Middle Ages they made them into taverns.

Throughout most of the eleventh century, collective farming utilized a two-field rotation system of crops, meaning that only half the available land was plowed and seeded in any growing season while the other half remained fallow. This resting provided a primitive check on soil exhaustion. Alternating the crops sown in the fields also helped; planting barley or oats in a field that had just yielded a wheat crop replenished the soil with certain nutrients. Gradually northern farmers turned to a three-field system, in which only one-third of the arable land stood fallow, while the other two fields were planted with various cereals. With each growing season—of which northern Europe had two per year—the crop fields and fallow fields moved through a regular rotation for maximum efficiency. Labor was shared throughout. Each peasant family "owned" individual strips in each of the arable fields, but the work of plowing, tending the crops, and harvesting remained a communal activity.

A number of new technologies helped bring about a fairly dramatic increase in crop yields. The first was the introduction of a new type of plow. The soil of northern Europe is heavy and loamy, and the light scratch plow inherited from the Romans, while it worked well for the lighter and drier Mediterranean soil, was ill-suited to northern needs. The consequent introduction of a wheeled plow in the early tenth century made it much easier to pull the plow blade through the earth and made it possible to dig deeper furrows which assured that the planted seeds would not be borne away by the wind; later, the addition of a moldboard allowed for turning over the topsoil during plowing to expose the richer loam underneath. The greatest shortcoming of the three-field system was the cutback in the amount of grazing land available for cattle and sheep; to an extent, the clearing of more forestland to create open meadows alleviated this shortage, but clearing was still slow to catch on, in part because it went against the inclinations of the baronial overlord, who customarily guarded his forest- and hunting-rights jealously.

The most important new technology was the introduction of horses as draft animals. Horses moved faster than oxen, which meant that more land could be plowed in less time, and they also needed less pasture than oxen, making them more suitable for the three-field system. But the introduction of horses necessitated the invention of a new type of yoke, since the one used for oxen cut off horses' windpipes. The design of the new padded-collar yoke came ultimately from China—a striking example of the cultural reach of medieval civilization (and, of course, of Chinese civilization, too). An indigenous invention, however, was the horseshoe, which improved horses' traction. The new yokes and shoes allowed draft-horses to be harnessed in tandem—that is, one behind another instead of side-by-side—which improved drawing-power and made it possible to make even tighter turns at the end of the furlong. Thus farmers added more furrows per acre and increased the grain yield accordingly.

Harvesting, always a back-breaking labor, was done by means of long two-handed scythes or small single-handled sickles, depending on the crop. The difference mattered, since the stalks of straw that remained in the field were used not only as animal fodder but as the primary means of fertilizing the soil. Farmers set the whole field of grain-stalks ablaze, then gathered the ashes, mixed them with manure, and scattered the mixture over the fields. It was nearly as important to maximize the amount of leftover stalk in the field after harvest as it was to gather the grain in the first place.

Viticulture prospered roughly from the latitude of the Loire valley southward. Wine was drunk everywhere—after all, the liturgy demanded it—and the further south one went, the more that wine replaced ale as the staple drink of the masses. Efforts were even made to grow grapes in England, though the result was hardly to be borne: "a foul, greasy fluid that one has to strain through one's teeth while drinking it" is how one shocked continental visitor described English wine. There is no clear evidence of any major shift in viticulture technology in this period, whether one speaks of grapes or olives; since most products were produced and consumed locally, there was little reason to trade in bulk ordinary wines or olive oils. The major shift that occurred was in the production of high quality wines and oils for the aristocracy. Producing fine wines required not only a higher degree of knowledge but a dramatically increased commitment of manpower. Vines needed to be regularly pruned, weeded, and fertilized—sometimes over the course of two or three decades before premium quality wines could be achieved; in order to produce certain types of wines, different varieties of grapes had to be grafted together; special barrels were required and stone cellars had to be built for the proper aging of the wine. These refinements could only be made when farm labor became centralized and collectivized under the lords of the new manors. Indeed, the mere possession of superior wine was an indication of a manorial lord's social and economic status.

Agricultural innovations spread slowly over the eleventh century, but they nevertheless led to a significant increase in northern Europe's food production and created the first reliable annual surpluses that that part of Europe had known for centuries. Crop yields for wheat improved to perhaps four times the quantity of grain sown—that is, one bushel of seed produced four bushels of harvested grain. Of those four bushels, one had to be reserved for the next planting, one (and sometimes two) went to the lord of the manor as rent, and the remaining grain was either consumed, stored, or sold.[2] Surpluses meant safety from famine, but they also meant the possibility of trade; and the commercial economy of northern Europe, while hardly startling in its impressiveness, began a slow but steady growth.

A PEASANT SOCIETY EMERGES

Despite their depiction in popular tales and modern films, medieval peasants were not all alike. Characteristics of their social organization, material standards of living, gender roles, and legal rights varied widely from region to region. This hetero-

---

2. By contrast, the average wheat farm in America today produces roughly twenty-five bushels of wheat per bushel of seed.

geneity resulted as much from changes in geographical conditions from territory to territory as it did from ethnic or cultural traditions. The fertility of the soil, supply of fresh water, density of forestation, presence of wildlife, type of climate, and availability of mineral ores all shaped the nature of peasant labor and organization. When one adds to these elements the influences of varying ethnic customs and the differences in degrees of authority over the peasants held by the baronial lords, a far more dynamic (and confusing) picture of peasant life emerges.

Still, there were some constants. One of the most observable was diet. Northern peasants ate (but did not *enjoy*) a diet comprised chiefly of grains, vegetables, and wild fruit. By almost any standard the food was appalling. Finely milled wheat, which produced the best bread, usually went to the landlord as rent or to market in order to raise badly needed money, leaving only a mishmash of leftover grain, husks, and wheat-stems to produce the basic staple of peasants' lives.[3] Peasant bread was commonly known as *brown bread* or *black bread*, and it was both coarse and tasteless. Much grain went into the brewing of beer, which was the staple beverage among northern peasants, who drank two or three liters daily. Vegetables provided a supplement to the diet but they were not grown in great number or variety. Beans and root-vegetables predominated; corn, potatoes, squash, and tomatoes remained unknown until the discovery of the New World. Responsibility for growing vegetables fell almost exclusively to women; the men worked the big grain fields while their wives tended small private gardens alongside their individual huts. Vegetables did not store well and so did not have any market value (besides, all the farms grew essentially the same vegetables, which meant that there was little incentive to trade them); all were grown for consumption. A few herbs dotted these household gardens and offered some relief from the general tedium of the diet, but not much. Fruits could be gathered—again usually by women and children—in the manors' forests and meadows, but few places in the north actually cultivated fruit trees. Sugar was unknown at this time but honey was cultivated on a broad scale. Chickens provided eggs—the commoners' most consistent source of protein—and some meat, while cows and goats provided milk. But since no means of preserving the milk existed, it usually ended up as butter or cheese. Fish was common, but meat was rare. Only aged and sickly animals fell to the knife, usually in the autumn when peasants coldly assessed each animal's chance of surviving the winter. The most common form of meat was the tough, stringy flesh of the wild pigs that inhabited northern Europe's forests. Hunting these boar remained an exclusive privilege of the landlords, but the pigs' vast numbers made poaching relatively easy. Northern Europeans generally cooked with lard, obtained from these pigs.

Access to fresh water constantly determined the shape of most peasants' lives. Although a few windmills existed by this time, most peasants ground their grain at

---

3. Wild chestnuts were another food source. After the best chestnuts were harvested for the lord, his peasants were allowed to scavenge whatever they could find on the ground. The farmers then husked the nuts, dried them, and ground them into flour.

water-powered mills, the reason why most manors and villages stood near a river or running stream. Such water also provided irrigation for the crop fields, and caring for the hydraulic system remained a constant concern. Water was too precious to waste (hence they seldom bathed) and too unhealthy to drink. Primitive technology, rather than primitive manners, lay behind this. Most peasants had the right only to gather deadwood from their lords' forests—not to fell whole trees; hence they could hardly spare the fuel to heat a proper bath, and a cold-water bath in a cold climate was an invitation to disease, especially among a malnourished population. As for the beer that peasants drank in lieu of water, its alcohol content forestalled putrefaction; unlike water or milk, beer remained unspoiled for a relatively long time.

A fairly sharp division of labor existed between the sexes. Men performed the bulk of the heavy labor on the manor—plowing, planting, harvesting, milling, storing, butchering and carting—while their wives and daughters tended the domestic scene. Food preparation, child care, ale brewing, vegetable gardening, and cloth weaving filled most women's days. Wives generally had little property of their own and little right to control whatever they did have. By long-standing custom, a woman regarded as the legal property of her father since birth became at marriage the legal property of her husband. Harsh living conditions, poor food, the difficulties of childbirth, and the widespread custom of wife-beating resulted in a life expectancy much lower for northern women than men.

Numerous restrictions, both legal and cultural, shaped northern women's lives. Society both valued and feared women's sexual allure, but sexual prudishness was not necessarily characteristic of peasant culture. Degrees of permissiveness varied, of course. Society did not actually encourage young women to indulge their sexual nature, but absolute virginity prior to marriage was hardly demanded or expected. Indeed, in a world that needed to produce as many children as possible to offset the high infant-mortality rate (as many as one-third of all peasant children died within four years of birth), a young woman's bearing of a child out of wedlock frequently increased her desirability on the marriage market; her fertility, after all, was not in doubt. Clerical attitudes toward sex differed sharply. Monks and nuns were kept apart as much as possible, both by ecclesiastical decree and the maintenance of separate enclosures. Within parish churches, strict rules of decorum mandated female modesty in dress and comportment. In some northern areas, in fact, women were entirely banned from entering their parish church or even setting foot on its land, as the following example from the eleventh-century writer Simeon of Durham shows:

> There have been many women who in their audacity have dared to violate these decrees, but in the end the punishments they all received speak eloquently of the enormity of their crimes. One woman named Sungeova—the wife of Gamel the son of Bevo—was returning home with her husband one evening after some sort of entertainment [in the village]. She complained endlessly to her husband that there were no clean spots in the road, since it was filled with so many mud puddles. Finally they decided to cut through the yard

of the local church and to make amends for the transgression later on by giving some extra alms. But as they progressed Sungeova was seized by a sense of horror and cried out that she was losing her mind. Her husband silenced her and told her to hurry up and stop being frightened. But as soon as she passed the hedge surrounding the church's cemetery she fell senseless to the ground, and that very night, after her husband had carried her home, she died. . . . I could cite many other examples of how the audacity of parish women was punished by Heaven, but let this suffice for the moment.

The seasons of the agricultural cycle and of the ecclesiastical calendar governed most peasants' lives, whether male or female. Surprisingly few people saw a priest regularly; many counted themselves lucky to see one once a year, and in fact even as late as 1215 the Church had to pass a decree requiring the faithful to confess to a priest and attend Mass at least once every twelve months. Nevertheless, Church festivals punctuated the year with a continuous succession of saints' days observances, fasts, feasts, memorials, and celebrations. Itinerant priests, deacons, monks, and (later on) mendicant friars often presided over these festivities, but in many cases no clergy were present at all. Oftentimes a passing pilgrim would lead villagers in hymns and prayers. A sparse network of parish churches was established in the ninth century, especially under Louis the Pious and the first generation of lesser Carolingians that succeeded him; this network introduced some degree of institutionalized Christianity among rural folk, but rural priests were still poorly trained and few in number by the eleventh century.

Given the relative paucity of peasants' contact with clergy, it comes as no surprise that popular religious practices and beliefs frequently deviated from Catholic doctrine and continued to incorporate elements of their pre-Christian folkloric pasts. Divination, spell-casting, hexes and curses, and the use of magical amulets and herbal potions remained prominent features of popular Christianity. One of the best witnesses to this is a confessional handbook compiled around 1008 by a man named Burchard, who was the bishop of Worms in southern Germany. This handbook, just one part of a much larger compilation of canon law called the *Decretum*, was known as the *Correptor et medicus* ("The Corrector and Healer"). The book aimed to assist parish priests by preparing them for the resilient paganism still alive in peasant life. It warns of sorceresses, magicians, spell-inducing potions, witches, and all sorts of diabolical enchantments. Burchard supplies his priestly-readers with both the questions they should put to the peasants and the corresponding penalties they should impose upon the guilty.

> Have you ever tied knots,[4] performed incantations, or cast spells the way that certain wicked men, swineherds, oxherds, and huntsmen do? (They do this while intoning Satanic chants over scraps of bread and some herbs, all tied together with foul strips of cloth—and then they hide these talismans in trees, or

---

4. Tying patterns of knots in strips of cloth, yarn, or leather was an ages-old custom, a way of casting spells on people—something akin to the folk practice of sticking pins into effigies of a chosen victim.

throw them into crossroads, all as a means of supposedly curing their swine and cattle, or their dogs, of illness, or else as a way to cause illness in the herds of others.)

—[If so] you are to do penance for two years on all the appointed feast days.

Other forms of magical practice abounded:

Have you ever placed your child, whether male or female, on the roof of your house or on top of your oven, in order to cure him or her of some illness? Have you ever burned grain on the spot where a corpse has lain or tied knots in a dead man's belt, in order to place a hex on someone? Have you ever taken the combs that women use to prepare wool for spinning and clapped them together over a corpse [as a means of scaring off the dead man's spirit]?

—[If so] you are to do penance for twenty days on bread and water.

Or this:

Have you ever done what many women so often do? That is, they strip off all their clothes and smear honey over their naked bodies; then they roll their honeyed bodies back and forth over grains of wheat heaped on a sheet that they have spread out on the ground. Next they gather up all the grains of wheat that stick to their moist bodies and take them to a mill, where they turn the mill slowly in the direction opposite the sun and grind this wheat into flour. Then they bake bread from this flour and feed it to their husbands—who immediately fall sick and die.

—[If so] you are to do penance for forty days on bread and water.

Burchard never explains why magically inducing illness in a neighbor's ox merits a more severe penance than magically killing one's own husband, but we can surmise it had something to do with the relative replaceability of each.

Other aspects of peasant life stand out. The homes peasants lived in, for example, were small, dark, and filthy. A common form of construction utilized simple crucks, or parallel sets of curved beams joined at the top (picture two or three wishbones from a chicken placed one after another, with a bit of space in between), with the intervening spaces filled with timber slats and a simple plaster made up of mud, dung, lime, and straw. Windows were rare, flies plentiful. A hole cut in the roof allowed the smoke that accumulated from the central hearth-fire to escape, but it also allowed rain and snow to come in. A single door stood at the front. In wintertime the interior was made warmer, but smellier and filthier, by the presence of the peasant families' domestic animals—chickens, goats, sheep, geese, and, if room existed, even cattle. Families slept together on a single pallet that usually had a simple mattress of stuffed straw. Little privacy existed and most natural functions, including sexual couplings, were performed in front of the whole family.

Most villages had a church of some sort, even if there was not a priest in residence. These buildings, too, were modest, but they represented the symbolic heart of the community. They also provided the site for most village entertainments, where people drank and danced and tried to forget the difficulties of daily life. In medieval England, for example, the connection between churches and taverns was represented in the rustic tradition of a *church ale*—that is, a drinking party at which people filled themselves with as much beer as possible before tottering back to their huts.

The term *manor* originally applied only to the much larger house inhabited by the landlord for whom the serfs labored, but gradually it came to identify the whole village itself. The essential characteristic of manorial society was the near-total subordination of the peasants to the economic and jurisdictional authority of the landlord. Peasants were serfs—but most were not technically slaves.

Fine distinctions existed between classes of peasants, even though those distinctions may strike us as rather minor. Many manors housed a number of freemen—rent-paying tenant farmers who owed little or no service to the landlord at all—but freemen were relatively few in the eleventh and twelfth centuries. In eleventh-century England, for example, freemen made up no more than ten to fifteen percent of the peasantry. Beneath freemen were *villeins*—the most common status of northern peasant—who divided their labor between the landlord's fields and their own individual strips. So-called *half-villeins* received only half as many strips for their own use while owing a full complement of labor to the lord. They frequently rented out their services to other peasants to make up for their far more meager existence. *Cottars* or *cottagers* held no individual strips of their own and spent all their time working in the landlord's fields; in return, they received their huts and gardens, plus a set (but always small) portion of the lord's harvest. Lowest of all were *slaves*, who possessed no strips, no rights, owed all their labor to their lord, and survived on whatever food the landlord decided to give them.

The baronial *demesne*—the portion of the manor on which the peasants worked in return for their strips and tenements—included more than just the lord's share of the grain fields. It comprised parts of the meadow, woodland, and stream, measured by his right to a certain percentage of the hay produced, of grazing rights, of forest produce (timber, fruits, nuts, and absolute right to all the animals inhabiting the forest), and of the fish catch. The demesne included the manor's mills and ovens, too; peasants had to pay a fee in order to use them, and they were absolutely forbidden to use any others. These monopolized services were known in France as *banalities* (from Latin *bannum*, meaning "a command that must be obeyed").

Peasants fell under their lords' power in other ways, too. They owed an extra payment of a dozen eggs to the lord on Easter Sunday, and of a tributary goose on Christmas—the origins of our own practice of Easter eggs and Christmas geese.[5] The surviving family members of a peasant who died owed an extra tax to the landlord for the inconvenience caused him by losing the dead peasant's labor. A peasant girl who wanted to marry a peasant living on another lord's manor had to pay a fee for depriving the lord of the service of the children produced by the union; despite

---

5. The colloquial English phrase that a person's "goose is cooked"—to designate that someone is in trouble—originates here, too. The implication is that one's propitiatory gift has already been consumed and that one had better come up with another way of appeasing one's master or else expect the worst.

the popularity of the idea in novels and films, manorial lords did not have a right to sleep with a peasant bride on her wedding night.

Not all peasants lived under these draconian conditions, however. In the eleventh and twelfth centuries a wide scattering of so-called *free villages* came into existence, established by various figures (usually kings but also lesser nobles) in order to encourage clearing of the land and resettlement. One of the earliest of these was the village of Lorris in northern France, which King Louis VI (r. 1108–1137) established around 1115. It provided a model for many later communities. According to its founding charter:

> I [Louis] grant that anyone who lives in the parish of Lorris shall be required to pay only six pennies of rent for his house and for each arpent[6] of land he farms in that parish.
>
> No one in Lorris shall be required to pay any tariff or surcharge for his food, nor pay any tax for measuring the grain he produces by the labor of his own hands and his own animals, or for the wine he produces from his own vineyards.
>
> No one who farms in Lorris shall be vulnerable to losing his farm through fines, unless he has been fined for an offence against me the King.
>
> No one, not even I myself, shall have the right to demand a tallage[7] of the men of Lorris, nor to demand any other aid.
>
> No one in Lorris shall be compelled to work for me, except for once a year, in order to cart my wine to the city of Orléans. But even so, only those who possess wagons and horses and who have been explicitly summoned shall be required to do this.
>
> If anyone should desire to sell his belongings in Lorris he may do so, and with the proceeds of the sale he may freely and peaceably leave the village if he so desires, unless he is charged with a crime in the parish.

No fewer than twenty-nine other protections were specified in the charter, regarding timber rights, freedom to marry, the holding of fairs and markets, and many other matters. One of the most influential of these protections, one that had important repercussions for northern society as it was copied in other charters, established the free village as a safe haven for runaways from manorial farms.

> Anyone who lives in Lorris for a period of one year and one day without a claim for his return [by his original landlord], unless a warrant for his arrest has been issued by myself or one of my agents, from that day forward shall remain a free man and may not henceforth be disturbed.

From the time a manor-based peasant society emerged, elements already existed within it to weaken some of its bonds.

---

6. An *arpent* was a unit of land roughly equal to one-third of a modern acre.
7. *Tallage* was an arbitrary tax that manorial landlords could impose on their peasants at any time and in any amount, for any reason.

But farmers, whether serfs or free, did not comprise the entire population of manors. Other figures stood somewhat outside the manorial system while nevertheless contributing to it in indirect ways. Manors were set up by design as self-sufficient entities; everything needed to support the populace was ideally produced on the manor: food, clothing, tools, wine. Trade with the outside world was a benefit whenever there was a surplus of goods, but a manor that *depended* on trade for its livelihood was a manor that was not wholly independent—and hence not what the landlord desired for himself. To mitigate this potential weakness, landlords commonly tried to form ties with some of those tradesmen who formed a conduit with the outside world. Transient shepherds and professional woodsmen were two such figures. Shepherds, if they were lucky, owned their own flocks and spent the months between May and September in highlands well above most farms and hence outside the jurisdiction (de facto if not de jure) of the manorial lords. They lived in huts or tents, tended their sheep and goats, manufactured cheese, and gathered whatever they could of durable forest fruits like chestnuts. When the winter frosts approached, they led their flocks down toward the plains where they traded their cheeses and fruits, sheared their sheep, and sold their wool to the landlords. With the cash they earned they were able to negotiate terms for staying on as renters through the winter in the local village, before leaving again in the spring for the hills. Since herders tended to follow a variety of circuits year after year, they avoided becoming dependents of any given lord. Moreover, their contact with numerous villages made them distributors of news, gossip, and folklore—reason for their reputation as sly operators and mischief-makers. Woodsmen's lives followed roughly the same pattern. Their work was also seasonal but it was more inclined to fixed cycles than was flock-tending. Woodsmen engaged principally in woodcutting—whether lumber for construction or firewood for burning—and in the production of charcoal. They worked whenever possible in forests outside the domain of the local lords and brought their goods in to the village market whenever they had a sufficient quantity. Numerous trips were possible in a given year, and the demand for wood was constant. Like the shepherds, the woodsmen could spend the winter months on a manor, hiring out their services in return for room and board.

The essential thing to bear in mind is that the manors of the central Middle Ages formed the fundamental unit of society: Those who lived on a manor were bound together by legal, economic, social, and family ties. A farmer defined his identity by being a part of a specific family, a laborer for a particular landlord, a contributor to a unique rural community, and a member of a discrete parish. One's connections—or *connected-ness*, to use a better term—established who one was and the position one held in the world. The notion of Christendom so carefully promoted by the Carolingians, of a world made purposeful and orderly by membership in a larger cohesive whole, found its first concrete expression in the medieval manor and to a lesser extent in the free villages: a composite whole, an organic unity in which every life was given purpose by its function within the collective entity. The physical reality never lived up to the glossy ideal, but the ideal served a purpose nevertheless. The agrarian world that emerged from the rural-manorial reconstruction provided the essential material foundation for everything else that medieval civilization achieved.

CHANGES ON THE SEA

Changes in Mediterranean life were no less dramatic and far-reaching than continental change, although the general trend in the south was to reinvigorate an urban-commercial scene that had never altogether disappeared but had only abated. Far less *fundamental* change took place here. The decline of the south in the aftermath of the Carolingians had been extensive. Population levels fell sharply, in some cities (most notably, Rome itself) to a level only one-fourth their former size; extensive areas of these cities came to resemble "ghost towns." Buildings, without inhabitants to maintain them, fell into disuse and crumbled, and many towns took on the aura of vast ruins. But as with other periods of decline, it is easy to overstate the damage. Historians tend to have a flair for the dramatic and often rev up their rhetoric when talking about crises and catastrophes, so it is important to maintain a sober view.

Many factors contributed to the Mediterranean revival, but perhaps the most significant was the breakup of the Islamic empire. We have already discussed this somewhat, but a quick review and a bit more detail may prove helpful. The Islamic empire under the Umayyad caliphs (661–750) looked impressive as an entity on a map, stretching as it did from Spain to India, but it held myriad fault lines that kept imperial power and the process of Islamicization itself somewhat tenuous. By the end of the eighth century, the great bulk of the empire's population remained non-Muslim. Christians comprised by far the largest portion of the non-Muslim majority in the western half of the empire; a sizable Jewish population existed as well. Pagans were few, since the Qur'an enjoined pious Muslims to put them to death if they refused immediate acceptance of Islam. There is little reason to believe that those pagans who, under threat of execution, adopted the new faith, were any more authentically Muslim than the early Germanic converts who embraced Christianity because their kings ordered them to do so were authentically Christian. Relations between the Muslim rulers and their non-Muslim subjects remained tense. Just as tense, though, were relations with their Muslim but non-Arab subjects who saw no reason why adopting Islam had to entail political subjection to a foreign Arab elite. The Umayyad state consisted of a thin over-grid of an ethnically Arab military caste that monopolized political power, dominated the schools and mosques, and controlled the economy. Strong currents of animosity flowed underneath, however.

Matters changed dramatically with the replacement of the Umayyads by the Abbasids, who held the caliphate from 750 to 1258. The Abbasid dynasts were themselves Arab but they energetically promoted the advance of ethnic Persians at the caliphal court and in the leading Islamic schools. The resulting "Persianization" of the empire was symbolized by the transfer of the imperial capital from Damascus to Baghdad. To protect themselves against an Arab backlash, the Abbasids recruited soldiers on a large scale from the Turks who inhabited the central Asian steppe, and thus brought another non-Arab group into the center of Islamic power.

Many traditional Arab elites, especially those in the western reaches of the empire, deeply resented this eastward drift and responded by breaking away from the empire altogether and establishing independent states of their own. (The fact that the Abbasids sent out agents from Baghdad to assassinate all the remaining members of the Umayyad family did not help to ease tensions.) Secession followed secession, and the political unity of the Islamic world came to an end. The first splinter state to declare independence from Baghdad was Muslim Spain, in 756. Others followed quickly. The Rustamid dynasty, in modern-day Algeria, broke away in 779. The Idrisids established an independent state in Morocco in 789. The Aghlabids in Tunisia seceded in 800 and their armies quickly moved northward to conquer Sicily and parts of southern Italy. The Tulunids created an independent state in Egypt in 868, only to be quickly succeeded by a dynasty known as the Fatimids in 905.[8] Once the political fracturing began, there seemed no way to stop it. These smaller states, moreover, stood exposed to all of the ethnic, tribal, and religious tensions that roiled within them. Some states took harsher positions toward their Christian and Jewish subjects and began to impose stricter controls on them; some sought greater conciliation with their non-Arab Muslim subjects and opened the doors to power to them; some grew even more rigidly pro-Arab in their policies. Religious rivalries also came into play, as some of these dynasties—such as the Fatimids in Egypt—introduced and enforced Shi'ite Islamic practices, as opposed to the more mainstream Sunni Islam. In a brief period, in other words, the Islamic world faced a series of critical changes in and challenges to its way of life.

Few of the new princedoms were large enough or stable enough to be economically self-sufficient, a situation that led to the gradual erosion of the economic blockade that had long existed between the Muslim and Christian worlds. Under the Umayyads, trade with the Latin west had been forbidden, and this boycott—which, like all boycotts, had never been adhered to absolutely—was one of the principal causes of the economic and demographic decline of Mediterranean Europe. Commercial relations with Christendom did not reappear overnight; religious hatred is not so easily overcome. Another contributing element was the simple fact that Europe in the ninth and tenth centuries produced little that the Islamic states to the south were interested in. The consistent agricultural surplus produced by eleventh-century manors changed that, however. By the start of the eleventh century, more or less constant commercial contact was underway, and the reignition of

---

8. Some secessions occurred in the eastern reaches of the empire as well. The Samanids in Khurasan (what is today the eastern part of Iran and the western part of Afghanistan) broke away in 819 and the Saffanids (near what is today Pakistan) declared independence in 867.

the economy of Mediterranean Europe began. The first Christian cities to benefit from the breakup of the economic blockade—Venice, Pisa, Genoa, Marseilles, Naples, Palermo, and Barcelona—became the dominant economic powers in the Christian world in the twelfth and thirteenth centuries.

Developments in the Byzantine Empire also had important implications for the overall Mediterranean. Encroachments in the Balkans by numerous Slavic and Bulgarian peoples, and the establishment of a powerful new kingdom by the "people of Rus" (the early Russians) with its capital in Kiev drew Byzantine attention northward into the Eurasian land mass. Under the Macedonian emperors, whose dynasty lasted from 867 to 1025, Constantinople's might extended to the lower Danube while commerical and religious ties were established throughout the Black Sea. The Bulgar kingdom was established in the provinces of Transylvania and Wallachia, and while the Bulgars resisted Byzantine efforts to subdue them politically, they remained open to trade with Constantinople. Under their king Boris they converted to Orthodox Christianity in 865. Boris' son and successor Simeon (d. 927) lived in the Byzantine capital for several years and was educated in Byzantine law. Simeon's son Peter (r. 927–969) married the granddaughter of the emperor. But as the Bulgars fell increasingly under the cultural and religious sway of the Greeks, their political destiny did so, too. The greatest of the Byzantine Macedonian emperors, Basil II (r. 976–1025), ended Bulgarian independence by overrunning the region with a brutally efficient army that earned him the grim nickname "the Bulgar-Slayer."

At roughly the same time, Byzantium's influence began to stretch northward into Russia. This may have been inevitable, since the region of southern Russia—a large, open, and easily traversable plain—comprised one of the main conduits that had brought Asian nomadic groups into the western world. Most of the chain-reaction migrations that had led to Rome's fall and the rise of Germanic Europe can be traced to the region, so the Byzantines, if they hoped to stabilize their northern border, had to establish some sort of influence in the area. In the mid-seventh century, when Heraclius was fighting off the Muslims and Persians, an Asiatic group called the *Khazars* subdued all the territory from the lower Volga river to the mouth of the Don and Dniester rivers.[9] The Khazars treated the indigenous peoples with surprising tolerance, especially after their conversion to Judaism, but the local tribes nevertheless searched for aid against them. They turned to the Swedish Vikings who, unlike the Danish and Norwegian adventurers who had beset Europe, had raided eastward through the Baltic Sea and established settlements in northernmost Russia, around the city of Novgorod. By the middle of the eighth century, large numbers of Swedes had migrated to the south, assimilated with local Slavic groups, and began to call themselves *Rus*. By 878 the Swedish rulers in the north and the Swedish-Slavic Rus of the south had united and built a vast, though

---

9.   That is roughly the triangular region from Moscow to Stalingrad [Volgograd] to Odessa on a modern map—although those cities did not exist at the time or were little more than tiny settlements.

loosely organized, kingdom and established Kiev as their capital. Within another century, the last pockets of Khazar power were destroyed. The Kievan kingdom lasted until the arrival of the Mongols under Ghenghis Khan in the early thirteenth century.

The Kievan rulers did all they could to strengthen ties with Constantinople, which further drew Byzantine attention northward. Russia traded raw forestry products—furs, honey, wax, and slaves—for Byzantine wine, textiles, and jewelry. Russian expansion into the Crimea gave it control of an important grain-producing region whose exports helped feed the Greeks after they lost most of Asia Minor to the Turks in the eleventh century. Basil II, taking a break from Bulgar-slaying, negotiated a marriage alliance whereby his sister wed the Russian king Vladimir I (r. 980–1015) on the condition that the Russian ruler accept baptism into the Orthodox Church. Thus began the Christianization of Russia.

By the mid-eleventh century, the Byzantine empire was larger and stronger than it had been in five hundred years, but in the process it had reoriented itself away from Europe and the central Mediterranean, and toward Asia. The Byzantines' decision effectively to cede control of the sea-lanes to the Muslims and Latin Europeans opened the gates to the creation of a new maritime world.

A MARITIME SOCIETY EMERGES

The society that emerged in southern Europe in the eleventh and twelfth centuries differed little, in any fundamental sense, from the Mediterranean society of earlier times. It remained a world based on urban life, in which industry and commerce reigned supreme and a person's social position was determined as much by the role he played in communal life as by birth or inheritance. A land-based aristocracy did indeed exist and its members dominated the rural zones that surrounded each urban center, but within the cities themselves the real sites of political-economic power and social-cultural influence lay among the mercantile, financial, and industrial elites.

The revival began with a pronounced eastward focus. This was, to an extent, traditional, since the eastern half of the Mediterranean had always dominated commercial life. The recovery of Byzantine might—much of it at the expense of splintering Islam—also played a key role. By the middle of the eleventh century, Byzantine conquests and reconquests had doubled the empire's size from its eighth-century nadir. Armies organized by the *theme* system had pushed far into the eastern and southern regions previously lost to the Umayyads, and they restored Byzantine rule over all of Asia Minor, Armenia, Syria, and the northern half of Mesopotamia. This restoration brought the ancient trading cities of Antioch, Edessa, Melitene, and Trebizond back into the Byzantine fold and restored the empire's direct contact with the transcontinental trade routes. But Byzantine armies had also moved far northward and westward until by 1025 they had conquered the entire Balkan peninsula, taking all of what is today Greece, Albania, Macedonia, and a large portion of today's Bulgaria. With this newfound strength, the Byzantines stood once again in a position to participate fully in Mediterranean trade.

But in a different way from before. Greek military advances had taken place almost entirely on land. Ever since the Muslim armies had overrun Egypt in the seventh century, the Byzantines had failed to maintain any significant presence on the sea. A defeated maritime empire had become a successful land-based one. So when the empire reestablished commercial contact with the Latin west in the early eleventh century, traders from the west were able to dominate the shipping that went in and out of Byzantine ports. Venice seized the chance first, with the Genoese and Pisans close behind. These traders and financiers quickly built up a large seaborne commercial network. They brought Italian grain, wine, timber, textiles, and salt to the Byzantines, and their ships returned with eastern silks, spices, gold, and slaves. They traded for grain, oil, fruit, and wine with the Muslim states of Palestine, Egypt, Algeria, and Tunis (the Muslims of the Levant produced wine of good quality, but since their religion forbade drinking it they had plenty to trade with).

As the brakes on Mediterranean trade relaxed, more and more western cities joined in the action. Important new economic centers arose in towns like Amalfi, Gaeta, and Naples. In the western Mediterranean, cities like Marseilles, Montpellier, and Barcelona stirred to new life as they gradually opened ties with some of the western Islamic states. Southern Europe also began to reestablish links with the north. With new markets emerging and with the means to deliver their products increasingly available, northern traders began to cast about for resources that could produce a profit. Chiefly, all they could find at first were raw materials, especially minerals and wool. France, northern Germany, and Scandinavia began to mine iron; the people of southern Germany mined lead and copper; the English mined coal. Northern timber remained highly prized and made its way southward. But more than anything else the northern world produced wool. Most of the best of it came from England, whence it was shipped across the Channel to Flanders. The Flemish then produced finished cloth and sent it out along their own trade routes, selling some of it back to the English but also trading in the Mediterranean itself. Throughout most of the eleventh century relatively few people in the north could afford the higher-priced luxury goods of the south, and so little of those commodities sailed northward. The large salt pans that dot much of the Mediterranean coastline, however, produced great quantities of salt, which the north used for food preservation.[10]

---

10. Another note on food: In northern Europe, since few people ate fresh fish, the most common types of dried fish were *saltfish* and *stockfish*. Saltfish consisted of cod or haddock that were properly salted—a fairly long process. But since the normal practice of the north was not to gut or clean the fish before salting (so as not to risk the fish spoiling before the salting was complete), peasants often preferred stockfish, which were gutted, cleaned, and dried in the sun, without the use of salt. The trouble with stockfish, though, was their rock-like texture. Women preparing stockfish for dinner usually had to pound them with a mallet for an hour before they were edible.

A variety of new technologies made this east-west and north-south trade possible. Shipbuilding, in particular, underwent a significant change. As larger and
larger ships became necessary to deal efficiently with the increased volume of
trade, the traditional design of trade vessels had to alter. (The great slave-oared
warships of the ancient world had long since disappeared.) Until about 1100 most
western ships were of modest size, had relatively shallow hulls, and were guided
by an external steerboard that hung over the right-hand side of the ship—the origin of our term *starboard*. Control of the ship depended on the sheer physical
strength of the sailor manning the steerboard, a difficult matter on even a relatively tranquil sea like the Mediterranean. However, the development of a guiding rudder, firmly embedded in the keel, gave greater control over the vessel and
allowed shipbuilders to construct larger boats that were driven by enlarged
broadsails. Prior to this, ships had bobbed too wildly on the sea and were too easily upset by the winds to permit reliance on broadsails. Larger, stabler, and faster
ships thus made it possible to deliver larger cargoes in a cost-effective manner.
From the Muslims of Egypt, who had learned the technology in their trade contacts through the Red Sea and into south Asia, the Latins learned the use of lateen
sails—the triangular sails at a ship's bow—that helped control the drive produced
by broadsails. Until the advent of the astrolabe in the twelfth century and of the
compass in the thirteenth, however, navigation itself remained much as it had
been before, with ships steering by landmarks instead of the stars and seldom
sailing out of sight of land, but around this time Latin sailors did begin to draft
maps of the Mediterranean, which recorded distance, currents, and water-depths
and made navigation easier.

While reinvigorated commerce launched an economic boom, dangers increased as well. Piracy remained widespread throughout the Mediterranean and
threatened merchants with huge losses. Merchants were frequently people of real
courage, but few were willing to risk being cast into the sea or cut in two by a pirate's sword. Others might have possessed the physical bravery to resist attack but
lacked the capital to occasion attack. And so the Latins developed another new
technology: a financial instrument called a *commenda* contract. The earliest known
reference to a commenda dates to 976, in Venice, and the earliest surviving actual
document dates to 1073 (also in Venice); the device may have roots in earlier practices among the Muslims and Byzantines, however. In its typical form, a commenda contract was an agreement between an "investing merchant" (called a
commendator in Latin) and an "acting merchant" (or *tractator*) for a single commercial venture. The investing merchant provided the capital and the acting merchant
provided the service, and upon the end of the venture each partner received a previously agreed-upon portion of the profits. In case of commercial failure, the investing merchant assumed responsibility for loss of capital, while the acting
merchant lost his labor (and, in the case of pirate attack, possibly his life). It was a
crude instrument, but it linked those with capital but without the willingness to

An astrolabe crafted in Cordoba in 1154. The just-visible
Latin inscriptions were made in the fourteenth
century by a later owner.
Source: Giraudon / Art Resource, NY

face dangers at sea or in a foreign land, with those who lacked the capital but possessed the willingness to head into the fray. Later technologies such as the letter of credit, useful for those wary of carrying large amounts of money, and the policies issued by an embryonic insurance industry, gradually made international trade that much safer.[11]

Piracy was endemic since it was easy, profitable, and was technically not illegal. Even with the new advances in ship-design, it was no difficult matter to stop a

---

11.   These later devices were all in common use by the end of the thirteenth century. They too had Muslim and Byzantine antecedents. The English word *check*—as in a personal checking account—derives from the classical Arabic word *saqq*.

merchant vessel on the sea; all one had to do was cut down or set afire its mainsail and the ship could go no further. Stranded on the sea, a merchant had no option but to give up his goods and money. Moreover, pirates could attack with relative impunity. The sea beyond the harbors, being under no government's jurisdiction, was literally a place without law—and hence no activity there could be illegal. Most pirates were themselves merchants, and piracy was regarded as one of the natural risks of conducting business; a merchant assumed that risk in deciding to undertake maritime trade in the first place. So long as pirates did not commit unnecessary violence and did not attack ships in harbor, they were regarded as extra-legal (as opposed to illegal) nuisances. No particular opprobrium was attached to them or their way of making a living. As early as 1100 some figures even signed legal documents with the notation "I [John], pirate from Pisa."

Given the constancy of their contact with one another, Mediterranean cities grew into polyglot multi-ethnic emporia. A visitor to eleventh-century Venice, for example, would find the streets and markets filled with Greeks, Egyptians, Syrians, Maghribi Arabs, and a host of Jews from around the sea basin. Since rivalries and hatreds lurked just beneath the surface, most cities, as they grew in wealth and size, found it necessary to divide their civic territory into discrete neighborhoods. Merchants from abroad won special privileges that granted them the right to inhabit these merchant-residences, trade in the markets, and have access to the harbors. These privileges were jealously guarded. The maritime economy was far from being an entirely open market; monopolies were secured whenever possible, wages and prices determined by negotiation and enforced by law. Rather than enjoying an atmosphere of tolerance and free exchange of goods by merchants eager simply to do business together, the cities of the south were rife with tensions; if anything, these towns had an atmosphere of controlled violence. Riots and street-fights were common. Urban institutions that could keep such violence in check were slow to develop and were widely distrusted. Hence a social code of *honor* developed among the urban elites, a notion of being true to one's word and willing to exact personal justice. A merchant proved his honorable nature by fulfilling his contracts with his clients and being willing to hire thugs to wreak revenge on anyone who meddled in his affairs or sullied his reputation of being a person who delivered what he promised.

Most Mediterranean cities operated as communes or urban republics, with elected officials serving set terms of office: executive officers, treasurers, public utilities managers, judges, rudimentary police corps, sanitation engineers, etc. Most positions tended to circulate among a clique of leading families within each city; but the social and political scene was often complicated by the presence of older landed families who controlled much of the farmland surrounding each municipality. Whenever one refers to the leading magnates of a city one is talking about a diverse group made up of rural aristocrats, well-to-do merchants, professionals (such as bankers or lawyers), and members of leading artisanal guilds. Each of these groups had their own privileges and customs, which made administering the cities quite a challenge. Nevertheless, southern cities from the late eleventh century on witnessed quite explosive growth, as shown most clearly by the ever-expanding fortified walls that surrounded each site.

The reignition of commerce gave a strong impetus to the rise of these new commercial elites. Scores of newly wealthy and influential families emerged in the cities and seized the reins of urban government. While the urban commune required some time to develop fully, its earliest forms can be seen as early as the mid-eleventh century in northern Italy. Government began to follow principles of representation, and many cities established permanent embassies with their most important overseas trading partners. These cities provided a pattern for the development of northern cities as well, as the revival of Mediterranean trade gradually stimulated the growth of an urban-industrial sector in the feudal world of northern Europe. We will trace the details of these parallel and intersecting developments in the next chapter.

SUGGESTED READING

Texts

Guibert of Nogent. *Memoirs*.

Ordericus Vitalis. *Ecclesiastical History*.

Otto of Freising. *The Deeds of Frederick Barbarossa*.

Suger of St. Denis. *The Deeds of Louis the Fat*.

Source Anthologies

Davis-Weyer, Caecilia. *Early Medieval Art, 300–1150: Sources and Documents* (1986).

Lopez, Robert S., and Irving W. Raymond. *Medieval Trade in the Mediterranean World* (2000).

Pullan, Brian S. *Sources for the History of Medieval Europe from the Mid-Eighth to the Mid-Thirteenth Century* (1966).

Studies

Bartlett, Robert. *The Making of Europe: Conquest, Colonization, and Cultural Change, 950–1350* (1993).

Biddick, Kathleen. *The Other Economy: Pastoral Husbandry on a Medieval Estate* (1989).

Duby, Georges. *Rural Economy and Country Life in the Medieval West* (1968).

Fossier, Robert. *Peasant Life in the Medieval West* (1988).

Freedman, Paul. *Images of the Medieval Peasant* (1999).

———. *The Origins of Peasant Servitude in Medieval Catalonia* (1991).

Geary, Patrick J. *Phantoms of Remembrance: Memory and Oblivion and the End of the First Millennium* (1995).

Génicot, Léopold. *Rural Communities in the Medieval West* (1990).

Goetz, Hans-Werner. *Life in the Middle Ages: From the Seventh to the Thirteenth Century* (1993).

Haddad, Yvonne H., and Wadi Z. *Christian-Muslim Encounters* (1995).

Kaegi, Walter E. *Byzantium and the Early Islamic Conquests* (1995).

Kennedy, Hugh. *The Prophet and the Age of the Caliphates: The Islamic Near East from the Sixth to the Eleventh Centuries* (1986).

Lopez, Robert S. *The Commercial Revolution of the Middle Ages, 950–1350* (1971).

Miller, Edward, and John Hatcher. *Medieval England: Rural Society and Economic Change, 1086–1348* (1978).

Moore, R[obert] I. *The First European Revolution* (2000).

———. *The Formation of a Persecuting Society: Power and Deviance in Western Europe, 950–1250* (1987).

Morris, Rosemary. *Monks and Laymen in Byzantium, 843–1118* (1995).

Raftis, J. A. (ed.) *Pathways to Medieval Peasants* (1981).

Reynolds, Susan. *Kingdoms and Communities in Western Europe, 900–1300* (1984).

Rösener, Werner. *Peasants in the Middle Ages* (1992).

CHAPTER 9

A New Europe Emerges: North and South

The "great change" of the eleventh century did not create a new Europe—it created two new ones. The north developed as a rigidly hierarchical society in which status was determined, or was at least indexed, by the extent to which one owned, controlled, or labored on land, whereas the Mediterranean south developed a more fluid, and therefore more chaotic, world in which industry and commerce predominated and social status both reflected and resulted from the role that one played in the public life of the community. In other words, individual identity and social community in the north were established on a personal basis whereas in the south they were established on a civic basis. In the north, social identity for most people was defined by the relationships he or she had: as the vassal of Lord A, or the lord of vassal B, the tenant of landlord C, the husband of woman D, a member of parish E, under the authority of bishop F. In the south one was a citizen of a particular municipality, and was little else; social position for most was determined by what they accomplished with their free citizenship. Generalizations like this are always heavy-handed and we must be careful not to press the point too hard, but the fact remains that by the start of the twelfth century northern and southern Europe were very different places indeed. The Europeans themselves noticed it and commented on it.

Political dominance belonged to the north. Germany, France, and England had large populations and large armies that made them, in the political and military senses, the masters of western Europe. Organized by the practices known collectively as *feudalism* (which we will discuss in this chapter), these kingdoms emerged as powerful states with sophisticated machineries of government. Their kings and queens were the leading figures of the age; their castles and cathedrals stood majestically on the landscape as symbols of their might; their armies both energized and defined the age. Moreover, feudal society showed a remarkable ability to adapt to new needs by encouraging the parallel development of domestic urban life and commercial networks; in some regions of the north, in fact, feudal society may even have developed in response to the start of proto-urban trends. But southern Europe took the lead in economic and cultural life. Though the leading Mediterranean states were small in size, they were considerably wealthier than their northern counterparts. The city of Palermo in the twelfth century, for example, alone generated four times the commercial tax revenue of the entire kingdom of England. Southern communities also possessed polyglot urbane cultures that made them the intellectual and artistic leaders of the age. Levels of general literacy in the south far surpassed those of the north, and the people of the south put that learning to use on a large scale. Science, mathematics, poetry, law, historical writing, religious speculation, translation, and classical studies all began to flourish; throughout most of the twelfth century most of Latin Christendom's best brains flocked to southern Europe.

So too did a lot of the north's soldiers. One of the central themes of the political history of the twelfth century was the continual effort by the northern kingdoms to extend their control southward in the hope of tapping into the Mediterranean bonanza. The German emperors from Otto I on, for example, struggled ceaselessly to control the cities of northern Italy, since those cities generated more revenue than all of rural Germany combined. The Capetian kings of France used every means at their disposal—from marrying southern heiresses to leading crusader armies into Languedoc—to push the lower border of their kingdom to the Mediterranean shoreline. And the Normans who conquered and ruled England established outposts of Norman power in Sicily and southern Italy; the English kings also hoped or claimed at various times to be, either through money- or marriage-diplomacy, the rulers of several Mediterranean sites. But as the northern world pressed southward, so too did some of the cultural norms and social mechanisms of the south spread northward. Over the course of the twelfth century, the feudal kingdoms witnessed a proliferation of cities modeled in large degree on the municipalities of the south. Contact with the merchants and financiers of the Mediterranean led to the development of northern industry and international trade (which helped to pay for many of those castles and cathedrals mentioned earlier). And education spread as well, culminating in the foundation of what is arguably medieval Europe's greatest invention: the university. The relationship of north and south was symbiotic, in other words, and the contrast between them was more one of differences in degree than of polar opposition. The interplay between these two worlds, and between the urban-republican and rural-hierarchical elements within both of them, provides the focus for this chapter.

THE RISE OF FEUDAL SOCIETY

Feudalism is a term that our popular culture more or less automatically associates with the medieval world, or at least the northern part of it. We do so at our peril, however, for a simple reason: Feudalism never existed. How can this be? Have historians simply been wrong all this time? Is feudalism somehow a giant hoax that has fooled everyone who has studied the Middle Ages, a convenient fiction created by frustrated medievalists intent upon imposing order on a disordered world? Hardly. While feudalism as a coherent, conscious, and cogent plan for how to model society never existed, eleventh- and twelfth-century society in northern

Europe certainly possessed and became characterized by *feudal relations*—that is to say, relationships that were based on the idea of mutual obligation and service in the public arena. The nature of those relations differed considerably, however, between England, France, and Germany, and often did so even within those realms.

The basic idea has a long genealogy. A hierarchical notion of social organization, whether expressed as the relations between patron and client or between chieftain and warrior, extends far back in both the classical and Germanic traditions. Individuals desiring protection or a position in society could attach themselves to powerful figures who possessed either great wealth, social stature, or political might and thereby acquire privileges that would otherwise be beyond their reach. In continental Europe people increasingly became identified, and their positions in society determined, by the nature of their relationships with powerful others who had lands to bestow in return for recognition of their lordship. Among the ancient Germans, according to Tacitus, a warrior established his worth by the extent of his service to his chieftain and received in turn a measure of status and legal protection—although it certainly stretches things a bit to trace feudal relations all the way back to the first century. It is wrong to assume, too, that these relationships necessarily originated between established and mighty great lords on the one hand, and weak though ambitious minor ones on the other. During the long disintegration of the Carolingian Empire, vulnerable warrior-landholders sought such protective relationships from each other just as much as dislocated peasants sought out well-armed landlords who might protect them from the dangers that abounded. In fact, as early as 847 the three sons of Louis the Pious, in a rare moment of accord, urged that "every free man in the realm should choose the lord he prefers—whether that be one of us three or one of our faithful subjects." Such relationships offered neighboring barons a means of resolving disputes of one kind or another without taking recourse to drawn swords. But the relationships were also often fragile and filled with suspicion. For example, when Rollo, the leader of a large Viking band that had agreed to foreswear further invasions of France in return for the grant of lands to settle (what became known as the duchy of Normandy), formalized his feudal relationship with the late Carolingian ruler Charles the Simple in 911, he objected to the expected ritual that he, as the enfeoffed partner in the relationship, should express his gratitude by kissing Charles' foot. All sorts of trouble broke out.

> But Rollo was unwilling to kiss the king's foot, which prompted the bishops to say: "Whoever receives such a fief needs to kiss the king's foot." Rollo replied: "I've never bent my knee before anyone and I will not kiss any man's foot!" Nevertheless, he was moved by the pleadings of all the Frankish soldiers, and so he ordered one of his [Viking] warriors to kiss Charles' foot in his place. This soldier immediately grabbed the king's foot and lifted it to his lips while standing abruptly upright and kissed it while the king fell over backwards.

Things usually went more smoothly than that. After all, by entering a feudal relationship a warrior received legitimacy, assistance, and a recognized position in society.

A Flemish writer named Galbert of Bruges recorded the homage ceremony performed in 1127 between the local count, named William, and some local knights.

> These men performed their homage in the following way: First the count asked each one if he was willing to become completely his [William's] man. Each replied: "I am so willing." Then each man clasped his hands together and placed them between the count's hands, where they were then kissed. Each man who performed this act of homage then pledged his fealty to one of the count's agents, in these words: "I swear by my faith that I will from this point on remain faithful to Count William and will stay entirely true to this vow of homage to him against every other person, doing so in good faith and without deceit." Each man then swore his oath on the relics of the saints. Finally the count, who held a ceremonial wand, granted investitures to everyone who gave these assurances of their homage and fealty.

These passages introduce us to some new vocabulary: *fief, homage, fealty,* and *investiture.* Generally speaking, these terms designate the principal elements of the feudal relationship; but interpreting their meaning is a tricky business, for feudal customs did not become clear in their specific legal meaning until fairly late into the twelfth century. A fief was usually a quantity of land—sometimes an individual estate, or, as in Rollo's case, an entire duchy—that the lord assigned to his vassal in return for that vassal's service. The lord, in making the bequest, gave his vassal a means of support and legitimated his possession of the land.[1] The vassal who received the fief could usually parcel out smaller parts of it to other knights who would then become the vassals of the first vassal (who was, to them, their lord). This process became known as *subinfeudation.* A fief did not necessarily have to be a piece of land, though: it could be a government position, an annuity, a tax exemption, or a set of economic privileges. The oaths of homage and fealty that formalized the relationship guaranteed the allegiance of the person receiving the fief to the person who bestowed it. One became literally someone else's "man."[2] The lord then performed an act of investiture by handing over to his new "man" a clod of earth that symbolically represented the fief being granted. As in any type of contract, the specifics of feudal relationships varied tremendously from occasion to occasion as lords and vassals kept trying, naturally enough, to negotiate the best deals for themselves. Bishop Fulbert of Chartres, writing in the year 1020, described the general expectations of lord-vassal ties in this way:

> Anyone who swears fealty to a lord ought always to keep six things in mind: to do no harm, to pose no threat to safety, to behave honorably, to be useful, to make things easier, and to be practical. "To do no harm," meaning that he ought never to cause his lord bodily injury; "to pose no threat to safety," meaning that he ought never to harm his lord by betraying his confidence or the defenses on which he depends for security; "to behave honorably," meaning he ought never to undermine the lord's work of doing justice or any of his other

---

1. The English word *lord* derives from the Anglo-Saxon word *hlaford,* which meant "bread-giver."
2. *Homage* is linked etymologically with the Latin word *homo,* meaning "man."

acts that pertain to his honor; "to be useful," meaning that he ought never to bring harm to the lord's property; "to make things easier," meaning that he ought never to make difficult those things which his lord can do easily; and "to be practical," meaning he ought never to make impossible for his lord that which is possible.

But while it is proper that a faithful vassal should avoid injuring his lord in these ways, he does not deserve his fief if all he does is to avoid inflicting harm; some type of positive good must be done as well. Therefore it remains that a vassal ought faithfully to advise and assist his lord in all six matters mentioned above if he wishes to be considered worthy of his benefice and secure in the fealty he has sworn. The lord, for his part, ought to act similarly toward his faithful vassal in all six matters—and any lord who fails to do so will rightly be considered guilty of bad faith, just as a vassal, if he should be found avoiding or conspiring to avoid his obligations to the lord, would be considered guilty of treachery and perjury.

Fulbert's protestations aside, the most striking aspect of these relationships is their negative character. They are far clearer on what the members of the contract may *not* do to each other than on what they may do or must do. This suggests that in their earliest form, feudal relations were loose alliances between equals or near-equals instead of hierarchically determined and legally precise arrangements between superiors and inferiors. The Latin word used for "fiefs" in the tenth and eleventh centuries *precaria*, from which the English word *precarious* derives, drives home the point. The loose and amorphous quality of these relationships would change, however, in the twelfth century when feudal relations took on a more clearly articulated hierarchical quality.

At all times, though, a vassal's chief obligation to his lord was military service. The better service one could render, the greater the fief one could expect to receive. Feudal society thus developed, in other words, as a military regime—a society organized for war. And wars certainly did abound. But it is not at all clear that the growing network of feudal relations was the cause of all that violence; the aim of feudal connections, after all, was to control violence and pacify the countryside by ending disputes that had lasted decades, even centuries, over who governed any given territory. The collapse of the Carolingian Empire had left the notion of political legitimacy wide open. Feudal relations formed a way of rebuilding a institutional framework to establish a new standard of legitimacy. But a vassal's military service to his lord was sharply limited. By the end of the eleventh century, a norm had developed that put the service owed at just forty days per year. For the rest of the year, each vassal remained on his fief, governing its people, watching over its manors and villages, collecting taxes, and dispensing justice.

A vassal's second chief obligation was to attend his lord's court. In the first place, merely by answering a summons to attend court, the vassal was recognizing the lord's authority; but there was more to it than that. The lord's court provided the chief venue for making judicial decisions and debating political matters. The lord was required to ask his vassals' advice on important affairs of state, but he was not obliged to follow it. Vassals also owed their lord a variety of special payments called *reliefs*. These varied from place to place but were commonly used to defray the costs of certain public ceremonies and special projects such as the construction of a lord's new castle, the marriage of his daughter, the knighting of his son, or the ransoming of a lord taken captive by an enemy.

The system sounds fairly straightforward, but human relationships tend to become very complicated. Two vassals of one lord might, because of the equal amounts of service they perform, hold fiefs of comparable size and wealth, and therefore appear to be social equals. Yet one may have an aristocratic lineage extending back before Charlemagne, while the other may be a talented commoner raised to noble status by his knighting. Would society regard the patrician and the parvenu equally? Would they receive equal honor at court? Would their families be likely to intermarry? Other types of complications arose. Nothing prevented a man from becoming the vassal of multiple lords, thereby building up a whole string of fiefs. But what if his lords went to war with one another? On whose side would he fight?—and if he fought for one, would he necessarily forfeit the fiefs he held from the other?[3] Complications such as these, coupled with regional differences of nationalities, languages, customs, and geography made the feudal world a widely variegated and diverse place.

By the middle of the twelfth century, a new class consciousness gradually developed, a kind of *esprit de corps* that bound the feudal knights, culturally speaking, into a loose fraternity. This awareness of themselves as an elite brotherhood took the form of a distinctive code of behavior known as *chivalry*. Chivalry, like feudalism itself, meant different things at different times, but its foundational idea remained constant: No knight should violate his sense of honor by taking unfair advantage of another knight. In practice, this promise meant that knights were expected to fight fairly and openly on the field of battle and not to resort to ambush or treachery. A knight who struck down another was expected to spare his life; the vanquished knight was to be held in honorable captivity until he was ransomed. (A knight who struck down a common soldier, however, was free to butcher him if he wished.) In tournaments, spectacular occasions filled with contests, revelries, music, and mock fighting, knights contended with one another to win glory and renown;[4] tournaments also served as recruiting stations for lord-vassal relationships, where a landless knight seeking a fief and position in society could prove his prowess against others and thereby win the attention of an approving lord. Tournaments were among the most popular and important ceremonies of life. Chivalry also aimed to distinguish the

---

3.   This is the origin of *liege lordship*. Knights serving several lords were required to identify one of them as his "liege lord"—that is, the lord who took precedence over all others.
4.   The fighting was not always playful or staged. At a tournament in 1247 at Neuss, in western Germany, eighty knights were killed over the course of the festivities.

"true" rural nobility from the *nouveau riche* merchants who sought to set themselves up on country estates and join the aristocratic ranks: The ability to fight with exemplary bravery and honor, to trace one's descent from generations of Christian warriors, to display superior breeding and comportment, were useful tools of social exclusion.

The Church played a role in cultivating the chivalric ethic, too, although the Church was horrified by tournaments and constantly forbade them, a prohibition that everyone happily ignored. The emerging class of knights was a class of soldiers, after all, not of gentleman farmers; and soldiers, by training and (presumably) inclination, wage war. Indeed they had to, since their privileged positions were explicitly justified by their military service. The Church, responding to public demand, strove to tame their excesses and did so in part by promoting the cult of chivalric knighthood. A chivalrous knight, they preached, was one who fought to defend the poor, to promote justice, and to defend the faith, not merely to win renown as one who was good at swinging a sword or a battle-axe at someone else's head. The chivalric element of knighthood, in other words, derived from the *purpose* and *manner* of one's fighting and not from the fighting alone. Toward this end the Church supported the popular *Peace of God* movement, which aimed to protect peasants, pilgrims, clergy, women, and children from baronial attack, and later the *Truce of God*, which forbade fighting during certain seasons of the liturgical year (especially Lent and Advent) and on major feast days. Knights who cared more for action and booty than for Christian piety largely ignored such prohibitions, but the ideal of a "Christian knight" did gradually catch on over the course of the twelfth century. Here is how one cleric of the time, John of Salisbury (d. 1180), described such ideal knights:

> Now, just what is the function of these duly "ordained" soldiers? It is to defend the Church, to attack infidelity, to respect all clergy, to defend the poor against injury, to bring peace to the land—and then, as their oaths of fealty command, to shed their own blood for their brethren, even to lay down their lives for them, should it be necessary. Loud "Hosannas!" to the Lord are ever in their throats. The sharp swords in their hands are to bring punishment upon the [pagan] nations and reprove their people, to set their rulers in chains and their noble fighters in irons.
>
> What purpose does all this serve? Is it in order to gratify the knights' passion [for violence]? their vanity? their greed? their personal lust for glory? Not at all! It is rather that they might carry out the just judgments entrusted to them. In this way, each knight obeys not his own promptings but the commands of the Lord God, His holy angels, and His appointed rulers [on earth], to promote justice and the public good. . . . Knights who do these things are in fact saints.

The chivalric ethic thus sought one way to Christianize Europe's military caste, and to the extent that it did so it helped to promote peace and stability. But in the process, as we shall see in Chapter 10, it also militarized the Church itself, a phenomenon given its most notable expression in the Crusades.

THE FIRST GERMAN EMPIRE

Now that we have discussed some of the more general aspects of feudalism and chivalry we will turn to the specifics of how these elements played out in the principal feudalized states of the north. Then we will briefly examine the unique case of Spain (parts of which were, at one time or another, among both the most- and least-feudalized territories in all of Europe) and finish with the experiences of southern France and Italy.

When we turn to Germany, we encounter an immediate problem of terminology, for the territory that today comprises Germany was not called *Germania* in the eleventh century but was regarded as the easternmost reach of *Francia*. This had been one of the last regions added to the Carolingian Empire—remember that it had taken Charlemagne thirty-four years to defeat the Saxons—and was therefore also one of the last parts of Europe to be added to the world of Latin Christendom. By the eleventh century, this region extended only a bit further east than the upper reaches of the Elbe river; the border then stretched in a south-southeasterly direction to include the embryonic city of Vienna, then dropped abruptly south to reach the Adriatic Sea.[5] This geography meant two things: first, the area had a particularly thin veneer of meaningful Christianity among its rural peasantry; and secondly, its governmental traditions had never accorded well with the Carolingian system of appointing landed counts to administer the territory. Instead, the peoples of this region recognized the authority of traditional indigenous leaders (*duces*) who could trace their lineages back far into the tribal (meaning pre-Christian and pre-Carolingian) past.

As Carolingian power waned, the local strength of these *duces* (henceforth *dukes*, for simplicity's sake) increased accordingly. The last Carolingian in the east, Louis the Child, died in 911, which freed the dukes of Bavaria, Franconia, Saxony, Swabia, and Thuringia to elect their own "king of eastern Francia." They chose Conrad I, the duke of Franconia (r. 911–919). Not much is known about this arrangement but it may be the earliest example in the east of local lords electing to obey a superior lord in return for that over-lord's recognition. It is hard to tell what the relationship was since Conrad was on the scene so briefly, and besides, the dukes who elected him hardly listened to a word he said. After his death, the duke of Saxony, named Henry "the Fowler" for his love of hunting, succeeded to the throne (r. 919–936). Henry is the founder of what later became known as the *Saxon dynasty*, which survived as over-lords of "eastern Francia" until 1024. Henry had been Conrad's own personal choice for a successor, but the dukes and magnates formalized matters by acclaiming him as king since they wanted to avoid establishing the notion that the kingship was not theirs to award. They lived to regret their decision, though, because Henry proved quite successful at subduing the more inde-

---

5.   In other words, the area included roughly what is today eastern Germany and Austria and part of the Czech Republic, but excluded what is today Poland, Slovenia, Hungary, and all of the Balkans.

pendent-minded magnates. He also extended royal power eastward by fighting against the Slavs and Magyars. This policy of eastward expansion—what German historians refer to as the *Drang nach Osten*, or "Push to the East"—was a smart move. Henry understood that the best way to keep the East Frankish magnates in line was to increase his own personal wealth so that he could hire soldiers to serve him and free him of dependence on his ducal vassals. By moving into eastern Europe, he was able to place numerous Slavic and Magyar territories under his own personal lordship and to amass a large fortune. In the seventeen years he ruled, the number of manors owned by the crown increased from a mere five estates to nearly six hundred.

By far the most successful and most lucky of the Saxon kings was Henry's son Otto I "the Great" (r. 936–973). He inherited his father's aggressiveness and continued the eastern expansion, but Magyar and Slavic resistance grew accordingly and threatened to turn the tide against him. He needed a larger army but knew that he could not rely on his vassal-magnates to the west. Then, suddenly, his lucky day arrived. An enormous silver lode was discovered near Goslar in the Harz mountains, in the heart of Otto's Saxon duchy, and he became all at once the wealthiest man in northern Europe. Mercenary knights and would-be vassals flocked to him, and with these forces he was able to inflict a crushing defeat on the Magyars in 955 at the battle of Lechfeld. His power extended further and further eastward as he enfeoffed his new vassals and built a secure chain of fortified border towns. Otto also quickly brought some of the rebellious duchies to his west to heel and replaced the dukes in power there with several of his sons. His sons, though, rebelled against Otto on their own. Stung by this ingratitude, Otto initiated a dramatic new policy in the East Frankish variety of feudalism: He began to install archbishops, bishops, and abbots in his fiefs. Presumably churchmen would not have any children, ungrateful or otherwise, to inherit the fiefs and lead rebellions from them. Otto retained strict control over ecclesiastical appointments, and he used his influence to establish several important new bishoprics in the east, most notably at Magdeburg and Prague. In taking up this policy, Otto began to pattern himself after Charlemagne and to view himself as the great emperor's direct successor.

Otto's support of the German Church lead to the German Church's support of him. Throughout the tenth, eleventh, and twelfth centuries, the German prelates remained the most loyal of all the crown's subjects—even to the point, as we will discuss in detail in the next chapter, of supporting the German ruler against the pope himself. Like Charlemagne before him, Otto devoted himself to the cause of Christianizing the pagans under his control. Many pagans remained; in fact, they may even have made up fifty percent of his East Frankish and eastern European subjects. Court-directed missionary campaigns scoured the countryside for the rest of Otto's long reign.

Otto's last grand campaign was his effort to gain control of Italy. He succeeded in 961, when he invaded the peninsula at the request of Pope John XII (r. 955–964), who wanted Otto's help against a local political rival. Early in 962, John gave Otto

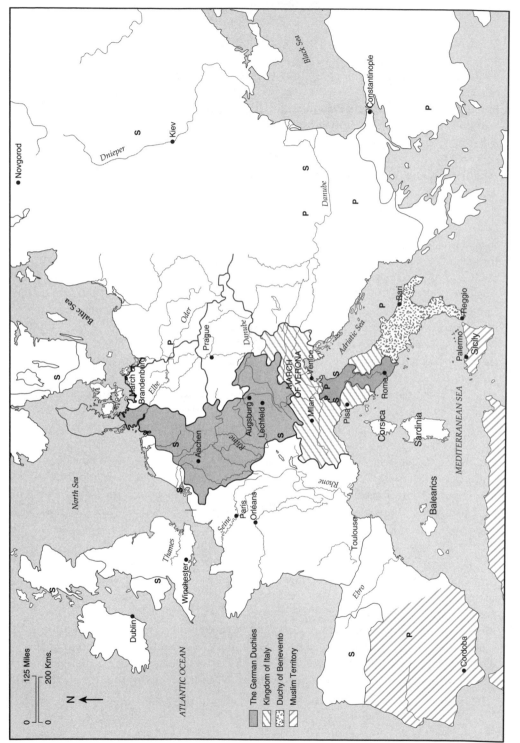

The Ottonian Empire, ca. 960.

the reward he had promised him as an enticement to march southward: the imperial title. Otto was now literally the successor of Charlemagne. Neither John nor Otto could agree on what this meant, however, and their brief alliance quickly fell apart. Otto believed (and all his successors as German emperor throughout the rest of the Middle Ages did, too) that as emperor he controlled the papacy just as he controlled the Church within Germany. From the pope's point of view, though, the title of emperor meant only that the person who held it was obligated to serve the pope whenever the Holy See required. As we shall see later, it took several centuries to resolve this dispute.[6]

The reigns of Otto II (r. 973–983) and Otto III (r. 982–1002) were far less dramatic and impressive. Both men struggled against redoubled German rebellions— the princes and dukes remained determined to resist a strong, centralized imperial power—and were consequently always on the defensive. Otto II and Otto III were both keenly interested in securing their power over Italy, since the resurgent Mediterranean economy made an irresistible target. Concern with Italy, in fact, became a hallmark of German imperial interests for the next three centuries. But three fundamental problems continually frustrated them: the desire of the Italians not to be under German control; the phenomenon that nearly every time a German emperor went to Italy, a rebellion of magnates broke out back in Germany; and the simple fact that the German empire and Italy have a slight geographical obstacle between them—the Alps.

The three "Ottonians," as they are generally known, had dreamed big. With their wealth, talent, and good fortune, they had managed to effect a *translatio imperii*—a more or less universally recognized "transfer of the empire" from the western Frankish heartlands to the easternmost reaches of continental Latin Europe. This transfer meant more to contemporaries than just the rise of a new imperial dynasty in a slightly different locale. It implied a continuity, a steadfastness of the divine purpose, that deserved respect and obedience. It encouraged the idea that God Himself had a plan for human history, for its unity, and for its ultimate salvation under the joint leadership of emperor and pope. Otto II married a Byzantine princess named Theophano in the hope of linking—symbolically, to be sure, but also with an eye to an actual dynastic union—the new German empire and the older Greek one. (Recall that Charlemagne had offered his hand in marriage to the Byzantine empress Irene in the same hope.) Otto III, who spent most of his early life in Italy and was tutored by Greek scholars who had come westward with his mother, maintained throughout his life a dreamy vision of apocalyptic imperial grand (re)union. One of his non-Greek tutors was a brilliant French cleric named Gerbert of Aurillac—arguably the greatest ecclesiastical mind of the tenth century—who perhaps unintentionally inspired Otto III to view himself as

---

6. Otto's formal title was "emperor" (*imperator*) alone, without a territorial or legal specification. His realm became formally known as the "Roman Empire" in 1037; and in 1157 it began to be called the "Holy Roman Empire."

*Emperor Otto II, accompanied by personifications of the four regions of his empire.
Tenth century. Otto II of Germany (973–983) is shown enthroned, receiving the
tribute of the four principal regions of his empire (Lotharingia, Bavaria, Saxony,
Burgundy). The classical influence and pretension of the Ottonian court are clear.
Source: Giraudon/Art Resource NY*

Charlemagne incarnate and, ultimately, as the successor of Constantine the Great.[7]
It is difficult to judge. Otto III was a quixotic personality, one whose dreams of glory
far outstripped his actual abilities. A sense of his mystical view of his own and the
world's future can be seen in a strange episode: On the Feast of Pentecost in the year

7.   In 999 Gerbert was elected pope. Significantly, he took the name of Sylvester II (999–1003). The first
Sylvester had been the pope during the reign of the emperor Constantine.

1000 Otto personally exhumed Charlemagne's body from its tomb at Aachen, be-lieving that he was somehow magically imbuing himself with the spirit of the great ruler. In reality, probably the only thing he experienced was a heady dose of methane. Still, the action illustrates Ottonian ideology rather well. This ideology survived, though in a rather toned-down form, through the next two centuries of German imperial rule.

Otto III died childless in 1002 and a contested succession ensued. The dispute illustrates an essential fault line in medieval German politics: None of the princes, as individuals, wanted to elect a strong emperor, yet each prince who was elected wanted immediately to establish as much power over the others as possible. The princes' choice fell ultimately to the duke of Bavaria, Henry II (1002–1024), a distant relative of the Ottonians. Compared to his predecessors, Henry had comparatively little interest in Italy, but this may have been due to circumstances. Like so many emperors, he found himself facing rebellion after rebellion as soon as he came to the throne. In his case, he may have suffered from the nobles' fear that his relative lack of interest in Italy meant a heightened interest in centralizing his power over Ger-many itself. The most important aspect of Henry II's reign is the fact that he brought westward into the German heartlands the Ottonian policy of enfeoffing and elevat-ing the archiepiscopal, episcopal, and major abbatial territories of the imperial realm and raising them to the status of the throne's closest allies, vassals, and de-pendents. Theocracy, not democracy, thus emerged as the dominant element of Ger-man politics.

The three Ottos and Henry II are often credited with inspiring a cultural revival known, predictably, as the *Ottonian Renaissance*. Like the Carolingian revival before it, the Ottonian version was a modest affair, limited primarily to the imperial court itself. Otto II's Byzantine wife, Theophano, deserves much of the credit for it, since she brought with her from Constantinople a stable of painters, sculptors, poets, and scholars who found work in the imperial capital and at the handful of new schools established by the court. For the most part their works, while highly accomplished, served chiefly propagandistic purposes: They exalted the majesty of the new dy-nasty, its power, its enjoyment of divine favor, and its joint Roman-Carolingian-Byzantine inheritance. By far the most interesting person in this renaissance was a nun named Hrotsvitha von Gandersheim. Entirely unconnected with the imperial court (although Otto I had founded her convent), she wrote lively and polished verse; much of what survives is rather conventionally didactic in content, since her poems were intended for the religious education of the novice nuns under her care, but the language with which she extols the virtues of chastity, piety, and obedience is often quite impressive. She also wrote a long narrative poem on the greatness of Otto I, but by far her most important and interesting works are a half-dozen ex-tant plays. Hrotsvitha modeled her plays on the comedies of the Roman writer Terence, the most popular of the Roman playwrights throughout the Middle Ages; but she turned the tables on him, so to speak, in the depiction of female characters. Like most Roman writers Terence had filled his plays with the stock female characters/caricatures—the shrewish wife, the conniving seductress, the whiny girlfriend, the clever servant-girl. Hrotsvitha's plays instead celebrate women as heroic figures, although, the plays being intended for audiences of nuns and novices, her figures' heroism usually takes the form of submission to God, dedication to modesty, and acceptance of martyrdom. Nevertheless, she possessed a genuine talent for witty dialogue and solid stagecraft.

An important shift in political practice came with Conrad II (r. 1024–1039). Conrad, the founder of the new *Salian dynasty*, opposed the popular ecclesiastical reforms of his time since he feared they would lead to the establishment of a Church independent of governmental control. This position estranged many of the higher clergy who had been the mainstays of the empire since Otto I. Conrad turned instead to the lay nobility and tried to make himself into a kind of feudal populist— which sounds like an oxymoron. The great magnates of Germany, despite their supposed vassalage to whoever wore the imperial crown, held their principalities by hereditary right but steadfastly resisted the rise of such attitudes among *their* vassals, the lesser princelings, counts, margraves, and knights. Conrad championed the hereditary principle for these lesser nobles in the hope that, having won their support, he could use them to counterbalance the influence of the great magnates; he also turned to talented urban commoners and placed them in administrative positions within the central government. These officers held the title of *ministerialis* (pl. *ministeriales*), and they played roles of ever-increasing importance in German politics through the end of the twelfth century. But the most important aspect of Conrad II's reign was the fact that it marked the turning point in Church-State relations in Germany. As the Church reform movement gained speed, the German rulers from Conrad on commonly became viewed as the enemies of reform, opponents to be overcome.

Henry III (r. 1039–1056) drew upon both Conrad II's policies and the more conservative notions of the Ottonians. He pacified the magnates by easing up on the campaign for hereditary rights among the lower nobles (perhaps because he was the greatest magnate of all: When he came to the throne he controlled all but two of the duchies in Germany), although he increased his dependence upon the ministeriales. Henry mildly championed the Church reform movement—in 1043 he personally delivered a Peace of God sermon at Constance, in lower Bavaria—but only to the point where it did not impede the authority of the emperor himself. Henry also used his armies to further the Drang nach Osten and managed to force the kings of Poland, Bohemia, and Hungary to recognize his feudal overlordship. At the same time he secured a measure of control over Burgundy to the west, and northern Italy, thereby creating a vast and contiguous empire. An important semantic shift can be dated to Henry III's time. The word *empire* (Latin *imperium*) began to take on a fixed geographical meaning; prior to this it had a jurisdictional meaning only, referring to a "right to rule" by whoever had it, over whatever territory the possessor happened to have. After Henry III's reign, however, the term referred to a specific place—the land mass composed of Germany, Burgundy, and northern

Italy—under the centralized and increasingly professionalized administration of a single ruler. Under his son Henry IV (r. 1056–1106), the contest between the new, centralized Empire and the reformed, centralized Church would reach its dramatic climax.

A great change had taken place in German governance under these men. Feudal relations linked landholders together in a kind of power grid that had originated as a network of personal relationships, but by the late eleventh century the German government had evolved into an institutional and territorial state. The empire, as an organic polity, existed as something beyond the group of individuals who exercised power within it. Two chief reasons lay behind this. First, the wealth of the Saxon rulers freed them from dependence on the counts and princes to their west and south, who claimed to have inherited political autonomy from family links with the old Carolingian line. The new dynasts were thus able to expand into central and eastern Europe with a new corps of followers. Second, they parceled out these new territories as ecclesiastical fiefs instead of direct bequests to their new loyalists. This way, the Saxon kings earned the support of the German clergy while still providing "career paths" for the men who had conquered the new territories for them. As ministeriales—civic officials engaged in the day-to-day administration of the ecclesiastical fiefdoms—these laymen soon developed a conception of themselves as a distinct legal class, an intrinsic element of the state, and they began to compose and codify the evolving customs of their activities. The German state as a permanent institution living according to its own laws—not as a group of people possessing individual privileges of governance—marked an enormous conceptual leap in political theory and action.

THE RISE OF CAPETIAN FRANCE

Western Francia at the end of the Carolingian era stood in even greater disarray than the German territories to the east. Here the Vikings had attacked longest, most often, in greatest numbers, and with deadliest effect. Here too the internal strife between warlords reached its zenith, until what had once been a single Frankish kingdom had devolved into a messy sprawl of hundreds of petty principalities. The closer one got to Paris, the greater the mess. Large independent duchies, such as Rollo's duchy of Normandy established in 911 or the duchy of Aquitaine under Ramnulf I (d. 867), had already broken away and gave only the slightest lip service to their vassalage to Paris. But in the central regions near Paris the independent states grew smaller and smaller. The royal desmesne itself was one of the smallest in France. In 987 when a local baron named Hugh Capet finally overthrew the last Carolingian ruler and took over the government for himself, the royal desmesne consisted only of the cities of Paris and Orléans and the thin strip of land that connected them. Hugh Capet led a local family that had first risen to prominence a hundred years earlier when one of his ancestors fought off a Viking raid on Paris. Hugh's reign lasted only nine years (r. 987–996) and he failed to accomplish much during it, but the *Capetian dynasty* that he founded went on to rule France for over three hundred years. For nearly half that span the Capetians were arguably the poorest and weakest royal family in western Europe: They could not purchase loyalty since they had practically no land to give away as fiefs, neither could they command loyalty since their baronial neighbors were on the whole wealthier and more powerful than they. The great nobles of southern France never even bothered to appear at the Capetian court until well into the twelfth century.

The first Capetians proceeded cautiously since they could not risk giving any of the magnates a reason to get rid of them. Instead, they focused on administering their own demesne. Hugh, his son Robert II "the Pious" (r. 996–1031),[8] and grandson Henry I (r. 1031–1060) developed a tightly centralized system of governing the royal lands and showed little hesitation in seizing ecclesiastical revenues whenever they could. This practice helped solidify their control of their own lands but did little to extend the reach of their power. Two innovations, however, changed that. First, each new ruler ensured his son's succession by crowning him as coregent during the reigning king's own lifetime. This early inheritance helped guarantee an orderly passing of the crown and gave the inheriting son several years of valuable experience before taking over the reins of government for himself. (Whether out of good biological luck or sheer doggedness, the Capetians never failed to produce a male heir through eleven straight generations.) Early inheritance gradually eroded the Frankish custom of elected kingship that had started to emerge during the Carolingian decline and freed the monarch from having to curry favor among the electing nobles, who generally were willing to accept a permanent Capetian dynasty precisely because of the family's weakness. Better a weak monarch who left them alone, they reckoned, than a powerful one who tried to lord it over them.

The Capetians' second innovation was hardly a new practice but one which they pursued with extraordinary dedication: aggrandizement through marriage. They scoured the French countryside in search of estates, counties, and principalities, whether large or small, that had fallen into the hands of childless young widows or unwed noble daughters; holding out the offer of social prestige through a union with royal blood, they married as many heiresses as they could to their various brothers, sons, nephews, and cousins in order to bring the women's dowries under Capetian family control. Many baronial families—the smaller ones at first—leapt at the chance to link their families with the royal line, and so long as the Capetians limited their efforts to exert power to those lands that belonged to their family, the more powerful barons voiced little complaint. The process was a slow one, but it worked. In the course of three or four generations, the royal demesne

---

8. Hugh Capet's grandfather had briefly held the throne in the early tenth century and is known as Robert I.

had increased substantially, even though it consisted of a far-flung sprawl of discontiguous territories. But by the start of the twelfth century, under Philip I (r. 1060–1108) and especially under Louis VI "the Fat" (r. 1108–1137), the monarchy had become strong enough to overrun some smaller baronies and so begin the process of linking together the demesnal lands into a patchwork quilt. As this quilt grew, the kings parceled out fiefs to those willing to perform fealty and homage. Louis VI was the first Capetian to issue charters from his own royal chancery, a sure sign of the growing recognition of the king's central authority. Prior to this development, Frankish kings had commonly affixed their seals to documents that had been prepared by the parties involved in any particular dispute or transaction. The change was more than symbolic: Henceforth the king did not merely confirm decisions made by others; he effectively made the decisions himself and handed them down from his own court.

But the great lords of the south still held out. These figures—the lords of Poitou, Aquitaine, Gascony, Quercy, Toulouse, and Auvergne, among others—offered only token allegiance to the crown and generally went their own independent ways. At least they never openly rebelled, as the German magnates seemed to have done every chance they could against the Saxon and Salian emperors. The Capetians' big chance came in 1137 when Duke William X of Aquitaine offered his daughter and heiress Eleanor to Louis VI's son, the soon-to-be Louis VII (r. 1137–1180). Aquitaine was the largest and wealthiest of the southern principalities and the center of a vibrant court culture. Poetry, music, some science, and philosophy all thrived here, making it one of western Europe's great cultural centers. Eleanor herself was an exceptional character: intelligent, proud, energetic, and strong-willed. She was also renowned for her beauty:

Were all the lands of Europe mine
Between the Elbe and the Rhine,
I'd regard them all as worthless charms
Could [Eleanor] lay in my arms

ran a popular song.

Eleanor's marriage to Louis VII was unhappy, although Louis was clearly in love with her in his way. He had a gentle and meek nature—as his father's second son he had never planned to be king nor had he been trained for it—and he ill-suited Eleanor's passionate, cosmopolitan character. She is reported to have once complained that Louis was more fit for a life of endless daily prayer than for one of long nights in a queen's bed. In the aftermath of Louis' disastrous attempt to lead a crusade (1147–1149), the marriage was annulled and Eleanor married Count Henry of Anjou, the soon-to-be King Henry II of England. The Capetians' advance southward had stalled. Nevertheless, they had managed to reorganize and centralize monarchical power over much of northern France, to introduce a fairly comprehensive system of feudal relations, and to raise the prestige of their family and throne.

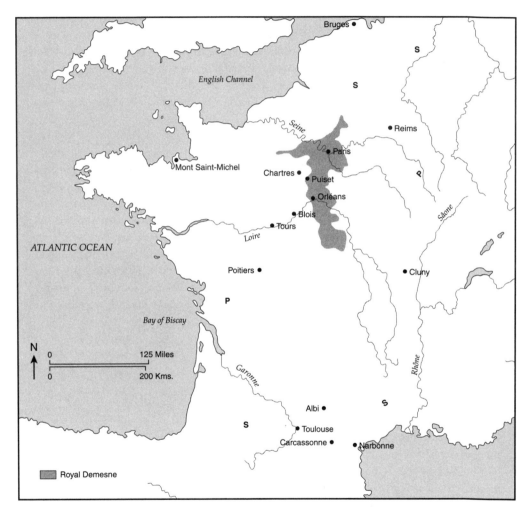

Capetian France, ca. 1100.

A charter by Louis VII of France, showing the royal seal. The text reads, in part: "A number of Jewish converts to Christianity recently approached me who, led on by the Devil, declared their desire to return to the Jewish faith. Recognizing the terrible ignominy this would bring to the name of Christ and the contempt it would show for the Christian religion, I decreed that so presumptuous a crime must be prohibited by the awesome weight of a royal command. And therefore I declare and affirm by my royal authority that henceforth any Jew who has been renewed in Christ by grace of baptism yet presumes to return to his old error shall not be suffered to remain anywhere in my kingdom. If any such be caught, they are to be sentenced to capital or corporeal punishment. . . . Done at Paris in the year of the Lord's Incarnation 1144. . . ."
Source: Réunion des Musées Nationaux / Art Resource

For all his pious dedication to the Church, Louis VII did take action to limit its legal jurisdiction within France. The Second Lateran Council of 1139 had prohibited clergy from participating in trials involving torture or capital punishment (such as murder, rape, or arson), but within France many churches continued to do so nonetheless. Louis issued dozens of charters to individual churches condemning their activity and subjecting them to heavy fines, which resulted in a significant broadening of the recognition of royal power. The central court remained inchoate, however. Since the Capetians were itinerant, the government traveled with them, a practice that made it difficult to develop highly evolved institutions. Few royal officials emerged with clearly articulated duties; instead, particular tasks were doled out on an ad hoc basis. No central treasury existed. No central archive existed. Individuals seeking royal justice often had to spend months seeking the royal court, which might be anywhere in the realm. Until a permanent center of administration was established—which would not be until the very end of the twelfth century—French government would remain more chaotic and fluid, more personal and susceptible to influence, than in most kingdoms.

THE ANGLO-NORMAN REALM

A united kingdom of England was a long time a-borning. Under Alfred the Great in the ninth century, an awareness of England as a unified whole, with centralized institutions of government to match, came briefly into being, but the need to placate the Danes stood in the way of realizing that dream. The creation of the Danelaw itself had annexed over one-third of England proper to the kingdom of Denmark, and over the course of the tenth and early eleventh centuries still more of England fell under Danish control. Resistance to the Danes centered on the old line of Wessex kings, but the English generally recognized the vast military superiority of the Danes and preferred to compromise and pay tribute rather than take the field against them. Who could blame them? The Danes were renowned for their ferocity and fearlessness—an image that they carefully cultivated in order to keep their subjects in line. Their popular sagas commemorated savage heroes like Bui of Børnholm who once, when he received a vicious swordblow that sliced off his chin and lips and loosened most of his teeth, merely spat the useless teeth to the ground and said with a laugh: "I suppose the women of Børnholm won't be so eager to kiss me now!" Later in the saga Bui, after a profitable raid on England, was forced to abandon ship in a storm. Even though he had since suffered having both of his hands chopped off, he refused to part with his treasure chest—so he stuck his arm-stumps through the chest's handles and leapt with a laugh into the sea.

In 1013 the Danish king Swein set sail for England, having decided to put an end to Wessex and all of non-Danish England. He brought with him his seventeen-year-old son and heir Canute. The Wessex king Ethelred the Unready[9] fled to Nor-

---

9. In Anglo-Saxon *unræd* means "ill-advised" or "poorly counseled."

mandy with his two sons, and all of England surrendered. Swein died the following year, and Canute, needing to secure his Danish crown, returned briefly to the
continent. When he arrived back in England in 1015, he found that Ethelred had returned and with his elder son Edmund Ironside was trying to organize English resistance. Canute quickly defeated the English, probably had Edmund killed, and
after Ethelred's death married his widow Emma. (The fact that Canute was already
married seems not to have bothered him; we do not know what either of his wives
felt about the matter.) Canute thus became the undisputed ruler of a united England (r. 1016–1035)—but of an England itself united, dynastically, with Denmark.
Later conquests added Norway, parts of Sweden, and Estonia to his realm and
earned Canute the self-proclaimed title of *Emperor of the Northern Seas* under which
title he attended the 1027 imperial coronation of Henry II of Germany in Rome;
Canute was the first Scandinavian ruler ever to receive an invitation to the papal
court.

Canute was a Christian, nominally, though he may have been more intrigued
or amused by the faith than genuinely committed to it. When he lay on his
deathbed in 1035, he begged his Christian clergy to perform memorial masses for
his soul; but after these clerics had tearfully left the room, Canute ordered a group
of pagan priests to have a series of human sacrifices made to appease the Nordic
deities. Whatever his beliefs, he lavished money on the English church as a way to
ease his acceptance by the Anglo-Saxons, restoring many crumbling foundations
and creating many new ones. At the same time he retained iron-fisted control over
ecclesiastical appointments and saw to it that the Church served his ends as well as
God's. He issued a new codification of English law as well, one that recognized and
confirmed Anglo-Saxon customs and privileges.

England seemed poised to join a Scandinavian confederacy-in-the-making; the
island's commercial ties had centered on the North and Baltic seas since the ninth
century anyway. But Canute's two sons possessed none of their father's talent or
drive, and while they squabbled over the Danish throne after their father's death,
the Anglo-Saxon *witan*, or nobles' council, recalled Ethelred's second son from Normandy and placed him on the throne. Edward the Confessor (r. 1042–1066) would
be the next-to-last Anglo-Saxon king of England. He was a capable and pious man
of nearly forty, but conditions in England were not in his favor. Having lived in
Normandy since the age of three and being half-Norman himself (his mother
Emma had been a Norman princess prior to marrying Ethelred [and Canute]) he
understood Norman ways and institutions better than English ones; he spoke
Norman-French better than Anglo-Saxon; and he was accustomed to the feudal
model of royal-noble relations instead of the "first among equals" tradition of the
English aristocracy. Still, most Englishmen accepted him as the legitimate heir of
Alfred's royal Wessex line.

Not everyone did, however. Some powerful magnates kept their distance from
Edward and offered only the most tenuous displays of loyalty. When Edward, in
the 1060s, appeared likely to die childless, these barons began to prepare openly for

a fight for the crown.[10] By the time of Edward's death in 1066 two main rivals remained: Harold Godwinson, the earl of Wessex, the legally crowned monarch (1066) and Duke William of Normandy, the bastard son of one of Edward's cousins who claimed (probably spuriously) to be Edward's own choice as a successor. Both men had spent several years courting support from influential figures within England and without, and they finally settled the matter in a dramatic battle at Hastings in southern England. William had sailed his army across the Channel and landed unopposed while Harold was busy fighting off a Norwegian invasion in the north of England. Hearing of the Normans' landing, Harold quickly led his soldiers on a forced march down the length of England. At Hastings William's army routed Harold's exhausted men, and on Christmas Day 1066 William was crowned king of England (r. 1066–1087) in London's Westminster Abbey. Norman rule got off to a rather shaky start since the new conquerors were not only despised by the general populace but were also enormously outnumbered by them. At William's coronation, in fact, nerves ran so high that when the crowd inside Westminster Abbey let out a shout as the crown settled on William's head, the company of Norman soldiers stationed outside the building feared the Anglo-Saxons had begun a counterattack—and so they went on a rampage, slaughtering citizens in the street and setting fire to a good portion of central London. William himself, a chronicler informs us, stood shaking and sweating at the head of the Abbey, not knowing whether to expect an assassination attempt, to attack his own marauding troops, to join in the mayhem, or to flee for his life. In the end, the soldiers rioted for a day or two before William could restore order. The task of finding a way to govern then began.

Given the Normans' small numbers, only two real options existed: Either they could adopt Anglo-Saxon ways, creating goodwill and assimilating into English society as quickly as possible, or they could compensate for their small numbers by the application of brute force, thereby compelling Anglo-Saxon submission. True to his nature, William chose the latter. He had grown up in a violent world—before he had even turned eighteen he had survived at least three assassination attempts back in Normandy—and believed that nothing inspired obedience and loyalty as well as fear. On top of this, he had a monstrous temper whenever he felt that he had been offended or his rights had been trammeled. During one of the many rebellions that had marked his rule in Normandy prior to 1066, for example, the people of Alençon had taunted William by covering the wooden walls of their town with animal hides soaked in vinegar. This was done in part to protect their walls from William's flaming arrows, but it also mocked William illegitimate origins (his unmarried mother had been the daughter of a leather-tanner). Enraged by the insult, William had stormed the town, sacked it thoroughly, and ordered the right hand and right foot of every adult male inhabi-

---

10. According to some reports, Edward took a vow of celibacy just prior to his marriage.

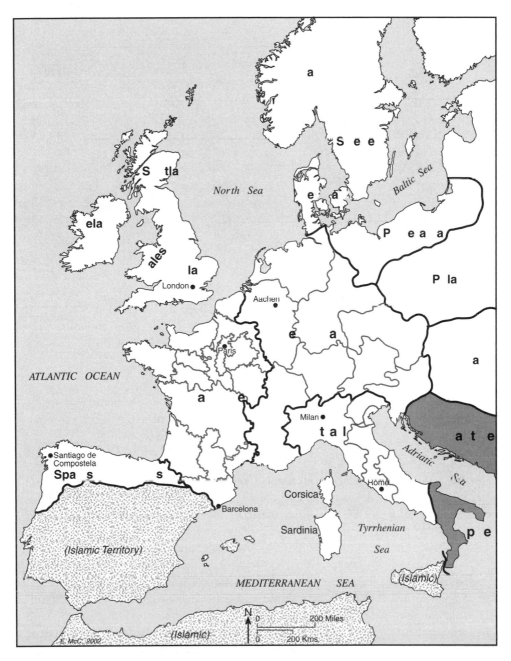

a

S e e

S tla

ela

ales

la

e a

P e a a

P la

North Sea

Baltic Sea

London •

Aachen •

e a

a

ATLANTIC OCEAN

Paris •

a

e

Milan •

t a l

Santiago de
Compostela •

Spa s s

Barcelona •

(Islamic Territory)

Corsica

Sardinia

Rome •

Tyrrhenian
Sea

Adriatic
Sea

a t e

p e

(Islamic)

MEDITERRANEAN SEA

N

0   200 Miles

0   200 Kms

(Islamic)

E. McC. 2002

Medieval kingdoms

Detail of a battle scene from the Bayeux Tapestry. Late eleventh century. The magnificent tapestry was woven around 1080 to commemorate the Norman victory over Harold at the Battle of Hastings. The tapestry, consisting of connected panels of embroidered linen, extends over seventy meters and is fifty centimeters in height. This detail depicts the Saxon foot soldiers confronting the Norman cavalry. Source: Giraudon/Art Resource NY

tant cut off. He was not a man to settle for reasoned compromise, if an alternative existed.

He spent several years subduing pockets of resistance, of which there were many, especially in the north of England. These tended to be relatively small rebellions led by lesser nobles, since many of the local aristocratic families had died out, emigrated, or been replaced by Danish warlords during the turbulent years immediately prior to William's conquest. Nevertheless, resistance occasionally proved dogged enough to require strong measures, and William ordered Alençon-type punishments on numerous villages and towns in northern England. He confiscated lands on a grand scale, driving indigenous baronial families into ruin and parceling out the estates to his own followers. Much of the land he kept for himself; ultimately, somewhere between one-fifth and one-fourth of all the real estate in England belonged personally to him. Whether the lands remained part of the royal demesne or whether he granted them out as fiefs, William built fortified strongholds everywhere in order to keep an eye on the locals and to serve as physical emblems of Norman power. (The most famous of these structures is the Tower of London.) He was especially careful to construct a network of castles across the southern districts of Kent and Sussex in order to ensure an easily defended retreat path to the Continent, should the need for one ever arise.

Unlike the Capetians' first haphazard efforts at creating feudal links with their followers, the distribution of fiefs in England took place rapidly and according to a plan. Since all the land belonged to the king by right of conquest, so were all fiefs held either directly or indirectly from the throne. William distributed lands to approximately 180 leading nobles—mostly Normans but with a few Anglo-Saxons thrown in—who rendered the greatest amount of service to the throne and became known as *tenants-in-chief*. But the need to prevent these great landholders from obtaining potential power-bases from which to challenge the king led William to divide these large fiefs into many separate territories. Thus the earl of Percy, for example, held a tenancy-in-chief that was scattered among no fewer than forty counties from Cornwall to Northumbria. The sprawl of his (and other chief tenants') lands over so wide a territory had two important repercussions for Anglo-Norman England. First, there was relatively little sub-infeudation. Fewer than eight hundred lesser nobles held fiefs from the tenants-in-chief, and virtually none of them held territories large enough for further sub-infeudation. This meant that the total number of enfeoffed nobles in England was a manageable corps of about one thousand families, a large enough population to help control and govern the realm but not so large a group that the royal administration could not keep an eye on all of them. Second, the tenants-in-chief had to professionalize the maintenance of their own territories since they could hardly run them all themselves. Large corps of bailiffs, stewards, sheriffs, reeves, and other officials soon dotted the landscape and provided avenues for modest advancement by diligent locals. Just as significantly, the realm-wide basis of major tenancies meant that the chief tenants themselves remained concerned for the well-being of the entire kingdom rather than their own parochial corner of it—since those parochial corners did not exist. This fact contributed significantly to the development of the English parliament, since the nobles came to represent the kingdom itself and not just their own privileged group-status within it.

The new regime proved both generous to the Church and dismissive of it. As had been their practice in Normandy, the Normans in England actively supported churches and monasteries and lavished lands, annuities, and privileges upon them. Such generosity no doubt sprang from a genuine commitment to the faith but also owed much to a cold-eyed recognition of the Church's utility in fostering social cohesion; since all the land in England was the king's so too were all the lands bestowed in such large measure on ecclesiastical houses. Ultimately the crown gave roughly one-fifth of England's land to religious houses, but such gifts served to strengthen the monarchy more than the Church since the crown made it clearly understood that the churches themselves were in fact vassals of the king. William and his successors kept firm control of all ecclesiastical appointments and never hesitated to confiscate from any disobedient house the lands they had been granted after the conquest. When Pope Gregory VII (r. 1073–1085) tried to remind William that England was technically a fief of the Church given to him by the papacy (an arrangement agreed to by William in order to secure papal approval of his invasion), the king responded by issuing a declaration known as the *Triple Concordat*, which asserted that without royal permission no authority claimed by the papacy could be exercised within the kingdom of England. For the time being, the Holy See could do nothing about William's intransigence.

The centralization of power under the monarchy drove a wedge between the new rulers and the Anglo-Saxons. English political custom prior to 1066 had been based on a high degree of local independence, with social cohesion resulting from a common culture, language, and religious practice. But the Norman settlement did away with much of earlier tradition. Norman French replaced Anglo-Saxon as the language of court and government (for two hundred years after 1066 no king of England could speak English or would admit to it if he could). Old English as a written language virtually died out; driven underground, it survived largely in oral usage. By the time the French monopoly was broken and English resurfaced in the thirteenth century, it appeared in writing in a vastly different form—the so-called *Middle English* familiar to us in the works of Chaucer and Langland. French architectural styles and French musical style also came to the fore and altered English tradition. The old Saxon liturgy and calendar of saints' cults declined as well, to be replaced by the new liturgy and practices emanating from the continental church reform movement. Such changes angered the English, who continued to resent their foreign rulers long after they had stopped rebelling against them. Nearly the last act of William's long reign confirmed and codified the subordinate position of the English in Norman society. In 1086 William ordered the compilation of an inventory of all the land and property in England. It was an enormous enterprise—the first such inventory in European history—that symbolized the ruthless efficiency of Norman centralism. It measured the farms, counted the sheep in each flock, inventoried the tools available, named the peasant tenants, and cataloged the rents due from each. It is a treasure-trove of information that, under computer-analysis, is now revealing fascinating insights. Among other things we could point to, this survey, known as the *Domesday Book*, drove home one powerful specific statistic: Well more than three-fourths of the people in the countryside (that is, excluding the urban populace) were legally classified as *serfs*.

Fearing perhaps that his sons would rip his dominion apart if he did not apportion it to them himself, William's will divided his possessions carefully. The eldest son, Robert, received the duchy of Normandy; William II, better known as William Rufus (r. 1087–1100), became king of England; and young Henry inherited a lump sum of money and a handful of grand estates. William Rufus and Henry easily outdid Robert in cunning and ambition. Whereas Robert's greatest dream was to be a chivalrous knight par excellence and a faithful servant of the Church,

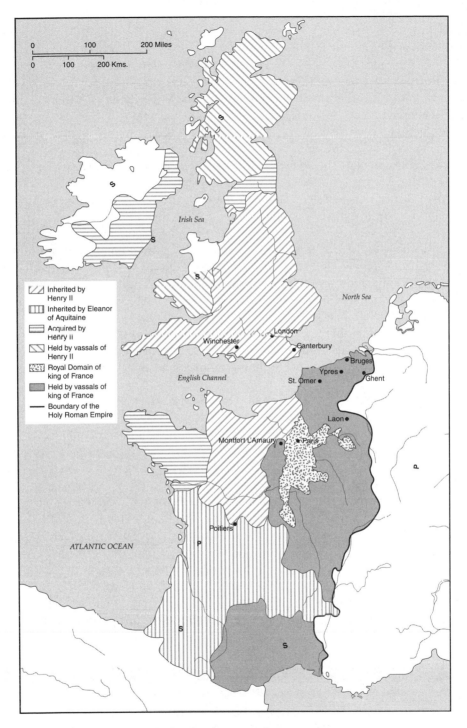

England and Normandy, ca. 1100.

his younger brothers had eyes only for the acquisition of power. When Robert in 1095 pawned his duchy to William in order to raise money for his participation in the First Crusade (1095–1099), his days as an independent ruler were over. William quickly took advantage of Robert's long absence and put Normandy under his autocratic control. Surviving accounts assure us that virtually all of William Rufus' subjects hated him. "He went to bed every night a worse man than he had been when he awoke, and he awoke every morning a worse man than he had been when he went to bed the night before," wrote one contemporary. He probably was not as bad as all that. The animosity resulted as much from a growing consciousness of the changes introduced into England by the feudal system as it did from William Rufus' personal demeanor or behavior. After all, while he was certainly capable of physical violence, he never came near his father's level of brutality. What irked his subjects was instead his hyper-legalistic bent, his penchant for taking advantage of the smallest legal details in order to manipulate and control his subjects. For example, William Rufus quickly seized on a vassal's tiniest failing to perform his feudal duties to the crown as an excuse to negate the entire contract, confiscate the fief, and reaward it to a more subservient vassal. This meant that even the newly installed Norman barons did not feel secure in their holdings and that the crown regarded its feudal nobles in a far more servile light than did the nobles themselves. The strain of initiating a new social and political system became clear in William Rufus reign. No one mourned when he died in a hunting accident in 1100.

But few people celebrated when the crown passed to Henry I (r. 1100–1135), for he was a cruel and dissolute sensualist.[11] Conspiracy addicts have tried for centuries to implicate Henry in his brother's death, but the greater likelihood is that Henry—who was part of the hunting party when William Rufus died—simply saw his chance and acted quickly. He left his brother's body lying in the woods, dashed to Winchester to seize the royal treasury, then raced to Westminster Abbey to be crowned king by the bishop of London. Though never a very admirable person, he turned out to be a rather successful king. He threw Ranulf Flambard, William Rufus' most hated tax-collector, into prison, recalled the popular exiled archbishop Anselm of Canterbury, and married Matilda, a descendant of the ancient Wessex line, in order to placate the Saxons. He presided over the formation of the *Exchequer*, the fiscal accounting office of the royal treasury.[12] He introduced a more or less comprehensive system of itinerant justices, called *justices in eyre*, who staged regular courts throughout the kingdom and gave commoners an opportunity to voice

---

11.   He is known to have sired at least twenty-two illegitimate children by as many mistresses; and he once worked out his anger with a certain townsman by personally heaving him over the city walls. In 1125 he discovered that several workers in the royal mint were adulterating the coinage with base metals; Henry ordered them to be castrated.

12.   The Exchequer derived its name from the checkerboard table-covering used by the department's auditors, who would tabulate sums by moving markers up and down its columns. The checkerboard worked in a manner analogous to an abacus, knowledge of which had entered Latin Europe via the Islamic world.

grievances. Administration proved surprisingly to be Henry's true calling, and his reign marks the beginning of the centralized English state.

His reign ended in tragedy, however, and was followed by a period of strife known as the *Anarchy*. As so often in the Middle Ages, what triggered the trouble was a succession crisis. Henry, for all his amorous efforts, produced only two legitimate children: a son and a daughter. The son, William, had been carefully trained to take over the reins of government but he drowned at sea in 1120. Henry was grief-stricken and at a loss for what to do: His daughter Matilda had been married at the age of eleven to the German emperor Henry V, and her succession meant the absorption of Norman England into the German Empire. But Matilda was widowed in 1125, which made her a viable successor to her father. Matters seemed temporarily settled. Her new marriage to Geoffrey of Anjou, the Normans' traditional enemy, however, upset things again.[13] Barons, churchmen, and townspeople were divided, at Henry's death in 1135, whether to accept Matilda and Geoffrey as regents for their new son Henry or to throw their support to a rival, Stephen (r. 1135–1154), the son of William the Conqueror's daughter Adele. Stephen won, but the struggle lasted throughout his reign. By 1154 the imperfect nature of England's feudal system and the shortcomings of its embryonic centralized administration were abundantly clear.

THE SPANISH KINGDOMS

Spain also underwent a radical transformation in the eleventh and twelfth centuries. This is hardly surprising since the Iberian peninsula was the site of the greatest, longest, and most continuous interaction between Muslims, Christians, and Jews. The Arab conquest of 711 had been the last of the great Muslim victories, and it had brought under their control a site ideally suited to the culture they imported. The large highland plain of the peninsula's interior consists of arid soil that receives much sun and little rainfall; although it provided good pasture and scrubland for herding, it did not offer much by way of agricultural potential until the Arabs and Berbers arrived with their centuries-long traditions, born in the desert, of managing scarce water resources through new crops and effective administration of wells, aqueducts, and irrigation systems. With these innovations, the land bloomed as never before. The more fertile and urban coastal plains provided access to industry, commerce, and civic tradition. The Spanish Muslims also took advantage of their links with the North African Berbers and quickly began to trade for, and then wholeheartedly to plunder, the large supplies of gold, spices, and slaves available in sub-Saharan west Africa. With the sudden influx of capital and cheap labor, Muslim Spain—called *al-Andalus* ("the land of the Vandals" in a dismissal of Visigothic claims to political legitimacy)—began a rapid ascent as one of the western world's

---

13.   Her second marriage was a stormy one, which may have been due to a difference in ages that was the reverse case of her first marriage. When she married Geoffrey, Matilda was twenty-five while he was only fifteen. He seems to have resented her treating him like the adolescent he was.

wealthiest and most cosmopolitan realms. Its zenith was reached during the reign of Abd ar-Rahman III (r. 912–961), whose capital city of Cordoba rivaled Constantinople and Baghdad as one of the most splendid and prosperous cities in the world. Its population stood at well over one hundred thousand.

Al-Andalus became famed for its agricultural abundance—wheat, rice, citrus fruits, olives, and grapes, especially—and for manufactures like leather, wool, cotton, silk, steel, and paper. Its population of roughly eight million was diverse and highly skilled. A thin over-grid of thirty thousand to fifty thousand Arabs made up the political and military elite who dominated the courts, the schools and mosques, and the urban mansions. Beneath them was a class of roughly a half-million Berbers brought up from North Africa; they provided the corps of civic officials, lesser military commanders, and lower clerics. The great bulk of the population consisted of indigenous Hispano-Romans and Visigoths (all Christian) and Jewish professionals (merchants, physicians, scribes, scholars, and financiers). By the tenth century, a sizable population of black slaves also existed; tax records put their number in Cordoba alone at over eight thousand.

Islamic law defined the subject Christians and Jews as *dhimmis*, or "protected communities," which meant that so long as they did not proselytize or practice their faith in public they were legally protected from persecution. Nevertheless, Muslim Spain was not a utopian haven of tolerance. Tensions regularly bristled across religious lines, and while Christians and Jews did not normally face outright persecution from the state, they did have to contend with occasional pogroms, severe restrictions on their actions, and considerable popular violence. The Muslims generally aimed at winning the religious contest by attrition: By cutting the Christian majority off from the rest of the Christian world and restricting Christian education and evangelization, they hoped slowly but ultimately to Islamicize the peninsula. Similar measures aimed at discouraging the survival of Judaism. The Muslims succeeded to a large degree with the Christians, less so with the Jews. By the middle of the ninth century, the Christian bishop of Seville even had to arrange for the Bible to be translated into Arabic since his parishoners could no longer understand Latin. Growing numbers of subject-Christians fled al-Andalus in the ninth and tenth centuries, emigrating principally toward Barcelona in the northeast and toward Santiago de Compostela in the northwest.[14]

Religious and ethnic tensions grew steadily over the tenth and eleventh centuries. One reason was the rise of the Abbasid dynasty and the Persianization of the Islamic world. In 929 Abd ar-Rahman III became the first Arab regional governor to assume the title of *caliph*, thus rendering permanent the break with Baghdad begun two hundred years earlier. At first the implications of this assumption for Spain

---

14.   In the mid-ninth century Christians discovered in Santiago what they believed to be the body of St. James, one of Jesus' original twelve apostles. News of the discovery quickly spread throughout Europe, and Santiago became one of the most popular pilgrimage sites of Latin Christendom. The city also inevitably acquired a symbolic role as a center of Christian resistance to Islam.

were minimal, but upon Abd ar-Rahman's death in 961 a storm of political rivalries broke out. Did his assumption of the caliphal title imply that the throne had to pass to his son? Was the selection of the next caliph to be left to the *ummah*, or community? Could anyone claim the title arbitrarily, just as Abd ar-Rahman seemed to have done? Al-Andalus began to split into a variety of political factions which, given Islam's nature, took on religious significance. The breakaway caliphate itself began to break into rival petty princedoms. The faltering of Muslim Spain's good fortune appeared to many to be the result of religious failure—a failure specifically to rid the peninsula of non-Muslims. As a consequence, the treatment of subject Christians and Jews worsened, and refugees to the Christian-held north regaled their listeners with tales of brutal Islamic oppression. These tales, though frequently exaggerated, became believable enough when a renegade Muslim prince named Ibn ab-Amir (but better known by his nickname *al-Mansur* "the Conqueror") sacked Barcelona in 985 and Santiago de Compostela in 997.

Spurred on by reports of oppression and encouraged by the political fracturing of al-Andalus, the Christians of northern Iberia began a counteroffensive beginning with the campaigns of King Sancho III of Navarre (r. 1000–1035) and culminating in Ferdinand and Isabella's victory over Granada in 1492, this reconquest of Iberia—the so-called *Reconquista*—dominated the political history of the rest of medieval Spain. It was a fitful series of sporadic regional conflicts rather than a single, fully conceived campaign. The recapture of Toledo in 1085 marked a decisive turning point. Toledo had been the capital of the old Visigothic kingdom and the metropolitan see of the Christian Church in Spain; moreover, its location at the center of the peninsula had important strategic consequences. On the local level Muslims, Christians, and Jews continued to interact as they had done before, sometimes peacably and sometimes not, in the marketplace and in the courts, within a context of ongoing military action along an ever-shifting frontier. Intra-religious relations were confusing and often contradictory, but as the border delineating Christian-ruled lands from Muslin-controlled ones moved southward, an awareness of the groups' mutual dependence fostered a willingness to put up with one another. This atmosphere, which the Spanish refer to as *convivencia*, was hardly the same thing as what we mean by the English word *tolerance*, but Spain did nevertheless represent the region of the greatest substantial non-violent contact between the three religious groups.

Two twelfth-century literary texts, both of which originated in earlier oral tradition, illustrate the difference between northern Christian and Iberian Christian attitudes toward the Muslims. *The Song of Roland*, a French knightly epic or *chanson de geste* (literally a "Song of Deeds"), depicts the heroic exploits of a Carolingian nobleman named Roland. There is a kernel of truth in the legend. During Charlemagne's first campaign into Muslim Spain a famous ambush occurred at the Pyrenean mountain pass at Roncesvalles (Roncevaux, in French), during which a group of Basque renegades attacked the Carolingian rear guard, led by Roland, and massacred it. Over the generations French popular memory turned this minor episode into an epic of over four thousand lines of verse, depicting the unbelievably heroic—if gore equals heroism—efforts of Roland and his outnumbered men to defend the pass. Ignoring all the facts of the real event, the *Song of Roland* identifies the Muslims, not the Basques, as the foes of the Christians and portrays them as devious cheats, cowardly and immoral pagans. Roland and his small band go down fighting, determined that to die in battle against the Muslims is the surest way to win the favor of Charlemagne, all of Christian society, and even of God Himself. At Roland's death he is rewarded by having God's angels lift his soul to paradise; the murderous knight has become a saint. In sharp contrast stands a contemporary epic from Christian Spain called the *Song of the Cid*.[15] In the form it has come down to us, it too represents a much-elaborated tale of an heroic Christian knight that has a certain basis in fact. It celebrates the adventures of the warrior Don Rodrigo Díaz de Vivar, a leader of the early *Reconquista*. Rebuked and banished by his Christian king, Alfonso VI of Léon (r. 1065–1109), the Cid led a life of roguish exile on the Muslim-Christian frontier, fighting sometimes on behalf of the Christians, sometimes for the Muslims, and sometimes just for himself, while garnering a reputation for feats of arms and an idiosyncratic noble uprightness. The poem is filled with characters and scenes as complex as the Cid's own personality, with sympathetic portraits of all three religious groups. Don Rodrigo has Muslim friends and Jewish compatriots as well as more than a few Christian enemies. While hardly a paean to cross-cultural amity, the *Song of the Cid* depicts a society that is worlds away from that of the *Song of Roland*. Religious rivalry certainly played a role in Iberian life but it did not necessarily define it; and through its first phase the *Reconquista* was motivated as much by everyday concerns for local power and social order, and who would command it, as it was by religious strife. Don Rodrigo ended his life as frontier-ruler (*al-sayyid*) of Muslim Valencia, in eastern Spain, where he enjoyed considerable popularity with his Islamic subjects. His most implacable foes were a group known as the *Almoravids* (1056–1147), a fundamentalist reform sect within western Islam led by south Moroccan Berbers who believed that the Christian advances in Iberia resulted from the failure of Muslims to adhere rigidly enough to Islamic law. Their much stricter posture toward non-Muslim subjects added to the urgency of the Christian reconquest, which took on more explicitly religious overtones. The eventual supplanting of the Almoravids by an even stricter Islamic group called the *Almohads* (1130–1269) resulted in an even more radical suppression of Christians and Jews in Spain and North Africa and raised the *Reconquista* to the status of a crusade.

As the reconquest gained momentum in the twelfth century, the Christian lords leading it found it as difficult to maintain a united front as did the Muslim princes they were supplanting. By 1139, when an independent kingdom of Portugal was declared, a half-dozen autonomous Christian states had emerged: Portugal, Léon, Castile, Navarre, Aragon, and Catalonia. Each possessed its own language, laws,

---

15. The nickname *El Cid* derives from the Arabic term *al-sayyid*, meaning "lord" but carrying with it a connotation of descent from the Prophet.

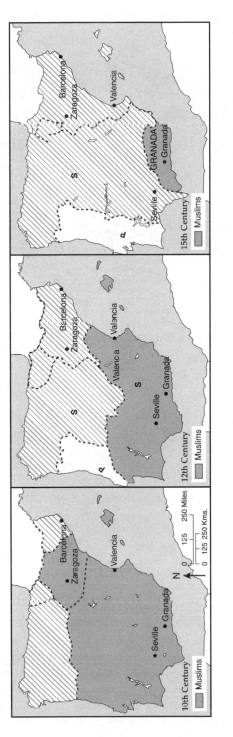

Muslim and Christian Spain, ca. 1100.

A king with his scribes, issuing charters. This is a page from the Liber feudorum
*("Book of Fiefs") prepared for the rulers of the kings of Aragon; it is a record
of the fiefs granted to royal vassals as the border of the* reconquista *continued
to push southward. Source: Scala / Art Resource, NY*

and customs, and each in its own way confronted the problem of how to assimilate
a newly conquered Muslim majority (not to mention a large Jewish and an Arabized Christian minority) into its expanded realm. For some, a modified version of
feudalism sufficed. Knights received fiefs along the advancing border both in order
to shore up defenses and to promote settlement along the frontier; but these knights
tended to be young upstarts, fighting men looking for a place in society rather than
members of the more established noble families of Christian lands further north.

The knights' background meant that the feudal ties that connected the conquering kings with the soldiers fighting on their behalf differed from the relations between those kings and the older aristocratic families who were more or less behind the lines. Moreover, the need to encourage settlement of artisans, merchants, urban laborers, financiers, teachers, and civic officials led to the continual awarding of local privileges and guarantees of autonomy (called *customs* or *usages* in Spain) that made for a bewildering but dynamic political and social scene. Dependent as they were on their conquered majorities, the rulers of the Christian kingdoms had to adapt their policies and institutions to meet local needs, in the process creating a kaleidoscopic frontier world. A telling insight into the Christian rulers' success is the fact that as the Christian border moved further southward a large-scale migration of Spanish Muslim farmers and craftsmen moved northward, believing that their lives would be better as much-needed subjects of a Christian state than as residents of a declining al-Andalus. Muslim subjects of Christian Spain continued to live under Islamic law and under the jurisdiction of their *muhtasib* (police chief) and *qadi* (civil and religious judge).

The borders dividing Muslims and Christians—both the borders separating their states and those separating their social interactions within any one state—remained porous. Given the fact that the political boundaries between Christian Spain and al-Andalus were constantly shifting, with any given town often conquered, lost, and reconquered a half-dozen times, local inhabitants had to find ways of continuing stable daily lives regardless of who was in power. Local bilingual Mozarabs and Jews played crucial roles in sustaining these relations, serving as linguistic and cultural interpreters and promoting the notion that religious rivals could find a common ground. As the conquering Christians encountered the Muslim libraries and schools, they began to encourage the translation of their works into Latin. Word of the intellectual riches available in Spain quickly spread through the rest of western Europe, and soon a parade of eager scholars arrived to advance the work of translating. One of these was an Italian scholar named Gerard of Cremona (d. 1187):

> He had been trained since childhood in various philosophical schools and had come to know everything that was available in Latin. But he developed a passionate interest in the *Almagest* [an astronomical work written in Alexandria by the Greek scientist Ptolemy in the second century] and since he could find no copy of it anywhere in the Latin world he went to Toledo. There he saw the enormous abundance of books in Arabic on every subject imaginable; pitying the backwardness of the Latin scholars in these subjects, he learned Arabic in order to translate the books himself. . . . For the rest of his life he toiled in order to pass on to the Christian world all that he thought the best, on whatever subject.

A surviving catalog of Gerard's works shows that he translated three books on alchemy, twelve on astronomy, three on dialectic, four on geomancy, seventeen on geometry, twenty-one on medicine, and eleven on philosophy. Most of these were Arabic translations of Greek originals (that is, Gerard produced translations of translations), but soon Latin scholars began to learn the Greek language itself and to produce more faithful renditions. Other renowned translator-scholars included Adelard of Bath, Herman of Carinthia, and Rudolph of Bruges, whose very names testify to the wide repute of the Spanish schools. The gradual recovery of Greek—in addition to increased Mediterranean trade—led to more scholarly contact between Latin Europe and Byzantium and thereby to the gradual decline of the Spanish translation schools as centers of intellectual life; but through most of the twelfth century the Spanish schools, combined with similar sites established in Sicily and southern Italy, were the intellectual nerve-centers of the Latin Christian world.

As Gerard's catalog suggests, most of this early work focused on the sciences. In order not to challenge orthodoxy, cultural and religious prescriptions had restricted Muslim intellectual life. The empirical sciences like astronomy, mathematics, or medicine posed no threat to Islamic teaching and therefore received the support and encouragement of the Muslim state, but fields like philosophy were another matter altogether. Muslim scholars had produced numerous translations of the works of Plato and Aristotle, among others, and had written extensive commentaries on them, but very little original philosophical work had been done. Moreover, those scholars who had ventured into these fields were regarded with disapproval by most of their contemporaries. Even a figure like Ibn Rushd (known in the west as *Averroës*), the greatest Aristotelian scholar of his age, was a marginal figure in the Islamic intellectual world. Distrusted for his insistence that since certain passages of the Qur'an contradicted the truths derived from Greek philosophy, those passages were therefore not be read literally, but were instead to be interpreted metaphorically, Ibn Rushd was something of an intellectual outcast. Summoned before the local Almohad ruler to answer charges of apostasy, Ibn Rushd lied and swore that he had never even read the works of Aristotle, much less actually translated or commented upon them. As the Christian scholars who translated Ibn Rushd, and then Aristotle himself, into Latin discovered, philosophy could be a dangerous thing in Christendom as well.

A kaleidoscopic image of society thus started to emerge in Spain by the twelfth century. A pluri-ethnic and multi-religious land, it embraced both a knightly and feudalistic structure in the rural regions of the upland plains, a looser and more free-flowing land-tenure along the battlefront, and a strongly localized communal scene along the Mediterranean coast and in the urban settlements along the shifting frontier. Reconciling and harmonizing the different traditions that made up Spain's political, social, religious, and cultural legacy proved difficult over the centuries but contributed much to making it one of the more dynamic and intriguing, if more than usually puzzling, worlds of medieval Europe.

THE ITALIAN SCENE

Change gripped the Italian peninsula as well. By the middle of the twelfth century, Italy too had well-developed traditions of communalism and of monarchy, of liberal near-egalitarianism and of hierarchical paternalism. As a natural crossroads for the cultures that made up the Mediterranean basin, Italy displayed surprising degrees of tolerance across religious and ethnic lines along with often astonishing degrees of repression and violence. In a general sense the political and social traditions of the Italian peninsula from the eleventh century on reversed the basic pattern established throughout continental Europe—within Italy the communal-urban model dominated in the north whereas the feudal-monarchical model became (with some modifications) the norm through most of the south. By the middle of the twelfth century, however, both northern and southern Italy witnessed dynamic economic growth intellectual advance, and institutional development.

The communal-urban pattern of the northern peninsula represented to a certain extent merely a revival of the normative style of life that dated back for centuries. The terrain of Italy, with its coastal clusters of merchant-settlers and its rugged mountains that divide the interior into discrete rural units, accounted for much of this traditional localism. But a nexus of forces released in the eleventh century ignited the rise of the urban communes; these forces included a fast-rising birth rate, increased agricultural production, the liberation of trade following the breakup of the Islamic empire, and the rediscovery of Roman law. As the population of northern Italy grew, so did the demand for food. Some of the technological advances in farming mentioned earlier—the wheeled plow, crop rotation, the use of horses as draught animals instead of oxen, and so on—produced higher yields than before. But even more important for northern Italy was the extension of arable land made possible by the draining of marshes and fens, the clearing of forests, and the irrigation of arid lands. Many of these newly developed areas existed outside of or marginal to the established estates of the old aristocratic families and the ecclesiastical estates of the great monasteries, which made it possible for a large class of individual landholders to develop, small farmers who held their lands freely without the manorial ties characteristic of northern Europe. But these new sites needed an influx of capital in order to become productive, and they provided impetus to the development of banking and financial interests within the cities. Moreover, the increased volume of agricultural produce provided incentives for the entrepreneurial merchants, who now had a steady supply of goods to trade on the opening Mediterranean market. In other words, the agricultural renaissance of northern Italy eroded the last vestiges of manorialism and created a proto-capitalistic rural economy amid a sprawl of merchant cities, whereas the agricultural renaissance of northern Europe occurred largely as the consequence of manorialism.

Prosperity meant a steady stream of people into the cities. Established municipalities like Milan, Genoa, and Pisa became even larger, while tiny hamlets like Padua or Verona became, by the start of the twelfth century, established cities in their own right. South of Rome new coastal communities like Gaeta and Amalfi competed with ancient establishments like Naples and Rome itself. Slowly but steadily the shipping lanes of the Mediterranean became filled with Italian merchant vessels carrying goods from one end of the sea to the other and making Italy the leading economic force of the eleventh and twelfth centuries. The German emperors retained their claim to overlordship of northern Italy and were usually (and begrudgingly) recognized by the Italians whenever the imperial army happened to cross over the Alps; but most of the time the cities had de facto independence. Organizing themselves into communes (urban republics with administrative jurisdiction over the surrounding rural zones) they enjoyed near-complete autonomy—a fact recognized even by the German imperial chronicler Otto of Freising:

> In governing their cities and administering public life they are as wise as the ancient Romans themselves. They love liberty so much that they are governed by consuls who eschew arrogant power instead of by monarchs. . . . These consuls are chosen from among each of the cities' classes and are replaced in office virtually every year so that none of them, driven by lust for power, becomes a tyrant. As a result, since virtually the whole land is divided among the cities, each city requires its bishop to reside within the town itself; more than that, hardly any nobleman or magnate can be found anywhere who does not recognize the city's authority. Because of their ability to hold sway over all these lands and leaders, each city is accustomed to refer to the rural lands belonging to the lay and ecclesiastical lords as the city's own *contado*. In fact, in order to make sure they keep their aristocratic neighbors in line, these cities do not hesitate to bestow knightly status and noble titles upon citizens of low birth, even mere tradesmen whom other nations avoid like the plague when it comes to public respect and honors. But because of all this, these cities surpass every nation on earth in wealth and power.

Otto did not hide his envy, but he also made a point of emphasizing that Italian republicanism ran contrary to what northern Europeans regarded as the naturally and divinely appointed order of things—a hierarchical society of landed lords ruling the peasant masses. He singled out for criticism the Italians' tendency to obey their German master only when the imperial army was in town.

> Nevertheless these city-dwellers, forgetting the noble traditions of their past, show signs of their barbaric flaws. They boast that they live "according to the rule of law" but they do not obey true law, for they show little if any respect for the princely orders to which they ought to defer and which they should willingly obey. They do not even live according to the integrity of their own laws [i.e., recognizing imperial overlordship] unless they confront [the emperor's] authority in the person of his vast army. And while they will occasionally force a citizen to "obey the law" and will sometimes force an opponent into submission "according to the law," they themselves routinely remain hostile to the very person whom they ought to accept as their own kindly ruler, when all he is doing is to demand what is rightfully his.

Civic institutions developed quickly; indeed, their workings resemble those of a modern municipality: a central administrator akin to a modern mayor (called a *podestà* in medieval Italian) who served a one-year term of office, an elected council of legislators, commissioners of public water works, directors of road maintenance, tax assessors, judges, public health officials, and police corps. The structure of communal government varied a bit from city to city, but the broad outlines remained similar enough that northern Italy quickly spawned a large class of professional municipal administrators who passed from commune to commune, serving terms of office in each before moving on to the next job in the next city.

The laws they lived by, and which so irked Otto of Freising, were hybrids made up of local customs and privileges, but they came to share a common core. In the late eleventh century a complete and intact manuscript of the *Corpus iuris civilis* (the "Corpus of Civil Law" compiled by the emperor Justinian in the sixth century) was discovered in a library in Pisa. While knowledge of Roman law had never died out entirely in Italy—in partial form it had never ceased to be taught at the law school in Ravenna, for example—it had survived in practice only in bits and pieces. The rediscovery of the complete Corpus immediately excited legal scholars, and the book became a subject of academic study, but it eventually began to be put into practice by the communes, too. After all, what the Corpus represented was a comprehensive legal code for the administration of municipal republics based on industry and commerce. What could be handier? From roughly the middle of the twelfth century on, Roman law began to be implemented in northern Italy and coastal Spain, and from there it spread to other parts of Europe.

A very different scene developed in southern Italy. A tug-of-war between native Lombards, the Byzantines, and the North African Muslims had long dominated this region's political fortunes. The arrival of Norman adventurers in the 1020s broke the stalemate, however. These were men of the same stock as the Normans who in 1066 sailed across the English Channel under William the Conqueror. They seem to have come to Italy first as pilgrims passing through on their way to the Holy Land, but local leaders soon enlisted them to fight as mercenaries in the three-way struggle. By the 1040s, the Normans had begun to fight for themselves and to carve out zones for their own rule. A frontier atmosphere predominated as northern barons eager for glory, plunder, and independence hurried to the lower peninsula. The most successful of these was a cattle-rustler turned prince named Robert Guiscard (d. 1085), who knitted several of these independent Norman baronies into a larger unit. The papacy saw the potential value of having an adventurer like Guiscard to serve as a foil against the claims of the imperial Germans and appointed him a vassal of the Holy See. Meanwhile Guiscard's younger brother Roger "the Great Count" began to establish a Norman power-zone in Sicily, where he had started to campaign as early as 1061. The Sicilian conquest was complete by 1091 and Norman-style feudalism was imposed. Roger the Great Count died in 1101 and left Sicily in the hands of his wife Adelaide; she retired from the scene when their son Roger II reached manhood and took over the government in 1112. Roger II also inherited Guiscard's peninsular territories in 1129; thus was created a vast new realm at the very heart of the Mediterranean. On Christmas Day 1130, Roger II assumed royal status with a grand coronation in his capital of Palermo.

This Norman-Sicilian kingdom ended when the dynasty's direct line died out in 1194. But while it lasted, it stood out as one of the wealthiest and most powerful kingdoms in Latin Europe, thanks to the trade that passed through Sicilian harbors. As in England, the Normans governed their realm with a heavy hand. Feudal

A view of the Italian city of San Gimignano. Cramped for space within the town, urban eiltes built high-towered residences to show off their wealth and power: medieval McMansions.

practices and institutions did not fit well in Mediterranean Europe, where they ran counter to traditions of local autonomy in the countryside; the urban coastal centers also were accustomed to their own communal ways; and the polyethnic and multi-religious nature of the kingdom made for a cosmopolitan but also continually tense social scene. Historians have frequently romanticized the extent to which the Norman-Sicilian kingdom managed to harmonize these antagonisms. If Muslims,

Mosaic from the central apse of the cathedral at Monreale, Sicily. Twelfth century. The mosaics of Norman Sicily are among the most splendid produced in the whole Middle Ages. Here we see an image of Christ Pantocrator standing majestically above a scene of an enthroned Madonna and Child who are flanked by angels, apostles and saints. Elements of Greek artistic tradition (in the portraiture as well as in the Greek lettering) combine with some Islamic elements (in the elaborate geometric tracery) to produce a harmonious and powerful work of art. Source: Giraudon/Art Resource, NY

Greeks, Lombards, Sicilians, and Normans, town-dwellers, country rustics, and royal administrators found it possible to live together and to prosper, this was more the "harmony" of people who got along because they knew that they would face serious reprisals if they did not, than it was an oasis of mutual respect. Nevertheless, for at least a few generations, these communities from around the Mediterranean did share a common ground that was not, for once, a battlefield.

SUGGESTED READING

Texts

Anonymous. *The Poem of El Cid*.

———. *The Song of Roland*.

———. *The Usages of Barcelona*.

Galbert of Bruges. *The Murder of Charles the Good*.

Hugo Falcandus. *The History of the Tyrants of Sicily*.

John of Salisbury. *Policraticus*.

Ordericus Vitalis. *The Ecclesiastical History*.

Otto of Freising. *The Deeds of Frederick Barbarossa*.

———. *The Two Cities*.

Source Anthologies

Amt, Emilie. *Medieval England, 1000–1500: A Reader* (2001).

Shinners, John. *Medieval Popular Religion, 1000–1500: A Reader* (1997).

Strayer, Joseph. *Feudalism*.

Studies

Abulafia, David. *The Two Italies: Economic Relations between the Norman Kingdom of Sicily and the Northern Communes* (1977).

Barber, Richard W. *The Knight and Chivalry* (1995).

Bartlett, Robert. *The Making of Europe: Conquest, Colonization, and Cultural Change, 950–1350* (1993).

———. *England under the Norman and Angevin Kings, 1075–1225* (1999).

Bisson, Thomas. *Cultures of Power: Lordship, Status, and Process in Twelfth-Century Europe* (1995).

———. *The Medieval Crown of Aragon: A Short History* (1991).

Bloch, R. Howard. *Medieval Misogyny and the Invention of Western Romantic Love* (1992).

Chibnall, Marjorie. *Anglo-Norman England, 1066–1166* (1986).

Crouch, David. *The Reign of King Stephen, 1135–1154* (2000).

Duby, Georges. *The Chivalrous Society* (1978).

———. *Medieval France* (1991).

———. *The Three Orders: Feudal Society Imagined* (1980).

———. *William Marshall: The Flower of Chivalry* (1985).

Dunbabin, Jean. *France in the Making, 843–1190* (1985).

Fleming, Robin. *Domesday Book and the Law: Society and Legal Custom in Early Medieval England* (1998).

Freedman, Paul. *The Origins of Peasant Servitude in Medieval Catalonia* (1991).

Gerber, Jane S. *The Jews of Spain: A History of the Sephardic Experience* (1992).

Glick, Thomas F. *From Muslim Fortress to Christian Castle: Social and Cultural Change in Medieval Spain* (1995).

Hanawalt, Barbara A., and Kathryn L. Reyerson. *City and Spectacle in Medieval Europe* (1994).

Jones, Philip J. *The Italian City-State: From Commune to Signoria* (1997)

Keen, Maurice. *Chivalry* (1984).

Lopez, Robert S. *The Commercial Revolution of the Middle Ages, 950–1350* (1976).

Loud, Graham. *The Age of Robert Guiscard: Southern Italy and the Norman Conquest* (2000).

Matthew, Donald. *The Norman Kingdom of Sicily* (1992).

Poly, Jean-Pierre, and Eric Bournazel. *The Feudal Transformation, 900–1200* (1991).

Reilly, Bernard F. *The Medieval Spains* (1993).

Reynolds, Susan. *Fiefs and Vassals: The Medieval Evidence Reinterpreted* (1994).

———. *Kingdoms and Communities in Western Europe, 900–1300* (1984).

Skinner, Patricia. *Family Power in Southern Italy: The Duchy of Gaeta and Its Neighbours, 850–1139* (1995).

CHAPTER 10

THE REFORM OF THE CHURCH

The reform of the Church in the eleventh and twelfth centuries is one of medieval Europe's great success stories. Considering the depths to which the Church had sunk in the tenth century, the fact that by the end of the eleventh century it was able to re-create itself so completely in terms of its institutional, doctrinal, intellectual, and spiritual life is deeply impressive. The medieval reform and its aftereffects is arguably the most revolutionary chapter in Church history; even the Protestant Reformation of the sixteenth century, some have argued, effected less fundamental change in Christian life. The reform began at the local level and worked its way up the social and ecclesiastical hierarchy, gaining momentum as it progressed, until at the end of the eleventh century it reached the highest echelons of Church and State. As a result it both reflected and catalyzed the upsurge of religious enthusiasm of the age. The more the Church reformed, it seemed, the more thoroughgoing the people expected the reform to become, until finally the stage was reached, with the pontificate of Gregory VII (r. 1073–1085), when the reform movement's own goals were surpassed and an entirely new ordering of society was proclaimed. In other words, what began as a reform turned into a revolution of sorts. The end result was a Church as radically different from what it had been before as Europe's social and political orderings and institutions were, as outlined in the preceding two chapters.

The reform of the Church is both an exciting and a cautionary tale. The reformers, guided by aspirations for a more meaningful and independent spiritual life, gradually became enthusiasts for a type of spiritual purity that endangered those people outside the orthodox Christian order. On a popular level, champions of peaceful pilgrimage to holy shrines evolved speedily into armed crusaders determined to rid the world, or at least certain corners of it, of the "enemies of Christ." Anti-Semitic violence became widespread, though sporadic, in feudal Europe, and anti-Semitic prejudices (the same hatred, though with less of the violence that sprang from it) abounded in the south. Within the Church itself, proponents of ecclesiastical freedom from State control gave way to ideologues who proclaimed the authority of the reformed Church over the State and every aspect of life within it. And the culmination of the reform came in the bloody struggle for supremacy between the reformed Church and the equally reformed feudal monarchies.

There is no question that reform was badly needed. For all its achievements, the Church had never established itself as a freestanding institution; ever since Constantine convened the Council of Nicaea in the early fourth century, the churches of Christendom had lain under the more or less direct authority of the secular state. The Carolingians had continued the practice by every means at their disposal. Indeed, Charlemagne had made his view of things—the only view that mattered, as far as he was concerned—perfectly clear in a series of letters he sent to Pope Leo III, in which he articulated the general policy that it fell to the emperor to maintain the Church materially, organizationally, and spiritually. The sole responsibility of the pope, he asserted, is to serve as a kind of personal example of ideal Christian devotion: to provide a model of piety, prayer, modesty, virtue, and obedience. But the Holy See is literally powerless.

The Carolingians' successors viewed it as their right to lord it over their local churches; and as we saw in Chapter 9, they hurried the Church's decline by their pillaging, their simony, and their general lack of concern for maintaining orderly spiritual life. A gathering of bishops at a Church synod in Trosle in the tenth century lamented the ruin of the briefly thriving Christendom of Charlemagne's time:

> Our cities are depopulated, our monasteries wrecked and put to the torch, our countryside left uninhabited. . . . Just as the first human beings lived without law or the fear of God, and according only to their dumb instincts, so too now does everyone do whatever seems good in his eyes only, despising all human and divine laws and ignoring even the commands of the Church. The strong oppress the weak, and the world is wracked with violence against the poor and the plunder of ecclesiastical lands. . . . Men everywhere devour one another like the fishes of the sea.

As civil society decayed, so did the local churches, which local warlords seized as sources of revenue. Simony—the sale of ecclesiastical offices—ran rampant, as did the practice of barons simply installing themselves, their friends, or family members, in ecclesiastical positions without regard for whether or not those people were capable of, or even interested in, actually guiding the spiritual lives of their communities. The rot reached as high as the papacy itself by the tenth century, when the Holy See was kicked around, bartered, and sold like a trophy among the families conspiring to dominate local Roman politics. The absolute nadir was reached with the pontificate of John XII (r. 956–963), an indolent and cruel sensualist who became pope at the age of eighteen and spent his seven years in office engaged in orgies of sex, violence, incest, arson, and murder. No one mourned when he died (reputedly of a heart attack after a strenuous bout of lovemaking with a married woman). Few of his contemporaries were much better, and the dismal nature of the situation can be glimpsed from the mere cataloging of what befell those popes who came immediately before and after him: John VIII (r. 872–882) was knifed to death; Stephen VI (r. 896–897) was strangled while rotting in a prison cell; Benedict VI (r. 973–974) was smothered while he slept; and John XIV (r. 983–984) was probably poisoned in the papal retreat at Castel Sant'Angelo. Another pope named Formosus (r. 891–896) died a natural death but suffered a cruel post-mortem humiliation: His successor, Boniface VI (896), accused Formosus of having been a heretic and a usurper, and decided, perversely, to place him on trial. Boniface ordered Formosus' body to be exhumed. The dead pontiff was brought into the synod, propped up in the witness chair, convicted on all counts (his inability to testify in his own defense was taken as evidence of his guilt), and then his corpse was stripped naked and thrown into the Tiber river. Before throwing the body into the river, though, Boniface cut off the finger on which Formosus had worn the papal ring; he kept the finger as a memento of his bizarre triumph. Boniface himself lasted on the throne only a few days after this, before he too was dispatched.[1] Clearly, something needed to be done.

THE ORIGINS OF THE REFORM

As seen earlier, Church reform began at the grass-roots level, with masses of commoners protesting the violence of the age and the corruption of the churches by the warlords. The attack on the churches and the oppression of the poor, they proclaimed, was an offense against God and nature. Outraged by what they saw happening at all levels, and anguished by doubts about the efficacy of the corrupted clergy's sacraments, they demanded change in large, though unorganized, numbers—protesting made possible by the clustering of the rural populace under manorialism. Rural workers demanded that the lords release their stranglehold on the churches. These "Peace of God" rallies, as they became known, were the first mass peace movement in western history, and the workers regarded the "freedom of the church" (*libertas ecclesie*) an essential component of that peace.

These protests followed a monastic lead. Since monasteries were often wealthy, they were singled out for attack by the post-Carolingian warlords. Tiring of the abuse, Latin monks demanded protection and used, as we saw before, techniques like liturgical cursing in order to persuade grasping barons to grasp less. The first monastery to receive a guarantee of its freedom was the abbey of Cluny, near the Aquitanian-Burgundian border, in or around 910. Duke William IX of Aquitaine, in founding the abbey, made a sweeping declaration of its privileges and immunities, and relinquished forever control of the monastic house, its lands, possessions, clients, and tenants. Most importantly, he recognized its right to freely select its own abbot and declared that

> the monks gathered there are not to be subject to my authority or to that of my relatives, neither to the splendor of the royal sovereignty nor to that of any earthly power. In fact I warn and admonish everyone, in God's name and that of all His saints, and by the terrible Day of Judgment, that no secular prince, no

---

1. Shocked by his behavior, a Church synod declared Boniface VI's pontificate null and void after he had been only fifteen days on the throne. Indeed, they claimed, his pontificate was never valid since he had twice been defrocked on moral charges before being installed in St. Peter's.

count, no bishop, nor even the pontiff of the aforesaid Holy See is to attack the property of these servants of God, nor alienate it, harm it, grant it in fief, or appoint any prelate over it against these monks' will.

Cluny's success inspired other houses to demand the same freedoms from their masters, and many of those that managed to win out placed themselves under the authority of the abbot of Cluny, so that by the start of the eleventh century, Cluny governed a network of several dozen monasteries, both male and female, and the Cluniac abbot was the single most powerful figure in the Latin Church.[2]

The village and manorial protests—the Peace of God movement—took Cluny as a model of sorts, and starting around 985 demanded the same basic freedoms for their parish churches. They had three things going for them. First, the fact that the protesters were now concentrated in clusters of manorial settlement meant that the lords needed to listen: After all, a crowd of several hundred, and sometimes several thousand, passionate and torch-bearing protesters represented a genuine threat to baronial safety. Second, the protesters appealed to the power of the saints whose relics were the centerpieces of each church, just as the rebel monks invoked the power of the saints in their liturgical curses. Devotion to the saints stood at the center of commoners' spiritual lives, given the paucity of untainted priests in the tenth and eleventh centuries, and by invoking the power of the relics against the warlords, the Peace of God enthusiasts significantly raised the emotional pitch of their movement; in other words, it was not only the people of any given parish who were outraged by local tyrannies but the saint himself, or herself, whose relics adorned the local church. These first two factors were enough to ensure the movement's partial success. Thugs who had won their positions in society by seizing the churches found that they could win popular support by becoming champions of ecclesiastical reform, a gain that frequently more than made up for whatever they lost in relinquished ecclesiastical revenues. Their role as reformers added an element of religious legitimacy to their emerging social status under the twin influences of feudalism and manorialism.

But then the third factor weighed in. The bishops of Europe's developing cities scurried to seize the reins of the reform movement and provide it with organization, energy, and ecclesiastical blessing. Promoting the reform certainly raised their profile. In theory the urban bishops had always had jurisdiction over their entire dioceses, but in practice very few early medieval bishops had ever had any meaningful control over the countryside (that is, control over ninety percent of their flocks) because of the small, primitive, and isolated nature of the cities themselves. A bishop's real power seldom reached much further than the municipal gates, leaving the rural countryside far more under the indirect influence of the monasteries and the great abbots. To counter this influence, urban bishops had long relied on a network

---

2. Cluny grew extremely quickly as enthusiastic monks flocked to it. A new building was soon required, and before the end of the tenth century Cluny had started construction on a massive new church and enclosure that was easily the largest in Europe. It was destroyed during the French Revolution, and only a portion of one transept of the church remains.

of surrogate "rural bishops"—also called "core-bishops" (after the Latin term *corepiscopi*)—who oversaw the country churches. By taking control of the Peace and Truce of God, the municipal bishops aimed to supplant the power of both the rural abbots and the core-bishops. An ecclesiastical revolution was in the making, one in which bishops, for the first time, were the dominant figures in the Church.[3]

By the start of the eleventh century, the reform movement was clearly in the hands of these bishops. Their strategic first step was to undermine the authority of the core-bishops, who enjoyed considerable popularity with the rural faithful. As early as the middle of the ninth century, a group of bishops gathered at Reims, in northern France, and compiled an enormous collection of forged documents—mostly letters from early popes (some of whom, like Evaristus I and Telesphorus I, were virtually unknown figures of the second century)—which supposedly proved the absolute authority of bishops over core-bishops (and thus, of town over countryside). Some of the faked letters even rejected the very notion of a "core-bishop" as a legitimate representative of the Church. For good measure, the reformers at Reims also composed papal letters that supposedly recognized the independence of all bishops from their respective archbishops. All bishops come under the direct and unique jurisdiction of the papacy, these letters claimed. Europe's archbishops were outraged, but the pope in Rome could not have been happier. Thus from the very start of the reform, the fates of Europe's bishops and of the papacy were united. The Reims documents formed the basis of episcopal privilege for six hundred years, until they were discovered to be forgeries in the Renaissance; but throughout the rest of the Middle Ages they were believed to be the legitimate work of an ancient Church scribe named Isidore Mercatus, and hence they are now known as the *Pseudo-Isidorian Decretals*.

Some readers may be surprised to find devout ecclesiastical reformers engaged in wholesale lying (but it may be exactly what others would expect). The great Church Reform was in many respects a "golden age" of forgery, with scribes on all sides churning out reams of phony papal letters, land grants, charters of immunity, and conciliar decrees. Forgery had always been a common phenomenon of medieval life. Poets everywhere scribbled mediocre verses and ascribed them to Virgil and Horace. Historians waged wars on their pages that never occurred in life. Would-be philosophers and theologians wrote volumes of nonsense and placed Cicero's or St. Augustine's names on the title page. The most tireless forger of all, Ademar of Chabannes, even altered the Holy Gospels by inserting the name of his favorite saint, the third-century St. Martial, into the text as one of Christ's original twelve apostles. Some scholars have estimated that as much as fifteen percent of the writing that survives from the mid-ninth to the mid-eleventh centuries is either completely or partially faked.

---

3.   As an index of how important this shift was, one should note that with the exception of the miserable politicos who abused the office in the tenth century, the great majority of those who held the papacy in the preceding five centuries had previously been monks; in the second thousand years of Christian history, virtually every pope has been a bishop before ascending to the Holy See.

The explanation, however imperfect it may seem, is that medieval people felt differently about the "truth" of a text than we do. We believe a document—a land deed, for example—to be authentic if it is the actual, specific, physical record produced by the appropriate juridical authority and bearing his or her signature and seal. Its "truth," in other words, is a function of its material existence. But in the Middle Ages the "truth" of a document lay in its *content* rather than its mere physical form. If what a document said was true, then the document was in fact a true one. Consider a convent that has been sacked by a rogue army. As the abbey went up in flames so too did the title-deeds of its landholdings, including (for example) a charter from Charlemagne by which he granted the convent ownership in perpetuity of a certain woodland. Charlemagne's gift was the "true" event, not the now-disappeared parchment record of it. Therefore the nuns who rebuilt their abbey in the wake of the assault did not think they were in any sense "lying" by producing an eleventh-century counterfeit which stated "I, Charlemagne . . . grant" the woodland to the abbey, or in signing it with Charlemagne's supposed signature, or in putting a date of "November 807" on it even though it was perhaps written in June 1034.

The reformers who produced the *Pseudo-Isidorian Decretals* firmly believed that the ancient popes they "copied" had either said what the bishops claimed they had said, or that they would have said what the bishops claimed if only they had had the opportunity. Therefore, there was no dishonesty even in inventing letters for unknowns like Telesphorus I. The reformers' ideas about forgery were certainly self-serving, but it is important to recognize that they believed they were only re-creating a parchment tradition to buttress a living ecclesiastical tradition that had always been there in the first place. Whatever their origin, the *Decretals* certainly proved to be a highly effective weapon. By the middle of the eleventh century, the rural "core-bishops" had virtually disappeared from the scene and the urban-based bishops had begun to found cathedral schools attached to their mother churches that enhanced and accelerated the reform. Opposition remained, of course. The roughly two dozen archbishops whose authority was cast aside by the *Decretals* put up a particularly stubborn resistance. But the primacy given by the *Decretals* to the papacy guaranteed their ultimate success. The very first pope to be informed of the *Decretals'* existence, Nicholas I (r. 858–867), received them enthusiastically and made them the foundation of papal claims to independence from the State and primacy over the entire Church. Every pope who followed him did the same.

The papacy itself was the last part of the Church to be reformed. The avaricious aristocrats of Rome saw to that; after all, by controlling the papacy they were controlling the single most important element of the city's economic life, for not only was the Holy See itself wealthy in terms of estates and tax revenues, but it represented the chief tourist attraction of Christian pilgrims. What finally brought about papal reform was a curious counterplay of headstrong personalities. Whatever people thought about the papal office prior to the reform, most Latin Christians still identified closely with the city of Rome as the symbolic center of Christendom. Pilgrimages to Rome were wildly popular and so were such songs as:

O Roma nobilis, orbis et domina,
Cunctarum urbium excellentissima,
Roseo martyrum sanguine rubea,
Albis et virginum liliis candida. . . .

[Noble Rome! Mistress of the world!
Most excellent of all the cities of earth,
Glowing with the red of the martyr's blood
And shining with the lily-whiteness of the virgins . . .]

Therefore, what happened to the Holy See mattered powerfully. And by the middle of the eleventh century reformist pressures began to focus. In 1044 the reigning pontiff Benedict IX (r. 1032–1044) decided, for whatever reason, to resign from the office. Could such a thing be done? Benedict, in any case, offered the position for sale to Sylvester III, who died very shortly thereafter and forced Benedict back into the job. Undeterred, Benedict tried again and sold the post to Gregory VI (r. 1045–1046), an earnest reformer despite his own simony. But several months into Gregory's pontificate, Benedict decided that he wanted to be pope again, and so he declared Gregory a corrupt usurper and announced that he was, after all, still the sole legitimate pope. This was too much for most Christians, and the German emperor Henry III massed his army and marched on Italy and summoned a council at the city of Sutri, just north of Rome, in 1046. Henry's council declared both Benedict and Gregory deposed and installed another pro-reform candidate as Clement II (r. 1046–1047). Clement was not a popular figure, however, and died a sudden death. Henry tried again and installed Damasus II (1048), who died even quicker. Finally deciding that enough was enough, Henry appointed his own cousin, Bishop Bruno of Toul, who took the name of Leo IX (r. 1049–1054) and wisely surrounded himself with a large corps of imperial bodyguards.

Leo IX is generally regarded as the first "reformed" pope. He certainly was a charismatic and talented figure. Leo recognized two things from the very start: first, that the papacy could not be properly reformed so long as it remained mired in Roman factional politics; and second, that the papacy needed to be seen by the faithful in order to secure the gains of the reform. Consequently, he avoided Rome as much as possible, although he made sure to sprinkle enough bribes around the city to buy support from the local magnates in his absence, and then he went on the road with his entire curial retinue, traveling all across the Continent. The importance of these journeys should be noted. Leo IX was literally the first pope to be seen in the flesh by any Christians beyond those relative few who made the pilgrimage to Rome. What a marvelous climax to the populist-driven reform movement, actually to set eyes upon the now-reformed head of the Church! Leo put on quite a show wherever he went. His entry into any given city was preceded by days, if not weeks or months, of advance notice. The gathered crowds ultimately saw a spectacle beyond their imagining: a parade of chanting clergy, colorful banners, trumpets and drums, relics and holy objects carried in triumph, a cavalcade of armed and mailed knights, and then finally, in triumph, the robed and tiared Holy Father on a brilliant golden throne carried on the shoulders of a crowd of papal servants. For the tens of thousands who saw him, *this* was the glorious culmination of four generations of reforming efforts. Leo's journeys were more than an itinerant propaganda campaign; they were a triumphal celebration.

Everywhere he went, Leo staged large-scale Masses, pronounced Peace and Truce decrees, and offered all the faithful the opportunity to air grievances about their local churches and ecclesiastical leaders. All clergy tainted to any degree with simony, he declared, could remain in office if they publicly confessed their faults and swore to dedicate themselves to the reformed Church. These acts of contrition and forgiveness were performed in front of the crowds, which served two purposes: first, the people themselves got to hear the confessions of their clergy, and second, the pope got the pleasure of having the faithful see the priests, bishops, and archbishops kneeling before Leo himself in order to be reconciled to the Church and restored to office. Leo, in other words, used the reform-celebration itself as a means for establishing papal authority over the episcopacy. Henceforth, everyone understood that the bishops served as the legitimate leaders of the Church *because* the Holy Father himself had publicly bestowed their office upon them. The papacy now stood at the head of a new hierarchy and determined its legitimacy. The boldness of Leo's move surprised many bishops who had long championed the reform and the ideas contained in the *Pseudo-Isidorian Decretals,* but who casually ignored the *Decretals'* assertions about papal power; until Leo, the pope, after all, was some figurehead in Rome whom hardly anyone ever saw. The case of the archbishop of Reims is instructive. He was a pro-reform cleric who eagerly welcomed Leo to his city precisely because he wanted to complain to the pope that he had had to pay too much for his archbishopric and was not being given a free hand to enjoy all the revenues due to him from his office. Could Leo do anything to help? Yes, said Leo; then he sacked him on the spot.

THE PAPAL REVOLUTION

Leo IX's pontificate marked a turning point for the Church. He was not around long enough to finish rooting out corruption, but he certainly brought the reform into its final phase. He drove simoniacs from office, helped to end the practice of clerical marriage, and improved priestly training and education. His last significant achievement was the creation of the College of Cardinals. Recognizing that the Church was intellectually ill-equipped to deal with all the issues confronting it, Leo decided to create a special body of advisors to the papacy—theologians, lawyers, philosophers, historians, scientists, and diplomats who could lend expert counsel. These figures, handpicked by the pope (as they still are today), became the College of Cardinals. They figured prominently in the effort to resolve many of the long-pressing doctrinal issues that had never been wholly settled within the Church. For example, whereas everyone agreed that simony was evil, did that necessarily mean that the sacraments performed by clergy tainted with simony were invalid? The cardinals produced "position papers" on a variety of responses to the problem, laying out all the arguments they could muster; the Holy See then used these in order to come to its ultimate conclusion.

Another issue was the celibacy of the clergy. Was lifelong chastity a fundamental requirement or merely an ideal encouraged for all those who were interested in it? Ever since its inception, the Catholic Church had been filled with well-meaning clerics who believed that celibacy was not a specific requirement; at various times in the past married clergy—that is, clergy who were either legally and fully married or who lived in common-law marriages with concubines—may have been in the majority. But others argued from the start that only those willing to vow themselves to the celibate life were fully qualified for the priesthood. As the reform movement reached its culmination, this issue too had to be resolved. Surrounded by the cardinals, the papacy began establishing itself as the decision-making center of the Church on all doctrinal issues.

In 1059 a synod at Rome made two decisions that started to turn the reform movement into a revolution. The pope at the time was Nicholas II (r. 1059–1061). Under his leadership the council condemned the practice of *lay investiture*—that is, the tradition by which secular rulers installed all clergy in their offices. The ritual by which a lay prince "invested" a priest or bishop with the insignia of his office suggested that the ecclesiastical authority was subordinate to the secular, and therefore the practice now stood condemned. The synod next promulgated the *Papal Election Decree* (1059), which asserted that henceforth and for all eternity the only way for any individual to become the legitimate pontiff of the Holy Catholic Church was to be freely elected to the position by the College of Cardinals. This decree removed the Holy See from the clutches of the Roman magnates, but it also declared the papacy's independence from the imperial power. Emperors had dominated the Church ever since Constantine, the synod declared, and in so doing planted the seed of corruption that took seven centuries to root out. Only by assuring the Church's full liberty from state-manipulation could the purity of the great reform be maintained.

These actions directly challenged state authority, especially that of the Germans who held the imperial title. Each side prepared for the inevitable clash by courting intellectual, diplomatic, and military support. The reformist emperor Henry III had died in 1056; his infant son Henry IV (r. 1056–1106) inherited the imperial title but could do no more than watch his authority be undermined until he reached adulthood. The Church swung into action by allying itself with Robert Guiscard, the leader of the Normans in southern Italy, and trying to win support among the secular German princes who were always interested in policies that would weaken the emperor. The papal alliance strengthened the position of the Norman rulers who were in the process of subduing the southern regions, and by this alliance the Holy See hoped to rein in these rowdy upstarts, but relations only worsened between Rome and the Byzantine Empire whose forces the Normans were removing.

Matters came to a head during the pontificate of Gregory VII (r. 1073–1085), which coincided with Henry IV's reaching adulthood and taking control of his government. Both were headstrong men to whom the notion of compromise was anathema. Henry was kept busy for two years putting down rebellions by various princes, during which time he and Gregory maintained cordial though tenuous relations. But Henry deeply resented the papacy's actions during his minority of pressing for more radical reform of the churches and encouraging the princes to undermine imperial power, while Gregory feared that it was only a matter of time before Henry would attempt to attack the crowning achievements of the reform by contesting papal independence from the emperor. In 1075 Henry finished dealing with his rebels and prepared to confront Rome, and Gregory responded with a preemptive strike that surprised everyone, including the most ardent pro-reform enthusiasts. Gregory penned a declaration called the *Dictatus Papae* ("Dictates of the Pope") in that year. This was a list of twenty-seven single-sentence statements about papal power. For example:

> The pope alone has the power to instate and depose bishops.
> The pope alone may use the imperial insignia.
> All secular princes are to kiss the pope's foot alone.
> The pope's name alone shall be spoken in all churches.
> The pope has the power to depose emperors.
> The pope himself may be judged by no man.
> The pope may release subjects from their vows of fealty to men who are unjust.

No one knows for certain what Gregory intended by the *Dictates*: Were they a dogmatic assertion, or a sort of ecclesiastical "wish list"? Were they an outline for a book that he planned to write? Were they a collection of random thoughts? All that we know is that the *Dictates* triggered an angry reaction from Henry, who viewed them as an unprecedented attack on imperial rights. (The other monarchs in Europe did not like the *Dictates* either, but were generally willing to stand by and let Henry lead the fight against them.) Letters passed back and forth between emperor and pope, and the vitriol of their language increased with every exchange. Finally, by the end of 1076 both the emperor and the pope had declared each other excommunicated and deposed from office. Rejoicing in Henry's apparent deposition, the German nobles rose up against him once again and this time they were joined by a number of the empire's important ecclesiastical vassals as well. Henry temporarily defused the situation in 1077 by making a pilgrimage to Canossa, in northern Italy, where Gregory was staying. Dressed in penitential rags, Henry stood barefooted for three days outside Gregory's palace window begging forgiveness for his sins and pleading to be restored to the Church. It was a personal humiliation—people came from miles around to watch—but it was politically quite clever. Gregory, as a priest, could not refuse to forgive a penitent sinner, and Henry knew that Gregory's forgiveness of him would of necessity put an end to the rebellions against him, since rebels against a good son of the Church would themselves become the Church's enemies. Gregory was furious at having been caught unawares, but all he could do about it, since there were so many witnesses to Henry's abasement, was to enjoy the spectacle for a few days before granting absolution.

The war of words continued for several more years, and finally in 1081 Henry decided to put an end to the struggle by invading Italy. As the German army entered Rome, Gregory took refuge in his fortress at Castel Sant'Angelo, which Henry soon surrounded. The pope was effectively imprisoned. But Gregory had sent word to his Norman ally Robert Guiscard of Henry's approach, and Robert came hurrying to the rescue.[4] Henry's forces wanted nothing to do with the Normans and fled north to Tuscany. For two years an unsteady peace existed, as the German imperials cut down pro-papal communes in the north of Italy and the Normans routed rebels in the south and prepared to resume their march on Constantinople, while Gregory stayed cowering in Castel Sant'Angelo. But in 1084 Henry pounced on Rome again. Robert rode northward in a fury, only to find that Henry had once again vanished. Guiscard then indulged himself by letting his soldiers sack the Eternal City. They pillaged Rome as it had never been pillaged before, and when the smoke finally cleared and the Normans marched southward, a chastened Gregory VII had to go with them under protective custody from the Roman mobs who demanded the pope's head. Gregory soon caught sick and died at Salerno in 1085.

This was the dramatic climax of the investiture struggle but not its end. So long as Henry IV lived, there were no signs of compromise coming from Germany, although the first popes after Gregory VII were careful not to aggravate relations by pressing too hard on papal claims.[5] The Holy See shifted its focus from debates with secular authorities to efforts to secure papal supremacy over the

---

4. When the pope's messengers went in search of Robert, they found that he had headed eastward, having decided to conquer the Byzantine Empire. He had, in fact, actually made it halfway to Constantinople and had already defeated the main imperial army when the pope's plea reached him. Confident that he could always come back to Constantinople after taking care of Henry, he gave up the mission and headed back to Italy.

5. The investiture struggle formally ended in 1122 when the emperor Henry V (r. 1106–1125), the son of Henry IV, reached a compromise with Pope Calixtus II (r. 1119–1124). The settlement, known as the *Concordat of Worms* (the German city where the accord was finalized), allowed ecclesiastical appointments to be made by the Church alone but gave secular princes the right to participate by "investing" appointees with the lands and appurtenances that accompanied the position. The delicate issue of papal supremacy versus imperial supremacy was sidestepped. It would flare up anew in later centuries.

The German emperor Henry IV, facing rebellion from his nobles, pleads with Countess Matilda of Tuscany to help persuade Pope Gregory VII to end the rebellion. This image appears in an eleventh-century manuscript of the Life of Matilda, Countess of Tuscany. *Source: Giraudon / Art Resource, NY*

Church itself. The key issue here was to assert papal jurisdiction over the episcopacies, since the Church was now one in which the bishops were the leading figures. Monastic life continued to thrive and attracted thousands of new recruits, but it was clear by the end of the eleventh century that the true centers of Christian life had shifted to the cities and that bishops had replaced abbots as the dominant figures in shaping Christian devotional and institutional life. In fact, it is worth noting that there were more assertions in the *Dictatus Papae* about papal authority vis-à-vis bishops than there were assertions about the pope's power over the emperor. Urban II (r. 1088–1099) devoted himself to completing the work of reform by traveling widely, holding councils and public ceremonies à la Leo IX, championing—and gaining popular support for—the notion of the Holy See's supremacy as foremost of the bishops. Urban was less charismatic than Leo, but he helped finalize the reform movement and establish beyond a doubt that after nearly eleven hundred years the Roman pontiff finally stood at the head of a united Church.

CHRISTENDOM AND THE EAST

Urban II was also the pope who began the crusades, the first major effort of the reformed Church to flex its muscles. The crusades were a series of campaigns led by the papacy to regain the Holy Land, especially Jerusalem, which had been under Islamic rule since 639. What distinguished these campaigns from earlier wars was their unique status as the only wars officially sanctioned by the Church. To participate in the fight against Islam was not only justified by the Church but was considered a positive spiritual endeavor. In short, this sort of armed struggle actually *pleased* God, and those who, with penitent hearts and devout motives, gave their lives to the struggle received a *plenary indulgence* from the Church—that is, their sins were forgiven and they were granted admission to heaven. The roots of the crusades are long and tangled.

Let's begin with the speech delivered by Urban II at the Council of Clermont on 27 November 1095, the speech that triggered the movement. The text, considerably reworked, was preserved by a chronicler named Robert the Monk.

> O you Frankish people, people from across the mountains, people especially chosen and beloved by God—as is shown clearly by so many of your deeds—and set apart from all other nations by the condition of your country, by your Catholic faith, and by the favor of the Holy Church! To you our discourse is addressed, and for you our exhortation is intended. We wish you to know what a grievous cause has led us to your country; what grave peril—one that threatens you and all the faithful—has led to our being gathered here.
>
> From the limits of Jerusalem and the city of Constantinople a horrible tale has spread and has time and again been brought to our ears: namely, that a race from the kingdom of the Persians—an accursed race, a race utterly alienated from God, a nation which has not directed its heart and has not entrusted its spirit to God—has invaded the lands of the Christians of the Holy Land and has massacred them by sword, pillage, and fire. They have led some of them into their own country as slaves, and have murdered others by the cruelest tortures. They have destroyed outright many of God's churches and have appropriated others for their own religion. They have shattered altars, after first defiling them with their uncleanness. With force they circumcise the Christians, and the blood of these circumcisions they spread upon the altars or pour into the vases of the baptismal fonts. When they decide to torture people

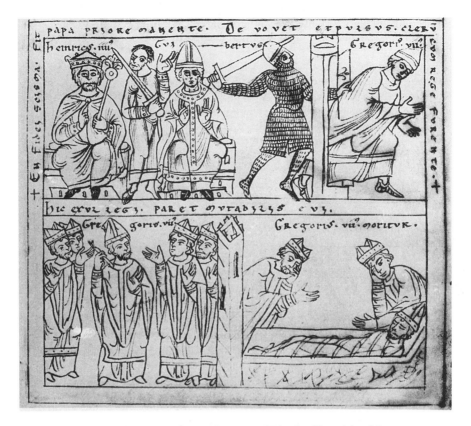

Derisive drawings of Pope Gregory VII in the Chronicle of Otto of Freising. In the top image, Gregory is expelled from the Vatican by Henry IV and his anti-pope Guibert. In the lower left, Gregory vainly excommunicates the emperor and anti-pope. In the lower right Gregory is place in his tomb, dead in exile.
Source: Foto Marburg / Art Resource, NY

to death, they puncture their navels, pull out one of their intestines, and bind it to a stake; then they beat and flog their victims around the stake until the viscera gush forth and the wretches collapse dead to the ground. Others they bind to posts and riddle with arrows. They stretch out the necks of others and hack through them with a single blow of their swords. What shall I say of the despicable rape of the women? No, no—to speak of it would be worse than to remain silent.

The kingdom of the Greeks lies dismembered by these people, and so much of its land has been lost that one could not traverse it all in two months' solid marching. To whom, then, has the duty of avenging these evils and recovering this land fallen, if not to you? You, upon whom God has bestowed more outstanding glory in arms, more greatness in courage, more vitality and strength than anyone else, all in order that you might bring down the brutes who resist you.

So let the deeds of your ancestors inspire you and incite your minds to acts of courage: the glory and greatness of King Charles the Great [Charlemagne], and of his son Louis, and of all your other kings who have vanquished the realms of the pagans, and have extended in those lands the reach of the Holy Church. Let the Holy Sepulcher of the Lord Our Savior, which is now in the hands of unclean nations, especially incite you, along with the holy places which are being humiliated and polluted by their filthiness. O most valiant soldiers, descendants of invincible ancestors all, do not fail us! Bear in mind always the valor of your fathers!

But if your love of your children, parents, and wives should get in the way, remember what the Lord says in the Gospel: "No one who prefers father or mother to me is worthy of me; no one who prefers son or daughter to me is worthy of me; anyone who does not take his cross and follow in my footsteps is not worthy of me." And also: "All those who have forsaken their houses, brethren, sisters, fathers, mothers, wives, children, and lands for my sake shall receive a hundred-fold and shall inherit everlasting life." Therefore don't let your possessions detain you, nor worry about your mundane affairs; for this land that you inhabit, enclosed as it is on all sides by the seas and surrounded by the mountain peaks, is too small for your vast population; neither does it abound in wealth; and it produces barely enough food for those who live here.

That is why you murder and devour one another; why you wage war on each other; and why you so often destroy each other. Therefore let your hatred go; let your quarrels end; let your wars cease; and put all your conflicts and arguments aside. Enter the road to the Holy Sepulcher. Win back the Holy Land from the wicked, and place it under your own dominion—for that land which, as the Scriptures say, "flows with milk and honey," was given by God Himself into the hands of the children of Israel.

Jerusalem is the center of the world. The land is fruitful beyond all others, like a paradise of delights. This land Our Redeemer has ennobled by His advent, beautified by His presence, consecrated by His suffering, redeemed by His death, and glorified by His burial. This royal city, we repeat, located at the center of the world, is held captive by His enemies and is being subjected to the worship of heathens who do not know God. She [Jerusalem] therefore desires and cries out for her liberty, and never ceases to implore you to come to her assistance. She asks this aid of you especially, since, as we have already said, God has bestowed upon you, above all other nations, great glory in arms. Accordingly, you should undertake this journey for the remission of your sins, and with the assurance of the eternal glory of the Kingdom of Heaven.

This is not exactly what Urban said, but it is probably not far off. More importantly, it reflects a number of the concerns and prejudices common to the European world in the crusading age.[6]

---

6.   Three other chronicles present versions of Urban's speech. They differ considerably. Of the four texts, Robert the Monk's version is regarded as the one most likely to proximate Urban's actual words.

The speech's horrific description of Muslim persecution of Christians, we know, is grossly overdone, yet it is true that Muslim treatment of subject-Christians and of Christian pilgrims en route to holy sites stiffened and coarsened considerably over the eleventh century, and that religious violence became far more pronounced. For the most part this violence was popular in nature—that is, it was something that happened at street-level rather than being an organized policy of the Islamic states. In Muslim Spain, as we have seen, the attacks of local warlords like al-Mansur on Christian sites like Barcelona (985) and Santiago de Compostela (997) signaled a change in religious relations. In Egypt the Fatimid caliph al-Hakim (r. 996–1021), whose hatred of Christianity and Judaism was intense, persecuted members of each faith with a heavy hand, and in 1009 sent an army to Jerusalem itself where they slaughtered the city's non-Muslim inhabitants and destroyed the Church of the Holy Sepulcher, the church built on what Christians believe to be the very spot of Christ's resurrection.[7] The Almohads of North Africa also repressed Christians and Jews brutally by liberally ordering imprisonments, maimings, and executions. But these official persecutions were not the norm. Popular hostility towards Christians, however, became commonplace over the eleventh century, leading western European Christians to conclude that some sort of rescue operation was justified.

Urban's speech also highlights the need for Christendom's elites to seek penance for their own predations on the poor. This call is an echo of the Peace of God and Truce of God demonstrations and of the Church's implied right to distinguish between justified and unjustified warfare. (Urban in fact concluded his speech by placing the entire kingdom of France under the Peace of God.) Only by turning their warlike instincts to a valid end, the Church maintained, could the knights of Europe attain forgiveness for their crimes. As an added enticement, the speech points out the relative poverty of northern Europe and the legendary riches of the eastern Mediterranean, which presumably would belong to the victors once they had vanquished the Muslim enemy.

It is worth emphasizing that this crusade-launching speech, while certainly anti-Muslim in its message, is not anti-Arab. The only ethnic group Urban mentions specifically is "a race from the kingdom of the Persians"—a reference to the Saljuq (or Seljuk) Turks. These were another nomadic people who emerged from the central Asiatic steppe in the tenth and eleventh centuries. The majority of Turks migrated south toward Baghdad where, once they embraced Islam, they were welcomed by the Abbasid court as a counterbalance against growing anti-Persian sentiment in the Arab-dominated states further to the west. The unruly warlike Saljuq segment of the Turkish mass headed west toward Constantinople, however, where they sought to establish themselves as an independent state. These Saljuqs

---

7. al-Hakim followed up on this in 1012 by ordering the demolition of every Christian church in his caliphate.

came to adhere to Sunni Islam, but their entry into the Levant further upset an already complicated ethnic, religious, and political situation. They scored a number of victories against the Byzantines in eastern Anatolia and in 1071 demolished the main Byzantine army in battle at Manzikert (modern day Malazgiv). Their leaders took the title of *sultan* ("power-wielder") and did not hesitate to use force to crush the Greek and Syrian Christians now under their dominion into obedience, although their anti-Christian violence probably had more to do with political expediency than religious antagonism.

The Byzantine Empire stood in dire need of assistance after Manzikert and appealed to the Latin west, where the battlefront against Islam was moving forward. After all, the *Reconquista* in Spain had been underway since the 1030s; the Normans had wrested southern Italy and Sicily from the Muslims in the 1060s and 1070s; and the Pisans, Genoese, and Catalans had begun to seize control of the Balearic islands, Sardinia, and Corsica by the 1080s. These Mediterranean powers, coupled with the emerging military might of feudal Europe, seemed increasingly capable of turning the tide. In the eleventh century much of the real power in Byzantium had devolved to local figures called the *dynatoi* (literally, "the powerful ones"). Their rise is somewhat analogous to the emergence of the *milites* who dominated western Europe in the wake of the Carolingian breakup, except the *dynatoi* were not necessarily military figures. Army officers certainly appeared among their ranks, but the class as a whole had as many regional bureaucrats, judges, bishops, magistrates, and well-heeled merchants and bankers as it had soldiers. What they had in common was ownership of land, most of which they acquired through purchasing individual farms from struggling peasants. This was a consequence of the shift in the empire's orientation away from the sea, which it lost to first Muslim and then Italian navies. Given the losses of territory to the various Islamic groups in the south and east, and to Slavic groups in the Balkans, the ability to hold and manage land at the local level increased in significance. The *dynatoi* often worked in collusion with the military officers of the *theme* system, whom they co-opted for local purposes. Thus they were able to resist imperial efforts to bring them to heel. As long as the empire was on the defensive, the *dynatoi* were able to become laws unto themselves. Thus the emperors had a real need to at least consider seeking help from the Latin west, both to defend against the Turks and to halt the decentralization of power to regional lords.

The Byzantines consequently appealed to the papacy to rescue eastern Christendom. They offered a tempting reward: the possible reunion of the Latin and Greek Churches. These churches had drifted far apart over the centuries. They spoke different languages, used different liturgies, and had different organization and relations with the State. There were also a number of overt theological differences, but these were relatively minor and did not necessarily stand in the way of maintaining the belief in, and hope for, a single Christian faith. But the two churches had split definitively in 1054 when reformers from Rome badly mishandled negotiations in Constantinople over the issue of papal supremacy that was

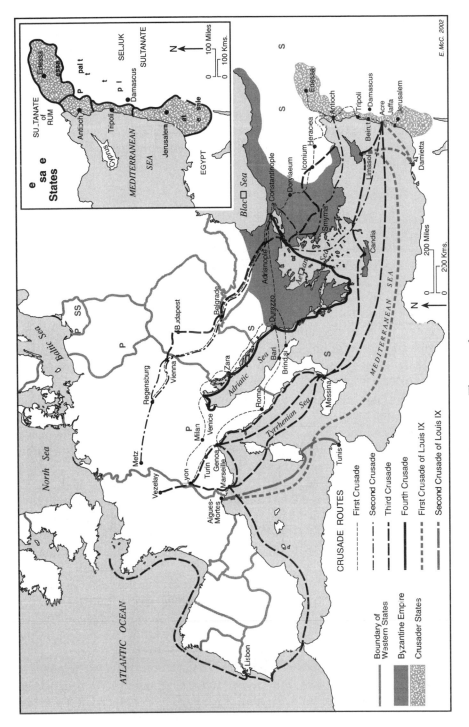

CRUSADE ROUTES

First Crusade

Second Crusade

Third Crusade

Fourth Crusade

First Crusade of Louis IX

Second Crusade of Louis IX

Boundary of
Western States

Byzantine Empire

Crusader States

The crusades

then reaching its climax in the west. Angry anathemas were hurled back and forth, and decrees soon went out announcing the permanent rift between the two churches. That is why the possibility of reuniting them, after the Byzantine emperor Alexius IV appealed for papal aid in 1095, proved irresistible.

The First Crusade (1095–1099) was the only fully successful one. A group of roughly thirty thousand knights, joined by perhaps as many attendants, servants, and hangers-on, formed the main army. They marched across central and eastern Europe and gradually convened at Constantinople, where a horrified Alexius IV cried out that he had only asked for some military aid, not another barbarian invasion. He had good reason to be frightened, for the crusaders had been preceded only a few months earlier by a ragtag mass of peasants led by an apocalyptic preacher named Peter the Hermit; these too were reported to have numbered as many as fifty thousand. Known as the *Peasants' Crusade*, this group was in thrall to the bizarre Peter, a popular preacher from central France who fancied himself a spiritual descendant of John the Baptist. Peter was a charismatic figure of electrifying eloquence who whipped his followers into a frenzy with warnings of the world's imminent end—but he also maintained that they, the peasants, must first lead a pilgrimage to retake Jerusalem as the necessary precursor to Christ's Second Coming. Peter's message was spread by a number of adherents, and peasants came from across France and Germany to undertake the journey to Constantinople. Along the way, however, hundreds engaged in large-scale slaughter of Jewish populations in the Rhine river valley, especially at Cologne and Mainz. When these zealots arrived in Constantinople, Alexius hurried to transport them across the Bosporus and into Asia Minor, where the Turks quickly decimated them.

The official crusader army was a different matter, though. They were in five main contingents, under Count Raymond of Toulouse, Geoffrey of Bouillon, Bohemond of Taranto (the son of Robert Guiscard), Count Robert of Flanders, and Duke Robert of Normandy (the eldest son of William the Conqueror), and had at least maintained some degree of military discipline. After securing promises that they would hold as Byzantine fiefs whatever lands they conquered from the Muslims, Alexius resupplied the crusaders and sent them on their way. After two years of hard campaigning through Anatolia and Syria, the crusaders finally reached the Holy Land and in July 1099 took Jerusalem itself. A horrifying bloodbath ensued as they ran through the city slaughtering civilians and setting fire to shops, homes, mosques, and synagogues. One participant, who exulted in the scene, wrote afterwards about the massacre of people huddling in the Temple of Solomon: "If only you had been there! For then you would have seen us wading ankle-deep in the blood of those we killed. What more can I say? No one was left alive, not even women or children." The bloody scene was not a freak occurrence. Religious zeal ran extraordinarily high among Europeans. The great Church reform had been pushed along by the masses, and had gained speed and fervor as it went. The enormous crowds that greeted Urban's original call to crusade were moved by a passion that they could scarcely control, and in fact it is plausible to view the Church's call for a crusade as an attempt to instill some sort of institutional control on this groundswell of popular enthusiasm, rather than as an attempt to stir up dormant feelings of piety and obligation.

Whatever the case, the crusaders who won the Holy Land confronted an immediate problem: What were they to do with it? No one wanted to turn it over to the Byzantines, as they had promised to do. Instead, since they viewed their crusade as a variant version of a pilgrimage, most of the crusaders, like regular pilgrims, returned home once they had reached their sworn destination. This left a tiny minority of Latin Christians in control of a coastal strip of land roughly five hundred miles from north to south, and one hundred miles from east to west at its widest point. They divided this territory into four principalities—the county of Edessa, the principality of Antioch, the county of Tripoli, and the kingdom of Jerusalem—which they then subdivided into fiefs for the remaining knights and began to administer as feudal states. Under its first king Baldwin I (r. 1100–1118), Jerusalem was the theoretical overlord of all four states, but in reality they operated as independent realms. Considering the brutality of the crusade itself, relations between conquerors and conquered were surprisingly peaceable. All four states built extensive networks of fortifications at strategic sites to ensure their control of the countryside. But even more important was the task of establishing good relations with the vast majority of Muslims under their jurisdiction. This happened rather quickly, since the crusaders recognized that they could not lord it over their new subjects and instead followed a general policy of guaranteeing as much local autonomy as possible: Muslim farms stayed in Muslim hands, Muslim villages continued to follow Islamic law, and the villagers continued to report to Muslim officials. Non-Latin Christians (such as Greek Orthodox, Monophysites, and Syrian Jacobites) and Jews retained their privileges of free worship and were in fact awarded various trade monopolies and local justiciarates in order to encourage their staying in place. On the whole, internal social and religious relations remained stable, and the crusader states prospered to such an extent that by 1184 the Muslim writer Ibn Jubair wrote that most of the crusaders' subject-Muslims preferred living under the Latins than under the Muslim rulers they had had before.

But the crusader states continually faced the problem of a shortage of Latin knights to defend the land against border attacks. Pilgrims from Europe came in large numbers every year, but few knights did—and few of those knights who came as pilgrims stayed as settlers. This meant that settlers remained vulnerable to attack from surrounding Muslim principalities, especially once those states began to mount organized joint campaigns. Once again, conflict came from encroachment by the Turks. In the 1120s a mighty Turkish warlord named Imad ad-Din Zangi rose to power in Mosul, along the upper Tigris river (in what is today northern Iraq). The people he led, like many new converts, were passionate in their devotion to a militant form of Islam and were convinced that the Arab world that had

*What the crusaders were after. The tomb of Christ at the Church of the Holy
Sepulcher in Jerusalem. The present chapel structure was built in the thirteenth
century. Earlier buildings were damaged or destroyed by various attackers, the most
notable being the Egyptian caliph al-Hakim in the early eleventh century.*
Source: Erich Lessing / Art Resource, NY

launched the Islamic empire had become corrupt and effete by adapting to western culture. Zangi began a relentless attack on the crusader states and the Arab
principalities that lived alongside them in relative peace. He led several campaigns
against Damascus, which the emir there successfully fought off thanks to his alliance with the crusader kingdom of Jerusalem. Zangi then turned his forces
against the county of Edessa, which he conquered in 1144. This sent shock waves of
concern through Latin Europe and eventually triggered the Second Crusade
(1147–1149).

The Second Crusade was a fiasco. France's king Louis VII (r. 1137–1180), urged
on by his adventurous wife Eleanor of Aquitaine, determined to lead the way. He
conscripted St. Bernard of Clairvaux, the highly respected abbot of one of France's
leading monasteries, to preach the crusade. Bernard initially hoped to keep this crusade an entirely French affair, but enthusiasm for the campaign quickly caught on
in Germany. The French troops gathered at Paris and set off for Constantinople be-

hind the advanced German contingent. Most of the German forces were cut down in Asia Minor, but Louis and his soldiers, accompanied by Eleanor and her Amazon-costumed ladies-in-waiting, made it safely to the Holy Land. By this time Zangi had been murdered by a political rival and his throne had passed to his son Nur ad-Din. While the crusaders were at Antioch, the count there, Raymond, pleaded with Louis to attack Nur ad-Din quickly, to dislodge him before he could settle into position, but Louis ignored Raymond's urging (possibly out of spite, since Eleanor was widely rumored to be conducting an affair with him) and moved instead to Jerusalem. Marshaling his forces there, Louis made the disastrous decision to attack Arab-controlled Damascus, the kingdom of Jerusalem's most important ally in the region. Caught between the advancing French and Nur ad-Din, the Damascenes sided with the Turks and helped to force the withdrawal of the French. Most of the crusaders returned home in shame, and Eleanor had her marriage to Louis annulled.

The Third Crusade (1189–1193) was full of drama. Once again, a reconfiguration of Islamic power in the region triggered the Latin response. In the aftermath of the Second Crusade, the kingdom of Jerusalem had sought to strengthen its position by advancing southward toward Egypt, which was then governed by a weakening Fatimid dynasty. The Latins took Ascalon in 1168 and attempted a full-scale invasion of Egypt, which was repulsed. The Fatimids feared another attack and pleaded with Nur ad-Din for help. He sent one of his ablest generals, a Kurd named Shirkuh, to Cairo; acting on Nur ad-Din's orders, Shirkuh murdered the caliph as soon as he met him and took over the government. When Shirkuh himself died a few years later, power passed to his nephew Al-Nasir Salah ad-Din (Saladin). Saladin quickly consolidated his power when Nur ad-Din died by marrying his widow in 1174. After a number of campaigns against rebels, during which he brutally suppressed Shi'ite communities, Saladin emerged as the sole ruler of the Muslim Middle East, and his dominion had the remaining crusader states surrounded. Saladin bided his time until he was fully prepared, then attacked. In 1187 he massacred the crusaders' army at the battle of Hattin and took control of Jerusalem. An immediate response came from Europe. The three leading kings of the feudal world—Richard the Lionheart of England (r. 1189–1199), Philip Augustus of France (r. 1180–1123), and the aged Frederick Barbarossa of Germany (r. 1152–1190)—mustered their forces with surprising speed. Frederick headed east first, in front of an army of perhaps fifty thousand soldiers, but so large a force moved slowly. His soldiers fought well and defeated the Turks at every turn. Unknown to them, however, the Byzantine emperor Isaac II had secretly allied himself with Saladin and did everything he could to hamper the crusaders' advance. Frederick himself drowned while crossing a river in Isauria, in south-central Asia Minor, and most of his army raced back to Germany in order to prepare for the political upheaval that was sure to follow.

The French and English forces, meanwhile, took the sea route. They wintered at Messina, Sicily, in 1190, and their respective kings quarreled fiercely most of the

The Siege of Antioch (1098). William of Tyre's Histoire d'Outremer *("History of Events Across the Sea") is one of our best sources for the first two crusades and the internal life of the crusader states between wars. Here the siege of Antioch—the most strategically important battle of the First Crusade—is depicted. Source: Art Resource, NY*

time. (It was widely rumored, and is still believed by many, that Philip and Richard were lovers.) They sailed to Acre the following spring, where they linked up with the remnants of the Latin army of Jerusalem. But Philip fell ill, and since his heart was never really in the crusade anyway he returned to Paris; this left Richard the Lionheart as the sole figure to confront Saladin. He spent two years campaigning. Aided by fleets from Genoa, Pisa, and Venice, he managed to win control of most of the coastal cities from Antioch to Jaffa, while Saladin remained in control of the interior. In the end, the two rulers decided on a truce: The Christian coastal cities remained free, and Saladin retained control of the rest of Palestine—with the special concession that Jerusalem itself was to remain open to pilgrims of all faiths. Saladin remained true to his word while he lived, but when he died only a few months after the crusade ended, his successors—known as the Ayyubid dynasty, which lasted until the middle of the thirteenth century—had a rather spotty record of recognizing non-Muslim rights. Richard, as is well known, was kidnapped by a local warlord in Austria while returning to England and held for ransom. During his absence, his brother John governed in his name, a situation that provided the basis for the Robin Hood legends.

There were many more crusades to follow, roughly one every generation, but the movement never had quite the vigor of these first three campaigns. Although actively promoted by popes and kings, the crusades began as a popular phenomenon—a wellspring of religious enthusiasm that drew upon and characterized the energies that had inspired the Church reform in the first place. By the eleventh century, Latin Christians simply demanded a different sort of world, one in which their faith was not persecuted, their Church not battered and abused, and their leaders not corrupted. They also were determined to bring the fight to the people who, for a variety of reasons, they regarded as the clear and implacable enemies of their faith. The emotional energy that lay behind the reform movement, both its positive and negative aspects, was remarkably intense. The same energy and enthusiasm contributed to the intellectual and cultural revival that accompanied the reform.

MONASTIC REFORMS

Christian monastic life has been one of continual reform and renewal. How could it be otherwise, when the very intent of the monastic vocation is the pursuit of an ideal spiritual existence? St. Benedict's establishment of his own order in the sixth century was itself an attempt to reform monastic practices that he regarded as outmoded and inadequate. Constant in all new orders and reforms was the effort to secure a more complete withdrawal from the world and a more perfect communion with God. Benedict's original program was exceptional in this regard and accounts for its popularity; but Benedictine monasticism veered off course during the Carolingian era by being drawn, often against its will, into the affairs of government. Abbots and monks filled the Carolingian court, conducted administration, ran the bureaucracy, and organized institutional changes, while leading efforts in the areas of evangelism, teaching, and ecclesiastical reform as well. They did a fine job of it, in general, but in so doing they inevitably were pulled away from their original vocation. The full-scale attack on the monasteries in the Carolingian aftermath only worsened matters.

The first substantial reform effort began with Cluny in the tenth century. Cluny did not alter the Benedictine program; it sought only to implement it more fully by achieving independence from the secular authorities. Its success was compromised, though, by its taking on the role of champion of monastic freedom, which inevitably engaged the Cluniac abbots in the affairs of the world. They lived like princes, and consorted with them. They traveled widely and moved in the highest circles of power and social influence. Nevertheless, throughout most of the tenth and eleventh centuries, the Cluniac houses were models of monastic devotion, discipline, and learning. Even so, there were voices of discontent. As Europe recovered, aristocratic families used Benedictine monasteries and nunneries as means for advancing their social status by dedicating some of their children to monastic life whether or not the children asked for it; every prominent family, it seemed, wanted to claim at least one monk or nun. Many of these individuals sincerely embraced the monastic life and found contentment, but inevitably others found themselves trapped in an existence they had not chosen. Most such religious went through the motions of monastic life with a spirit of detachment and resignation; others, though, rebelled and fled whenever possible. The rigorous monastic spirit seemed in danger. Moreover, the very success of the Cluniac reform undermined the movement. As Cluny grew wealthy, the monks did not need to devote as much time and energy to manual labor; instead, they took on tenants who did the farming while the monks remained in their chapels and libraries. By the start of the twelfth century, Cluny had the atmosphere of a highly discriminating private club whose members came from Europe's most powerful families. New cries for the renewal of monastic discipline began to be heard.

The two most important new monastic orders were the Carthusians, established in 1084, and the Cistercians, established in 1098. Both were Benedictine in spirit, but added features of ascetic discipline that set them apart from the mainstream. The first step was to limit entry into monastic life only to adults who freely chose it, and to submit them to a trial period in which they could undergo serious self-examination, to make sure of their calling. As a consequence, these new orders developed a degree of spiritual intensity that most Benedictine houses lacked. The Carthusians were noted for their austerity, as they still are today. (Indeed, they are the only order in the Catholic Church never to be reformed since their creation.) They lived in small, modest priories or charterhouses and worshiped in communal chapels, but to the extent possible they retained the tradition of individual asceticism. Carthusian monks lived in individual cells and engaged in near-constant meditation and prayer. A contemplative order by design, the Carthusians in the Middle Ages seldom produced noteworthy scholars or ecclesiastical leaders. The exceptional rigor of their life made them highly respected but it also kept their numbers down, since few felt up to the challenge. Their charterhouses—so-named after the first Carthusian monastery at Chartreuse in the French Alps—were intentionally small; an early tradition set the ideal number of monks in any one house at twelve, a symbolic re-creation of Christ's original group of Apostles. The Carthusians grew slowly: By 1300 there were only thirty-nine houses. Over a hundred houses were founded, however, during the fourteenth century.

Many more were drawn to the Cistercians. Founded at Cîteaux in 1098 by a group of idealistic monks who rebelled against the worldliness of the Benedictines, this order devoted itself to simplicity and austerity but without the extraordinary level of discipline demanded by the Carthusians. Their churches were unadorned, their houses unheated, their diet meager, and they were forbidden to speak unless it was absolutely necessary. The order was slow to attract followers at first, and by 1115 Cîteaux had only four daughter houses. But then an extraordinary young man entered the community: St. Bernard of Clairvaux. He was a man of exceptional gifts: a mystic, a brilliant preacher, a talented writer, an effective administrator, and a skillful advisor to popes and princes. His reputation for sanctity was widespread, and pilgrims flocked to his abbey in order to be healed of their ailments by his touch. People submitted their legal disputes to his judgment. Governments employed him as a diplomat, and we saw earlier that the papacy turned over the preaching of the Second Crusade to him. Bernard was the most admired churchman of his age, and his personal popularity ensured the popularity of the Cistercian order itself; Cistercians are frequently called Bernardines. By the end of the twelfth century Cistercian houses numbered over five hundred.

Another factor in the rapid rise of the order was its admission of peasants to partial membership. These peasant recruits were called *conversi*, and it was their task to work the monasteries' fields. Conversi took vows of obedience and chastity but were not tonsured. They observed spiritual services under the direction of the local abbot. The regular monks had little to do with them—but then, they also had little to do with each other. But it is clear that admitting peasants into the order assured its popularity, while it solved the perennial problem of a shortage of labor on Cistercian estates. So highly did people regard the Cistercians that the chronicler William of Malmesbury, writing in the 1130s, described the order as "the surest path to heaven." Their influence over twelfth century society was unusually broad. In founding new monasteries, the Cistercians tended to select sites that were on the outskirts of existing villages and manors, instead of seeking out distant isolation. Their proximity to established rural societies enabled them to interact with, influence, and frequently to dominate the secular world outside their walls. They helped clear land, affected the rural economy, and hired lay wage-earners (conversi), all of which enabled them to have a large impact on the secular world.

From 1115, when Bernard of Clairvaux entered the order, to 1210, when Pope Innocent III formally recognized the new mendicant order created by St. Francis of Assisi, the Cistercians were by far the most influential and inspiring order in the Church, intensely spiritual figures whom many regarded as the best exemplars of the Reform. They shied away from scholarship and dedicated their minds to contemplation and prayer. They led the movement to place reverence of the Virgin Mary at the center of Christian life (all Cistercian abbeys are dedicated to Her). Above all, they emphasized that the relationship between God and mankind is one of love and intimacy. Cistercian writing is powerfully emotional, as evidence by this passage from Bernard of Clairvaux's book *On loving God*:

> I remember a letter I once wrote to the holy Carthusian brothers in which I discussed [the] various types of love. . . . Let me repeat a portion of it:
> "One person might praise God because of His might, another because of His graciousness, and third because He is simply Goodness itself. The first is a mere slave fearing for himself, the second is merely greedy for more gifts; but the third is a true son rendering due honor to his Father. . . . Charity alone can turn the soul away from self-concern and love for the world, and towards the pure love of God. Fear and self-interest can never do that. They can only change the appearance and conduct, but never the object, of supreme desire. . . . The pure law of the Lord is love—the love that leads men to desire others' happiness. . . . Love is the eternal law through which the universe was created and by which it is ruled."

In order to avoid the worldliness of the Benedictines, the Cistercians renounced all benefices, rents, tithes, and tools, and earned their income solely from their land. This focused dependence on land forced them to pursue maximum efficiency, and consequently they built highly sophisticated systems of crop raising, animal husbandry, and mining, and turned themselves into some of Europe's best engineers. The monastery of Nuestra Señora de Rueda, founded in Aragon in 1202, constructed a dam on the Ebro river and built a massive waterwheel (*rueda*, in Spanish) that provided hydraulic power, giving the monastery indoor plumbing and one of Europe's first central heating systems. The monastery at Champagne mined the iron ore found on its land, constructed a blast furnace, and manufactured iron goods.[8]

The great Church reform had little direct, explicit impact on female religious. Women continued to seek out the conventual life, but there were fewer and fewer opportunities to do so in Benedictine orders. Money was the chief factor. As Europe prospered in the eleventh and twelfth centuries, more and more laypeople made pious bequests to churches and monasteries in their wills. This practice was as old as Christianity itself, but in the world after the first millennium there was a dramatic increase in the number of pious bequests that established endowments specifically for the performance of memorial masses for the benefactors. Masses require priests, which means that no women could fulfill these requests. As a consequence, the proportion of legacies left to convents decreased sharply; finite limits were placed on the number of nuns the Church could support. The Cluniac reformers did create a handful of affiliated nunneries, but the Benedictine strain of religious life entered a period of little or no growth.

Women responded eagerly, though, to the new orders. The original Carthusian Rule, called the Statutes, envisioned an all-male order but requests to create female chapters appeared quickly. Two convents were established in the twelfth century; nine more were added in the thirteenth; and four more appeared in the fourteenth. Most of these were new foundations, but several were established Benedictine convents that pressed for admission to the order. Carthusian nuns were exemplary in their discipline, devoting eleven hours a day to prayer and study; unlike their male counterparts, they sometimes engaged in a small amount of public ministry in doing work for the poor. Consecrated virgins all, Carthusian convents have never permitted widows to enter their order.

The Cistercian order, however, attracted women in remarkable numbers. The first convent was established in 1125 near Langres, along the river Marne in Burgundy. By the end of the thirteenth century they numbered in the hundreds, and some of the houses had hundreds of nuns. The nuns followed a strict regimen of prayer, meditation, and study; they worked in scriptoria and earned a reputation for excellent manuscript production. They also tended their own fields. Most

---

8. The monks also learned that the slag (a by-product of the refining process) was an excellent agricultural fertilizer; it became another source of revenue.

remarkably, in a small handful of Cistercian convents—such as that of Las Huelgas de Burgos, in Spain, founded in 1180—the abbesses possessed an ecclesiastical authority known as *vere nullius*, which empowered them to appoint clergy who could say Mass, hear confessions, and preach within the convents.

SUGGESTED READING

Texts

Abelard, Peter. *History of My Misfortunes*.

Bernard of Clairvaux. *Letters*.

———. *Five Books of Consideration*.

Comnena, Anna. *The Alexiad*.

Hildegard of Bingen. *Mystical Writings*.

Joinville. *Life of St. Louis*.

Psellus, Michael. *Fourteen Byzantine Rulers*.

Odo of Deuil. *The Journey of Louis VII to the East*.

Peter the Venerable. *Letters*.

Pope Gregory VII. *Letters*.

Villehardouin. *Chronicle*.

Source Anthologies

Constable, Olivia Remie. *Medieval Iberia: Readings from Muslim, Christian, and Jewish Sources* (1998).

Peters, Edward. *Christian Society and the Crusades, 1198–1229* (1975).

———. *The First Crusade: The Chronicle of Fulcher of Chartres and Other Source Materials* (1971).

———. *Heresy and Authority in Medieval Europe: Documents in Translation* (1980).

Skinner, John. *Medieval Popular Religion: A Reader* (1999).

Studies

Brooke, Christopher and Rosalind. *Popular Religion in the Middle Ages* (1985).

Bynum, Caroline Walker. *Holy Feast, Holy Fast: The Religious Significance of Food to Medieval Women* (1988).

———. *Jesus as Mother: Studies in the Spirituality of the High Middle Ages* (1982).

———. *The Resurrection of the Body in Medieval Christianity, 300–1300* (1998).

Chazan, Robert. *European Jewry and the First Crusade* (1996).

Crook, John. *The Architectural Setting of the Cult of the Saints in the Early Christian West. ca. 300–1200* (2000).

Fassler, Margot E., and Rebecca A. Baltzer. *The Divine Office in the Latin Middle Ages: Methodology and Source Studies, Regional Developments, Hagiography* (2000).

Flanagan, Sabrina. *Hildegard of Bingen, 1098–1179* (1989).

Head, Thomas, and Richard Landes. *The Peace of God: Social Violence and Religious Response in France around the Year 1000* (1992).

Lambert, Malcolm. *Medieval Heresy: Popular Movements from the Gregorian Reform to the Reformation* (1992).

Landes, Richard. *Relics, Apocalypse, and the Deceits of History: Ademar of Chabannes, 989–1034* (1995).

Maier, Christoph T. *Crusade Propaganda and Ideology: Model Sermons for the Preaching of the Cross* (2000).

Morris, Colin. *The Papal Monarchy: The Western Church from 1050 to 1250* (1989).

Newman, Barbara. *Sister of Wisdom: St. Hildegard's Theology of the Feminine* (1987).

Powell, James M. *Muslims under Latin Rule, 1100–1300* (1990).

Riley-Smith, Jonathan. *The Crusades: A Short History* (1987).

Robinson, I[an]. S. *The Papacy, 1073–1198: Continuity and Innovation* (1990).

Schulenburg, Jane Tibbetts. *Forgetful of Their Sex: Female Sanctity and Society, ca. 500–1100* (1998).

Tellenbach, Gerd. *The Western Church from the Tenth to the Early Twelfth Century* (1993).

Ward, Benedicta. *Miracles and the Medieval Mind: Theory, Record, and Event, 1000–1215* (1987).

Wilson, Stephen. *Saints and Their Cults: Studies in Religious Sociology, Folklore, and History* (1983).

CHAPTER 11

THE RENAISSANCES OF THE TWELFTH CENTURY

Latin Europe in the twelfth century crackled with energy. The reorganization of rural society, the reigniting of urban life, the creation of a stable feudal ordering, the growth of the economy, and the reform of the Church created an atmosphere of tremendous confidence and enthusiasm. All this change inspired some new thinking, even some new *ways* of thinking, that led to a flowering of intellectual and artistic life. This was a considerably greater phenomenon than either the Carolingian or Ottonian renaissances; those had been essentially court-centered occurrences that were very limited in scope. But the twelfth-century flowering was a popular phenomenon. Knowledge of law, learning, art, science, technology, and music flourished as never before and spread among tens of thousands (and perhaps, by 1250, even hundreds of thousands) of people. As the cathedral schools replaced the old monastic schools as centers of learning, they made education available to anyone willing to pay tuition—in theory. Interest in new technologies, new genres of literature, new philosophical systems, new architectural designs, new approaches to law, new mathematics, all increased dramatically. More than anything else, this new movement was dedicated to the idea of Reason. The cosmos is a rationally ordered place, scholars maintained, and God has given mankind the capacity to think it all out, to comprehend fully the mysteries of the universe. To do so is intellectually stimulating, of course, but it also enhances Christian faith—for what better way to love God than to appreciate the magnificent ordering He has given to everything? Reason and faith can be perfectly reconciled. And therefore *should* be.

Not everyone was delighted by this new thinking. Many figures in society felt that the intellectual achievements of the age were a sham, a mere passion for novelty instead of a dedication to truth. St. Bernard of Clairvaux himself sternly opposed the effort to introduce rationalism into Christian doctrine: God is a mystery, he insisted, and anyone who believes that he can think out God is guilty of hubris. Ideas that undermine religious faith, that disturb the social ordering, or that attack tradition are dangerous and need to be stopped. Figures like Bernard were not opposed to thinking per se but to the automatic assumption that reason is necessarily superior to faith or revelation as a means to knowing the truth.

The revival was long-lived and broad in scope. Scholars use the term *twelfth-century renaissance* to refer to the cultural and intellectual activity that enlivened Europe from 1050 to 1250. Two hundred years of exceptional intellectual and artistic achievement is, well, *exceptional* by any standard—and when placed in relation to the dark period that preceded it, one might argue that the twelfth-century renaissance was actually a greater achievement than the Renaissance of the fifteenth century. Like its more famous successor, the twelfth-century revival began with a passionate interest in the thinking and literature of classical times. Logic, the science of constructing arguments, of beginning with discrete facts or data and compiling them according to accepted rules into theories, lay at the heart of the matter. As early as the year 985 a writer like Gerbert of Aurillac (later Pope Sylvester II [r.999–1003]) attested to the importance of logical argument and the effective transmission of logic's conclusions: "Communicating effectively in order to persuade the minds of angry men and restrain them from violence is altogether useful. And for this reason I am energetically compiling a library [of classical writings], since the arguments must be prepared in advance." Intellectual reform, in other words, formed part of the Christian mission. Gerbert himself went on to make a number of advances in mathematics, including the popularization of the abacus.

But while the twelfth-century renaissance was a variegated affair, its most notable achievements were in philosophy and theology, the precise sites where the effort to reconcile reason and faith took place. So let us begin with the abstract and work towards the more specific. In the process we will see once again the knot of connections and cross-currents between the Latin, Greek, Muslim, and Jewish worlds as they collided with and nourished one another.

ARISTOTLE, ANSELM, ABELARD, AND IBN RUSHD

Aristotle was the most important philosopher of the twelfth century. It's true that he lived fifteen hundred years earlier, but his writings finally reached Europe in full only in the twelfth century, the ultimate example of a writer who had to wait for the recognition he deserved. Until the twelfth century only the handful of his works translated by Boethius in the sixth century had been known in the west. Gradually, more works became available from the Spanish and Italian translation schools, and by the end of the twelfth century direct knowledge of Greek made the entire Aristotelian corpus known. Rediscovering him was a revelation for medieval thinkers. What excited them was not his brilliant prose (Aristotle is as bad a writer as they come) but his empiricism and his logical method. Of course, people in Europe had thought logically before encountering Aristotle; but they learned from the old Athenian the rules of syllogistic reasoning, as well as systematic arguments regarding the nature of truth and the structure of knowledge. Aristotle provided them, in other words, with a new way of thinking. It was the medieval equivalent of discovering a completely new disk-operating system for one's mental computer.

As a systematizer, Aristotle was insatiably curious; he had investigated everything around him and had produced treatises on topics as diverse as botany, ethics,
logic, metaphysics, physics, poetics, politics, and zoology. Dante Alighieri, the medieval world's greatest poet, famously described Aristotle as "the master of those
who know," an inexhaustible source of knowledge. But what especially distinguished Aristotle's work and made it so appealing to medieval thinkers was his effort to harmonize his knowledge. He remained convinced that all truths were part
of a single Truth, that the universe was ordered and orderly, that things happened
for explicable reasons, and that the happiest state humankind can reach is to put itself in accord with the natural laws that govern existence. Aristotle delighted in the
physical world, less in a sensual than in an intellectual way, and this delight had a
special attraction for the people of the twelfth century who had grown weary of
heavy Augustinian moralism. A philosophy of existence based on sense-perception
inescapably validates the senses. With the rediscovery of Aristotle, philosophy became a matter of joy.

One of the earliest examples of sense-based thinking, and one that symbolically
represents the start of the philosophical renaissance, came from a northern cleric
named Berengar of Tours (d. 1088) who published a controversial work that argued
against transubstantiation. At that time, the Church had not yet dogmatically asserted the idea that the bread and wine of the Mass become completely and absolutely the body and blood of Christ, although popular belief tended in that
direction. Berengar argued that since our senses recognize no essential difference
between the bread and wine prior to their consecration and afterward, then it is logically impossible that such a change has taken place. The Mass is therefore merely a
symbolic celebration, not a renewed sacrifice. This conclusion set off an intellectual
firestorm, and theologians rushed into the debate. Lanfranc of Bec, who later became the archbishop of Canterbury, attempted to neutralize Berengar's argument
by emphasizing the difference between *substance* and *accidents*—Aristotelian terms,
both, indicating the difference between essence and mere external form. Lanfranc's
successor in Canterbury, St Anselm, took up the case, too, and in so doing made
sure that the debate over universals would dominate the philosophical activity of
the new age.

This needs a bit of explanation. By *universals* medieval philosophers meant
those ideal qualities that all members of a particular class or group share and that
define their essence. Consider, for example, two chairs. They may have different
shapes, be made of different materials, have different masses and weights, be of different colors, be used for different purposes, and yet there is no doubt that they are
both indeed chairs. They both possess some quality—let's call it *chairness*—that
identifies and defines their essence. But does *chairness*, the universal quality of all
chairs, actually exist? Or is it merely an abstraction, a concept that has a certain intellectual utility but no practical meaning? The meaning of this analogy for the debate raised by Berengar is obvious, for the question he raised centered on whether
or not the real essence of anything was determined by its physical characteristics.

Does the fact that something looks like, feels like, smells like, and tastes like bread necessarily mean that it *is* bread? But if those characteristics do not signify bread, then of what good are our sense-data? And if all our knowledge derives from our senses, how can we possibly know anything?

These are critical philosophical questions, and medieval thinkers devoted many thousands of pages to trying to puzzle them out. No one "won" the debate—that is not the way philosophy works—but as the debate progressed a number of major factions began to emerge. The *realists* insisted that universals really did exist as sensible and meaningful constructs, even if only in the mind of God. The *nominalists* held the opposite position, that universals were mere names or categorizing tools used by men to try to impose order on the world and were themselves essentially meaningless. Both positions were problematic. The realists, if they held true to their convictions, were vulnerable to charges of pantheism, since if individual people, for example, were real only to the extent that they formed part of the universal "mankind" in God's mind, then realism failed to distinguish adequately between God and His creation. The nominalists, on the other hand, if they traced the implications of their position out to their logical conclusion, were in the position of having to deny the Trinity, the Real Presence, and the divinity of Christ. Both schools produced a number of brilliant and challenging, if not altogether orthodox, thinkers: for example, William of Champeaux (d. 1121) and John Wycliffe (d. 1384) for the realists, and William of Ockham (d. 1348) and Jean Gerson (d. 1429) for the nominalists.

St. Anselm of Canterbury (1033–1109) was an important transitional figure from the Neo-Platonic and Augustinian model of the first half of medieval intellectual life to the Aristotelian model of the second half. Anselm was a realist who believed firmly in the power of reason to illuminate, though not to prove or authenticate, faith. "I believe in order that I might know" summed up his approach. Nevertheless, he was identified with the rationalist movement, and described the role of reason in explaining and supporting faith in these terms:

> I have been asked countless times, by mouth and by letter, to put down in writing the proofs of any particular teaching of our faith, as I have grown accustomed to do for those inquiring into it. I am told that these proofs give pleasure and reassurance. Those who ask this of me do not necessarily try to come to faith via reason; rather they live in the hope of being uplifted by learning that the things they believe by faith and instinct are true.

Anselm's most renowned contribution to western thought was the so-called *ontological proof* of God's existence. It is really quite clever:

1. By *God* we mean the greatest of all possible beings, the one being that it is impossible to conceive of anything else being greater than.
2. To exist in our minds alone, and not in reality, is a self-contradiction of the very definition of *God*.
3. Therefore such a being, since we can conceive of it, must exist in reality and not merely in our minds, for existing in reality is greater than existing only in our minds.

Nevertheless, for Anselm faith remained a basic instinct and an emotional commitment rather than an intellectual conviction. One cannot think one's way to God; but, beginning with faith in God, one can then think out a very great number of life's questions. Anselm was a beautifully subtle and moving writer.

By the time of his death, the cathedral schools were clearly on the rise. Anselm himself had begun his career as a monk and finished it as a bishop, unintentionally paralleling the seismic ground-shift taking place within the Church. The teachers at these cathedral schools were mostly itinerant, traveling from place to place and offering lectures and tutorials for cash; as their circuits spread, so did their reputations. They traveled in search of money, renown, libraries, patrons, and, since many of their new ideas were deeply upsetting to established orthodoxies, personal protection. The greatest of these wandering scholars was Peter Abelard (1079–1142). The son of a Breton nobleman, Abelard showed his intellectual promise early in life and even before he finished his elementary studies was already challenging his teachers. (In the often raucous atmosphere of the cathedral schools, students could challenge their teachers to public debates on any given question. Abelard did so and defeated his teacher William of Champeaux, who tried to defend his extreme realist position. William's teaching career never fully recovered from the humiliation, while Abelard's was launched.)[1] Abelard was the most brilliant member of his generation—and he knew it. His first book was his most audacious and important. Entitled *Sic et Non* ("Yes and No"), it assembled texts from the Bible, the Church Fathers, papal letters, and conciliar decrees that contradicted one another on such fundamental questions as "Is God omnipotent, or not?" and "Did God create evil, or not?" Abelard's point was that the Church could not rely solely on the authority of tradition to resolve such basic questions of faith since the tradition itself was imperfect; instead, he argued, a rigorously logical and scholarly approach was needed. "Diligent and constant questioning is the fundamental key to all wisdom," he wrote in the book's majestic preface; "by doubting we come to inquiry, and by inquiring we come to the truth." Having shown the need for a rational reconstruction of Christian thought, Abelard then devoted himself to the task with fervor, teaching to large crowds in Paris and writing a stream of philosophical and exegetical works. Crowds flocked to his lectures, with some students traveling hundreds of miles to hear him: "The dangers of travel meant absolutely nothing to them," wrote one commentator; "they all came in the firm belief that there was nothing he could not teach them." If we can take Abelard at his word, some of these students were so aflame with enthusiasm after his lectures that they occasionally lifted him onto

---

1. A similar episode occurred in 1113 when Abelard attended a series of lectures delivered in a local synagogue by the theologian Anselm of Laon—until they acquired facilities of their own, the early schools sometimes rented space in established synagogues—that left him unimpressed. Anselm, the leading theologian of his time, was lecturing on the *Book of Kings* but, complained Abelard, "while he may have kindled a fire, he filled the room with far more smoke than light." He challenged Anselm on the spot. Abelard was given one week to prepare a lecture on an obscure passage from *Ezechiel*. Instead, Abelard lectured on the passage the very next morning, and did so with such brilliance that he was driven out of town by the students loyal to Anselm. Abelard moved on to Paris.

their shoulders and carried him home while chanting his name through the streets of Paris.

But that is not all he devoted himself to. As he later described in his autobiography *The History of My Misfortunes*:

> At that time there was in Paris a certain young girl named Héloïse. She was the niece of a canon named Fulbert who, since he loved her dearly, was eager to do all he could to help her progress in knowledge of letters. She was hardly among the least of women in her physical beauty and was among the greatest in the abundance of her learning.

Abelard agreed to tutor Héloïse, found her irresistible, and soon seduced her. But what began as a sexual conquest turned into genuine love. When she became pregnant he offered to marry her, but she refused since marriage would effectively end his career as a scholar (since all scholars were regarded as clerics, whether or not they took holy orders). In a cruel blow, uncle Fulbert learned of Héloïse's pregnancy and hired a group of thugs who attacked Abelard one night as he lay asleep and castrated him. The humiliation of his wound, which quickly became known throughout Europe, led Abelard to renounce the world and enter a monastery. At Abelard's urging, Héloïse became a nun. They continued to correspond throughout the rest of their lives—their letters survive and have been frequently translated—but they seldom met face to face. Their baby was given to Abelard's sister.

Castration did not end Abelard's misfortunes, however. His books kept getting him into trouble. He was the sort of person who enjoyed flirting with heterodox ideas and tweaking the noses of accepted authorities, and his writings came under attack from conservative quarters. His chief nemesis was St. Bernard of Clairvaux, who pursued Abelard with considerable zeal. It was Abelard's whole approach, rather than any particular set of his ideas, that infuriated Bernard. To Bernard, the rationalization of faith was tantamount to the trivialization of it. God cannot be bound by the laws of syllogism, he insisted, and to suggest otherwise is to commit a heinous crime of pride. Worst of all, to Bernard, Abelard was urging young students to hold the basic tenets of faith up to questioning. "The faith of the common people is being held up to scorn; the secrets of God Himself are torn open; the most sacred matters are discussed with reckless abandon . . . [Abelard] approaches the dark cloud that surrounds God not as Moses did—that is, alone—but surrounded by a whole crowd of his disciples!" Abelard was certainly the better scholar, Bernard perhaps the better man. But they spoke fundamentally different languages, and their conflict illustrates the tensions existing in Latin Christendom as a result of the new learning. In the end, several of Abelard's books were condemned at councils headed by Bernard; Abelard died at Cluny while en route to Rome to appeal his case to the pope. Abelard and Bernard made peace with each other before Abelard's death, but it is important to emphasize that at stake in the dispute between them was more than a clash of personalities and egos. What truly separated them was an irreconcilable chasm—so it seemed in the twelfth century—between the truths that are attained by logic and those that are received by the revealed authority of the

Church and its traditions. As Lanfranc of Bec, the archbishop of Canterbury in the late eleventh century, put it: "Any time a disputed topic can be best explained by means of the new [i.e., Aristotelian] logic I always cover up the logical method as much as I can with the traditional formulas of faith because I don't want to appear to place more trust in the new method than I place in the truth and authority of the Holy Fathers."

The campaign to introduce logic in theological questions continued, however. Abelard's pupil Peter Lombard (1100–1160) carried on his master's work and wrote the *Four Books of Sentences*, which became the standard textbook for the study of theology for the rest of the Middle Ages. Few medievalists nowadays bother to read the *Sentences*, but from the twelfth to fourteenth centuries they were the core text of theological study at virtually every university in Europe; hundreds of scholars and would-be scholars wrote commentaries on them. The book's influence is most clearly shown in the establishment of the Church's final doctrine on the sacraments, a doctrine that rose directly from the commentaries on Lombard's book. Until this time there had never been universal agreement on the number of sacraments, or on which priestly acts were sacramental.[2] Lombard and the theologians who learned from him argued that there were seven distinct acts established either by Christ himself, the Church, or tradition, that held sacramental force: baptism, confession, confirmation, last rites, the Mass, marriage, and ordination. All these rites, with the exception of marriage, had played a part in priestly life down through the centuries, but not all had always carried sacramental authority.[3] The influence of the *Sentences* reached its highpoint when the Fourth Lateran Council in 1215 formally recognized the seven sacraments as official Church doctrine.

Perhaps the greatest commentator on Aristotle in the twelfth century was the Spanish Muslim writer Ibn Rushd (1126–1198), who is known in the west as Averroës. Aristotle challenged and worried the Muslim world as much as the Christian, and perhaps more so, for Islam was based on the idea of the unique, absolute, and perfect revelation of God to the Prophet Muhammad; nothing more than the Qur'an was needed, and even to suggest otherwise smacked of heresy. Islam had brilliantly adapted to most of classical culture once it had made contact with it, but its embrace of classical philosophy had always been wary. Medieval Islam produced several philosophers of genuine brilliance, but these figures had been marginalized, suspicious characters in their own lifetimes, like al-Kindi (d. 866), al-Farabi (d.950), and Ibn Sina (Avicenna, d. 1037). They are renowned as brilliant

---

2. A sacrament, you will recall, is a priestly rite by which divine grace is bestowed upon the faithful; this grace—and hence the rites that confer it—is essential to salvation. Baptism, for example, is a sacrament whereas a simple priestly blessing, while a rather nice thing, is not.

3. Marriage entered the sacramental canon in order to resolve a contradiction in Christian life. Lombard's commentators, following his lead, pointed out that the Church had long preached the superiority of lifelong celibacy as the Christian ideal, but if everyone was celibate the faith would obviously die out. The only rational solution was for the Church to legitimate a certain type of sexual activity (married intercourse) as a positive spiritual act—the procreation of more Christian souls.

scholars today but in the Middle Ages they were pariahs. Ibn Rushd was perhaps the least controversial of them, but he got into trouble nonetheless. He was also a world-class intellectual snob. He believed that Greek philosophy, and specifically Aristotelian logic, could harmonize with and elucidate the great teachings of the Islamic faith, "for truth does not contradict truth, but stands in accord with it and bears witness to it." But what should one do when logic appears to contradict Qur'anic assertion? Ibn Rushd cautiously suggested that certain verses of the Qur'an could not be read literally but needed to be interpreted metaphorically. But since not all humans are capable of making such fine distinctions, Ibu Rushd insisted that philosophical learning had to be kept under wraps, made available only to those individuals who were capable of appreciating the subtleties of higher thought. Philosophy was for the elite only.

> Anyone who is not a scholar needs to take these [Qur'anic] passages in the literal meaning; a metaphorical interpretation of them is, for such a person, a waste of effort since it leads to a failure of faith. . . . Metaphorical interpretations ought to be laid out only in scholarly books, because if they are laid out only in scholarly books they will be read only by scholarly men.

But while Ibn Rushd's elitism may seem distasteful, his understanding of Aristotle was sublime. In a long series of books, he brought to light many aspects of the old philosopher's teaching. His influence within the Muslim world remained minimal, but in the Latin Christian world his commentary on Aristotle's *Metaphysics* had a dramatic impact.[4]

Reconciling reason and faith is difficult—and perhaps not even necessary. After all, faith is by definition an irrational act; it means believing something *despite* the fact that rational arguments cannot be made on its behalf. But in the highly charged and confident atmosphere of the twelfth century, Latin Christians remained convinced that it was possible, in the aftermath of Europe's great reform, to explain the world, to understand man, and to prove God. The results of their efforts are thrilling to behold.

LAW AND CANON LAW

The revival of law was the second great achievement of the twelfth-century renaissance. This is hardly surprising: The lawlessness of the tenth and eleventh centuries spawned as great an interest in legal reform as in ecclesiastical reform. Feudalism and manorialism, as they developed, addressed some of these concerns but in real-

---

4. Ibn Rushd is in fact the only figure in all of Islamic history to have spawned a Christian heresy. A group of theologians in Paris in the thirteenth century, most notably Siger of Brabant (d. 1284) and Boethius of Dacia (d. 1277), became so enamored of his work that they stumbled into a heterodox position known as *Latin Averroism*. They adopted his conviction that philosophy was an end in itself, regardless of its theological consequences; and they further endorsed his ideas about the "agent intellect" (a kind of collective consciousness that every individual human participates in) and the eternity of matter (the doctrine that all matter experiences transitions but remains eternal, without beginning or end). Such teachings contradicted fundamental tenets within both Islam and Christianity.

ity they raised as many problems as they solved. Old customary codes no longer fit the ways of twelfth-century life, especially when they confronted the problem of multiple customs. How could the Capetians, for example, built a stable kingdom if "France" consisted of hundreds of individually governed districts each with its own system of laws? In point of fact, nearly every fief in feudal Europe had its own set of customs, although there were naturally many similarities between them. Moreover, ancient western tradition had maintained a principle known as *the personality of the law*, which held that every person was entitled to live under the laws or customs of his or her ethnic group. A free Gascon scholar, in other words, still lived according to Gascon legal traditions even if he or she lived in Burgundy; Milanese merchants residing in Marseilles were judged by the customs of Milan; the Jews of London lived according to Jewish law and answered to Jewish officials. One generally carried one's law with one (provided of course that you were a freeman). The growing passion for rationalized order demanded something different than the personality of the law. But there was a problem. Until the twelfth century most people in Latin Europe had a different conception of law than we do. *Law* to them was not a body of regulations and privileges to be created, modified, or repealed as the jurisdictional authorities deemed fit. Law was by definition permanent and unchanging; if a way of doing things could be altered at will, it was not law. In other words, the twelfth century thought of law in general the way that we think of the *laws of nature* or *laws of physics*, sets of permanently fixed rules to which we must conform our lives—not vice versa.

Two factors brought on change. Feudalism contributed the idea of *territorial rulership*, the notion that a governing authority has jurisdiction over an *area*, not only over a group of individuals. The early medieval kings had people-based, not land-based, power. Thus Clovis was *rex Francorum* ("King of the Franks") not *rex Franciae* ("King of France"); Alfred the Great was *rex Anglorum* ("King of the Angles") not *rex Angliae* ("King of England"). In theory, Alfred would still have been "King of the Angles" even if they had all moved to Iceland. But with the rise of feudalism and manorialism, the idea of direct jurisdiction over land gradually developed. Feudal titles reflected this change. The man who granted independence to the monastery of Cluny in 911 was William *dux Aquitaniae* ("Duke of Aquitaine"). The victor at the battle of Lechfeld in 955 was Otto *dux Saxoniae* ("Duke of Saxony"). The man who conquered England in 1066 was William *dux Normanniae* ("Duke of Normandy"). The emphasis on territory instead of the ethnicity of the territory's inhabitants undermined the doctrine of the personality of the law. But the process was slow, given the conservatism of agrarian societies.

The second factor had a quicker influence. As mentioned earlier, the rediscovery of the *Corpus iuris civilis* in the late eleventh century sparked immediate interest among legal scholars. Discovered at a library in Pisa, the manuscript of the *Corpus* made its way to Florence when a Florentine army, after an attack on Pisa, carried it off as war booty. From there knowledge of it spread across northern Italy. By 1100 a legal scholar named Irnerius lectured at the school in Bologna on the complete text.

Most significantly, Irnerius taught Roman law *as a system*, an organic whole, not merely as a compilation of various bits of legislation, which is how scraps of Roman laws had been known and passed on in earlier centuries. By glossing the text of the *Corpus*—explaining obscure words, relating various parts of the text to one another, and showing how the system evolved over time—Irnerius emphasized that Roman law had an organic and inextricable relationship to the society that spawned it and that it, in turn, regulated. Law as represented by the *Corpus*, in short, is a constantly evolving social creation, not a static body of immutable customs. The fundamental principles on which law is based, such as an individual's right to private property, Irnerius and his successors argued, do not change, but as social systems and practice develop over time, it is necessary for the specific legislation that implements those principles to develop as well. Students interested in law flocked to Bologna, which quickly became the premier site for legal study and training for the rest of the Middle Ages.

The impact of the *Corpus* was pervasive. For the urban south it provided an immediate blueprint for administering society, even though obviously many of the specific laws that were contained in the *Corpus* had to be jettisoned as no longer appropriate. As one moved northward into feudal Europe, the direct incorporation of the Roman law decreased, but even there the rulers made explicit attempts to introduce the system into the emerging urban areas of those realms. Municipal charters from the twelfth and thirteenth centuries in England, France, and Germany were clearly an amalgamation of Roman principles and specific local needs, as shown by the language of King John of England's (r. 1199–1216) charter creating the borough or city of Ipswich in the year 1200:

> We grant and by this present charter confirm that we grant to the townsfolk of Ipswich the borough of Ipswich with all its appurtenances, liberties, and customs. . . . We also grant them immunity from the customs in force throughout our realm and throughout our seaports . . . and immunity from criminal and civil jurisdiction outside the borough of Ipswich, on any issue except those in relation to foreign tenures. . . . We establish that in regard to all lands, holdings, and possessions within the said borough of Ipswich justice shall be administered to them according to the laws of Ipswich. . . . We also forbid anyone in our whole realm to exact [taxes] from the men of Ipswich, on penalty of £10 to the royal [treasury]. We altogether wish and command that the townsfolk of Ipswich shall have and retain the aforesaid liberties and customs securely and peaceably. . . . [Towards this end] we direct and command that our said townspeople [of Ipswich] . . . shall elect two or more law-abiding and circumspect men of their town . . . who shall faithfully and honorably hold the administrative office of that town, and that as long they conduct themselves honorably in that office they shall not be removed, unless the common people of that town so desire.

But the impact of the *Corpus* shows as well in the systematization of laws throughout Europe. North and south, the states of Latin Europe began to codify and standardize their legal codes along the lines of the *Corpus*. One or two examples will suffice. A jurist in the court of England's king Henry II—tradition attributes it (falsely) to his chief justiciar Ranulf Glanville—complied the first major treatise *On the Laws and Customs of England* in 1188–1189 and proudly compared England's legal tradition with Rome's. Henry Bracton's even more comprehensive treatise from around 1260 incorporated further elements from the *Corpus* and is most famous for its hairsplitting attempt to integrate the old Roman maxim *Quod principi placuit legis habet vigorem* ("What is pleasing to the prince has the force of law") with the Anglo-Saxon custom of the king being altogether under the authority of the law:

> Whatever is properly described, defined, and approved by the advice and consent of the magnates and the common agreement of the realm has the force of law, so long as the authority of the prince or king is first taken into account.

Citations from the *Corpus* dot the municipal code (called the *Usatges*) of Barcelona from the mid-twelfth century, while in 1268 King Alfonso X of Castile published his monumental work called the *Siete Partidas* ("Book in Seven Parts") that offered a minutely detailed blueprint for administering a highly feudalized realm along Roman legal principles. This plan required efficient central administrations, and the emergence of the very idea of the State can be traced to the expansion of Roman law. Such ideas were also put forth by France's Philip Augustus and Germany's Frederick Barbarossa in their attempts to consolidate authority over their often truculent barons. In the twelfth century, in other words, the originally private and personal authority of feudal privileges bound by vow and tradition transmuted into a modern notion of government as a public authority endowed with the power to legislate, create, annul, and adapt law as it saw fit.

The Church got into the act as well, since the reform of ecclesiastical law (known as *canon law*) was a vital component of the overall reform movement. For the Church's inner governance, the bulk of the content of the *Corpus* was naturally of little direct value, but its structural model proved highly valuable. As early as the late eleventh century, canonists were busily at work sifting through conciliar decrees, papal proclamations, the writings of the patristic Fathers, and episcopal letters, organizing them by topic, trying to resolve contradictory items, omitting what had become outdated. One of the earliest of these sources was the reformer Ivo of Chartres who in the 1090s produced two important compilations, to one of which, called the *Panormia*, he added a preface that is Latin Christendom's first treatise on jurisprudence since ancient times.[5] Ivo's works had great influence over the northern churches for nearly fifty years, whereas other canonists' works in Italy—such as that of Anselm of Lucca—predominated in Mediterranean Europe. Sometime around 1140, a scholar-monk named Gratian, who taught canon law at Bologna, published a massive compilation that he called the *Concordance of Discordant Canons* but which soon became known simply as the *Decretum*. Gratian's work harmonized

---

5. Ivo did not know the entire *Corpus*, but he was familiar with enough of it to understand its organizational principles.

both the northern and southern traditions and quickly became the standard text of canon law. His *Decretum* was influenced by Aristotle as well as the *Corpus*, and in his greatest innovation he cast his work in dialectical form, organizing his material around a series of specific questions or problems that any churchman might expect to confront over the course of his career, and then supplying the appropriate legal responses, along with citations of their origins. Here is one example.

> A certain noble lady learned that her hand was sought in marriage by a nobleman, to which she consented. But a different man, who was not noble and was in fact a slave, presented himself to her and pretended to be the noble. He married her. But then the first man, the noble one, arrived on the scene, intending to wed her. The noblewoman complained that she was the victim of deception and wanted to be joined in marriage to the first man, the nobleman.
>
> *Question: Was she already married? If she had believed that the man who wed her was a freeman and only afterwards learned that he was a slave, may she legally withdraw from the marriage?*

Gratian's comprehensiveness and pragmatic approach made his compilation by far the most useful; his use of hypothetical issues also made his text surprisingly readable, a feature that it still shares with the numerous commentaries made on it by later canonists.[6] It is important to emphasize that the *Decretum* was a book to be used in everyday life, not just to be studied by scholars in remote libraries, and it was this characteristic—one that it shared with the *Corpus*—that made it so central to the revival of medieval life. These books were not merely products of cultural change, they were engines of it.

By the end of the twelfth century, the intellectual revival of Europe was far advanced and clearly based on three essential texts: the *Sentences* for theology, the *Corpus* for secular law, and the *Decretum* for canon law. With these texts one could say that the medieval world had become in an important sense re-Romanized. When we turn to science, however, we will see that the influence of the Muslim, Greek, and Jewish worlds was greater than that of the Roman.

THE RECOVERY OF SCIENCE

Knowledge of the sciences had never been very sophisticated or widespread in the early Middle Ages. The Romans themselves had not made many significant advances in science, being generally more interested in technology and applied knowledge. Therefore most of what was known in the early medieval centuries was limited to whatever had been translated from the Greeks by a handful of pre-Carolingian scholars or else written down from various folk traditions. The seventh-century Spanish bishop St. Isidore of Seville (d. 636) summarized most of

---

6. Some of the hypothetical problems he invented were not, considering the pre-reform history of the Church, all that hypothetical. Consider, for example, the question: "What should be done if the pope fornicates on the altar of Saint Peter's basilica?"

this information, and added some implausible bits of his known, in his encyclopedic compilation called the *Etymologies*. The book is filled with what appears to us as nonsense—for example, Isidore suggests that human beings weep more easily when kneeling in prayer because of the fact that the knees and eyes of an infant in the womb are closely juxtaposed—but by the standards of the ancient world his credulity was not egregious. Isidore had intended his encyclopedia to be a summation of all knowledge up to that point, and for several centuries scholars in the west were generally content to assume that Isidore had in fact succeeded in his aim—with the result that virtually no original work was done in the area of science for four hundred years.

The roots of the scientific recovery in the west lay far to the east, in Baghdad. The Muslims under the Umayyads had scarcely begun to assimilate Hellenic learned culture by the time they were overthrown by the Abbasids. Jihad, not geometry, was first in their minds. Apart from translating a few alchemical works, they had explored very little of the great Greek tradition. The Abbasids, however, dedicated their court with equal zeal to the assimilation of Greek and Persian learning, and under the caliphs Harûn al-Rashîd (r. 786–809) and Al-Ma'mûn (r. 813–833) they began to gather scholars, manuscripts, and translators on an enormous scale and established a "Library of Wisdom" (*khizanat al-hikma*) in their new capital.[7] Most of the scholars at the "Library of Wisdom" were ethnically Syrian, Armenian, or Arab Christians—primarily Nestorians[8]—who had already assimilated Greek science and philosophy into a Christian worldview. A type of spiritual vocabulary had developed among these scholars that enabled them to bring this knowledge into the new vehicle of the Arab tongue. But not only Greek knowledge. The Baghdad scholars translated the Persian scientific tradition as well, bringing astronomical, mathematical, alchemical, and botanical works out of Sanskrit and Pahlavi. As these newly Arabized texts circulated throughout the empire, more schools, libraries, and translation centers were established, and Islamic science began to take on a more specifically Arab Islamic cast (especially as one moved westward). But a sense of intellectual pragmatism—as opposed to religious "openness" or toleration—still predominated; thus the ease with which Christian figures like Gerard of Cremona or Adelard of Bath (see Chapter 9) could move among the translation centers of al-Andalus was not unique to Muslim Spain but was characteristic of Islamic higher learning from the start. Surprisingly few Muslim scholars in the Middle Ages could read Greek (or Sanskrit or Pahlavi). Once the works of the

---

7. It later became known as the *bayt al-hikma*, which means "House of Wisdom."
8. Nestorians took their name from Nestorius, a fifth-century bishop who had emphasized a distinction between Christ's human and divine natures. Mary was mother of the human Jesus, Nestorius argued, but could in no way be construed as the "mother" of the divine Christ. Condemned at the Council of Ephesus in 431, Nestorius and his followers went into exile in Egypt. Driven out of Egypt a few years later, the Nestorians settled in Persia and slowly spread out from there throughout central Asia. They were the first Christians to reach China, for example. Their familiarity with so many cultures gave them a well-deserved reputation for assimilation and tolerance.

ancients had been Arabized, they were only read and commented upon in Arabic. Scholars commonly regarded the ancient languages as debased.

The Islamic world created or popularized at least four landmark institutions for the advancement of western science: the library, the observatory, the *madrasa* (a "school of religious law") and the paper mill. Libraries, we have seen, came to dot the empire: There were state libraries in Baghdad, Cairo, Damascus, and Seville, and innumerable private libraries. Patronage of science became a hallmark of Muslim nobility, an emblem of one's cultivated nature, and in order to attract scholars to one's court one had to possess a library in which they could work. For those engaged in astronomical research one also needed an observatory—fewer in number than libraries, but impressive in scale. Islamic observatories had permanent staffs, fully equipped libraries, charts, computational tools, and observational equipment. Too often, however, these observatories were built primarily for the casting of the horoscopes of the patrons (a residuum of pre-Islamic paganism) and were seldom used for pure research. Madrasas were another story altogether. A madrasa was the primary institution of higher education in the Islamic world; it was where Muslim men studied the Qur'an, the hadith, the *shari'a* [Islamic laws], and the commentaries upon them under a variety of legal experts. Although geared specifically toward religious instruction, the madrasas also taught at least two sciences— mathematics and astronomy—since these were necessary to the observance of Islamic law.[9]

A strong though still under-appreciated Jewish element factored into the efflorescence of science. Jewish scholars were among the leaders in Greek-to-Arabic and Arabic-to-Latin translations, and they were also active in producing original works of their own, most of which were never translated out of Hebrew in the Middle Ages. Even prior to the rise of Islam, there were scores of original mathematical and astronomical treatises penned by Jews, primarily in the cities of Byzantium. Most of these early works are anonymous. An exception is an early medical encyclopedia by Asaph "the Physician" that draws equally on Greek medicine and Talmudic teaching; it dates from around 600 and was probably written in Syria.

By the twelfth century, Jewish scholars had established a clear preeminence for themselves in medicine and in some branches of philosophy. Like so much of the intellectual outpouring of the twelfth-century revival, their medical writings were intended for practical use in society; such use is shown most clearly by the common practice of Jewish scholars—the astronomer Abraham ben Hiyya is a good example—of not translating books out of Arabic but of transliterating them into Hebrew letters. Most Jews of the southern half of the Mediterranean basin, from Spain to Syria, spoke Arabic and/or another local vernacular rather than He-

---

9. Complex rules governed the system of inheritance, for example, which made instruction in arithmetic and algebra necessary, while the requirement for daily prayer at set times created a need for some understanding of basic astronomy and spherical geometry. The latter were also helpful in determining the direction of Mecca, toward which all Muslims must turn when they pray.

brew. Hebrew was the language of liturgy and scholarship—as Latin was for Christians—but it was not necessarily the everyday tongue of the common laborer or shopkeeper; nevertheless, most Jews would have received enough education in their synagogue to read Hebrew letters.[10] Jewish physicians were highly prized at Islamic and Christian courts, even though Christian law technically forbade them to practice on Christian patients (Islamic law had no such strictures), and many Muslim and Christian students flocked to study with Jewish physicians. Interestingly, Jewish physicians in the Middle Ages made very few contributions to medical knowledge—that is, they did little "original research"—but in terms of treating illness they were peerless until the mid-thirteenth century when the establishment of the medical school at the University of Montpellier in southern France put Latin Christendom for the first time on roughly the same level of scientific sophistication.

The first signs of a Latin scientific revival appeared in the field of medicine in the late eleventh century in Italy, specifically at the southern city of Salerno. This city had long had close links with Islamic Sicily, and scholars there learned a good deal of Muslim medicine (which the Muslims themselves, of course, had largely derived from the Greeks). Salerno, in fact, quickly emerged as the first center for advanced medical study in Latin Europe, just as Bologna emerged as the center for legal studies. The best known of the Salernitan medical scholars were Constantine the African, a monk-translator at Monte Cassino in the second half of the eleventh century, and "Trotula," who lived sometime in the twelfth century.[11] "Trotula" may have written an influential work called *The Diseases of Women*, the first gynecological treatise in Western history; throughout the Middle Ages women commonly served as midwives and providers of basic health care to other women, but "Trotula" was the first, and for a long time virtually the only, woman-practitioner actually to put her knowledge into writing. Like Constantine, she subscribed to the traditional model derived from the second-century Greek physician Galen, who posited that the human body is composed of four fluids called *humors* that govern our health and disposition. Galen identified these humors as blood, phlegm, choler (yellow bile), and melancholy (black bile). It is a combinatorial theory of medicine: The interactions of these humors, and the fluctuations of their temperatures and degrees of moisture, react with the workings of the various organs to produce health or illness. "Trotula," like all medieval physicians, followed the Galenic model but added to it empirical knowledge that she had gathered from her practice. It is possible, too, that she learned more about anatomy through dissection—which we

---

10. As the huge trove of records in the Cairo *geniza* shows, medieval Jews commonly wrote everyday documents like business contracts, shopping lists, personal letters, wills, diaries, memoranda, and receipts in Hebraicized Arabic. These records have been exhaustively studied by Shlomo Goitein in his five-volume work called *A Mediterranean Society*.

11. Traditionally identified as Trotula of Saxeino or Trotula de Ruggiero, the existence of this woman has recently been questioned. The doubt is justified but I shall nevertheless speak of the author of *The Diseases of Women* as "Trotula," for convenience.

know was performed at the medical school in Salerno in the twelfth century. "Tro-tula's" book moves back and forth between theory and practice, with light touches of autobiography added for good measure.

> God distinguished the human race beyond all other creatures by granting it an extraordinary virtue . . . the freedom to reason and think. . . . Since women are by nature weaker than men it stands to reason that illnesses plague them more frequently; this is especially true regarding the procreative organs. But since these organs happen to be in, as it were, a recessed location, women's modesty, not to mention the delicacy and sensitivity of these organs, commonly prevents them from bringing their troubles to male doctors. For that reason I, out of sym-pathy for their situation and at the urging of a certain prominent lady, began to study in earnest the maladies and complaints that women are vulnerable to.

"Trotula" writes of diet, hygiene, skin care, menstruation, and pregnancy. Also how to avoid the latter—and it is in some of her precise recommendations that we per-ceive the survival of folk medicine within the broader Galenic theory.

> Galen notes that "women with narrow vulvas and small wombs ought not to marry, for they risk death if they become pregnant." But since not all women can avoid [marriage and pregnancy], they need help. If a woman fears death and so seeks not to conceive, she should wear next to her naked flesh the womb of a virgin she-goat. . . . She might also try removing the testicles from a weasel—without killing it—and wear them upon her bosom wrapped in the skin of a goose or some other animal skin. Then she will not conceive.

Despite such passages, *The Diseases of Women* is filled with much valuable informa-tion, especially on the use of medical herbs and ointments, and it became the stan-dard text on women's health at Salerno. By the thirteenth century, however, a new medical school opened up at Montpellier in southern France, and as it rose to prominence Salerno and "Trotula" declined in influence.

More solid achievements were made in mathematics, geometry, and astron-omy. Translators from England were especially important here. In the 1120s Ade-lard of Bath, who learned Arabic in Sicily, translated an Arabized version of Euclid's work on geometry and al-Khwarizmi's treatise on trigonometry. Al-Khwarizmi (800–847) is usually credited with having introduced "Arabic numerals"—which actually originated in India—to the west. That might seem at first like a relatively modest development; but European mathematics had long been hampered by the use of Roman numerals, whose inherent limitations become obvious if one tries to multiply *mccxlviii* by *dcciv* instead of *1248* by *704*. Al-Khwarizmi also wrote a book called *The Restoration and Opposition of Numbers* that was translated by an-other Englishman, Robert of Chester, around 1150. So significant was this work that later Arab mathematicians referred to it simply as "Reckoning," which in Arabic is *al-jibra*—now the bane of many a Western adolescent.

The greatest Latin mathematician of the Middle Ages was Leonardo Fibonacci (1170–1230). He made his mark in 1202 when he published his *Book on the Abacus*, in which he explored the possibilities of decimal-based mathematics. He developed a sequence of numbers known as the *Fibonacci sequence* that was to have important implications. It goes like this:

1, 1, 2, 3, 5, 8, 13, 21, 34, 55, 89, 144, 233, 377, 610, 987 . . .

In the sequence, each number is the sum of the two numbers that precede it. Fibonacci developed the algebraic formula to express this sequence; it is called a *recursion relation*. The significance of the formula, for our purposes at least, is that it describes a surprising number of natural phenomena. The formula, when mapped on a graph, corresponds exactly with the spiral arrangement of petals on flowers, the curve of snail shells, the twisting array of branches around the trunk of a tree. The ratio of pine leaves on opposed spirals of a pine cone is always 5:8; of bumps on a mature pineapple 8:13; of seeds in the center of a sunflower 21:34—all of which are adjacent Fibonacci pairs. The number of rabbits produced in a litter under ideal conditions is always a Fibonacci number. Moreover, once one progresses several places into the sequence, the ratio between the adjacent numbers of the sequence becomes constant and approaches a quantity that the ancient Greeks called the Golden Mean: 1.618.[12] Many other correspondences exist—and so Fibonacci's discovery did much to affirm the medieval certainty that they lived in a rationally ordered world. His formula was later used by Renaissance artists and architects to design the curves and ratios they used to create what they regarded as perfect balance and proportion.

In astronomy the most important developments were the translation of Ptolemy's *Almagest*, at Palermo in 1160, and again at Toledo in 1175. Medieval astronomers preferred the Toledan version since it came equipped with the Arabic commentary. But meanwhile the widespread use of the astrolabe, a device for measuring the position of stars and planets in the night sky, made possible much more precise mapping of planetary positions. The astrolabe had been known as early as the late tenth century: in fact, Gerbert of Aurillac, Pope Sylvester II, was one of the first figures in the west to study it. But the astrolabe was not widely applied until the twelfth century when it helped to advance astronomical knowledge and made navigation easier and more reliable.

Several technological developments emerged around this time as well. One of the most important was a new type of mill. Latin Europe had been limited to water mills for centuries; hydraulic power was plentiful but problematic. Mills obviously could only be located along major waterways, which placed a clear limit on human settlement; mills also strengthened the hierarchical structure of feudal-manorial society, since one often had only to control a strategic waterway, mill, or bridge in order to maintain effective power over an entire community. This is one reason why we see lords and vassals, in feudal contracts, speaking quite precisely about water

---

12. To the Greeks the Golden Mean was an ideal ratio to create visual beauty. Imagine a line segment AB. At some point along that line there is a point X. The ideal proportion is reached when AX is to XB as XB is to AB, which is a ratio of 1.618. This Golden Mean was used throughout Greek architecture (it governs the proportions of the Parthenon, for example) and sculpture (the Venus de Milo).

rights. But in the twelfth century, the first windmills began to appear in Europe. Knowledge of their design probably was brought back to Europe by the soldiers of the First and Second Crusade, for we know that the people of Palestine, Syria, and Iraq had developed windmills at least by the late tenth century. Windmills could be constructed anywhere and were less vulnerable to seasonal change than water mills. They allowed free farmers to remain free by giving them the chance to mill their grain without having to go to a manorially controlled mill; in their own small way, windmills were often emblems of resistance to feudal control of the country-side.

Other new technologies that appeared included the start of a silk-weaving industry, the first efforts to build mechanical clocks, the first experiments at optics and the grinding of lenses, the distillation of spirits (brandy out of wine, chiefly, but there are signs of something like a rough whiskey being made in Ireland and Scotland), the introduction of the magnetic compass for navigation, the development of the galley as the main seagoing ship, the construction of stone castles and churches (which we will discuss in Chapter 14), the appearance of vernacular poetry and polyphonic music.

THE RISE OF THE UNIVERSITIES

It seems a natural consequence that all this intellectual activity would sooner or later find some sort of institutional organization; ideas exist, after all, in order to be shared with others—or else they are no good as ideas. But how to organize the new learning of this time? The twelfth century was a time of great intellectual vibrancy and curiosity, but perhaps as a consequence it was also a time of considerable intellectual disorder. The only hope for coming to some sort of meaningful agreement about all these new discoveries was if the scholars themselves learned from one another. This seemed a reasonable hope, since the medieval mind was so powerfully geared toward the idea that all knowledge interrelated with all other knowledge.

The origins of the new schools that came to dominate European intellectual life are somewhat obscure. Certain models date back to classical times: Both Plato and Aristotle had founded academies in Athens where they regularly gave lectures, and in Roman times there had been organized centers of study at places like Alexandria and Antioch. In Islam, the institutions of the *majlis* and madrasas (Qur'anic bookstores and schools, usually attached to a mosque) also provided certain precedents, while Jewish synagogue schools provided another model. And of course, Christendom had its enormous network of monastic schools. By the twelfth century these were largely disdained, however. The monastic vocation was still deemed a noble one—but that was part of the problem; monastic life had become monopolized, it seemed, by the aristocracy, and monasteries, no matter how reformed and holy, were commonly regarded as sanctified country clubs. Moreover, monastic education was too limited in scope; it aimed only to help the student become a better monk. Therefore a new type of school was needed, one where all the new learning in philosophy, science, art, mathematics, music, and "humane letters" (*litterae humaniores*) could be studied.[13]

At first these new ideas circulated through Europe via itinerant scholars like Peter Abelard, but eventually it became clear that a more permanent educational system needed to be devised. Once again the bishops took the lead. By attaching schools to their cathedrals they achieved a variety of goals: They placed themselves in a position to attract and observe the most talented young people for entry into the priesthood; they assured themselves of an important additional source of revenue; they raised their social profile by being the providers of social advancement; and they exerted a degree of control over the new learning as it emerged under their watchful eyes. The medieval cathedral schools—and the universities they would evolve into in the thirteenth century—differed from all their forerunners in several critical ways. They offered standardized curricula; those curricula were taught by organized, incorporated bodies of professors; and, in their most radical innovation, they bestowed formal degrees upon those students who completed the curricula. Henceforth, education was an empirical, legal fact, not merely a state of mind.

And so the schools began to grow. The school at Angers, in the Loire valley, produced scholars like the trouble-making Berengar of Tours and the reformers Robert of Arbrissel and Marbode of Rennes. Constantine the African and "Trotula" made Salerno the best place to study medicine. Irnerius single-handedly established Bologna's reputation as the premiere site for legal study. But these were just the "marquee" names; thousands of scholars in hundreds of towns filled lecture halls across Europe, teaching tens of thousands of students. Even in a small town like Bergamo, in northern Italy, the cathedral school had nearly two dozen full-time faculty by the middle of the century, a company capable of handling approximately six hundred full-time students. Schools in larger cities were even larger, both in absolute numbers and in the ratio of students to teachers. To the extent possible, the schools always retained their professional mission—the preparation of clergy—but they were quick to open their doors to other ideas and goals as well. One frequent problem was that most of these schools were led by a single master (Latin *magister*), normally appointed by the bishop, with the majority of tutorials and lectures conducted by the cathedral canons, whereas most of the new advances in legal, philosophical, and scientific scholarship were being made by the itinerant scholars who, while they never really sang for their supper, were usually willing to lecture for it. Consequently, schools began to offer more or less permanent positions to these scholars in return for their services as popular teachers. William of Champeaux was one of these early scholars-in-residence. Others included Peter Abelard, who took William's job from him, and scholars like Hugh of St.-Victor. Schools had to compete for these celebrity faculty, much as today's universities do.

A school that had the foresight and means to attract more than one scholar—a philosopher and a legal theorist, for example, with perhaps a couple of grammarians,

---

13. The "humane letters" were not part of the universities' curriculum until the late thirteenth century.

mathematicians, astronomers, and physicians thrown into the mix—soon confronted a problem: how to manage the inevitable rivalries between them? Academicians have been prima donnas from the start, and dealing with their scholarly egos has been a problem for school administrators for just as long. More importantly, how did a school establish uniform standards of service and expectations? The answer lay in creating a formal university. The word *university* derives from the Latin term *universitas*, which was the word for a "commercial guild." That is, a *universitas* was a legal corporation that established its own standards, regulated itself, and enjoyed certain legal privileges. The *universitas* established its own criteria for what it expected of its students, and it rewarded those students who satisfied those criteria by bestowing on them a formal recognition of their achievement—just as a mercantile guild recognized a journeyman who learned all the skills of a certain trade by elevating him to the status of master and admitting him into the guild. Thus originated university curricula and degrees.

As self-governing institutions, universities stood outside the jurisdiction of the cities that gave them a home, just as cities themselves existed outside the jurisdiction of the feudal districts in which they were located. This "town-gown" distinction led to frequent conflict, since every university attracted students from across Europe, and consequently each university was often a microcosm of whatever political tensions and conflicts engulfed Europe. Arguments and general rowdiness were common and local city officials were relatively helpless to do anything about it, since university students were keenly aware of their legal privileges. In frustration, people sometimes resorted to vigilante justice, which possibly explains the origin of the three most famous universities in Europe. In 1200 a group of German students at the University of Paris rioted in the city streets—possibly over an ongoing dispute between England's King John and Germany's Otto of Brunswick—and a Parisian mob, led by the local police commissioner, counterattacked, leaving one student dead and many more wounded. The university's English students and masters, fearing that Paris was becoming too hostile, fled back to England in search of a spot where they could establish a school of their own. They joined a small cathedral school in the town of Oxford, and thus began Oxford University. But only nine years later, in 1209, a group of drunken Oxford students assaulted a local girl of the town, which led the citizens to rise up in arms against them and drive them out. The hooligans looked about for another refuge, a place to start yet another school for themselves. Thus began Cambridge University. Other universities sprang up quickly; these also were not wholly new institutions, but were cathedral schools of long standing that simply received a new legal status: Padua in 1222, Naples in 1224, Toulouse and Angers in 1229. By the year 1300 there were nearly two dozen universities in Latin Europe, and by the year 1500 there were seventy-nine.

Whether established by pope, emperor, king, count, or commune, universities were overwhelmingly episcopal institutions. The bishops were their nominal

Teaching novice monks. This painting comes from the cover of
a Latin vocabulary and grammar textbook from thirteenth century
Austria. Note that the teacher appears to be female. Guiding
students through the trivium *(grammar, rhetoric, dialectic) was*
frequently done by women religious.
Source: Erich Lessing / Art Resource, NY

heads, although usually the officer who ran each bishop's chancery was the fellow who performed their day-to-day administration (and that is why university heads today are commonly called *chancellors*). In an effort to provide a greater degree of continuity and standardization between the degrees offered by each university, the papacy was quick to take action. The Holy See bestowed the title of *studium generale* ("general school") upon schools that met its standards of mastery within each of the subjects studied. Not surprisingly, the emperor insisted on his ability to establish a

Medieval Universities
- ● Established before 1300
- ○ Established after 1300

SCANDINAVIA

SCOTLAND
○ St. Andrews (1413)

North Sea

Baltic Sea

Rostock (1419)

POLAND

IRELAND

ENGLAND
Cambridge (1209) ●
Oxford (1167) ●

Leipzig (1409)

Cracow (1397) ○

Cologne (1388) ○
Louvain (1425)

Erfurt (1379) ○

Prague (1347) ●

ATLANTIC OCEAN

Paris (c. 1150) ● ● Sorbonne (1253)

Heidelberg (1385) ○

GERMANY

Vienna (1365) ○

Angers (1229) ● ● Orleans (1250)

FRANCE

Bordeaux (1441) ○

Cahors (1332)

Grenoble (1339) ○

Vicenza (1204) ●

HUNGARY

Pavia (1361) ○

Padua (1222) ●

Orange (1365) ○

Piacenza (1248) ○

Montpellier (1289) ●

Avignon (1303) ○

Bologna (1158?) ●

Toulouse (1229) ●

Pisa (1343) ○

Florence (1349) ○
Perugia (1308) ●
Siena (1247) ●

Adriatic Sea

Coimbra (1308) ● Salamanca (1218) ●

Valladolid (1230) ●

Lérida (1300) ○

Rome (1244) ●

ITALY

Lisbon (1290) ●

SPAIN

Valencia (1245) ●

Naples (1224) ●
Salerno (9th Cent.?) ●

PORTUGAL

Seville (1254) ●

Tyrrhenian Sea

MEDITERRANEAN SEA

N

0   200 Miles
0   200 Kms.

E. McC. 2002

Medieval universities

studium generale also, and until the end of the Middle Ages both figures did so. The recognition mattered. Receiving one's degree from a *studium generale* gave one the right to teach one's subject anywhere; degrees from lesser institutions were less portable. With this new system of accreditation, the rationalization of education caught up with the rationalization of thought itself that so distinctively character-ized the twelfth-century renaissance.

Whatever the subject, lecturing by gloss was the primary method of teaching. A *gloss* was a commentary upon an authoritative text: thus a professor of canon law would teach his subject by reading a passage from Peter Lombard's *Sentences*, then commenting on it at length, pointing out grammatical nuances, fine stylistic points, allusions to literary texts, references to earlier canonical collections or to patristic lit-erature, and quotations from Scripture, and then drawing attention to parallel or contrasting passages elsewhere within Lombard's own text. Then he would move on to the next passage, and repeat the entire process, and so on until he had read and glossed the entire text. A law professor would do the same with the *Corpus*, a medical professor with a text of Galen or Hippocrates, a philosophy professor with a text of Aristotle or Plato. This method served at least two fundamental purposes: it retained the authority of the texts themselves, assuring that they provided the bedrock for all subsequent thought, and it offered a way for students to procure working copies of the texts. Books were still too expensive for most (non-noble) stu-dents to afford easily. The method of reading out a single paragraph a day, and commenting carefully upon it word by word and line by line, gave students a chance to write out their own copies. The method may strike modern readers as hopelessly dull, but in the twelfth century it generated extraordinary intellectual excitement: The newest and most advanced ideas in every field were being circu-lated in the most efficient way possible. The new schools were raucous, lively, exu-berant places, in sharp contrast to the earnest toilsome quiet of the monastic schools.

So raucous, in fact, that they caused a good deal of trouble. Most students be-gan their college careers around the age of fifteen, provided that they could prove mastery of Latin. The trivium and quadrivium remained the basic curricular struc-ture, although faculty were allowed a certain amount of freedom to innovate and to introduce new texts. After a year or two, students were encouraged to ask ques-tions during their professors' lectures and to debate them publicly on certain occa-sions. After four or five years a student, then aged twenty, took a set of oral examinations which, if he passed, earned him a bachelor's degree. This qualified him to serve as an assistant lecturer, much like a teaching assistant in an American graduate school today. After two or three years of assistant teaching, during which time he would continue advanced studies in specialized topics, the student would proceed to another set of oral examinations, after which he was required to present a public lecture and engage in a disputation with a panel of scholars. At the dispu-tation the student was required to argue his points with detailed references and, when called for, quotations from the texts he had studied. If he passed this hurdle, he received a master of arts degree and was licensed to teach or become a clerk. Few opted to continue on for a Ph.D. since it required so many more years of study (by statute, law required at least six more years, medicine eight, and theology twelve).

Two observations stand out. First, educated people in the Middle Ages had prodigious memories. With books so rare and their contents so highly prized, it should not surprise us—and yet it does—that medieval scholars could retain so many volumes of text in their heads. The poet Dante Alighieri reportedly could recite the entire text of Virgil's *Aeneid* (over three hundred pages of verse, in modern editions) from memory. Well-disciplined monks had little difficulty in reciting the entire Psalter. The itinerant scholars who contributed so much to the intellectual revival of their age traveled with only the library in their memory lobes. When Peter Abelard compiled his *Sic et Non*, with all its contradictory passages from the patristic Fathers, Church councils, papal decrees, and Biblical verses, he wrote most of them out from memory. Studying in the Middle Ages involved spending as much time memorizing texts word for word as it did analyzing them logically, and indeed most scholars would have insisted that the latter is not truly possible without the former.

An important consequence of this learning-by-memorization method, though, is that medieval scholarship remained conservative even when it was most radical. It is true that university students read a body of materials that was exponentially broader in scope than what monastic students were exposed to, but the fact that those broader studies became focused and anchored upon their own set of authoritative texts—Lombard's *Sentences*, the *Corpus*, Gratian's *Decretum*, Aristotle's *Works*, Euclid's *Geometry*, Ptolemy's *Almagest*, Galen's *Medicine*, or whatever—meant that medieval scholarship never became so daring as during this initial twelfth-century era when the new canon was formulated. Once the curriculum was established, however, basic innovation became less and less frequent. Intellectual life in the thirteenth century was in many ways a brilliant culmination of what the twelfth-century innovators had accomplished, but it was in some respects less fundamentally exciting. We need to temper our sense of the radicalism of the age with a sense of the strictures that still remained on scholars.

Second, while most tuition was not prohibitively high and while teaching methods were designed partially to help students provide themselves with copies of the books they would need, the time spent on university education meant that young men who came from rural or urban working families were effectively excluded. To support a young man from age fifteen to his early twenties—during the height of his youthful strength and energy, when those qualities were sorely needed in the fields or shop—was more than most lower-income families could afford. Thus even though medieval education was theoretically open to anyone (male, that is) who could pay the tuition, in point of fact it remained a virtual monopoly of the middle class and the lower nobility. (The upper nobility generally disdained the

Marble sculpture of the twelfth century, from the tomb of a notable scholar,
Giovanni da Legnano, depicting students listening to a lecture.
Source: Scala / Art Resource

universities and preferred to hire private tutors for their children.) The schools were engines of social mobility, particularly if one received an advanced degree in law, medicine, or theology. To encourage such mobility and to secure a sufficient pool of talent for administrative and professional needs within the city, many towns began to offer scholarships to urban youths. Wealthy individuals endowed scholarships or hostels for housing students who were either of a particular nationality or following a particular course of study; The Collège de Sorbonne began as a hostel created by the wealthy Parisian Robert de Sorbonne for students wishing to study theology at the University of Paris.[14]

---

14. Presumably if they all lived together they could encourage each other to avoid temptation. Robert seems to have regarded four acts as particular temptations to watch out for, to judge from the statutes he designed for his college: a preference to dine alone instead of in the main hall, a desire to wear loud clothing, an interest in maintaining contact with secular persons, and a wish to possess a key to the pantry.

Universities commonly housed students by their nationality regardless of their course of study. This practice had the effect of sometimes making universities miniature Europes—and they often reflected on the university site some of the political tensions that existed between the European states at any given time. If France and the German Empire were at war, for example, then there was a good chance that the French colleges and German colleges were taunting one another at universities all across Europe. This is one reason why universities from their very inception acquired reputations as havens for young troublemakers, rowdies who needed only the prospect of a weekend free of classes and a visit to a local tavern in order to start hellraising. Of course, the rigors of their studies—and the pursuit of some of the other things that are on the minds of young men in their late teens and early twenties—no doubt added fuel to the fire. *Aliqua nunquam cambiunt* ("Some things never change").

COURTLY LIFE, LOVE, AND LITERATURE

The universities were not the only places where cultural and intellectual life flourished. The other principal site of these energies was the aristocratic courts. By the twelfth century, the chivalric code had evolved into a sophisticated cultural practice that expected far more of a knight than prowess in arms. A knight was understood to be an ideal form of secular Christian—pious, magnanimous, charitable, learned, polite, and cultured as well as brave. To the twelfth-century chivalric mind, Lancelot (minus that naughty business with Queen Guinevere) was the ideal knight, whereas the brutish Roland had been the measure of perfection to eleventh-century knights. Twelfth-century knights were still expected to be unsurpassed warriors, but they were now expected to be so much more besides. Their representations in the popular literature of the age represents this shift. New genres emerged to tell of their exploits; in an even greater innovation, court poets began to sing the glories of their chivalric heroes in their vernacular tongues.

The chivalric code was based on courtesy, not in the sense of "politeness" but of "courtliness." Courtly manners, deportment, and values became the fashion of the age, and added a civilized veneer to the warrior essence of the knightly class. The ability to split a pagan's skull with a battle-ax may have been the chief prerequisite for entry into the best society in Clovis' or Charlemagne's time, but twelfth- and thirteenth-century Europe demanded more refined achievements. After all, the pagans were gone and the Muslims were the chief trading partners of the Christians in the south. The courtly lover was expected to be daring and pious, to dedicate himself to the praise of his beloved, and to strive for the greater glory of her fame and his own reputation for steadfast loyalty by performing heroic exploits. Lyric poetry was a suitable genre for professing great love, but narrating the exploits performed in love's service was the purview of *romance*. These verse narratives tell of secret meetings between lovers, stolen kisses, narrow escapes from discovery, rousing chases through forests and fields, tournaments, battles against enemies and mythological

Illuminated initial from English copy of the Letters of Pope Gregory I. Twelfth century. English scribes in the Middle Ages were particularly well known for the vitality and fluidity of their draftsmanship. This example, from a twelfth-century copy of the Letters of Gregory I, shows a noble warrior—identifiable from his stance on top of a common foot-soldier, plus his brandishing of a fine sword—fighting a two-headed dragon. It is a brightly colored image, filled with hues of airy blue, green, gold, light copper, and red.
Source: Giraudon/Art Resource, NY

beasts. The best of them, such as *Lancelot, Yvain,* or *Erec and Eneid* by Chrétien de Troyes, or *Eliduc* by Marie de France, still make wonderful reading today.[15]

One of the more interesting components of courtly love was its use of social inversion: the lover usually falls in love with a woman who is his social superior and is hence unattainable; in fact, as often as not, she is the wife of the lover's lord—as with Lancelot and Guinevere. Although always erotically charged, these love-relationships are usually sexless; the most a lover can hope for from his beloved is a chaste kiss or the delight of being allowed to carry the beloved's handkerchief or a lock of her hair. This chasteness represented what courtly culture regarded as a perfect form of love: a man's physical love for a female—straightforward lust—they held to be essentially self-love, a desire for one's own pleasure, and hence a love that is inward-turned; the ordinary shared love between husband and wife was something to be treasured, but its mutuality was its imperfection. On the other hand, *courtly love*—a pure love given absolutely to a woman without hope or expectation of anything in return—was an idealized Christian love, a love that poured out unconditionally. The courts believed that it ennobled one's spirit to love in this way; it made one a better man. Hence these courtly loves were made public and the topic of song and celebration. In the case of Lancelot, falling in love with Arthur's wife was not wrong at all; turning that ideal love into an active sexual relationship, though, was an unpardonable crime that led to everyone's ruin.

Europe had always retained a panoply of well-developed vernacular cultures and literatures, but these had been passed on orally. For centuries Latin had held sway as *the* language for all forms of writing—liturgical and exegetical works, legal contracts, scientific treatises, poetry and drama, histories, letters, law codes, or whatever—since Latin was the only language known by all educated people. Latin was the common tongue that held Christendom together and gave it, in a linguistic sense at least, a cohesive identity. A poem written by a Scotsman could be read and appreciated by an audience in Vienna; a stage drama by Hrotsvitha von Gandersheim could be performed by nuns in Aquitaine; a medical treatise written in Salerno could be studied in Denmark. To medieval minds, the only things worth writing down, since writing materials were expensive, were things that could be read by everyone. A history written in a local vernacular dialect—and it is important to bear in mind that Europe's vernacular tongues were all small regional dialects rather than the large national languages that we think of today—could not be read by anyone outside one's small region, and hence was of little practical value.

---

15. Marie's most popular tale was the light-hearted *Lanval*, which tells of a knight at King Arthur's court (Lanval) who is passionately loved by a fairy princess. Lanval returns her ardor but is under her strict orders never to reveal her identity. All is well until Queen Guinevere develops a passion for him too. When Lanval declines her advances, an incredulous Guinevere accuses him of having "no desire for women" and brings charges against him for having treated her dishonorably. At the trial, Lanval breaks down under Arthur's questioning and informs the court of his true love. The fairy princess (who is never named) appears, forgives Lanval for having broken the gag order, and whisks him off to the misty island of Avalon. The story was hugely popular and was retold by other poets. The identity of Marie de France has never been known, although it is generally assumed that she lived at the court of Henry II of England and his wife Eleanor of Aquitaine.

These facts explain the prejudice against vernacular literature that was common from the start of the Middle Ages until the twelfth century: A poem written in early Catalan dialect was an inferior poem—not necessarily because Catalan was an intrinsically "inferior" language to Latin, but because the simple fact that only Catalans could read it made it of less universal import.

Attitudes began to change toward the end of the eleventh century and especially over the course of the twelfth. Most of the earliest vernacular writings were works that by their very nature were not intended for universal application: A physician writing a health regimen for a patient, for example, hardly needed to keep the interests of all Christendom in mind and was concerned only that his patient adhere to the diet and exercise schedule he was prescribing. Similarly, letters between businessmen discussing what items to buy at the Champagne fairs, in what quantities, and at what prices, were hardly intended for a wide audience; in fact the narrower the audience the better, in this case. Much of the earliest vernacular writing we have is of this private nature, and a lot of it makes fascinating reading.

Vernacular poetry, fables, legends, histories, and popular songs had been passed on orally for generations. Indeed, considering that most of this material was not written down until the twelfth century, it is surprising how much has survived. Every story is changed in its telling, though, so it is difficult to know how closely the written-down versions correspond to the earliest oral renditions either in terms of content, or in the tongues employed. In fact, it seems clear that much traditional literature was intentionally reworked and reformed in the writing, since the decision to preserve that literature on parchment was often related to embryonic nationalistic schemes fostered by the emergence of the new states of the central Middle Ages. Poets of the age continued to write in Latin (Peter Abelard was himself a Latin poet of note, even though he also wrote some vernacular love songs), and much of their work is quite good; but the vernacular poetry of the time quickly surpassed the Latin in both quantity and quality.[16] Apart from the court poets of the Carolingian Renaissance, the only Latin poets with anything like a wide reputation these days are the anonymous "Goliardic poets"—chiefly university students and itinerant scholars who took time off from their studies to pen ribald verses on the glories of carefree drinking and womanizing. This material is entertaining as light verse, but most of it is negligible as poetry.[17]

---

16. It is worth noting that hardly any non-specialist in medieval history can even name a single Latin poet of the Middle Ages, whereas almost everyone has at least heard of the great vernacular poets like Geoffrey Chaucer and Dante Alighieri.

17. An example:

My intention is to die
      In a tavern, drinking.
Wine will be at hand, for I
      Want it when I'm sinking.
Angels who look on will cry,
      Their eyes with tears a-blinking:
"Save this drunkard, God on high
      —he's absolutely stinking!"

Vernacular literature focused on a handful of principal genres: epic poetry, lyric poetry, verse romances, prose fables, and religious drama. Epic poetry perhaps had the longest genealogy; it dated back to the earliest centuries of the medieval period, to the arrival of the Germanic tribes in the west. These violent poems are known today as *chansons de geste* ("Songs of Great Deeds") and they typically tell a rousing tale of derring-do, usually against almost impossible odds, by a central warrior hero. Each Germanic tribe had its own repertory. The now-fragmentary *Song of Hildebrand*[18] is one of the oldest, and it illustrates the themes of struggle, bravery, and grim fate that were characteristic of the genre. *Hildebrand* is the earliest written epic; it can be traced to the scriptorium at Fulda, in lower Saxony, around the year 800, and it is believed by many to have been a personal favorite of Charlemagne's. The oldest surviving Anglo-Saxon epic is *Beowulf*, which happens to survive in its entirety. Handed down orally for generations, it found its way into print sometime around the year 1000. The closest thing to a national epic for the Franks is the *Song of Roland*,[19] a vast celebration of slaughter and revenge.

Scores of these *chansons de geste* survive from across feudal Europe, and it is no coincidence that the bulk of them were finally put into writing during feudalism's formative period. The *chansons de geste* helped to celebrate the great role of the warrior elites who defended society and gave it leadership; they present us with a militarized and stratified world in which the links between lord and vassal are the bedrock of social cohesion and survival. Scholars now group these songs into several cycles, each dealing with the same character or set of characters. The so-called "Charlemagne Cycle," of which the *Song of Roland* is part, consists of over twenty epic songs in which Charlemagne has a role. His role in *Roland* is large; in others it is considerably smaller. An "Alexander Cycle" gathers together several *chansons* whose narratives feature the character of Alexander the Great, the ancient Greek emperor who was a popular figure in the literature of the Middle Ages. The *Song of Hildebrand* is representative of the "German Cycle" of epics about ancient Germanic heroes. The last main grouping is the "Arthurian Cycle" of epic stories about the legendary figure of King Arthur and his knights at Camelot. Most of the *chansons de geste* make exciting reading and show considerable poetic craftsmanship.

A different type of vernacular poetry predominated in southern Europe. Here poets extolled the virtues of love, rather than the feats of the battlefield, in lyric poems of great subtlety and beauty: They praised beauty, sensitivity, constancy, and gallantry. Often with a welcome erotic element. The lyric poets were known as *troubadours*. The word derives from the Occitan verb *trobar*, meaning "to compose," which suggests that the southern poets prided themselves on being original authors of their verses as opposed to the "mere scribes" who wrote down the ancient *chansons* of the north. That may be overly fanciful, but it is clear that troubadour poetry

18. See the discussion in Chapter 3.
19. See the discussion in Chapter 6.

differed dramatically from northern verse in content, form, language, and theme. The earliest troubadour poet whose works survive was William IX, the duke of Aquitaine and count of Poitou (r. 1071–1126), and the grandfather of Eleanor of Aquitaine. He left behind a number of fine love songs, a few bawdy lyrics, and this delightful *jeu d'esprit* that suggests that there really was a pervading sense of difference from and rivalry with the feudal north:

I'll write a verse now just for fun,
One not about me or anyone,
One not about a youth in love.
Or anything along that course.
  I'm writing it out in the sun
  While riding on my horse.

I cannot say when I was born,
I am not happy but I'm not forlorn,
Still I'm ill at ease and unsure of
What I'm going to do next.
  Bewitched by an enchantress, I'm feeling torn;
  In fact I'm rather perplexed.

I can't tell real life from a dream
And must be told when day would seem
To have begun. My heart's a-scream
With bitterness and confusion;
  I care so little I might blaspheme—
  Just a stab at resolution.

I have a lady-love, fine and pure,
But who she is I am not sure
And where she lives is anyone's guess.
But she treats me in a way I can endure.
  Anything!—as long as the Normans on their tour
  Stay out of Poitou, I confess.

I adore this woman, though I have not yet
Laid eyes on her; I'm told she does not set
Much store by what I think—but I don't let
That bother me. I never forget
  There are some others, three or four
  That I'm just as faithful to—maybe more.

I feel ill: like death has me in its hold,
And I know nothing except what I'm told.
I wish a doctor would be so bold
As to tell me what's going on, like a man of honor.

If he cures me, I'll give him gold;
If not, then he's a goner.

My verse is done, and if you please
I'll send it off now, at my ease;
There is a man up in Anjou
Who claims to know a thing or two
    About all manner of poetry;
    But I don't believe it at all—do you?

Troubadours delighted in poking fun at their own works in this way, but the bulk of their verse consists of genuine expressions of love and desire, longing and loneliness.

Not all the troubadours were from Mediterranean Europe, nor were they all men. Reinmar von Hagenau, the court poet at the ducal palace in Vienna in the 1190s, composed some fine lyric verse like this wedding song:

An end to my yearnings seems nowhere in sight,
And so to my beloved do I turn, as is right.
Her I will love every day that I live,
Knowing that she, only she, has the power to give
Joy to my sorrow; and it's a marvel to me
That she can do this so effortlessly.

I now know no joy that depends not on her,
And there is no one else of whom I can say:
"She, only she, is my Easter Day."
My heart to her I entirely confer.
She lives in my, and I in her, breast—
As God, to Whom no one can lie, will attest.

Perhaps the best of the female troubadours, of whom we are familiar with roughly two dozen, was a woman known only as the Countess of Dia, even though only four of her poems survive. She was born around 1140. Like many other women troubadours, she deals with a painful theme:

I have been of late in fretful mood
Over a knight who once was mine.
I want it always understood
That I loved him with a love sublime.
But now I see I've been betrayed
Because I wouldn't make love with him.
In my naked nights and in day, full arrayed,
I dwell on this mistake so grim.

Stage plays were another strength of vernacular culture. Itinerant players were a frequent sight in medieval Europe, traveling from town to town, even village to village, and putting on productions of farces, musical pageants, and religious dramas. In fact, although the roots of western drama reach back to pagan Athens, its development in Europe was closely linked to that of the Christian church. The dramatization of Biblical stories by stage-players was a popular means of religious education for the illiterate rural world; it was certainly easier to get labor-hounded peasants to watch a play than it was to get them to sit through a sermon. In fact, in most medieval villages the open space—it seems too optimistic to call it a *green*—in front of the local church was the usual site for performing stage plays when a touring troupe passed through. Since plays were not an official church ceremony, they did not need to be performed in Latin, and in any case it made better sense, given their pedagogical function, to have them in the vernacular. These Biblical dramas are called *mystery plays*.[20] Related to them, though rather later in time, are the so-called *morality plays*, in which personified human attributes (Pride, Lust, Patience, Charity, etc.) disputed between themselves, and the *miracle plays*, which were dramatized versions of saints' lives. The earliest surviving mystery play is the anonymous twelfth-century Anglo-Norman work called the *Jeu d'Adam* ("Adam's Play"); better known are the German Passion Plays, especially the one at Oberammergau; and the English dramas that comprise the Wakefield Cycle and the so-called N-Town Cycle. The stagecraft of these early works is often highly effective. Here, to offer the briefest of illustrations, are a few lines from the English *Noah's Flood*. In the scene, the rains of the Great Flood have just begun and Noah and his children are pleading with Noah's wife—who will not get aboard the ark unless she can bring her friends (here called *gossips*, in an archaic English usage), and they are preparing to drink a farewell toast to each other before they drown.

GOSSIPS: The flood comes fleeting in full fast,
            On every side that spreadeth full far.
            For fear of drowning I am aghast;
            Good Gossip, let us draw near.
            And let us drink ere we depart,
            For oftentimes we have done so.
            For at one draught thou drink a quart,
            And so will I do, ere I go.

NOAH'S WIFE: Here is a pottle of Malmsey[21] good and strong;
            It will rejoice both heart and tongue.
            Though Noah think us never so long,
            Yet we will drink atyte.[22]

JAPHETH: Mother! We pray you all together—
            For we are here, your own childer—

---

20. The term refers to the players, not the plays; it derives from the medieval French word *mestier*, meaning the métier or trade of the performers.
21. Roughly, two quarts of sweet wine.
22. *Atyte*: meaning "at once."

	Come into the ship for fear of the weather, For His love, that you bought!
NOAH'S WIFE:	That will I not for all your call But[23] I have my Gossips all!
SHEM:	I'faith, mother, yet thou shall, Whether thou will or nought. [*He drags her aboard.*]
NOAH:	Welcome, wife, into this boat. [*She slaps him in the face.*]
NOAH'S WIFE:	Have thou *that* for thy note![24]
NOAH:	Aha, Mary! This is hot! It is good for to be still. Ah, children! Methinks my boat remeves[25] Our tarrying here me highly grieves. Over the land the water spreads. God do as He will.

The single most popular vernacular work of the Middle Ages was the *Romance of the Rose*. It was begun by Guillaume de Lorris sometime in the 1230s, and he completed about four thousand lines of verse narrating a dream-vision in which the poet wanders through an enchanted walled garden filled with personifications like Lord Mirth, Lady Gladness, Friend, Villainy, and of course Love. The poet-narrator falls in love with a perfect rose at the center of the garden—the rose itself being an allegorical symbol for perfect womanhood—and the "story" of the poem, to the extent that it has one, is of the narrator's journey to reach the rose. Lorris died leaving his poem unfinished, but his work was taken up by Jean de Meun, who probably qualifies as the most enthusiastic literary heir in western history. De Meun added another eighteen thousand lines to the poem, thereby making it as long as Homer's *Iliad* and *Odyssey* combined (and to some readers, making the reading of it seem to last as long as the Trojan war). Lorris was an elegiac, lyrical idealist with a delicate poetic touch. De Meun, though stylistically gifted, was a scholastic theorist of love, determined to elaborate an entire system of human emotions and psychological states. What began as a dreamy love-vision became, in de Meun's hands, a kind of *summa amatoria*, an encyclopedic road-map of the human heart. The poem's popularity, which continued right through the Renaissance, was nothing short of phenomenal and provides a good example of the passion for complex order that characterized the High Middle Ages.

---

23. *But*: meaning "unless."
24. *Note*: meaning "trouble."
25. *Remeves*: meaning "sails off" or "starts to move."

Far less ambitious than the *Romance of the Rose*, but also far more fun to read, were the rambunctious popular fables known as *fabliaux*. These were witty, irreverent, and often salacious, short stories in verse. Fabliaux were a chiefly French phenomenon and a decidedly urban one. Bourgeois attitudes toward aristocrats, the Church, peasants, work, leisure, sex (and more sex), food and drink, and the human body itself[26] are on full display here. Merchants, tradesmen, free farmers, bakers, millers, and butchers are the professions most often represented, and the fabliaux give us a glimpse of their lifestyles. Adultery and seduction (or attempted seduction) are the two most common themes; interestingly, the adulterers are far more often wives with lovers than they are husbands with mistresses, and a surprising number of seducers (or attempted seducers) are priests. But this is the post-reform Church, so most of their seductions fail. The fabliaux indulge in broad and often heavy-handed humor, but in general they are stories told with wit and style; most of them are a pleasure to read even today, and they provide an intriguing glance at urban life and its real or imagined foibles.

Suggested Reading

Texts

Abelard, Peter. *History of My Misfortunes.*

———. *Sic et Non.*

Abelard, Peter, and Héloïse. *Letters.*

Anselm of Canterbury. *Prayers and Meditations.*

Bernard of Clairvaux. *Five Books on Consideration.*

———. *On Loving God.*

———. *Sermons.*

Bracton, Henry. *On the Laws and Customs of England.*

John of Salisbury. *Policraticus.*

Lombard, Peter. *Sentences.*

de Lorris, Guillaume, and Jean de Meun. *The Romance of the Rose.*

Trotula. *The Diseases of Women.*

Troyes, Chrétien. *Complete Romances.*

Source Anthologies

Bogin, Meg. *The Women Troubadours* (1976).

Doss-Quinby, Eglal, Joan Tasker Grimbert, Wendy Pfeffer, and Elizabeth Aubrey. *Songs of the Women Trouvères* (2001).

Hanning, Robert, and Joan Ferrante. *The Lais of Marie de France* (1978).

Somerville, Robert, and Bruce C. Brasington. *Prefaces to Canon Law Books in Latin Christianity, 500–1245: Selected Translations* (1998).

---

26. In some *fabliaux* that I don't dare to quote from, the characters' genitalia talk to one another, detach themselves from their owners, adopt more flattering dimensions, and happily go their own merry ways.

Spade, Paul V. *Five Texts on the Medieval Problem of Universals: Porphyry, Boethius, Abelard, Duns Scotus, Ockham* (1994).

Thorndike, Lynn. *University Records and Life in the Middle Ages* (1944).

Studies

Benson, Robert L., and Giles Constable. *Renaissance and Renewal in the Twelfth Century* (1982).

Berman, Harold. *Law and Revolution: The Formation of the Western Legal Tradition* (1983).

Biller, Peter, and Anne Hudson. *Heresy and Literacy, 1000–1500* (1994).

Clanchy, Michael T. *From Memory to Written Record: England, 1066–1307* (1992).

———. *Abelard: A Medieval Life* (1997).

Cobban, Alan B. *The Medieval Universities: Their Development and Organization* (1988).

Colish, Marcia L. *Medieval Foundations of the Western Intellectual Tradition, 400–1400* (1997).

Evans, G. R. *Bernard of Clairvaux* (2000).

Gies, Joseph and Frances. *Leonardo of Pisa and the New Mathematics of the Middle Ages* (1969).

Grant, Edward. *Physical Science in the Middle Ages* (1971).

Haren, Michael. *Medieval Thought: The Western Intellectual Tradition from Antiquity to the Thirteenth Century* (1992).

Jaeger, C. Stephen. *The Origins of Courtliness: Civilizing Trends and the Formation of Courtly Ideals, 939–1210* (1985).

Keen, Maurice. *Chivalry* (1984).

Keiser, Elizabeth B. *Courtly Desire and Medieval Homophobia: The Legitimation of Sexual Pleasure in "Cleanness" and Its Contexts* (1997).

LeGoff, Jacques. *Intellectuals in the Middle Ages* (1993).

Lindberg, David C. *The Beginnings of Western Science: The European Scientific Tradition in Philosophical, Religious, and Institutional Context. 600 BC to AD 1450* (1992).

Luscombe, David. *Medieval Thought* (1997).

Makdisi, George. *The Rise of Colleges: Institutions of Learning in Islam and the West* (1981).

Marenbon, John. *The Philosophy of Peter Abelard* (1997).

McGinn, Bernard. *The Calabrian Abbot: Joachim of Fiore in the History of Western Thought* (1985).

Morris, Colin. *The Discovery of the Individual, 1050–1200* (1972).

Morrison, Karl F. *History as a Visual Art in the Twelfth-Century Renaissance* (1991).

Muscatine, Charles. *The Old French Fabliaux* (1986).

Partner, Nancy. *Serious Entertainments: The Writing of History in Twelfth-Century England* (1977).

Paterson, Linda. *The World of the Troubadours: Medieval Occitan Society, ca. 1100–ca. 1300* (1995).

Rosenthal, Franz. *The Classical Heritage in Islam* (1975).

Sirat, Colette. *A History of Jewish Philosophy in the Middle Ages* (1990).

Southern, Richard W. *St. Anselm: A Portrait in a Landscape* (1990).

Stock, Brian. *The Implications of Literacy: Written Language and Models of Interpretation in the Eleventh and Twelfth Centuries* (1983).

Weinfurter, Stefan. *The Salian Century: Main Currents in an Age of Transition* (1994).

Woolf, Rosemary. *The English Mystery Plays* (1972).

CHAPTER 12

THE PAPAL MONARCHY

The conflict between Gregory VII and Henry IV, for all its drama, hardly ended the struggles between the reformed Church and the new states of the medieval west; the conflict was in fact merely a prologue to what was yet to come. The Concordat of Worms in 1122 had more or less resolved the specific issues of ecclesiastical appointments and investiture, and in its aftermath a general lull existed in Church-State tensions. The crusades provided a venue for joint action and made the contestants willing to set aside their dispute for a time. Besides, Europe's booming prosperity and atmosphere of excitement in the twelfth century disinclined people to drag out old conflicts at a time when they could instead devote themselves to reinventing and, they thought, mastering their world. But the conflict could not be ignored forever. Too much was at stake, and when the tensions renewed they did so with just as much intensity of feeling as before; the issues, though, were different this time around.

The Concordat had generally confirmed the so-called Two Swords theory of ecclesiastical-governmental relations. This was a doctrine first articulated centuries earlier by Pope Gelasius I (r. 492–496), according to which it was understood that God had created both the ecclesiastical power (*sacerdotium*) and secular royal authority (*imperium*), and that He intended for them to work in harmony with one another—the first having dominion over spiritual life and the latter having jurisdiction over earthly and mundane matters. It was essentially a refinement of Christ's dictum that one should "render unto Caesar what is Caesar's, and unto God what is God's." A simple enough theory in principle but a messy one in the details. For example: Since twelfth-century Europe was now governed by territorial law instead of personal law, could a French citizen convicted of a crime appeal his case to the papacy—that is, to an authority outside France itself? If an English priest committed a crime against the king's law (for example, if he murdered someone), was he to be tried by the king's court or by the local bishop's, and by English law or by canon law? A German abbot was undeniably a member of the Church, but he was also a citizen who used German roads and bridges, was defended by German soldiers, and bought and sold goods at German markets and fairs. Was he therefore liable to taxation by the state? If not, why not?

These were the sort of issues debated in the second round of the Church-State conflict, rather than high-minded disputes over the superiority of pope over emperor, or vice-versa. And while the new struggles were more commonly wars of words between diplomats and legal scholars than conflagrations between armies, they were intensely dramatic nonetheless and on their outcome rested the ultimate development of European political society.

CHURCH AGAINST STATE ONCE MORE

The first king to renew the debate was England's Henry II (r. 1154–1189). He was an exceptional ruler, devoted with equal determination to exerting ruthless power and providing justice for his subjects. His claim to the throne came through his mother Matilda, the daughter of Henry I (r. 1100–1135), which parentage made him the duke of Normandy and count of Maine as well; but as the son of Geoffrey Plantagenet, the count of Anjou, he was also lord to the French territories of Anjou and Touraine. Finally, as the husband of Eleanor of Aquitaine, who had divorced France's Louis VII in the aftermath of the Second Crusade, he controlled Aquitaine, Poitou, and Auvergne. These holdings, plus some other territories he later seized on the Continent, made him the master of nearly half of France as well as king of England. Historians commonly refer to his enormous realm as the *Angevin Empire*, although Henry never held or claimed an imperial title. That was the only limit on his ambitions, though. Henry was determined to expand his authority on the Continent and ideally to stretch it all the way to the Mediterranean littoral. He cared little for England and valued it chiefly as a source of revenue and the place that provided him with a royal title; he much preferred his French lands and never bothered to learn to speak English. (Neither did his sons Richard the Lionheart [r.1189–1199] or John [r.1199–1216].)

Henry was dedicated to the rule of law and providing justice for his subjects. This program probably owed more to political pragmatism than high-minded principle, for the English were more likely to obey a foreign king who served them well than one who did not, but it is praiseworthy nevertheless. Effective central government had declined under his predecessor Stephen (r. 1135–1154) to the point that local barons and sheriffs had become essentially laws unto themselves. It took Henry nearly twenty years to bring them to heel; by 1170 he had suspended from office all the sheriffs in the realm and conducted a kingdom-wide inquest into popular grievances against local officials. Such actions earned him the respect of the commoners, as did his efforts to develop a single law code for the entire realm, one that applied to all non-noble citizens and was based as much as possible on customary practices (hence its name, the *Common Law*). He increased the corps of itinerant justices who traveled throughout England holding public inquests and hearing appeals. Royal justice was fairer, quicker, and less costly than the seigneurial courts of the local barons, whose judicial functions declined accordingly just as their military functions were increasingly taken over by salaried common armies.[1] Henry also regu-

---

1. Vassals could commute their military service by paying a special relief called *scutage* (literally, "shield-money"). Most were eager to do so, since they preferred to spend their time building up their economic might and local political power.

larized the use of trials-by-jury and did away with the old rural tradition of trial-by-combat.

Ironically it was his concern for justice that got Henry into trouble with the Church. During the 1130s and 1140s England's ecclesiastical courts had greatly enlarged their jurisdiction until they impinged upon cases normally reserved for the royal courts. The royal curia was determined to rectify the situation but had to wait for the right moment. There were a variety of important issues at stake. First was the restoration of royal rights; the court simply could not afford to let the Church take over the function of providing justice. Second was a question of perceived fairness. What, for example, would happen to a person convicted of murder or rape in an ecclesiastical court? The king's law was clear: Both were capital crimes. But the Church could hardly order anyone's execution, and so it normally condemned murderers and rapists to excommunication and banishment. The existence of two standards of justice violated the sense of rational order. Third was the issue of criminal clergy, priests who violated royal law. The curia insisted on its right to punish those who broke the king's law. Fourth, if the Church controlled royal courts, what was to prevent convicts from appealing their cases to Rome? This possibility threatened the very sovereignty of the Angevin dynasty.

In 1162 the archbishop of Canterbury, the primate of the English Church, died, and the court saw its opportunity. Henry appointed his best friend and chief adviser Thomas Becket, the royal chancellor, to the post. But Becket—to everyone's surprise, including his own—experienced an spiritual epiphany when he was consecrated as archbishop and became instantaneously an implacable foe of royal designs. Henry was hurt and outraged by what he regarded as open treachery. Angry words were volleyed on both sides and by 1164 their quarrel had grown so bitter that Becket had to flee to France for his own safety. An attempt at reconciliation in 1170 fell apart when Henry, angered by reports that Becket's first action after returning to his cathedral at Canterbury was to order the excommunication of several of the king's supporters, flew into a rage. In his wrath he reportedly cried out: "Will no one rid me of this miserable priest?" Four of his household knights, believing that they had been given an oblique order, rode to Canterbury and murdered Becket as he was celebrating Mass at the altar.

Becket's martyrdom shocked Europe. He was, after all, the first prominent Christian leader to be killed by the State ever since the European recovery and Church reform had taken root. A popular cult focused on his martyrdom arose instantly and his canonization became formal within three years. Miracles were reported to occur at his tomb, and Canterbury quickly became England's most popular pilgrimage site. For centuries, pilgrims came from all over Europe to pray at his shrine. (We will meet the most famous group of them in a later chapter.) Henry was genuinely remorseful for his unintended complicity in the murder and even submitted to a penitential flogging by the Canterbury canons, but he refused to relinquish his jurisdictional claims. In general, he and most of the English kings who followed him in the Middle Ages retained control over ecclesiastical appointments and regained full jurisdiction over the royal courts, but the ecclesiastical courts retained the deciding hand in all cases regarding those who could claim "benefit of clergy."

The second site of renewed Church-State tensions was the German Empire. The emperor Henry V (r. 1106–1125), who had agreed to the Concordat of Worms in 1122, died only three years later without an heir. The German prelates favored as emperor the devout, and hopefully therefore malleable, duke of Saxony named Lothair. They engineered his election, and Lothair ruled for twelve years (r. 1125–1137) but remained rather ineffectual since (as was by now the clear fate of all German emperors) he could never win the support of most of the secular princes. He did, however, produce a daughter whose marriage to Henry the Proud, the duke of Bavaria, opened up a dynastic and ideological rift that would dominate imperial and northern Italian politics for several centuries. The daughter, Gertrude, brought to her husband both the imperial title and the duchy of Saxony—and these, combined with Henry's own Bavarian principality, made him easily the most powerful of all the German princes. Thus when Lothair died in 1137, very few of the princes wanted Henry as emperor, and so they elected instead the relatively weak duke of Franconia Conrad III Hohenstaufen (r. 1138–1152), who set to work immediately to attack Henry the Proud and cut him down to size. Civil war engulfed most of Germany for nearly twenty years as Henry and his followers—known as the *Welfs* (from Henry's family name)—fought against the Hohenstaufen family and their supporters—known as the *Waiblings* (from the Hohenstaufen family's favorite hunting lodge at Waiblingen). In one way or another this Welf-Waibling rivalry, which is better known by the Italianate version of their names as the struggle between the *Guelf* and *Ghibelline* parties, played a role in almost all subsequent imperial politics both within Germany and northern Italy, even long after people had forgotten what the original designations meant.

Conrad III's reign corresponded almost exactly with Stephen's reign in England and had much the same anarchic character. Upon his death the elector-princes, still favoring a weak emperor, selected Conrad's nephew Frederick Barbarossa (or "Frederick Red-beard"), whose reign from 1152 to 1190 made him the contemporary of England's Henry II. Frederick tried to reconcile with his Guelf opponents, but had mixed success. His most important action was to reestablish direct control over northern Italy. He rode south with a large army and bludgeoned every city that did not welcome him with open arms. The pope at that time, Hadrian IV (r. 1154–1159), rode north to greet him.[2] Their meeting at Sutri was tense, but pope and emperor joined forces to combat a new problem: a revolutionary leader named Arnold of Brescia. John of Salisbury gives a sharp thumbnail sketch of the man.

> [Arnold] held priestly status, was a canon regular, and he disciplined his body through denial and an absence of possessions. He had sharp intelligence, was

---

2. Originally named Nicholas Breakspear, Hadrian IV is the only Englishman ever to have been pope.

steadfast in the study of Scripture, spoke eloquently, and vigorously preached contempt for the world. But as everyone says, he was also a born troublemaker and rabble-rouser, and everywhere he went he stirred up the people against the clergy. He had been the abbot at Brescia, and when the local bishop, who had traveled to Rome and was returning from there, arrived back at Brescia he found that Arnold had so roused the minds of the local citizens against him that they were scarcely willing to permit their own bishop to re-enter the city. Because of this Pope Innocent I deposed Arnold as abbot; Arnold then went to France and studied under Peter Abelard. . . . He gave bishops no rest, attacking them for their avarice and their shameful money-grubbing, for leading sin-stained lives, and for trying to build God's Church through the shedding of blood.[3] . . . He won the whole city [of Rome] over to his side while the pope was abroad in France. . . . Arnold's followers practiced chastity, and this, to-gether with their reputation for honesty and self-discipline made them popular with everyone but especially with religious women. . . . He openly attacked the cardinals with the charge that their College, on account of its hubris, avarice, hypocrisy, and manifold wickedness, was not a church of God but a business-house and a den of thieves. . . . He said that the pope himself was not what he claimed to be—that is, an apostolic man, a shepherd of souls—but a man of blood who maintains his power by fire and slaughter, a desecrator of churches, and an oppressor of the innocent who does nothing but feed on the world's flesh and fill his own purse by emptying those of everyone else.

Arnold's party had taken over Rome in the hope of reestablishing the ancient Re-public and thus doing away with both pope and emperor. This rebellion in Rome marks the first clear indication of widespread and passionate dissatisfaction with the direction taken by the new Church and the new Europe. The Church, Arnold in-veighed, having freed itself from the corruption that came through control *by* the State, had become corrupted once again, but in an even more malignant and noxious way, by assuming control *of* the State, and the bishops who once were loving shep-herds of Christian souls had turned themselves into power-drunk potentates. Cities themselves, man's natural social and political unit according to Arnold—the com-munities in which men may speak for themselves and control their own destinies, places that formed the foundational units of the early Church itself—have fallen vic-tim to warlords and episcopal bullies. Only by restoring true republicanism, by top-pling corrupt and anachronistic hierarchies, Arnold preached, can a truly Christian society be created. Arnold and his followers believed that stripping the Church of all its wealth and political authority could establish a truly Christian commonwealth and secure human happiness; in other words, only a Church that was wholly di-vested of earthly concerns could possibly fulfill its spiritual mission. Hadrian and Frederick joined forces and put Arnold's rebellion down quickly, and Arnold himself was hanged—but his ideas long survived him and became prominent elements in heterodox reform movements of the thirteenth and fourteenth centuries.

---

3.   He is referring to the crusade movement. The Second Crusade had recently gone awry when Arnold attempted his revolution.

Arnold's suppression and Hadrian's rapprochement with Frederick signaled an important change in the papacy's relations with the free cities of Europe, especially within Italy, for it seemed to many that the Holy See had in fact become the enemy of the most cherished republican ideals—namely, an independent episcopacy, communal autonomy, and a reformed Church uninterested in wealth and power. The next pope, Alexander III (r. 1159–1181), tried to improve relations by championing the Lombard League, an alliance of northern communes against Barbarossa's depredations. Barbarossa tried to crush the League, and scored his greatest success when he flattened the city of Milan itself; nevertheless, the League defeated the German forces decisively at Legnano in 1176, a battle that forced the emperor, the pope, and the communes to come to terms. A final agreement was reached with the *Peace of Constance* in 1183, which recognized the de facto autonomy of the communes, their right to self-government, to select their own officials, collect their own taxes, and administer their own laws. The communes, for their part, recognized the suzerainty of the emperor—a suzerainty that they generally maintained simply by the payment of annual tribute.

After this peace, Frederick's difficulties with the Church abated somewhat. He was an old man, and as he aged he became more devoted to a pious life. His life ended when he responded to the news of Jerusalem's fall to Saladin in 1187 and put together a massive army that led the first wave of the Third Crusade. Frederick drowned while crossing an Anatolian river, and his forces quickly disbanded and raced back to Germany to prepare for the next round of imperial politicking. The subsequent phase of the imperial-papal struggle owed much to the results of those maneuvers.

THE CONSOLIDATION OF PAPAL AUTHORITY

Toward the end of the twelfth century, as the Church reform came to its conclusion, many of the ideals and energies that had propagated it in the first place began to wane. The reform had begun with an identification of the Church as the outraged innocent, the spiritual house of God being trammeled by a self-serving and greedy secular world. Christians had rushed to its rescue in the tenth and eleventh centuries and won it the freedom it needed; but then, toward the end of the eleventh century and throughout the twelfth, when the reform reached the papacy, figures like Gregory VII, Urban II, and Alexander III changed the rules of the game by openly proclaiming the Church's supremacy to and sovereignty over the secular world. Church and State, in other words, were no longer separate; they were still one, but with their historical roles reversed. The papacy itself had become a massive bureaucracy whose hallways teemed with lawyers—canon lawyers, to be sure, but lawyers nonetheless. Church supremacy over secular society made necessary the means to wield it; consequently an elaborate financial machinery, judicial system, bureaucratic structure, police network, and standing army all became elements of the new Church. Not everyone was pleased by this militancy, as the example of

Arnold of Brescia showed. Could the Church, and specifically the papacy, dominate and administer the world without being corrupted by it? The leading figures in the papal curia believed that it could. More importantly, they believed that it *had* to. The idea of the "papal monarchy" rested on the conviction that the stability of Christian society required the oversight of an impartial arbiter. The very fact of the Church's disinterestedness in worldly affairs made it the perfect and necessary judge over them. The fact that the Holy See had had a territorial base in the Papal State since the seventh century meant that it had quite a bit of experience in secular administration; but it now began to take those powers abroad. As the examples of England's Henry II and Germany's Frederick Barbarossa show, the campaign was a bumpy one, but during the pontificate of Innocent III (r. 1198–1216), the medieval papacy reached the high point of its political power and international prestige. Innocent was by far the single most powerful pope of the Middle Ages.

At first, the conditions did not seem right for so large an ambition. The wars of Alexander III to win papal control, or at least to break imperial control, over northern Italy, combined with the burgeoning bureaucracy of the papal court itself, left the papacy deeply in debt in the 1180s and 1190s. Relatively few members of the curia received a salary; most lived off fees that they exacted for their services. But since no general standards existed to determine what those fees should be, the opportunities for bribery were widespread. Persons filing petitions with an office of the curia or appealing to the papal court had to grease the palms of an apparently endless sequence of officials. So lucrative were some of the clerkships that popes like Alexander III began the practice of granting (for a fee) the "expectancy" of the office—in effect, selling the position like a future share on the bond or stock market.[4] Thus a certain conundrum existed: Papal prestige ran at an all-time high, but the reputation of the curia—the lawyer-officials who ran the pontiff's administrative machinery—stood at a low level indeed. Popular satires were written all across Europe ridiculing the corruption of fee-crazed papal bureaucrats, the most famous of these being the "Gospel According to the Mark of Silver" and the mock-hagiographic "Life of the Blessed Martyrs Albinus [Latin for 'silver'] and Rufinus ['gold']."

When Lothario dei Segni became Pope Innocent III in 1198, he was the youngest cardinal in the Church, only thirty-seven years of age. He was also the most brilliant. He had written two still-underrated books, *De contemptu mundi* ["On Contempt for the World"] and *De sacro altaris mysterio* ["On the Sacred Mystery of the Altar"], and had received a thorough legal training at Bologna. *De contemptu mundi* does not have the tone and message that its title might lead one to think. It is a subtle work that both evokes and expands upon St. Augustine's distinction between *use* and *enjoyment*; the world we inhabit is the supremely beautiful creation of a loving God, but it is the Creator, not the creation itself, that we ought to focus our own love

---

4. Since these expectancies were for offices that were technically administrative rather than ecclesiastical, selling them escaped the charge of simony.

upon. Compared to God Himself, this world is as nothing and we ought not to let it distract us from our true mission in life of loving and serving Him; we should, in short, use the world to advance God's cause but not enjoy the world for its own sake.

It is in this light that we must consider Innocent's enormous political ambition, for even though he had an aristocratic background and an autocratic temperament he did not seek power for power's sake. His voluminous writings show a genuine and complex, if at times contradictory, commitment to the ideal that only the Holy See can arbitrate between secular leaders, resolve secular disputes, administer secular concerns, and gauge secular actions and behaviors—precisely because of its lack of interest in them. The papacy possessed, he argued, a "fullness of power" (*plenitudo potestatis*) that entitled it, and in fact required it, to involve itself in every aspect of human life in which moral or spiritual matters were at stake. That is a rather large catchment area, and Innocent seldom hesitated to press his claims. Nor did he bother to elucidate a large, carefully developed, all-embracing theory about papal might; he simply produced a justification for every action whenever one was needed.

To take a particular example: Like many churchmen, Innocent had ambivalent feelings toward the economic bonanza that Europe was enjoying. The improved standard of living certainly pleased everyone in a general way, but the embryonic system of capitalism that was emerging raised important moral questions. Capitalism, after all, depends on the use of credit in order to function. Banks loan money to manufacturers, manufacturers loan money to merchants, merchants loan money to business partners or to customers, all in order to keep the cycle of manufacturing, marketing, and consumption moving. But credit also involves the payment of interest, which is where the problem lay. From the Church's point of view, the charging of interest was intrinsically immoral since it entails profiting directly from someone else's economic need; to offer money to someone who needs it only on condition that the person in need will repay more than the amount borrowed is extortion (the specific term the Church used is *usury*), and the Church tried everything it could to stamp it out—all to no avail.

Nevertheless, the issue illustrates Innocent's concerns and methods: The Church has a right and obligation, he insisted, to involve itself in any human activity that has a moral component. Such a claim cast a wide net, one that Innocent used to full advantage. Asserting his claim of *plenitudo potestatis* he tried not only to end the practice of charging interest but to set what he deemed the just price of goods and services and to determine the fair wages of workers, to articulate a specific code of sexual conduct within marriage and to regulate the prostitution trade, to control social contact between members of different ethnic and religious groups, to limit what he regarded as the excessive liberality of some of Europe's schools and universities, and to establish standards for social dress and comportment. Moral renewal, Innocent felt deeply, had to be a constant, ongoing process at a personal, daily level, and it was the Church's responsibility to be at the center of it all and to urge it on.

One of his dearest desires was to lead a successful crusade, which he saw as part of the call to personal moral renewal. Jerusalem still lay under Muslim control, and the modest tolerance that marked Saladin's treatment of Christians after the Third Crusade ended with his death in 1193. Innocent planned the preaching and recruitment for the new campaign meticulously. It was decided that the crusaders would take the sea route rather than trek across eastern Europe and Anatolia—since the Byzantines could not be trusted—and so plans were laid for the crusaders to gather at Venice. But the commanders-in-charge had overestimated the number of recruits they could bring and found themselves unable to pay the Venetians for all the supplies and steerage for which they had contracted. The leading magistrate (*doge*) of Venice, Enrico Dandolo, agreed to forgive the crusaders' debt and transport them to the Holy Land if they would stop en route at the Dalmatian city of Zara, which the king of Hungary had seized some years before, and restore it to Venetian control. Seeing no other option, the crusaders did so. When news reached Rome of the crusaders' sidetrack action, Innocent flew into a rage and excommunicated the entire crusading army. Zara, after all, was a Christian city. The crusaders-in-exile wintered in Zara, and while they were there an embassy arrived from the Byzantine prince Alexius, who had recently been driven from Constantinople by a palace coup. Alexius promised the crusaders that if they helped restore him to his throne he would provide them with ample soldiers, supplies, and money to complete their conquest of Jerusalem. He was lying, of course, but the crusaders believed him since they saw no alternative. They therefore set sail for Constantinople, which they conquered and sacked in April 1204. The crusade commander, Count Baldwin of Flanders, quickly got rid of Alexius and became the new emperor; he and his successors ruled until 1261, during which time the forced reunion of the Latin and Greek churches was proclaimed. Given this unexpected outcome, Innocent relented and rejoiced in the involuntary return of the Greeks to Latin authority. The Greeks, for their part, felt otherwise.

The Latin empire that Baldwin and his successors ruled was hardly an empire at all; it consisted of little more than the cities of Constantinople and Adrianople plus the thin strip of land that connected them and a few outposts on the Anatolian coast. Most of Asia Minor remained in Turkish hands. Three Byzantine rump states were established at Nicaea, Epirus, and Trebizond, and the bulk of the western portion of the empire (including most of the Aegean and eastern Mediterranean islands) was divided up by Venetian armed companies and French barons. On the whole, the Latin Christians treated their Orthodox subjects more harshly than they did their Muslim ones in the Holy Land. They introduced feudalism with a heavy hand and displaced tens of thousands of indigenous farmers; they held monopolies over the most lucrative commodities moving through eastern ports; they pillaged Orthodox churches and monasteries and attempted to compel obedience to Rome. Innocent III, to his credit, was horrified by the reports of the despoliation of the eastern churches but was not so stricken that he could not reconcile himself to the notion of a reunited—even if an unwillingly reunited—Christendom.

Innocent III confirms the establishment of the Franciscan order. This fresco by Giotto di Bondone depicts Innocent handing the official Rule of the order to St. Francis. Source: Scala / Art Resource, NY

In his relations with the European heads of state, Innocent showed himself to be a skillful politician, deftly playing one ruler off another. His first challenge was in dealing with the Norman-Sicilian realm. In 1186 Frederick Barbarossa had married his son Henry VI (r. 1190–1197) to Constance, the aunt of Sicily's young king William II (r. 1166–1189). William, hoping to emulate his adventurous ancestor Robert Guiscard, had been planning to conquer Constantinople and wanted a German alliance in order to avoid an invasion from the north while he was on campaign. The pope at that time, Urban III (r. 1185–1187), saw no reason to oppose the match since he assumed, along with everyone else, that William would produce an heir to the Sicilian throne. But in 1189 William died unexpectedly and childless, leaving his aunt Constance and her Hohenstaufen husband as the rulers of Sicily and southern Italy. The Papal State stood surrounded by imperial territories, and these were now governed by the Holy See's most implacable Hohenstaufen enemy. When Innocent III came to the papal throne, Henry VI was dead but a son—named Frederick—had already been born, thus assuring the dynastic linkage of the northern and southern territories. Innocent played on Constance's well-founded fears of a baronial refusal to recognize her son's rights and persuaded her to recognize the Holy See as feudal overlord for Sicily; when Constance herself took ill, she made her three-year-old son Frederick a ward of the papal court. Innocent had won at least a respite from immediate danger as he waited for Frederick to reach maturity.

Innocent's warnings to Constance about baronial revolt had not been alarmist. Throughout the Middle Ages the succession of a minor to a royal title almost always inspired at least some aristocrats to break away and form an autonomous principality. The fact that Frederick was only three meant that ambitious princes had at least a dozen years at their disposal for doing mischief in Germany. Two figures soon emerged to claim the throne for themselves: Otto of Brunswick led the Guelf party, while Frederick's uncle Philip of Swabia was the Ghibelline candidate. Aiming to minimize the Hohenstaufen power-base, Innocent initially supported Otto after extracting from him promises never to attempt to unite Sicily with the empire and to renounce all the royal controls over the German Church left standing by the Concordat of Worms. But when Otto reneged on his promises, Innocent quickly absolved the German princes of their oaths of loyalty to him and began negotiations with Philip Augustus of France for a retaliatory strike. Otto patched together a hasty pact with England's unreliable king John, but the alliance was smashed in a decisive battle at Bouvines by Philip Augustus' forces in 1214. This defeat effectively ended Otto's reign, as the German magnates grudgingly recognized young Frederick as the heir to the throne, and also started the French campaign of driving the English from their continental possessions. Eighteen-year-old Frederick, for his part, vowed to adhere to all the concessions originally granted by Otto to Innocent. By deft diplomacy and a bit of luck, Innocent had succeeded in securing Frederick's crown, winning recognition that Sicily was a papal fief and would forever remain separate from the empire, and securing the renunciation of all remaining royal rights over the German Church.

Innocent scored similar successes in his dealings with England and France. Relations between those two kingdoms hardly improved in the aftermath of the Third Crusade. While Richard languished in his Austrian prison cell and John ineptly took over his government, Philip, a much keener strategist than either of them, was hard at work plotting to drive the Plantagenets from France[5]. Since the dispute was between

---

5.   The family name of the Plantagenets comes from the Latin *planta genista* ("broom bristles"). Tradition maintains that the name derives from an ancestor who liked to decorate his cap with springs of straw.

a feudal lord and his vassal, Innocent had no direct right to intervene, so he invented one. Whenever there is a threat of war, he argued, there is a threat of sin being committed, and for this reason the pope is obliged to take action. Innocent wrote scores of letters to each sovereign, trying to micro-manage the Anglo-French conflict. As Philip reconquered territory after territory from the English—in the end he regained all the continental territories except for part of Gascony—John's authority in England grew weaker and weaker. The disputed succession to the archbishopric of Canterbury in 1206 showed the extent of John's weakness and of Innocent's willingness to use every weapon at his disposal. The cathedral canons had elected one candidate to the office; the suffragan bishops had chosen another, and John had put forth a third. All three candidates sent embassies to Rome, but Innocent rejected them all and appointed instead Stephen Langton, an English cardinal whom Innocent had met years before when studying theology in Paris. The canons and bishops acquiesced, but John loudly refused to recognize Langton or let him into the country. When the conflict escalated, Innocent took extreme measures: He excommunicated John, freed his vassals from their feudal ties, helped Philip Augustus prepare an invasion of the island, and placed the whole of England under an interdict.[6] Faced with rebellion on all sides, John capitulated in 1213 and in a desperate attempt to stay in power agreed to give the kingdom of England to Innocent and receive it back from him as a papal fief. Innocent rewarded John's return to obedience by condemning *Magna Carta*, the charter confirming the king's obligations to his vassals and restricting his claims upon them.

Philip Augustus proved much harder to bring to heel. Innocent had clashed with him earlier over the issue of Philip's marriage to a Danish princess in 1193. Philip, according to biased sources, married the young woman, named Ingeborg, but found on the wedding night that her breath was intolerably bad, and so he had her put away and ordered a council of French bishops to declare the marriage annulled (even though he kept her dowry); he then remarried and raised a family. Ingeborg appealed to Rome and Innocent tried for several years to get Philip to return to her. When all else failed, Innocent imposed an interdict on France—but Philip was shrewd enough to recognize that Innocent needed him to provide muscle for the papacy's struggles with England, Germany, and Sicily, and the pope would therefore never take direct action to stir up the French nobles against their king. So he bided his time. When Philip's second wife died in 1213, he did agree to restore Ingeborg to her queenly throne, but he never surrendered to Innocent's authority the way that Europe's other monarchs had done and in the process he won Innocent's grudging respect. Philip's victory at Bouvines against a German force led by Otto of Brunswick, (the princes' candidate for emperor, as opposed to the papally supported Frederick II), marked the turning point in Innocent's political influence, and it made Philip, for the time being, the most powerful monarch in Europe.

---

6. An *interdict* is a ban on the performance of all sacraments within a proscribed territory. Although an interdict could in theory be imposed by any bishop, in the past usually only popes had been willing to use this extreme measure. Innocent used it often, and it usually worked.

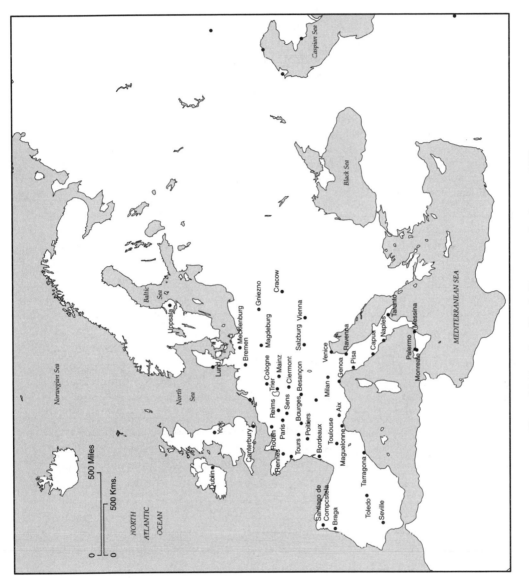

The archbishoprics of Latin Europe, under Innocent III

In 1215 Innocent embarked on his greatest achievement of all: He summoned to Rome a general council to complete, finalize, and codify the reform of the Church. This was the *Fourth Lateran Council*, and it was by far the largest, busiest, and most imposing gathering of clerics since the Council of Nicaea in 325. More than four hundred bishops and eight hundred abbots, with all their retinues, were in attendance, along with the Patriarchs of Constantinople and Jerusalem.

> The Council began at daybreak on St. Martin's day [11 November] with the pope celebrating Mass in the Church of Our Savior, also known as the Church of Constantine. The only people admitted were cardinals, archbishops, and bishops; but when the Mass was ended and the various bishops and abbots (who wore no mitres, unlike the bishops) had taken their seats, then many thousands of people—it seemed like ten times a hundred thousand—clerics and commoners alike, all streamed into the church. In no time at all so many had poured in that even the church's immense size could hardly hold them. Then the lord pope, a man wiser than all others and filled with the spirit of wisdom and understanding, stood on a raised platform above his cardinals and ministers and sang the *Veni Creator*.

Most of the council's work had been accomplished beforehand; the convocation was mainly a ceremonial send-off for all the ecclesiastical legislation that had been drawn up earlier. With this council the Catholic Church reached full maturity. It organized the papal bureaucracy into the offices that it would retain for centuries: the *Chancery*, which dealt with records and bulls; the *Camera*, which administered papal finances; and the *Datary*, which headed the Holy See's judiciary wing. The council also formally established the seven sacraments of the Church: baptism, confirmation, confession, the Mass, marriage, ordination, and last rites. It decreed that all baptized Christians had to confess their sins and receive communion at least once a year (a requirement that tells us much about the extent to which medieval commoners participated in the Church's sacramental life). It placed a moratorium on the establishment of new religious orders; it forbade clergy from participating in secular trials-by-ordeal. It condemned the practice of clerics' charging fees for their performance of the sacraments. It enacted measures to enforce clerical celibacy and obedience. It required that every monastery in Christendom undergo an annual visitation by its presiding bishop to ensure proper liturgical observance, monastic obedience, and moral uprightness. It ordered Europe's Jewish and Muslim populations to wear distinguishing badges on their clothing so that no one would inadvertently trespass interreligious social and legal borders. It ordered all bishops to operate schools attached to their cathedrals and to preach in them regularly.

The Fourth Lateran Council lasted only three weeks, in which time it issued an historic body of legislation. Innocent stood at the pinnacle of his power.

THE REVIVAL OF HERESY

In the twelfth century, widespread heresy returned to Latin Europe. There is little record of heterodox or dissenting religious groups in the preceding centuries and this scantiness has led some historians to suggest that heresy all but vanished under the Carolingians and then suddenly reappeared four hundred years later; this conclusion in turn inclined them to believe that the sudden new outbreaks of heretical views must have been the result of foreign influence—ideas brought back by traders, crusaders, or pilgrims to the Greek and Muslim East. But a more likely explanation is that the late- and post-Carolingian world faced such dire threats of invasion, pillage, disease, and famine that religious deviance seldom got mentioned in the surviving texts. Who cared about theological hairsplitting when the Vikings were burning the village? Besides, the most common religious problem was probably apostasy—that is, newly Christianized people reverting to their original paganism—which does not come under the category of heresy, and hence those few chroniclers who set to work in the tenth and eleventh centuries seldom mentioned any heresy astir in Christendom.

But full-fledged heresy came back with a vengeance, literally, in the twelfth. It first reappeared in various guises in the Mediterranean cities and spread northward. The influx of new philosophical ideas from the translation centers, itinerant scholars, cathedral schools, and universities certainly played a role in shaping some of these new heresies, or in supplying some of their vocabularies, but it is a mistake to think of twelfth-century heresies as movements of intellectual dissent. They were instead, like the very energies that began the Peace of God campaigns and the entire reform effort, popular movements and grassroots expressions of social and spiritual discontent. A single, simple ideal propelled most of these heretical groups: a desire for what they regarded as the *apostolic life*. Only a Church that was made up of the simple ritual and moral purity of Christ's first followers, they believed, could be a true church "of Christ." Hence their heresy often consisted more of rejecting ideas and practices of the reformed Church that they regarded as superfluous than it did of replacing those ideas and practices with contrary ones of their own. Many protestors did not even recognize the necessity of a sacramental priesthood—after all, they reasoned, the overwhelming majority of believing Christians had been effectively priestless for twelve hundred years anyway, so what did priests matter? The people developed their own traditions of devotion, a kind of lay piety. They gathered in small groups to pray, sing hymns, and recite psalms; those who knew how would read out passages from the Bible. The devotional style was more congregational than most people today realize. The Church, as it reformed, responded to the situation in a number of ways, and the very proliferation of cathedral schools, ideally for the training of new generations of priests, was the spearhead of the response. But until there were sufficient clergy to meet society's needs, other volunteers stepped into the breach, often assuming an anticlerical stance since it seemed to many of them that the Church's slow response was the result of a lack of concern for town dwellers' needs.

The *Waldensians*, also known as the *Poor of Lyons*, were one such sect. The Waldensians were a lay spiritual movement founded around 1173 by Waldes, a well-to-do merchant from Lyons. Waldes experienced an apostolic conversion in that year after listening to a reading of the *Life of St. Alexis*. Taking to heart Christ's injunction that the wealthy ought to give away all their money to the poor if they wish to please God, Waldes placed his wife and daughters in a convent, hired two priests to translate the Bible into French so that he could read it, and gave away the rest of his wealth. He then dedicated himself to preaching to the urban masses. Waldes and his followers were orthodox in their dogmatic beliefs, although they did place greater emphasis on three themes than the mainstream clergy did: the need for Christians to adopt voluntary poverty, the need for vernacular translations of the Bible, and the need for the Waldensian brethren to engage in public preaching. These were difficult issues for the Church. It was true that Christ had proclaimed "Blessed are the poor," but did that mean poverty was *required* of Christians? or that the mere possession of wealth was proof of spiritual unworthiness? The fact that the Church itself was exceedingly wealthy suggested that the Waldensian stance entailed a criticism of the ecclesiastical order. The issue of translating the Bible into the vernacular formed another sticking point. The Church had preached from the very start that Christians ought to read the Bible for themselves, but that they had to read it in the universal Church language. There were two reasons for this stance: First, the danger of errors and misinterpretations working their way into faulty translations was large; second and more important was the conviction that the faith, and the book on which it was based, needed to be supra-national. Christians from Portugal to Norway, from Scotland to Hungary, from Ireland to Poland, would be more closely bound together into a religious community if they were all reading the same version of Scripture. The proliferation of vernacular Bibles would unravel the sense of religious unity holding together the medieval world. The last issue, that of public preaching by the Waldensian brothers, seemed to undermine clerical authority. Christ had, after all, established a sacramental priesthood with the unique authority to bind and loose, to preach and to teach. If any layman, however pious and orthodox his beliefs, could interpret the Bible for the masses—then what need of a priesthood?

The Waldensians' activities soon roused the opposition of local clerics, and in 1179 Peter Waldes appealed unsuccessfully to Pope Alexander III for approval of his order. Believing that he had been commanded by God to preach, Waldes decided to disobey the papal command to cease his activities, and his order continued to grow in popularity. Condemned as heretical in 1184, the Waldensians were inspired to sharpen their critiques of the Church, which some of them began openly to refer to as the "Whore of Babylon." The rhetoric escalated rapidly on both sides, and Waldensian communities took root over a wider area, especially within central Europe and southern France. The Waldensians are a perfect example of the new type of heresy that spread: one bereft of fanciful ideas and calling only for simplicity, purity, good words, good deeds, kind hearts, and a putting away of unnecessary pomp. At the same time we ought not to romanticize them as dewy-eyed naïfs crushed by a heartless bureaucracy; they could give as good as they got when it came to spewing venom. Most of the Waldensian groups were suppressed during the thirteenth century, but a handful of Waldensian churches survive even to this day, primarily in Switzerland.

An even more significant lay order was established by women known as the *beguines*. These women too sought to imitate the earthly life of Christ and His first apostolic followers: to renounce wealth, embrace simple virtues, perform charitable acts, preach the need of repentance, and anticipate the arrival of the Kingdom of God. The beguines appeared sometime in the twelfth century and by the early thirteenth had become a significant social force with communities established in cities across the Low Countries, France, and Germany. They were women who wanted to live a religious life but were either unable to become nuns or were uninterested in the calling. Most beguines were unmarried, either never having married or having been widowed, and they lived in communal homes called *beguinages*; those who had families continued to live with them but spent their daytime hours involved in the order's works. The beguines lived by manual labor, chiefly spinning and weaving, and by providing elementary education. They vowed themselves to chastity and poverty but possessed no general administrative structure and claimed no priestly or prophetic authority. Beguines lived as a communal sisterhood, praying, working, teaching, and ministering to the sick as best they could; but they were not an intellectual order and produced no substantial body of writing through which we can know them. Most of our information about them comes from clerical groups overseeing their activities, some of whom admired the sisters wholeheartedly and some of whom eyed them with deep suspicion.

Beguinages proliferated rapidly after Pope Gregory IX (r. 1227–1241) gave formal approval to their activities in 1233. The German city of Cologne alone had nearly sixty such communal houses. A 1328 report on the beguinage of St. Elizabeth in Ghent, which was so large that it formed a separate district of the town, yielded the following observations:

> It is surrounded by moats and walls and in the center of it stands a church, next to which is a cemetery and a hospital. . . . The women have also built many houses for themselves, and each sister has her own garden. . . . Two chaplains reside there, at the sisters' expense. . . . They live together in these houses in a state of considerable poverty, owning nothing but their clothing, a bed, and a chest; they rely on no one but live by the labor of their hands, washing wool and cleaning the clothes that are sent to them by the townspeople. They make enough money from this that, given their simple ways, they can still pay their dues to the church and give the rest away in alms. . . .
>
> During the week they habitually rise early in the morning and gather together in the church, each sitting in the seat assigned to her so that any absences will be noticed. They hear Mass and recite their prayers, then return to their little houses and spend the rest of the day in quiet labor. . . . They never cease praying as they do their work; each house appoints two suitable women to recite the *Miserere* and other familiar psalms, plus the *Ave Maria*. . . . At night, after Vespers, they return to their church for further prayer and meditation until the bell is rung, sending them to bed. On Sundays and holy days they devote themselves to the Lord's service with Masses, sermons, prayers, and meditations.

No one may leave the beguinage on these days without the explicit permission of the headmistress.

The Capetian kings gave special protection and support to the beguine movement after its approval by the Holy See. A hospital dedicated to caring for ill beguines was established at Valenciennes in 1239; the beguinage in Paris was reported to house nearly four hundred women. But the very success of the beguines began to work against them. Through pious gifts, they amassed sizable fortunes despite their dedication to poverty. Envious people resented the special privileges and protections granted them by ecclesiastical and secular authorities. Some of this resentment may have been caused by the confusion generated by other, less devout, lay male groups that called themselves *beguins* or *beghards* and who wandered through many urban communities begging for alms but without necessarily performing the charitable acts of the female beguines. By the latter part of the thirteenth century, public opinion began to turn against them. Finally, at the Council of Vienne in 1312, Pope Clement V forbade the building of new beguinages and prohibited new members to join. Beguines already established were allowed to live out their lives, but the movement ended with the death of the last sister sometime in the middle of the fourteenth century.

Dissident groups that broke into open heresy were numerous. By far the most significant of these were the *Cathars*, also known as the *Albigensians*.[7] They numbered in the tens of thousands and dominated certain areas in southern France, especially around Toulouse, although large Cathar communities existed in northern Italy, Catalonia, and the Rhineland as well. The Cathars were a dualist sect, meaning that they believed in the existence of two eternal and equally powerful gods, one good and one evil. Satan, the evil deity, created the physical universe. By a primeval trick, Satan entrapped human souls—the creation of the good and loving God—in their physical bodies, with the result that human beings became the battleground upon which the cosmic struggle between Good and Evil takes place. The Cathars believed that only the destruction of the physical could liberate one's spiritual essence; hence they forbade sex, practiced self-flagellation, ate severely restricted diets, rejected the use of medicines, and generally engaged in a highly asceticized deathwatch. They condemned marriage, denied Christ's humanity, and rejected transubstantiation. But they believed in the cyclical reincarnation of souls: If one led a life of proper self-denial, one would return after death in a more spiritually enlightened form until finally one achieved permanent release from embodiment and reunion with God. The Cathars took as the most concise statement of their beliefs the prayer "Our Father": It emphasizes God's power and mankind's dependence upon Him, the need for repentance, and the requirement to forgive one's enemies; what it does not emphasize, of course, is the role of Jesus as the

---

7.   The word *Cathar* derives from the Greek term *katharós*, meaning "pure." The name *Albigensian* derives from the southern French town of Albi, which was one of the Cathars' chief strongholds.

earth-born messianic savior. A Cathar liturgy—the so-called "Lyon Ritual"—survives and gives us an indication of some of their central beliefs. Admission to the Cathar faith came about through a rite known as *melioramentum* (literally, one's "improvement"). In it, the postulant stands before an Elder who leads him or her through a triple recitation of the Lord's Prayer, followed by the following words spoken by the Elder:

> We give you this holy prayer in the hope that you will receive it from us, from God, and from His Church; that you will continue to recite it day and night for the rest of your life, whether alone or among friends; and that you will never eat or drink without first reciting it. . . .
>
> Dear brother, do you wish to dedicate yourself to our faith? [Repeated three times.] . . .
>
> Do you dedicate yourself to God and His Gospel? . . .
>
> Do you promise that from this day forward you will never eat meat, eggs, cheese, or animal fat; that you will subsist only on the fruits of water and wood [i.e., fish and vegetables]; that you will not lie, swear, kill, nor give your body over to any type of pleasure; that you will never travel alone when it is possible not to; that you will never sleep unless fully clothed in breeches and shirt; and that you will never abandon our faith out of fear of fire, water, or any manner of death. . . .

After which the community performed a laying on of hands, which completed and formalized one's conversion.

Unlike other heretical groups, the Cathars possessed a modicum of organization, although their practice remained inconsistent and fluid. They had a handful of quasi-bishops whose most important activity was the appointment of the "Perfects," the main clerical body. The Perfects traveled itinerantly, teaching, preaching, fasting, and promoting the Cathar system of values: the condemnation of property, the evil of sex, and the need for repentance. Below them came the bulk of the believers. But the Cathars had many sympathizers among the Catholic masses who never fully embraced their rigorous teaching, so it is difficult to estimate the actual number of heretics. One reason for their popularity was clearly their strong anticlericalism. The Cathars believed firmly that the Catholic Church had lost its way, had surrendered its spiritual mission, had become obsessed with luxury, wealth, and the concerns of the mundane world—and that the more the Church had "reformed" in the twelfth century, the worse matters became. As summarized in *The Inquisitor's Handbook* by Fr. Bernard Gui, the main tool used by the Church in its struggle with the Cathars:

> They maintain that virtually the entire Roman Church is a den of thieves, the Whore of Babylon described in the *Book of Revelations*. They reject the Church's sacraments so adamantly that they regard the holy water of baptism to be no different than river water, and the Host of Christ's Sacred Body no different than common bread. . . . They consider Confirmation and Confession to be meaningless and frivolous. They teach that Marriage is a lie and that there is no salvation in it if the married couple produces children. They

deny the Resurrection of the flesh and propound some nonsense about our souls being angelic spirits cast down from heaven by the sin of pride . . . and about how these souls, after living through seven earthly lives, will final complete their penance and return.

The Church took little action against the Cathars for two or three generations, being more concerned with completing the reform effort and dealing with the Church-State struggles it spawned. The Waldensians, in fact, were the first group to preach against this new sect. When Innocent III came to the throne in 1198 he decided to act. His first impulse was to organize a preaching campaign to teach the heretics the errors of their ways and bring them back into the bosom of the Church. But in 1207 Innocent's personal legate Peter of Castelnau was brutally murdered by a band of Cathars acting, apparently, at the instigation of Count Raymond of Toulouse, a Cathar sympathizer. That is when things turned nasty.

THE ALBIGENSIAN CRUSADE AND THE ORIGINS OF THE INQUISITION

The word *inquisition* conjures up powerful images, usually of beefy sadists and hooded hypocrites, red-hot pincers and screaming voices rising from dark dungeons. But the word itself simply means an "official inquiry." The public hearings that Charlemagne's traveling lords (*missi dominici*) staged were inquisitions; so were the hearings that produced the information in William the Conqueror's *Domesday Book*. Episcopal visitations to the churches within their dioceses were inquisitions, too. The idea of an inquisition had its roots in Roman law; it was a process by which it was incumbent upon the appropriate magistrates to gather evidence of a possible crime and, if such a crime was found, to prosecute it. The Romans considered this process preferable to their older custom of *denunciation*, in which a citizen publicly accused another person of a crime after the fact. Certain crimes, the Romans reasoned, were so pernicious to society at large that authorities had both a right and a duty to take action even before a specific charge had been filed against a specific individual. The inquisition, as defined in Roman law and as initially practiced by the medieval Church, was the direct forerunner of our modern probable-cause hearings.

The recovery of Roman law added to the Church's developing notion of inquisition, and the outcropping of heresy in the twelfth century provided the justification for using it. The Church "inquisited" (to coin a new word) the Waldensians and beguines by having the appropriate bishops inquire into the groups' beliefs and practices. The idea behind this inquiry was that the Church first had to understand what the suspected persons or groups actually believed and did before it could effectively administer them, and that the way to do this was simply to ask them. Once a person's or group's beliefs became known, then the Church could take appropriate action—which usually meant preaching the orthodox doctrines to them in order to show the falsity of their ways. Most churchmen believed that reasoned argument alone was sufficient to guide most heretics back onto the true path.

Thus when Innocent III confronted the problem of the Cathars, he promoted a campaign of inquisition, argument, and preaching. Eventually he came to rely especially on the Order of Preachers (the Dominicans) created by Saint Dominic in 1205. The preachers had no success, however, and sadly reported to Innocent that the whole south of France might be lost to heresy soon. But the gratuitous murder of the papal legate by an underling of the Cathar-sympathizing Count Raymond of Toulouse changed Innocent's approach. He decided that force was necessary. The question, though, was who would provide it? Innocent turned to Philip Augustus who, as Raymond's feudal lord, would presumably have some influence over him, but Philip demurred. He was already busy fighting John of England, and he certainly did not want to establish a precedent of attacking a vassal without just cause; Raymond, after all, had not done anything to Philip. But Philip, like all the Capetians, was eager to stretch his direct power farther to the south and did not mind at all the prospect of someone else toppling Raymond. Therefore when Innocent proclaimed a crusade against Raymond and all the Cathars of the south, Philip agreed to let all his vassals who wished to join, do so.

The so-called Albigensian Crusade was a horribly bloody affair. To Innocent and his crusaders, the Cathars were the overt enemies of Christ Himself, a threat to Christendom even worse than the Muslims, while to the Cathars the Catholics were deluded servants of Satan, the champions of all things physical and therefore evil. An ugly war of words further poisoned the atmosphere while the armies prepared for battle and made any compromise or negotiated settlement impossible. The crusaders gathered in northern France under the leadership of a new papal legate, Arnold Amalric, and began marching south in the spring of 1209. The first major battle was one of the worst. In July of that year the crusaders besieged the Cathar stronghold of Béziers, near the Mediterranean coast above Narbonne. Having breached the walls, the crusaders stormed in. At that moment someone suggested to Arnold Amalric that many devout and obedient Catholics still lived in the city. Arnold replied grimly: "Kill them all! God will know His own!" More than seven thousand people were slaughtered that day. Innocent rewarded Arnold by appointing him the new archbishop of Narbonne.

Simon de Montfort, a middling baron and ambitious zealot, then took over the leadership of the crusade. He used Béziers as a base from which to launch annual campaigns throughout southern France; he took town after town, and each victory was followed by a massacre of heretics. In 1212 Simon began to attack Count Raymond himself, who had briefly submitted to Rome in 1209 but had since given his support back to the Cathars. King Peter of Aragon, in northeastern Spain, then became involved since he was Raymond's brother-in-law and had a claim to overlordship of Toulouse. Peter was already one of the champions of Christendom, having just led the Christian forces to victory in the most decisive battle of the Spanish *Reconquista* at Las Navas de Tolosa. So the leader of one crusade fought the leader of another, and at the battle of Muret in 1213, Simon defeated Peter and left him dead on the field. Simon then captured Toulouse itself in 1218 and became the undisputed master of southern France. Not for long, however. The towns of the regions, whether heretical or orthodox, were sickened by his brutality and staged a rebellion. Simon was killed in a skirmish only a few months later and no one mourned his passing.

When Simon's son and heir proved unable to hold onto Toulouse, he surrendered the county to the French crown. This brought the Capetians themselves into the fray, and finally King Louis IX (r. 1226–1270) put an end to the Albigensian Crusade by annexing Toulouse and Poitou to the Capetian domain, thus realizing the dynasty's long-held dream of a Mediterranean outpost. The Treaty of Meaux-Paris, signed in early 1229, formally ended the crusade. The powerful lords who had supported the Cathar Church were destroyed; mopping up the rest of the heretics could be left to the inquisition.

The rise of the inquisition and the use of the crusade against the perceived internal enemies of Christendom mark a symbolic end to the great reforming era of the eleventh and twelfth centuries. What an extraordinary change had taken place in these two hundred years. Latin Europe had gone from a divided and war-torn backwater to an energized, highly developed, prosperous, reformed, and intellectually reinvigorated society. Moreover, it was a society that pursued several clear lines of development: one line of strong rural economy, social stratification, and monarchical authority restricted by the rights and privileges of an aristocratic class of chivalrous elites, and another line of urban manufacture and commerce characterized by social fluidity, individual freedom, intellectual and cultural exchange, interethnic contact, and communal-republican government. Geographically, the first line predominated in but was hardly exclusive to northern Europe, while the second was characteristic of yet hardly unique to the Mediterranean south. In the process of this development, western Europe had not only declared its freedom from the Byzantine east and the Muslim south but had attempted to take the fight to them, to regain control of the Mediterranean basin from the Byzantines and Muslims, and to establish the suzerainty of Latin Christianity over them.

Large ambitions entail large risks, however. In the process of creating a single Christian world under the leadership of the "Two Swords" of the papacy and the European secular powers, a great many people became disaffected. The Church had lost its way, many believed; it had become too concerned with lands and taxes, with borders and rights, and too little concerned with sermons and sacraments and service and souls. The State, in becoming regularized and professionalized, all too easily slipped into tyranny and neglect of local traditions. Hence voices called out for resistance. The Church, for its part, responded with the inquisition—an institution that, although we know what it devolved into, began as a teaching program, a campaign to understand how people fell into error, and then to correct them. But the Church had misjudged the severity of the problem. By the end of the twelfth century, tens of thousands of people in Europe were not only in disagreement with the Church but were convinced that it represented an actual bar to salvation, an evil that had to be rooted out by violence if necessary.

Suggested Reading

Texts

Gui, Bernard. *The Inquisitor's Handbook.*
Innocent III. *On Contempt for the World.*
John of Salisbury. *Pontifical History.*
Villehardouin. *The Conquest of Constantinople.*

Source Anthologies

Peters, Edward. *Heresy and Authority in Medieval Europe* (1980).
Tierney, Brian. *The Crisis of Church and State, 1050–1300* (reprint, 1988).
Wakefield, Walter L., and Austin P. Evans. *Heresies of the High Middle Ages* (1969).

Studies

Arnold, Benjamin. *Princes and Territories in Medieval Germany* (1991).
Arnold, John. *Inquisition and Power: Catharism and the Confessing Subject in Medieval Languedoc* (2001).
Cohen, Mark R. *Under Crescent and Cross: The Jews in the Middle Ages* (1994).
Constable, Giles. *The Reformation of the Twelfth Century* (1998).
Costen, Michael. *The Cathars and the Albigensian Crusade* (1997).
Given, James. *Inquisition and Medieval Society: Power, Discipline, and Resistance in Medieval Languedoc* (1997).
Kedar, Benjamin Z. *Crusade and Mission: European Approaches toward the Muslims* (1984).
Kieckhefer, Richard. *Magic in the Middle Ages* (1989).
———. *Repression of Heresy in Medieval Germany* (1979).
Lambert, Malcolm. *Medieval Heresy: Popular Movements from the Gregorian Reform to the Reformation* (2002).
Le Roy Ladurie, Emmanuel. *Montaillou: Catholics and Cathars in a French Village, 1294–1324* (1978).
Moore, R[obert]. I. *The Formation of a Persecuting Society* (1987).
Morris, Colin. *The Papal Monarchy: The Western Church from 1050 to 1250* (1989).
Pegg, Mark. *The Corruption of Angels: The Great Inquisition of 1245–1246* (2001).
Pennington, Kenneth. *Popes and Bishops: The Papal Monarchy in the Twelfth and Thirteenth Centuries* (1984).
Peters, Edward. *Inquisition* (1989).
———. *The Magician, the Witch, and the Law* (1978).
Powell, James M. *Innocent III: Vicar of Christ or Lord of the World?* (1994).
Russell, Jeffrey Burton. *Dissent and Order in the Middle Ages: The Search for Legitimate Authority* (1992).

Sayers, J. E. *Innocent III: Leader of Europe, 1198–1216* (1995).

Simons, Walter. *Cities of Ladies: Beguine Communities in the Medieval Low Countries, 1200–1565* (2001).

Waugh, Scott L., and Peter Diehl. *Christendom and Its Discontents: Exclusion, Persecution, and Rebellion, 1000–1500* (1995).

Webb, Diana. *Pilgrims and Pilgrimage in the Medieval West* (1999).

PART THREE

THE LATE
MIDDLE AGES

❧

The Thirteenth and
Fourteenth Centuries

CHAPTER 13

POLITICS IN THE
THIRTEENTH CENTURY

S tatecraft and notions of political identity developed significantly over the thirteenth century. A constant tension between a centralizing royal ambition and a
centrifugal aristocratic localism characterized French, English, and German politics, and each state responded to that tension in its own creative way. France
emerged as the largest and strongest of the centralized monarchies, mostly at England's expense. England developed the most effective and modern parliamentary
form of government, whereas Germany's analogous *Diet* served essentially a conservative function as a guarantor of baronial privilege. For northern Europe, therefore, the thirteenth century was less a time of political experiment and innovation,
as the eleventh and twelfth centuries had been, than it was a time of maturation
and ripening. Her political institutions developed an exceptional degree of practical sophistication and theoretical underpinning. In the Mediterranean, the communes went through a series of refinements and changes, in some cases
strengthening their republican and mercantile character, in others lessening it in
favor of a growing despotism based on control of land. In all these changes, the
fundamental goal—at least among the theorists—was still to find a right ordering
of the world, to create a polity that was in accord with local circumstances and traditions but also with an understanding of God's design of and for the world. Rebellions and reform movements usually carried the banner of trying to uproot
injustice and restore a divinely ordained order. Conditions varied from place to
place, and therefore so too did political structures and practices, but the goal of establishing a state based on natural and divine law, one in which each individual,
class, religious and ethnic group held its natural and essential position, remained
more or less constant.

By the end of the thirteenth century, most of the states of Europe had the fundamental institutions and political traditions that they would retain for the next five
hundred years. Lots of detail changed in the intervening centuries, but the basic
structures remained remarkably steady. The German Empire, which had entered
the eleventh century as Europe's strongest monarchy, limped out of the thirteenth
century as the weakest, while France took the opposite course and the Capetians
found themselves, especially during the reigns of Louis IX (r. 1226–1270) and Philip

IV "the Fair" (r. 1285–1314), unexpectedly the dominant monarchs in the west. In the Mediterranean, three commercial and political superpowers arose: Venice, Genoa, and the Barcelona-based confederation known as the *Crown of Aragon*. A fourth major power, the Angevin kingdom of Naples (which included Sicily), owed its influence more to its close alliance with the papacy than to its own innate political or commercial might; nevertheless, it played a crucial role in the political development of the Mediterranean in this century, and in some senses it formed the linchpin for many of the diplomatic maneuverings of the age. "Whoever wishes to control the Mediterranean must control Sicily," wrote the Catalan chronicler-adventurer Ramon Muntaner. As we shall see, most of the leading southern states, plus a few of the northern ones, too, attempted exactly that.

The theme of the third part of this book is the climax of medieval civilization in the thirteenth century and its painful disintegration in the fourteenth. It is a dramatic story. The zenith of medieval life was quite all-encompassing: In terms of political strength, economic prosperity, intellectual achievement, cultural vitality, and what for lack of a better term I can only call "social energy" (which I hope will become clear over the next few chapters), Latin Europe in the thirteenth century—that is, from 1199 (the start of Innocent III's pontificate) to 1300 (the year of Boniface VIII's great Jubilee)—was an exceptionally exciting place. Although they were never lacking major problems, the people of that era had a degree of cultural confidence that is striking. To many, it seemed that they truly had figured out the riddle of God's ordering of the cosmos, that they had cracked the Great Code, and that they could consequently see the whole of creation as a single rational order in which everything had its place. This was the age of enormous majestic cathedrals, of scholastic *summas*, a time when an English friar believed that he could write—if only someone would give him the funding!—the encyclopedia to end all encyclopedias, which would explain literally everything about the world, and a time when an Italian poet could write a spiritual epic that ordered the universe according to his own will and in which he brought himself before the face of God.

But the disasters of the fourteenth century, both long-simmering and sudden, brought an end to such confidence and forced the people of medieval Europe to question the most basic assumptions of their lives: Was there in fact a rational order to the universe? Is there any observable purpose in life? Can one in fact truly know anything for certain? If so, how? Can one necessarily assume that any given social or political system is more natural than another? Is it even possible that the Church itself is in error, and that there are other avenues to knowing God? If so, how can we discover them? The forced confrontation with these questions over the course of the fourteenth century brought the medieval period to an end—not all at once, of course, but gradually. As we shall see in our epilogues, aspects of medieval life not only lingered on into the Renaissance but in fact formed part of its very core.

THE RISE OF REPRESENTATIVE INSTITUTIONS

Representative institutions of government form, along with universities, one of our most important medieval legacies. By the end of the thirteenth century or the very beginning of the fourteenth, nearly every state in Europe had some sort of representative assembly, possessing something more than mere advisory power. The ability to check the authority of the ruler, whether king, count, doge, urban magistrate, or *podestà*, is the essential characteristic of representative government—without that ability there is no meaningful representation. In most cases, the first check placed on a ruler was financial. When a ruler lacked funds to carry out his schemes or conduct his administrative business, he had to turn to the people for support in the form of taxation. But people seldom willingly paid taxes, and so they began to demand something in return for their support, such as a voice in determining how the money would be spent. As the power and reach of centralized bureaucracies grew in the twelfth and thirteenth centuries, so too did their expenses, which led to continuous increases in taxation; these in turn contributed to the rise of representative institutions. But that is hardly the only explanation. After all, the subjects of the contemporaneous *Song* emperors in China also hated paying taxes yet they never developed a representative tradition. The reasons for the rise of parliamentarianism in the medieval west are more complex, and can be traced back in various ways to the multi-cultural roots of medieval civilization itself.

From the Greco-Romans the medieval world inherited the twin notions of *individual rights*, such as the right to property, and of *public duty*, a citizen's obligation to serve the state that preserves those rights. Civic-mindedness, in the classical sense, implied an understanding of the state as a corporate entity, an organic institution comprised of the people being governed (or at least of those people holding the legal status of citizenship); this definition explains the classical notion of law as a social creation that evolves over time rather than as an eternal, unchanging set of divinely appointed precepts. As the conditions of human life change, so too can, and in fact *must*, the laws governing those lives change. And the changes must spring from the people themselves; rulers are magistrates and functionaries—they enact the will of the people rather than impose their own wills upon them.

The ancient Germanic tradition played a role as well. Tacitus' *Germania* described in some detail the Germanic practice of holding assemblies of the tribal leaders before all major decisions affecting the tribe were made:

> The chiefs alone deliberate minor matters, but on important issues the whole tribe is consulted once the chiefs themselves have discussed the issues amongst themselves first. They assemble on fixed days, usually at the new moon or the full moon, unless something unexpected necessitates their sudden meeting. . . . When enough of them have gathered they sit down fully armed. Silence is commanded by their priests, whose responsibility it is to keep order. Then the king or tribal chief—who holds his position by right of age, noble birth, distinction in battle,

and eloquence—is heard, but his is only a power to persuade, not an ability to dictate. If his ideas displease the people they reject them with loud shouts. . . .

Tacitus' description is somewhat fanciful: Writing in the first century of the Roman Empire, he intentionally idealized the supposedly democratic character of the Germans in order to inspire his own countrymen to restore the Roman Republic; but it is clear nevertheless that the early tribes had a tradition of some sort of majority rule on issues that affected the entire community. Military necessity, rather than high-minded notions of parliamentarianism, probably drove the tradition—a warrior society, after all, will not last long if the warriors are disaffected with their commanders—but the tradition existed nevertheless.

Christianity contributed a strong notion of community, one derived less from the Scriptures themselves—which, to the extent they discuss politics at all, appear to endorse monarchical absolutism—than from the daily practices of the earliest Christian groups. Most of the surviving evidence suggests that the first Christians lived in communes, held their goods in common, and resolved disputes as a deliberative group. The most important direct influence on medieval developments was the evolution of cenobitic monasticism in the west. These were the first Christian communities that were consciously and deliberately established *as* communities. The monastic Rules provided the earliest models of a constitutionally organized, self-governing ministate in which each individual had an established place, rights, and duties.

The interplay of these traditions over the centuries contributed to the development of the medieval assembly, with different traditions playing greater or lesser roles at different times and in different places. But the evolution of parliamentarianism was hardly a triumphal march of the progress of liberty through history. The reality was far more disjointed and uninspiring. From Carolingian times onward, medieval rulers usually called assemblies for specific reasons and only when they had exhausted all other means of acquiring whatever precise monies or favors they were seeking. Thus a parliamentary tradition was built up only incrementally and grudgingly, as a last resort.

ENGLAND AND FRANCE

England and France provide an interesting contrast. By around 1300 both had established parliamentary traditions, but in England the parliamentary principle resulted in a significantly restrained monarchy while in France it largely strengthened the royal hand. Clearly it was not the rise of representative government per se that weakened the English crown; the loss of the continental possessions played a more direct role in that. But the two developments were closely interrelated. Just as obviously, the culmination of Capetian power owed most to the enormous growth of the Capetian royal demesne achieved by driving the English from the land and extending royal authority southward during the Albigensian Crusade.

Let us take the English example first. Henry II (r.1154–1189) had left England with an enormous empire, a highly developed body of law and a judicial system capable of carrying it out, and a strongly centralized government that had few checks on it other than the customs written into the feudal contracts that bound the king to his vassals. Conditions changed dramatically during the reigns of his sons Richard the Lionheart (r.1189–1199) and John (r.1199–1216). Richard, as we have seen, was an absentee ruler who spent no more than six months of his ten-year reign in England. But he was a popular ruler nonetheless. As a heroic crusader he won respect throughout Christendom for himself and the English soldiers who fought under him. In his absence the government ran efficiently despite John's meddlings and abuses; and besides, the sheer fact of Richard's absence meant that he could not inflict on the English the more despotic elements of his personality. His military ventures were costly, however, and when he died the royal coffers were nearly empty, a situation that emboldened the feudal barons to assert themselves in a way they had not dared to do under Henry II.

John was another matter altogether. He was vain, greedy, and cruel, capable of brilliant strategy but unreliable and inept in action. He had the unfortunate habit of seducing his vassals' wives and daughters. He also had the poor luck of being pitted against two of the most capable politicians of the Middle Ages: Philip Augustus of France and Pope Innocent III. John was no match for either of them, let alone for both of them. But that is not to say that he did not try hard. John labored long hours at the minutiae of administration, sitting in court, hearing appeals, overhauling the Exchequer, searching for ways to streamline and improve the bureaucracy. He deserves credit for recognizing, in a way that his father and brother had not done, that the urbanization of English society held out the greatest promise for long-term growth. England's towns were multiplying rapidly in size and number, the merchants were organizing into guilds and developing international trade connections, and the commercial economy was gaining ground on the rural as a percentage of realm-wide revenue production. John did his best to encourage this trend by granting numerous municipal charters and developing a unified commercial tax code. He tried to raise money as well by insisting on higher feudal reliefs from his barons and charging fees for favors granted by the crown.

These new demands for money need not have been his undoing but for the fact that they took place within the context of the inept loss of the continental possessions that provided the bulk of the king's revenue. Townsmen and barons alike complained that they were being forced to pay for the crown's own folly. Moreover, it was humiliating for the English, who had single-handedly battled Saladin to a stalemate, to be driven from France at such astonishing speed; the king's own subjects began to call him names like "John Soft-sword" and "John Lack-land." John followed nearly every loss with new demands for higher taxes and reliefs in order to raise yet another army to take to France. The Capetian victory at Bouvines in 1214 was the last straw. The barons gathered together with Stephen Langton, the archbishop of Canterbury whom Innocent III had forced John to accept, to plot a rebellion. In the spring of 1215 they occupied London. John had no choice but to relent, and when he met with representatives of the rebels at Runnymede (a meadowland then outside London but now near the site of Windsor Castle) he agreed to sign *Magna Carta* or the "Great Charter."

Magna Carta is something of a disappointment to read. Although it is commonly regarded as one of the foundational documents of western parliamentary government, it has none of the stirring rhetoric and idealism of the American *Declaration of Independence*. It reads, in fact, like a memo composed by an accountant.

> If any of my earls, barons, or any other tenant-in-chief of mine owing military service should die, and if at his death his heir should be of legal age and owe feudal relief to the crown, then he shall receive his inheritance upon payment of the relief: specifically, the heir or heirs of an earl shall pay £100 for a whole earldom; the heir or heirs of a baron shall pay £100 for a whole barony; and the heir or heirs of a knight shall pay 100 shillings, at most, for a whole knight's fee.

This extract is about as high-flying as the charter's rhetoric gets. But it is important to remember that Magna Carta is a conservative document rather than a revolutionary one; it confirmed and guaranteed old privileges; it did not create new ones. It outlawed specific abuses of which John was guilty (in fact, its greatest utility is as a sort of legal indictment of John's feudal crimes), but it did little to extend the rights of the ruled in any significant way. Even its assertion that no extraordinary taxes were to be levied without the consent of the Great Council was only a restatement of old custom. Magna Carta's most famous clause stipulated that "No free man shall be arrested, imprisoned, dispossessed, outlawed, or banished, or in any way destroyed, neither will we proceed against him nor command against him except by the legal judgment of his peers or by the law of the land." This is the earliest expression of the notion of *due process* in customary law and is worthy of notice, even though the notion was already well-established in Roman law. Indeed, the most significant thing about the Magna Carta is its symbolism rather than its content: The mere fact that the king was *forced to sign* a document guaranteeing certain rights of the governed gives the Great Charter an important place at the start of the development of representative government.

John was succeeded by his nine-year-old son Henry III (r.1216–1272), an ineffective monarch by any standard. Certainly the odds were against him from the start, given his long minority during which the barons did all they could to wrest authority away from the crown. But even when grown to manhood, Henry remained something of a child, a spoiled simpleton who surrounded himself with fawning, scheming, false friends who made much of their supposed affection for the king while plotting to enrich and empower themselves at his expense. His reign is the era of the real foundation of parliamentary government in England.

Like his predecessors, Henry was more French than English. Both his parents were French, and he surrounded himself at court with mostly French advisors. He married Eleanor, the daughter of the count of Provence, and spoke French at home and at court. This habit is significant because English society at the time was developing a keen sense of itself as a unique culture separate from the Continent, possessing its own language, literature, legal traditions, political institutions, and social organization. This was the era of Robert Grosseteste and Roger Bacon in English science, of *Sir Gawain and the Green Knight* in English letters, of Henry Bracton in English law. A decidedly un-English king, especially one as poorly suited to the job as Henry, was not the best thing for England at that time. Consequently, Henry never had a substantial reservoir of public goodwill on which to draw during difficulties. Adding to his woes, he was a deeply devout man whose piety took the particular form of an almost obsequious obedience to the Holy See in both political and personal matters. So badly did Henry mismanage affairs that even the English clergy rose in rebellion against him—not, as in the Becket affair under Henry II, because the king opposed the pope, but because the king so completely *obeyed* him.

Henry III was constantly in debt and sought new ways to improve his income. So long as his international ambitions remained in check, the barons were able to help the king keep within his means; but in 1250 the throne to the kingdom of Sicily became vacant and the papacy offered the crown to the highest bidder. Henry was determined to acquire it for one of his sons and spent several years in fruitless and expensive adventures trying to get it. In 1258 the barons reached the end of their patience and staged a kind of coup d'état that established an aristocratic oligarchy that severely checked the power of the king; in effect they created a constitutional monarchy. The barons forced Henry to agree to the *Provisions of Oxford* in that year, which established a baronial council under the leadership of an official called a *justiciar*, who ran the government in the king's name. The first justiciar was Simon de Montfort, a younger son of the man who had led the Albigensian Crusade, and the governing council took the name of *Parliament*. Both the outraged king and the Parliament sought support among the leaders of urban society, which gradually opened the door to the involvement of the commoners in governmental matters.

Simon de Montfort summoned a Parliament in 1265 that, for the first time, included two knights from every English shire and two burghers from every English town. This is usually considered England's first true Parliament. The representatives of the shires and towns brought considerable political acumen and experience with them since they had been actively governing themselves at the local level for some time. They did not gather for each meeting of the Parliament, but their presence became more common as the decades went on. It was not until the fourteenth century that a more or less permanent House of Commons joined the great lords in the composition of Parliament.

It was Henry III's son and heir Edward I (r.1272–1307) who deserves most of the credit for that union. Edward was an energetic and resourceful ruler who recognized that the inherent strength of an English monarch now rested upon his Englishness and his dedication to the rule of law. He excelled at both. Edward saw Parliament as a means of increasing his popularity with the English people and in so doing increasing his *de facto* personal power—even if that meant at the expense of increasing the *de jure* authority of the Parliament over the crown. Edward fought many wars, chiefly in Wales and Scotland, and needed lots of money to do it. He convened Parliaments so frequently that they became almost commonplace. But the people appreciated their newfound importance in the administration of the realm, just as they enjoyed Edward's continued successes on the battlefield. For his role in developing Parliament, and especially for his work at codifying English law, he is sometimes referred to as the English Justinian.

Under Henry III the barons had usurped many royal privileges, especially lucrative jurisdictional powers. They forbade royal sheriffs from entering their shires and compelled tenants to appeal their cases before the more expensive private baronial courts. Edward put a halt to such abuse by appearing to condone it: He agreed to recognize and affirm in perpetuity any baronial privilege whose grant from the crown could be proven by charter. At these *Quo warranto* hearings Edward's nobles were asked "by what warrant" they claimed any particular jurisdiction. The nobles forfeited any privileges for which they could not produce a royal charter, but they secured confirmation of authorities that often had been in dispute for generations. Edward thus strengthened his hand by clarifying the judicial map and establishing a clear precedent that the crown is the final arbiter of justice. He followed this success with a new statute called *Quia emptores* that prohibited subinfeudation—all with the aim of limning the extent of baronial authority and privilege, just as Magna Carta had limned that of the throne.

The French experience contrasts sharply with the English. The Capetians came to power—if we can call it that—in 987 as arguably the poorest and least significant monarchs in the west. Nearly two hundred years later, matters had improved quite a bit, but the personal, political, and territorial setbacks of Louis VII's reign undercut much of what had been achieved. It was only under Louis' son Philip Augustus (r.1180–1223) that France and her monarchy came to prominence. Philip increased the French national territory fourfold. Most of this expansion came at England's expense, of course, but Philip added significant amounts of land by the traditional Capetian practice of opportunistic marriage, confiscation of vacant fiefs and those of rebellious vassals, and manipulation of the confused pattern of land-tenure in the south after the Albigensian Crusade. But for all his battlefield success, Philip himself was not a great or avid military leader. He far preferred diplomatic maneuvers and political intrigues to risky military solutions to a problem.

He also turned Paris into the de facto capital of France. It had long been the largest city in the realm (by Philip's death it had a population of perhaps fifty thousand), but he established it as the permanent seat of government with permanent offices, archives, and courts. He built an imposing palace near the cathedral of Notre Dame, widened and paved the city streets, constructed heavy walls around the city, and began work on a massive fortress—the Louvre—just outside the western-facing walls to protect the city from attack coming up the Seine valley, Paris' most vulnerable approach.

Philip was succeeded by his son Louis VIII (r.1223–1226) who, apart from his participation in the Albigensian Crusade, is remembered chiefly for granting away large sections of the territories won by his father as *apanages*. An apanage was a land

grant made to the younger sons of the royal family as compensation for not inheriting the crown. These were not fiefs—that is, the grants were not made on condition
of feudal obligations of service; instead it was assumed that a sense of family loyalty would make the receiver of the apanage a loyal servant of the crown. But
legally, there was nothing to compel such service, so apanages were technically independent provinces. Louis probably had little choice about his land grants: For
one thing the Capetian demesne had grown so large that even the corps of baillis,
seneschals, and provosts was stretched thin in trying to administer it. For another,
the Capetian family brood kept growing larger, and it evidently seemed expedient
to Louis to forestall a rebellion by the landless lesser royals by giving them something. But the long-term consequences of the apanage system were grievous.

Upon Louis VIII's early death, the kingdom fell into the hands of his widow,
Blanche of Castile, who governed on behalf of their young son, also named Louis.[1]
France was lucky in this, for Blanche was one of the most capable politicians of the
Middle Ages. She was the daughter of Alfonso VIII of Castile (r.1158–1214) and his
wife Eleanor (the daughter of Eleanor of Aquitaine and Henry II of England), and
she inherited from both sides a haughty and determined temperament. She was in
fact rather domineering. Louis IX's biographer Joinville relates how much the
young king both loved and feared his mother. Blanche, for example, positively detested Louis' wife Margaret of Provence, whom she regarded as an idiot, and
loathed the idea of her son sleeping with her. Louis gave standing orders to his servants that whenever he was planning to spend the night with his wife (kings and
queens often had separate bedchambers in those days), they were to keep watch
outside Blanche's door and start beating the palace dogs whenever the queen-
mother left her chamber in search of her son. The dogs' howling was Louis' signal
to sneak back to his own rooms.

Blanche ran France during Louis' minority as firmly as she tried to run his sex
life after he grew up. As was usual during a regency, many nobles rose up in a series
of changing coalitions to wrest greater independence from the crown. Blanche herself took the field to lead armies and conduct sieges against them all. She proved to
be a skillful negotiator as well, and she was able to pass on to her son, when he
reached maturity in 1234, a unified and generally obedient kingdom. She remained
his chief political advisor until her death in 1252 and in fact once again took over the
government in her son's name when he departed on a crusade in 1248.

Louis IX (r.1226–1270), or St. Louis, is widely regarded as medieval France's
greatest king. With a realm that reached from the North Sea to the Mediterranean,
from the Atlantic Ocean to the Rhone River, he was certainly the greatest Frankish
ruler since Charlemagne. His personal virtues were many: He was pious and hard-
working, deeply concerned with bringing justice to his subjects, brave in battle, and

---

1. The Capetians had many talents, but a gift for names was not one of them. Between 1060 and 1322
every single king of France was named either Philip or Louis. Obviously, they were following the pattern
of the Carolingian family in creating a small pool of sacralized Christian names.

capable of enormous generosity. At the same time, though, he was rabidly anti-Semitic, so obsessed with detail that he often lost sight of his larger aims, and was frequently blinded by idealism. He was also given to uttering pious platitudes, as when he once advised his son "to win the love of the people in the realm—for I'd rather have a Scotsman govern them, if he did it well and justly, than have the world think you did a poor job of it."[2]

Louis did not substantially alter the administrative structure he had inherited, but he did work hard to redress some of the complaints raised by his subjects about over-aggressive baillis and seneschals. He believed that his subjects were just as entitled to their rights as he was to his, and promised to correct abuses. He did this by creating yet another body of royal officials—this time inspectors known as *enquêteurs*—whose responsibilities were somewhat similar to those of the old Carolingian *missi dominici*; they traveled throughout the realm holding open courts and listening to local grievances. Reports of abuses made their way back to Paris, and Louis then took appropriate action. His reign did not contribute in any direct way to the development of representative institutions; indeed in his reign there was no such thing, and even the nobles had at best an advisory role at court. But Louis' emphasis on the legal rights of every citizen certainly helped to pave the way for parliamentary developments under Philip IV the Fair (r.1285–1314). An important development in the royal court did occur on Louis' watch, though. Given the enormity of the royal demesne, the sheer number of cases appealed to the royal court had increased dramatically, such that a permanent site for the court became necessary; up to this time, the royal court and all its officials usually traveled with the king in his retinue. The caseload by Louis' time demanded a fixed site where appellants could turn for timely justice. Louis established a permanent court in Paris that met whether or not the king or major nobles were present; professional jurists handled the bulk of the cases, but for appeals that involved a great feudal lord, a company of his peers was summoned. This Parisian court was called the *Parlement*.[3]

Louis' two greatest adventures were his leadership of the Sixth and Seventh Crusades—1248–1250 and 1270, respectively. Both were dismal failures. He spent four years intricately planning his first campaign, even going to the trouble of building a vast new port at Aigues-Mortes (literally "Dead-Waters," in reference to the calmness of the recessed bay) in the south of France as an embarkation point for his army of twenty thousand. Louis left the government of France in his mother's hand—and he took the precaution of taking his wife Margaret with him, rather than leave her at Blanche's mercy. After wintering at Cyprus, he launched his attack on Egypt and quickly captured the port city of Damietta, but his forces were routed when they tried to advance inland and Louis himself was taken captive. After being

---

2. Among other pieties Louis had a noteworthy horror of profanity. He once ordered a foul-mouthed goldsmith in Caesarea to be bound to an upright ladder and buried in the viscera of butchered pigs up to his nose, so that he might fully appreciate the filthiness of his speech.
3. It is important not to get confused by the similar-sounding names. The *Parliament* in England was the representative legislative body; the *Parlement* in Paris was the chief royal judicial institution.

ransomed, Louis sailed to the Holy Land and spent three years helping to rebuild the fortifications of the few remaining Latin Christian outposts. In 1254 he returned to France—two years after his mother's death—convinced that his failure had been due to his own sinfulness, and he dedicated himself to purifying both himself and his administration. It is in fact during the post-crusade years that he instituted his corps of royal *enquêteurs*. His last crusade ended almost as soon as it began. An unlikely rumor had spread abroad that the Muslim ruler of Tunis wanted to convert to Christianity, and Louis, for whatever reason, responded to the news by deciding to send a crusade against him. His forces landed at the shore near Tunis, and Louis, who had evidently taken ill with dysentery, died almost immediately. The troops disbanded on the spot and returned to France.

Louis' successors Philip III (r.1270–1285) and Philip IV the Fair[4] (r.1285–1314), followed his policies of increasing the centralization of government and reining in the abuses of aristocrats and lesser royal functionaries. But money grew into an obsession with the crown in the latter decades of the thirteenth century, owing to an increase in warfare. Philip III fought in Spain against the Catalans. Philip IV struggled to add Flanders to the Capetian realm (but was repulsed in 1302), fought an indecisive series of wars with Edward I of England for control of Aquitaine, and conducted numerous successful small campaigns against the vulnerable border-territories of the disintegrating German Empire.

Philip IV used almost any means he could think of to raise money, and he found a way to justify each action. He first set about reorganizing his court and wresting private justice from the nobles who, like their English contemporaries, still possessed extensive jurisdictional powers. The French Parlement came to consist of three distinct chambers dedicated respectively to receiving complaints, conducting investigations, and adjudicating cases.[5] It is possible that the idea for some of these reforms came from the officials of the reconquered English territories; such certainly was the case with Philip's financial reforms. Professional finance ministers replaced tax farmers and aristocratic sinecures at both local and royal levels; they increased the efficiency of the financial machinery and rooted out some of the most egregious corruption. But the new regime was not immune to corruption of its own kind. Royal finances previously had been under the care of the Templar knights in Paris who conducted an annual audit of all the *baillis* and *prévôts* in the realm, but by 1300 the kingdom had increased far beyond the ability of the Templars to deal with the accounts—and Philip was the sort who, when confronted with administrative inefficiency, leapt immediately to accusations of embezzlement and thievery. He brought ludicrous charges against the Templars and began to seize their enormous real estate and capital holdings. The trial of the Templars became an elaborate circus that lasted ten years and ended with the formal suppression of the order by

---

4. His nickname refers to his reputedly exceptional good looks, not his fair-mindedness (of which he had little).
5. That is, the *chambre des requêts*, the *chambre des enquêts*, and the *chambre des plaids*.

the papacy in 1312, but by that time the Templars' wealth had long since been pocketed by Europe's kings as the other monarchs were quick to follow Philip's example.

Philip ordered the arrest of every Jew in France in 1306, following the example of England's Edward I who had done so in 1290, and after confiscating all their property and loan accounts, he expelled them from the kingdom. Anti-Jewish sentiment had been on the rise over the thirteenth century for three reasons: the uncertainties many felt about the development of the new money economy and the popular prejudice that associated Jews with it; the rise of popular reform movements within Christianity that expected the long-resistant Jews to recognize finally the truth of the "real" Christianity revealed by those reforms; and frustration over the continued failure of crusade efforts—which many Christians attributed to divine vengeance for not having put Europe's own spiritual house in order before attempting to liberate the Holy Land. Philip capitalized on all these sentiments when he ordered the Jewish expulsion and found himself more popular than ever as a result of it. He also drew enormous loans from various Italian banks and defaulted on them, bringing several financial houses down in the process.

This background provided the context for the development of France's representative institution, the *Estates General*. In 1301, in desperate need of money, Philip pressed the French churches for revenue, only to encounter the stern resistance of Pope Boniface VIII and a handful of French bishops. Philip charged one bishop with treason and imprisoned him in the hope of scaring the others into compliance. When the bishops held fast, Philip decided to take a chance on the anticlerical sentiment brewing among the populace. He summoned a meeting of a representative assembly in 1302, the Estates General, to endorse his ecclesiastical policies and vote him the tax money he needed to support an army. This was France's start down the road to constitutional government. It is ironic to note that virtually the first action taken by the assembly was to declare that the pope was a heretic and criminal, subject to the jurisdiction of the French crown. In contrast to the English example, then, the French parliamentary tradition developed as a means of strengthening royal power and enabling it to do things that it otherwise was incapable of.

GERMANY, ITALY, AND THE PAPACY

German, Italian, and papal relations in the thirteenth century were dominated by the struggle to undermine, and if possible to destroy and replace, the power of the Hohenstaufen family. Innocent III had done all he could to this effect already, but the situation now hinged on young Frederick II's (r.1215–1250) willingness to live up to his promises to keep Sicily and the empire separate, to relinquish control of the German Church, and to recognize the rights of the German magnates. He reached adulthood in 1215 and made it clear from the start that he would follow his own path. He was an odd personality, and people were clearly in awe of him. Most of his biographers have emphasized his unique character; in the Middle Ages he was referred to as *Stupor mundi* ("The Wonder of the World"), and most commentators since then have taken much the same line. But sometimes oddness is simply odd. At least in regard to his royal policies Frederick was thoroughly conventional: He sought to enrich himself and his family, to centralize and extend his authority, and to emphasize the rule of law—but more out of a wish to exert power than to express commitment to a social ideal. What set Frederick apart from his contemporaries was his personal flamboyance and the catholicity of his interests. Having grown up in Sicily, he had a rather more cosmopolitan character than his Salian predecessors: He was a troubadour poet, knew five languages including Greek and Arabic, kept a harem, maintained a zoo of exotic animals, fancied himself something of a scientist, favored Arab-style robes and turbans to Christian tunics and caps, and described himself as the devoted champion of the Christian Church (while he remained a freethinker in terms of religious belief). To the papal court he was simply the Antichrist incarnate.

Frederick spent his first years in power consolidating his hold over Italy. Germany interested him little. He promised Pope Honorius III (r.1216–1227) that he would lead a crusade to the Holy Land, but ignored the promise as much as he did others. Only after the next pope Gregory IX (r.1227–1241) excommunicated him for violating his oath did Frederick finally agree to go. His crusade of 1228 was a curious affair. He sailed to Palestine but refused to fight the Muslims, whom he viewed with favor, having grown up among so many in Sicily. Through a series of extended negotiations with the sultan of Egypt—al-Kamil, who was then the titular ruler of Jerusalem—Frederick somehow convinced the Muslim strongman to give him the Holy City without a fight, plus Bethlehem and Nazareth and other cities associated with Christ, together with a corridor from these sites to the seacoast. Frederick agreed to guarantee freedom of religion for everyone in these lands whether Muslims, Christian, or Jewish, and not to aid any subsequent crusade coming out of Europe. Frederick crowned himself king of Jerusalem in March of 1229; the Church responded by excommunicating him again.

After several months of wrangling, Frederick and Rome patched up their relations, and Frederick turned to the task of restructuring his Italian dominions—which included the northern communes that he had temporarily forced into submission. With the *Constitutions of Melfi* (1231) he established a uniform legal code that emphasized the king's absolute legislative and judicial power. He was also willing, even eager, to relinquish most of his claims to Germany; more than any other emperor, Frederick regarded Germany as a remote and insignificant place compared with the Mediterranean. His *Constitutions in Favor of the Princes of Germany* (also 1231) sweepingly ceded royal rights to the princes; among its twenty-three clauses are the following:

> No new castles or cities will be built by us or by anyone else to the prejudice of the princes.
>
> No new markets will be allowed to interfere with the interests of previously established ones. . . .

The serfs of the princes, nobles, *ministeriales*, and churches will not be admitted into our cities.

Lands and fiefs belonging to the princes, nobles, *ministeriales*, and churches, but which have been taken from them by our cities, shall be restored to them and preserved forevermore. . . .

We will never cause to have any money minted within the land of any prince that should prove injurious to his own coinage.

The jurisdiction of our cities shall not extend beyond their [current] city-limits unless we possess special jurisdictional rights in the region . . .

No one shall be forced to contribute to the fortification of our cities unless he is specifically bound under law to render that service.

These were exceptional concessions, for they granted away many of the very privileges that had made rapid urban development possible in the first place. Frederick in effect was giving up a strong German monarchy in return for a guarantee of the princes' leaving him alone in the south. The magnates were quick to take him up on his offer, and the political dissolution of Germany began in earnest. By the end of the thirteenth century, the former empire was comprised of scores of essentially autonomous principalities with their own laws, customs, currencies, and institutions. The empire itself remained in theory, but with one or two exceptions no figure ever again held meaningful authority over the princes for the rest of the Middle Ages. The princes themselves met in an assembly called a *Diet* to select a new emperor whenever the previous one died. After Frederick II, they usually made a point of electing the weakest candidate they could find, in order to make sure that the empire *as* an empire never came back. The Diet thus came into existence, ironically, to guarantee the political fragmentation of the empire and to serve as institutional guardian of the rights of the autonomous princes.

Frederick found it much harder to assert his authority over northern Italy than to relinquish it over Germany. The Lombard League that had defeated his grandfather Frederick Barbarossa in 1176 was re-created with papal help in the 1230s, and the Guelf-Ghibelline contest began anew. On-again off-again wars gripped the peninsula, and upon Frederick's death in 1250 most of the communes were still independent. So despised was Frederick by most churchmen by that time that he was often loudly castigated as the Antichrist. He remains the most frequently excommunicated ruler in European history. Frederick left behind a son, Conrad, who had an eventful but ultimately insignificant reign of only four years. Thus ended the Hohenstaufen dynasty—that "brood of vipers," in the words of Innocent IV (r.1243–1254)—that had begun by threatening the survival of the Papal State and ended with the virtual dissolution of the German Empire. A long interregnum (a nice word for "civil war") followed in Germany during which no one won universal recognition as emperor.

The interregnum lasted until 1273 when the Diet agreed to elect Rudolf of Habsburg (r.1273–1291), an altogether inconsequential princeling, as emperor. Rudolf was intelligent enough to recognize that he owed his election to the fact that he was too weak to even *hope* to control Germany—and so he did not try to. Instead, Rudolf and his Habsburg successors focused on extending their personal patrimony further into eastern Europe. The magnates did not oppose this strategy, since it did not affect them directly, but neither did they exert themselves strenuously to help the crown bring the strategy to fruition. The painstaking slowness of the Habsburg hegemony in eastern Europe was one of the principal reasons for their longevity on the imperial throne. It took several centuries before their personal demesne was sizable enough to provide them with the resources that would give them any real influence over the German princes.

The problem of what to do with Sicily remained. Since it was technically a papal fief, Rome tried to dispose of it to its own advantage by awarding the royal title to Charles of Anjou, the ambitious younger brother of France's Louis IX. But a bastard son of Frederick II named Manfred still was on the scene and enjoyed considerable popularity with the local population. It took Charles, with French and papal support in the form of crusade-revenues and recruits, several years to defeat Manfred and install himself in the realm. By 1266 he was on the throne. But Charles, who had a grimly cruel streak, was enormously unpopular, as were the rest of the Angevins. In 1282 the citizens of Palermo started a riot that quickly escalated into an island-wide rebellion. In a matter of weeks the French were driven from the island entirely and took refuge in Naples. While they plotted a counterstrike, the Sicilians offered their throne to Peter, the ruler of the Crown of Aragon confederation centered in Barcelona. They chose Peter because he was Manfred's son-in-law and therefore the closest thing to a legitimate Hohenstaufen successor, but more especially because the Crown of Aragon was quickly emerging as one of the three dominant military powers in the Mediterranean. The Catalans—the dominant group in the Crown of Aragon's maritime expansion—were a match for the Angevins. For twenty years the Angevins and the Catalan-Sicilian allies fought for control of the island; when this "War of the Sicilian Vespers," as it is known, finally ended in 1302, the island had won a shaky independence from the Angevin mainland but had also started to slide into an ingrained poverty and factional strife from which it never fully recovered.

THE NEW MEDITERRANEAN SUPERPOWERS

Three states dominated the Mediterranean in the thirteenth century: Genoa and the Crown of Aragon in the western half of the basin, and Venice in the eastern. Other communities certainly played important roles in the economic and diplomatic contests of the time, but increasingly as the century wore on they generally did so in association with, or under the leadership of, one of these three.

Genoa had already secured a degree of prominence by the late tenth century, when her merchants were among the few willing to risk attack by Muslim navies. The Genoese began by bringing Italian goods to southern France, and vice-versa, but they were constantly exposed to pirates operating out of Corsica and Sardinia. In 1016 Genoa allied with her rival city-state of Pisa and together they drove the

Muslims from those two islands. The Genoese went on to begin raiding Muslim ports in eastern Spain and along the western part of North Africa, opening up commercial networks there while the Pisans focused more on colonizing Corsica and Sardinia. When the Normans under Robert Guiscard and Roger the Great wrested Sicily and southern Italy from Islamic control in the 1050s and 1060s, the western Mediterranean basin was almost wholly opened up, leaving the Genoese and Pisans as the dominant commercial powers.

The crusade movement accelerated Genoa's growth, since her merchants sailed eastward with cargoes of supplies and reinforcements for the crusaders inching their way down the Levantine coast; and once the crusader-states of Antioch, Tripoli, and Jerusalem were established, the Genoese (and the Pisans) won lucrative trading and shipping privileges with them. Genoa built her fortune by bringing eastern silks, slaves, spices, and sugar to western ports like Marseilles and Narbonne. By the middle of the thirteenth century, the amount of annual trade passing through Genoa was three times the size of the regular income of Louis IX from his enormous demesne in France. By that time, too, most of the Genoese had become staunch Guelfs, opposed to the Hohenstaufen rulers. Consequently, the commune avidly endorsed papal designs and gave material and moral support to Charles of Anjou in Sicily. The War of the Sicilian Vespers frustrated Genoese plans somewhat since it placed their rivals the Catalans in power at the strategic nexus of trans-Mediterranean trade. As the Catalan star rose, the Genoese began to decline. The collapse of Hohenstaufen aims in the 1280s, however, allowed Genoa to eclipse Ghibelline Pisa and assume a more dominant role in northern Italy. The city remained a vital center until well into the fourteenth century.

Catalonia began as a polity during Charlemagne's time when he established it as the *Spanish March*—the outpost province where the Carolingian Empire met the Muslim caliphate. As a result, Catalonia traditionally looked northward to France, in terms of trade and culture, more than it did to the rest of Iberia. The breakup of al-Andalus gave Catalonia a prominent role in the *Reconquista*, but many Catalans in the eleventh century traded with their Muslim neighbors and in fact fought for them as mercenaries (like the Cid, for example). In the twelfth century the successive counts of Barcelona, the nominal leaders of the largely autonomous towns that made up the province, urged the Catalans to maritime expansion. A marriage alliance linked Catalonia with the upland feudal kingdom of Aragon and initiated the "Crown of Aragon" confederation. The Albigensian Crusade effectively ended Catalonia's traditional links with the French regions of Foix, Toulouse, and Provence, and under James I the Conqueror (r.1213–1276), the Crown of Aragon moved aggressively southward to conquer the Muslim kingdom of Valencia and eastward into the Mediterranean to seize the Balearic Islands. James' son Peter was the ruler recruited by the Sicilians to aid them against the Angevins, a move which then brought Sicily into the confederation as well. Later additions included parts of Greece, conquered in the first years of the fourteenth century, and Sardinia, which the Crown seized in 1325.

The various parts of the Crown of Aragon were governed separately: Aragon proper as a feudalized rural monarchy, Valencia as a Roman-law kingship, Catalonia as a conglomerate of urban republics, Sicily as a constitutional monarchy overseeing a sprawl of independent communes. In the thirteenth and early fourteenth centuries, the Crown emerged as one of Europe's wealthiest and most influential states. With such a polyglot mixture of ethnicities, languages, laws, and religions, it was the site of a cosmopolitan culture and a good deal of bewilderment. While ethnic and religious tensions still bristled, a greater degree of willingness to live with one another prevailed here between Muslims, Christians, and Jews than anywhere else in Europe. The Crown of Aragon was also the first European state to acquire paper-making technology, which allowed it to develop a considerably more literate population than elsewhere in the west, and its government to amass an enormous archive of records that required an advanced professionalization of its civil service. At its height, the Crown of Aragon was one of the best governed states in Europe.

Venice was the greatest of the three superpowers, and her might was exclusively in the eastern Mediterranean. The city was already a thriving port by the year 1000. It had been founded in the early fifth century when merchants and artisans in northeastern Italy fled the Huns by moving out to the small islands in the malarial marshes of the lagoon at the uppermost reaches of the Adriatic. Theirs was a hard-scrabble existence, and since they were incapable of producing their own food they had to live by trade. In fact, trade virtually defines and sums up medieval Venetian history. "Merchandise passes through this great city like water through a fountain," is how one medieval commentator characterized the place. The Venetians purchased the agricultural produce of the north Italian mainland and shipped it to the Dalmatian coast, Greece, and Palestine, and brought back eastern textiles, metalwork, and spices. The Venetians also perfected a method of producing salt by evaporating the sea water they drained from the marshes to give themselves a larger habitable area; salt was universally used as a food preservative, and its production generated large amounts of capital. Venice retained her independence from the peninsula throughout the early Middle Ages, although during Justinian's reconquests in the sixth century the city came briefly under the authority of the Byzantine exarchate at Ravenna; when Greek authority in most of Italy disappeared with the arrival of the Lombards, Venice retained her commercial links with Constantinople, which allowed the city to prosper when most of the west fell into decline. Indeed, Venice had a virtual monopoly on trade with Byzantium until the First Crusade altered the geopolitical and commercial traditions of the east.

The establishment of the Crusader States benefited Genoa and Pisa, but embarrassed the Venetians because those states were created at the expense of the Byzantines. Still, Venice could hardly stand idly by while her rivals reaped all the rewards of the new east-west trade. Thus they contributed naval support to follow-up operations like the assault of Jaffa in 1100 and the capture of Tyre from the Fatimids of Egypt in 1124, and received extensive trade privileges in return. Similar actions led

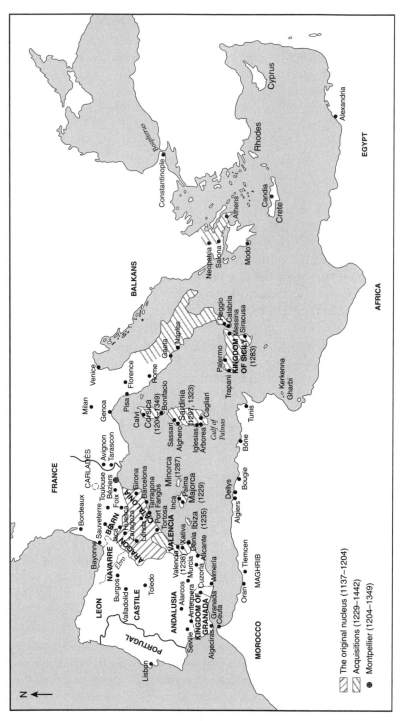

The Crown of Aragon under Peter the Great

The original nucleus (1137–1204)

Acquisitions (1229–1442)

● Montpellier (1204–1349)

to similar results in a half-dozen Syrian port cities. Consequently, Venice's relations with Constantinople suffered. Venice attacked the Byzantine-held island of Corfu in 1122–1123 and again in the 1170s. They had clearly decided that their long-term interests were better served by trade with the Latin and Muslim east than with Constantinople itself, although they never entirely relinquished commerce with Byzantium. A crucial turning point came in 1202–1204 with the re-routing of the Fourth Crusade, first to Zara and then, calamitously, to Constantinople itself. Although Baldwin of Flanders quickly took the title of *Latin Emperor* in the east, the Venetians remained enormously influential and at various times were the real powers behind the throne. In 1222 the Venetian doge and city council even considered moving the seat of their government to Constantinople, so strongly did the maritime republic view itself as the "Third Rome." The collapse of the Latin Empire in 1261 did not end Venice's eastern hegemony. The city had trade links throughout the Aegean and Black Seas, and even further east. By 1261, in fact, the Venetian merchants Niccolò and Maffeo Polo—the father and uncle, respectively, of the merchant-adventurer Marco Polo—had already established trade links with the Mongol leader Kublai Khan in China.

BYZANTIUM AND ISLAM IN THE THIRTEENTH CENTURY

A number of dramatic changes affected the east at this time, most of them political and military in nature. One of the ironies of the thirteenth century is that in this part of the medieval world, despite the regular arrival of crusaders from the west, religion played less and less of a role in determining relations among Catholics; Orthodox Christians; Sunni and Shi'ite Muslims; Palestinian, Ashkenazic, and Sephardic Jews; and others. This down-playing resulted less from an increase in tolerance and mutual respect across religious lines than from a sense of resignation, a reluctant recognition that after centuries of preaching, pleading, haranguing, enticing, coercing, threatening, and sometimes fighting by all sides, none was going to effect the mass conversion of the others. As at other times in the east's past, ethnic differences mattered more since they were frequently the determinative factor in political events.

Those events had not gone well for the Byzantine Empire ever since the start of the crusades. The Comneni dynasty—Alexius I (r.1081–1118), John II (r.1118–1143), Manuel I (r.1143–1180), Alexius II (r.1180–1183), and Andronicus I (r.1183–1185)—were for the most part rulers of considerable skill, but they were tainted with blame for having summoned the crusades in the first place and then for not finding a way to put an end to them. The best they could do, so long as the crusades took the land route through Constantinople in the twelfth century, was to negotiate agreements with the crusaders for the return of conquered lands to the Empire in exchange for supplies, guides, and military assistance. The crusaders, as we have seen, never intended to live up to those agreements, but neither did the Byzantines. The distrust that built up between the powers, plus their ongoing competition for control of shipping lanes in the eastern seas, contributed more than any theological differences to the permanent religious and cultural rift that opened up between the Catholic and Orthodox worlds.

Latin rulers had coveted the empire, or at least parts of it, for some time. Robert Guiscard and his Normans had attempted to conquer the Empire, and came close to doing so, in the eleventh century. Much of the German policy of advancing into southeastern Europe and Venice's attempts to secure control of parts of the Dalmatian coast came at Byzantium's expense. When the soldiers of the Fourth Crusade finally took Constantinople in 1204, it was not altogether a freakish occurrence but the realization of a long-held goal.

Others had had eyes on Byzantium, too. Groups of Arabs, Syrians, Turks, Armenians, and Kurds all directed armies against Byzantium in the eleventh and twelfth centuries and carved away enormous swaths of land in Palestine and Asia Minor, while armies of Bulgars, Slavs, Pechenegs, and Cumans wrested away territories in the Balkans, along the north shore of the Black Sea, and in the Pontic and Caucasus regions. By the mid-twelfth century, the Empire was only two-thirds the size it had been in the mid-eleventh. After 1204, the surviving Byzantine rump-states (that is, those regions not conquered by the Latin armies) were less than half the total area of what the Empire had been in the mid-twelfth. Three of these rump-states survived: the *Principality of Epirus*, made up of what is today northern Greece and Albania; the *Empire of Nicaea*, a narrow strip of land comprising the corridor from the island of Rhodes in the south, due north to the city of Pergamum, then veering to the northeast to include the cities of Nicaea and Heraclea Pontica;[6] and the *Empire of Trebizond*, consisting mainly of a coastal strip of land on the southeast shore of the Black Sea and centered on its capital of Trebizond.[7]

A new dynasty called the *Palaeologi* finally drove the Latins from Constantinople in 1261 and restored most of what the Byzantine Empire had been in 1204—territorially speaking, that is. In terms of economic might, military strength, political influence, and cultural and intellectual output, Byzantium never fully recovered from the Fourth Crusade. It survived largely by skillful diplomacy, playing one international rival off another whenever it could, and buying off enemies when it could not. In the early fourteenth century a renegade band of soldiers from the Sicilian branch of the Crown of Aragon moved into Greece and established an independent duchy at Athens. Other zones came under the direct political authority of Venice. The only things keeping Constantinople alive were the strength of its fortifications and the fact that there were other powers on the scene that locals had to pay immediate attention to.

The most important of these were the Turks and the Mongols. In order to put these groups into perspective, it is useful to consider the basic divisions that had

---

6.   Today called Bergama, Iznik, and Eregli, respectively.
7.   Today's city of Trabzon.

occurred in the geopolitical structure of the Islamic realm. In the tenth and eleventh centuries, as we have seen, the Islamic empire began to fracture into a sprawl of independent caliphates, emirates, and sultanates. The religion itself continued to thrive, thanks in no small part to waves of reform movements analogous to those that swept through Christian Europe, and by the twelfth century Islam had in fact become the majority religion in all the territories under Islamic political control. But regionalism carried the day politically. From the *taifa* principalities in what remained of Muslim Spain, across the North African coast, through Palestine, across the Arabian peninsula and stretching all the way to central Asia, the Muslim world was a huge array of separate states. However, they fell into three main groupings that provided a basic structure for economic activity and cultural interaction. Farthest to the west was the relatively self-contained unit made up of rump al-Andalus and the emirates of the western half of North Africa (a region known as the *Maghrib*). Ethnically, Berbers dominated here even though the ruling elites continued to be of mainly Arab descent. This area retained the closest ties with Christian Europe, most especially with the Crown of Aragon. Farther to the east lay a territory defined by the Fatimids of Egypt and their allies and client states in Syria and western Arabia. This region had the highest percentage of Shi'ite Muslims, and had the closest dealings with the commercial empires of the Venetians, Genoese, and Catalans, plus the remaining sites still under Christian rule in the Holy Land; it also had the largest aggregate Jewish population. The region centered on the great metropolises of Cairo and Damascus. At its easternmost reach was the congeries of states comprising what is today southern Iraq and most of Iran. Still under the nominal authority of the Abbasid dynasty (until 1258), these states showed the greatest degree of Persian influence in their religion and culture, and Baghdad remained the gravitational center of their political, economic, and cultural lives.

In the eleventh and twelfth centuries, the arrival of the Saljuq Turks added a dynamic new element to the Islamic world. Initially enticed into the Islamic empire by the pro-Persian Abbasids who sought allies against the expected pro-Arab backlash, the Turks had settled principally in Iraq and Syria, but a large restive group of them had pushed farther northward and westward and were in fact the group that wrenched control of eastern and central Asia Minor from the Byzantines and triggered the events that led to the First Crusade. The rise of militant local rulers like Zangi, Nur ad-Din, and Saladin in the central Islamic zone occurred at least as much in response to the Turkish threat from the east as from the crusaders' threat from the west. The Ayyubid dynasty founded by Saladin ruled Egypt—and the bulk of the Middle East, at least in name—from 1169 to 1252. But Muslim military success in the east was offset by losses in the westernmost zone. Despite the brief recoveries that took place under the Almoravids (1056–1147) and Almohads (1130–1269), the Islamic world here was clearly on the defensive. Within Spain the Reconquista continued apace, and in North Africa incursions were made by the Catalans, the Genoese, the Normans, and the Sicilians.

The Saljuqs continued to press against Byzantium in the twelfth and thirteenth centuries, and were greatly aided by the creation of the Latin Empire of Constantinople which turned the remainder of Byzantine energies away from the Islamic world and toward regaining control of their own state from their increasingly remote coreligionists. But then the Mongols arrived.

The Mongol Empire was the creation of a single man, a bloodthirsty warrior named Ghenghis Khan (1167–1227). The Mongols were not a single people but a loosely confederated group of nomadic tribes that originated in east-central Asia. By 1206 they had been united, by force, under Ghenghis Khan, who had ambitions of world domination. Of the peoples he conquered he demanded three things: the payment of tribute, the mandatory military service of all adult males, and unquestioned obedience to the laws he laid down. The slightest resistance brought brutal, even sadistic, retaliation. The Saljuqs at Bamian, for example, fought valiantly against the Mongols and slew Ghenghis' grandson in the process; after finally taking the city, Ghenghis ordered the execution of every living creature—human and animal—within the city gates for revenge. But extreme savagery was not necessarily the norm. Those who did submit in due time were generally allowed to live at peace[8]—but it is important to bear in mind that the Mongol expansion into China, central Asia, Russia, the Islamic world, and eastern Europe came at the expense of an estimated twenty million lives.[9]

In the 1220s the Mongols pressed westward into Georgia and southern Russia, but upon Ghenghis's death in 1227 they retreated, as was their custom, for a meeting of the Mongol elders to select the next Khan. Their return to eastern Europe about ten years later sent tremors of terror throughout the Latin Empire in Constantinople. A few leaders in the west dreamed of converting the Mongols to Christianity and using them as an ally against the Muslims. Popes Honorius III (r.1216–1227) and Gregory IX (r.1227–1241), and France's Louis IX, sent emissaries to the Mongols offering them aid against the Muslims if only the Mongols would first convert and accept vassalage to Europe's great leaders. The Khans scorned such overtures, although they did allow Christian missionaries like the Franciscan friars Giovanni Piano and William of Rubruck to live among them. Giovanni wrote an extraordinary ethnographic study that is still one of our chief sources for understanding Mongol culture, and William's diplomatic letters home describe court life under Mangu Khan with fascinating detail. The Mongols never got any farther into Europe than Hungary in 1241.

But their sweep into the Islamic world was dramatic. They laid waste to much of Iran and Iraq, and in 1258 they sacked Baghdad itself, for centuries the very heart

8.   Not always, though. The Turks who lived in Samarkand surrendered their city as soon as Ghenghis Khan approached in 1221 and agreed to join his army. He ordered every one of them butchered anyway, saying that people who would desert their own cause so readily were clearly people he could not rely upon.
9.   Legends abounded their bloodthirstiness. It was reported that when the Mongols ran out of water while crossing Gobi desert they survived by slaying horses and drinking their blood.

of Muslim culture; some sources attribute over one hundred thousand deaths to this single action. A cadet branch of the Mongol ruling family reigned over the region until 1336, and it and its followers were gradually Islamicized.[10] The Mongols made attempts to extend their power further westward, but they were defeated in Syria by an army composed of *mamluks*, or military slaves, recruited from Egypt by the local Ayyubids. Having gotten rid of the Mongol menace, the leaders of the mamluks then deposed the Ayyubids who had hired them and seized power for themselves. The so-called *Mamluk dynasty* in Egypt thus ran from the middle of the thirteenth century until 1517; it was they who finally overran the last Latin Christian outpost in the Levant, the city of Acre which fell to them in 1291.

SUGGESTED READING

Texts

Anonymous. *The Chronicle of San Juan de la Peña.*

Froissart, Jean. *Chronicle.*

Joinville. *Life of St. Louis.*

Muntaner, Ramon. *Chronicle.*

Paris, Matthew. *The Major Chronicle.*

Rubruck, William of. *Journey of William of Rubruck.*

Source Anthologies

Amt, Emilie. *Medieval England, 1000–1500: A Reader* (2001).

Tierney, Brian. *The Crisis of Church and State, 1050–1300* (1964).

Studies

Abulafia, David. *Frederick II: A Medieval Emperor* (1988).

———. *The Western Mediterranean Kingdoms, 1200–1500: The Struggle for Dominion* (1997).

Arnold, Benjamin. *Princes and Territories in Medieval Germany* (1991).

Baldwin, John W. *The Government of Philip Augustus: Foundations of French Royal Power in the Middle Ages* (1986).

Bartlett, Robert. *The Making of Europe: Conquest, Colonization, and Cultural Change, 950–1350* (1993).

Bisson, Thomas N. *The Medieval Crown of Aragon: A Short History* (1991).

Brentano, Robert. *Rome Before Avignon: A Social History of Thirteenth-Century Rome* (1991).

———. *Two Churches: England and Italy in the Thirteenth Century* (1998).

Burns, Robert I., S. J. *Jews in the Notarial Culture: Latinate Wills in Mediterranean Spain. 1250–1350* (1996).

———. *Muslims, Christians, and Jews in Crusader Valencia: Societies in Symbiosis* (1983).

---

10. The Mongol ruling family converted in 1295 and ordered the conversion of their followers, another example of a top-to-bottom conversion model.

Crouch, David. *The Image of Aristocracy in Britain, 1000–1300* (1992).

Duby, Georges. *France in the Middle Ages, 987–1400* (1991).

———. *The Knight, the Lady, and the Priest: The Making of Modern Marriage in Medieval France* (1984).

———. *The Legend of Bouvines: War, Religion, and Culture in the Middle Ages* (1990).

Freedman, Paul. *The Origins of Peasant Servitude in Medieval Catalonia* (1991).

Haverkamp, Alfred. *Medieval Germany, 1056–1273* (1992).

Housley, Norman. *The Italian Crusades: The Papal-Angevin Alliance and the Crusades Against Christian Lay Powers, 1254–1343* (1982).

Huffman, Joseph P. *The Social Politics of Medieval Diplomacy: Anglo-German Relations, 1066–1307* (1999).

Jordan, William Chester. *Louis IX and the Challenge of the Crusade* (1979).

Kaeuper, Richard. *Chivalry and Violence in Medieval Europe* (1999).

Larner, John. *Marco Polo and the Discovery of the World* (1999).

Leopold, Antony. *How to Recover the Holy Land: Crusading Proposals of the Late 13th and Early 14th Centuries* (2000).

Nirenberg, David. *Communities of Violence: Persecution of Minorities in the Middle Ages* (1996).

O'Callaghan, Joseph F. *The Cortes of Castile-León, 1183–1350* (1988).

Prestwich, Michael. *English Politics in the Thirteenth Century* (1990).

Richard, Jean. *Louis IX: Crusader King of France* (1992).

Sedlar, Jean W. *East Central Europe in the Middle Ages, 1000–1500* (1994).

Stacey, Robert C. *Politics, Policy, and Finance under Henry III, 1216–1245* (1987).

Strayer, Joseph R. *The Government of France under Philip the Fair.*

Waught, Scott L., and Peter D. Diehl. *Christendom and Its Discontents: Exclusion, Persecution, and Rebellion, 1000–1500* (1995).

CHAPTER 14

ART AND INTELLECT IN THE THIRTEENTH CENTURY

The intellectual and artistic production of the thirteenth and early fourteenth centuries, arguably the high point of medieval cultural life, was the grand culmination of the twelfth century's hectic energies. In virtually every artistic medium—architecture, painting and sculpture, poetry, drama, music, and dance—Europe produced a nearly dizzying array of masterpieces, works that can still astonish us with their creative power. From the cathedrals at Durham, Chartres, Cologne, Venice, or Barcelona, through the poetry of Chrétien de Troyes, Bernat de Ventadorn, Wolfram von Eschenbach, Guido Cavalcanti, Dante Alighieri, and the anonymous author of *Sir Gawain and the Green Knight*, to the dream-visions of Hildegard of Bingen (the most original woman writer of the Middle Ages), the anonymous authors of the great mystery and morality plays, the stories of Christine de Pizan and Giovanni Boccaccio, the bawdy adventures of the fabliaux, and the polyphonic music of Léonin and Pérotin, medieval Christendom at its height was bursting with talent, dazzling audacity, and the confidence to accomplish enduring art.

All this creative energy flowed into well-established genres and overflowed into several new ones. In literature the dominant forms were those of traditional epic and lyric poetry and drama, but also the new genres of verse romance and prose fable. By the end of the thirteenth century, the Catalan lay evangelist Ramon Lull had written Europe's first novel—an unencouraging debut work called *Blanquerna*. In ecclesiastical architecture the heavy sternness of the Romanesque style, with its massive walls and columns, dark interiors and dank atmosphere, gave way to the soaring elegance of the Gothic, which emphasized light, color, majesty, and transcendence, while the sculpture and painting that adorned the churches steered away from the (literally) fantastic playfulness of Romanesque allegory and abstraction toward the idealized naturalism of Gothic style that paved the way for the heightened realism of the Renaissance of the fifteenth century. Medieval music, whether love-longing troubadour songs or liturgical motets, grew in complexity and sophistication to include two- and three-part harmonies and a plethora of new instruments.

Intellectual life showed the same vitality and ambition. Philosophers and theologians brought to fruition the great rationalization of intellectual thought and religious belief begun by the neo-Aristotelians of the twelfth century. An entire intellectual movement begun in the cathedral schools and universities, and hence called *scholasticism*, confidently asserted its ability to provide rational proofs and explanations for literally every tenet of Christian faith. The greatest of the scholastics, St. Thomas Aquinas (1225–1274), nearly lived up to the boast. The scholastics may have been, in a sense, less original than the great thinkers of the twelfth century, more summarizers and systematizers than bold creators, but their achievement in synthesizing faith and reason and providing a comprehensive blueprint for the rational organization of the cosmos is enormously impressive. They personify, in fact, the general medieval outlook we have been tracing in this book—the belief in the fundamental cohesion and orderliness that lay behind and give meaning to the anarchic heterogeneity the world presents us with. The modern world has largely rejected the scholastics' synthesis, but their achievement still deserves respect.

The greatest intellectual originality occurred in the sciences. By the start of the fourteenth century, advances in fields like medicine, astronomy, optics, physics, mathematics, and geometry, and in their applications, had opened up whole new worlds of inquiry and had given Latin Europe a decided scientific and technological advantage over the rest of the then-known world. Scientists like the Englishmen Robert Grosseteste (1170–1253) and Roger Bacon (1214–1294)—the latter one of the most colorful figures of the age—accelerated the rise of empirical and experimental science that, for both good and ill, has dominated much of modern intellectual life in the west. "Whoever wishes to rejoice in the universal truths that underlie the visible phenomena [of the world], and to do so without a hint of uncertainty, must first learn to dedicate himself to experiment," Bacon wrote. His experimentation, his certainty, and his joy all characterize the intellectual and artistic life of the medieval world at its zenith.

SCHOLASTICISM

Scholasticism is, like feudalism, one of the traits most closely associated with the Middle Ages in our popular culture, and like feudalism its common repute is vaguely but decidedly negative. The word itself conjures up images of dry-as-dust encyclopedias of abstract theological minutiæ, and of arcane arguments carried to absurd lengths. "How many angels can fit onto the head of a pin?" is a good example of a stereotypical scholastic question. (This particular question was a supposedly clever way of inquiring whether or not angels were corporeal beings.) Simply and specifically, the word *scholasticism* refers to the philosophical and pedagogical method utilized by the faculty of the cathedral schools and universities. It was indeed a *method* more than a universally accepted set of ideas. Scholastic philosophers disagreed with one another in hundreds of ways, but they did agree on a foundational principle: Whether one began, in Platonic mode, with overarching theories and worked one's way down to empirical specifics, or if one proceeded, in Aristotelian fashion, from raw empirical data and painstakingly collated them into general and universal theories, one would in fact find that the cosmos had a divinely ordained rational ordering. Everything that happens, scholastics were convinced, happens for a reason, and every idea, fact, occurrence, physical being, and social construct has a place in that ordering. God has given us the ability to perceive and understand that cohesive unity, and man's duty is to arrange his life in such a way that it emulates and harmonizes with God's evident intention.

The scholastics argued, like their twelfth-century forebears, that faith and reason were completely reconcilable. While none of them maintained that faith and reason were the same thing, most would have asserted that faith had a profound rational component and was thus a rational activity, a commitment to truths whose truth could be demonstrated. This is quite a different position from that of the Church Fathers in the earliest centuries of Christianity, the figures whose ideas had dominated the first thousand years of Christian thinking. They had maintained that faith was by definition an irrational activity—a profession of belief that could not be proven to be true. As the third-century writer Tertullian described it:

> What does Athens have to do with Jerusalem? Where is the meeting ground between the Academy and the Church? . . . Enough of these efforts to produce a quasi-Christianity based on Stoic, Platonic, and dialectical ideas! We don't want an *argument* for believing in Jesus Christ, and we don't need a *logical analysis* in order to appreciate the Gospels!

He summed matters up in his most often-quoted line about Christianity: "I believe it *because* it is absurd!" Attitudes had changed by the twelfth and thirteenth centuries, however, not least because of the Church's own attempt to codify, rationalize, and systematize its doctrine. The enormous elaboration of that doctrine by the scholastics occurred in part merely as an expression of intellectual excitement, the desire to play with ideas for their own sake and to take them as far as logical thought could go, but it was also done out of evangelical zeal. If Christian convictions could be rationally proven to be true, the scholastics believed, then the long-hoped-for conversion of the Jews and Muslims might at last be attained. What could possibly hold them back from accepting a demonstrable truth? And since these peoples had so long excelled at philosophy, what delight in beating them at their own game! It is no coincidence that one of the greatest works of the scholastic movement (by Thomas Aquinas) was entitled *Summa contra gentiles*, or "Summary [of Arguments to be Used] against the Non-Christians." The enormous cultural confidence of medieval Europe at its zenith is nowhere clearer than in its conviction that the universal victory of Christianity was at hand—or at least that the tools to effect it were.

Although the scholastics, who came to be associated especially with the University of Paris but were to be found throughout Europe's universities, never devised a comprehensive syllabus or platform, they generally agreed on three basic assumptions about the nature of Truth: that it was to be found through Argument, that it was to be found through recognized Authority, and that it was Additive. The first aspect, the argumentative, is the rationalistic element: the belief that by posing questions and proposing logical answers to them, and then subjecting the answers themselves to further questioning, one gradually arrives at truth. This technique explains the unappealing formalistic appearance of most scholastic texts. They proceed not as long discourses of seamless prose but as bare-bones outlines of numbered questions and answers; they have the aesthetic charm of computer instruction manuals.[1] But in a sense this comparison heightens their utility: One can proceed directly to the most specific question one has and confront it as an independent whole, without relying upon what has gone before or comes after. The second order of Truth is that derived from authority. Chief among the recognized authorities, of course, was the Bible in Jerome's Vulgate version, followed by the writings of the Latin and Greek Fathers, especially the Four Latin Doctors. But appeal to authority, even to the Bible itself, never sufficed to prove a point for the scholastics, who regarded such measures at best as corroborating evidence for an argument from Reason. Despite their divinely inspired nature, all authoritative texts were, after all, human productions and therefore fallible. Peter Abelard's *Sic et Non* had amply shown that fact, although none of the scholastics was very keen about mentioning *his* name again. Finally, the scholastics regarded all truth as additive—that is, all truths in all areas of human experience and knowledge are harmonious and reconcilable. There exists an essential *unity of truth*, and any apparent contradictions or inconsistencies in human knowledge are the result of imperfections in our understanding, not of flaws in nature.

Not everyone was enthusiastic about the scholastic program. St. Bernard of Clairvaux, as we have seen, implacably opposed what he regarded as a devilish attempt to subordinate faith to mere human reason. Scholars coming out of the Franciscan order especially tended to favor the more traditional Platonic-Augustinian approach to philosophical matters. Revelation took precedence over reason, they maintained. God *is* rational but He is also more than that, and unquestioning acceptance of the scholastic method reduced God's majesty and mystery. A good example of this countermovement was St. Bonaventura (1221–1274), who studied philosophy and theology at the University of Paris and was a close friend of Aquinas in their university days. Bonaventura rose to be the Governor General of the Franciscan Order and was a leading member of the College of Cardinals. To him, one's capacity for love and goodwill had more significance than one's rational faculties for achieving union with God: "If you ask how [divine things] may be known, my answer is: turn to grace instead of doctrine, desire instead of knowledge, the groaning of prayer instead of the labor of study—in a word, to God instead of man." But man's intellect is not without value. Bonaventura insisted that reason is an unparalleled tool for investigating and understanding the physical cosmos and should be cultivated; but we ought not to let our enthusiasm lead us into thinking that we can think-out God. In one of his most important books, *The*

---

1. But then, some might argue that that is their closest modern analog!

Mind's Road to God, he elaborated his view about the glorious power, but also the limitations, of human reason. Our intellectual capacity carries us far down that road, he argued, but the last stage of the journey depends solely on our capacity for nonrationalized love.

The scholastic movement is most closely associated with Dominicans like Albertus Magnus (d. 1280) and his most brilliant student Aquinas. Thomas Aquinas (d. 1274) was the son of a Norman-Italian aristocratic family that expected him to enter the Benedictine order and take his rightful honored place in society as an abbot. He surprised them, though, by choosing to be a Dominican priest, vowing himself to poverty and the life of the mind. His personality was that of an absent-minded academic; in many ways he resembled the great German metaphysician of the nineteenth century, Georg Wilhelm Friedrich Hegel, who was renowned for being in such a cogitational fog that he once walked into a lecture hall in his stocking feet, not having noticed that his shoes had come off in the mud outside the building. Aquinas reportedly was once so lost in thought on a philosophical point that he never felt the cutting and poking of a surgeon operating on his infected ear.

Odd though Aquinas may have been as a personality, his teaching and thinking were brilliant. He began his career at the University of Naples and later taught, in two separate stints, at the University in Paris. Between teaching jobs he served as an advisor to the Holy See, specifically regarding the effort to reunite the Latin and Greek Churches. Students flocked to his lectures and he quickly earned a reputation not only for vast knowledge and subtle argument but for an ability to get the students enthusiastic about what he called the "wonderfulness" of every topic. He also had an exceptionally busy pen: His writings fill thirty volumes. (He wrote so fast, in fact, that he developed his own personal shorthand system so that his secretaries could keep pace with him.) The two works that have established his reputation as the greatest of the scholastics are the *Summa contra Gentiles* that we mentioned before and the *Summa theologica* ("Theological Summary"). The first aimed to provide rock-solid logical arguments both for Christian beliefs and against the prevailing notions of the non-Christian faiths—be they Judaism, Islam, paganism, or one of the Christian heresies then so common. Since the *Summa contra Gentiles* was meant to be a sort of handbook that evangelists could carry with them and consult whenever they disputed matters with non-Christians, it is a shorter and rather elementary work—a kind of evangelical crib-sheet. But it makes fascinating reading, not least for the way it illustrates the extent to which Christian scholars truly understood the subtleties of the other faiths. The *Summa theologica*, by contrast, is an immense work of synthesis. Aquinas' aim was literally to prove every tenet of Catholic Christianity without recourse to Biblical authority, papal decree, conciliar pronouncement, or appeals to trust in faith. His method could hardly have been more thorough. He begins with a question—"Does God exist?"—and offers an array of every possible logical argument that might prove the existence of a deity. He then offers every logical argument *against* his initial propositions. He then reverses course once more and details all the arguments

*A seminar made in heaven. This fourteenth-century painting by Francesco Traini
depicts St. Thomas Aquinas (center) surrounded by Christ (top),
Aristotle (left), and Ibn Rushd (Averroes, right), plus a number of lesser scholars.
It resides in the church of Santa Caterina in Pisa.
Source: Scala / Art Resource, NY*

against the rebuttals; and so on, back and forth constantly until he has utterly exhausted every conceivable pro and con argument. Then, having reached the conclusion that God does indeed exist, he moves on to the next question and repeats the entire process.

The *Summa theologica* is not an easy book to read. It is of enormous length, mind-numbing detail, highly technical language, and has virtually no stylistic elegance. Aquinas exerts no effort at all to make the reading experience a pleasant one. To pick just one example, here is how he starts his discussion of the question "Does human law bind a man's conscience, or merely his actions?" [That is, does obeying a law require us to accept that law as right in the solitude of our own minds, or merely to obey it mindlessly in terms of our actions?]

> Laws are deemed to be just by their *end-result* (namely, when they result in the common good), by their *author* (that is, when a given law is promulgated within the jurisdiction of the lawgiver), and from their *form* (that is, when the law places an equitable burden on its subjects in proportion with their position in society and is done so for the common good). For since every individual is a part of a community, so does each man, all that he is and all that he possesses, belong to the community as well—since anything that is an intrinsic part of something else belongs to that something else. So too does nature inflict a burden on the individual part in order to save the whole—and for this reason human laws that impose proportionate burdens are just and binding in conscience and are therefore legal laws.

That is as plainspoken (and as riveting, in terms of narrative flow) as the *Summa theologica* ever gets.

But scholastic works like these are tremendously important as cultural phenomena. The mere conceit that a rational proof can be given for *everything* taught by the Church is a stunning example of intellectual pride and cultural confidence. Few people would even suggest the possibility of such a thing today. But in the thirteenth century, medieval Christendom was bursting with just that sort of certainty. The Church had been reformed, society brought under the papal monarchy, the Latin and Greek Churches brought within reach of reunification, and intellectual life revitalized; universities were proliferating, economic prosperity was abundant, governments were professionalized, centralized, and kept in check by representative institutions. Who could doubt that the Christian world had finally achieved its perfect, natural, and divinely ordained ordering in a perfect, natural, and divinely ordered cosmos?

Aquinas experienced a mystical vision in 1272 in which he perceived that the divine truth whose perfect ordering he was so busily proving in his *Summa* was actually something quite different, larger, stranger, and inexplicable. He emerged from this revelation with the conviction that "everything I have written seems to me to be mere straw." He never completed the book, and seems to have given up writing theology and philosophy altogether. He gave himself over to pious simplicity and died soon after, spending his last months seeking "to be serene without frivolity, and mature without self-importance."

Aquinas was canonized in 1323 and given the title of *Angelic Doctor*. But even in his last years, there was a considerable backlash in intellectual circles against his brand of unshakeable rationalism. Most of the Franciscans and secular clergy—those churchmen most at work in the regular world, instead of ivory-tower academics like Aquinas—were opposed to what they regarded as the heartless theorizing of the scholastics. Nevertheless, Aquinas's extraordinary achievement survived the challenge, and the *Summa theologica* is second only to St. Augustine's

City of God as the most important philosophical and theological work of the Middle Ages.

THE GOTHIC VISION

The exuberant confidence of the scholastic writers was shared and expressed by the artists of the age, who enjoyed a period of extraordinary creativity. The sheer ubiquity of artistic opportunities accounted for much of this creativity. Towns, castles, cathedrals, smaller churches, urban mansions, and universities were sprouting up everywhere, giving artists of every variety the opportunity to develop and perfect their techniques. Major new developments occurred in lay and ecclesiastical architecture, decorative tapestry, painting, and sculpture; the courts of urban magnates and rural lords provided venues for vernacular literature and popular song. Cathedrals rang with new sacred music in polyphonic style. Court fashions favored sumptuous designs in dress and needlework. Poets sang lyrics, players performed theatricals, musicians played in courts and fairs and on village greens. Europe practically hummed with creative energy.

It is hardly surprising that the great churches and aristocratic courts were the sites where most of these energies were at work. As the leaders of reformed Europe, they were naturally the principal patrons of art; nor is it surprising that much of the art they commissioned aimed at glorifying their centrality to medieval life. A common theme of medieval art was the cohesion and unity of society under the leadership of the great powers. "Christendom," the ideal vision since Charlemagne's time, had become a meaningful cultural and religious reality (or at least medieval leaders liked to think so) and was deserving of praise and celebration.

As theology was "Queen of the Sciences" (in Albertus Magnus's phrase), architecture, and specifically religious architecture, was the dominant art form. From one end of Europe to another, tens of thousands of cathedrals, churches, abbeys, and monastic chapels were constructed in the twelfth and thirteenth centuries. In France alone, workers mined more stone for building churches in these two hundred years than the slaves of ancient Egypt quarried in three thousand years of pyramid-, temple-, and palace-building for the pharaohs. In Mediterranean Europe, workers turned first to the already-quarried stone of the old Roman ruins, which they simply dismantled. The Colosseum in Rome, for example, which in the eleventh century had been used as an enclosed meadow for pasturing sheep, lost much of its stone for use elsewhere. Quarrymen, stone masons, architects, engineers, and construction workers of all types had little difficulty in finding employment. Even today literally thousands of churches from this era survive, in whole or part, across Europe.

As anyone knows who has visited them, Europe's cathedrals were immense. This was construction not on the large but on the colossal scale. Nothing like these buildings had been attempted in a thousand years; even the enormous monastic abbey at Cluny owed its size to accretion rather than original design. The largest church in pre-reform Europe had been Charlemagne's imperial church at Aachen; modeled on the Byzantine basilica at Ravenna, its central sanctuary—an octagonal shape—measured a mere fifty feet in diameter, roughly the size of a typical lecture hall in a modern university. The interior of London's great Westminster Abbey, by contrast, which William Rufus had built in two years (1187–1189), measured two hundred and forty feet by eighty feet—ten times the square footage of the Aachen sanctuary. Twelfth- and thirteenth-century churches were also very tall, as architects and engineers mastered the technological challenge of supporting the weight of such structures. The Gothic cathedral at Beauvais—a stunningly beautiful building—is tall enough that it could hold a fifteen-storey modern office tower inside its central nave.

Two styles predominated: the *Romanesque* in the eleventh and early twelfth centuries and the *Gothic* from the middle of the twelfth to the early fourteenth. The Romanesque took its name from its use of rounded stone archways, such as the ancient Romans had used. But Romanesque buildings looked only superficially like Roman ones; they shared a building technique rather than an aesthetic style. The Gothic style, by contrast, does not refer in any direct way to the early Goths. The word itself was coined in the early modern period, which spurned all things medieval, and was meant to imply crudeness of style. Fortunately, the word no longer has that meaning for us. Gothic architecture's most distinctive characteristic is the pointed arch. In the Middle Ages the style we call Gothic was known as the *French Style* since French artists were the first to employ it. But Gothic churches were built everywhere from Portugal to Hungary and from Sicily to Sweden.

Early medieval churches had been primarily of a type known as a *basilica*, usually rectangular in basic shape with a flat or only slightly sloping wooden roof. Its floor plan was dominated by a central *nave* divided into aisles by rows of stone columns. When one stood in the nave and looked toward the main altar one was invariably facing eastward—that is, toward Jerusalem. At the eastern end of the basilica, a *transept* intersected the nave at a right angle to give the overall floor plan the rough shape of a cross. The altar stood at the intersection of the nave and transept. A small rounded *apse* then extended beyond the altar, forming, as it were, a curved head to the cruciform floor plan.

Romanesque churches developed out of the basilican style; they retained both the eastward orientation and the cruciform shape, which in fact they made more pronounced by increasing the size of the transept and apse in relation to the nave. Romanesque architects also increased the size of the choir, which was located just east of the transept but before the apse, and gave a new rectangular shape to the apse in order to put it in greater harmony with the rest of the building. Their most important innovation, though, was the roof. Basilican roofs had been strictly functional: They were flat, wooden, and undecorated. (They were also a constant fire hazard.) Romanesque engineers found a way to replace these roofs with rounded stone vaults called *barrel vaults* that extended down each aisle of the nave. The transept formed another barrel vault, and the intersection of the transept vault and aisle vaults formed a new structure called a *cross vault* that was, in an engineering sense, the structural key to the entire church. Cross vaults were of great weight and generated enormous forces of downward and lateral thrust. In order to support this weight and thrust, the exterior walls of Romanesque churches had to be massive. Few windows were possible, since a window represents a weak point in any wall, and early Romanesque churches could therefore be grimly dark. But the oppressiveness of the atmosphere was lightened by the introduction of ceiling painting, wall paintings, sculptured capitals,[2] hung tapestries,[3] gold and silver ornaments, and the incense and music of the Mass.

These churches were also innovative on their exteriors. Unlike their usually bare basilican ancestors, Romanesque churches had elaborate sculptures surrounding portals and extending along their exterior walls. The sculptures normally formed a carefully planned program of images. The main western portal, for instance, might have had a network of images designed to emphasize the theme of God's majesty, while a different portal—for example, the northern, which was traditionally used by pilgrims—might carry images emphasizing the theme of penance. Symbolism and occasional abstraction, rather than strict realism, frequently predominated here. Human figures were often presented in full human size in columnal sculptures, for example, but in unnaturally elongated form. Romanesque portraiture was seldom naturalistic or true-to-life. The main point of presenting, for example, an image of the biblical King David was to emphasize his abstract, and therefore universally significant, kingly quality rather than his specifically individual David-ness. Thus a Romanesque sculptor might aim for an image that expressed authority, sternness, or the status of lawgiver; this image was more important than a supposedly "realistic" portrait of the actual man. Another new feature of Romanesque exteriors was the use of towers. These often soared above the main body of the church, helped increase the sounding power of the bells they contained, and gave the exterior of the building a new uplifted character.

The transition from Romanesque style to Gothic in the middle of the twelfth century resulted from a host of factors. On an engineering level, new ways were developed to increase both the height of the church and the number and size of the windows that ran the length of the nave. These innovations both encouraged and responded to the heightened emotionalism of popular piety as expressed not only by pilgrims but by the townsfolk whose labor made the new churches possible in the first place. After all, building a cathedral required the backbreaking work and financial support of thousands of people over periods of years, sometimes several generations. A Gothic cathedral was not merely a construction project, it was an act of mass faith that required no less a commitment of devotion than of money. One witness to the popular support for the construction of the great Gothic cathedral at

---

2. Capitals are the decorative connection points where an arch meets the columns that support it.
3. Tapestries on the walls also helped to keep out some of the cold.

Basilica de la Madeleine, Vezelay. There were many local variations on the Romanesque and Gothic styles of architecture. In this example, the abbey of La Madeleine in Vezelay (1104), the barrelvault of the nave was replaced by a new style that utilized a groined-vault and transverse arches. The redistribution of weight and stress that this involved made possible the introduction of more windows, thus creating a more open and airy effect. Source: Scala/Art Resource, NY

Chartres in the 1140s, marveling at the sight of hundreds of townsfolk marching off to the quarry, cutting stone, and hauling it back over great distances, described the scene this way:

> When these faithful people . . . set out on their path amid the blowing of trumpets and the waving of banners, it is a marvel to relate that their work went so easily that nothing at all could discourage them or slow them down, neither steep mountains nor rushing waters. . . . It came as no surprise that mature

*Statues from the "Royal Portal," Chartres Cathedral. Ca. 1145. These elongated yet
still somewhat naturalistic portrayals of four kings and queens of Judah are
representative of Romanesque sculpture at its best. Their formal poses and idealized
features are complemented by a faintly naturalistic element in the drapery of their
robes. Source: Giraudon/Art Resource, NY*

adults and the elderly took on this labor to atone for their sins—but what inspired even adolescents and young boys to pitch in? Who brought these children to that supreme Guide? . . . The vast project begun by the adults will be
left for the youth to complete; and complete it they will, for they were there to
be seen, organized into teams with their own little leaders, tying themselves
with ropes to stone-laden wagons and pulling them as though they weighed
nothing, with backs erect (unlike the hunched and bowed shoulders of the
elders) and moving with astonishing speed and agility. . . . When they arrived

back at the church site, they circled their wagons around it like a spiritual encampment, and all through the night that followed this army of the Lord kept
watch with psalms and hymns. Candles and torches were lit at every wagon;
the sick and hurt were led away and had the relics of the local saints brought to
them for their healing.

The cathedrals became symbols of civic pride; their grandeur reflected the prosperity, piety, and public spirit of the people—so much so that neighboring towns frequently competed with one another to see who could build the more impressive
edifice. The magnificence and centrality of cathedrals were also intended to reflect
the importance of the bishops who formed the backbone of the Church. A Gothic
cathedral, always the largest building in a city and the first building visible to one
approaching the city, represented a summation and harmonization of artistic genres
and expressions. It comprised architecture, sculpture, painting, drama (in the form
of the Mass), and music. It was a living art work, a complex vision whose majesty
derived from its harmonization of its component parts. Each cathedral was in its
way a free-standing *summa theologica*.

The chief characteristics of Gothic style were the pointed arch, ribbed vaulting,
and the *flying buttress*. The pointed arch dispersed the weight and thrust of the
archway in a new way and thus posed an engineering problem, but it achieved a
pleasing new effect—a heightened sense of verticality and openness. The introduction of the ribbed vault—ceilings composed not of solid archways of stone but of a
network of arched stone ribs that fanned out over the aisles, with the areas between
the ribs filled with plaster—dramatically decreased the weight of the roof and
made it possible to raise the churches' overall height and to introduce still more
and still larger windows. But while the ribbed vaults solved the problem of weight,
they helped little with the lateral thrust of the heightened walls and roofs. Thus the
flying buttresses—external supports strutting outward from the walls at regular
intervals, like the legs jutting out from the torso of a caterpillar—resolved this difficulty. It took several decades for church builders to perfect these new methods
and to bring them into aesthetic balance, but once they had done so the effect was
astonishing. Gothic cathedrals like those at Amiens or Reims in France shimmer
with light and color, and the strong vertical lines established by the raised roofs,
pointed arches, and tall, slender columns have the effect of drawing one's spirit up-
ward toward heaven, while heavenly music rings down upon one from the elevated choirs. Combining as it does such an array of arts, each so wonderfully
realized and all placed in such harmony with one another, a Gothic cathedral, in
the course of celebrating a High Mass, continues to offer an unparalleled spiritual
and aesthetic experience.

SCIENCE AND TECHNOLOGY

Scientia meant something different in the Middle Ages from what *science* means for
us today. Our modern English word made its first appearance only in 1340, when it

The nave (central aisle facing the altar) of Durham Cathedral.
A good example of Romanesque style.
Source: Scala / Art Resource, NY

had the simple meaning of "knowledge." But scientia implied something larger and grander. It evoked images of God's magnificence and the harmony of His creation. Scholars used to translate scientia as "natural philosophy," a term that was intended to rouse the notion of systematized knowledge—and it is a pretty good rendition. The great "scientists" of the thirteenth and early fourteenth centuries made important individual discoveries and helped to promote the notion of the Grand Design of the universe. This notion was to be the dominant Western attitude until the troubling scientific dissolution of the early modern period.

The catalog of achievements in medieval science and technology is impressive. The fields of anatomy, astronomy, botany, chemistry, geography, kinetics, linguistics, magnetism, medicine, oceanography, optics, pharmacology, and zoology, to name only a few, all enjoyed significant advances in their theoretical understanding and practical application. At the level of technology, medieval engineers and inventors developed eyeglasses, astrolabes, mechanical clocks, and magnetic compasses. It is difficult to answer the question "what did people in the Middle Ages really know?" in terms of science, because there is no easy way to tell how widely spread any given bit of knowledge might have been. In terms of astronomy and cosmology, for example, almost every university-educated person in the thirteenth century knew that the earth was round, but the majority of town dwellers and rural workers probably did not. The prevailing popular cosmological model posited an immobile earth at the center of the universe, with all the planets and non-fixed stars revolving around it in concentric circular orbits; but the theory of a rotating earth was also extremely well known (it simply was not regarded as proven). Medical science was hampered by cultural and ecclesiastical restraints on dissection, although by the thirteenth century the leading physicians at schools like the University of Montpellier were known to perform occasional dissections. Figures like Arnau de Vilanova (d. 1311) wrote numerous treatises on the various organs and their functions.

The two most important scientific figures of the thirteenth century were both Englishmen: Robert Grosseteste (1168–1253), the first Chancellor of Oxford University, and Roger Bacon (1214–1292), who was one of the first, and certainly one of the most outspoken, champions of the experimental method as the key to advancing scientific knowledge.

Grosseteste was born into a poor Suffolk family and received an excellent education through England's network of provincial patronage, rather than through formal schooling. Wealthy patrons eager to show their sophistication frequently retained scholars on their estates, providing them with libraries, equipment, and above all the leisure time needed to educate themselves and each other. Grosseteste was fortunate enough to receive such patronage and enjoy the company of other self-taught scholars. His first big break came when he entered the household of the bishop of Hereford, under whose guidance he added a strong foundational knowledge of law and medicine to his already excellent background in science. Ultimately, Grosseteste went on to the University of Paris to earn his degree in theology; sometime around 1214 he returned to Oxford and took up residence as University Chancellor, a post he held for about a decade. He lectured, broadly and brilliantly, on topics as varied as astronomy, linguistics, music, and optics, and earned a reputation as a preacher as well. Like many self-taught people who had to struggle for years for his education, he had little patience with students who did not take their studies seriously. Increasingly drawn to the Franciscans whom he found to be consistently the best scholars at the university, he devoted himself to preaching and lecturing to the friar-scholars about five years after arriving in Oxford. (He never actually joined the order, however.) In 1235 he was appointed bishop of Lincoln. His single best-known discovery was in the field of optics: By refracting light through a lens, he produced the first accurate description of the color spectrum and the first solid explanation of the cause of rainbows.

Façade of Chartres Cathedral. One of the most celebrated examples of Gothic architecture.
Source: Vanni / Art Resource, NY

Interior of Sainte-Chapelle, Paris. The stained-glass windows of the Sainte-Chapelle (1246–1248) are a fine example of the vibrancy of Gothic art. The pointed arches and ribbed vaulting of the Gothic style can also be seen clearly.
Source: Giraudon/Art Resource, NY

Grosseteste was a serious-minded, earnest scholar and preacher; but his student Roger Bacon was a phenomenon, a brilliant ambitious scientist with a prickly contrarian's personality. In fact, he was an intellectual bully who never met a man he could not offend. Bacon came from a wealthy non-noble family that could afford to give him an education. He boasted later in life that prior to becoming a Franciscan in 1252, he had spent over two thousand pounds (an enormous sum) on books. He studied at Oxford with an eye to winning a doctorate in theology, but he felt that

A drawing by Villard de Honnecourt (d. 1250) of the flying buttresses
used at Reims Cathedral. Source: Giraudon / Art Resource, NY

theology—the "Queen of Sciences"—could only be done properly if one had first mastered all the fields of philosophy and science, and he spent so long in what he considered essential preparatory work that he never got very far in theology itself. He taught for a while at Oxford, then moved to Paris for more advanced work. Like many scholars of the age, he was a passionate student of Aristotle, but Aristotle was still frowned upon by the conservative masters of Paris. Bacon had virtually no patience with anyone with whom he disagreed or whom he regarded as an inferior intellect—which left him with very few friends. His students, though, loved his brash brilliance. He was an enormous success as a lecturer; unlike most university teachers he encouraged his students to ask questions, to make sugges-

Choir of Gloucester Cathedral. A example of florid late Gothic style, the choir of Gloucester Cathedral (1337–1357) is a beautifully controlled riot of color, light, vertical thrust, and fanciful vaulting. Source: Scala/Art Resource, NY

tions, to challenge everything he taught them. He was a refreshing change to the dour seriousness of figures like Grosseteste or Aquinas, and he clearly enjoyed his success.

Bacon's chief goal was to do for the sciences what the scholastics were trying to do for theology, to synthesize all knowledge into a harmonious system. This meant nothing less than acquiring a full mastery of subject after subject, from astronomy to zoology, and Bacon threw himself into the gargantuan task with typical aplomb. But he did more than read the works of other scientists; he himself was a passionate champion of experimentation—the setting up of experiments, the gathering of data, and the work to deduce general laws from them.

Anyone who wishes to rejoice with certainty in the natural laws underlying natural phenomena must first learn to dedicate himself to experimenting—for

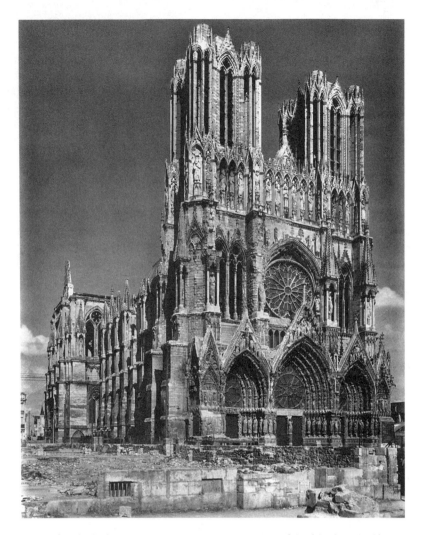

Façade of cathedral at Reims. A more ornate version of Gothic than at Chartres.
Source: Foto Marburg / Art Resource, NY

so many authors write so many things (and so many people believe them!) solely on the basis of logical deduction without the benefit of direct experience, and such reasoning is wholly false. For example, it is widely believed that the only way to split a diamond is by daubing it with goat's blood, and [deductive] philosophers and theologians continue to spread this falsity. Yet a bloody jewel-cutting of that sort has never been accomplished, though it's been tried ever so many times; but a diamond can be cut without blood [by an ordinary gem-cutter] at any time. . . . Let all things [in science] be verified by experience.

In this way, he developed the principles for creating the first rudimentary telescope and the thermometer; he also determined the chemical composition of gunpowder. He laid out, two hundred years before Leonardo da Vinci, schematic designs for airplanes, automobiles, and motorized boats. It is important to bear in mind, however, that by the word *experiment* Bacon and his contemporaries meant something closer to our use of the word *observation*. Real controlled experiments, in the modern sense, were still a thing of the future. Still, Bacon advanced the frontiers of knowledge in dramatic ways. The more he learned, the greater the scorn he heaped on others, especially theologians (whom he generally regarded as stupid and useless—and said so). The Franciscans grew worried, since they feared reprisals from the theologians who winced under Bacon's withering criticism. Moreover, at least one of Bacon's theories was troubling. Bacon loved science and believed it held the key to understanding the cosmos. He maintained, in fact, although he never used this terminology, that there was a single master code in control of the universe, a genuine physical analog to what priests in the pulpit constantly referred to as "God's plan." A properly trained scientist like himself, Bacon insisted, but not the "idiot jackasses" he saw all around him, could crack that code and understand the universe's deepest secrets. He was convinced that such a discovery was God's intent for mankind—why else would He have given us the capacity to reason?—but he also came to believe that scientific knowledge could prove to be dangerous if it fell into the wrong hands; Bacon in fact ultimately concluded that Antichrist himself, when he appeared, would be a scientist. It is through science, evilly employed, that the work of Satan will be done. There was nothing intrinsically heretical in such an idea, but since it was the Franciscan order that was so closely associated in people's minds with scientific research, it did not seem wise to Bacon's superiors to let him continue his work. In 1257 he was ordered into an abbey in Paris—essentially house-arrest—and his books were submitted for censorship by the Ministers General of the order.

Bacon appealed to Rome for help for several years without luck, but in 1265 the new pope Clement IV (r.1265–1268) took interest in Bacon's plight and was especially intrigued by Bacon's project of writing a massive encyclopedia of all science, a kind of *summa scientifica*. Clement told Bacon to start writing and to send some sample excerpts to him. But Clement died in 1268, leaving Bacon stranded. He came to recognize that even if he could find another papal champion, he would never live long enough to complete his great work. He reconciled with his Franciscan superiors, returned to England, and spent his last two decades in quiet study. He continued to write and to work in his laboratory, but his greatest accomplishments were behind him. He died in 1292.

The study and practice of science at the medieval zenith thus paralleled other aspects of medieval cultural and intellectual life: It was approached, at least by its new innovators and enthusiasts, as a comprehensive whole, an organic system that could be understood by reason and confirmed by observable data. The cosmos made sense, the scientists triumphantly declared, and God's glory was made manifest. The interconnectedness of all things, an ages-long intuitive belief of human beings, had been proven to be the case by the thinkers of the thirteenth century, and in that interconnectedness lay the ultimate balance, stability, and beauty of Creation.

But there was a darker, less rational, yet still vaguely scientific aspect to Creation as well, an aspect best approached through magic. The term *ars magica* ("magical art"), throughout the early and central Middle Ages, meant any sort of spell, incantation, potion, use of amulets or stones, or any other type of sorcery that invoked the power of demonic spirits—not necessarily Satanic spirits, as people often think, but forces beyond the realm of the normal visible material world. Early medieval magic had numerous cultural roots: Greco-Roman, Germanic, and Celtic. It is very difficult to sort out which belief derived from which source. We discussed some of these early beliefs when we examined folkloric practices that remained in early medieval culture even after Christianization. Many such practices survived conversion since in common opinion they did not contradict Church teachings in any obvious way. Thus we find early medical texts prescribing such unlikely cures as spitting into the mouth of a frog as a means of relieving oneself of toothache; the recommended treatment for gallstones was to smear the afflicted person's abdomen with the blood of a goat that had been slaughtered by a virgin and gathered up in clean cloths by a troop of naked boys.[4] The idea behind such practices was to invoke the assistance of another spirit/demon/life-force through a ritual that was not in itself scientific but which could nevertheless resolve a scientific (in this case a medical) problem.

By the thirteenth century, scholars' attitudes toward *ars magica* had changed significantly. Specifically, they now distinguished between two general varieties of *artes magicae*. Scholars deplored base folk-beliefs that they regarded as demonic—anything involving incantations or the summoning of spirits, for example—but they upheld the scientific validity of what they called *magica naturalis* ("natural magic"). Natural magic worked in slightly different ways from magical art, according to different writers, but in a general sense it can be defined as the power of the miraculous that is everywhere in God's creation—and it is the role of science to learn how to harness whatever aspects of the miraculous power God sees fit to allow us to reason out. It is *magica naturalis* that splits light into a spectrum of dazzling colors after passing through a prism, for example, but it is the science of optics that figures out the precise mechanism of how to behold the miracle and what to do with the knowledge attained by it. *Magica naturalis*, scholars believed, was one of the forces that held together the great ordered cosmos, so studying it was essential to the thirteenth-century dream of synthesizing all knowledge. Writers as sober as John of Salisbury and Thomas Aquinas believed in natural magic. Pope Boniface VIII (r.1294–1303) eagerly submitted to being treated with amulets, gemstones, and incense for his dys-

---

4. These prescriptions appeared in a book called *De medicamentis* ("On Treatments") by Marcellinus Empiricus, who lived near Bordeaux around the year 400.

pepsia. The world was literally a magical place to thirteenth-century scientists, and God's glory was revealed in every minute bit and working of it.

ASPECTS OF POPULAR CULTURE

Not all creative life took place in noble courts, university libraries, or ecclesiastical settings; much of the most exciting cultural vitality was centered in taverns and village greens, in workshops and rural fairs. Rural and urban commoners possessed cultural lives of uncommon richness, if the surviving evidence is representative. For most of the Middle Ages very little is known of popular culture above the material level—the type of tools people used, the clothing they wore, the buildings they lived in, etc.—but by the thirteenth century we know a surprising amount about peasants' and town-dwellers' popular songs, dances, folktales, festivals, games and sports, diets, occasionals fads, and unflagging vices. The character of the age determined this, to an extent: "Study *everything*," Hugh of St. Victor wrote to an earnest young scholar who had asked him for advice, "eventually in life you will come to understand that nothing is superfluous." As the passion to know spread, and as literacy spread with it, people began to write down more things than they had done in earlier times. A new technology made this task easier and more affordable: papermaking. Paper mills were part of the booty of the Spanish *Reconquista*, and as the knowledge of papermaking spread through Europe in the thirteenth century, it allowed people to set down in ink a record of the most mundane details of life: private letters, diaries, grocery lists, sketches and doodlings, silly poems, or whatever. It is often through such haphazard records as these that we reconstruct the popular life of the commoners.

Festivals and holidays punctuated the commoners' lives, so it is not surprising that much of our knowledge of their popular pastimes is centered on them. Whether people tilled the land or toiled in a shop, medieval life was one of hard labor for most of them, but it was not unremitting gloom. Approximately one hundred days out of each year were Church-proclaimed holidays during which there was to be no work.[5] Fasting usually preceded feasting—in part as a spiritual exercise, in part as a way to increase the appetite—and prayer services were usually followed with much singing, dancing, games, and drinking. It is impossible to offer a comprehensive view of medieval popular culture since it varied so much from locale to locale, but it may be worthwhile to point out almost at random a few particular examples of how the people celebrated, rested, and enjoyed themselves.

---

5. These would have been: the approximately fifty Sundays of each year, the twelve-day season from Christmas to the Feast of the Epiphany, Holy Week (Easter), the major saints' festivals (the Annunciation, 25 March; Sts. Peter and Paul, 29 June; All Saints, 1 November), the moveable feasts like Pentecost, Holy Trinity, and Corpus Christi; plus whatever patron saints' days were celebrated locally in each region, town, or village. On manors it was also common to observe the birthdays, saints' days, or wedding-days of the lords' family members as well.

Popular music had its roots far back in various traditions, as we saw in an earlier chapter with forms like the chansons de geste and the love lyric. By the thirteenth century, we find even highly respected composers of Church music writing secular pieces; they had probably always done so in the past but had never deigned to attach their names to their secular works. There were probably two reasons why it suddenly became acceptable to "admit" to composing secular music: The love that this music so frequently celebrated (courtly love) had been Christianized and made acceptable, and the music itself became much more sophisticated. French composers like Philippe de Vitry and Guillaume de Machaut were among the first to adapt the motet form, as developed by ecclesiastical composers like Léontin and Pérontin at the Church of Notre Dame in Paris, to secular topics.[6] Genres were fluid, performances more so. Professional musicians like *jongleurs* or minstrels proved their talent not only performing songs as written but by improvising new lyrics and harmonies on the spot to please a particular audience. Cleverness and audacity were valued equally—along with the discernment to know when to employ them—in poking amiable fun at a local character, offering gentle bawdy humor, or criticizing current events. Performers were lionized and pilloried with roughly equal frequency. The Franciscan chronicler Salimbene tells of his admiration for one musically gifted friar:

> Brother Henry of Pisa was a handsome fellow, medium height, always generous, courteous, charitable, and cheerful. He knew how to get along with everyone . . . [and he could] compose the sweetest and most charming songs, both in harmony and in plainsong, and he was a marvelous singer . . . Once, hearing a certain young woman going through the cathedral at Pisa while singing in the vernacular tongue
>
> *If you care no more for me,*
> *I will care no more for thee.*
>
> he at once began to sing this hymn, using the exact same melody
>
> *Christ divine, Christ of mine,*
> *Christ O King and Lord of all.*

Yet Salimbene is also careful to report that numerous Church authorities have warned of the dangers of *all* music, even ostensibly religious music:

> no matter if it is instrumental or vocal. . . . Remember that Orpheus, with his lute, followed his desire straight to hell itself. Note too that one hardly ever finds a man in this world with a light voice and a grave life. . . . I have known innumerable men and women, the heightened sinfulness of whose lives corresponded exactly to the increased sweetness of their voices.

---

6.   The motet (which derives its name from the French word *mot*, meaning "word") was perhaps the most important musical form to emerge in the thirteenth century. It originated in the practice of adding a sung text that rose above the melodic line of plainchant, thus introducing "two-part" harmony or polyphony. Vitry and Machaut were the first to set secular vernacular texts to such form and quickly expanded it to include more voices and melodic lines.

Most professional musicians came from the lower or middle orders of society. The most prominent exception to this rule were the German *Minnesänger*. They were troubadour poets in the courtly love tradition (*Minne* is Middle High German for "courtly love") who flourished from the late twelfth to the early fourteenth centuries, especially in the Rhineland and in Bavaria; they were typically drawn from the German aristocracy.[7] So long as it remained an aristocratic art form, the *Minnesang* retained its allegiance to traditional themes of a knight's perfect love for an unattainable lady and of loving service without earthly reward, but the rising importance of the German towns and early bourgeoisie meant that the old forms were given new life and thematic elements toward the start of the fourteenth century. The greatest of the *Minnesinger* poet-composers was Walther von der Vogelweide (d. 1230), who was a favorite of emperor Otto IV (r.1208–1215) and of Frederick II.

Many hundreds, even thousands, of popular lyrics survive for which we do not have any corresponding music. They were not necessarily sung, and were not necessarily associated with any particular festival or occasion. Then as now people wrote songs to commemorate the everyday events of life, like this example from thirteenth-century England—about a young man's infatuation with his first love, a girl named Alison.

Bitweene Merch and Averil,	
When spray biginneth to springe,	
The litel fowl hath hire wil	
On hire leod➤ to singe.	*In her language*
Ich libbe➤ in love-longinge	*I live*
For semlokest➤ of alle thinge.	*the loveliest*
Heo➤ may me blisse bringe:	*She*
Ich am in hire baundoun.➤	*power*
An hendy hap ich habbe yhent,➤	*A lucky chance I have received*
Ichoot➤ from hevene it is me sent:	*I know*
From alle➤ wommen my love is lent,➤	*all other / withdrawn*
And light➤ on Alisoun.	*alights*

Female lyricists expressed their longings as well, as in this excerpt from a *trobairitz* (woman troubadour) from southern France:

Handsome beloved, so attractive and fine,
When shall I hold you in my arms?
If only I could lie with you a single night,
    and give you a passionate kiss!
Know this:

---

7. By the start of the Renaissance these figures had evolved into the *Meistersingern* ("Mastersingers"). The Mastersingers were urban-based guild musicians, not court-based nobles.

I would long to embrace you like a wife embraces a husband,
If you would only swear to do everything I ask.

We know a fair amount about the popular dances of the noble courts, but far less about the dances of the townsfolk and peasants. Dancing was one of the chief entertainments in feudal courts from the twelfth century on, despite repeated attempts by the Church to ban the dangerous practice. (Dancing, as everyone knows, leads to lechery.) Most dances among the commoners were ordinary rounds and processionals. Carols, which consisted of a closed ring of men and women dancing around a focal object—a tree, perhaps, or a haystack, a maypole, or a fountain—were the most popular.

Commoners in the thirteenth century had a wide array of popular games and sports to select from, to keep themselves entertained. Wrestling was enormously popular since it cost nothing and required as few as two people; yet whole teams were often drawn up, often with surprising results, as the following passage from the history of Roger of Wendover relates regarding a match in 1222.

> On the Feast of St. James the townsfolk of London gathered together just outside the city, at the hospital established by Queen Matilda, to have a wrestling match with the inhabitants from the whole district surrounding the city; in this way they all hoped to find out who was stronger, the townspeople or the rustics. After they had been at it for a long time, with loud shouts coming from both teams, the Londoners overthrew their opponents and gained the victory. Among those who were defeated was the seneschal of the Abbot of Westminster, and he went away brooding on how he could get revenge for himself and his companions upon the townsfolk. He finally settled on this plan: he sent word throughout the whole district for everyone to gather at Westminster on St. Peter's Day [for a rematch] . . . and he promised the prize of a ram to whoever proved himself the best [individual] wrestler. In the meantime, however, he gathered together [from throughout the kingdom] a throng of powerful and skilled wrestlers, in order that he might ensure his team's victory. The Londoners, expecting another victory, came to the match in high spirits.
>
> When the match began, each side commenced to throw the other about for quite some time. But then the revenge-seeking seneschal, together with his rustic companions and provincials, pulled out their weapons and began to beat and assault the unarmed Londoners, until they caused considerable bloodshed among them.

Drawings in manuscripts depict games that look remarkably like the modern games of baseball, tennis, and hockey; card games of great variety; numerous board games (such as chess—almost exclusively an aristocratic or upper bourgeois game); and the unsurprising array of balls, dolls, wooden swords, and other bric-a-brac of childhood.

The point of this is simply to remind us (as we all need reminding on occasion) that medieval people were not only soil-tilling serfs and shop-working artisans, busy maids, praying monks, fighting knights, patient wives, scheming princes, and crouched scribes. They sang and danced, they had favorite sporting teams, they enjoyed theatricals, they had private likes and dislikes. They were fully human, fully flawed, fully complicated—and therefore all the more interesting to study.

SUGGESTED READING

Texts

Aquinas, St. Thomas. *Summa contra gentiles.*

——— *Summa theologica.*

Bacon, Roger. *Opus Majus.*

St. Bonaventura. *The Mind's Road to God.*

de France, Marie. *Lais.*

de Meun, Jean. *Romance of the Rose.*

de Troyes, Chrétien. *Complete Romances.*

Source Anthologies

Bogin, Meg. *The Women Troubadours* (1976).

Bosley, Richard N., and Martin Tweedale. *Basic Issues in Medieval Philosophy: Selected Readings Presenting the Interactive Discourses among the Major Figures* (1997).

Doss-Quinby, Eglal, Joan Tasker Grimbert, Wendy Pfeffer, and Elizabeth Aubrey. *Songs of the Women Trouvères* (2001).

Flores, Angel. *An Anthology of Medieval Lyrics* (1962).

Hanning, Robert, and Joan Ferrante. *The Lais of Marie de France* (1978).

Studies

Baldwin, John W. *The Scholastic Culture of the Middle Ages, 1000–1300* (1971).

Bony, Jean. *French Gothic Architecture of the Twelfth and Thirteenth Centuries* (1983).

Calkins, Robert G. *Medieval Architecture in Western Europe from AD 300 to 1500* (1998).

Colish, Marcia L. *Medieval Foundations of the Western Intellectual Tradition, 400–1400* (1997).

Cross, Richard. *Duns Scotus* (1999).

Drury, John. *Painting the Word; Christian Pictures and Their Meanings* (1999).

Erlande-Brandenburg, Alain. *The Cathedral: The Social and Architectural Dynamics of Construction* (1994).

Jaeger, C. Stephen. *The Origins of Courtliness: Civilising Trends and the Formation of Courtly Ideals, 939–1210* (1985).

Keen, Maurice. *Chivalry* (1984).

Keiser, Elizabeth B. *Courtly Desire and Medieval Homophobia: The Legitimation of Sexual Pleasure in "Cleanness" and Its Contexts* (1997).

Kieckhefer, Richard. *Magic in the Middle Ages* (1990).

Kolve, V. A. *The Play Called Corpus Christi* (1966).

Lacy, Norris J. *Reading Fabliaux* (1993).

Muscatine, Charles. *The Old French Fabliaux* (1986).

Paterson, Linda. *The World of the Troubadours: Medieval Occitan Society, ca. 1100-ca. 1300* (1995).

Radding, Charles M., and William W. Clark. *Medieval Architecture, Medieval Learning: Builders and Masters in the Age of Romanesque and Gothic* (1992).

Southern, R[ichard] W. *Robert Grosseteste: The Growth of an English Mind in Medieval Europe* (1992).

Williamson, Paul. *Gothic Sculpture, 1140–1300* (1995).

Woolf, Rosemary. *The English Mystery Plays* (1972).

Yudkin, Jeremy. *Music in the Middle Ages* (1989).

CHAPTER 15

DAILY LIFE AT THE MEDIEVAL ZENITH

Despite the idealizing visions of the theologians, political theorists, architects, artists, and scientists, medieval society continued to be, at street level, remarkably dynamic and changeable. A monolithic medieval society never in fact existed; regional and local differences in social organization, religious practices, laws and currencies, dress and diet norms, dialects, prides and prejudices, remained strong. What united the medieval worlds, more than anything else, was the simple *desire to create* a unity, an eagerness to think in collective instead of individualistic terms and to define the essence of things by their relation with other things. This desire both preserved individuality and fostered a sense, however vague or indirect in practice, of cohesion. But it would be a mistake to exaggerate the degree to which such organic cohesion was actually achieved in daily life. More people in medieval Europe believed in unity than actually lived it.

Europe was now a surprisingly crowded place. Its population around the year 1300 was somewhere between seventy five and one hundred million, easily twice and perhaps even three times what it had been around the year 1000. Proportionally, the urban population was clearly in the ascendant: a handful of megalopolises existed—Constantinople, Milan, Venice, and Palermo all had populations of a hundred thousand or more; at least a dozen cities like Barcelona, Cologne, Mainz, Florence, London, Marseilles, and Paris had between thirty and seventy thousand. Even rural villages were growing in size. A farming town of four thousand people was not uncommon. As cities and villages grew, they tended to clear the surrounding countryside since they needed the lumber for constructing and heating their buildings. Hence cities were not only larger and more numerous in an absolute sense, but they also stood out more sharply on the landscape. A traveler could eye most cities at a distance of several miles, especially their towering cathedrals. In order to support this increased population some changes in the land became necessary. Medieval engineers perfected the methods of draining fens and marshland. In northern Italy a vast network of canals, dams, embankments, and reservoirs helped control the runoff waters of the Alpine heights. In Spain the ancient Roman irrigation systems were revived. The people of the Low Countries constructed their so-called *Golden Wall*, a chain of breakwaters and dikes from

Flanders to Frisia in order to help reclaim land from the Zuider See. Half of what is today Holland, plus about a fifth of today's Belgium, used to be underwater; the land literally came to light thanks to medieval engineers and workers, and the burghers who paid for the project.

The urbanization of Europe had far-reaching consequences. Cities, after all, are more than sites of commerce and administration. They are social organisms that themselves promote further organization; most city dwellers, then as now, maintained membership in a variety of other social networks and local linkages: parish churches, trade guilds, neighborhood assemblies, ethnic or religious ghettoes, local schools, religious confraternities and prayer groups, sports teams, or even the gathering of regulars at the local tavern. The creation of these communities demanded and catalyzed change. For example, the needs of urban life—contracts, receipts, deeds, government reports, judicial summonses and decisions, letters and libraries—tend to foster a need for, and therefore an increase in, general literacy. This need both contributed to and resulted from the proliferation of schools in urban centers. But cities also offer the opportunity of anonymity; most readers of this book will know what it is like to feel alone in a crowd of several thousand people. So for medieval townsfolk, and for new immigrants to the cities anonymity was a new sensation indeed, one that elicited fundamental questions of identity and position. The conception of one's own identity changed significantly once one was freed, for good or ill, from the relationships that defined one's identity and social role in a smaller and rural setting. As a consequence of this anonymity, and the general proliferation of literacy, cities in the High Middle Ages witnessed the otherwise inexplicable rise in popularity of the genre of *autobiography*. St. Augustine may have invented it in the fifth century with his great *Confessions*, but no such analogous work was even attempted, that we know of, until the twelfth century. Peter Abelard's *History of My Misfortunes* seems to have revived the form; in the thirteenth and fourteenth centuries, it became surprisingly popular.

As laboratories of cultural interaction, cities created the atmosphere for testing social assumptions and traditional behaviors. Many gender roles were questioned; some were changed. Ideas and technologies passed from one group to another. But resistance to such changes also ran strong, and in a backlash reaction medieval Europe became obsessed with the notion of labeling and identifying people so that one knew who was one dealing with. Ethnic and religious groups were increasingly forced to wear identifying badges—Jews, for example, had to sew circular badges of yellow cloth on their outer garments—but the passion for identifying people went beyond religion and was something larger than mere prejudice. Bakers wore certain kinds of hats; priests wore clerical collars; students wore academic robes; members of individual guilds had signifying collars, badges, robes, and rings to identify their trade, pilgrims carried staves and rucksacks that betokened their status. Statutes called *sumptuary laws* laid down strict rules for dress standards that differentiated the classes: The well-to-do wife of an international merchant, for example, might be allowed to wear a silk garment with twelve silver buttons and an embroidered hemline two palm-widths from the ground, but the wife of a modest tavern-keeper, regardless of how much disposable cash she had, had to resign herself to a woolen garment with a half-dozen brass or even wooden buttons and a plain hemline four palm-widths from the ground.[1] Everyone had a pigeonhole and had to live in it. But even here the idea was less to atomize society than to bind it together by having everyone play their appropriate role and not pretend to anything else. What medieval society, consciously or not, aimed for was a vision of civilization that was best defined, in a very different context, by the twentieth-century poet W. H. Auden: Civilization, he said, is measured by "the degree of diversity attained and the degree of unity retained." That, above all, was the goal of the medieval worlds, and it was best attained in the cities of the thirteenth century.

Economic Changes

The most important innovations in economic life at the medieval zenith were the development of the guild system and the banking industry. A *guild* was analogous to a modern trade association, if one is talking about the artisanal crafts, or a cartel, if one is discussing the merchants who sold the craftsmen's goods on the regional or international market. Merchants were the first to organize—a *guilda mercatoria* existed at Saint-Omer, in far northern France, by the 1090s; artisanal guilds did not become common until after 1200. To survive in a world where robbery and rogue barons ruled the day, merchants took refuge in numbers and banded together against extortion; they also came together for mutual protection when traveling. Whatever the spark that ignited their formation, guilds proliferated with exceptional speed throughout the twelfth and thirteenth centuries, from the Mediterranean to the Baltic and from England to the borders of Byzantium.[2] Large cities like Cologne, Lübeck, Milan, Paris, or York had dozens of guilds apiece, often one for each major manufacture. Once established, guilds set norms for commodity pricing, the quality, quantity, and means of production, and the wages to be paid to the various workers who produced the goods. The earliest guilds were usually comprised of all the merchants in a given city, regardless of the commodities they dealt in, and they began to form in the late eleventh century.[3] Membership in an urban guild amounted to a general business license; the development of separate guilds for individual industries occurred over the course of the twelfth century,

---

1. An example from the municipal laws of London (1281): "No woman of the city may henceforth enter the marketplace, walk on the king's highway, or leave her house for any reason, wearing a hood trimmed with anything other than lambskin or rabbitskin—upon penalty of the sheriff's confiscating that hood—unless that woman is one of the [noble] ladies entitled to wear fur-trimmed capes (the hoods of which they may trim with whatever fur they deem proper). This law is enacted because many shopgirls, nurses, servants, and women of loose morals do now go about bedecked in hoods trimmed with squirrel-fur or ermine, as though they were in fact true ladies."
2. German and Scandinavian guilds commonly went by the name of *hansas*.
3. There were precursors to the guilds in the religious confraternities (called *caritates*) of the Carolingian period. These were sworn associations of laymen who dedicated a portion of their lives and livelihoods to the notion of religious community but without taking full monastic vows.

each with its own statutes, privileges, guild hall, and governing protocols—although it was common to find many of the same merchants on the rolls of more than one guild.

Guilds had considerable influence over society. Craft guilds controlled entry into their industry by setting strict regulations for awarding apprenticeship contracts, advancing workers to journeyman status, and recognizing craft mastery and admission into the guild. Heavy fees were required along the way, and even heavier penalties were meted out to those who scoffed at the regulations. Merchant guilds, by contrast, required proof of no particular technical skill like the artisanal organizations, but admission was conditional on any number of factors that changed from time to time and from place to place: Wealth, family connections, social standing, ethnicity, political affiliation, and commercial contacts all figured into the calculus.

Guilds served both commercial and social functions. Commercially, they acted as loose monopolies controlling the economic life of a city; in this guise they came to play highly influential, and frequently determinative, roles in urban politics. On a social level, guilds became organized charitable institutions that helped to establish schools and hospices, provide food for the poor, assist in evangelical activity, and to care for guild members who fell upon hard times. The rules of the wine and beer merchants' guild at Southampton in the thirteenth century, for example, established that

> whenever the guild is in session the lepers at [the hospital of] La Madeleine shall receive in alms from the guild eight gallons of ale, as shall the sick in [the hospitals of] God's House and St. Julian's. The Franciscans shall receive eight gallons of ale and four gallons of wine; and sixteen gallons of ale shall be distributed to the poor from whatever spot the guild meets at. . . . If any guild member should fall into poverty and cannot pay his debts, and if he is unable to work and provide for himself, he shall receive from the guild one mark [of silver] every time the guild meets in session, in order to relieve his suffering.

Admission into merchant guilds was carefully screened; applicants had to be people of good standing and repute in the community, had to meet basic income standards and pay regular dues. Inheritable membership kept many cities' guild memberships fairly constant and left trade in the hands of a coterie of highly influential families.

Artisanal guilds were more fluid. Individual craftsmen like blacksmiths, coopers (barrel makers), carpenters, tailors, stonemasons, or glassblowers would take on apprentices to whom they taught their crafts. Urban youths began their apprenticeships quite early in life—often as young as eight years of age, depending on the trade—and lived in the master's home and worked in his shop until they had learned the fundamental skills needed for the job. This education commonly took seven years. Having completed his apprenticeship, a young worker then moved on to *journeyman* status. At this level he was now a paid employee with greater legal rights and social standing; a journeyman usually worked for his master for several more years, refining his skills and forming the business connections that would ultimately help him set up his own shop. In theory, artisanal apprenticeship was available to anyone who convinced a master of his potential and could come up with the money to pay for his room and board and instruction. Movement across class lines was therefore possible, and a former serf could rise, if he was very lucky, through the rank of journeyman to master craftsman. Few people of low origin, however, were able to break into the merchant ranks.

Women and girls were indirect beneficiaries of the apprenticeship system, or at least they could be. Since most town dwellers lived and kept shop in the same building, an artisan's wife, sisters, daughters, or nieces who lived with him could learn his techniques just by watching him teach his apprentices. Women generally did not have the legal power to go off and start their own businesses, but they could inherit them. And since townsmen in the Middle Ages tended to take young wives—sometimes as young as twelve or thirteen, in order to take maximum advantage of child-bearing years (although such cases were extreme even by medieval standards)—many urban women found themselves running shops and businesses inherited from their fathers or dead older husbands. In some regions, women, if they knew a particular trade like ale-brewing but happened to marry a man who followed a different trade, could legally open their own shops and run them themselves, provided that their husbands approved of the venture. By the late thirteenth century, some trades in fact were dominated by women—ale-brewing and tavern-keeping, silk-spinning, and haberdashery, for example. Women practiced many trades and were full-fledged members of many guilds. Female artisans were found most frequently in textile guilds (as weavers or cloth-finishers, usually), in brewing, in candle-making, and in baking guilds. Widows could usually inherit their husbands' guild memberships, but membership was often nullified if a woman remarried. In Paris alone by the end of the thirteenth century, women held memberships in 80 of the city's 120 trade guilds, and 6 of those 80 were designated as female-only guilds.

With the rise of guilds, medieval cities became centers of industrial production for the first time; prior to roughly 1200, most craft work and manufacturing was done domestically, with each family producing most of what it needed in terms of material goods. Some small-scale production of goods for general sale had always been present, but organized mass production of specialized commodities by individual businesses was a new development. It is likely that industry of this sort was the creation of the merchants who wanted to find a way of guaranteeing the supply of certain commodities for which they had markets abroad. The raw materials for those industries did not have to exist locally: Flemish textile merchants, for example, purchased raw wool from England and brought it to the weavers in Flanders, and then sold the woven cloth on the international market. In this way the merchants made healthy, and at times enormous, profits since they owned the commodity from start to finish; the craftspeople did not own the goods they produced in their shops, but only worked on them in return for a set wage paid by the merchants.

In order to reduce the cost of transporting goods on the international market, merchants in the twelfth and thirteenth centuries developed the institution known as the *fair*. These were large-scale commercial emporia established throughout Europe where merchants would bring their goods to sell on the wholesale market. Most fairs lasted only a week per year, but the largest ones met annually for as many as three weeks. Many merchants traveled in a regular circuit from fair to fair instead of trekking laboriously from city to city. In order for a fair to be successful, it had to be held at a site which had a suitable infrastructure for the transport of enormous quantities of goods; hence, fairs most commonly lay along navigable waterways or at the intersection of major trade routes. The most famous medieval fairs were those held in the county of Champagne, just east of Paris. Four locations in Champagne were fair sites, which meant that the county annually staged at least four, and sometimes as many as six, fairs per year, which generated enormous sums of tax and toll revenue for the local count. The danger of carrying the large sums of money needed for this sort of commerce led to the development of bills of exchange or letters of credit; these functioned very much like our modern checks, although they were not necessarily drawn upon banks. Groups like the Templars, before their dissolution in the early fourteenth century, served as financial service units, holding depositors' funds and settling accounts. Individual moneylenders and currency changers also played an important role here. Jewish merchants often specialized in finance of this sort, since they were exempt from the Church's strictures against charging interest on loans. Christians and Jews bought from and sold to each other openly in the markets, but there were strong objections, from religious leaders on both sides, to their entering joint commercial enterprises as business partners. Such partnerships did happen with some frequency nevertheless.

The development of banking techniques and institutions was no less impressive. Banking—the word comes from the Latin *banca* which denoted a money changer's "bench" or "counter"—has an obscure origin. The principal functions that we associate with banking (deposit-holding, moneylending, and currency exchange) had all been performed by individuals on an ad hoc basis in earlier times, and historians agree that true banking began only when two or more of these activities became the normative functions of a settled capital concern made up of a sworn association of financiers—a guild of the moneyed, in other words. At this point agreement ends, since historians see the confluence of these elements in different places and at different times. By definition, however, banks require money, and western Europe did not develop a money economy until the late tenth century or even later. Since the first areas to develop money economies were the Mediterranean city-states and the German empire, it is likely that the origins of banking should be sought in either of those areas. The southern cities probably engaged first in currency exchange and deposit-holding, while the empire may have had the lead in combining moneylending and exchange; this conjecture is based on the fact that the empire experienced a sudden influx of specie under the Ottonians and could draw upon their sizable Jewish population to provide loans and serve as contacts

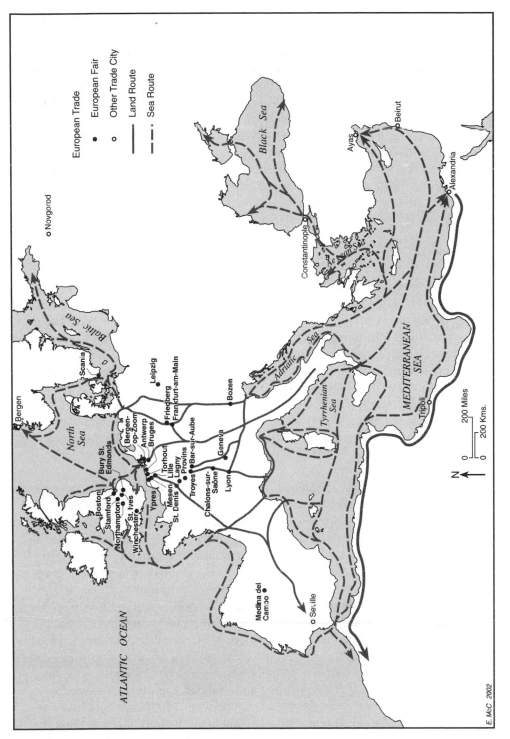

First trade routes

E. McC 2002

with foreign merchants, whereas the southern cities reignited commercial networks that had merely gone into abeyance.

The popularity of the commercial fairs gave further impetus to the development of banking, for funds had to move frequently and often over long distances in order to meet obligations. The ability to deposit money in a bank in one city, only to draw on that amount from another office of that bank in another city, eased the problem of transferring funds considerably. Certain cities earned reputations as major financial centers: Bruges, Cahors (in southwestern France), and Florence were three of the most prominent. But by the thirteenth century, most major cities had within their confines either banks of their own or offices of foreign banks. Many of these banks had quite fantastic sums of capital at their disposal: Loans from the Riccardi bank in the city of Lucca, for example, kept the government of England afloat for nearly twenty years during the reign of Edward I (r. 1272–1307).

PEASANTS' LIVES

The overwhelming bulk of the medieval population continued to work the land. After the proliferation of collective manors in the tenth and eleventh centuries, relatively few major structural or technological changes took places in rural life in the twelfth and thirteenth. The agrarian scene was not altogether static, however. In order to provide more food for the urban and international markets, manors across Europe grew significantly in size. Since there were no major advances in farming methods to increase the yield per acre of farmland, landowners chose instead to produce more farmland: They felled forests, drained marshlands, and brought meadows under the plow. This clearing meant more work for more peasants, and the populations of manors and villages increased accordingly. But the rhythms and workings of daily life continued on much as they had done before—with at least two important changes.

In England there was a pronounced movement away from lease farming, which had become quite common over the course of the twelfth century. Peasants had frequently become rent-payers, commuting their manorial services into fixed rents that they owed to their landlords in return for the right to work the landlords' lands, use his tools and animals, and appeal to his authority for the settlement of disputes. By the start of the thirteenth century however, large numbers of landlords decided they could make greater profits by commuting their tenants' rents back into required services and selling their manors' produce directly on the market for themselves; they traded the security of steady rental income for the higher risk but greater potential of marketing their own produce. This new style of commercialized farming did not carry the components of private justice and local administration that the earlier manifestations of manorialism had possessed, since those functions were now performed by the developed and professionalized government. This shift clearly hurt the peasants, who were thus driven back into classical serfdom, but there was little they could do about it short of abandoning the land and heading for the city. In this way, English manors became rather more economic institutions than the essentially social institutions they had earlier been. Not all manors underwent such a change, of course, but enough did so to create a decidedly different atmosphere in the countryside. The strong development within England of royal government, of shire courts, and of the corps of royal officials administering more and more aspects of social life meant that the traditional administrative and judicial roles earlier played by landed nobles were eroded; these changes also left them with only their economic function of managing farmland. This shift in the nobles' role is illustrated by the sudden proliferation of handbooks on estate management—self-help books on how to turn an old social institution into a profitable new professional business. The most famous of these works was the treatise *On Husbandry* by Walter of Henley written in the 1270s; the works are enlightening in the way they show how little most rural lords actually knew about farming. Some of Walter's suggestions on how to manage a profitable farm include:

> You should pay no more than a penny in order to have three acres of cropland plowed, and four pennies for one acre of meadow. . . . It should take no more than five men to harvest and bundle two acres of wheat in a single day. . . . Since many workers do not measure their productivity by the number of acres they have worked, you should always organize field-workers into bands of five men—if you use women workers, you should count each as half a man—and know that five bands (that is, twenty-five men in total) should be able to harvest and bundle ten acres in a full day's work, a hundred acres in ten days, and two hundred acres in twenty days. . . . Therefore, determine the number of acres you need to have harvested and inform [your field-workers] of the number of days they have to work, and pay them the appropriate number of day-wages. If they take longer than the set number of days to complete the harvesting, do not pay them for extra days, for it is their fault if they have not gathered the whole harvest or worked as hard as they should have done.

Walter goes on to educate landlords about dairymaids:

> A good dairymaid should always be loyal and of good reputation, personally clean, knowledgeable of her craft and of everything that pertains to it. She should never allow an underling to steal any milk, butter, or cream, on account of which the amount of cheese produced [for market] will be lessened and the dairy farm's profits decreased. And she should be adept at making cheese and knowing how to preserve the dairy's various vessels, so that new ones need not be purchased every year.

and about swineherds:

> A swineherd should be kept on all manors that maintain herds of swine, and those swine should always be kept in forests, woods, wastelands or marshes— any place where they will not feed on the grainfields. But if the winter frost is harsh and the swine must have some food from the grainfield, then the swineherd must build a pigsty in a marsh or wood, so that the food may be brought

to them day and night [rather than letting the herd roam through the grain-field]. . . . Any landlord who maintains a herd of swine for a year on the food of his grainfield alone . . . will suffer a net loss for the year of one hundred percent.[4]

On the Continent in general, but especially in France, the Low Countries and eastern Germany, peasants not only continued to be rent-payers instead of service-providers but the practice of commuting services into rents actually expanded over the thirteenth century. In the Low Countries and in eastern Germany this was prob-ably due to a shortage of farm laborers: Landlords who wanted to have their lands worked at all had to offer the best terms available—and peasants almost always preferred to pay a set rent and sell their surpluses on the markets by themselves. Within France, however, the explanation is a bit more complicated. French nobles, despite the centralizing efforts of the Capetians, never lost their jurisdictional roles in the countryside and valued greatly their roles as social leaders and wielders of power; they preferred to retain that position. Moreover, the cult of chivalry ran strongest in France, and it taught that a true nobleman—a chivalrous lord whose sense of honor represented the backbone of aristocratic society—should never sully his hands with commerce; to do so would be unspeakably "common." Far better to retain one's honor by fulfilling one's duty as a ruler of men than to enter the com-monplace world of the market, even if that meant missing out on some of the enor-mous profits available there. In Spain the advance of the *Reconquista* both created a need for new farmers to settle the frontier lands—they generally insisted on freeholdings—and created an opportunity for former service-owing peasants to renegotiate the terms of their tenure in return for agreeing to stay on the land and commute their services into rents. So a higher preponderance of freeman farmers became the norm on most of the Continent.

The physical appearance of peasant villages and homes had changed little from the eleventh century. Homes were still one- or two-room hovels built on rubble foun-dations, with thatched roofs and timber frameworks plastered with mud and straw. A good insulator, thatch kept rain from entering the house and kept the warmth of the central hearth from escaping, but it was also highly flammable and susceptible to infestation by vermin.[5] Floors were usually nothing but packed earth covered with straw. Furniture was sparse and simple, the two essential items being a bed and a table. The beds were usually quite large, since families tended to sleep together for warmth. Perhaps the most important innovation in peasant homes by the thirteenth century was the introduction of chimneys, which reduced the intense smokiness of houses in earlier centuries and also provided a check against flames. Peasants still housed their animals in their homes during foul weather, with the expected results abounding everywhere. The straw strewn on the floors had to be changed regularly.

---

4.   That is, the swine will consume twice as much in grain as they themselves will provide in capital on the market.
5.   Peasant homes in Mediterranean Europe tended to have tile roofs instead.

The peasant diet remained limited—mostly grains, root vegetables, and fruit—but it had improved considerably from the eleventh century thanks to the introduction of beans and peas that provided protein and, more importantly, iron; most medieval peasants suffered from chronic iron deficiency (although they did not know it), which left them weak with anemia. This was especially true of women, since menstruation, pregnancy, and breast-feeding drain iron from women's bodies (and they need more iron than men do in the first place). By the thirteenth century, peasants were able to add a fair amount of inexpensive meat to their diets, chiefly pork and rabbit. Ale and wine remained the principal beverages, even for children. Peasants typically drank a gallon of (rather weak) ale a day in northern Europe; southern peasants preferred wine and drank it in comparable quantities. Ironically, peasant diets were probably healthier than the ostentatious meat-orgies of their landlords; nobles shunned grains and vegetables as "common" food and ate meat (fowl, red meats of all kinds, and fish), white bread, and wine almost exclusively—although fruits remained a popular after-dinner treat. Heart disease, digestive trouble, scurvy, intestinal infections from decomposed proteins, gout, and tooth rot were consequences that most peasants were spared.[6]

Daily work remained segregated by gender. Men worked the land, tended the draught animals and herds, repaired tools and fences; women generally milked the cows, made butter and cheese, spun yarn and wove cloth, cooked, and tended to the children. Men and women tended to share certain tasks and worked together at haymaking, sowing, threshing, sheep-shearing, and roof-thatching. The work was hard and dangerous. Coroners' rolls from thirteenth-century England, for example, give grim evidence of the often daily occurrence of serious woundings on peasant farms: digits or limbs severed by farm implements, bones crushed by draft animals or falling stones, legs burned when cloaks brushed against hearth fires, children drowned after falling down wells. Crime was also common.

> . . . . On 2 October 1270 Amice, daughter of Robert Belamy of Staploe, and Sibyl Bonchevaler were carrying a tub full of grout between them in the brewhouse of Lady Juliana de Beauchamp in the hamlet of Staploe in East Socon, intending to empty it into a boiling leaden vat, when Amice slipped and fell into the vat and the tub [capsized] upon her. Sibyl immediately jumped towards her, dragged her from the vat and shouted; the household came and found her

---

6. Peter of Blois, a well-traveled writer of the twelfth century, memorably bemoaned the food in aristocratic courts in a letter to a friend: "I am amazed that anyone accustomed to a scholar's life in places of quiet repose can ever endure the annoyances of life at court. . . . The bread is like lead, full of bran and only half-baked, un-kneaded and un-leavened, and made from the dregs of a beer barrel. The wine is spoiled, sour, and full of mould, thick, greasy, rancid, and tasting of tar. I myself have seen wine served to noblemen that was so full of dregs that they had to filter it through their teeth in order to drink it. . . . The beer at court is wretched to drink and disgusting to look at. Meat, since everyone demands it, is purchased whether or not it is fresh. They buy fish that are four days old—and the fact that it reeks doesn't lessen its price one bit. As for the servants, they care nothing whatsoever whether a guest lives or dies; their only concern is to pile meat on their masters' tables. Those tables, in fact, are usually so heaped with putrid meat that if it were not for the fact that those who eat it exercise regularly, most of them would die even sooner than they already do."

scalded almost to death. A chaplain came and Amice had the rites of the church and died by misadventure [early] the next day. . . .

. . . . On 24 May 1270 Emma, daughter of Richard Toky of South-hill, went to Houleden in South-hill to gather wood. Walter Garglof of Stanford came, carrying a bow and a small sheaf of arrows, took hold of Emma and tried to throw her to the ground and deflower her, but she immediately shouted and her father came. Walter immediately shot an arrow at him [Richard], striking him on the right side of the forehead and giving him a mortal wound. He struck him again with another arrow under the right side and so into the stomach. Simon of South-hill immediately came and asked him why he wanted to kill Richard, and Walter immediately shot an arrow at him, striking him in the back, so that his life was despaired of. Walter then immediately fled. Later Emma, Richard's wife, came and found her husband wounded to the point of death and shouted. The neighbors came and took him to his house. He had the rites of the church, made his will, and died at twilight on the same day.[7]

Among the factors that made peasant life difficult was a shortage—or rather, an uneven distribution—of metals for farm tools and domestic vessels. Western Europe has sprawled pockets of mineral ores that were accessible with medieval technology, but the cost of mining the ore, refining the metals, producing the worked tools, and distributing them on the rural market, made them prohibitively expensive for peasants in many parts of Europe. One such region was southern France, where some peasants had to rely on wooden spades and pitchforks until the start of the fourteenth century. Even the relatively wealthy Templar estate at Sainte-Eulalie-du-Larzac had only a single metal cauldron and hook and a few simple drills and files; most of its other tools were made wholly of wood. A metal scythe was something only to be dreamed of. Nevertheless, other areas in the west had an abundance of metal goods at affordable prices, especially after the rich coalfields in Flanders began to be worked in the twelfth century and the coal shipped by river barges, making available an inexpensive and potent fuel to refine iron ore.

Peasant life had its pleasures and entertainments, too, as discussed in the last chapter. The day-in, day-out schedule of grinding labor was punctuated with times of rest, spiritual nourishment, or just a few hours of extra sleep. Village life was hardly filled with rollicking fun, but it was not unremittingly grim. The most common forms of entertainment were dances and bonfires, cockfights, wrestling matches, and simply drinking and conversing in taverns.

TOWNSFOLKS' LIVES

Urban life at the medieval zenith is difficult to summarize since the character of cities varied so much and since most cities were themselves remarkably complex and diverse. Naples was quite a different place from Hamburg; Vienna was not like Montpellier or Lisbon; citizens of Milan would hardly have recognized people from

---

7. Quoted from *Women's Lives in Medieval Europe: A Sourcebook*, ed. Emilie Amt (New York, 1993), p. 189.

Edinburgh or Copenhagen as fellow urbanites. These attitudes may have been more a matter of parochialism than anything else; people tend to identify themselves rather fiercely with their home cities.[8] Townsfolk in the Middle Ages took great pride in their cities, as evidenced by their passionate commitment to cathedral building and vast public projects like bridges, aqueducts and sewers, ever-expanding town walls, bell towers, harbors, hospitals, and private endeavors like urban palaces, guild halls, and commercial warehouses. But civic pride shone through in other ways as well. The mid-twelfth to mid-fourteenth centuries were a great age for the writing of municipal documents: Earnest citizens wrote long, detailed histories of their cities, government officials commissioned reports on demographic changes, public works projects, crime levels, and popular religious movements within the town walls; artists made cities themselves the subjects of paintings; poets sang the praises of their urban settings. Cities, as legal "persons" possessing the right of self-governance, had their own seals made and strove to outdo one another in the splendor and beauty of their designs.

On a social level the dominant feature of urban Europe was the development of a new class: the burghers or bourgeoisie. (The words derive from the German term *Burg*, meaning "town." German cities established in the Middle Ages can usually be identified by the suffix *-burg* appended to their place name: Hamburg, Strassburg, Regensburg, etc.) The bourgeoisie were the free artisans and merchants who controlled the economic life of the community and usually its political life as well. The middle class was broad and fluid, with a wide range of income levels and social or legal privileges. As cities grew and prospered, town dwellers took considerable pride in themselves and their labors; they clung tightly to the legal privileges accorded to them—a Barcelonan traveling through Clermont retained the rights given him by Barcelonan law—and came to develop prickly, and sometimes outright hostile, attitudes toward the rural society that surrounded them. Merchants generally regarded feudal aristocrats as pampered dullards who drew their living off a society that they no longer served in a meaningful way; to the nobles, merchants were uncultivated nouveaux riches who thought they could buy their way into proper society. Tensions between town and countryside were generally less virulent in England and Italy than they were in Spain, France, and Germany, but even in Italy municipal records frequently itemized special explanations of legal clauses for individual aristocrats with a dismissive comment that the explanation was being done "because he is a knight and is therefore presumed to be ignorant of the law."

Prior to the "great change" of the eleventh and twelfth centuries, most people in Europe seem to have accepted a great degree of immutability in the world; political systems and social structures were ordained by God, they felt, and were therefore not expected to change fundamentally. Since the bonds that held feudal society together were sacred oaths and since sacred oaths could not, by definition, be

---

8. I myself will forever defend Minneapolis against the criticisms leveled at it by bigoted fools. *Salve magna parens.*

altered, it came as an unexpected shock to feudal kings that the reliefs owed them by their vassals in 1066 were not the same thing, in absolute value, in 1266. Such nonnegotiable oaths were one reason why kings were always short of money and therefore worked so hard to encourage the growth of towns, where the culture was based on the idea of change. A serf could flee his landlord and become a free citizen. A simple laborer could rise to become a master craftsman or (rarely) a great merchant. An educated boy of low birth could become a civic official or even enter the royal government. A simple shop girl could end up as the owner of her own business. Change was the order of the day, and change allowed people to prosper.

But townsfolk did not endorse every type of change. The main functions of the guild system were to control all aspects of industrial production, prices, costs, and wages. Cities were quick to zone themselves into discrete neighborhoods: Slaughterhouses and butcher shops, for example, tended to be concentrated in a single area of each city; textile weavers had neighborhoods of their own; most Mediterranean cities had their own "Genoese Street" where the residing merchants from Genoa lived; Jews in every city had their own segregated district. German cities like Cologne passed laws defining what sort of clothes one could wear, depending on one's income level and not just on the basis of what one's trade or profession was. Much of this sort of clustering and tagging came from the natural desire of people to be around people like themselves, but some resulted from civic action. The forced concentration of butcheries into certain areas of a city, for example, helped to contain animal smell and waste. Establishing discrete zones or streets for the shops of spice merchants made it easier for buyers to compare prices and quality and for tax collectors to gather their revenues. Laws set standard days and times for different types of activities. Social codes regulated the interaction of ethnic and religious groups. Cities, in sum, were not oases of free movement and action, but they did possess a significantly higher degree of fluidity than the countryside.

Since they lived and died by trade, cities jealously guarded their commercial rights and property. Especially in the Mediterranean, cities were willing to go to war with one another in order to protect their trade networks—consider Venice's redirection of the Fourth Crusade to Zara, for example. Milan, Florence, Bologna, Siena, Pisa, and Genoa seem almost always to have been in conflict with one another or else engaged in vicious factional struggles. Merchants and merchants' companies in England, along the Seine and Rhine river valleys, and across the Baltic coast regularly fought with one another in the courts and in the streets to secure their access to markets. The importance of property can be seen in the number of municipal laws that detailed property rights. Crimes against property were not taken lightly. In some Flemish towns, for example, thieves were punished by having their ears nailed to the wheel of a cart, which was then rolled through the streets. In Strasbourg thieves were occasionally thrown into the sewer.

German cities were unique. Most of the larger towns became established as self-governing bodies in the twelfth century, and especially in the eastern reaches, they were often built from a plan, unlike the helter-skelter accumulation of buildings in most cities elsewhere; they were laid out with streets on a gridiron pattern that made the movement of goods easier. German cities also cooperated with one another to an unusual degree. They organized themselves into leagues and their merchants worked together as a kind of super-corporation. The most famous of these were the *Hanse* and the *Swabian League*. The Hanse was a cooperative venture centered on the Baltic city of Lübeck; its merchants operated as a cartel, owning commercial rights and trade routes throughout the Baltic Sea and beyond. By the end of the thirteenth century the Hanse had offices and warehouses in over one hundred and fifty cities—from London in the west to Novgorod in the east.

Most medieval cities were formed, from a bird's-eye perspective, of an expanding series of concentric circles, with each walled section representing a phase in a city's growth. At the center of each city lay the cathedral and the main market square. The city hall, clock tower, and main guild halls stood nearby. Narrow, twisting streets angled off from the city center in no organized way and were lined with shops. Shops tended to be clustered together by type, as mentioned above, and one can still find in European cities streets named for the commodity sold along it in the Middle Ages. Grouping businesses in this way made a certain sense. One always knew where to find a bakery, for example, in a strange city—one simply asked for directions to Baker Street.[9] Shops were marked by street signs whose image identified the type of shop: An apothecary shop, for example, usually bore a sign with a mortar and pestle. There was no point in writing "Apothecary Shop" on a sign: Too many people were illiterate and would not be able to read it. One frequently had to step down from street level in order to enter a shop, since town roads were usually kept in repair simply by adding a new surface on top of the old one. Urban homes were built above shops. These were usually of two or three rooms; as in the countryside, people slept together for warmth. In Geoffrey Chaucer's *Reeve's Tale*, the main character—a miller from Trumpington, near Cambridge—slept in bed with his wife, grown daughter, baby granddaughter, and two university undergraduates who rented from him. (You can probably supply the rest of the plot yourself.)

Medieval cities could be foul places. The only way to get rid of human waste was to dump it into the street.[10] Refuse from the shops was thrown there, too: spoiled vegetables, fish entrails, chicken feathers, sawdust from carpenters' shops, dyes from textile shops, ashes from metalworkers' furnaces. Street sweepers worked at night, sweeping all the waste into a channel cut into the center of the street, through which a stream of water ran. Only the largest of cities had sewer systems

---

9. The city of Montpellier, for example, was divided into a handful of trade neighborhoods: Some of these were the neighborhoods of *Corraterie, Draperie, Flocaria, Fustaria, Herberie,* representing respectively the leatherworkers', drapers', wool-weavers', wood-carvers', and produce merchants' districts.

10. Louis IX of France once had the contents of a chamberpot poured on his head as he strolled through Paris early one morning. He stormed to the door of the house and demanded to know who had done it. It turned out that the guilty person was a university student who had risen early in order to study. Louis was so impressed by the young man's dedication that he gave him a scholarship. (This is not recommended as a way of financing a college education.)

which emptied into rivers. In England, charcoal dust was often scattered in the streets, then swept up; it absorbed some of the ever-present odors. Without modern streetlights, and with houses stretching out over the confines of the shops underneath them, cities were pitch dark at night and therefore unsafe. Most cities had organized night patrols by the thirteenth century—the precursors of modern police forces—but they supplied only the slightest check on crime. Most towns therefore imposed strict curfews and forbade people to be out after nine o'clock; anyone caught violating the curfew was usually assumed to be a thief or, if a woman, a prostitute, and was subject to arrest.[11]

Although they were increasingly crowded, most medieval cities still had ample open space, either in the form of public squares and parks or bits of garden behind individual shops and houses. The gardens had practical as well as aesthetic value: A city besieged by an enemy army had to be able to produce at least a modicum of food to help it survive. Some cropland therefore existed within most city walls, and animals were pastured in the open areas behind homes. As pork became more common to medieval diets, most cities had substantial pig populations.[12] (Pigs were also useful as primitive sanitation workers, since they ate much of the food scraps and refuse otherwise hurled into the streets.) Open spaces also provided areas for children to play. It is true that under the apprentice system, childhood ended sooner in the Middle Ages than it does today, but medieval children did indeed have childhoods filled with games, toys, silly songs, and all the traumas of playground power politics. By the start of the thirteenth century, urban Europe even had access to popular books on child care written for worried parents. The homes these children lived in were simple and noisy, placed as they were immediately above shops and busy streets, but they could be rather grand in the case of a successful merchant. In 1308 a carpenter in London contracted to build a house for a fur merchant to the following specifications:

> a hall and a room with a chimney, with a pantry between them; also a sunroom above the said room and pantry. A window [will be installed] at one end of the hall, above the sitting-bench, as will a set of steps and porch leading from ground level to the floor level of the said hall. [Also to be built are:] two enclosed cellar rooms underneath the hall and situated at either end of it; an additional cellar space to be used as a sewer, which will contain two pipes connecting it to the city sewer; a stable twelve feet in width between the hall and the kitchen, with a sunroom above, and with an attic built atop that room.

---

11. The *curfew* itself was a medieval invention. The word is of Old French origin (*coevure fu*) and means "to cover a fire." It signaled the hour, usually between eight and nine o'clock, at which all home fires were to be extinguished. Cities were thus thrown into a complete, almost eerie, darkness until sunrise, and it made them dangerous places indeed.

12. Pork meat was usually salt-cured or smoked to preserve it, or ground into sausages. Suspicions about the quality of sausages were rampant. Jacques de Vitry, a Dominican preacher of the thirteenth century, writing in his handbook on how to deliver a successful sermon, recommended the use of a joke as a surefire way to win an audience. His example: A certain Parisian was talking to his butcher one day and tried to persuade him that, as a good and loyal customer for the last seven years, he should be entitled to pay less for the shop's sausages. The butcher replied: "Seven years? And you're still alive?"

At the end of this sunroom another kitchen with a chimney [is to be built], and there will be a windowed sitting room at least eight feet in length adjacent to the hall.

Parish churches were everywhere. In Paris alone there were over one hundred and sixty by the 1270s; London had approximately the same number.[13] In most towns, churches were often only a few streets apart. Most were small neighborhood churches, and not all were permanently staffed; but the buildings were there for people to use. Local residents could stop in for a moment of prayer while going about their daily business. These churches were mostly unadorned except for wall paintings, since portable items were vulnerable to theft. Neighborhoods tended to take their names from their churches. Thus *St. Mary's* in Munich referred both to a specific church and the section of the city it served. Urban sports teams frequently organized themselves along the same lines. Cemeteries were initially placed well outside the walls, but urban expansion by 1300 had progressed to such an extent that most of the largest cities in Europe had at least one, and usually more than one, cemetery within their confines, and they raised serious public health concerns.

The fluidity of their populations and the constant arrival of new immigrants gave medieval cities much of their lively strength and resilience, but during times of economic downturn the same features could create an atmosphere of hostility and suspicion. In most cases this atmosphere resolved itself in localized altercations of shopkeepers and tenants against particular individuals or groups suspected of causing trouble or of profiting from the temporary bad times. Exorbitant interest rates or a run of defaulted loans, for example, could trigger outbursts of violence against foreign moneylenders: Flemings, northern Italians, and Jews of any provenance were the most likely targets of this sort of attack since they were the groups most commonly associated with commercial finance. But as cities grew beyond their means with immigrants from the countryside, urban society began to dissociate the established urbanites from the parvenus. Many cities began to redivide by social class and economic distinction, with wealthy enclaves being established (often with protective walls, gates, and armed guards) to separate the merchant elite and urban patriciate from the toiling masses. In times of particular crisis, charismatic opportunists and fiery ideologues could rise up from the crowd and vow to lead them in revolt against the foreigners and elites who were living off their labor. Here is one example of a populist tyrant from Forli, a small town in the Papal State, who seized power by appealing to the urban crowd to overthrow their traditional rulers (in this case, members of the Church) and to seize the government for themselves:

> In the Romagna district at this time [the early fourteenth century] there was an impious dog of a Patarine who rebelled against the Holy Mother Church [which held overlordship over the town]. . . . His name was Francesco Ordelaffi

---

13. For comparison, London had approximately ten times as many drinking establishments.

and he was a despicable character, a mortal enemy of all priests. . . . He was a faithless and stubborn tyrant who, when he heard the church bells ringing on the occasion of his excommunication [by the priests of Forli], ordered other bells to be rung while he pronounced his own excommunication upon the Pope Himself and all His cardinals. Worse still, he set afire straw effigies of them in the marketsquare. . . .

Here is how he treated the priests: The bishop, once he had pronounced Francesco's excommunication and had been outrageously insulted in return, stayed absolutely away from the city; but this freed Francesco to force most of the remaining clergy to celebrate a Mass even despite the interdict that had been placed on the town. No fewer than fourteen clerics—seven monks and seven priests—were martyred, for Francesco ordered the first group hanged by the neck and the second group flayed alive [once their Mass was completed].

Nevertheless it must be said that he was absolutely devoted to the people of Forli and was much loved by them. He made a show of tremendous philanthropy, found husbands for many orphaned girls and found employment for countless others, and together with his friends provided for all the poor. . . .

Such occurrences of tyranny were rare during the thirteenth century but became all too frequent during the calamities of the fourteenth.

Most cities had their own distinct Jewish quarters. Jews lived and had their shops in these districts, although they could move freely through the city in order to conduct their business. These districts were more than mere neighborhoods; they were mostly autonomous legal entities that governed themselves, collected their own taxes and fees, ran their own courts, and maintained their own buildings. In some cities the Jewish quarters were actually encircled by their own protective walls; the local rabbi held the key to the gate. The quarters needed the walls and locked gates, frankly, for anti-Semitic violence was common. The Church's position regarding the Jews had not changed from earlier centuries: Jews were to be treated with fairness, and it was in fact the special responsibility of the Church to protect them against popular prejudice and violence. As summarized by Pope Innocent III in 1199:

No Christian may use violence in order to force a Jew to receive baptism . . . for no one who has not willingly sought baptism can be a true Christian. Therefore let no Christian do a Jew any personal injury—except in the case of carrying out the just sentence of a judge—or deprive him of his property, or transgress the rights and privileges traditionally awarded to them. Let no one disturb the celebration of their festivals by beating them with clubs and hurling stones at them; let no one force from them any services which they are not traditionally bound to render; and we expressly forbid anyone . . . to deface or violate their cemeteries, or to extort money from them by threats of doing so.

But such a declaration was itself a recognition that those things occurred. Nor were Jewish sufferings always the spontaneous result of temporarily uncontrollable mob passions. Institutionalized anti-Semitism existed as well. In the city of Toulouse, for example, a representative of the large Jewish community was legally required to go

The Gothic cathedral at Strasbourg includes this portal sculpture of
"Synagoga," a personification of Judaism that frequently appeared in
the twelfth and thirteenth centuries. She is blindfolded, her body is
twisted unnaturally, and the staff she carries (now partially missing) is
broken. She provides a counterpoint-in-defeat to the triumphant figure of
"Ecclesia," the personification of Christianity, who is unfailingly clear-eyed,
ramrod straight, with a powerful staff and a victorious aspect.
Source: Foto Marburg / Art Resource, NY

to the cathedral every year on Good Friday in order to be publicly slapped in the
face by the bishop. In Béziers city dwellers had the right—which they jealously
guarded as long as they could—to stone Jewish homes during Holy Week. Alfonso
X of Castile (r. 1252–1284) wrote in his vast legal code called the *Siete Partidas* ("The
Seven Categories") that whereas "a synagogue is a place where God's name is

praised" and therefore no Christian may "deface one, steal anything from one . . . bring animals into one, loiter in one, or in any way try to prevent the Jews from performing their devotions in one," still Jews were forbidden to speak against Christianity in any way or even to appear in public on Good Friday. Moreover, Jews who had sexual relations with Christians were to be put to death, as were Christians who converted to Judaism.

Within the constraints placed on them by Christian society and their own Talmudic law, medieval Jews had exceptionally vital and cosmopolitan lives. A twelfth-century Jewish traveler named Benjamin of Tudela wrote a memoir of a journey he made from central Spain to the Holy Land and back again, in which he celebrates the sprawl of thriving Jewish communities he encountered, while lamenting the agonies of anti-Semitism he also discovered along the way. His book, called the *Itinerary*, is a remarkable document that provides us with detailed information about Jewish communities of all sizes and their rabbinical leadership. He records, for example, that the Jews of Narbonne numbered approximately four hundred and were divided into three synagogues. The chief local rabbi, Kalonymos, proudly owned heritable property awarded to his family in perpetuity by the city rulers themselves in recognition of the Jews' importance to civic life. Long a center of learning, Jewish Narbonne boasted of an organized network of schools that guided study for the devout from childhood through advanced age; some classrooms were attached to the synagogues themselves, others were found in the teachers' own homes. One school, dedicated especially to educating Jews from outside Narbonne proper, neighbored the viscount's own urban palace.

Benjamin's *Itinerary* was not a unique book, however. Many Jewish travelers composed memoirs or travelogues. These texts are not well known since they were intended for Jewish audiences and were consequently written in Hebrew; they were in other words cautionary texts warning merchants of the dangers lurking throughout Christendom, and few of them have been translated into English.[14] But they also extolled places and individuals of tolerance and peace.

One observation driven home by such travelogues and other texts is the cultural rift that differentiated northern Ashkenazic Jews and southern Sephardic Jews. This rift—really better described as separate lines of development—began in the late Carolingian era but became pronounced in the late eleventh and early twelfth centuries. The northern Jews, who had been invited into the Rhineland and other areas by Carolingian promises of tax benefits and legal protections in return for their financial expertise and commercial contacts, had been widely resented by the locals from the moment of their arrival as privileged outsiders given almost exclusive rights to earn comfortable livings off the labors of the Christian poor. Surrounded by hostility and living at such a remove from the rest of the Jewish world,

---

14.   Petahiah of Regensburg, from twelfth-century Germany, would be another example. His *Tour* has never been translated. For the original Hebrew, see *Sibbuv R. Petachiah*, ed. Ludwig Grünhut (Frankfurt am Main, 1905).

Ashkenazic Jews in the twelfth and thirteenth century developed a brilliant but inward intellectual culture based on biblical exegesis and legal study. Their liturgical poetry, much of it staid and powerful, reveals a persistent emphasis on exile and martyrdom that is understandable given their predicament, but which heightened their isolation and their predilection for living apart from the urban majority. Northern Jewish intellectual life focused strongly on the study of the *Talmud* and showed little interest in secular topics or in developments from non-Jewish society. Considering the cruelty visited upon them with the preaching of every crusade, it is small wonder that they turned so energetically inward and embraced conservative tradition.

The southern Jews, or Sephardim, had more liberal lives and were open to all the influences of the Mediterranean. On the whole they fared better with their non-Jewish neighbors than did the Ashkenazim, but it would be a mistake to picture them enjoying lives of tolerated ease. The Jewish quarters of southern cities were usually less segregated than their northern counterparts; they existed more often as zones of legal jurisdiction than as walled-off and gated enclosures. Jews moved freely through the south—though seldom alone if they could manage it, for safety's sake—and non-Jews passed through and did business in Jewish *calls* (as many of these districts were named). Many local governments passed laws restricting or even forbidding Christian interactions with Jews, as did the local churches, but people ignored these strictures whenever it pleased them: Christians and Jews frequently entered into business partnerships, consulted each others' physicians and jurists, played together as children, shopped in each others' markets, and studied each others' writings. Indeed one of the chief hallmarks of Sephardic cultural life was its involvement in the intellectual and artistic developments taking place throughout the Mediterranean. The Sephardim excelled in lyric poetry, music, mathematics, medicine, and philosophy.

The greatest Jewish scholar of the Middle Ages, Moses ben Maimon (1135–1204, known in the west as Maimonides), came from an eminent family of scholars, rabbis, and judges in Seville, but he had to flee central Spain after the arrival of the Almohads. He traveled throughout the Mediterranean before finally settling in Cairo and setting to work on his extraordinarily voluminous writings, which range from biblical exegesis to legal study, science, medicine, and philosophy, all of which betray his familiarity with developments in the Christian and Islamic schools of the time. His *Letter to Yemen*, written in 1172, includes a brief biographical introduction.

> I am a simple scholar from Spain whose former high station has been brought low by exile. For even though I have always dedicated myself to studying the commandments of the Lord I have failed to attain the great learning possessed by my ancestors. Evil times and suffering have overtaken my family and we have not been able to live in peace. We have had much labor but little rest—and how could I study the *Torah* when I was constantly being expelled from city after city and country after country? Nevertheless I tried to follow in the paths of

A page from the Mishneh Torah, *the massively learned compilation of Jewish law by R. Moses ben Maimon (Maimonides), the greatest Jewish scholar of the Middle Ages. This fourteenth-century copy includes a miniature portrait of Maimonides (center). Source: Giraudon / Art Resource, NY*

those who have reaped before me, picking up whatever grains of learning I could, whether ripe and plump or withered and decayed. Only now I have found a place of refuge.

From that refuge Maimonides produced a dazzling amount of scholarship, the most significant being the *Mishneh Torah* (a vast compilation of Jewish law with commentary), the *Guide for the Perplexed* (an analysis of the relationship between reason and faith, focusing especially upon the contrast between the God of the Hebrew Scriptures and the understanding of the divine power as known to the pagan Greeks), and the *Book of Commandments* (his effort to enumerate the traditional 613 commandments given to mankind by God). Maimonides wrote almost all his works in Arabic (only the *Mishneh Torah* was composed in Hebrew, among his major works), and his use of Arabic reflects the Sephardic openness to non-Jewish culture—after all, he had learned most of his philosophy by reading the works of the Greeks as prepared by their Arabic commentators—and the general preeminence of Arabic philosophy and science prior to the establishment of the Latin universities.

To sum up the character of medieval cities, they were boisterous places indeed, with all the admirable and regrettable qualities that spring from boisterousness. Despite their shortcomings, cities remained popular places; as the Middle Ages progressed, the migration of country dwellers consistently picked up pace. Cities offered higher degrees of legal and social freedom, a chance to learn a trade and make money, a means to an education, and a vibrant religious and cultural life. Their popular appeal was, if anything, too great for their own good, since the mass movement of people into cities inadvertently created some of the conditions that would make the catastrophes of the fourteenth century possible.

THE QUESTION OF LITERACY

The question of popular literacy in the Middle Ages is a difficult one to answer since there is no clear way of studying it. The mere existence of written materials from any time period, even the vastly increased existence of them hardly proves anything. What does it mean to be literate, anyway? Is a society a literate one if it *can* read, but *doesn't*?[15] These questions become even more difficult when we turn to the past. Medieval people are frequently described in legal documents as being either *literatus* or *illiteratus*, and *sciens* or *idiota* (meaning "literate," "illiterate," "knowledgeable," and "uneducated," respectively)—but it is unclear whether these terms refer to the ability to read, the ability to read *and* write, the ability to read and/or write *in Latin* as well as the vernacular, or the ability to read and/or write *in only the vernacular*. Sometimes the documents appear to describe the ability to *speak* Latin without suggesting anything at all about the ability to read it or write it. At other times the terms appear to describe the extent of a person's formal education—whether or not someone has attended a university or not, or has completed a degree or not—rather than the person's capabilities vis-à-vis a written page of text. For all these reasons, medieval literacy remains a particularly difficult issue to study.

The best answer to the question of how widespread literacy was, is probably "Further than most people think prior to studying the Middle Ages, and less than

---

15.   In the United States today, for example, books are available in enormous quantities in libraries and bookstores everywhere, yet only 2 percent of all adult Americans read books with any degree of regularity; moreover, one-third of the children in the United States are raised in homes that do not have books, and video stores outnumber bookstores and public libraries by quite a high degree.

most people think after studying them for a while." Certainly in the early medieval centuries—that is, in the era of the pre-Carolingian Germanic kingdoms—the ability to read was seldom to be found; hardly anyone who was not a monk could read—and few enough of the monks could. The Carolingian Renaissance marked an important turning point, but less in terms of the number of literate people than in the simple standardization of monastic curricula, the preservation and circulation of texts, and the regularization of orthography. These developments provided a firm basis for later advances in literacy. Most peasants continued to be illiterate until the thirteenth century, and to have a shaky speaking knowledge of Latin. They of course spoke their vernaculars in day-to-day living, and probably knew only enough Latin to follow what the priest was saying during the Mass and to recite their prayers and creeds (the priests' sermons were invariably delivered in the vernacular). The rise of peasant freeholding in the twelfth century probably did the most to extend peasant literacy; since their freedom depended on written privileges and deeds, it was very much in their interest to be able to know what the documents said. But this was a very limited reading ability. Chances are that no more than a handful of peasants in any given rural village could read. Peasants certainly understood the significance of written texts and recognized their authoritative value, but the actual ability to read them probably eluded most rural folks until well into the thirteenth century.

The cities were a different matter. Conducting most business, and certainly anything involved with long-distance trade and credit, was virtually impossible without knowing how to read and write. The rise of urban schools, and the great number of itinerant scholars who hired themselves out as tutors, gives clear evidence of increased literacy. Giovanni Villani, the chronicler of fourteenth-century Florence, proudly notes that his city has six municipally run schools that excel in teaching reading and basic mathematics and that they have an average of eight to ten thousand students enrolled in them annually. Merchant guilds frequently stipulated that a school diploma and a proven capacity to read, write, and perform mathematical calculations in Latin were prerequisites for membership. Merchants, financiers, and city councilmen in northern cities like Hamburg and Munich frequently established scholarships for local youths to ensure their university education. By the thirteenth century, it seems safe to suggest that at least ten percent of the adult urban populace throughout Europe could read and write well, and could do so in both Latin and the vernacular, and that another ten percent could probably read and write at a very basic level. But some parts of Europe had better-educated populations than others. England and the Crown of Aragon seem to have had the highest literacy levels among large states in absolute numbers, although smaller polities like Venice and Bruges probably surpassed them proportionally. Roughly half of all German city councilors had some degree of university education by the early fourteenth century, yet it was not uncommon to find urban councils and courts in which the only literate magistrate was the scribe who wrote up the council's actions. Records have been found from thirteenth-century Sicily, for example, in which court proceedings were dated to the wrong year, under the reign of the wrong king, under the auspices of illiterate judges, performed by *idiotae* lawyers, and attested to by witnesses who could not sign their names to the settlements they were witnessing—all in the same document. Among women, few at the artisanal level knew how to read beyond an elementary level, but the wives and daughters of merchants were often very well educated in areas like literature and music, and were comfortable reading in either Latin or their vernacular tongue. Some schooling in letters was available for women who could afford it at abbey schools run by Poor Clares, the female wing of the Franciscan Order, at some beguinages, and in some hospices (most notably those run by Cathar heretics in areas around Toulouse). Medieval universities, of course, were all-male enclaves that excluded women from higher learning.

At the twelfth- and thirteenth-century medieval zenith, in other words, Latin Europe was decidedly a text-based society, one in which the written word became authoritative, and it was well on its way to becoming a truly literate society as well. If not everyone knew how to read, most at least valued the ability and envied those who had it.

Sex and the City (and the Town, and the Village)

But everyone knew about sex. The Church talked about it incessantly; poets sang about it; physicians wrote about it and prescribed all manner of ways to do it. Prostitutes made it available in every city, town, and village. And anyone who has ever spent time working on a farm knows that sex is everywhere every day.

Medieval people were less prudish about sex than we usually think. It is true that the Church tried hard to promote chastity as the ideal that all Christians should strive for, whether they were married or not, and that it fulminated loudly and often against the sins of the flesh. Legal systems and social codes also strove to control sexual behavior—less so, perhaps, for moral reasons than for practical ones such as concerns over inheritances, property interests, household organization, social status, and public health, all of which were affected by peoples' sexual activity. The dominant, normative ideas about sex and sexuality came of course from the Church. From the time of the Church Fathers on, the dangers of sex were a consistent theme of Sunday sermons, Church decrees, and theological treatises.[16] But there is an irony in this, since Jesus himself said very little about sex, or at least the writers of the Gospels felt that his teachings on sex were not of sufficient import to

---

16.   A Carolingian bishop in Orléans was once asked by a parishioner when he and his wife should absolutely abstain from sexual intercourse in order to remain in a state of spiritual grace. The bishop suggested a moratorium on sex *at least* on every Sunday, Wednesday, and Friday; on every five-day stretch prior to the couple's receiving of communion; on the eve of all the major feasts of the ecclesiastical year (and then on the feast days themselves, naturally); throughout the eight-day vigil prior to Pentecost; and throughout the entire forty-day seasons of Advent and Lent. In addition, intercourse was to be avoided during the wife's menstrual period. This meant abstaining from sexual activity between 200 and 250 days of each calendar year. We do not know the parishioner's response.

write down in great number. The Gospels do quote him saying that celibacy is a gift from God and that whoever can receive this gift should do so. But it was far from clear whether a statement like that necessarily meant that all sex is intrinsically evil, or that any particular type of sexual activity was more or less pleasing in God's eyes than another. Jesus may have lived an abstinent life—but did that mean that those who believed in him had to do the same? His own chosen favorites, the twelve apostles, were not universally sexless. St. Peter himself had a wife.[17]

The simple truth is that most of the sexual morals associated with early and medieval Christianity were pagan in origin.[18] Christianity simply adapted itself to a set of cultural ethics already in place, and it was able to do so precisely because Jesus seems not to have considered the issue to be all that significant. He appears to have had more important things on his mind (such as money: He comments more directly on money than on any other aspect of daily human life). From where, then, did the western European emphasis on virginity, married heterosexual intercourse, the avoidance of masturbation, the disapproval of homosexual activity, the horror of prostitution, and the danger of sexual profligacy come? The answer is: the pagan Romans and the pre-Christian Germans. Despite the well-known stories of orgies at the imperial court and the supposedly Olympian sexual appetites of rulers like Tiberius, Caligula, and Nero—not to mention some of their wives and daughters— the Roman world was actually renowned for its sexual modesty. That, in fact, is why some of their writers paid so much attention to the sexual exploits of the ruling class: The rulers' actions were completely out of step with the values of the common culture. The early Germans brought with them into western Europe a near mania about controlling sex. Their societies placed high premiums on modesty and virginity, strict heterosexuality, and married fidelity (although they did allow for the practice of concubinage, but largely to keep in check the dangerous predilection for promiscuity). Certain circles in Roman society allowed for some types of homosexuality, but the culture on the whole disapproved of it. Early Germanic laws are unforgiving on the subject.

Church doctrine about sexual matters began to coalesce during the fourth and fifth centuries—precisely during the period when the Roman, Germanic, and Christian cultures confronted one another en masse. The very general principles laid out in the Gospels easily accorded with the detailed Roman and Germanic sexual codes, and Christian teaching became far more specific in regard to what it approved of and what it condemned. But then as now, there was always a difference between what the Church preached and the State proclaimed, and what people actually did. The history of sex cannot be written from the law codes alone. But since medieval people did not leave diaries filled with intimate details of their sexual

---

17. Matthew 8:14–15 describes Jesus healing Peter's mother-in-law of a fever.
18. Consider the cases of St. Jerome and St. Augustine, two of the principal architects of the Christian code of sexual ethics: Both of them were horrified by and disgusted with their own sexual profligacy *before* they became Christians. They then simply cast a Christian veneer onto their preexisting system of values.

lives for us to read—out of scholarly interest alone, of course—we must try to reconstruct those lives from whatever material is at hand.

Medical writings provide one viewpoint, and in fact a rather consistent one. Whether the writer was an early female physician like the "Trotula" author or a later male one like Arnau de Vilanova (d. 1311), moderate sexual activity was regarded as a boon to health for both men and women, but excessive activity was deemed dangerous. Sex literally drained the body not only of reproductive fluids but also of the fundamental humors that comprise our very being. Physicians warned especially against the harmful effects this draining had on men; since women received the fluids that men expended in sex, they were invigorated by the activity. A sexually voracious woman, it was widely believed, could literally drain the life out of a man, given enough time. On the other hand, the fundamental danger presented to women was the pregnancy that resulted from sex. Giving birth was an absolutely life-risking experience. Since women in the Middle Ages often married soon after they reached puberty, it was common that a woman's first experience of pregnancy and childbirth occurred when she was only fifteen or sixteen. The strain of childbirth on a body that was itself often still a child's had the expected result: a high mortality rate. It has been estimated that as many as one out of every three medieval women died in their first childbirthing.[19] The children fared little better: As many as one out of every four children died before their first birthday.

Medical writings often describe methods of contraception, but they could only *describe* them, since recommending them would violate the teachings of the Church. The most common method was *coitus interruptus*,[20] but other methods included primitive cervical caps made from clumps of wool or cotton soaked in honey, condoms made from animal tissue, and herbal formulas designed to prevent the implantation of a fertilized egg into the uterus.

Sexual activity was ideally confined to husbands and wives, but not exclusively. Concubinage remained widespread and legal into the tenth century and was not uncommon into the eleventh. Prostitution provided another avenue for sex, especially after the urban revolution of the eleventh and twelfth centuries. Medieval society had complicated attitudes about prostitution; they hardly approved of the practice from a moral point of view, but their moral view had little to do with the notion of sex per se. What they feared above all about prostitution, apart from the spread of certain diseases, was its likelihood to result in miscegenation—the mixing of the races. The children borne by prostitutes had unknown fathers, so it was impossible to know for certain the ethnicity of anyone. As prostitution flourished in the cities, the problem grew apace. If you were a decent hard-working merchant in Bremen, there was no way to know for sure if the decent-looking civic

---

19. Those who survived tended, not surprisingly, to be physically vigorous enough to repeat the process. Ample evidence exists of women of all classes giving birth to ten or more children in the course of a lifetime; but these were the survivors. In general, mortality rates for both the mothers and their offspring increased the further north one looked.
20. At last, a piece of Latin I don't have to translate for you!

official who asked for your daughter's hand in marriage did not have, somewhere in his genetic background, a trace of peasant blood, or a criminal's blood, or Jewish blood, or the blood of a leper. This question of paternity is why cities tried hard to regulate prostitution: Some, for example, established separate prostitution houses for the use of different ethnic, religious, and social groups. As a public health measure, there were always separate prostitution houses for lepers (the women who worked in them were those who had already contracted leprosy).

In the countryside, absolute chastity prior to marriage was not the norm. One problem in trying to make chastity the norm was the shortage of priests, for even after marriage became a sacrament in 1215, most country-dwellers did not see a priest much more than once a year, and many went many years without seeing one. (The long interdicts frequently imposed on kingdoms by the popes from Innocent III on down did not help matters.) Thus peasant couples commonly lived together for years before marrying and the children they produced were considered legitimate. Even among young women, virginity until marriage was not always absolutely expected; in fact a young woman's having a baby out of wedlock sometimes increased her value on the local marriage market, since it dispelled any doubts about her fertility. And fertility was a widespread concern. Rural society needed lots of children to share the labor, and the high mortality rate of children meant that women had to produce as many children as possible; but apart from the physical hardship of teenage motherhood, the lean diet of most peasants also meant that most would-be mothers did not receive the nutrients they needed in order to be fertile. So-called barren women abounded in the Middle Ages, and diet was the chief factor for most of them.

Male sterility was often considered a spiritual rather than a physical problem, especially when it occurred to a young man. Popular folk beliefs attributed male sterility to spells cast by demons and spirits, and it was treated by counterspells, incantations, and potions. But a man's sterility did not negate his marriage, whereas a woman's barrenness was legal cause for the husband to divorce her. Male impotence was a different matter. A wife could sue for divorce if her mate was impotent—but the courts required proof of his impotence, for which they usually appointed one or two local prostitutes to try to stimulate him into arousal, while a court notary watched.

In the east many people had sexless lives forced upon them. Byzantine and Muslim aristocratic society employed large numbers of eunuchs as personal attendants.[21] The Arabs had no pre-Islamic tradition of utilizing eunuchs, but adopted the practice after taking over the regions of Palestine, Syria, and Persia, where

---

21. Greek and Islamic law distinguished between two types of eunuchs: males who were physically whole but sexually impotent, and males who had been castrated. Castration usually occurred at birth, and was performed intentionally in order to create a class of these preferred servants. Castration was not restricted to slaves. It was frequently performed on the offspring of political enemies—to end a family's claim to a piece of land or to a political office. Ignatios of Constantinople, for example, was the son of the Byzantine emperor Michael I (r. 811–813); he was castrated (at the age of 16) when a palace coup deposed his father. Some parents even had their sons castrated precisely in the hope that they could rise up the social ladder by entering aristocratic or even imperial service. Byzantine law officially forbade this type of castration, but Leo VI (r. 886–912) relaxed the penalty for it to the point that the practice remained common.

eunuchs had played prominent roles in society for many centuries. Muslims generally used eunuchs solely as harem guards and servants. A harem, contrary to notions made popular by Romantic writers and artists in the nineteenth century, was not a hothouse of erotic delights provided by scantily clad sex-slaves; the word meant simply the private area of a home, the part off-limits to visitors. Eunuchs, being incapable of sexual activity, tended to the daily care of the female members of a nobleman's home. Law did not restrict the use of eunuchs to the nobility, and eunuchs were occasionally found in commoners' homes as well, tending to the care of the four wives allowed to a man by Islamic law. Among the Byzantines, however, eunuchs played a wider range of roles and often rose to positions of enormous political and religious importance. The Greeks used eunuchs as personal aides (the word *eunuch* derives from the Greek phrase for "bed maker"), tutors, business managers, political advisors, and spiritual advisors. Justifiably or not, they believed that eunuchs who were well-treated by their employers displayed a higher degree of loyalty than other attendants—presumably because the eunuchs had no families of their own to provide for. Unlike the Latin west, the Orthodox Church had no particular difficulty in accommodating eunuchs. Several monasteries—such as that of St. Lazaros in Constantinople—were founded solely for eunuch-monks, and at least a half-dozen Patriarchs of Constantinople were eunuchs.[22] The Byzantine state likewise opened its doors to talented eunuchs: Justinian I appointed a eunuch named Narses (d. 574) as general of his army; it was Narses who quelled the Nike Rebellion which nearly forced Justinian from office, and who led, along with Belisarius, the reconquest of Ostrogothic Italy. Eunuchs like Eutropius (d. 399), Samonas (d. 908), and John the Orphanotrophos (d. 1048) held a variety of prominent civic positions and served as imperial advisors.[23] The arrival of the Komneni dynasty in the eleventh century and the hard-edged militarism they brought to the empire, however, led to a decline in the use and prominence of eunuchs.

Medieval attitudes toward homosexuality were overwhelmingly negative, although outright persecution of homosexuals was sporadic. Prohibited in the Hebrew Scriptures and by Paul's Letters in the New Testament, homosexual activity was likewise condemned by civil authorities from the time of Theodosius in the fourth century.[24] The *Codex Theodosianus* declared homosexuality punishable by death by sword, and the same penalty was imposed by the *Codex iuris civilis* of Justinian in the sixth century.[25] Not all the western kingdoms forbade sodomy

22. The most notable of these were Germanos I (r. 715–730), Methodios (r. 843–847), Ignatios of Constantinople (r. 847–858, and again 867–877), and Eustratios Garidas (r. 1081–1084). Germanos is a saint in the Orthodox Church; Ignatios is a saint in both the Orthodox and Roman Catholic churches.
23. The term *orphanótrophos* means "director of an orphanage." Orphanages were numerous in the Byzantine empire and under state protection. More than mere group homes, orphanages frequently included schools, hospitals, and elderly hostels as part of their operation.
24. Jesus himself said nothing about homosexuality, according to the Gospels, and in fact said little about any kind of sexual activity at all.
25. These laws did not condemn all forms of homosexual relations; instead they focused on the exclusive enjoyment of the passive role in homosexual intercourse. They also showed a degree of leniency by recognizing the propensity for sexual experimentation by youths under 16.

explicitly, and most of the known cases of prosecution for homosexuality involved prominent individuals for whom there may have been political motivations in their arrest. In other words, people were seldom arrested and punished for homosexuality alone; rather, charges of homosexuality were commonly added to a list of other charges as a final dollop of vitriol. The Church's position was adamant. St. Augustine had declared that "of all the sexual sins, that which is against nature is the worst"; and the eleventh-century reformer Peter Damian dedicated an entire book—the *Liber gomorrhianus*—to describing the horror of homosexual activity among monks. The notion of *plenitudo potestatis* in the post-Reform papacy added to the Church's role in setting norms for sexual behavior, and condemnations of homosexuality were constant and ubiquitous. But just as medieval people commonly ignored or found ways to elude the Church's positions on the use of interest, the setting of prices and wages, and economic interaction with non-Christians, so too did many people find ways around the religious and civil prohibitions of homosexuality. But it is wrong to interpret such maneuvers as signs of tolerance; instead, the willingness to put up with a degree of homosexual presence in society probably meant only that there were other problems confronting the medieval world that were more important.[26]

The Middle Ages was hardly a paradise of carnal delights, but neither was it puritanical in its attitudes or actions. Unless one became a professed cleric vowed to chastity, sex was not something to be denied, squelched, and obliterated from life; it was, however, a powerful, and hence potentially disrupting, force in society. This meant that it needed to be regulated and managed, like everything else in life. But given such regulation, sex was for the most part regarded by society as natural.

Suggesting Reading

Texts

Benjamin of Tudela. *Itinerary.*
Maimonides. *Book of the Commandments.*
———. *Guide for the Perplexed.*
———. *Mishneh Torah.*
Salimbene. *Chronicle.*

---

26. Probably the most famous of homosexual couples in the Latin west were Richard the Lionheart of England and Philip Augustus of France; but not everyone agrees on the nature of their relationship. The only direct evidence of it is this passage from the *History* of Roger of Hovedon:

> Richard, the duke of Aquitaine and the son of the king of England, stayed with King Philip of France, who held him in such esteem that they ate together every day at the same table from the same dish, and at night they did not keep separate beds. [Philip] loved [Richard] as his own soul; in fact the two of them loved each other so much that the king of England [Henry II, Richard's father] was utterly astonished by the passionate attachment between them, and wondered what it might mean."

Villani, Giovanni. *Chronicle.*

Walter of Henley. *On Husbandry.*

Source Anthologies

Amt, Emilie. *Women's Lives in Medieval Europe: A Sourcebook* (1993).

Dean, Trevor. *The Towns of Italy in the Later Middle Ages* (2000).

Harvey, P. D. A. *Manorial Records* (1984).

Lopez, Robert S., and Irving W. Raymond. *Medieval Trade in the Mediterranean World* (1997).

Murray, Jacqueline. *Love, Marriage, and the Family in the Middle Ages: A Reader* (2001).

Studies

Bartlett, Robert. *The Making of Europe: Conquest, Colonization, and Cultural Change, 950–1350* (1993).

Bennett, Judith M. *A Medieval Life: Cecilia Penifader of Brigstock, c. 1295–1344* (1999).

Bizaguet, Armand. *The Dawn of Modern Banking* (1979).

Boswell, John. *Christianity, Social Tolerance, and Homosexuality: Gay People in Western Europe from the Beginning of the Christian Era to the Fourteenth Century* (1980).

———. *The Kindness of Strangers: The Abandonment of Children in Western Europe from Late Antiquity to the Renaissance* (1988).

Brooke, Christopher. *The Medieval Idea of Marriage* (1989).

Brundage, James A. *Law, Sex, and Christian Society in Medieval Europe* (1987).

Burns, Robert I., S. J. *Muslims, Christians, and Jews in Crusader Valencia: Societies in Symbiosis* (1983).

Clanchy, M. T. *From Memory to Written Record: England, 1066–1307* (1993).

Duby, Georges. *Rural Economy and Country Life in the Medieval West* (1968).

———. *The Knight, the Lady, and the Priest: The Making of Modern Marriage in Medieval France* (1983).

Dyer, Christopher. *Standards of Living in the Later Middle Ages: Social Change in England, c. 1200–1520* (1989).

Elliott, Dyan. *Spiritual Marriage: Sexual Abstinence in Medieval Wedlock* (1993).

Epstein, Steven. *Wills and Wealth in Medieval Genoa, 1150–1250* (1984).

Hanawalt, Barbara A. *Growing Up in Medieval London: The Experience of Childhood in History* (1993).

———. *The Ties That Bound: Peasant Families in Medieval England* (1986).

Herlihy, David. *Medieval Households* (1985).

Howell, Martha C. *Women, Productivity, and Patriarchy in Late Medieval Cities* (1986).

Jones, Philip. *The Italian City-State: From Commune to Signoria* (1997).

Karras, Ruth Mazo. *Common Women: Prostitution and Sexuality in Medieval England* (1996).

———. *Sexuality in Medieval Europe: Doing unto Others* (2005).

Liu, Xinru. *Silk and Religion: An Exploration of Material Life and the Thought of People, AD 600–1200* (1999).

Mirrer, Louise. *Women, Jews, and Muslims in the Texts of Reconquest Castile* (1996).

Nirenberg, David. *Communities of Violence: Persecution of Minorities in the Middle Ages* (1996).

Paterson, Linda M. *The World of the Troubadours: Medieval Occitan Society, c. 1100–c. 1300* (1993).

Payer, Pierre J. *The Bridling of Desire: Views of Sex in the Later Middle Ages* (1993).

Piponnier, Françoise, and Perrine Mane. *Dress in the Middle Ages* (1998).

Reyerson, Kathryn L. *Business, Banking, and Finance in Medieval Montpellier* (1985).

Rösener, Werner. *Peasants in the Middle Ages* (1992).

Shahar, Shulamith. *Childhood in the Middle Ages* (1990).

———. *The Fourth Estate: A History of Women in the Middle Ages* (1983).

Swanson, Heather. *Medieval Artisans: An Urban Class in Late Medieval England* (1989).

CHAPTER 16

CHANGES IN RELIGIOUS LIFE

Religious life reached its peak in the thirteenth century. The soaring cathedrals that dominated the landscape were built with passion as well as stone, and the high emotional pitch that attended their construction spilled out into the streets, so to speak, in mass popular processions, in crowds huddled around market-place preachers, and in large-scale pilgrimages to holy sites. Sermons, songs, and popular art celebrated a new emotionalism that emphasized God's mercy; Christ was transformed from the angry judge of earlier centuries into a loving savior still very much at work in the world as evidenced by his continued reappearance in the mystical visions granted to his followers. Most originally of all, Christ's mother Mary came almost to center stage in popular devotion. She had always been a prominent figure in western Christian belief, but until the twelfth century she had never received the attention she had long enjoyed in the Orthodox east. Worshipers made up for this delay by granting Mary a centrality in devotional life that was extraordinary; at times she appeared almost to displace her Son in people's hearts.

One hallmark of late medieval piety was its popular emphasis on *imitatio Christi*, or "the imitation of Christ." By the hundreds of thousands, if not more, pious faithful set out not only to believe in Christ and live by his precepts but actually to emulate his lifestyle. Religious confraternities existed by the handful in almost every city of any size: Guilds practiced congregational worship and organized charity; beguinages bulged with new aspirants; pilgrimage routes swelled with chanting crowds of penitents; and market squares filled with popular preachers calling believers to renounce their sinful lives and take up the cross of reform and salvation. Renouncing their own wealth, property, and position, preachers traveled the city streets and rural countrysides in small groups, evangelizing as much by their example as by their words. The leading Church figures in this movement were the *mendicant orders* that were established by the dozen. The best known, then and now, were the Dominicans and the Franciscans, but the idea they represented proved to be so popular that other groups sprang up so quickly and in such great numbers that the Church finally felt compelled at the Fourth Lateran Council (1215) to forbid the establishment of any new monastic or clerical rules. The movement was in danger of getting out of hand.

What motivated most of these people was the conviction that the Church needed help. Society was developing so quickly, with rising populations everywhere and with demands for spiritual and social services keeping pace, that the Church's resources were stretched thin. Try as it might, it simply could not reach all the people who yearned for spiritual instruction and guidance. The mendicants felt that the Church, in becoming fully established, had also become static, and the *plenitudo* of its *potestatis* left it in the distressing situation of administering the world rather than ministering to it. The mendicants therefore envisioned themselves as itinerant clerics free of the parish church and the remote monastery; they wanted to be churchless servants of the Church, meaning that they wanted to avoid the deepening mundane responsibilities of the other clergy—tasks like tending to the parish church building and schools, overseeing curricula, organizing festivals, raising money for various causes, and all the other things that a parish church did on the days between its Sunday services. The mendicants wanted only to bring the faith to the people, no matter where the people were. Not everyone could attend a parish church with regularity; especially in the countryside where many churches were unstaffed. Must these people be left alone? The mendicants wanted to travel as Christ and his apostles had done, preach as they had done, tend to the sick as they had done. They did not seek to challenge or supplant the established clergy but only to assist them. But as is often the case when people receive assistants they have not requested, friction often arose between the established clerics and the popular new mendicants.

The impetus for these Church changes—a heightened emotionalism, a humanized Christ, a prominent Mary, the *imitatio Christi*, and the rise of the mendicant orders—came from the populace just as the impetus for the Gregorian Reform had done. As medieval confidence and prosperity reached their peak, the faithful poured their spiritual energy into a new theology of love that stressed kindness and mercy, penitence and forgiveness, and the desire to know God better by imitating the life of His Son. As a sign of His approval of this enthusiasm, God rewarded many of those who led the reform with wave after wave of mystical visions that gave the believers a foretaste of the transcendence of paradise. Although always cautious about unchecked popular enthusiasms, the Church responded to popular demands and desires by endorsing the new emphasis of God's mercy to the penitent, by advocating (within limits) the *imitatio Christi*, and by recognizing and encouraging the mendicants. By championing the opening up of the mendicant orders to women, in affiliated orders rather than as an intrinsic part of the main order, the Church provided women with an opportunity to serve as representatives of the Church in the world, and tapped into a long-unused resource of energy, skill, and dedication.

THE IMPORTANCE OF BEING PENITENT

It may seem ironic that this wave of celebrating God's love coincided with a strong new emphasis on penitence. Sermons by parish clergy and mendicant preachers alike called people to sorrowful repentance as often as they urged hearers to rejoice in God's love. Devotions like confession, praying the rosary, and performing the Stations of the Cross became regular features of religious life. But the importance of penitence and the celebration of God's loving-kindness went hand in hand. The widespread popular assumption of the early Middle Ages, as discussed in Chapter 4, was that in all likelihood only professed monks and nuns would receive eternal life since they were the one people who devoted themselves entirely to God; the stern judging Christ of that era demanded no less. This belief had never been an official doctrine of the Church, but since most Churchmen in those centuries were in fact monks, the majority would probably have gone along with the belief. At some point in the "great change" of the tenth and eleventh centuries, however, popular assumptions began to reflect a more optimistic attitude that God will reward all those who strive after good and show genuine remorse for their wrongs. A change in the doctrine of penance clearly had something to do with this shift. Until the late tenth century, penance, frequently in the form of penitential pilgrimage, was a penalty that one paid for sins already committed, but at some point around the turn of the millennium, the notion caught on that one could in fact perform penances as a matter of everyday devotion and spiritual discipline. These did not need to be dramatic actions like mortification of the flesh but could be simple observances like reciting a hundred *Our Fathers* while tending to one's daily affairs or attending an extra Church service. If one's penitential regimen exceeded one's sinfulness, a person could in effect compile a "treasury of merits" that would earn favor in God's eyes.[1] This is one reason for the enormous increase in the popularity of pilgrimage in the eleventh century—a development that led directly into the Crusade movement. After the Early Middle Ages, penance and love became two sides of the same coin. Christians repented their sins because they loved God and wished to please Him; God loved His people and so redeemed those who were penitent.

Among the strongest advocates for penance and the promise of God's forgiveness were the *Dominicans*. Their order was popularly named after its founder, the Castilian cleric Dominic de Guzmán (1170–1221), but it is officially known as the *Order of Preachers*.[2] (To this day a Dominican has the initials *O.P.* after his or her name.) From early in his career, Dominic desired to be more than a neighborhood priest; he wanted to be an evangelist at work in the world. In 1205 he traveled to Rome to request that he be sent as a missionary to the Mongols then advancing westward out of Asia. The pope at that time, Innocent III, had another idea: He charged Dominic to preach to the Cathar heretics in southern France. (The Albigensian Crusade did not begin until 1209.) Dominic took up the task with great zeal. He organized a group of close associates and spent the next decade living among the

---

1. The belief in Purgatory, a sin-cleansing way-station where devout but imperfect souls might be absolved of their guilt and prepared for God's salvation, became a commonplace of Christian devotion at just this time.
2. They were also informally known as the *Black Friars*, in reference to the identifying black cowls they came to wear.

heretics, learning their beliefs and practices, preaching to them, and trying to teach them the falseness of their doctrines. He viewed heresy as an educational problem, not a crisis of Evil Incarnate at work in the world. He was convinced that heresy arose not because human beings are wicked but because they do not receive the religious instruction and pastoral guidance they need, and that most clergy, tied to their heavy parish duties, simply could not devote the time needed to keep the rustic faithful within the Church's fold. Dominic and his followers united a deep spiritual emotion with a highly developed and confident rationalism, confident that the combination of warm heart and engaged intellect would suffice to win back the heretics. As it happened, the Dominicans' earliest efforts earned the respect of some Cathars, but they reconverted few to Catholic orthodoxy.

In 1215 Dominic attended the Fourth Lateran Council in order to have his associates recognized as a formal order within the Church. The Council agreed, and in late 1216 Pope Honorius III signed the charter of the Dominicans' formal establishment. From the start, they were a scholarly preaching and teaching order. They stressed educational training for their members and the conviction that human error arose through ignorance rather than wickedness. Dominicans also embraced the *imitatio Christi* in the sense that they took vows of poverty, but this practice never played as central a role in Dominican thinking or observance as it did in other mendicant groups. As part of their training, all Dominicans were required to master three texts: the Bible, Peter Lombard's *Sentences*, and the *Historia Scholastica* of Peter Comester, all three of which they carried at all times.[3] Ideally, they were to produce these books by their own labor in the *scriptorium*, but as Dominican schools became better established the provincial boards governing the order began to supply them. These three books were the key works needed by an itinerant preacher, they felt, to buttress any exposition of Church doctrine. Dominicans spent the first two years of their training studying the liberal arts, then three years studying science (which they called *natural philosophy*), before moving on to another three years of theological study at a Dominican-associated university such as the University of Paris.

Dominicans usually worked in pairs or small groups as they traveled from village to village. Since they were outside the usual clerical structure of the Church, they were required to seek the permission of the local bishop before beginning their work in a diocese. Once that permission was granted, they went to work preaching to crowds, answering questions and relieving doubts, hearing confessions, and especially debating those with differing or heretical views. Knowledge and rational persuasion, they hoped, when coupled with a modest and pious lifestyle, could do more to keep Christ's flock in line than any number of crusades and episcopal excommunications. Nevertheless, in time it was the Dominican friars who became especially associated with the inquisitions.

---

3. Peter Comester (literally, "Peter the Eater"—in the sense of a devourer of books) was a twelfth-century scholar whose *Historia* was essentially a survey of biblical history. He died in 1178.

The order was popular from the start. Dominic died in 1221, only six years after getting formal recognition for his order, but even by then there were well over five hundred Dominican brethren. Those attracted to the order tended to be people of a scholarly bent, and those with an interest in law were especially prominent. One of these was Ramon de Penyafort, a Catalan canonist who wrote the first constitution for the order and who was perhaps the greatest lawyer of the thirteenth century. The constitution called for almost exclusive attention to study; everything else in Dominican training was to take a backseat. The curricula were carefully devised, with the books to be read, and those to be avoided, figured out in detail. The list of prominent Dominican scholars in the thirteenth century is impressive (Albertus Magnus and St. Thomas Aquinas stand out especially), but the list of their evangelical successes is not. This was not through lack of effort, though. Dominicans marched far and wide, often into openly hostile territory, in order to spread the Word of Christ: into the Baltic regions, the Holy Land, Russia, central and southern Asia, Tibet, Mongolia, and China. They worked tirelessly against both popular heresies like Catharism and against intellectual heresies that popped up in the universities. But the number of their converts, or of reconverts back to orthodoxy, remained small. To many of their critics, the Dominicans' method *was* their message—cold, calm intellectualizing, in an age that was pulsing with emotion. In the thirteenth century, they had a widespread popular reputation for academic dryness: great minds in bloodless bodies, theological bean counters. What else could one expect from a group of lawyers? One of their most vocal detractors, the Catalan physician and religious reformer Arnau de Vilanova (d. 1311), published a series of blistering essays against what he regarded as the incompetence of these "pseudo-religious pseudo-theologians." His rhetoric was over the top, but it reflected a widespread prejudice.

Women were part of the Dominican order almost from the very start. St. Dominic established the first female chapter in 1213 at Prouille in southern France; it was made up in part by noblewomen he had converted from Catharism. Before he died, he had created three more houses in Bologna, Madrid, and Rome. Dominican nuns were not itinerant preachers like the Dominican friars; they remained cloistered but participated in the preaching effort by helping to produce the books used by the brethren. By the 1340s, there were nearly 150 Dominican convents across Latin Europe, and women comprised more than ten percent of the overall order's membership—which by the 1340s was nearly fifteen thousand. There were a handful of attempts in the thirteenth and fourteenth centuries to dissociate the female Dominicans from the male wing of the order since the Dominican *Constitution* stipulated that every convent had to have a company of at least six male brethren residents to supervise the nuns' lives; as the Dominicans rose in social status, and especially as they came to dominate the universities, fewer brothers wanted to settle for the career-ending position of convent supervisor. In the end, however, the authority of St. Dominic's initial desire for the order carried the day.

As the thirteenth century progressed, the Dominicans began to show a decided preference for living in large communities; and since they were also increasingly associated with the universities, this meant that by the 1270s and 1280s their convents were almost exclusively to be found in Europe's largest cities. Many teams of friars continued to work in the countryside, especially as they became involved in the inquisitions, but by 1300 they had become a decidedly urban—almost cosmopolitan— elite order.

THE IMPORTANCE OF BEING POOR

A second popular passion of the age was for what its practitioners called *evangelical poverty*. This differed from regular run-of-the-mill poverty in that it was *chosen*, and was chosen for specifically religious reasons. Many Christians have always had ambivalent feelings about money. Money, if one has it, adds comfort and pleasure to life and enables one to do good works. Yet Jesus himself had shown no personal interest in money and seems to have been content to beg for his food and lodging. On the other hand, he did *say* a lot about money—and most of it was not very sympathetic. The evil of money, in general, is that it binds one's interest to the things of this world, and Jesus preached that the next world, the world of God's kingdom, is the only one that matters. In his most telltale teaching, Jesus instructed the rich young man who had come to him asking what he must do to earn salvation, "Go and sell your possessions and give the money to the poor." When the young man turned dejectedly away, Jesus said to his disciples: "It is easier for a camel to pass through the eye of a needle than for someone rich to enter the kingdom of Heaven" [Matthew 19:21–24].[4] "Get rid of all money," lectured Peter Damian in the eleventh century, "for Christ and money do not go well together in the same place."

Many faithful grew frustrated by the Church's increasing involvement in and concern for money matters. A Church that sought to govern everything needed the resources to do it, and so the Church became increasingly attentive to the raising of clerical taxes, the management of ecclesiastical estates, the administration of parish finances, and the collection of fees for its social services. A popular, yet unfairly easy, joking criticism of the Church's concern for money was a simple anagram that, in Latin, spelled out the phrase "Avarice is the root of all evil."

Radix Omnia Malorum [est] Avaritia.

The Church's teachings about money and its own relationship with money formed the basis of a whole series of crises in the medieval period. In the eleventh century the issue of simony had taken center stage; in the twelfth clerical taxation became the hot-button issue; and in the thirteenth the scholastics' focus on usury and theories of the "just price" were the focal points of thinking about money.

---

4. The image of a camel passing through the eye of a needle is a bizarre one and may have resulted from a simple spelling error. The word for "camel" in biblical Greek is *kámelos*, but the word for "rope" is *kámilos*. It certainly makes more sense to picture someone trying to thread a rope through a needle's eye than to push a camel through one. The expression also appears in Mark 10:25. It is possible therefore that the two Gospel writers—both of whom make frequent mistakes in Greek—just made a spelling error.

By the early thirteenth century, a passionate debate had arisen on the very notion of ecclesiastical wealth. The issue, to some critics, was not the way in which the Church's money was accumulated or the use to which the Church's money was put, but the very existence of such money. If the ideal Christian life was the *imitatio Christi*, how could the Church justify its own constant concern with raising taxes, building cathedrals and palaces, employing armies, managing universities, financing crusades, collecting fees, gathering rents, and running law courts? The very success of the Church in achieving what it regarded as its appropriate role in European life was the problem. This attitude, in part, lay behind the twelfth-century heresies like Waldensianism and Catharism, the conviction that the established Church, perhaps unintentionally but no less definitively, had vitiated its spiritual authority by becoming one of the powers of this world. The Church in the thirteenth century was wealthy and, according to non-heretic reformers, was *ipso facto* spiritually lost, or at the very least in danger of becoming so. The only solution was to revive the idea of Christ's own personal poverty.

To renounce money when one has none is not exactly a great virtue. What drove many of the people who emphasized the importance of poverty was a sense of guilt, or maybe simple dissatisfaction, over their own relatively comfortable position. Most champions of evangelical poverty in the thirteenth and fourteenth centuries that we know anything about were all people who had been born into a certain degree of material and financial comfort; in this sense they were analogous to the middle-class figures who initiated the ascetic and monastic movement in the fourth and fifth centuries. They found ample numbers of followers among the poor who relished the idea that "no kings, no princes, no prelates of the Church and none of the clergy or anyone who has wealth can be saved," but the impetus toward creating a theology of evangelical poverty came first and foremost from those who renounced their own riches. *Imitatio Christi*, if it was to be genuine, meant an absolute commitment to hardship, to poverty and want, that these people of means desired for themselves and believed to be necessary.

The best known of these renouncers was St. Francis of Assisi (1181–1226), the founder of the Franciscan Order—formally the *Order of Friars Minor* (O.F.M.). It is difficult not to feel affection for Francis. He was the son of a well-to-do merchant, and after a carefree youth (and a brief, unremarkable career as a crusader) he experienced an intense religious transformation in his early twenties. He decided to renounce his inheritance and dedicate his life to evangelical poverty and serving the urban poor. His family was alarmed by his odd behavior: He dressed in rags, lived in a rough shack, gave away whatever money or food was given him by sympathetic passersby, tended to a local leper community, prayed and sang hymns constantly. Worse still, he talked to animals: Passersby sometimes overheard him telling flocks of birds in a tree how fortunate they were to be the creations of a loving God and to inhabit His beautiful world. Perhaps Francis was simply practicing for his vocation to come. In 1209, after attending Mass at a small chapel in Assisi, he decided to start preaching to people. Francis was not a priest, however, and needed to get permission before he could deliver sermons, and so he went with about a dozen followers to Rome and presented his case before Innocent III. Innocent was a haughty theocrat and hard-nosed politician but he was also a person of deep piety and he recognized a special quality in Francis. He granted the license to preach and directed Francis to compose a Rule for his new order.

The Franciscan Order was formally established in 1210. Its members dedicated themselves to living the *imitatio Christi*, preaching, and serving the poor. They traveled in pairs, begged for their food, and worked with tireless devotion. Popular response was immediate and overwhelming. People rushed to join the order, and the Franciscans were received with open arms everywhere. By Francis' death in 1226, the Friars Minor had established missions throughout all of Europe, across North Africa, through the Holy Land, and had started to reach far into Asia. It was a Franciscan mission led by Friar John of Pian (Giovanni Piano) that traveled to the court of Ghenghis Khan. Francis himself preached to the Ayyubid sultan in Egypt. Francis was as disorganized a person as one might ever imagine, and for years he avoided writing a Rule for his group; when he did finally produce one it was so vague and shapeless as to be effectively useless. He was not opposed to the life of the mind, but he much preferred the gifts of the heart. His sermons and various other writings—he excelled at poetry—do not dazzle one with ideas and insights, but they reverberate in the heart. His most famous poem is his *Canticle of the Sun*, which loses most of its magic in translation but is still worth a reading.

> *Most High, All Powerful, and Good Lord,*
> > *We give You praise and glory, honor and blessing;*
> > *To You alone do these things belong.*
> > *Not one of us is fit to call on You.*
> *Praise to you, my Lord, for all You have created,*
> > *Above all for Brother Sun*
> > *Who brightens the day and fills it with his light;*
> > *He is so beautiful, so radiant and splendid,*
> > *And speaks to us of you, O Most High.*
> *Praise to you, my Lord, for Sister Moon and the stars;*
> > *You have set them in the heavens—shining, elegant, and lovely.*
> *Praise to you, my Lord, for Brother Wind,*
> > *For air, clouds, fair weather and foul*
> > *Through which you give nourishment to all Creation.*
> *Praise to you, my Lord, for Sister Water.*
> > *So healthful and simple, precious and pure.*
> *Praise to you, my Lord, for Brother Fire*
> > *Through whom You light up the dark;*
> > *He is lovely and joyful, mighty and strong.*
> *Praise to you, my Lord, for our sister, Mother Earth*
> > *Who sustains us and keeps us*

And brings forth fruits, grasses, and bright flowers.
Praise to you, my Lord, for those people who out of love for You
   Offer forgiveness, endure weakness and trouble;
   Bless those who keep Your peace.
   You, Most High, shall give them their crowns.
Praise to you, my Lord, for Sister Death,
   From whom no man escapes.
   Woe to those who die in sinfulness, but blessed are those
   Who give themselves to Your Will.
   Death can do them no harm.
Praise and bless the Lord, and give Him thanks, and serve Him with humility!

Even more than the Dominicans, the Franciscans pledged themselves to lives of simplicity and service; they sought to promote Christ by example rather than argument, to win converts by loving them rather than lecturing them. "Preach the Gospel at all times," wrote Francis in one of his most memorable lines; "when absolutely necessary, use words." If the Dominicans had a collective reputation for braininess, the Franciscans were generally regarded as kindhearted sweet souls—or to their detractors (like the Dominicans themselves) as pious simpletons.[5] The reputations of both orders changed markedly in the fourteenth century.

To the Franciscans, evangelical poverty was their defining characteristic, the emotional rallying post to which they clung for their identity. Francis' Rule and the will he left behind at his death emphasized the need to relinquish all wealth as a spiritual necessity even more than as an institutional policy, for the order was becoming wealthy in spite of itself. People of all walks of life who were in one way or another moved by the good works of the Franciscans made pious bequests to the order, offering them lump sums of money, buildings to use as chapter houses, farmlands, and investment properties. Though they had nowhere near the wealth of monastic orders like the Benedictines or Cistercians, the Franciscans soon found themselves with uncomfortably comfortable incomes. Francis, in his last years, distanced himself from his own order with the lament that he was "Francis, but not a Franciscan." In 1220 he formally resigned his leadership of the group and went off

---

5. Episodes like the following contributed to the Franciscans' reputation for simple-mindedness; it comes from the *Chronicle* of Fr. Giordano Gianni: "In the year of Our Lord 1219 . . . Brother Francis convened a meeting of the [Order] . . . and commissioned brothers to preach in France, Germany, Hungary, Spain, and those regions of Italy into which the friars had not yet penetrated. . . . The German mission was comprised of some sixty friars, led by Brother Giovanni of Parma. When they arrived in Germany, a place whose language they could not speak, they simply answered '*Ja*' whenever anyone asked them if they wanted a place to stay or something to eat or anything else. . . . Since saying this word procured them such kind treatment they decided to answer '*Ja*' to every question put to them. Thus when they were asked if they were heretics who had come to Germany in order to spread the same evils with which they had already infected Lombardy, they answered '*Ja*.' This resulted in [their leaders'] being thrown into prison while the others were stripped of their clothing and forced to stand on village greens while the locals made fun of them. This led the friars to conclude that their efforts in Germany were in vain and so they returned to Italy, where they spread such horrible stories about the Germans that no friars thereafter would travel there except for those who desired martyrdom."

to live once again as a hermit. After his death—which was mourned throughout Europe—the new leaders of the order tried to establish a revised Rule that moderated the anti-wealth austerity that Francis had desired. The new Rule allowed for collective ownership of property by the order itself, but the friars remained individually bound by vows of personal poverty. Many friars rejected this compromise out of hand and insisted that to be a Franciscan meant to obey Francis' desire absolutely and to reject all money and all property, both individually and collectively. These dissenters were voted down, and many broke away from the order and established rival groups that would carry on the mission of evangelical poverty. The most famous of these splinter groups became known as the *Franciscan Spirituals* (or *Spiritual Franciscans*). By the turn of the fourteenth century, they were outspoken critics not only of the main Franciscan order but of the entire Church, mired as it was, they preached, in luxury and dead to spiritual responsibility. Their virulent anticlericalism led to their condemnation as heretics in 1323.

The Franciscan movement remained popular through the rest of the Middle Ages, although it no longer enjoyed the near-exultant popularity of its early years. Franciscans preached widely and effectively; they ran hostels and tended to the poor and sick; they gathered alms to feed the starving. But they also began to assume more staid and traditional roles within the Church: They studied and taught at the universities; they pursued scientific research at aristocratic courts; they built convents and chapter houses; they patronized the arts. They remained a favorite of the town masses, but seldom rose to leadership positions in the Church. It looked briefly as though their stature might change when Honorius IV (r. 1285–1287), the first Franciscan to become pope, ascended to the Holy See, but his pontificate ended quickly.

Like Dominic, St. Francis established an affiliated order of female mendicants. A young woman from Assisi named Clare, the daughter of a wealthy merchant family, came under the spell of Francis' preaching, and in 1212 she organized a group of young women who wanted to devote themselves to pious works. Francis established the women at the nearby church of San Damiani—and hence the women became initially known as *Damianites*, although the sisters soon took the name of *Poor Clares*. Like the male Franciscans, the Poor Clares followed the *imitatio Christi* and advocated evangelical poverty. They did not work in the world, however, and were cloistered like Dominican nuns. The Rule that Clare wrote for her sisterhood was the first female-authored Rule in Christian history. It begins with a recognition of the authorities to whom the sisters are bound.

> The manner of life that Blessed Francis laid down for the Order of the Poor Sisters is as follows: namely to observe the Holy Gospel of Our Lord Jesus Christ by living in complete obedience, without any possessions of one's own, and in perfect chastity.
> I, Clare, the unworthy servant of Christ and the spiritual seedling of Blessed Francis, do swear obedience and reverence to the Lord Pope Innocent [III], all his canonically elected successors, and to the entire Roman Church. Just as I

and my fellow Sisters promised to obey Blessed Francis from the very moment of our conversion, so now do we swear the same inviolable obedience to all his successors.

Moreover, all the Sisters who follow us shall forever be obliged to obey the successors of Blessed Francis and of Sister Clare and all the canonically elected abbesses who succeed her.

The order received formal approval from the papacy in 1258. The Poor Clares were highly respected, and many women joined, but they were never as popular as uncloistered groups like the *beguines* who continued to draw large numbers of recruits. During Clare's lifetime, the nuns at San Damiano refused all gifts and endowments, but later convents received modest awards from benefactors. The Poor Clares, however, did not suffer the painful split in their order that the male branch endured.

THE HUMANIZATION OF CHRIST AND THE CULT OF THE VIRGIN

Among the most interesting developments in lay piety were a sharp change in spiritual style and the popular attitude toward the figures of Christ and his mother Mary. Christ as the stern Judge or the awe-inspiring King of Heaven, the two images of Christ that predominated in early medieval devotion, gradually gave way under lay influence to a kinder, gentler Christ in the twelfth and thirteenth centuries. Increased focus was given to his loving-kindness, his mercy for all believers. Medieval artists still portrayed Christ as an enthroned king—a quick look at the portals of most Romanesque churches will show that—but they began also to present a more humanized figure: one who cared for his followers and healed the sick, one who preached a gospel of love and forgiveness, a devoted son, an inspiring teacher, a suffering man on a cross. These changes did not necessarily entail any new developments in the theology of who Jesus was, but they did reflect a new style of devotion, a new emphasis on the ways in which he was like the rest of humanity. Thus Christ became a more approachable figure. The straight and narrow road to heaven was broadened by this new sort of Christ, and the possibility of salvation was extended to more and more of his flock.

This change did not occur only in representations in art. Medieval sermons also focused increasingly on Christ's humanity; saints' lives described more episodes of saints encountering the tender-hearted Jesus in mystical visions. New devotional rites like the Stations of the Cross—a Lenten service during which believers circulate past paintings and statuary depicting the events of Christ's Passion—focused attention on the human suffering he endured. Even the Mass itself changed. Through the early centuries of the Church, parishioners themselves seldom ate the bread or drank the wine of the Mass; they only witnessed their elevation and transubstantiation into Jesus' body and blood. Usually only the priests conducting the ceremony partook of the sacraments. But by the thirteenth century the common people themselves began to consume them, bringing home the idea that Christ so loves mankind that he makes himself available to all in this most intimately tangible of ways.

These were not subtle changes, nor were they merely an attempt by theologians to make Jesus more likable. This refocusing of his personality was, like the very Church Reform it was a late aspect of, a popular demand. Even when actively developing its notions of papal absolutism and its own universal authority over society, the Church here proved highly responsive to popular concerns and ideals. Behind the humanization of Christ was the same sort of religious enthusiasm, or at least the same degree of enthusiasm, that lay at the root of the crusade movement. In 1233 a mass revival movement known as the *Great Alleluia* arose in Italy, and news of it traveled quickly around Europe. It resembled in some ways the Peace of God gatherings of the tenth and eleventh centuries, but unlike them it was a joyful, even raucous, event celebrating God's love and the near certainty of salvation for those who believe in Him. It was also directed, whether by design or default, by Franciscan preachers. As recorded by the Franciscan chronicler Salimbene de Adam (1221–1289), who witnessed the event when he was twelve:

> 1233 was the year of what later came to be called the "Great Alleluia," a celebration of happiness, joy, thanksgiving, rejoicing, praise, and merrymaking— above all a time of peace and calm, when all weapons were cast aside . . . even the knights and foot soldiers went about singing songs and sacred hymns. This pious spirit ran throughout all the cities of Italy; I myself witnessed [it] in my native city of Parma. . . . Enormous crowds of men, women, boys, and girls flocked to the city from the surrounding villages carrying banners [depicting their local saints] in order to hear our preachers and sing praises to God. They sang, in fact, with "the voice of a God, not of a man" [Acts 12:22] and walked with the air of a man who has been saved. . . . Everyone carried tree branches and lighted candles, and there was preaching morning, noon, and night. . . . The crowds stopped in every church and square, where they lifted their hands to God in praise, and blessed His Name for ever and ever. In fact, they were incapable of stopping their praises, since they were so drunk on God's love. . . . They did everything without anger, discord, quarrel, or bitterness.

What might have triggered such actions? No events of any unique drama or significance that we know of occurred in that year or the one preceding it. It is highly likely, though, that the Alleluia had something to do with the popular assimilation of the great achievements of the Fourth Lateran Council in 1215, and it was almost certainly related to the fast developing canonization movement for St. Francis, who had died in 1226. The Fourth Lateran represented to many the final step in the Church's long road to reform (even though it represented to others, as we have seen, the first step in its decline), and it symbolized the Church Triumphant. In Francis thousands of people had seen a reflection of Christ himself—a gentle, loving, lovable, pious, and absolutely approachable person. The reputed miracle of Francis' receiving the stigmata (the sudden appearance on his body of marks corresponding to the wounds that Christ received on the Cross) only added to the connection. To many, Christ seemed almost to have come yet again, in the person of Francis, to remind his people that he loved them and that heaven awaited them. So they rejoiced.

Closely related to this humanization of Christ, and in fact preceding it by several generations, was a dramatic new emphasis on the role of the Virgin Mary in Christian life. She had been revered as the model of female piety and virginity by the Church at large at least since the late fourth century.[6] But unlike the Greek east, where she was revered as the God-bearer and the Queen of Heaven, Latin Christians in the early medieval centuries did not place any special emphasis on Mary. Local saints were of considerably more significance to them. But starting in the late eleventh century, then picking up momentum throughout the twelfth, and reaching fever pitch in the thirteenth, was a widespread popular cult focused on Mary's direct role in helping one earn salvation. Thousands of churches were named in her honor; countless sermons emphasized her role as a mediator; miracle stories proliferated about her continuing action in this world; sculptors, painters, and mosaicists portrayed the story of her life in loving detail; sea-captains named their ships after her; musicians wrote love songs to her; mystics claimed to have had numberless visions of her and to have spoken directly with her. Not only did Mary appear more frequently in Christian devotion, she appeared in new guises or roles. By the twelfth and thirteenth centuries, she was no longer solely an ideal image of virgin chastity; she was called upon as an intercessor, a healer, the Queen of Heaven, the ideal mother, the steadfast friend, the supreme protector of the sick (especially of women). Summarizing all these new roles, she became to Christians everywhere simply and lovingly "Our Lady." The connection between the reverence for "Our Lady" and the aristocratic courts' chivalric dedication to the "My ladies" of courtly love is obvious.

Signs of Mary's new significance were everywhere: the new devotional practice of the rosary; the proliferation of images of the *Pietà*;[7] feast days in her honor added to the ecclesiastical calendar; the heightened number of references to her in the liturgy. By far the most popular of hymns to Mary was the *Salve Regina*.

> *Hail, Queen and Mother of Mercy;*
> *Hail, our Life, our Comfort, our Hope.*
> *We, Eve's exiled children, call to You;*
> *With sobs and cries we call to You*
> *From this valley of tears.*
> *Come to us now, dear Advocate;*

---

6. It was St. Jerome, especially, who brought Mary permanently to the forefront. A rival writer of the time, named Helvidius, had suggested that Mary, after giving miraculous birth to Jesus, had had a normal (i.e., sexual) marriage with her husband Joseph. This sent Jerome into a ballistic rage and inspired him to write a short but blistering book called *Against Helvidius*. It demolished Helvidius' position, and Mary's perpetual virginity was never questioned thereafter.
7. Literally the "Sorrowful Mother," this is the portrayal of the mourning Mary holding the dead Jesus on her lap. Michelangelo's sculpture of this theme is probably the most familiar.

Turn Your loving eyes upon us now,
And when this, our earthly exile, is over,
Lead us to Jesus, the fruit of Your womb,
Oh kind, Oh pious, Oh sweet Virgin, Oh Mary.

In Castile, Alfonso X spent thirty years supporting the production of a magnificently illustrated work called the *Cantigas de Santa Maria* ("Songs of Holy Mary") that gathered, recorded, and illustrated over four hundred popular songs in her praise. Many of these take the form of psalms and hymns; others are versified miracle stories:

> Let me tell you about a miracle, one that I heard that the Mother of the Most High King performed for an abbess who was utterly devoted to Her. The devil had led this woman into sin and caused her to become pregnant by a man from Bologna.... The nuns [at that abbey] were overjoyed at the rumor, for the abbess had always been strict with them, and they hated her. They sent a complaint to the bishop of their diocese, who was in Cologne. He summoned [the abbess] to his presence, and she went to him happily and smiling.... Then the bishop said to her: "My lady, I have heard of your sin and have come to let you make amends before me." But the abbess immediately ran away from him and went to pray to the Mother of God. Blessed Mary came to the abbess like a spirit in a dream and lifted the child from inside her; then She had it born and raised in Soissons.... When the abbess awoke and found herself childless she ran to the bishop. He looked at her carefully, and asked her to disrobe. And as soon as he saw her [childless] body he praised God and rebuked the nuns who had accused her.

This curious story leaves one wanting to ask many questions. But the most important aspect of Alfonso's collection of songs is its representation of the enormous outpouring of love that Christian heaped on Mary at the medieval zenith. For a brief time, Mary seemed nearly to crowd Jesus himself off the stage in popular devotion. He quickly moved backed into the spotlight, of course, but when he did it was in his new, humanized form. Medieval faithful now loved him more than they feared him, and that was partially due to the fact that they loved his mother so much.

MYSTICISM

Related to all the developments described above was the phenomenon of mysticism, the reputed experience of immediate, tactile contact with God. Throughout the centuries, some believers have always claimed to have experienced something greater than the everyday general sense of God's love. Their experience was qualitatively and enormously different. It changed their souls and thereby changed the world. It left no doubts. It created urgencies, and could not do otherwise. Mystical experiences have peppered this book: Constantine's vision of the Cross in the night sky; the voice heard by St. Augustine telling him to "take up [the Bible] and read"; the revelations granted to St. Boniface as he went on his lonely

This fresco of the Virgin Mary, from the church dedicated to her in Assinou, Cyprus, illustrates the kindliness and loving nature attributed to her by the faithful during the height of the so-called "Cult of the Virgin" from the twelfth to the early fourteenth centuries.
Source: SEΓ / Art Resource, NY

missions to the early Germans; the multiplicity of visions and voices surrounding Hildegard of Bingen in her abbey; the "letter from God" that Peter the Hermit waved before his rabid crowd of peasants on their brutal crusade; St. Bernard of Clairvaux's dreams of the Virgin Mary; the stigmata received by St. Francis. All these experiences represented a kind of puncturing of the fabric that separates this world from the next heavenly one: the sudden irruptive presence of the divine in our lives.

So the mystical experience was hardly a new idea, nor was it controversial. After all, God, being God, can by definition do anything He desires—and if He wants to speak to a person, He obviously can. Medieval faithful were far more comfortable

Tympanum on the north portal of Chartres Cathedral, depicting the death (bottom left, burial (bottom right), and coronation as Queen of Heaven (top) of the Blessed Virgin. Source: Erich Lessing / Art Resource, NY

with the idea of mystical experience than we are today. But in the thirteenth and fourteenth centuries it seemed as though God was literally let loose in the world on a kind of mystical rampage. Thousands upon thousands of people from all walks of life and from all parts of Europe began to have direct, personal revelations in which they literally saw God, or heard His voice, or felt His physical presence. Others encountered Jesus, or Mary, or one of the Archangels (Gabriel and Michael were the most common), or the Dove of the Holy Spirit itself. These experiences were accompanied by hypnotic trances, swoonings, passionate cries, and physical transformations. They were above all highly emotional experiences; very few of the thirteenth and fourteenth century mystics claimed to have received any sort of intellectual enlightenment from their encounters with God. Most, in fact, appear to have been profoundly puzzled by what happened to them—and it was precisely this reaction

Madonna and Child statue. The sweet character of this sculpture exemplifies the approachability of the Virgin, which made her the intercessor par excellance of the High Middle Ages. From the treasury of the Sainte-Chapelle, Paris.
Source: Erich Lessing / Art Resource, NY

that made other people believe so readily in the honesty of these mystics' experience.

Late medieval mysticism was profoundly Christocentric. It was God as Christ who, more than anyone else, appeared to people; it was Christ's voice (or those of His representatives) that resounded in people's ears. The Virgin Mary was close behind. She too was seen, heard, and palpably felt by thousands of passionate believers.

*Portal sculptures of the Annunciation (left) and Visitation (right) at Reims
Cathedral. Two of the most popular images of Mary.
Source: Scala / Art Resource, NY*

Mother and child appeared to be everywhere. One of the most interesting features of the mystical wave that poured over Europe was its catholicity: It occurred to members of every ethnicity, social class, age, gender, and educational
level. The very ubiquity of the phenomenon is the hardest thing to explain about
it. After all, if such radical experiences were felt only by a certain group of people in a certain part of Europe, modern skeptics might easily and legitimately
search for scientific explanations like the local proliferation of hallucinogenic

mushrooms.[8] But no easy explanation fits here. This was a wave of exuberant, sensuous, transformative contact with God that hit everywhere.

To try to understand this phenomenon, scholars often differentiate between *mysticism* and *mystical theology*. Mysticism was the immediate personal revelation of Divine Presence felt by individuals. A dramatic example was the middle-class Englishwoman Margery Kempe (the first woman in Western history to have written an autobiography), who experienced literally hundreds, if not thousands, of mystical revelations. Here she is on pilgrimage to Jerusalem:

> And when this Creature, riding on an ass, finally beheld Jerusalem she thanked God with all her heart and prayed that since He had seen fit, in His mercy, to bring her to behold His earthly city of Jerusalem He would also grant her the grace of seeing the Heavenly City of Jerusalem as well. Our Lord Jesus Christ, answering her prayer, granted her wish. . . . Then they went to the Temple in Jerusalem. . . . The aforesaid Creature wept and sobbed uncontrollably, as though she were seeing Our Lord suffering His Passion with her own eyes. For in fact, she *did* see Him standing there before her in her soul. . . . And when they went up to Mount Calvary she fell to the ground, unable either to stand or kneel, and she rolled and writhed her body, spreading her arms out and crying loudly as though her heart had burst open; for in the city of her soul she truly *saw* Our Lord's Crucifixion. Before her very face she saw and heard, in mystical sight, the mourning of Our Lady, of Saint John, Mary Magdalene, and of countless others who loved Our Lord.

Margery did not consciously choose to have visions; they simply came to her, almost against her will. The involuntary quality of these revelations are a hallmark of most mystics.

Mystical theology was a rather different matter. By this term we mean either the learned, "scientific" study of mysticism by late medieval writers, or the actual pursuit of mystical experience via study. Mystical theology can be localized, to an extent. It occurred or was pursued primarily within Germany, primarily by members of the Dominican order. This dominance seems to have resulted from the Dominicans taking on the task of overseeing the *beguinages* of northern Europe; there they came into contact with beguine practices, and some writings, that were clearly mystical in nature. In the effort to ensure the strict orthodoxy of beguine spiritual life, the friars had a powerful element of mysticism introduced into their own rigorous work. Many of these German Dominicans flirted with heterodoxy after their experiences. One fellow, known as Meister Eckhart, described his contact with God as a sensation of losing his being in Him like a drop of water in a barrel of wine; it's a poetic image, and he may have intended it only as a poetic image, but to unmystical Dominicans it smacked of pantheism. Heterodox or not, Dominican mysticism

---

8. Some have tried to explain mysticism by the prevalence of ergotism, the disease that results when people eat tainted bread. Grains (especially rye) that are stored on wet ground instead of an elevated floor in a grain storage compartment can grow a particular fungus that, if ingested, produces hallucinations and fevers. But mystical visions proliferated even in parts of Europe where rye was not grown or eaten.

often worked against the very intellectual activity that was the hallmark of the order. St. Thomas Aquinas is a non-German example of this mysticism: His long years of dry-as-dust study finally culminated in a glorious vision of God, but his mystical experience convinced him that all his writings were worthless. He put down his pen forever and spent his last years in dream-like contemplation.

The Church had an uneasy relationship with the epidemic of divine revelation. It certainly validated the notion of God's ability to make Himself known to whomever He wished, and it certainly urged all believers to pursue a relationship with Him; but at the same time the Church remained suspicious of such wide-ranging claims of divine contact. It is one thing to accept the idea that God *could* appear to anyone anywhere and at any time if He so chose to do; it is quite another to accept that the person sitting next to you in a crowded tavern is seeing God and hearing His voice at that very moment (especially if he or she starts behaving like Margery Kempe). Most mystics, therefore, were carefully watched and tended to by a member of the clergy who heard their confessions, listened to their descriptions of their revelations, and frequently wrote those revelations down—sometimes in bowdlerized form—for episcopal or even papal review. Thus a large body of mystical literature survives. Moreover, recognized mystics acquired great influence in society and within the Church. A woman like St. Catherine of Siena (1347–1380), the daughter of a wool dyer and his wife (who bore an astounding twenty-five children, Catherine being the twenty-fourth), received visitors and letters from across Europe, asking her advice on spiritual and moral questions. Catherine, moreover, fearlessly addressed popes, kings, queens, and urban leaders and castigated them for failing to live up to their Christian responsibilities. Nearly four hundred of her letters survive.

If the surviving literature is representative, mystical revelation seems to have occurred more to women than to men in the High and Late Middle Ages. It may be that female mystics were regarded with greater suspicion than male ones, and hence the record of their revelations is more abundant; but it is also likely that mysticism, by virtue of its non-intellectual (and in many cases anti-intellectual) nature, simply was in greater accord with female religious experience in the Middle Ages—that it represented, in other words, an intensified version of a type of spirituality that had always belonged to women. The fact that Church tradition left women with fewer options for fulfilling a religious calling also is likely to have played a role. The thirteenth and fourteenth centuries provide a roll call of women whose ecstatic experiences gave them considerable influence over social and religious life: Marie d'Oignies (d. 1213) is traditionally regarded as the foundress of the beguine movement; Juliana of Mont-Cornillon (d. 1258) began the popular call for an official Feast of Corpus Christi, which the Church initiated in 1247; Hadewijch of Flanders (d. ca. 1245) described her visions in a long series of poems, letters, and narratives that utilized the vocabulary of courtly love to reflect upon her "mystical marriage" or "mystical bridal-union" with Christ; Bridget of Sweden (d. 1372) used her mystical authority to criticize the Holy See itself for its shortcomings, doing so even while residing at the papal court; Catherine of Siena (d. 1380) followed in Bridget's path and publicly railed against the "stench of corruption" that surrounded the papacy; Julian of Norwich (d. 1420) wrote the *Revelations of Divine Love*, perhaps the most moving of mystical memoirs, and became a cult figure; Margery Kempe, also of England, offered a minutely detailed record of a life forever changed (and quite possibly unhinged) by Jesus' irruptive presence in her life. The writings of these women contrast sharply in tone with the spiritual writings of their male contemporaries; their language is sensual, vibrant, filled with passion.[9]

But whether female or male, late medieval mysticism offered a dynamic new vitality to religious life. Like the Great Alleluia, the preaching of the Franciscans, the humanized Christ, and the cult of the Virgin, the emphasis was on love and the understanding that love alone can bring. In the words of an anonymous English mystic known only as the "Solitary of Durham":

> I have found an understanding greater than that of the ancients because I have sought Your Commandments, O God. This is the reason why the Psalmist was able to write that he understood God's ways—for he did not write "It is because I have gone to the schools and have studied under learned men"; instead he wrote "It is because I have sought Your Commandments." And truly it is so—for there is a genuine understanding and knowledge of Holy Scripture which the Lord promises to give to those who walk in His ways. . . . Let the meek hear this and rejoice in it: that there is an absolute knowledge . . . that is learned from the Holy Spirit and is made manifest in good works. . . . The layman often knows this, while the cleric does not; the simple fisherman knows it, while the rhetorician does not; and the simple old woman knows it, while the Doctor of Theology does not.

Few of the mystics thought of themselves as rebels against the Church; most indeed championed orthodox doctrine, though a doctrine enlivened with the pulse of an enflamed heart. Nevertheless it is easy to detect in the phenomenon of mysticism an element of dissatisfaction with the world and the institutions that governed it.

---

9. Newcomers to this literature often focus on its fantastic elements, but the consistent trait in mystical writing is the simple, though surpassingly powerful, expression of love. This is how Julian ends her book—the final revelation of what all her previous encounters with the divine meant:

> I have begged repeatedly to understand what God meant by these visions, ever since I had them. Finally, after more than fifteen years, I received the answer, for I heard in my soul the following words: "Would you like to know the Lord's message in all this? Then learn this well: Love was His message. Who showed this message to you? Love did. What did He show you? Love. Why did He show it to you? Out of Love. Hold on to this [idea] and you will forever grow in your knowledge and understanding of Love; otherwise you will never know or learn anything."
>
> And this is how I learned that Love was Our Lord's message. I saw with certainty that even before God created us He loved us, and that His Love has never slackened, and that His Love shall endure forever. All the works He has done have been done out of this Love; in this Love He has created all things for our good use; and in this Love our lives are everlasting. We began to exist at the moment of our creation, but the Love that made us was in God from the beginning of time. Our truest beginning is therefore in His Love, and all of this we shall see in God, without end."

SUGGESTED READING

Texts

Anonymous. *The Cloud of Unknowing*.

Catherine of Siena. *Letters*.

Francis of Assisi. *The Little Flowers of St. Francis*.

———. *The Rule of St. Francis*.

Hilton, Walter. *The Scale of Perfection*.

Julian of Norwich. *The Revelation of God's Love*.

Kempe, Margery *The Book of Margery Kempe*.

Meister Eckhart. *Sermons*.

Rolle, Richard. *The Fire of Love*.

Thomas of Celano. *The Life of St. Francis*.

Source Anthologies

Armstrong, Regis J., O.F.M. Cap. *Clare of Assisi: Early Documents* (1994).

Campbell, Karen J. *German Mystical Writings: Hildegard of Bingen, Meister Eckhart, Jacob Boehme, and Others* (1991).

Lynch, Cyprian J. *A Poor Man's Legacy: An Anthology of Franciscan Poverty* (1988).

McElrath, Damian. *Franciscan Christology* (1980).

McGinn, Bernard. *Visions of the End: Apocalyptic Traditions in the Middle Ages* (1979).

Petroff, Elizabeth A. *Medieval Women's Visionary Literature* (1986).

Shinners, John. *Medieval Popular Religion, 1000–1500: A Reader* (1997).

Studies

Brooke, Rosalind B. *The Coming of the Friars* (1975).

Burr, David. *Olivi and Franciscan Poverty: The Origins of the 'Usus Pauper' Controversy* (1989).

Farmer, Sharon, and Barbara H. Rosenwein. *Monks and Nuns, Saints and Outcasts* (2000).

Finucane, Ronald C. *Miracles and Pilgrims: Popular Beliefs in Medieval England* (1977).

Hamilton, Bernard. *Religion in the Medieval West* (1986).

Harvey, Barbara F. *Living and Dying in England, 1100–1540: The Monastic Experience* (1993).

Kieckhefer, Richard. *Unquiet Souls: Fourteenth-Century Saints and Their Religious Milieu* (1984).

Lambert, Malcolm. *Franciscan Poverty* (1998).

Lawrence, C. H. *The Friars: The Impact of the Early Mendicant Movement on Western Society* (1994).

Little, Lester. *Religious Poverty and the Profit Economy in Medieval Europe* (1978).

MacVicar, Thaddeus, O.F.M. Cap. *Franciscan Spirituals and the Capuchin Reform* (1987).

McNamara, Jo Ann Kay. *Sisters in Arms: Catholic Nuns Through Two Millennia* (1996).

Moorman, John. *A History of the Franciscan Order: From Its Origins to the Year 1517* (1997).

Ozment, Steven. *The Age of Reform, 1250–1550: An Intellectual and Religious History of Late Medieval and Reformation Europe* (1980).

Rubin, Miri. *Corpus Christi: The Eucharist in Late Medieval Culture* (1993).

Swanson, Robert N. *Religion and Devotion in Europe, ca. 1215–ca. 1515* (1995).

Szarmach, Paul E. *An Introduction to the Medieval Mystics of Europe* (1984).

Ward, Benedicta, O.P. *Miracles and the Medieval Mind: Theory, Record, and Event, 1000–1215* (1982).

Warren, Ann K. *Anchorites and Their Patrons in Medieval England* (1985).

Waugh, Scott L., and Peter Diehl. *Christendom and Its Discontents: Exclusion, Persecution, and Rebellion, 1000–1500* (1995).

Ziegler, Joseph. *Medicine and Religion ca. 1300. The Case of Arnau de Vilanova* (1998).

CHAPTER 17

THE CRISES OF THE
FOURTEENTH CENTURY

By almost any standard, the fourteenth century was a calamity. War, famine, disease, economic decay, political chaos, spiritual crisis, and social unrest dogged the whole century. Fear that the world was coming to an end again became widespread—and perhaps for the first time ever those fears were not entirely irrational. It was the lengthiest and most thoroughgoing time of trouble since the collapse of the Carolingian world, and quite understandably a rather different society emerged at the end of it, one that remained recognizably medieval in its outlines but contained a number of new elements that have become associated with the modern age: a greater valuation of individual rather than communal experience, an emphasis on reason and method rather than faith and tradition, a heightened confidence in the beneficence of science, and an increased suspicion of established authority. Medieval historians have long argued the question of precisely when the Middle Ages ended and the modern world began, and the debate shows no sign of ending soon. Some insist on a date as early as Dante's starting to write *The Divine Comedy* in 1312; others suggest that the turning point was the arrival of the Black Death in 1348; many prefer the year 1453, when the Byzantine Empire fell to the Ottoman Turks in the east and the Hundred Years War between England and France ended in the west; while more than a few insist that western Europe remained essentially medieval until Martin Luther began the Protestant Reformation in 1517. (Many modern historians, for their part, insist that only the French Revolution of 1789 finally liberated the world from the Dark Ages.) To a certain extent, the long life of this debate owes something to scholars' love of disagreement; but more importantly it highlights the essential fact of the matter—that the medieval world did not suddenly end at all but slowly evolved into something else. The fourteenth century, with all its agonies, was the period of the most intense and painful evolution from the medieval to the modern world.

The troubles do not mean that the century was without positive achievements. In some respects the fourteenth century was in fact medieval Europe's greatest age. In terms of government the modern state fully emerged with all the now-familiar lineaments of power: professionalized bureaucracies, resident embassies, intelligence networks, and the very idea of statecraft. In literature the medieval world's three greatest poets appeared: Dante Alighieri, Geoffrey Chaucer, and Francesco Petrarca. So did the first novel ever written—Ramon Lull's *Blanquerna*—and the first professional female author to live entirely by her pen, Christine de Pizan. In art the greatest of all medieval painters, Giotto di Bondone, introduced techniques that would characterize painting throughout the Italian Renaissance. A powerful new wave of mysticism, led chiefly by urban women, reinvigorated spiritual life. Philosophers like William of Ockham and Duns Scotus pared away the worst excesses of scholasticism and paved the way for much of modern philosophy. Advances in technology—especially in ship design, navigation, timekeeping, and cartography—prepared western Europe for its physical expansion into Africa, the New World, and ultimately into Asia, while developments in mathematics, accounting, and business procedures, though certainly less dramatically interesting in themselves, helped create the entrepreneurial tools and attitudes whereby Europe became able to dominate the global economy.

On the whole it was a fascinating century. Seldom before had Europe faced such dramatic challenges or responded to them so creatively. The fourteenth century, in sum, formed a bridge between the worlds of the Middle Ages and the Renaissance, and above all it shows how the latter was in many respects actually the culmination, not the repudiation, of the former. The Renaissance—or the early part of it, at any rate—was in many ways everything that medieval civilization had striven for. The history of the fourteenth century explains why. In this chapter we will discuss the various crises that occurred during the century, and in the chapters that follow we will examine some of the responses that the people of western Europe devised, and some that they just blundered into.

ECONOMIC DIFFICULTIES

The troubles began slowly and raised no general alarm. The boom years from roughly 1050 to 1300, after all, had witnessed impressive gains in wealth, material culture, and population increase, but the growth had been a steadily gradual affair rather than an exhilarating period of explosive growth, and consequently the slow cooling of the economy around 1300 did not seem at first to be a particularly serious problem.[1] Several factors accounted for the decline. One of the most important, though perhaps the least dramatic to relate, was a shift in climate. The remarkably fair weather of the twelfth and thirteenth centuries took a decided turn for the worse in the fourteenth: Chroniclers' comments, tree-ring examination, and pollen analysis all indicate that over the course of the fourteenth century Europe's average annual temperature declined approximately two degrees Celsius—which may sound like very little at first, but if one considers current projections about the possible effects of global warming, in which the average annual temperature shift is

---

1. Western Europe's population tripled between 1050 and 1300, and historians have been quick to seize on this fact as evidence of the supposedly explosive growth of the medieval economy (since premodern populations increased only when economies—and especially food supplies—grew enough to allow the numbers of people to rise); but any statistician could easily tell you that this figure works out to a modest, if unusually steady, increase of less than two percent a year.

only one degree Celsius, a rather different impression emerges. As the temperature dropped, shortening the summer growing season and affecting the resilience of certain vegetal species, the wind and rain increased. This meant that crop yields declined precipitously and the agricultural economy began to contract. As food supplies dwindled, costs rose accordingly and cut into the amount of capital that people had available for other purchases or investments. This inflation in turn added to the gradual constriction of the commercial economy.

Just as significant were changes in the geopolitics of the Mediterranean world. The decline of the Byzantine Empire meant more than the shrinking of a state on a map: It meant the interruption of trade routes to central and eastern Asia. The rise of the Mamluks in Egypt, the appearance of the Ottoman Turks in Anatolia, and the dominance of the Mongol *il-khans* in what is today Iran and Iraq signaled a new era in Mediterranean connections, one in which religious loyalty and ethnic fidelity mattered more than commercial ties. The fall of Christian-held Acre in 1291, for example, sharply curtailed western Europe's direct economic connections with the Levant.[2] Consequently, the movement of goods and services between east and west began to slow, to the detriment of both the Christian and Muslim worlds. European interest in circumnavigating Africa and of exploring westward into the Atlantic, in fact, originated in the desire to avoid the roadblock of the Islamic world and to tap directly into the trade with eastern Asia that had long sustained Europe's economic growth. One sign of the effects of these changes in the sea basin was the proliferation of so-called *recovery treatises* in the fourteenth century. These were books dedicated to mapping out strategies for reestablishing a western role in the eastern Mediterranean, in the hopes of reviving trade and restoring religious balance. The bulk of the recovery treatises were written by merchants, the most famous being Marino Sanudo Torsello.

A more immediate cause of the sputtering economy was an observable absence: Since the eleventh century there had been few significant changes in the technology of agriculture. Developments like the wheeled plow, the rotation of crops, the introduction of the horseshoe, and the use of natural fertilizer that had made possible the agricultural revolution of the eleventh and twelfth centuries had had no follow-up, and farming still was conducted in 1300 roughly the same way it had been done in 1100; but with a considerably larger population to feed, there was little surplus left to generate fresh capital. As a consequence, food production fell perilously close to subsistence level. Signs of trouble had already emerged by the middle of the thirteenth century when occasionally low yields revealed how perilous was the balance between Europe's population and its food supply. Apart from territories beset by war, the tentativeness of the food supply became evident first on the farmlands most recently brought under cultivation during the economic expansion of the twelfth century. The less-established farmers of these lands frequently did not have the means to survive successive poor harvests. Tenant farmers unable

---

2.   The Venetians retained a strong presence in the east after the fall of Acre, and the Catalans a considerably lesser one, but merchants from few other places continued to figure in the east.

to pay their rents thus began to slip into debt, and landlords who depended on rents for their income began to rely increasingly on urban financiers for credit. Even whole governments became entangled in the credit crisis, England being the most notable example. The cycle of indebtedness was hardly inexorable, but the string of bank failures and commercial collapses in the first half of the fourteenth century is nonetheless striking: The famed Bardi and Peruzzi banks of Florence (the two largest financial houses in Europe) collapsed spectacularly in the 1340s. They were soon followed by the Riccardi bank of Lucca, whose massive loans to Edward III had kept the English government afloat for years. Many more houses collapsed in turn. Ironically, as the economy faltered, the strength of some local governments increased. This increase was due in part to the fact that people with capital who lacked sound commercial enterprises in which to invest began to put their money in municipal bonds, especially at first in northern Italy and eastern Spain. This subsidy aided the further development of the state as an institution in those lands and also accounts for the rise to prominence of certain families like the Medici and the Visconti, financiers who became the rulers of Florence and Milan, respectively, in the Renaissance. They came to view the right to govern the city-state as collateral for the revenue they had loaned to it in the form of bonds.

An important demographic trend resulted from and contributed to the economic malaise: large-scale migration of rural populations into the cities. Europe's overall population growth from 1050 to 1300 had been primarily due to an increase in the number of rural folk, but as economic forces made agrarian life more parlous around 1300, hard-pressed farmers and their families began to migrate to the cities in large numbers in search of work. Many cities doubled in size, and some even tripled, over the course of just one or two generations. Few cities were capable of absorbing such large numbers of people: With manufacturing in decline, there were few employment opportunities and the cities began to swell with crowds of poor, unemployed, and untrained people. The available statistics are sobering. Census records from a single county within Normandy—Beaumont-de-Roger—estimate the 1313 population at over one hundred thousand, a level not again reached by that county until the twentieth century. Giovanni Villani, the author of a renowned contemporary history of Florence, estimated the number of destitute beggars in that city to be around seventeen thousand. London and Paris became bloated with poor wretches and developed reputations as centers of crime and vice, especially prostitution.[3] The *Calendar of Letters* for London in 1309 contains the following notations:

---

3. In 1393 the city government of London, trying to find ways of reducing the disorder caused by unchecked prostitution in the streets, passed the following ordinance: "Since so many different riots, fights, and arguments have broken out, and so many men been killed and murdered, on account of their constant consorting in taverns with common whores (especially Flemish ones) . . . we order . . . that all such women who pass through or reside in the city or its suburbs . . . are to restrict themselves to the districts assigned to them—namely, the bathhouses on the further side of the river Thames—or else suffer the punishment of forfeiting their bodies and cloaks." It is unclear how forcing prostitutes to walk through the streets topless would decrease their trade or why Flemish prostitutes were so much more dangerous than others.

These are the articles of law that our Lord the King [Edward II] has commanded to be kept in his city of London, in order to preserve the peace.

First, it is forbidden—since so many murders, robberies, and homicides have been recently committed in the city both night and day—that anyone should walk the city streets after the curfew bells at St. Martin's are rung while carrying a sword, buckler or any other weapon unless he is a baron. . . .

Second, no tavern keeper may keep his inn open for selling wine or beer after the curfew; neither is he to allow anyone into his tavern or house—lest he risk answering for the King's Peace, under the aforesaid penalties. . . .

Third, no one is to maintain a fencing school [within the city limits] either by day or night, on penalty of forty days imprisonment. And since so many murderers, once arrested, are treated with excessive leniency—and since this gives encouragement to so many others—it is ordered that no sheriff or other royal official may release a prisoner without the prior knowledge of the city's warden, mayor, and aldermen. Moreover each alderman is empowered to search his precinct with diligent care for all criminals, and if any be found [the alderman] shall bring them before [the city council] for punishment. . . .

Fourth, no foreigners or strangers are to maintain lodgings within the city. Only those who are freemen of the city or who can produce an acceptable character witness from their home city and are prepared to produce similar guarantors of their good behavior among the citizens here may enter and reside in the city. . . .

Cities suffered just as greatly as rural areas during food shortages, and perhaps even more so. Forced by circumstance to rely on grain imports, cities experiencing interrupted food supplies became concentrated areas of discontent. Thousands of starving laborers clustered together within a town's walls can become a force of considerable violence. Food riots were increasingly common in the late thirteenth and early fourteenth centuries; less dramatically, protests against the exorbitant prices caused by shortages of one kind or another became almost daily occurrences in the largest—and therefore most vulnerable—cities like Cologne, Florence, London, Mainz, Marseilles, Milan, Naples, Palermo, Paris, and Vienna.

As urban life grew difficult, crowds of laborers formed factions in the attempt to force change. These sometimes took the form of organized political groups under legitimate authorities (the aggressive companies allotted to the London aldermen, for example) while at other times they amounted merely to street gangs (as in the armed urban gangs—called *comitive*—in fourteenth-century Palermo) distributing vigilante justice. One clear symptom of this factional violence was the growing effort to segregate and dispel foreigners, as the London record also reflects. Increasing suspicion and harassment of foreigners led many trading companies to sever ties with former markets, and as economic troubles grew so did the likelihood of war.

Even more than the periodic outbursts of crime and riot that they caused, urban crowding and poor access to fresh water and proper sewage posed serious dangers to public health. Masses of human waste poured into the streets or along the banks of rivers (the two most common dumping sites) were a clear invitation to disease, especially dysentery and cholera. Lack of adequate housing left thousands of town dwellers exposed to the weather, one result of which was a noted increase in the spread of tuberculosis (then called consumption) that medical authorities struggled to halt.[4]

THE GREAT FAMINE

The Great Famine was a series of devastating crop failures that appeared first in Mediterranean Europe and became ever more severe as they advanced northward. Few areas were spared. Recent scholars estimate that the sustained food shortage afflicted a total area of roughly 400,000 squares miles in northern Europe alone (nearly one-third of the continent's land mass), stretching from the Alps to southern Scandinavia and from England to Poland. The Mediterranean famine was more scattered but no less dire. Altogether, somewhere between thirty and forty million people were affected by the famine; not all died, but most experienced more or less continuous hardship punctuated by periods of outright crisis. Given the climatological changes taking place, it is difficult to tell if the southern and northern phenomena were related. Nevertheless, it is clear that a dramatic agricultural crisis hit the Mediterranean world in 1311 and lasted for at least the next three years—years in which rural production declined so low that Sicily, long one of western Europe's greatest wheat producers, forbade the export of grain lest its own people starve— only to be followed, starting in 1315, by a seven-year stretch of consistently miserable yield in the north. It takes no great insight to imagine the effects of eleven consecutive years of interrupted food supply. People died slow and painful deaths; prices for available food rose significantly; hoarding became common, charity less so; animals were sacrificed for the sake of their meat and to avoid wasting precious winter grain on them; public prayers for relief grew more desperate; laws governing manorial duties grew more stringent; efforts to control prices and wages became more concerted and successful. A disturbing contemporary English poem called *On the Evil Times of Edward II* regales the reader with references to cannibalism, infanticide, pervasive fear for the future, and the hatred engendered by despair. The poem is negligible as poetry, but as an expression of bitterness and fear it has impressive power.

Weather changes alone do not account for the decline in food production. Just as significant was the fact that over the course of the thirteenth century much European farming had become highly specialized, with a strong trend toward monoculture (that is, the production of a single crop for mass export instead of the more varied, self-sustaining production of the classical medieval manor). Places like

---

4. The most commonly prescribed treatments for consumption were varieties of hot baths. One English medical text from the 1380s, the *Breviarium Bartholomei*, suggests the following: "Take several blind puppies, remove their viscera, and cut off their limbs, then boil them in water. The patient should then bathe in this water for approximately four hours after every meal. While in the bath he should keep his head completely covered and his torso completely wrapped up in a lambskin, to protect him against a chill."

Sicily, which had previously produced, in addition to wheat, large quantities of flax, barley, citrus, olive oil, cotton, alum, indigo, and animal products, drifted slowly into the mass production of wheat alone for export. Sites like Bordeaux and Burgundy, by contrast, focused less on grain and animal husbandry and more on the production of the wines for which they were famous. But while monoculture was lucrative during times of economic growth, it resulted in misery when either the market declined for the privileged crop or when climatological changes occurred that had uniquely harmful effects on that crop. In 1315 and 1316, two years of ruinously bad weather were marked by such incessant rain that, in the words of one contemporary, "whole buildings, city walls, and even castles were undermined" by the soaked and washed-away earth, and the effect on viticulture was devastating: "There was no wine [produced] in the entire kingdom of France," he wrote simply.

Freak interruptions in food production like this could be overcome, of course, but their effects were long felt. When grain becomes so dear that people resort to cannibalism, they are not likely to set any food aside to feed their animals. The slaughtered cattle, horses, and sheep may provide an immediate source of sustenance—and yet they leave the farmers exposed to further trouble once the crisis has passed, for without cattle or horses to pull the plows the peasants can hardly begin farming again. Animal losses reached dangerously high levels during the famine. At a single priory in northern England, that of the Austin canons at Bolton, the estate's herd decreased from three thousand animals in 1315 to only nine hundred in 1317. A less obvious consequence of the cold wet weather, but one which had long-term effects, was a sharp reduction in the production and distribution of salt—the main food preservative in the Middle Ages.[5] The crisis phase of the famine ended in 1322, after seven years of misery, but its effects continued throughout most of the century.

THE BLACK DEATH

A malnourished population living in squalid conditions is not likely to succeed at warding off disease, especially when the disease is the Black Death. This was the *bubonic plague*, an infectious disease affecting the lymphatic system, that originated in eastern Asia.[6] The advance of the Mongols under Ghengis Khan was probably responsible for carrying the sickness westward. It had probably never before existed

---

5.   Most salt came from salt pans, areas of coastal flatland that held shallow water after the tide receded. Normally the heat of the sun sufficed (with a bit of human help) to evaporate the water, leaving the salt behind for people to gather and refine. Cool wet weather meant that these areas failed to dry up, and little salt was therefore available.
6.   Bacterial in nature, the bubonic plague developed a related form known as the *pneumonic plague* that attacked the lungs; it was not actually a separate disease, but only the pneumatic stage of a lung infection. The disease could also cause septicemic poisoning of the bloodstream and enteric infection of the bowels. The name *Black Death* refers to the large black sores and bruises left on the bodies of those it killed.

Famines continued long after the period of the Great Famine (1315–1322). This manuscript painting depicts the rationing of grain in the Orsanmichele, near Florence, in 1335. The distribution was organized by the grain merchants guild of the city. Note the image of Madonna and Child to the right, to whom prayers are raised for an end to the famine.
Source: Scala / Art Resource, NY

in the west; famous reports of "plague" affecting the eastern Mediterranean in earlier centuries were most likely different diseases altogether.[7] But even if these earlier epidemics had been bubonic plague, the bacterium that caused them (which

___

7.   For example, the "plague of Athens" in the fifth century B.C. that Thucydides described so vividly appears to have been typhus, and the sixth century plague of Justinian's time, which originated in eastern Africa, has never been fully identified.

mutates easily anyway) had never reached western Europe before, which meant that the populace there had no biological means of fighting it off; several centuries were required before the necessary antibodies developed in the general population—and consequently waves of the plague continued to beset Europe until well into the eighteenth century.

The Black Death was arguably the worst natural disaster in western history. It arrived in Latin Europe—first appearing in Messina, Sicily—in November of 1347, struck Marseilles, in southern France, early in 1348, and from there it spread throughout the continent. Exact numbers are of course impossible to reckon, but scholars all agree that by the time the Black Death's rampage ended, it had killed as many as thirty-five million people in less than three years—somewhere near one-third the entire population of Europe. It indiscriminately attacked young and old, men and women, rich and poor, and it left piles of corpses from Portugal to Scandinavia and back east to Russia. Because of the nature of its transmission, however, it had the highest mortality in the cities. The bacterium that caused the disease was carried by fleas which inhabited the bodies of rats, who were themselves immune to the disease. And since rat populations tended, then as now, to reside in centers of human population, the plague literally exploded onto the urban scene with deadly force.[8] It carried off most of its victims within three days. Many contemporaries bore witness to the horrifying scene. Michele da Piazza described its arrival in Sicily:

> At the start of November [in 1347] twelve Genoese galleys . . . entered the port at Messina. They carried within them a disease so deadly that any person who happened merely to speak with any one of the ships' members was seized by a mortal illness; death was inevitable. It spread to everyone who had any interaction with the infected. Those who contracted the disease felt their whole bodies pierced through with pain, and they quickly developed boils about the size of lentils on their thighs and upper arms. These boils then spread the disease throughout the rest of the body and made its victims vomit blood. The vomiting of blood normally continued for three days until the person died, since there was no way to stop it. Not only did everyone who had contact with the sick become sick themselves, but also those who had contact only with their possessions. . . . People soon began to hate one another so much that parents would not even tend to their own sick children. . . . As the deaths mounted, crowds of people sought to confess their sins to priests and to draft their wills . . . but clergy, lawyers, and notaries refused to enter the homes of the ill. . . . Franciscans, Dominicans, and other mendicants who went to hear the confessions of the dying themselves fell to the disease—many of them not even making it alive out of the ill persons' homes.

---

8. A discomfiting fact of human history is that there is generally one rat for every person in any given city. In Boston, where I now live, the ratio is estimated to be two-to-one. The reason we don't see more of them is that they generally dislike us as much as we dislike them and stay hidden during the day (except, of course, for places like Boston, where the rats have real attitude).

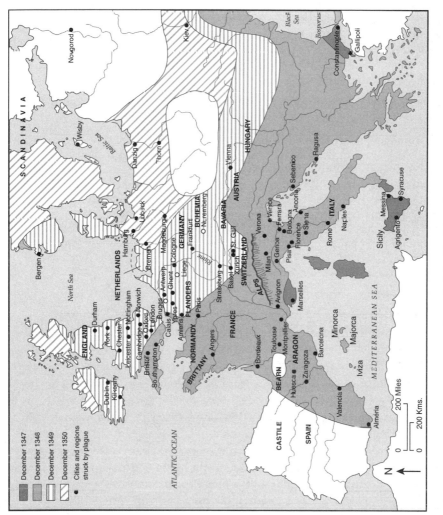

Spread of the Black Death

Jean de Venette, describing the epidemic in Paris, related a widespread reaction to the crisis:

> Some said that the pestilence was the result of infected air and water . . . and as a result of this idea many began suddenly and passionately to accuse the Jews of infecting the wells, fouling the air, and generally being the source of the plague. Everyone rose up against them most cruelly. In Germany and elsewhere—wherever Jews lived—they were massacred and slaughtered by Christian crowds and many thousands were burned indiscriminately. The steadfast, though foolish, bravery of the Jewish men and women was remarkable. Many mothers hurled their own children into the flames and then leapt in after them, along with their husbands, in order that they might avoid being forcibly baptized.

In England, Henry Knighton traced out some of the plague's less expected consequences:

> At the same time sheep began to die everywhere throughout the realm. In a single pasture one could find as many as five thousand carcasses, all so putrified that no animal or bird would go near them. . . . Sheep and cattle wandered aimlessly through meadows and crop fields, for there was no one to go after them and herd them. As a result, they died in countless numbers everywhere, in ditches and hedges. . . . Moreover, buildings both large and small began to collapse in all cities, towns, and villages, since there was no one to inhabit and maintain them. In fact, many whole villages became deserted: everyone who lived in them died and not a single house was left standing. It is likely that many of these sites will never be inhabited again.

A Spanish Muslim historian named 'Ibn Khaldun summarized the plague (which, of course, also decimated the Byzantine and Islamic worlds) in this way:

> It was as though humanity's own living voice had called out for oblivion and desolation—and the world responded to the call. God inherits the earth and whoever is upon it.

It would be difficult to exaggerate the horror people felt. Death seemed to rule the world. There were many eerie reports of death ships drifting aimlessly in the Mediterranean, North, and Baltic seas, their entire crews perished, with the victorious rats feasting on their corpses and cargo.

People tried everything they could think of: medicines, quarantines, prayers, parades of self-flagellation, folk cures based on herbs and pagan-rooted incantations. Fearing tainted food supplies, they intentionally starved themselves; fearing vulnerability to the disease as a result of malnutrition, they gorged themselves on every available morsel. Many turned passionately in prayer to the Christian saints, while others desperately invoked pagan spirits, fairies, and folkloric cures.[9] Charla-

---

9. This latter point is the origin of the nursery rhyme "Ring around the Rosey." The "ring of roses" was the rose-colored circle that grew around the infected boils. The sick tried to cure themselves with the folkloric treatment of gathering pocketfuls of posies—but the result was always the same: "Ashes to ashes, we all fall down."

The personification of the Black Death strangling a victim in his bed. The manuscript containing this image is in the University Library in Prague, Czech Republic. Source: Wener Forman / Art Resource, NY

tans sold serums supposedly guaranteed to protect those who drank them. Others claimed to possess magical powers that could drive the evil spirit of the plague away.[10] Thousands went into voluntary exile, avoiding all human contact; still others, giving up all hope, gave themselves over to licentiousness. The faculty of the medical school at the University of Paris studied the epidemic and confidently

10. Thus the children's tale of the Pied Piper, who claimed to be able to play (for a price!) a magical tune on his pipe that would hypnotize all the rats in the city, so that the piper could lead them away to drown in a river.

reported to King Philip VI that it was the result of an unfortunate alignment of Mars, Jupiter, and Saturn in the night sky. Their recommendations?

> Eat no poultry, waterfowl, suckling pig, old beef, or fatty meat. . . . We prescribe instead broths made of pepper, cinnamon, and other spices. . . . Sleeping during the daytime is dangerous; one should awaken either at dawn or shortly thereafter. . . . Eating fruits, either dried or fresh, is harmless provided that they are accompanied by wine; without the wine, however, they may do harm. . . . Fish should be avoided, as should exercise. . . . Olive oil might kill you. Fat people should get as much sun as possible. . . . Diarrhea is serious and bathing is dangerous. Regular enemas should be had, in order to keep the bowels clear. And of course, sexual intercourse with women is lethal. Avoid all coitus and do not sleep in any woman's bed.

(For the record, the plague befuddled most Muslim and Greek physicians as well. Islamic law [*shari'a*] at the time even rejected the very idea of contagion, although at least one commentator—Ibn al-Khatib, of Granada—cautiously noted the epidemic's infectious nature.) In some instances desperate townsfolk, knowing that rats transmitted the disease but not knowing how else to get rid of them, even resorted to intentionally burning down their entire towns in order to drive the rodents away. The inevitable result, however, was merely to hasten the spread of the sickness to neighboring villages.

The consequences of the Black Death were considerable and long felt. Perhaps the most immediately observable consequences were economic. The sheer number of fatalities, and the concomitant fear of contact with any others, destroyed agricultural and industrial production and severed trade and distribution networks. For reasons outlined in the discussion of the effects of the Great Famine, these sorts of economic disruptions can have very long-term effects. The loss of draught animals meant a prolonged difficulty in restarting agricultural production; the heavy losses of sheep meant the interruption of the supply of raw wool for the textile industry. The emptying of whole villages and districts led to the ruin of vineyards. (It can take as many as twenty years for grapevines and olive trees to reach full productive capacity.) Between 1347 and 1350 European commercial life virtually ground to a halt. But once the initial wave of death passed, a twin inflationary and recessionary spiral ensued. Workers in the towns who had survived could now demand higher wages, since there was so great a shortage of labor. Combined with the general scarcity of goods, these demands led to rapid increases in prices and wages. A rather different pattern emerged in rural areas. There, peasant farmers who had weathered the storm could demand lower rents, since their decreased numbers meant that the landlords particularly depended on them to get the land working again. But so many people had died overall that even a truncated food production more than adequately met immediate needs; thus food prices dropped. Low prices hurt the farmers even more than the lowered rents helped them. So urban workers generally profited from the plague (if they survived) while rural farmers remained stuck in poverty.

*The Annals of Gilles de Muisit includes this miniature painting
of people struggling to keep up with the burial of plague victims
in Tournai, France.*
Source: Snark / Art Resource, NY

Western governments were hard-pressed to deal with the crisis in any useful systematic way. Providing health care was the least of their concerns, since that was not considered to be any part of government's responsibility in the Middle Ages. Whatever medical care there was came through private physicians or church-run hospitals. But maintaining public order was a governmental matter, and its need rose sharply as the plague ran its course and crowds ran riot in the streets. Here the problem was twofold: taxation and factionalization. Royal governments and local communes both tried to capitalize on the increased wages of urban workers by imposing heavy new taxes upon them. Workers complained that they were being singled out to finance the recovery. Making matters worse, many governments tried to halt the rise in inflation by imposing wage controls and freezing the prices for manufactured goods. These measures triggered a series of urban revolts across the Continent. The most famous was the so-called *Ciompi Revolt* in Florence in 1378. The Ciompi were the textile workers (spinners, fullers, weavers, dyers, etc.) employed by the powerful wool merchants' guild. The guild members had attempted to lower workers' wages and raise cloth prices by ordering a reduction in cloth production to a drastic level that was only one-third

Fresco from a Sicilian palace, showing "The Triumph of Death." This terrifying image of Death riding roughshod over a crowd that includes kings, bishops, friars, merchants, laborers, noble ladies and peasant laborers graphically illustrates the fear and pessimism that gripped western Europe in the wake of the Black Death and the endemic wars and famines of the fourteenth century. Perhaps there is an element of wishful thinking on display as well: The middle-class figures and social leaders seem to be getting the worst of it, while the lower-class figures to the right cower in fear and supplication. Source: Scala/Art Resource, NY

what it had been even before the plague arrived. This reduction resulted in thousands of suddenly jobless workers. They took to the streets, raided shops, destroyed machinery, and ransacked warehouses. The revolt was short-lived, though, as guild leaders quickly allied themselves with municipal officials and forcibly restored order.

The Ciompi experience also illustrates the growing problem of urban factionalism. The problem emerged first and most fully in Italy. Propertied figures who feared the growing restlessness of the urban workers began to form varying alliances, sometimes with other merchants or financiers (as in Florence or Milan) and

A procession of flagellants, who performed public penance and scourged themselves to compensate for the sins of the town members that, presumably, helped bring on the plague. Source: HIP Art Resource

sometimes with local rural aristocrats (as in Palermo) in order to combine governmental controls in the courts and strong-arm tactics in the streets to keep the crowds in line. But these allied groups often vied with one another for power within any given city. Such power struggles helped prepare the way for the factional strife of the early Renaissance and the gradual emergence of the Renaissance tyrants. In England and France urban factionalism often resulted in increased popular support for the monarchy as the only power capable of restraining the excesses of local factions, despots, and cartels.

Conditions in the countryside grew troubled as well. All across northern Europe, peasants were resentful that what they had hoped would be their gain from the epidemic—decreased rents for tenants and increased wages for rural laborers—turned instead into increased dependence on the landlords. The collapse of agricultural prices bore much of the responsibility for that, but so did the landlords' success at reimposing their traditional privileges over the rural classes. The first sign of trouble appeared in northern France, where a peasant insurrection

known as the *Jacquerie* broke out in 1358.[11] The French nobles had lost a major battle against the English in 1356, during which the French king John (r. 1350–1364)
was taken prisoner. Even though the rules of chivalry demanded that the nobles
pay their king's ransom, they tried instead to shift the burden onto the peasants by
a series of heavy taxes and forced loans. Already smarting under the collapse of
food prices in the wake of the plague, the peasants rose up in great violence, mur-
dering landlords and their families indiscriminately, burning down manors,
churches, monasteries, courthouses, and record offices everywhere they went. The
nobles responded quickly and with equal brutality and suppressed the rebels in a
few months.

In England, the landlords who made up much of the House of Lords joined
forces with representatives of the urban merchants who made up the House of
Commons to secure passage of the Statute of Labourers in 1351, the statute froze rural rents at artificially high levels just as it froze urban wages at artificially low ones.
This freeze deeply angered the lower orders in town and country, but their resentment simmered relatively quietly for a while. What led them ultimately to take action was the imposition by Parliament of a series of poll taxes in the 1370s. Most
earlier levies in England had been indirectly indexed to taxpayers' incomes,[12] but
the poll taxes imposed a standard duty on every adult in the realm regardless of
income—which meant that the levy fell heaviest on those with the least amount of
money. This tax finally drove the peasants over the edge, and in May 1381 they began a mass protest known as the *Peasants' Revolt*. Crowds of angry peasants
marched on manorial residences (primarily in Essex and Kent), burning local court
and tax records, sacking baronial homes, and driving nobles into flight. Led by a
small group of charismatic figures—the best known was Wat Tyler—they gradually
converged on London and entered it on June 13. They besieged the royal officials in
the Tower and began to plunder and set fire to a good portion of the city; they went
so far as to sack the palatial home of John of Gaunt (the most powerful nobleman in
the kingdom) and to murder Simon Sudbury, the archbishop of Canterbury and
chancellor of the realm. A nervous young King Richard II (r. 1377–1399) met the rioters and agreed to honor their demands, provided that they dispersed. Those demands included the abolition of serfdom and an immediate decrease in rents.
Richard probably had no intention of living up to his promises (and in fact he never
did), but he did succeed in getting most of the rioters to return to their homes. The
remainder were quickly subdued by the kings' men, and Wat Tyler himself was put
to death.

In the wake of the Black Death, other, less dramatic, changes took root in society. One was a noticeable shift in the average age at which people married. In the

---

11.   The name derives from the disparaging nickname *Jacques Bonnehomme* (or "Jack Good-man") that
French nobles often used to describe their peasants.
12.   These were not income taxes *per se* but taxes on household property, both moveable and immoveable.
Since the amount of property one owns is usually linked, albeit loosely, with one's income, the revenues
generated by the English levies provide a rough index of income trends.

thirteenth century, urban and rural males tended to marry rather late, in their late twenties or early thirties, since they often had to wait for their fathers to die in order to inherit enough land or capital with which to support a family (sons, after all, did not receive dowries). Common women, by contrast, were usually married while still in their teens in order to allow the greatest number of fertile years for child-bearing. After the Great Famine and Black Death, however, whether out of concern for life's uncertainty or in order to benefit from some of the economic opportunities available, rural and urban men began to marry earlier, at an age closer to that of their wives. It is tempting to attach greater significance to this phenomenon than it deserves, but it is a fact that surviving marriage manuals from the second half of the fourteenth century place less emphasis on husbands' rights to beat their wives into submission and place a greater value on fair and affectionate treatment within the marriage tie. Women still had nothing even approaching equal rights within marriage, but some of the most egregious disparities between husbands and wives seem to have lessened. One example of this gentler, though still patronizing, attitude comes from a marriage manual written by a Parisian merchant to his bride in the year 1392:

> Care for your husband—for his whole person—with love, and I pray you will keep him in clean linen, for that is your responsibility. Since it is man's responsibility to tend to the affairs of the world, a husband must do his part by coming and going, journeying here and there in rain and wind, in snow and hail, often drenched, occasionally dry, sometimes sweating, sometimes shivering, hungry, homeless, uncheered, and without a decent sleep. But this does not deter him so long as he retains the hope of a wife's tender care of him when he returns—the comfort, happiness, and pleasure that she will give him or will arrange to have brought to him. [These include:] to have his shoes removed before a good fire; to have his feet washed; to be given fresh shoes and stockings, and plenty of good food and drink; to be well served and cared for; to be invited to a good bed with clean sheets and nightcaps, heaped with good coverings—and then at last to be soothed by those joys and delights, those intimate, loving, and private acts that I shall not name. . . . It is without doubt, fair sister, that such care makes a man love his wife and want to return to her and be with her and to spurn all others. And so I advise you to bring such cheer to your husband in all his comings and goings, and not to stop. Also, to be kind toward him and bear in mind the old proverb: "There are three things that drive a man from home—a leaking roof, a smoking chimney, and a scolding wife." Therefore, dear sister, I pray that you will keep yourself in your husband's love and good grace, being always unto him gentle, amiable, and sweet tempered.

The manual further describes at great length how a good wife should go about hiring and treating servants, running a household, tending a garden, planning meals, and organizing games. Its patronizing tone is obvious; being a merchant's manual, it reads at times like a contract. Nevertheless it is suffused with a tone of affection for and celebration of domestic pleasures that earlier manuals noticeably lacked.

Women took on slightly more active roles in commercial life after mid-century as well, especially in the Mediterranean cities. As the economy and population started to grow again, numerous opportunities became available for women with manufacturing skills. The urban labor shortage meant job opportunities for women as well as men, and the towns quickly started to fill with young females fleeing the still depressed conditions of the countryside. Since the most common women's manufacturing skills were in cloth production and brewing (tasks they had grown up performing in their rural homes), women gradually assumed a somewhat larger role in these industries. Tavern-and inn keeping offered other avenues for economic independence. By 1400, in the city of Florence, no fewer than 15 percent of the city's population comprised households headed by single women. Still, restrictions remained. Most textile guilds, for example, relegated women to the primitive parts of the industry; they performed the slow tasks of carding and spinning while the men did the more skilled and lucrative jobs of weaving and dyeing; but still, skilled women could become apprentices and even earn licenses as master craftsmen.

WAR EVERYWHERE

As if famine, plague, and economic collapse were not enough, the fourteenth century also suffered from almost incessant warfare. In terms of the sheer number of conflicts, this may in fact have been the most war-filled century in Europe's history to date. For the most part the conflicts were small but they were ubiquitous. Place your finger almost anywhere on a map of fourteenth-century Europe and you will have a good chance of pointing at a war zone. In Germany, the emperor Henry VII of Luxembourg (r. 1308–1313) led his armies into Italy in the hope of putting an end to the Guelf-Ghibelline struggles; after his death a contested imperial election between Louis the Bavarian and Frederick of Austria brought the war home to Germany itself for another twenty years. Further to the east, two brothers, Wenceslas and Sigismund, wore the crowns of Bohemia and Hungary, respectively, and through their ineptitude kept both realms in a state of confusion, war, and rebellion.[13] The Angevin rulers of the kingdom of Naples continued their war against Catalan Sicily, while the Catalan-Sicilians themselves sent armies eastward to conquer Greece. The Crown of Aragon waged war to the east against Genoese-controlled Sardinia and to the south against Murcia and Granada, while Léon-Castile pressed

---

13. This is not the "Good King Wenceslas" of the well-known Christmas carol. *He* was a tenth-century figure who died a martyr's death in 935. The fourteenth-century Wenceslas was incompetent and a hopeless alcoholic, whereas his brother was mentally ill. In fact, a common joke of the time was that Wenceslas was only sober in the mornings while Sigismund was only sane in the afternoons—which explained why the brothers could never agree on any sensible regional policies.

the final stages of its part of the *Reconquista* against Muslim Spain. The French had a violent struggle with the Flemish, and afterward with the Burgundians. The English fought against the Scots under King Edward II (1307–1327) and then against the Scots, the Welsh, and the Irish under Edward III (1327–1377). The English then initiated the century's major conflict—the Hundred Years War (1337–1453)—against the French. In the aftermath of defeat there, the English then went to war against themselves in a civil conflict known as the War of the Roses (1453–1485). In Scandinavia a knot of dynastic rivalries and misalliances led to a dizzying sequence of two- and three-front wars between Norway, Denmark, and Sweden in every possible recombination. Meanwhile, the Ottoman Turks continued to advance on the rump Byzantine Empire, while dynastic and religious rivalries continued to rip apart the states of Muslim North Africa.

The most significant of these conflicts, the Hundred Years War between England and France, lasted from a decade after Edward III's accession to the final French victory outside Calais in 1453; it was the longest war in Western history. What mattered most about the Hundred Years War was the way in which it was fought, rather than the tale of who defeated whom, for it was the mechanism of warfare itself that triggered the greatest amount of social and political change. And the extraordinary events at the war's end illustrated some of the far-reaching religious changes that had occurred as well.

The war was a long time coming. France and England had had a strained relationship ever since 1066, because of the dual relations between their monarchs. As the English realm turned into the Angevin Empire in the twelfth century, more and more French territories fell under London's control. But then in the thirteenth century, the rapid expansion of the Capetian realm came largely at the expense of the English. As England's continental holdings lessened, her need to establish sure control over the rest of the British territories—Wales, Scotland, and Ireland—increased, in order to guarantee access to certain raw materials and commercial markets (not to mention the need to get rid of violent neighbors). England appeared to be on the defensive and, territorially speaking, in decline. The sad spectacle of Henry III's hapless reign (r. 1216–1272)—a king whose effectiveness is reflected by the fact that Dante's *Divine Comedy* relegated him to the purgatory of pious idiots—highlighted this decline. The successes of Henry's son Edward I (r. 1272–1307) represented only a partial recovery from that nadir; but even so, the disastrous reign of Edward II (r. 1307–1327) made England's perilous position all the more clear.

But luck changed when Edward III inherited the throne in 1327. From his unfortunate father, Edward inherited the throne of England; from his mother, Isabelle of France, he held a legitimate claim to the French throne as well. It happened this way. Philip IV, the Fair, the man who had set in action the dissolution of the Templars and who had shocked Europe by issuing an arrest warrant for Pope Boniface VIII, had died in 1314. His crown passed to his first son Louis

X (r. 1314–1316), then to his second son Philip V (r. 1315–1322), and then to his third son Charles IV (r. 1322–1328), each of whom died without a legal heir. Charles' death put an end to the Capetian dynasty that had ruled France since 987. But Philip IV had a fourth child, his daughter Isabelle who had married Edward II of England. Edward III therefore claimed the French throne as the nearest surviving relative of Philip IV. Technically, he was correct, and the crown should have been his. However, the idea of an English king of France was as much anathema to the French in 1328 as the idea of a French king had been to the English in 1066—only this time the French were in a position to do something about the situation. The Estates General quickly found a rival to Edward: Philip VI (r. 1328–1350), the founder of the *Valois dynasty*. Philip was the son of Philip IV's younger brother Charles, and he and his successors eagerly stepped into the self-styled role of preservers of all things French. The Hundred Years War, then, would continue beyond Edward III and Philip VI and would engulf (with many peaceable lapses) the reigns of the next five generations on each side of the family dispute.

Of course, other factors played a role. The Franco-Flemish war mentioned earlier resulted from a struggle to control the wool trade that passed between England and the Continent, while struggles to dominate the wine trade that passed through Gascony (another English-held French territory) provided another source of contention. Edward's claim to the French throne offered England an irresistable opportunity to put an end to nearly three hundred years of Anglo-French bickering, and the Hundred Years War began, within England, as a very popular affair indeed. It was a fascinating struggle, one in which England won nearly every battle, yet in which the French ultimately triumphed.

The most important thing about the Hundred Years War, though, was not its outcome but the way in which it was fought. At the start of the conflict, both sides still relied heavily on feudal military might, with armored aristocratic cavalry providing the most important fighting force. But the English quickly recognized that they had to change their tactics significantly: The French, after all, outnumbered them at least twelve-to-one. The idea of meeting the French in pitched battle between knights on an open field seemed ludicrous. Therefore, the English gradually began to implement several new tactical lessons they had learned from their struggles with the Scots, Welsh, and Irish. Those Celtic fighters, faced with England's mounted knights, had fought back with some very simple and inexpensive yet highly effective new weapons: the longbow, the crossbow, and the stake.

Most earlier bows had been mobile cavalry weapons, designed to be slung over a knight's shoulder as he rode into battle and shot as he galloped over, around, and through the melee. These bows were relatively short in length and had limited force. Longbows, on the other hand, were conceived as weapons of the infantry and were much longer and more powerful than their horse-bound precursors. By the thirteenth century, the highland Celts had learned to carve longbows as long as six feet out of yew trees.[14] Their force was so great that the arrows they launched could pierce a suit of armor at a distance of two hundred yards. Accuracy at such a distance was poor but hardly mattered, since one could produce more than a hundred such bows and equip the men to shoot them for less cost than that of the single mounted knight they aimed at. Continuous volleys of hundreds of arrows could cover a large area and cut down considerable numbers of mounted knights long before they could arrive at the battlefield's center.

Those knights who survived the longbow volleys then had to contend with the crossbows. These were fearsome weapons, about the length of a modern sawed-off shotgun, that shot fat metal bolts called *quarrels*. Engaging the firing mechanism required great strength; with the first crossbows a bowsman had to bend at the waist, place the front end of the crossbow on the ground, step into a stirrup at the tip, attach the drawstring to a hook on his belt, and slowly straighten himself and arch his back until the drawstring finally engaged the trigger. Later a ratcheted iron gear, turned by a thick crank, drew the bowstring and provided the impetus for the bolt's flight. Like the longbow, the crossbow could shoot its missiles through a knight's suit of armor and could in fact pierce and shatter the thickest human bones that lay behind it. The crossbow was the first weapon in Western history to be officially condemned by the Catholic Church for its awesome destructive force—the first attempt to stop the arms race. What horrified people especially was not the sheer deadliness of these weapons but the fact that with them any peasant or urban commoner could strike down any knight, a direct threat to the rules of chivalry and the whole social order those rules represented and served to legitimate.

The stake was a defensive weapon that consisted of a rough-hewn barricade of sharpened posts scattered about a battlefield. Its aim was to limit the maneuverability of mounted knights by goring the horses they rode. Without freedom of movement and the added force to his lanceblows provided by his horse's charge, a mounted knight became a much less lethal fighter.

Armed with these weapons and the willingness to use them, the English were initially able to tip the scales in their favor. The basic English strategy was to harass the French as much as possible with small bands of soldiers, led by nobles to be sure, but relying increasingly on common infantry armed with the new weapons. The English invaded, plundered, cut down vineyards, burned bridges, and disrupted trade, then fled before the French could amass their feudal armies and rout them. Surprisingly few pitched battles took place—yet whenever they did, the English usually won. The first major battle took place in 1346 at Crécy, when the French managed to cut off the English retreat route through Flanders. The English

---

14. The kind of tree mattered a great deal. Yew trees, when felled, offer lumber that comes in three distinct layers: under the bark lies a layer of white sapwood that is highly pliable and ideally suited to the outer shell of a bow, but immediately behind it is a hard core of red heartwood that remains remarkably rigid and gives enormous force to the drawn bow.

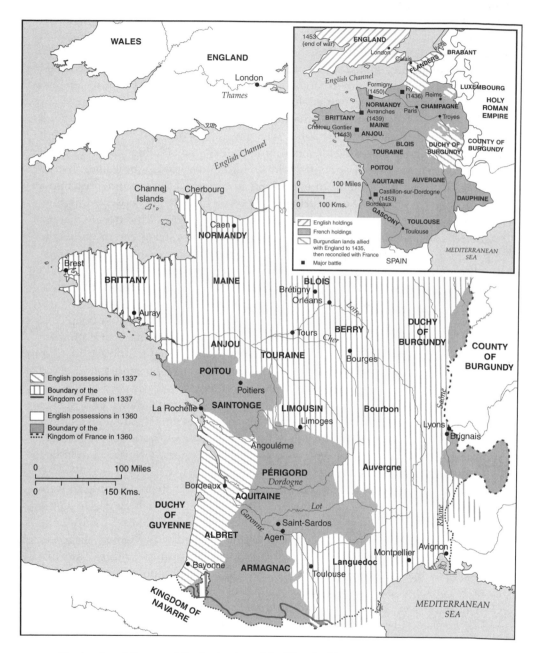

England and France at the beginning of the Hundred Years War, with inset of England and France at the end of the war

archers carried the day. According to Jean Froissart (1338–1410), the author of the greatest contemporary chronicle of the war:

> Then the English [longbow] archers stepped forward and shot their arrows with great might—and so rapidly that it seemed a snow blizzard of arrows. When these arrows fell on the Genoese [the French ally at the time] and pierced their armor, they cut the strings of their own weapons, threw them to the ground, and turned and ran. When the king of the French, who had arrayed a large company of mounted knights to support the Genoese, saw them in flight he cried out: "Kill those blackguards! They're blocking our advance!" But the English kept on firing, landing their arrows among the French horsemen. This drove the charging French into the Genoese, until the scene was so confused that they could never regroup again. . . . [When the slaughter ended] it became clear that the French dead numbered eighty banners, eleven princes of the realm, twelve hundred knights, and thirty thousand commoners.

The numbers are bloated, but the general picture is accurate. After Crécy the English forces, led chiefly by the heir to the throne—another Edward, known as the Black Prince—returned to their harassing strategy for several years. In 1356 another large battle took place at Poitiers with even greater results for the English, who not only defeated the French but captured their king and carried him back to London for ransom.[15]

Several temporary truces shortly followed, but the final phase of the war opened in 1415 when the new English king, the hot tempered Henry V, determined to conquer France outright. A bloody battle at Agincourt in that year, in which another fifteen hundred French nobles disappeared, opened the door for his conquest of the northern third of France. As the English prepared to march south and take the rest of the country, three fortunate things happened for the French: a death, a miracle, and a new alliance. First, Henry V contracted dysentery and died in 1422, depriving England of its most forceful leader since the war began. France's weak-minded new king Charles VII (r. 1422–1461) was ill-equipped to seize the opportunity this represented, but then the miracle happened. An illiterate seventeen-year-old peasant girl named Joaneta D'Arc [Joan of Arc, in Anglicized form] in 1428 began to hear heavenly voices telling her to persuade Charles to place her at the head of the French army and drive the English from the realm. Joan never professed to understand why God had chosen someone like her to lead an army, but she obeyed without hesitation. Charles, who may or may not have believed in her heavenly mission (historians still bicker over it), did assign her a military command. She

---

15. This led to the French tax revolt known as the *Jacquerie*. It is worth mentioning that French devotion to the ideals of chivalry remained so strong that a curious event occurred. The French ambassadors who forwarded the ransom money to London intentionally shortchanged the English, and bragged of their cunning to the king, John, after his return to Paris. John was so shocked by this betrayal of chivalric values that he insisted on returning to captivity in London until the French nobles came up with the rest of the money. What good was it, he wondered, to fight a war in defense of chivalry if the knights themselves failed to live up to its code?

cut her hair short, wore men's clothing and armor, and rode into battle. Almost in spite of herself she was surprisingly successful and scored some signal victories. Her courage and modest success helped persuade the French that they really could win after all—and given the mystical thrust of Joan's leadership, to believe that God was on their side.

In 1430 the Burgundians, who were allied with the English against the French, captured Joan at Compiègne and sold her to the English, who in turn accused her of witchcraft—largely a trumped-up charge—and turned her over to inquisitors. Joan's descriptions of her mystical voices were closely examined, along with her explanations for her supposedly unnatural habit of wearing male clothing, and she was condemned as heretic. She was burned at the stake in 1431.[16] She had not been on the scene long enough to change the course of the war, but her effect on improving French morale when it was at its lowest point was considerable.

What truly brought about the end of the war—the third piece of France's new luck—was the Burgundians' decision to break their alliance with the English and throw their support behind Charles VII. Burgundian motives are not entirely clear, but it is possible that Joan's success in rallying French morale convinced them that the war would simply continue on and on unless something was done to break the deadlock. Whatever their reasons, they defected from the English. No longer forced to fight a two-front war, the French were thus able to drive the English from their principal northern strongholds of Paris, Rouen, and Guienne. The exhausted English soon sued for peace, and the war finally ended in 1453 with the English in possession only of the port city of Calais and with the victorious French united enthusiastically behind their monarch.

Several important consequences of the conflict stand out. First of all, the new military tactics significantly hastened the demise of feudalism. From the eleventh century onward, what had justified a permanent, privileged aristocracy who controlled the lives of the peasantry that served it was the fact that the nobles provided the basic services that upheld social order: They defended the realm with their own lives; they oversaw the prosperous work of the rural economy, which was the backbone of economic life; and they provided the essential government services that maintained order. By the fourteenth century, however, the urban economy had emerged as the most essential aspect of the medieval world; the improvement of educational levels among the commoners meant that rulers did not have to rely on aristocrats for civil services, and the new techniques of warfare made it clear that henceforth the bulk of military service could be provided by commoners who needed only enough education to point their crossbows away from themselves before pulling the trigger. For the cost of maintaining a single mounted knight, a ruler could instead arm several hundred infantrymen, any one of whom could, with a

---

16. Noting the many irregularities in her trial, the papacy in 1455 reversed the sentence and formally proclaimed her innocent of all charges; in 1920 she was canonized as a martyr to the faith.

good shot, eliminate the knight in a moment.[17] The economy, civil administration, and military, in other words, had been revolutionized. Social revolution seemed close behind.

Although hereditary aristocrats retained their influence for centuries to come, their place in western Europe had changed significantly by the end of the fourteenth century. As outbreaks like the Ciompi Rebellion, the Jacquerie, and the English Peasant's Revolt indicated, masses of rural and urban commoners were willing to challenge openly the idea of maintaining privilege for a caste that no longer played its old indispensable role. Many now railed against not the *abuse* of privilege but the very *idea* of privilege. Why should a mere five percent of the population continue to have jurisdiction over the masses, control the land, monopolize the courts, enjoy exemption from taxes, dominate the Church, and be lauded by poets as the bulwarks of everything civilized in the world, when the bulk of the essential services in Europe were now provided by people of common birth? "When Adam delve and Eve span, Who was then the gentleman?" asked William Langland in his poem *Piers Plowman*; the meek-sounding question implied a radical idea—that when God created the world in all its perfection, there were no "gentlemen," no aristocrats, no privileged few living off the labor of the many. There was instead an absolute equality of mankind, and therefore the very notion of ordered hierarchy, perhaps the defining characteristic of the medieval mind, had no place in God's world. European society had entered a period of rapid change.

CHALLENGES TO CHURCH UNITY

Several important new developments appeared in western religious life at this time. In the thirteenth century the Church, with the papacy at its head, had pervaded medieval society, and the idea of Christendom—the Christian world as a unified organic whole that shaped and gave meaning to life—held sway as the dominant ideology, coloring everything from scholastic philosophy to economic theory, from artistic judgment to political policy. But by the end of that century there were already clear signs of a major shift in Latin religious life, a change not in doctrinal content but in spiritual style. The mystical phenomenon—it hardly seems right to call it a movement—injected a powerful new strain of spiritual energy among believers everywhere, and the various monastic reforms and new mendicant orders revitalized religious life. The aged Pope Boniface VIII (r. 1294–1303) celebrated these achievements (as well as himself) by proclaiming the Jubilee Year of 1300, a

---

17.   By the end of the Hundred Years War, gunpowder was also widely known (a German monk had described it as early as the late twelfth century, and Roger Bacon, the radical Franciscan, had determined its makeup in the thirteenth), but it did not have the same initial impact as the longbow and crossbow for the simple reason that whereas gunpowder itself was relatively inexpensive to produce, the cannons and handheld weaponry that employed it were not. Large-scale use of gunpowder by European armies did not become the norm until well into the sixteenth century.

sort of grand ball that the Church threw for itself, with pilgrimages, special services, the bestowal of indulgences, and festivities throughout Latin Christendom but focusing especially upon Rome. Popular response exceeded his wildest dreams, as no fewer than one million pilgrims from all over Europe made the journey to Rome, singing hymns, chanting, praying, celebrating masses, and incidentally bringing enormous sums of money into local coffers.

But only five years later a grimmer chapter suddenly opened in the Church's history. As we have seen, many Catholic faithful, both high-and low-born, had become dissatisfied with the Church's growing worldliness, its concern with crusades and taxation, its attempt to manipulate the international economy, its headlong push into politics, and its meddling with the intellectual activities of the universities. This anticlericalism had many roots and took many forms, but it frequently, if not usually, bore some relation to the centralization of ecclesiastical authority, which many began to believe had progressed beyond tradition and reason. Innocent III, around 1200, had envisioned a papal monarchy in which the Church would be involved in secular affairs as an impartial arbiter; Boniface VIII, around 1300, rejected the notion of disinterestedness and insisted on the Church's right to control whatever it wished to control. His pontificate marked a turning point in the history of the papacy. Much of whatever popular support for the Church was generated by his Jubilee was undone by his promulgation of two bulls: *Clericis laicos* (1296) and *Unam Sanctam* (1302). At first glance the texts appear relatively harmless, but their implications were considerable.

Clericis laicos dealt with taxation. Philip IV of France (r. 1285–1314) was chronically short of money to pay for his ambitious political schemes and decided to raise his income by heavily taxing the French clergy. Boniface responded immediately with his bull, which imposed a penalty of excommunication on anyone taxing clerical property without the Supreme Pontiff's direct authorization. The bull irritated Philip, of course, but it also angered many commoners in France and elsewhere because they regarded it as further evidence of the Church's quick action whenever it came to assuring its own well-being, whereas it was frustratingly slow in responding to the needs of the masses. But the bull touched a raw nerve with the churches, too, since state taxation of local churches was hardly new—but by tradition such taxation had been done with the consent of the clergy themselves. The pope seemed to be undermining the authority of the local clergy in order to maximize his own. Boniface and Philip reached a temporary compromise, but in 1301 Philip renewed the fight in an underhanded way by circulating a forged document that purported to be a new bull from Boniface, one in which the pope supposedly claimed direct temporal authority over the French king. Philip's timing was right. Popular outrage over Boniface's supposed claims broke out all over France.

Boniface responded by condemning the phony bull and issuing a genuine new one, *Unam Sanctam*, which made even more extravagant claims for papal power than did the French fake. *Unam Sanctam* was a short, bellicose, and utterly unapologetic declaration of papal supremacy over everyone, everywhere, and at all times. It offered little by way of argument or justification of its claims. It reads like a communiqué from a commander-in-chief—which of course is precisely what Boniface intended.

> We are compelled by our faith to believe and maintain—and we do firmly believe and candidly confess—that there is only one holy, catholic, and apostolic Church, outside of which neither salvation nor forgiveness of sins is possible . . . This one and only Church can have only a single body and a single head—namely Christ and His vicar St. Peter (and Peter's successor); it is not a two-headed monster. . . . We are told in the Holy Gospel that in Christ's fold are two swords, one spiritual and one temporal. . . . But both swords, the spiritual and the material, are under the control of the Church. . . . The spiritual authority judges all things but is itself judged by no one. . . . In fact we hereby declare, proclaim, assert, and pronounce that it is absolutely necessary to every single human being's salvation that he be subject to the Roman pontiff.

It was the tone that angered people more than anything else; after all, nearly every assertion in the bull had been made by earlier popes (most of whom had had the diplomatic sense to couch their claims in less blunt language). Boniface's pontificate ended in misery, as popular opinion swelled against him across the Continent. Philip tried to capitalize on the old man's unpopularity by dispatching a force of three hundred cavalry and a thousand infantry armed with a warrant for the pope's arrest—charging him, outrageously, with offenses that ranged from murder and black magic to every imaginable variety of sexual misconduct. Philip's men found Boniface at his residence in Anagni, south of Rome; they stormed the palace, broke down doors and windows, stole everything they could find that was of value, set fire to the building, and finally seized the pope in his private chamber. Their rough treatment proved to be too much for the eighty-five-year-old man, who died of traumatic shock while in the soldiers' custody.

Two years later, after the brief pontificate of Benedict XI, Clement V became pope (r. 1305–1314). Although duly elected by the College of Cardinals, he was not popular with the people of Rome, who took to the streets to protest. Clement was a Frenchman, and the rumor ran through Rome that his election had been engineered by the French king. The protests turned violent, forcing Clement and the majority of cardinals who had voted for him to run for their lives. They escaped to southern France, where they were granted residence at Avignon by Philip IV. Thus began the period known as the *Avignon Papacy* (1305–1378). The popes of this period—there were eight of them, all French—were viewed with suspicion and disdain by contemporaries, and their reputations have hardly improved over the centuries. Most of them were well intentioned, pious, and capable figures, but they were never able to shake off the imputation that they were in effect servants to the French king, doing his bidding in return for his protection. Moreover, the fact that the popes in Avignon built themselves a massive, foreboding, and downright gloomy palace behind thick stone walls and with omnipresent armed guards made it seem that they had in essence turned their backs on suffering Christendom. The popes seldom ventured into public and were generally seen only by courtiers and ambassadors, who

Papal palace at Avignon. Fourteenth century. The palace constructed for the papal court during its exile in Avignon (1305–1378) looks vaguely, when seen from the air, like a maximum-security prison—which in a sense it was. From ground level it is a massive, imposing stone pile. The popes brought their entire administrative machinery with them to southern France, and few of them ever set foot outside their fortified bunker. Source: Giraudon/Art Resource, NY

offered bribes to the guards and paid graft to palace officials in order to have their cases heard by the pontiffs. Financial corruption ran rampant, until it seemed that the concern with money, and the power that money makes possible, was the popes' only concern.

Most of the Avignon pontiffs don't fully deserve their bad reputations; they simply had the misfortune to stand at the head of the Church at the very time that the medieval world entered its most calamitous century. The Great Famine, the Black Death, the Hundred Years War, the dissolution of the German Empire, the stalling out of the crusade movement, the collapse of the medieval economy, the resurgence of heresy, the decline of Byzantium, and the rise of a newly aggressive Ottoman Turkish state formed a knot of enormous problems that even a healthy and popular papacy would have found difficult to deal with. But the popes did add to their own troubles in many ways. Their obsession with money—which in a few instances even reached the point of excommunicating poor communities whose taxes were past due—struck Latin Christians as cold and brutish behavior. Respect for the papacy began to fall, and popular anticlericalism rose accordingly. The humanist poet Petrarca described the Avignon Papacy as a new "Babylonian Captivity" of the Church and openly lamented the corruption and worldliness at the curia's center. Even more openly, St. Catherine of Siena (1347–1380) fearlessly criticized the papal court and its obsessions with money, wars, and political maneuvering. Her surviving letters to popes and princes, scholars and commoners, of which there are more than four hundred, are filled with plain spoken outrage at the Holy See's miserable condition.

Several attempts were made to return the popes to Rome; after all, is the pope truly the leader of the Church if he is not the acting bishop of Rome? Local conditions made that difficult, however, and the Avignon Papacy finally ended only through creation of yet another crisis. In 1377 Pope Gregory XI bravely ventured back to Rome but died early the next year. The Roman crowds took to the streets demanding that an Italian pope be elected, to wrest the Holy See from the control of the French. The cardinals, fearing for their lives, accommodated them by electing an Italian, Urban VI (r. 1378–1389); however, most of the cardinals then immediately raced back to Avignon, declared Urban's election null and void (since it had occurred only under the threat of mob violence), and elected another Frenchman who took the name Clement VII (r. 1378–1394). Thus began what is known as the *Great Schism*. From 1378 until 1417, when the dispute was finally resolved, there were two papacies—one in Rome and another in Avignon. Each had its own College of Cardinals, its own corps of court officials, its own money-making apparatus. And each, of course, ordained and consecrated its own order of bishops. Two separate churches were in the making, each regularly anathematizing the other and courting support from secular rulers by offering blessings, indulgences, praise, and a share of ecclesiastical revenues. When the first two rival-popes died, each church selected a successor, continuing the split into a second and third generation. The stakes were high, and the popes and their underlings looked for support wherever they could find it among Europe's elites. They were not particularly selective in deciding which politicos to back and be backed by. One of the Avignon-based popes, Benedict XIII (r. 1394–1423), enthusiastically supported as a champion of Christian order the drunken, boorish German emperor Wenceslas (r. 1378–1400)—a man who once, angered by a burnt dinner, ordered his cook to be roasted on a spit.

Resolving the Schism was difficult, for each side of the dispute could legitimately claim to have been canonically selected by the (or *a*) College of Cardinals. Even more fundamental was the question: Who has authority to judge the pope or popes? No one wanted to turn to the German emperor and risk reopening the Church-State conflicts, and the kings of England and France were too immersed in the Hundred Years War to give much attention to the papal rift; in fact they were benefiting from the split too much to want to rush to heal it. The jurisdictional problem was critical, since its resolution would establish a precedent for all future disputes within the Church. By the first years of the fifteenth century, many theologians began to advocate a universal church council as the only way out of the mess. Councils, after all, had been a common tradition within the Church for addressing all sorts of internal problems. But never before had a council been convened in order to pass judgment on the papacy itself. If such a council met, wouldn't its actions suggest that the Holy See was subordinate to it? If so, in what sense then is the pope the head of the Church? Who had the authority to summon such a council? Who would host it? The call for a council raised a host of constitutional questions—but the fact that a council was ultimately agreed to is an indication of how grave a problem the Schism had become. Over five hundred prelates representing both sides of the split met at the Council of Pisa in 1409. With great pomp the Council denounced both popes as "notorious schismatics and heretics guilty of perjury and bringing open scandal to the entire Church" and deposed them. In their place the Council elected a new pope, Alexander V (r. 1408–1409). But the first two popes, Gregory XII and Benedict XIII, stubbornly refused to recognize the Council's actions, leaving the Church in the humiliating position of having three popes. Popular frustration reached record levels, and political opportunists like the Neapolitan king began to move their armies into the Papal State itself. There seemed no other option, so a second council was convened at Constance in 1417. The Council of Constance deposed all three popes and elected Martin V (r. 1417–1431), effectively putting an end to the Schism.[18] But the Council of Constance also asserted in the strongest possible language the supremacy within the Church of an ecclesiastical council. The Council's decree *Haec Sancta* declared that a council "holds its power directly from Christ, and that all people, of whatever rank or dignity, even the pope himself, are required to obey it in all matters relating to faith, the end of the Schism, and the general reform of God's Church. . . . [Moreover] any person of whatever position, rank or title, even a pope, who stubbornly refuses to obey [a council] . . . shall be subject to its severe and just punishment." This was a far cry from Boniface VIII's *Unam Sanctam*. The so-called *conciliar theory* remained a lively debate within the Church for well over a hundred years and ultimately helped trigger the Protestant Reformation—since one of the specific points on which Martin Luther was officially condemned in 1521 was his assertion that a council has authority over the pope.

---

18. Two of the other three popes reluctantly accepted their deposings for the good of Christendom. But Benedict XIII angrily held out until his death in 1423, hurling excommunications and anathemas at everyone from his castle in Spain.

The Great Schism added powerfully to the disappointment and disgust felt by many Christians for the upper echelons of the Church. Piety continued to run strong and probably even increased in the face of so many troubles throughout the century, but many faithful began to turn away from regular church practice and to seek new expressions of their devotion. Lay confraternities began to flourish, groups in which the Scriptures were studied, hymns sung, and prayers led by educated laymen and laywomen. All-female houses of beguines remained popular too, following ideals of simplicity and service. Within the Church structure, signs of discontent were rampant. The Franciscan order split angrily over the notion of ecclesiastical wealth, with the most radical friars (the Franciscan Spirituals) demanding an ideal of "apostolic poverty." The Spirituals called upon the Church at all levels to abandon all property and wealth, and insisted that a refusal to do so would imply the negation of the Church's spiritual authority. This notion predictably horrified the Holy See; Pope John XXII (r. 1316–1334) condemned the renegade order, but its members had gained considerable popularity among the common people.

Discontent led many of those people into heresy. Two of the most significant heretical groups of the fourteenth century were the Lollards (or Wycliffites, after their founder John Wycliff) in England and the Hussites, followers of the religious and social reformer Jan Hus, in Bohemia. John Wycliff (1330–1384) was the Master of Balliol College at Oxford University and a popular preacher. He was a prolific writer and original thinker, but he might never have caused a stir had he not been pulled into politics by King Edward III in 1374. Edward appointed Wycliff to serve on a commission to negotiate with papal representatives regarding the relationship between the English Church and the perogatives of the monarchy. Like other monarchs of the time, Edward hoped to capitalize on the Avignon Papacy's unpopularity by winning an extention of his control over ecclesiastical appointments and ecclesiastical revenues. Wycliff came away from the experience disillusioned with both the clerical and secular powers, and he began to entertain a number of beliefs that put him at odds with both. He argued that the exercise of authority on earth, whether ecclesiastical or political, is a gift from God and not an intrinsic right of those individuals and institutions that wield it; such authority is external to those individuals, not a constituent element of them. From this it follows—and this is where Wycliff got into trouble—that the moral right to exercise authority depends on the moral worthiness of the person in power. A secular or clerical authority whose personal behavior is at odds with God's just expectations effectively nullifies his own legitimacy as an earthly power. By this logic, a secular ruler may justifiably usurp the authority and confiscate the property of unworthy clergy (an idea that no doubt made Edward III smile); but so too might a righteous populace justifiably usurp the authority and confiscate the property of an unworthy king (at which point the smile presumably left Edward's face).

Wycliff had a predilection for provocative ideas and he enjoyed the shock value of what he said and wrote. But it is by no means clear that he endorsed political or ecclesiastical revolution, even though many of his readers believed him to have done so. His arguments linking moral worthiness and earthly dominion can be read as nothing more radical than a call for those with power in the world to improve their moral lives. Nevertheless, his followers, who became known as *Lollards* (from a medieval Dutch word *lollaerd*, meaning a "grumbler"), seized upon his ideas and soon surpassed them. The Lollards, who came chiefly from the artisanal classes and played an important role in fomenting the Peasants' Revolt of 1381, opposed the subordination of the English Church to Rome, the temporal authority of the clergy, the doctrine of transubstantiation,[19] the demand for clerical celibacy, and the veneration of religious images. The Lollards also demanded that, in order to remain valid ministers of God's word, all clergy had to attend regularly to their parishes' needs (a notion that Wycliff, an absentee-rector of several rural parishes, might have balked at), and they insisted most especially on the need to have English translations of the Bible available to all believers.

The Catholic Church had always been opposed to vernacular translations of the Scriptures and had squelched earlier efforts in this area with a heavy hand but not out of a desire to keep God's message from the people. There were three main reasons for prohibiting translations of Scripture: first of all, the belief that St. Jerome's Latin Vulgate was itself a divinely inspired rendition, and therefore not to be tampered with; second, the conviction that one of the chief strengths of Christianity was its transcultural nature, and that as long as all Christians read the Scriptures in the same language and spoke to each other in the same tongue, that transcultural element would not be lost; and third, the belief that it mattered a great deal, even if only as a matter of individual spiritual discipline, for the faithful to come to the Bible's language, not vice versa. But Wycliff produced a complete English version of the Bible—hardly a model of accuracy and not even the first such version—that circulated widely, if surreptitiously, throughout England. His ideas had considerable appeal.

And not only to the English. King Richard II (r. 1377–1399) married a Czech princess named Anne, and this union resulted in heightened contact between their two realms; Wycliff's ideas soon circulated throughout the Czech territories—known as *Bohemia* in the Middle Ages—and he became briefly one of the most popular authors in the land. Among his most avid readers was the Czech nationalist and earnest reformer Jan Hus (1372–1415). Hus was a professor of theology at the University of Prague (the first university established in eastern Europe) and served as confessor to the Bohemian queen. He shrank from some of Wycliff's most radical views but generally endorsed the main thrust of his ideas. Even so, Hus might never have been a public figure were it not for his entanglement in politics. Bohemia was technically part of the Holy Roman Empire and was as independent-minded as most of the provinces. Two matters thrust Hus into the political spotlight in 1409. First, the emperor Wenceslas (the one who got very angry when his dinner was overcooked) ordered a reorganization of the University of Prague in

---

19.   The Catholic doctrine that in the Eucharist the material essence of bread and wine is fundamentally and absolutely changed into the body and blood of Christ.

"Despair," an allegorical painting by Giotto di Bondone, depicting one of the cardinal sins. Although painted in 1305, it illustrates powerfully one of the dominant elements of the fourteenth-century atmosphere. The fresco appears in the Scrovegni Chapel in Padua. Source: Art Resource

which a majority of the leading positions went to ethnic Czechs. The disgruntled German faculty stormed away and founded a rival new university at Leipzig where they spread rumors that Prague was in the grip of heretical Wycliffites led by Hus. Second, several of the Leipzig faculty ventured to the Council of Pisa, which was then involved in the embarrassing business of turning a Church torn between two popes into a Church torn between three. The king back in Prague supported one of the popes, the Archbishop of Prague supported a second (to whom he owed his archbishopric), and Hus was inclined toward the third. Disgust over the situation started to drive Hus into a closer adherence to Wycliff's heretical views.

Hus finally was summoned to answer charges of heresy at the Council of Constance. His trial was hardly a fair one, since he was allowed only to give one-word answers to the questions put to him; he wrote many letters to friends and supporters back in Prague in which he bemoaned not being allowed to explain himself. In the end he was condemned on thirty of forty-five specific charges and was burned at the stake. Although he died in the conviction that he was a good Catholic, Hus' execution was later regarded as the martyrdom of a proto-Protestant.

The problems confronting the Church in the fourteenth century proved too much for it. Even though many of those problems were not of its own making, the Church had to adapt to appallingly difficult conditions. It might have made some better choices at particular moments, but the Church's great misfortune was that Latin Europe went into a tailspin precisely at the point of a fundamental constitutional crisis within the Church—and that until the crisis was resolved, no proper campaign to address the troubles of the age could be forthcoming. The keen disappointment felt by millions helped to pave the way for the Protestant Reformation in the early sixteenth century.

SUGGESTED READING

Texts

Froissart, Jean. *Chronicles.*

Kempe, Margery. *The Book of Margery Kempe.*

à Kempis, Thomas. *The Imitation of Christ.*

Langland, William. *Piers Plowman.*

Wycliffe, John. *On Simony.*

Source Anthologies

Goodich, Michael. *Other Middle Ages: Witnesses at the Margins of Medieval Society* (1998).

Hudson, Anne. *Selections from English Wycliffite Writings* (1997).

Shinners, John. *Medieval Popular Religion, 1000–1500: A Reader* (1997).

Stouck, Mary-Ann. *Medieval Saints: A Reader* (1999).

Strauss, Gerald. *Manifestations of Discontent in Germany on the Eve of the Reformation* (1971).

Van Engen, John. *Devotio Moderna* (1988).

Studies

Allmand, Christopher. *The Hundred Years' War: England and France at War, ca. 1300–ca. 1450* (1988).

Geremek, Bronislaw. *The Margins of Society in Late Medieval Paris* (1987).

Goodich, Michael E. *Violence and Miracle in the Fourteenth Century: Private Grief and Public Salvation* (1995).

Guenée, Bernard. *States and Rulers in Later Medieval Europe* (1985).

Hillgarth, J[ocelyn]. N. *The Spanish Kingdoms*, 2 vols. (1976–1978).

Jordan, William Chester. *The Great Famine: Northern Europe in the Early Fourteenth Century* (1996).

Kaminsky, Howard. *A History of the Hussite Revolution* (1967).

Kedar, Benjamin Z. *Merchants in Crisis: Genoese and Venetian Men of Affairs and the Fourteenth-Century Depression* (1976).

Langmuir, Gavin L. *History, Religion, and Antisemitism* (1990).

Miskimin, Harry A. *The Economy of Early Renaissance Europe, 1300–1460* (1975).

Mollat, Michel, and Philippe Wolff. *The Popular Revolutions of the Late Middle Ages* (1973).

Nicholas, David. *The Later Medieval City, 1300–1500* (1997).

Nirenberg, David. *Communities of Violence: Persecution of Minorities in the Middle Ages* (1996).

Ozment, Steven. *The Age of Reform, 1250–1550: An Intellectual and Religious History of Late Medieval and Reformation Europe* (1980).

Platt, Colin. *King Death: The Black Death and Its Aftermath in Late Medieval England* (1996).

Renouard, Yves. *The Avignon Papacy, 1305–1403* (1970).

Sedlar, Jean W. *East Central Europe in the Middle Ages, 1000–1500* (1994).

Sumption, Jonathan. *The Hundred Years War*, 2 vols. (1999).

Waugh, Scott L. *England in the Reign of Edward III* (1991).

Ziegler, Philip. *The Black Death* (1969).

CHAPTER 18

SIGNS OF A NEW ERA

Even at its zenith the medieval world showed signs of strain. It was after all an age of great achievement but not one of universal euphoria. Poverty still afflicted many lives; ignorance and prejudice still throve; governments still abused power; criminals still preyed on victims; husbands still beat their wives; zealots still persecuted those they disagreed with. Most markedly of all, popular prejudices hardened against those who did not fit well into the complex medieval mosaic—groups like the Jews, homosexuals, and lepers were increasingly singled out for exceptionally harsh treatment. By the end of the thirteenth century, some European governments, led by England, began to order the expulsion of Jews from their realms; most of the others followed suit over the course of the fourteenth. Spain, the final holdout, did the same in 1492. These social fault lines, these signs of strain, did not lead inevitably to the dissolution of the medieval sense of unity nor did they necessarily reflect a dissolution already underway. It took the catastrophes of the fourteenth century, which we discussed in Chapter 17, to break apart more or less permanently the mentality of High Medieval civilization. But during the second half of the thirteenth century, if not before, there were ample telltale signs that another wave of change (and a deeply troubling one at that) was on its way, one that would question and alter the grand schematic ideals of papal monarchy, scholasticism, and the belief in the world's ultimate orderliness.

Some of these changes are reflected in the writings of five people: a philosopher, William of Ockham (1288–1348); a political theorist, Marsilius of Padua (1275/80–1342); two poets, Dante Alighieri (1266–1321) and Geoffrey Chaucer (1340–1400); and the literary woman-of-all-trades Christine de Pizan (1364–1430). The first two knew each other and influenced each other's work, while the latter trio were separated by three generations and would most likely have had nothing very pleasant to say to one another, yet each of the five championed worldviews that were at odds with mainstream medieval certainties and pointed the way to modern doubts. Christine's writings betray a backward look longing for a lost security. These writers were not prophets—there were plenty of *those* around, mostly predicting doom and gloom—but they did exemplify a changed consciousness, an awareness that High Medieval certainties were anything but certain, and a conviction that while Truth, Justice, Love, and Joy still existed as absolutes, the paths to them were less smooth and less clear than earlier generations had believed. These writers did not cause, but they certainly reflected, a shake-up of the medieval mentality that began in the rocky period around 1300.

WILLIAM OF OCKHAM

William of Ockham, a small village in Surrey (southwest of London), was born around 1288. We know virtually nothing about his background and early life, but he probably received his primary education at a nearby Franciscan school because he joined the order before his fourteenth birthday (a very early age). It is likely that he then moved to the larger Franciscan school in London to begin his philosophical training. Around 1306 he moved on to Oxford, where he quickly impressed everyone with his exceptional intellect. After finishing his philosophy degree, he stayed on to lecture in logic. Philosophy at Oxford had been dominated by Franciscans since the says of Robert Grosseteste, and the teachers there had little patience with the scholastic system-building of the Dominican philosophers in Paris. Ockham was an eager champion of Franciscan particularism, its emphasis on the reality of discrete individual objects and the need to erect theories on the basis of their hard factuality, as opposed to the general Dominican preference for abstractively creating theories that were then used to organize and interpret the individual objects.[1] The danger of creating elaborate systems of theory, Ockham learned from masters like Henry of Ghent and John Duns Scotus, was that they can have the unintended effect of limiting God's power. If a theoretical assertion of, for example, the nature of God's grace is accepted as fundamental truth, does that not in effect *bind* God to obeying the theory? Ockham was an audacious thinker, but not so audacious as to argue *that*. He insisted that God was too transcendent and mysterious to be encompassed by rational theorizing; at the same time, he remained convinced that everyday human existence and the physical world in which we live is too various, contingent, and diverse to lend itself to easy generalization. Far better, he believed, to begin with small, provable truths and to build one's way up from them, and not to accept any larger truth than it was absolutely necessary to accept by the laws of logic.

Ockham wanted in a sense to free God, to restore His awesomeness and mystery, by undermining our ability to speak with rational certainty about Him. He outlined his approach to philosophy in three main books: a *Commentary on the Sentences* [of Peter Lombard], the *Golden Exposition*, and the *Summary of All Logic*. His best known dictum—known as "Ockham's Razor"—aimed to pare away unwarranted leaps in logic. At first glance it appears harmless enough: *Nunquam ponenda est pluralitas sine necessitate. . . . Frustra fit per plura quod potest fieri per pauciora.*

---

1. These are large but not altogether meaningless generalizations. There were some Dominican empiricists and some Franciscan deductionists, but this general distinction between the ways these two orders approached the world were genuine (and it also helps to explain the often open enmity that existed between the orders).

("Plurality is not to be posited unless it is absolutely necessary. . . . It is pointless to explain by many words [or arguments] what can be explained by only a few.") The simpler the explanation, the better; and the humbler the truth being propounded, the greater its likelihood to be in fact true. What especially interested Ockham was the question of how we can *know*, absolutely, something to be true. He posited that there are two kinds of knowledge: intuition and abstraction. By *intuition* he meant, in general, sense perception: that which we perceive through our senses and which (since our senses can be deceived, as in an optical illusion) can be corroborated by the sense perception of others. For example, I *know* that the object I am holding in my hand [a pen] is real because my senses perceive it directly and my sense perception of it is corroborated by the sense perception of my wife (who is now giving me a very strange look because I've just asked her if she could corroborate the pen's existence). *Abstraction*, to Ockham, is the way our minds identify real objects by associating them with like objects we have perceived in the past. In other words, I know that this real object in my hand is a *pen* because my mind can associate it with other similar objects I have known, all of which are in accord with the abstract idea of a pen. In brief, intuition leads to a truth's reality, while abstraction leads to a truth's identity.

All of which sounds simple enough, and unprovocative. But Ockham pressed on from there by arguing that abstraction is fundamentally a function of individual human memory rather than a universally applicable set of unchanging classifying truths. I know that this object is a pen because my memory recalls other pens I have seen, held, and used. But what if I have in my hand an object whose like I have never before seen, held, imagined, read about, or heard of? If that is the case, Ockham insists, then I cannot possibly know what the object is, nor will I ever know. Even if I put the object to use—if I use it, for example, as a paperweight—I have merely imposed an identity of my own making upon it; I have not come to know its true identity. Its real self, its classificatory thing-ness, ceases meaningfully to exist. To Ockham, universals—the "pen-ness" of my pen, the "chair-ness" of the chair I am sitting on—have no existence outside the individual human mind. "No universal actually exists, outside the mind, in individual things; neither is a universal any part of an individual thing or any part of the existence of an individual thing," he wrote in the *Golden Exposition*.

The implications of Ockham's thinking were wide and account for much of the trouble he got himself into. On the one hand, his theories about knowledge opened him to the charge of asserting that no such thing as Truth (a universal, if ever there was one) exists. This would have been a dangerous assertion to make even if Ockham had not been a member of the Church, for if Truth does not exist, or at the very least cannot possibly be known to humans, then the Church, as the earthly preserver and promoter of God's Truth, becomes meaningless. Moreover, Ockham's theories, when coupled with his thoughts about God's all-surpassing freedom from constraint, suggest the possibility that God could condemn to damnation those who have lived in and for Christian truth (if it exists), or could reward with eternal salvation those who spent their lives attacking and abusing that truth. He came close in fact to saying exactly that: "It is entirely possible for someone to be accepted and loved by God without having any inherent supernatural form [divine grace] in his soul; and it is entirely possible for someone who possesses such [grace] in his soul to be rejected by God." Taken to their logical extremes, Ockham's ideas made human life morally meaningless.

In his defense, it is not at all clear that Ockham intended his ideas to be taken to their logical extremes. His "razor" doctrine, after all, insisted that one should progress from one idea or conclusion to another only when it is absolutely necessary to do so. What he wanted above all was to deflate the hyper-confidence of Dominican scholasticism and to insist on intellectual modesty when confronting the mystery of life. But every book that flowed from his pen raised new suspicions about his orthodoxy and his loyalty to the Church.

In 1324 he was summoned to the papal court at Avignon to answer charges of heresy. While there he met Michael of Cesena (d. 1342), the Minister General of the Franciscan order, who himself was under suspicion by Pope John XXII of being secretly a Spiritual Franciscan (recall that the Spiritual Franciscans had been formally declared heretical in 1323). Ockham became a close friend of Michael's and was drawn toward the Spirituals' doctrine of evangelical poverty; he certainly was quickly disgusted by papal politics. In 1328 Michael and Ockham fled from the court in advance of their expected guilty verdicts and took refuge in Munich with the German emperor Louis of Bavaria (r. 1314–1347), the last medieval emperor to attempt to exert real political control over Italy and to challenge papal authority.

Protected by Louis and encouraged by Michael, Ockham poured his energy into a long series of treatises, which argued that John XXII and his immediate successors were themselves in fact heretics in rejecting the doctrines of evangelical poverty. (For good measure, he accused John of seven distinct heretical opinions and seventy questionable ones.) The doctrine of evangelical poverty, he insisted, was self-evidently true and the Church, by opposing it, stood in danger of vitiating its spiritual authority. At the very least, the papacy's position represented an abuse of power that had to be corrected.

Michael of Cesena's death in 1342 and Louis of Bavaria's in 1347 tempered some of Ockham's fury, and in his last year he reconciled himself to the main Franciscan order and to the Holy See. He died in Munich, probably during the attack of the plague that struck in 1348–1349, and is buried in the Franciscan church there. But his philosophical work had given a significant boost to a new way of thinking that directly challenged, and in fact openly rejected, the mode of reasoning that had long been the accepted norm in Latin Europe. Ockham's influence could be seen immediately in his own pupils who carried on his new approach; one of them, Nicholas Oresme (1320–1382), was the first to challenge the normative view of cosmology by asserting that the movement of the planets can only be explained by assuming the rotation of the earth. Another pupil, Jean Buridan (1300–1358), utilized Ockham's method to argue that the planets and stars were composed of the same essential material as Earth and that planetary motion continued of its own accord through physical laws rather than through either Aristotelian "intelligences" or divine action. More than a century before Copernicus introduced the heliocentric theory, the followers of Ockham had shaken the very structure of space.

MARSILIUS OF PADUA

Marsilius of Padua, the last great political theorist of the Middle Ages, was one of the people whom William of Ockham met in Munich. We know even less about his early life than we know about Ockham's. He was born, depending on which source one uses, in either 1275 or 1280 in Padua (about twenty miles west of Venice), where he studied medicine at the local university. Sometime around 1300 he decided to give up medicine in favor of philosophy and went north to the University of Paris. He evidently made as much of an impression on the Dominican faculty there as Ockham made—at almost exactly the same time—on the Franciscans in Oxford, for by 1313 Marsilius was the rector of the university. He seemed destined for a brilliant academic career.

Soon after arriving in Paris, Marsilius read a controversial new book called *On Papal and Royal Power* by John of Paris (1250–1304), a lecturer at the university. Like many people of the time, John was dismayed by the renewal of Church-State tensions between Boniface VIII and Philip IV, and tried to help resolve matters by clarifying what he regarded as the proper demarcations between secular and ecclesiastical authority. Secular government, he argued, derives its authority from the community it governs, for unless there *is* a community there is no essential need for a government; the community's existence creates the need for secular authority and thereby legitimates it. Ecclesiastical authority, on the other hand, has little to do with secular matters precisely because it is not secular in origin. Having been ordained by God, priestly and papal power reign supreme over all spiritual matters, but *only* over spiritual matters. John wrote: "Royal authority existed and was exercised before there even was a papal authority; there were kings in France before there were Christians in it. Therefore neither royal authority nor its exercise come from the pope; they come from God and the people who select a king by choosing any given individual or royal family." Popes have no right to depose kings, he concluded; only the communities governed by them do. Papal claims to *plenitudo potestatis,* in other words, were invalid.

Marsilius found such thinking irresistible. As a native of northern Italy, he had grown up in a world riven by Guelf-Ghibelline, papal-imperial struggles that threatened the survival of the proud communal republics who, he believed (and he was probably right), did not really want *either* papal *or* imperial overlordship. Marsilius decided to take up John's position after his death in 1304 and to push it even further. More than anything, he wanted to provide a solid philosophical justification for the Italian communes' independence from both royal-imperial and papal authority. He drew heavily on Aristotelian political theory, much more so than John himself had done, and in the end produced Europe's first comprehensive theory dealing with the *notion of governance* itself, not merely the governing authority of any particular type of political power (monarchy, republic, theocracy, or anything else). It took Marsilius many years to trace out his ideas, but he finally published his theory, anonymously, in 1324 under the title *Defensor Pacis* ("Defender of the Peace").

It is a long and sophisticated piece of work, divided into two main sections with a third added on that represents an abridgment or summary of what the first two argue. The first section is the most purely theoretical and leans most heavily on Aristotle. In describing the fundamental principles of government, Marsilius makes the community being governed the active agent: Communities are organic systems that create the rules by which they live just as they create and legitimize the administrative figures and institutions responsible for enforcing those rules. If that responsibility is not met—if a government fails to perform its duty as determined by the community—then the community has the right to depose and punish its governors. Marsilius was no democrat; he was perfectly comfortable with the notion that the rights of different individuals and groups may vary within a community. He wanted above all to discuss communities themselves as entities, to make his theory fit all types of human societies. His theories were certainly radical. To assert that all rulers, regardless of the type or nature of their rulership, serve the ruled, and that they do so at the pleasure of the ruled, was to invert the quintessential medieval notion of political society.[2]

The second part of the *Defensor pacis* focuses on a single issue, what Marsilius calls the "pernicious pestilence" of the doctrine of *plenitudo potestatis*. Papal claims to jurisdiction over all matters of secular life, he insists, have no justification. Neither the Bible, the early councils, nor the teachings of the Church Fathers support such a claim; moreover, that claim runs contrary to the case presented in the first section of Marsilius book. This was his most radical point of all. The true Church is the community of all Christian believers, he argued, not the institution created and maintained by the clergy; as a community it is bound by the same ideas regarding community governance as any other. The clergy, he comes dangerously close to saying, are the creation of the community rather than of God; the papacy has no divine sanction behind it. The only legitimate way for the Church to operate, therefore, is for the clergy to be subject to the community of believers as represented in council. He falls short of calling for elected representatives of the faithful, and maintains that the community of Christians already have de facto chosen representatives in the secular authorities whom they have appointed for themselves; in a monarchy, that authority is the king and his corps of officials, in an urban republic it is the republican administration. These governors may or may not have been democratically elected in the modern sense of the term, but having sprung

---

2. Just imagine Charlemagne's response to being told that he was the servant of the people and could be deposed by them whenever they wished.

organizationally from the wishes and needs of the community they are the best representatives of the people. For this reason, Marsilius calls for the radical secularization of the ecclesiastical society. The Church was to be made wholly subordinate to the secular government even in spiritual matters.

Marsilius has sometimes been viewed as a sort of proto-Reformation thinker but in reality his doctrine is in one sense highly conservative. Although his vocabulary and rational method differ from earlier writers, the basic message of the *Defensor pacis* is perfectly Carolingian in outline, if one looks at it from the point of view of a monarchical community. The Church as an institution exists only as a tool to be used by the secular government. But Marsilius' work is a modern text if one bears in mind that Marsilius is more a champion of communities themselves—of whatever variety—than he is of any particular form of secular government. On this account his book was revolutionary and could easily be just as offensive to imperial claims of power as it was to papal ones.

Marsilius tried to keep his authorship of the book a secret but within two years of its publication everyone knew it was his, so he confessed. He resigned his position in Paris and fled to Louis of Bavaria in 1327, just in time to be offered protection before the inevitable condemnation of the *Defensor* and its author as heretical. Louis had good reason to object to Marsilius' ideas too, but he seems to have found the man more stimulating and engaging than offensive. (He was also practically useful. Marsilius helped to "stage manage" Louis' imperial coronation and acclaim by the Roman crowds in 1328.) To help secure his position at the imperial court, Marsilius even brushed up on his medical knowledge and became Louis' personal physician as well as his chief advisor on religious matters. Louis' court in Munich thus maintained for nearly twenty years the three most notorious anti-papal heretics in Europe: William of Ockham, Michael of Cesena, and Marsilius of Padua. Small wonder the popes of his era could not stand him.

DANTE ALIGHIERI AND GEOFFREY CHAUCER

The two greatest poets of the Middle Ages, Dante Alighieri (1266–1321) and Geoffrey Chaucer (1340–1400), were as diametrically opposed to one another in personality and outlook as one can imagine. Chaucer, coming later, knew and admired Dante's poetry but had little sympathy for the man who had written it. Dante, had he known Chaucer, would probably have disliked him as intensely as he seems to have disliked everyone. There is an irony in the way historians and literary critics refer to these men: Dante, one of the most severe and arrogant personalities of all time, is universally referred to by his first name, whereas Chaucer, as jovial, self-effacing, and life-loving an author as one could wish for, is always referred to more formally by his last. Dante is the centerpiece of all his poetic works and of some of his prose essays, too; everything revolves around *his* experiences, *his* emotions, *his* understanding, *his* point of view. His magnificent *Divine Comedy* tells the tale of his journey through Hell, Purgatory, and Paradise; his development from lost sinner to saved soul offers a unique and transcendent glimpse of the divine. Chaucer's equally magnificent *Canterbury Tales* also tells of a journey, but not his own. The tale he relates is the journey of a diverse group of pilgrims—including a knight, a priest, a miller, a merchant, a franklin [a landowner], and, most splendid of all, a lustily outrageous widow—on their way to pray at Becket's shrine in Canterbury. Both works are encyclopedic: Dante encounters most of the people mentioned in this book while on his journey, but we see them all through Dante's eyes; Chaucer gives us a generous cross section of English society, but whatever we learn of the poet's personality is refracted through the eyes of his marvelous characters. Different though they were, both writers illustrate some of the changes that were brewing in late medieval society, and the comparison of them is as interesting as the contrast between them—the one being the poet who forged his own salvation and literally saw God, yet never smiled, the other being the poet who celebrated the foibles of everyday life and wept over its sufferings, yet never stopped smiling.

Dante was born in 1266 in Florence, one of the great centers of republicanism and civic culture, and he died in 1321 in Ravenna, one of the few remaining symbolic centers of faded imperial glory. Both sites were fitting ones, considering the trajectory of ideas and events that marked Dante's life. He was the son of a merchant in one of the richest commercial cities in Europe. Pride in civic culture and in personal craftsmanship were dominant traits of the city, and Dante absorbed both. But Florence was engulfed—as was most of northern Italy—in continual strife between Guelph and Ghibelline factions. In the 1260s the last members of the Hohenstaufen family were still trying to retain power, and the papacy had recently allied itself with the Angevins to whom they awarded Sicily and southern Italy. Dante's family were staunch Guelfs (called "Whites" in Florence, in contrast to the Ghibelline "Blacks"), but by the time he came to manhood he tried to remain neutral, although he was widely assumed to have "White" sympathies.

Dante had some formal education but seems to have been largely self-taught. His great love was literature, both classical and vernacular. He claimed to be able to recite the whole of Virgil's *Aeneid* by heart. A few fixed biographical dates are known. He met the love of his life (more on her in a moment) in 1275; he began his Latin education two years later in 1277; his parents arranged a marriage for him in that same year; he wrote his first extant poems in 1283; he married his fiancée (not the love of his life, even though the marriage seems to have been a relatively happy one) in 1285; he fought in at least two military campaigns between 1286 and 1289. His great love died in 1290. After that, Western literature was never the same.

Dante was a courtly love poet who, true to the genre, dedicated his art to the praise of a woman he loved and could not have. Her name was Beatrice Portinari, a local Florentine girl with whom Dante fell in love when he was only nine years old and she only eight. They seem to have actually spoken only once, when she coyly said hello to him when they met crossing a bridge. Obviously this love was not the ordinary sort of human-to-human relationship; it was not meant to be. This was *courtly love*, a literary conceit in service to a spiritual ideal—that of a pure love given totally away. Such a love, courtiers and poets believed, purified and transformed one's self; it made one a better person; it ennobled the soul and enriched the heart. And, being cleansed of all worldly interest, of lustfulness, and of greed of gain, such love made one a better Christian. Courtly love poets customarily used extravagant language to praise their beloved's beauty, grace, purity, and gentleness. The poetry was religious, not erotic or amorous. But what Dante did with Beatrice was without precedent.

He put the remarkable musicality of his verse at the service of an outrageous idea. His Beatrice, he decided, was no mere "sweet little angel" to be placed on a pedestal for all to admire while the poet sang verses in her praise. Beatrice was, by Dante's conceit, the very representative of Christ on earth: salvation incarnate. He fills his love sonnets with Christological imagery and verifies the transformative nature of her every glance, her every sigh. In 1293 Dante selected thirty-one of his poems in Beatrice's honor, surrounded them with historical and literary-critical prose passages, and published the resulting book as *La Vita Nuova* ("The New Life").

Nothing like this had been done before—a text that commented on itself (a hypertext!). Given Dante's personality, some of this approach was probably the result of egomania, but it also served a greater purpose: Dante patterned his mix of poetry, history, exegesis, and exhortation on the Bible itself, as if to send the message that he was not merely writing love poetry but was in fact compiling a sacred scripture of a divine being, one whose very name meant "Bearer of Blessedness." But the extraordinary thing about Dante is that all his work, while it lauds the allegorical Beatrice and, by extension, God, aims primarily to praise his own genius for having conceived so grand an idea. He envisions and wills his own salvation by inventing his own means to that end. By placing himself at the center of his poetic universe, Dante celebrates God's eternality but even more so his own poetic immortality.

At the end of the *New Life*, he mentions a new vision he has received, a new way to engineer his salvation through this miracle-woman of his: "If I live a few more years I hope to write of her what has never been written before of any other woman." This vision evolved into Dante's great masterpiece, *The Divine Comedy*.[3] It took him many years to write, and tradition has it that he penned the last lines only a few days before his death in September 1321. Among its other attributes, the *Comedy* is without a doubt the single greatest poem ever written about a mid-life crisis; it begins with the middle-aged poet "lost in a dark forest" of confused ideas, desires, goals, and temptations. As he stumbles about in this opening section, the Roman poet Virgil, the author of the *Aeneid* and here the symbol of human reason, appears to him with a promise to lead him out of the darkness. That's the good news. The bad news is that the only way out of the forest is to pass, literally, through hell and purgatory and to witness the dire suffering of innumerable sinners. As the two poets proceed, the *Comedy* offers an encyclopedic view of medieval society: An end-

---

3. He called it simply *The Comedy*. *Divine* was added to the title by admirers of the poem in the Renaissance.

less series of popes, princes, lovers, philosophers, military heroes, failed priests, shady merchants, poets, urban officials, criminals, teachers, preachers, scientists, engineers, and artists pass by, each assigned his or her proper place and receiving his or her proper punishment or purgation. Both *Hell* and *Purgatory*, the first two part of this roughly nine-hundred page poem, are a sadist's delight. Dante not only designs and structures the afterworld, he apportions the eternal fates deserved by everyone in it. He even goes so far as to assign a place in hell for Boniface VIII even while the old curmudgeon was still alive on the throne in Rome.

At the end of *Purgatory* a remarkable event occurs. Virgil disappears and Dante, standing alone on the summit of Mount Purgatory,[4] has a sudden vision of Beatrice's arrival. She descends from heaven and guides him through paradise, or most of it anyway. It turns out that it was she who had sent Virgil to him in the first place, to offer her loving grace. Together Dante and Beatrice ascend through heaven, which the poet depicts as a winding spiral of spheres (rather like a simplified DNA molecule). Here too a litany of familiar figures follows: Saint Augustine is over *here*: Saint Francis is over *there*. The early martyrs reside happily in *this* place; the angels abide in *that* one. At every stage, Dante fills the heavenly choruses with magnificent song; the superb hymn to the Virgin Mary that he places in the mouth of St. Bernard of Clairvaux at the poem's climax may be the greatest of them all and serves as the capstone of the cult of Mary that began in the twelfth century. Dante's *Comedy* has a structural harmony that is remarkable, one that makes it in many ways a quintessentially medieval text; but it is also an outrageously subversive piece of work. When Dante finally encounters God Himself, in the poem's last lines, one almost has the feeling that even God is in heaven only because Dante has decided to place Him there.

The people of Dante's time were aware of the fact that he was producing an epic poem unlike anything ever attempted. He published the first sections, *Hell* and *Purgatory*, as soon as he finished them. But the outrage people felt over his audacity was balanced by the recognition, often a grudging one, that he was producing a genuine masterpiece. One of the civic leaders of Florence even urged him to translate the work into Latin, so that everyone in Europe could experience it. What little we know of papal attitudes toward the project suggests that successive popes viewed it with grave theological suspicion—how could they not?—but that they too were aware of its unique imaginative and literary power.

The Divine Comedy is one of the most difficult poems in the world, and Dante himself is, as a person, one of the least likable poets of all time. But his talent was astonishing and, for our purposes here, his vision was earth-shattering. While he made certain bows to Augustinian orthodoxies, he simply ignored at will the teachings of the Church of Innocent III and Boniface VIII and placed his own stamp on the universe. *He* was the touchstone, the foundational point, the last voice. *He* chose who was in paradise, in purgatory, and in everlasting torment. *He* decided that a

---

4. Purgatory, in the poem, is a multi terraced mountain—the inverse of Hell, which is a deepening well of concentric circles leading down to the pit, the very abode of Satan.

middle-class Florentine girl could guide humanity to heaven and into God's own presence. The Church blanched at his hubris but recognized that an indomitable spirit had been born.

Geoffrey Chaucer, by contrast, seemed to embrace everything without classifying it, to celebrate everyone without judging them. A generous spirit suffuses all his work, even when he is at his most sarcastic and critical. He was born in the early 1340s (the exact date is unknown) in London, the son of a wine merchant with close commercial links with France. Chaucer grew up speaking French and English, and he attended a local school in London where he began to study Latin literature (especially Ovid and Virgil, his two greatest loves) and science, in which he kept an amateur's interest all his life. In 1357 he entered court life as a page to the countess of Ulster, the daughter-in-law of King Edward III. He served with the English army in 1359–1360 during one of its raids into France, early in the Hundred Years War, and was quickly captured. The fact that Edward III personally paid Chaucer's ransom suggests that he was already attracting attention as a person of considerable talent. He served thereafter on a number of diplomatic missions on the Continent. In 1366 he married Philippa de Roet, the daughter of a French knight of Hainault; since Philippa was a lady-in-waiting to the queen of England (also named Philippa), Chaucer became even more prominent as a courtier. He became a favorite aide to John of Gaunt, the duke of Lancaster, as well. Except for a few periods when, given the political upheavals within England after Edward III's death in 1377, he was briefly out of favor, Chaucer remained a leading courtier and civic official in London for the rest of his life, and he served on roughly a half-dozen international diplomatic and commercial missions. He died on 25 October 1400 in a house he had leased in the garden of Westminster Abbey and was buried in what came to be known as Poets' Corner.

Apart from some short verses, his first significant poetic works were a translation of the *Romance of the Rose* (or at least part of it) and a long verse eulogy for John of Gaunt's dead first wife called *The Book of the Duchess*. For a first creative effort *The Book of the Duchess*, which Chaucer probably wrote sometime around 1370, shows remarkable talent. He uses a fictional first-person narrator, a favorite device throughout his career, one that allows him not only to tell a tale but, by refracting the tale through the peculiarities of the narrator's personality, to add layers of irony and touching but often hilarious modulations of tone and detail. *The Book of the Duchess* begins with the narrator's account of his own suffering: He has endured inconquerable insomnia for no less than eight years because of the pain he still feels from a lost love affair. One day, while reading Ovid, he learns of the existence of Morpheus, the ancient god of sleep, to whom he decides to pray for relief. A deep sleep immediately follows, in which the narrator has a dream that comprises the rest of the poem. In the dream the narrator has joined a hunt in the countryside, and while riding through the woods he encounters a black-clad knight who is weeping in grief. The narrator asks the knight the reason for his sorrow, and the knight tells of his own lost love, the Lady White (symbolically, the duchess of Lancaster whom Chaucer is eulogizing). The knight, in being drawn from his solitary grief by the narrator's tactful and gentle questioning, achieves a kind of cathartic release: He still mourns his loss but comes to feel grateful for having had the lady's love in the first place. Observing simply that "By God, hyt ys routhe!" ["By God, it's a pity"], the narrator leaves the knight and awakens from his dream, presumably ready now to move on in life without the weight of his own crippling woe.

Other works followed in a steady stream: a translation of Boethius' *Consolation of Philosophy*, a curious fragment called *The House of Fame* (which Chaucer may have intended as a lampoon of Dante's *Comedy*), a love allegory called *The Parliament of Fowls*, and a love tragedy called *Troilus and Criseyde*, which Chaucer adapted from a long poem by Boccaccio, in which the hero Troilus is loved but ultimately betrayed by the unfaithful Criseyde, who is herself the victim of political and familial manipulations. He also wrote several other lesser works.

Greatest of all his works is *The Canterbury Tales*, which he began to work on in 1387. The grand "General Prologue" describes the scene: Twenty-nine pilgrims meet at an inn in Southwark to begin a pilgrimage to Becket's tomb in Canterbury. Their host, named Harry Bailly, proposes that they entertain themselves along the way by telling four stories each—two on the way there, and two on the journey back.[5] Telling so many tales from some many narrative points of view is a technique that Chaucer learned from Giovanni Boccaccio, with whose works Chaucer became acquainted during his diplomatic errands on the Continent. Boccaccio's best-known work was *The Decameron*, a loosely connected set of one hundred short stories told by a party of ten narrators (one apiece per day over a period of ten days) who have temporarily fled the city of Florence because of plague. This technique accorded perfectly with Chaucer's gifts for narrative energy and characterization, subtle irony and broad comedy. The whole work begins with a passage that has become famous:

Whan that April with his shoures sote➤	*sweet showers*
The droghte➤ *of Marche hath perced to the rote,*➤	*drought / root*
And bathed every veyne➤*in swich licour,*➤	*vein / such moisture*
Of which vertu➤ *engendred is the flour;*➤	*By virtue of which / flower*
Whan Zephirus➤ *eek with his swete breeth*	*the west wind*
Inspired➤ *hath in every holt*➤ *and heeth*➤	*Breathed into / wood / heath*
The tendre croppes,➤*and the yonge sonne*	*sprouts*
Hath in the Ram his halfe cours y-ronne;➤	*run*
And smale fowles➤ *maken melodye,*	*birds*
That slepen al the night with open ye➤—	*eyes*

---

5. If this was actually Chaucer's full plan, there would have been 118 tales in the poem—a stupendously long work, since each tale was provided with a prologue of its own (some of which were even longer than the tales they prefaced); as it happened, Chaucer lived to complete only twenty-four prologues and tales.

So priketh hen Nature in hir corages—   Nature so spurs them in their hearts
Than longen folk to goon* on pilgrimages,*   long / go on
And palmeres for to seken straunge strondes,*   foreigners / shores
To ferne halwes, couthe* in sondry londes;*   far-off shires / known / lands
And specially, from every shires ende
Of Engelond to Caunterbury they wende,   make their way
The holy blisful martir for to seke,   seek
That hem hath holpen,* whan that they were seke.*   them / helped / sick

(The language is difficult to newcomers, but exposure seems worthwhile just once. The trick is to read it aloud, phonetically. The marginal notes should help.)

Chaucer himself intrudes upon the narrative several times, complicating the interpretation of the stories wonderfully; by himself reacting to the personal quirks of the characters who have themselves just told and reacted to their tales—not to mention the fact that the *other* characters also respond to the tales as they are told—he creates a constantly shifting kaleidoscope of interpretational levels. As a result, a tale that may appear at first to be crude slapstick comedy (the Miller's Tale, for example, appears on one level to be merely an elaborate fart joke) emerges at second glance as a piece of clever literary satire (the Miller's Tale is also a send-up of tales of chivalric jousts and knightly exploits to win the love of a lady), and at a third glance to be a deep lament for the capacity of human beings to deceive themselves (the Miller's Tale also sympathetically portrays characters who believe they are in control of their lives even as they meet inexorable fates and receive fitting punishments: images of Noah and the Flood abound in the poem).

History textbooks commonly praise *The Canterbury Tales* for presenting a "panoramic view of medieval society," or some such thing. There is some truth to such a view, but by itself it says too little. Chaucer is doing more here than trying to provide a cross section of medieval life, just as Dante is trying to do much more than provide a poetic architecture for Catholic orthodoxies. Chaucer's world is not only one of shifting and contrasting viewpoints, but one in which as far as human understanding is concerned there is *nothing but* shifting and contrasting viewpoints. The world shimmers with uncertainty and the impossibility of complete knowledge. Chaucer loves the world, its people, and their lives with tremendous passion, but he has no great confidence in our ability to make total sense of any of it. Personal experience seems to be all that we have, he says, and Truth—with a capital T—is always beyond our reach. This does not mean that life is without its joys. The world teems with the stuff of happiness, if only we know where to look for it. But laughter, love, humor, and impatience with cant—not pious conventionality and naive intellectualism—are our best ways of finding it.

One of Chaucer's greatest characters, the bawdy and outrageous Alisoun or "The Wife of Bath," in the prologue to whose tale she describes her five marriages and the delight she took (or, with typical Chaucerian irony, claims to have taken) in the merriment, sex, food, and wine that filled them all, offers the closest thing there is to a summation of Chaucer's view of life:

But Lord Crist! whan that it remembreth me➤	*I think*
Upon my yowthe➤ *and on my jolitee,*➤	*youth / joyfulness*
It tikleth➤ *me aboute myn herte rote.*➤	*tickles / my heart's root*
Unto this day it dooth myn herte bote➤	*good*
That I have had my world as in my lyme.	
But age, allas! that al wol evenyme,➤	*poisons everything*
Hath me biraft➤*my beautee and my pith.*➤	*bereft of / vigor*
Lat go, farewel! the devel go therwith!	
The flour is gone, ther is namore to telle:	
The bren,➤ *as I best can, now moste*➤ *I selle;*	*bran / must*
But yet to be right mery wol I fonde.➤	*will I try*

Like Dante, Chaucer is a medieval writer but one who is more remarkable for the ways in which he stands in contrast to, and perhaps in defiance of, medieval certainties. *The Divine Comedy* represents a supreme effort to impose unity and order on the cosmos, but in its very insistence on this theme it belies the awareness that that unity is no longer there. *The Canterbury Tales*, assuming that what we have of it is representative of Chaucer's overall intentions for the work, surrenders even the attempt to assert unity and order, and it dares us to recognize that human life is an utterly unpredictable pilgrimage toward a goal that we, like Chaucer himself as well as his characters, may never live to reach. In light of such an awareness, a recognition of an unravelled world, Dante responds by willing an order of his own making upon the universe, whereas Chaucer reacts by celebrating, laughing at, bemoaning, and marveling at the individuals caught on the road to nowhere. But in the cosmos of both writers it is the experience of the individual that matters, that represents the only sure anchor in a world of unstoppable change.

CHRISTINE DE PIZAN

Christine de Pizan (1364–1430) was Europe's first professional woman of letters, a talented individualist who supported herself entirely by her pen. She was Italian, born in Venice to an astrologer in service to the Republic, but at the age of five Christine followed her father to Paris after he was hired as scientific advisor to the court of King Charles V (r. 1364–1380), and she spent the rest of her life in France. She was raised at court and given a solid education in languages and literature; growing up as a commoner (albeit a privileged one) amid aristocratic trappings, Christine combined the hard-working professionalism of the urban classes with the idealism of noble culture. Her lively demeanor and royal connections made her an attractive figure; she was courted by numerous suitors and at the age of fourteen was married to a nobleman from Picardy. Three children came in quick succession, and Christine might very well have ended up living a comfortable, if unremarkable, life as a patronness of a minor aristocratic court. But her husband died unexpectedly and left her with three children and an elderly mother to support, and little money to do it with. She was twenty-five. It seems that she began to write out of private need, an attempt to express her personal grief and fear; but she soon discovered that she had a talent for both verse and prose, and when friends urged her to publish her writings she found an admirer in Louis, the duke of Orléans (the brother of King Charles VI) who became her patron. Thus began a thirty-year career as a professional writer. She became famous after taking part in a literary debate over the popular *Romance of the Rose*, whose depiction of women she dismissed angrily as shallow and misogynistic. She never remarried or sought another career—even though she later lamented, in *The Book of Changing Fortune* (1403), that economic necessity had forced her "to become a man" who labored daily for survival—and poured out many volumes of prose and verse. The date of Christine's death is unknown, but probably occurred shortly after she completed her last known work, a poem called *The Song of Joan of Arc*, which appeared in late 1429.

Christine wrote in many genres: prose biographies, verse fables, essays, political commentaries, romantic ballads, short stories, courtly romances, literary satires, and moral treatises. Her works, like those of many prolific authors, are uneven in quality but all were popular in their time. No doubt one reason for that was her defense of French cultural and social superiority. Christine wrote during the darkest years of the Hundred Years War, when France suffered defeat after humiliating defeat at the hands of the English, and much of the power of her writing derives from her sense of moral urgency: The beauties and delights of life are to be celebrated but ought not to distract us from understanding that life is serious business. Whether urging the people on to repulse the English invaders and restore French greatness (in works like *On the Body Politic* [1407], *Of Arms and Chivalry* [1407], and *The Book of Peace* [1410]), skewering the fanatical esthetes of chivalric lore who love the idea of love more than the reality of flesh-and-blood women (in works like *Letter to the God of Love* [1399]), or praising the self-sacrificing zeal of Joan of Arc, Christine constantly insists on the value of the real, the here and now, the individuals present in our lives, the immediacy of emotion. The pain of her private losses never left her, and all her works carry the message that the time to be earnest is *now* because one can never tell when, given the world's unpredictability, our happiness will be snatched away from us.

The French defeat at Agincourt in 1415 broke her spirit, and she retired to a convent at Poissy, the birthplace of Louis IX. She continued to write, although less prolifically than before. Two heartrending works came first: *On the Prison of Human Life* (1416–1417), which bewailed the sufferings that so often characterize womens' lives in an unfair world, and *The Hours of Contemplating Our Lady* (1425), which Christine wrote to express her grief over the death of her son. Her last work was the rousing *Song of Joan of Arc*, which united her concerns for French society, the unfairness with which the world treats women, and the tragedy of frustrated love and idealism. Today her upbeat poetic satires and chivalric romances are more frequently read than her somber meditations—and they deserve to be read—but the focus on the upbeat can give a false impression of why she was so popular in her own time. Christine had the courage to describe the disappointments of life in unsparing terms and to insist that the only way to combat them was with honest emotion and honest relationships between people. And she insisted, almost relentlessly, that women deserve to be taken seriously. Social niceties and romantic fantasies are fun and should be enjoyed, but they should never blind us into thinking that they truthfully depict the reality of our solid and difficult humanity. If Christine's world is a harder and more difficult place that the romantic fairylands of many medieval tales, it has the benefit of being real and displaying the courage to demand to be taken for what it is.

Christine de Pizan, like the other writers in this chapter, pointed the way to a new era dawning. Her impatience with cant, her insistence on the significance of the individual, her conviction that life's real value can only be understood in terms of human relationships, her effort to overthrow earlier assumptions about the place of women in society—whether as individuals or as a group—and to demand a reordering of our values, and her philosophical pessimism all mark her as a figure of the Renaissance. Her writings are frequently dour, and will disappoint readers looking for lighthearted charm. She craved order and stability above all and was deeply depressed by the rapid erosion of those qualities all around her. Her work represents an urgent call for the people of France to return to (a rather conservative) political idealism, social order, emotional earnestness, and all that she regarded as the best in human nature. She certainly retained many medieval attributes—not least her political conservatism—but she had far more in common with those who came after her than before.

SUGGESTED READING

Texts

Alighieri, Dante. *The Banquet.*

———. *Complete Works.*

———. *The Divine Comedy.*

———. *The New Life.*

Chaucer, Geoffrey. *The Canterbury Tales.*

———. *Complete Works.*

———. *Troilus and Criseyde.*

Marsilius of Padua. *The Defender of Peace.*

Pizan, Christine de. *The Book of the Duke of True Lovers.*

———. *The Book of Peace.*

———. *The Path of Long Study.*

———. *The Treasure of the City of Ladies.*

William of Ockham. *Philosophical Writings.*

Source Anthologies

Blumenthal-Kosinski, Renate. *The Selected Writings of Christine de Pizan: New Translations and Criticism* (1997).

Bosley, Richard N., and Martin Tweedale. *Basic Issues in Medieval Philosophy: Selected Readings Presenting the Interactive Discourses among the Major Figures* (1997).

The Portable Chaucer.

The Portable Dante.

Studies

Aers, David. *Chaucer, Langland, and the Creative Imagination* (1980).

Bisson, Lillian M. *Chaucer and the Late Medieval World* (2000).

Brown-Grant, Rosalind. *Christine de Pizan and the Moral Defence of Women: Reading Beyond Gender* (2000).

Condren, Edward I. *Chaucer and the Energy of Creation: The Design and the Organization of the Canterbury Tales* (1999).

Gewirth, Alan. *Marsilius of Padua: The Defender of Peace* (1979).

Goddu, André. *The Physics of William of Ockham* (1984).

Jones, Terry. *Chaucer's Knight: The Portrait of a Medieval Mercenary* (1980).

Kolve, V. A. *Chaucer and the Imagery of Narrative: The First Five Canterbury Tales* (1984).

Leff, Gordon. *The Dissolution of the Medieval Outlook: An Essay on Intellectual and Spiritual Change in the Fourteenth Century* (1976).

———. *William of Ockham: The Metamorphosis of Scholastic Discourse* (1975).

McGrade, Arthur S. *The Political Thought of William of Ockham: Personal and Institutional Principles* (1974).

Pearsall, Derek. *The Life of Geoffrey Chaucer* (1992).

Richards, J. E. *Reinterpreting Christine de Pizan* (1991).

Willard, Charity C. *Christine de Pizan: Her Life and Works* (1984).

PART FOUR

TWO EPILOGUES

CHAPTER 19

CLOSINGS IN, CLOSINGS OUT

The late medieval world responded in a variety of ways to the crises it faced; not all ways were successful, nor were they all admirable, but it was clear that significant adaptations had to be made if Europe was to recover from the blows it had received. To many, Europe had in fact entered a new age. William of Ockham had rejected outright the quintessentially medieval belief in the ability of reason to decode the grand structure of God's ordered cosmos; in fact, he had attacked the very notion of order and insisted that only the hard, isolated, particular specific had any absolute meaning. Marsilius of Padua had argued passionately for the subjection of the Church to the secular state and for the political devolution of Europe itself. Dante and Chaucer had depicted worlds in which traditional structures of political and spiritual authority have failed; but whereas Dante resupplied a sense of order by imposing his own will on the universe, Chaucer chose to revel in the world's utter changeability, its wild variety and unpredictability. Christine de Pizan had a clear-eyed view of the latent harmfulness of medieval romance yet could not help but lament the passing of the world that had created it. Other figures also presaged an era of new values and attitudes. Jean Froissart (d. 1410) wrote his immense *Chronicles of France and England* (the standard edition today fills fifteen volumes) to eulogize the passing of aristocratic, idealistic, chivalric Europe and the rise of mass, mob-based, popular culture. The poet and early humanist Petrarca (1304–1374) decried the "barbarian" culture of the Middle Ages and looked forward to the start of a new era of enlightened thinking set free from the shackles of hidebound customs. Cries rose from Germany for the restoration of earlier certainties; one of the most passionate and comprehensive is an anonymous text from 1437:

> Almighty God and Father, Creator of Heaven and Earth, grant us the strength, grace, and wisdom to reattain the [former] ordering in our spiritual and secular lives. . . . All sense of obedience is dead, justice lies wounded, and nothing at all is now in its proper place—and that is why God has so justly withdrawn His grace from us. . . . Nothing can go well for very long when there is no proper ordering of Man's spiritual and earthly lives. . . . The lord emperor can no longer maintain his rightful station, which is continually diminished by the Electors [of the Diet] and other princes, with the result that our empire is sick, weak, and wounded. . . .
>
> There are numerous guilds in our fine imperial cities, but they have become too powerful and admission into them must be bought at a high price; moreover,

they pass laws among themselves—something that used to be the perogative of the cities. In fact in many cities they directly appoint the town council and determine how many guild-members shall serve on it. . . .

Another ill besetting our cities and countryside is the fact that individuals have more trades than are proper. One person is a vintner, yet he also sells salt and cloth. Another is a tailor, yet he engages in commerce. Everyone who is able to do so buys and sells anything at all, whatever they think will bring them a profit. But listen again to what our imperial law commands (our ancestors, bear in mind, were not fools): individual trades were created precisely in order that everyone should thus have a chance to earn his daily bread without trespassing upon another's trade; in this way the needs of the world are met and every man can support himself. . . .

All matters of citizenship and observance of law ought to be maintained by imperial authority, but the aristocrats, who still control most of the land, live almost as emperors in the own right upon their lands. These counts, barons, knights, and nobles . . . continue to reduce free farmers to dependence and bind them as serfs. . . . It is scarcely to be believed that such injustice still exists in the Christian world. . . .

The fifteenth-century English writer Thomas Malory devoted his years in various prisons (for crimes ranging from extortion, assault, and theft, to rape) to narrating in vivid style the tales of King Arthur and his idyllic court: a farewell to an idealized past in the face of ugly modern novelties.

But despite all the lamentations for the supposedly fast-vanishing medieval norms and manners, many of those traditions refused to go easily. In the realm of politics, a series of German rulers strove for decades to restore the imperial office to what it had been in the twelfth and thirteenth centuries; the feudal barons, though largely outmaneuvered in terms of political office and economic might, retained enormous influence in society and could still, when situations warranted it, bring governments to a halt. The Church, challenged and even derided on so many fronts, nonetheless offered the closest thing the west had to an umbrella-institution and a unifying ideology. Strict Catholic orthodoxy may have been on the wane, but not Christian zeal; the religious energy that had so long characterized medieval society still reigned supreme but now flowed through a plethora of channels.

Tough economic conditions prevailed from mid-fourteenth to mid-fifteenth century. The population of England, for example, fell nearly forty percent; moreover, this decline was matched by the decline in wool production and was surpassed by the decrease in wine production. Such decreases were felt throughout the Continent, and the weakened commercial and industrial base made it difficult for governments to find revenue. An impressionistic inventory of governmental incomes made by a Venetian writer compared governmental incomes in 1423 to what they had been only a century earlier. (See Table 19.1.) The specific figures are not to be trusted, but the general trend they illustrate is correct. Given these sorts of economic realities and the pained sentiments that surrounded them, it is not surprising to find that much of western Europe entered a period of retrenchment as the me-

Table 19.1 Comparison of State Revenues

Realm	State Revenues in 1320 (in Venetian ducats)	State Revenues in 1420 (in Venetian ducats)
Bologna	400,000	200,000
Brittany	200,000	140,000
Burgundy	3,000,000	900,000
England	2,000,000	700,000
Florence	400,000	200,000
France	2,000,000	1,000,000
Milan	1,000,000	500,000
Portugal	200,000	140,000
Spain	3,000,000	800,000
Venice	1,100,000	800,000

dieval world gave way to the early modern one. But retrenchment means more than a change in scale; it also involves an altering of priorities and a hardening of resolve. We see all these characteristics at play in the developments of the late medieval world.

THE LAST YEARS OF BYZANTIUM

The restoration of the Byzantine Empire in 1261 brought to power the last Greek dynasty, the Paleologoi. But *power* is hardly the right word to use since the restored rulers began with little and steadily lost whatever they had begun with; between 1400 and 1453, when the Ottoman Turks finally wiped out the last traces of the empire, the Byzantine state was little more than the city of Constantinople, an isolated municipality surrounded by hostile forces. The last two centuries of Byzantine history are essentially the history of a congeries of independent principalities—some Greek-led, others still Frankish-controlled—that paid a grudging lip service and occasional taxes to the Paleologoi in Constantinople. Even the Greek Orthodox Church, traditionally the principal bulwark of imperial power, paid little attention to the emperors. This inattention turned into open resistance when, throughout the fourteenth century and well beyond 1400, emperor after emperor desperately sought help from the west by again offering to subordinate the Orthodox Church to the papacy—the very stratagem that had initiated the crusades.

The empire's main weaknesses were economic and military. Control of the sea-lanes having long since passed into the hands of the Italians, the Saljuq Turks, and the Mameluks, the Byzantines suffered from commercial dependency. Forced to rely on others for the import and export of goods, they faced constant demands for more commercial privileges, more trading monopolies, more tax exemptions, from the foreign merchants who were in a position to set their own terms. The drain this dependence represented on imperial revenues made it impossible for the rulers in Constantinople to finance any sort of recovery, whether military or otherwise. Land revenues also declined because the local lords could simply refuse, with impunity, to send the rents and taxes they owed to the court. Late Byzantine economic policy took the form, symbolically, of selling off the family silver by granting out revenues, privileges, and exemptions left and right. At a certain point, the symbolic became real: One late emperor, John V, even found it necessary to pawn the imperial crown jewels to the city of Venice.

The military threat came in several waves. The Fourth Crusade and the period of the Latin Empire (1204–1261) had wreaked devastating violence on the country-side. As the westerners gobbled up whatever they could of Greek land and wealth, the Saljuq Turks and Egyptian Mameluks carved up the Holy Land and Anatolia between them, while most of the Balkans were taken over by the Bulgars and Serbs. The onslaught of the Mongols in the thirteenth century had shaken matters up even more by destroying the Abbasid caliphate, threatening the Bulgars (who in turn pressed further southward into Byzantium), and weakening the Saljuq Turks in Anatolia. The decline in Saljuq power enabled a rival group, the Ottoman (or Os-manli) Turks, to rise against them. The Ottomans had settled in northwestern Ana-tolia in the thirteenth century, under their leader Osman, as a semi-independent client nation under Saljuq control, but they quickly emerged as an autonomous power when Saljuq authority disintegrated. Keeping their main power base in western Anatolia, the Ottomans created a tightly organized army that in 1354 crossed the Bosporus and entered southeastern Europe to establish the first Islamic beachhead in Christendom since the conquest of Spain in 711. The Bulgars and Serbs, though no friends of the Byzantine state, rushed to the defense of the Ortho-dox faith. They were defeated in a quick series of clashes, though, the largest being the Turkish victory over the Serbs at the battle of Kosovo in 1389. The Ottomans then established a Balkan capital at Adrianople [modern Edirne] and proceeded thence to advance on Constantinople itself.

As Byzantium's demise grew imminent, western Europe's contacts with east-ern Europe increased. It was clear, after all, that the empire had long served as a buffer zone between the Christian world and the Islamic, between the European and the Asian, and in its impending absence the states of eastern Europe would be-come the buffer. Apart from Saxony and the East March territories of the German empire, Latin Christendom had had little to do with eastern Europe economically or culturally, but, starting in the fourteenth century and continuing into the six-teenth, the importance of relations with the east grew dramatically. Therefore, when Constantinople first appeared in serious danger of falling to the Turks, the west re-sponded, predictably, with yet another crusade. What was surprising, though, was the degree to which the westerners put aside their own squabbles in order to bring the crusade to pass. The English and French temporarily halted their Hundred Years War conflicts, the Burgundians joined in as well, and even the two rival popes (one in Rome, the other in Avignon, as a result of the Schism) set aside their differences. An army of about fifteen thousand soldiers, made up roughly equally of French, Germans, and Burgundians agreed to serve under the command of King Sigismund of Hungary, gathered near Budapest in the summer of 1396 and began to march southeast against the Ottoman stronghold of Nicopolis,[1] where they were joined by Venetian and Genoese auxiliaries. It took some time for the sultan, Bayezid, to march up from Constantinople, but when he arrived in September of that year he commanded a far superior force. What decided the battle, however, was another outbreak of chivalry among the French knights. They insisted on being placed in the front line so that they could lead the charge uphill against an enemy whose tactics they knew nothing about. As had happened to them as Crécy and Poitiers at the hands of the English, they were cut down by volleys of Turkish arrows and their horses were impaled by networks of spiked barricades. In the confusion that followed, Bayezid easily wiped out the rest of the crusaders. A second crusade effort in 1440 ended in another crushing European defeat at Varna, on the Bulgarian Black Sea coast.

This left most of southeastern Europe open for the Turks to take, with the grand culmination of seizing Constantinople now apparently inevitable. Ottoman goals were temporarily interrupted by the appearance of a rival in eastern Anatolia, where a warlord named Timur the Lame (known in the west as Tamerlane) had gathered together a mostly Mongol army in a last attempt to challenge Ottoman power. Timur eventually gave up on Asia Minor and focused on securing control over central Asia and Persia, a tactic that freed the Ottomans to close in on Constantinople. The imperial city fell to the sultan Mehmet II "the Conqueror" on 29 May 1453.[2] Repeated calls for western aid to recover the city failed.[3]

From the twelfth century onward, a renewal of interest in Greek learning and art had been growing in the west. The conquest of Constantinople in 1204 accelerated that interest by making available a tremendous number of plundered manuscripts and artifacts, but the final fall of the empire to the Ottomans in 1453 had little direct effect on the revival of Hellenism in the west since nearly everything that was

---

1. Modern Nikopol, on the lower Danube in Bulgaria.
2. The siege succeeded thanks in large part to some immense cannons Mehmet had had built for him by Hungarian engineers: The largest of these was reported to shoot cannonballs weighing twelve hundred pounds apiece. Even Constantinople's thick walls could not withstand a barrage like that.
3. Consider this excerpt from a speech by Pope Pius II in 1459. "We watched [the Turks'] power increase day by day, as their armies overran Hungary after they had already subdued Greece and the Balkans—so that now the faithful Hungarians suffer innumerable outrages. We feared that once the Hungarians fell the Germans, Italians, and rest of the Europeans would be next; this may still happen if we do not take care, and this would be a catastrophe that would surely result in the destruction in the Christian faith.
"We decided to take action to avoid this fate by summoning a Church Council where all the princes and people might come together in defense of Christendom. . . . But we are ashamed to find the People of Christ so indifferent. Some prefer to indulge in luxury and pleasure, while others simply dedicate themselves to their earthly greed.
"The Turks never hesitate to give up their lives for their vile faith—yet we cannot put up with the smallest expense or endure the smallest hardship for the sake of Christ and his gospel. I say to you truly, if Christians continue to live in this debased manner then we are all finished."

ever going to be transmitted westward had already been done so by then. What is observable, however, is a modest but significant migration of Greek-speaking peasants and urban workers westward. The peasants generally settled as tenant farmers in their new lands or sometimes ended up on the slave market (western qualms against the holding of Christians as slaves did not extend to Orthodox Christians); the latter figures, most of whom settled with their owners in Italy and Sicily, often found work as domestic servants and tutors, and helped to teach Greek to new generations of westerners hungry for Hellenism.

THE SEARCH FOR A NEW ROUTE TO THE EAST

The Ottoman advance, the Byzantine collapse, and the political upheaval of central Asia in the wake of the Mongols cut Europe off from southern and eastern Asia, with which it had had important and highly profitable commercial ties since the twelfth century. This development, coming as it did when the bottom had fallen out of the European macroeconomy, provided impetus to a long-held desire to secure direct relations with the east. The widely reported, if somewhat distrusted, reports of figures like Marco Polo of the willingness of the people in China to trade with the Europeans and of the immensity of the wealth to be gained by such contact made the idea irresistible. Many missionaries and merchant-adventurers made their way east in the years after Marco Polo's memoir-travelogue appeared, and they corroborated all his claims. The Franciscans, in fact, had established several churches in Beijing by the middle of the fourteenth century, and by 1400 eastern and southern China were dotted with dozens of Franciscan and Dominican houses. Possibilities for trade seemed promising, considering the welcome given to these first arrivals. But the Mongol and Ottoman domination of the eastern Mediterranean and central Asia meant that no hope existed for maintaining the traditional trade routes over land. A new way had to be found.

The chief problem was technological: How were the Europeans to reach the east? Europe's maritime tradition had developed in the context of easily navigable seas—the Mediterranean and the Baltic (and, to a lesser extent, the North Sea)—not of vast oceans. New types of ships were needed, new methods of finding one's way, new techniques for financing so vast a scheme. The sheer scale of the investment it took to begin commercial expansion at sea reflects the enormity of the profits that such east-west trade could create. Spices were the most sought-after commodity. Cinnamon, cloves, nutmeg, and pepper were so highly valued that European merchants would accept quantities of them as money if a fellow merchant was momentarily cashless. Spices not only dramatically improved the taste of the European diet (or, in the case of spoiled meat, could be used to hide the taste) but they were also used to manufacture perfumes and certain medicines. But even high-priced commodities like these had to be transported in large bulk in order to justify the expense and trouble of sailing around the African continent all the way to India and China.

Detail from a copy of Marco Polo's Travels. *Marco Polo (1254–1324) was a Venetian merchant who ventured east along the caravan routes and spent twenty-four years in the east, principally in China, as a trade-inspector for the great Mongol leader Kublai Khan. In 1295 he returned to Venice and served in her naval forces against the Genoese. Imprisoned for three years in Genoa, he dictated the memoir of his eastern adventures to a fellow prisoner. This book, known as the* Travels *or the* Book of Marvels, *was widely read. In this manuscript illumination Marco is shown, in the large ship at the bottom-center, departing from Venice (recognizable by the canals and the Piazza San Marco) on his way east in 1271. Source: Foto Marburg/Art Resource, NY*

The principal seagoing ship used throughout the Middle Ages was the *galley*, a long, low ship fitted with sails but driven primarily by oars. The largest galleys had as many as fifty oarsmen. Since they had relatively shallow hulls, they were unstable when driven by sail or when on rough water; hence they were unsuitable for the voyage to the east—even if they hugged the African coastline, they had little chance of surviving a crossing of the Indian Ocean. Shortly after 1400, shipbuilders in Majorca, Spain, and Portugal began to develop a new type of vessel properly designed to operate in rough, open water: the *caravel*. It had a wider and deeper hull than the galley and hence could carry more cargo; increased stability made it possible to add multiple masts and sails. In the largest caravels, two main masts held large square sails that provided the bulk of the impetus driving the ship forward, while a smaller forward mast held a triangular lateen sail that could be moved into a variety of positions to manuever the ship. It appears that the new design owed something to the Muslims it hoped to eliminate from the Asia trade; lateen sails had been used by Muslim fleets operating in the Indian Ocean for roughly a hundred years.

The astrolabe had long been the primary instrument for navigation, having been introduced in the eleventh century. It operated by measuring the height of the sun and the fixed stars; by calculating the angles created by those points, it determined the degree of latitude at which one stood. (The problem of determining longitude, though, was not solved until the eighteenth century.) By the early thirteenth century, western Europeans had also developed and put into wide use the magnetic compass, which helped when clouds obliterated both the sun and stars. The Majorcans of the thirteenth and fourteenth centuries were the premier mapmakers of the age, and their maps, refined by precise calculations and the reports of sailors, made it possible to trace one's path with reasonable accuracy. Certain institutional and practical norms had become established as well. A maritime code known as *The Consolate of the Sea*, which originated in the Catalan regions of the Crown of Aragon in the fourteenth century, won acceptance by a majority of seagoers as a normative code for maritime conduct; it defined such matters as the authority of a ship's officers, protocols of command, pay structures, the rights of seamen, and the rules of engagement when ships met one another on the sea lanes. Thus by about 1400 the key elements were in place to enable Europe to begin its seaward adventure.

But another problem remained: What could the westerners trade for the spices and silks of the east? The Chinese had little use for the heavy wool cloth produced in Europe, and they wove finer cottons and silks that the west could produce. Foodstuffs did not travel well over such distances and through such harsh climates, even if the west could produce them in sufficient quantities. These considerations left only metalwares (generally too heavy and bulky to be profitable) and gold or silver. Consequently the European traders who worked their way slowly along the African coastline after 1400 traveled with hoards of gold and silver aboard, along with the bulk commodities that they traded in Africa in return for yet more gold and silver. The effort to reach China represented a substantial drain on European supplies of precious metals, with concomitant implications for its currencies. It was not until the accidental discovery of the New World that the depleted reserves of precious metals were replenished.

The expansionist adventure had enormous consequences. Obviously, in the ultimate discovery of the New World by Christopher Columbus in 1492, an entire new chapter in global history was begun. But even before that epochal date, an important change had occurred. Throughout the medieval centuries, the geographical, economic, and cultural heart of European life had been the Mediterranean Sea. But with the start of the maritime expansion, the advantage had clearly begun to pass to the Atlantic seaboard states. It is hardly a coincidence that Europe's first explorers sailed out of Spain and Portugal, quickly to be followed by the French, the Dutch, and the English. They all enjoyed direct access to the sea, while the Mediterranean states remained in their own matrix of commercial and cultural ties that were, for the time being, made sluggish by the changes in the geopolitics of the region. The movement of the center of the European macro-economy from the Mediterranean basin to the Atlantic seaboard was an enormous structural shift that changed the economic and political ordering of Europe. That shift would not occur in full force until well into the fifteenth century, or even into the sixteenth, but the process had clearly begun around 1400 and it signaled the start of a new age.

CLOSING IN ON MUSLIM SPAIN

The thirteenth century had witnessed the most dramatic and substantial gains in the whole Reconquista. Led by three main powers—the monarchs of Portugal, the united kingdom of Léon-Castile, and the Crown of Aragon—Christians regained control of virtually the entire peninsula. The turning point had been the battle of Las Navas de Tolosa in 1212, a huge victory whose success was amplified by the constant internal fighting of the Almohad princes who survived. The Islamic forces never fully recovered, and the rest of the Reconquest was a slow piecemeal chipping away at what remained of al-Andalus. The end might have come quicker, except for the fact that 1212 marked the last time the Christian forces of Iberia mounted a campaign together or presented a unified front, for as the Christian-Muslim border moved further to the south the contest to partition the land to the north grew more insistent. Relations between Léon-Castile and Aragon-Catalonia were usually prickly in the extreme. Peter of Aragon's death in 1213 while fighting Simon de Montfort in the Albigensian Crusade—he fought less in defense of Catharism than in support of Toulousan independence—possibly averted a war between the two Iberian powers for control of the peninsula. With Peter's death Aragon-Catalonia passed to his young son, James I, the Conqueror (r. 1213–1276), and tensions between the realms were placed on hold while James grew to maturity in Montpellier under the care of the Templars there.

By the time James reached the age of majority, the Catalans had turned the eyes of the nascent Crown of Aragón eastward into the Mediterranean. James seized the Balearic Islands in the early 1230s and the Muslim coastal kingdom of Valencia in the late 1230s. From that point on, the Crown of Aragon concentrated on becoming a sea power; as we saw in Chapter 13, the Catalans became a Mediterranean super-power with a confederation of states reaching from eastern Spain all the way to Athens. This Mediterranean focus left virtually the rest of the Iberian peninsula to the Castilians and Portuguese. Castile's Fernando III (r. 1217–1252) pressed south-westward from Las Navas and took Córdoba in 1236 and Seville in 1248. By 1262 the forces of his son Alfonso X (r. 1252–1284) had captured Cádiz, the principal port opening onto the Atlantic Ocean. By immediately establishing trade links with Morocco, Castile signaled an early (though certainly very modest) interest in the idea of expanding via the Atlantic.[4] Castile and Portugal then agreed to a more or less peaceful partitioning of the western half of the peninsula, an arrangement that secured Castile's opening to the ocean and gave Portugal roughly the borders it still has today.

This progress sounds more straightforward than it was. In reality, fourteenth-century Spain was filled with dynastic struggles and civil wars that only seem placid when viewed in relation to the mighty dramas—Muslim versus Christian, Castilian versus Aragonese-Catalan—that dominated the thirteenth. The fact is that after the breaking of Muslim might after 1250 and the more or less permanent demarcation of borders between Castile and the Crown of Aragon, the Christian powers in Iberia had more to gain by avoiding conflict with each other. Portugal set her sights on Atlantic expansion, as the Crown had turned her eyes toward the Mediterranean, a move that largely left the inland peninsula to Castile. But it was precisely then that Castile fell victim to internal schisms and wars. The struggles began as a constitutional crisis between the legitimate but autocratic and detested king Peter the Cruel (r. 1350–1369) and a coalition of nobles led by Peter's bastard half brother Henry of Trastámara. Both factions looked abroad for support, and the Castilian problem thus became entwined in the Hundred Years War between England and France.[5] The conflict continued, like the English-French war, through several generations and was only brought to an end in 1479 when Isabella of Castile, the heiress of Peter's line, married Ferdinand of Aragon, who was the heir not only of Henry's line in Castile but also of the Crown of Aragon. Their union brought all of the Spanish peninsula together into a single state, with the exceptions of independent Portugal and the tiny Muslim remnant principality of Granada.

Although small, Granada had a large population since it had absorbed many of the Muslims who had fled the Christians' advance. Throughout the Reconquest Christians had attempted, for the most part, always to keep Muslims on the land and in the cities, but a large flight was to some extent inevitable as the reconquest entered its final stages. Being composed largely of refugees, the Granadan population developed a reputation for intransigency, a hardheaded determination to resist the final Christian advance no matter what. With such toughness, they held out for another two hundred years. Defeat finally came when Isabella and Ferdinand mus-

---

4.   The more immediate goal in seizing Cádiz was to cut off any Moroccan aid to Granada.
5.   The English allied themselves with Peter and his successors, which is not surprising when one considers the principle for which they were fighting against France in the first place—succession to the throne passing through the female line. The French, predictably, supported Henry and his successors

tered a huge force, crushed the last Granadan army, and received the surrender of Boabdil, the last Muslim ruler in Spain, in January of 1492—the same year in which they sponsored Christopher Columbus' first journey to the New World, and the same year in which they ordered all the Jews of Spain either to submit to immediate baptism or to be expelled from the kingdom.

The Expulsions of the Jews

The Spanish decree of 1492 is the end of the story of Jewish expulsion, not its beginning. Mass violence against Europe's Jews had emerged in all its horror with the First Crusade, when mobs in the Rhine river valley tortured and murdered thousands of Jewish men, women, and children. Zealous reform movements, like that affecting the evolution of the crusades, often result in waves of intolerance; the conviction that one is finally recovering and restoring the Truth can all too easily lead one to believe that those who reject that Truth stand in the way of the reform. But the roots of anti-Jewish violence are deeper, as we have seen. To many people of northern Europe the Jews were parvenus—prosperous Mediterranean urbanites who were brought north by later Carolingians eager to capitalize on their commercial connections, financial acumen, and organizational skills. Granted trade monopolies, tax exemptions, legal guarantees, and the personal protection of the counts and bishops, the Jews quickly emerged as leading figures in northern society—and also as focal points for the animosity and bitterness of those less fortunate. To many, the arrival of the Jews and the collapse of the Carolingian world appeared as no mere coincidences; the former was surely the cause of the latter. In this regard, Christian prejudice echoed the prejudice of those ancient Romans who had connected in their minds the sudden appearance of Christianity in Roman culture and the pronounced decline in Roman prosperity and peace; both prejudices resulted in persecution.

Over the course of the twelfth century, rumors regularly swept across Europe that Jews engaged in secret abominable rites whereby they desecrated the Holy Eucharist and massacred Christian babies, whose blood they either drank or used in Satanic rituals. Once again, the parallel with early Christian experience is interesting, for the pagan Romans accused the first Christians of the same sorts of crimes and used such beliefs as justification for persecuting them. A famous early case occurred in twelfth-century England. The murdered body of a young boy named William was found in the street in the city of Lincoln, and rumors quickly spread that the local Jews had killed him and used his blood in a bizarre Passover ritual (outbreaks of these rumors frequently corresponded with the period of the Jewish Passover or the High Holy Days, or with the Christian Holy Week). Mobs raced through the streets pummelling Jews and ransacking their shops. Similar scenes broke out with some regularity across Europe, but seem to have been most frequent and violent in France and Germany. The twelfth-century chronicler Rigord relates the following episode about the young king Philip Augustus:

He had frequently heard that the Jews who lived in Paris were accustomed, every year on Easter Sunday or at some other time during Holy Week, to sneak into hidden underground crypts and there to kill a Christian as a sort of contemptuous sacrifice against the Christian religion. . . . Philip inquired diligently, and when he came to know all too well about these and other iniquities of the Jews in his forefathers' days he burned with zeal . . . and commanded that all the Jews throughout his entire realm were to be seized in their synagogues and stripped of their gold, silver, and robes. . . . This was a foretelling of their expulsion from France, which by God's will soon followed.

Money was always a factor in anti-Semitic actions, and at times may have been the principle one in relation to state decisions about the Jews.

By the end of the thirteenth century—in 1290, to be exact—Edward I expelled all the Jews from England. His motives were complicated: He himself was deeply in debt to a number of Jewish financiers and banking houses (as he was to many other, non-Jewish ones as well) and found expulsion of his debtors easier than payment of his debts. It was certainly a popular move, since English town-dwellers were not very keen on seeing their tax money go into Jewish purses. And by expelling the Jews, Edward was also in effect cancelling the debts owed to Jews by all Englishmen. Those debts were considerable, and widely dispersed. Records from the Exchequer of the Jews show that most outstanding debts to Jews were from small landholders—the free farmers—and that farmers feared English land falling by default into Jewish hands. English law made this eventuality impossible, but either through well-placed rumor or of their own accord such fears spread nonetheless and caused widespread panic and a demand for action. Edward's popularity increased dramatically as a result of his expulsion order.

Other rulers were quick to take note. In 1292, Philip IV expelled the Jews from France and ordered the confiscation of all their bank accounts, property, and moveable goods; the expulsion order was not enforced, though, until 1306. (On a more local level, Charles of Anjou, the new king of Sicily, had driven the Jews from his counties of Anjou and Maine in 1288.) Expelled from England and France, the Jews migrated eastward to Germany where they were grudgingly received in the hope that their connections might foster an economic revival. But the arrival of the Black Death in 1348 put an end to those hopes, and many desperate crowds blamed the Jews for transmitting the disease and lashed out against them in violence. Jacob von Königshofen, a fourteenth-century chronicler, described what happened to the Jews in Strasbourg in this way:

On Saturday, St. Valentine's Day 1349, the town council of Strasbourg burned alive about two thousand Jews on a wooden platform in the middle of the Jewish cemetery. Those who agreed to be baptized were spared, and they say that there were about a thousand of these. . . . Every debt that was owed to the Jews was first nullified, and they had to surrender every surety and piece of collateral they held for all their loans. Moreover, the town council seized all the cash that the Jews had in their possession and distributed it to the urban workers in due proportions. In truth, it was their money that killed the Jews—for if they had been poor and if the nobles had not been in debt to them they would never have been put to the flames.

Forced to keep moving, thousands of Jews pressed on to Poland, where they enjoyed a period of welcome stability and fairmindedness under the rule of King Casimir III (r. 1333–1370).

The expelled Jews kept migrating eastward because of a basic cultural development. Having resided in the north since the ninth century, these Ashkenazic Jews had developed a distinct culture from the Sephardic Jews of the Mediterranean and felt more at home among their cultural brethren. Inevitably some did migrate southward into Italy and Spain, but the overwhelming majority preferred to march eastward, which may say as much about the cultural and religious rift between the Ashkenazim and the Sephardim as it says about the perceived degrees of tolerance available. The Mediterranean Jews, while hardly basking in a tolerant utopia, did fare better, and fared better longer, than their Ashkenzi cousins. The struggles of the fourteenth century marked the decisive turnaround in Christian-Jewish relations in the south. Mob violence became increasingly common over the century, and culminated in a massive outburst of hatred in Castile in 1391. This drive to separate the religions and cultures that made up medieval society, this centrifugal effort in state after state to replace the regulated and tension-filled yet creative and prosperous heterogenous model of society with a culturally, religiously, and ethnically homogenous world, was another sign that the medieval way of life was becoming something else.

CLOSING IN FOREVER: THE FORCED CLOISTERING OF WOMEN RELIGIOUS

In 1298, Pope Boniface VIII issued a bull entitled *Periculoso*, which ordered that every member of every female order within the Church was to be immediately and permanently cloistered. These sisters were henceforth to live entirely as monks did, without exception, physically removed from society in an enclosed Christian community with no contact with the outside world unless permitted under special circumstances by the abbess. Explicitly, the bull aimed to protect women religious from a dangerous world; since the Church could not protect women from men's all-too-common inclination to seduce or rape, nor men from women's perceived all-too-common inclination to tempt, the least it could do for its members was to protect them by enclosing them within cloisters. Although Boniface's language and argument were somewhat odd, his basic point was rather traditional. From the very start of the monastic movement in the fourth century, convents had been established as female counterparts to male monasteries; at the risk of making nonsense out of the monastic vocation, the Church could no more allow nuns to "live in the world" than it could allow monks to do so. To be "a nun in the world," Boniface suggested, was a contradiction in terms.

As it happened, *Periculoso* affected nuns rather little. Most of them *were* cloistered already, by choice, and had always been. This fact suggests that the bull was aimed at a different target altogether: the female lay confraternities, beguinages, and spiritual communities that had grown up around widely revered mystics. As early as the Fourth Lateran Council in 1215, the Church had been concerned about the proliferation of new religious orders and sought to stop it by forcing all new orders to adopt preexisting religious Rules. Enforcement of this decree was inconsistent—think of the Franciscans, for instance—but became more common as the thirteenth century wore on. The difficulty with female lay groups like the beguines was precisely the fact that they *were* lay and were therefore outside the administrative authority of the Church. Worse still, communities like these were becoming renowned for the extent and frequency of the mystical experiences enjoyed by their members. The communities' popularity increased accordingly, usually at the expense of the mainstream clergy, and there was no way of knowing whether these mystical revelations were valid or the likely origin of new heretical thought. But by exerting the authority granted under the idea of *plenitudo potestatis*, the popes gradually brought lay groups under the Church's control. Within Germany, for example, the beguinages gradually fell under the watchful eye of the Dominicans—with the unexpected result of inspiring a wave of Dominican mysticism.

The papacy, no matter how plenitudinous its power, could hardly outlaw mystical visions of God; but it could act to protect those who experienced such revelations from misinterpreting them. The best way to accomplish this was to turn all recognized female orders into nunneries under a recognized rule. This was the principle goal of *Periculoso*. It did not force individual beguines to take religious vows and wear religious habits; those who chose not to were free to "rejoin the world." But those who chose to remain were henceforth to live in cloistered seclusion.

The effort to close in on female religious went further. In 1311 at the Council of Vienne, Pope Clement V issued two new decrees, *Attendentes* and *De quibusdam mulierem*, which complained that many women who had opted to remain in their orders were not adhering to the new rules or recognizing ecclesiastical authority; they were wearing the habits and going through the motions but not living the true life of vowed members of the Church. Consequently, actions were taken that installed male clergy as heads of all female houses. These new heads were not resident, but they did possess visitation privileges and were empowered to enforce canon law over those who were disobedient. In time, the very word *beguine* came to have a pejorative sense, one tinged with suspicions of heresy.

There was an economic motive at work as well. Having been established by private endowments from pious aristocrats and royals, many of Europe's convents were quite wealthy. The same was true of male religious houses, of course, but female abbeys were wealthy in a different way. Generous grants to convents frequently took the form of endowments set aside for the specific use of an individual person or officeholder; thus a Frankish noble might bestow an endowment specifically for the place held within an abbey by a daughter. These positions, which continued on through the generations, were somewhat akin to endowed professorships within a modern university faculty; they created a clear, and sometimes enormous, discrepancy between the lives of endowed and unendowed members of a community. At the Benedictine convent of Harcourt in England, for example, the endowment supporting the abbess had increased to such an extent by the year 1400 that the possessor of the post was able to maintain, among other luxuries, a separate hunting lodge that staffed four falconers and a stable of over one hundred hunting dogs. The other sisters at Harcourt frequently starved to death. By bringing female religious houses under direct Church control, it was hoped that inequities like this could be ironed out.

Still, it is clear that at the end of the Middle Ages the Church showed much less willingness than before to allow women the freedom to pursue spiritual fulfillment on their own. Female mystics were celebrated and revered, but they had to pass muster; female lay groups were first eyed with suspicion, then effectively banned; convents that had been essentially independent for centuries were brought under ecclesiastical jurisdiction. Developments like these do not necessarily show a Church grown intolerant, but they do reflect one grown defensive. And that alone shows how far the world had changed from its medieval high point.

SUGGESTED READING

Texts

Anonymous. *Consulate of the Sea.*
Froissart, Jean. *Chronicles of France and England.*
à Kempis, Thomas. *The Imitation of Christ.*
Malory, Thomas. *The Death of Arthur.*
Robert of Clari. *The Conquest of Constantinople.*

Source Anthologies

Marcus, Jacob R. *The Jew in the Medieval World: A Source Book, 315–1791* (1979).
The Portable Medieval Reader.
The Portable Renaissance Reader.

Studies

Cahen, Claude. *The Formation of Turkey: The Seljukid Sultanate of Rûm—Eleventh to Fourteenth Century* (2001).
Fernandez-Armesto, Felipe. *Before Columbus: Exploration and Colonization from the Mediterranean to the Atlantic, 1229–1492* (1987).

Guenée, Bernard. *States and Rulers in Later Medieval Europe* (1985).

Harvey, L. P. *Islamic Spain, 1250–1500* (1990).

Kaeuper, Richard W. *War, Justice, and Public Order: England and France in the Later Middle Ages* (1988).

Makowski, Elizabeth. *Canon Law and Cloistered Women: 'Periculoso' and Its Commentators, 1298–1545* (1997).

Nirenberg, David. *Communities of Violence: Persecution of Minorities in the Middle Ages* (1996).

Phillips, J. R. S. *The Medieval Expansion of Europe* (1988).

Vryonis, Speros. *The Decline of Medieval Hellenism in Asia Minor and the Process of Islamicization from the Eleventh to the Fifteenth Century* (1971).

CHAPTER 20

The Renaissance in Medieval Context

There is little in the great Renaissance of the fourteenth and fifteenth centuries that surprises most medievalists, for despite all the changes that immediately preceded it, Renaissance Europe still appears, in its early stages at least, as a recognizably medieval place. As thoroughly medieval a character as Roger Bacon would have felt very much at ease discussing with the fifteenth-century Florentine humanist Giovanni Pico della Mirandola the ability of human reason to harmonize all truths into a single grand vision, or the view that mankind is the link connecting God and the physical world, or the limitless potential of human beings to achieve the loftiest goals when aided by a powerful individual will and God's grace. Bacon might even have bested the Italian in the debate. The merchants of thirteenth-century Barcelona or Montpellier, were they transported to the harbor of fifteenth-century Genoa, would certainly have recognized the place—the same goods, the same basic mercantile and financial practices, many of the same leading commercial and financial families dominating trade, the same basic structures and rhythms of daily living, although everything in a clearly diminished state. If anything, they might have smiled to see their former rival doing so poorly. And of course a figure like Innocent III would hardly have felt a stranger amid the Machiavellian politics of the Renaissance papal court.[1] On the whole, it seems more accurate to describe the early Renaissance as the medieval world with a difference, rather than as a different world altogether. In some ways, in fact, the Renaissance, or at least its first few generations, appears to be the culmination of much of medieval thinking and feeling.

The discovery of the New World in 1492 and the start of the Protestant Reformation in 1517 shattered once and for all the ideological and cultural unities that had held, or had purported to hold, medieval Europe together. The vast centering weight of Catholicism broke into a plethora of Christian interpretations, each for the time being utterly convinced of its own absolute rectitude; the tug of the New

---

1. He would, however, have been genuinely shocked by the sexual shenanigans that took place there under the Borgia popes.

World shifted the center of western commercial might and political dominion to the Atlantic seaboard states of England, the Netherlands, France, Spain, and Portugal; and the belief in the unity of truth received heavy blows from the explosion of new religious views, the reordering of the cosmos by experimental science, and the relativizing pressure of humanism itself. The western world after the middle of the sixteenth century was a dynamic and exciting place, but it was no longer predominately medieval in its outlook.

Still, Renaissance life was more than mere climactic medievalism. By 1400 in Italy, and later in the rest of Europe, a new sense of vitality and fresh thinking was alive, a willingness to be skeptical and embrace experiment, to try to fathom the world's increasing strangeness for its own sake. Politically, Italy in the Renaissance represented no sharp departure from its earlier experience. Sicily remained a Catalan satellite kingdom, poorer than before but essentially unchanged in its basic operations; the lower peninsula still answered to ambitious Angevin monarchs who were less skillful perhaps than those who had come before but were just as determined to fulfill what they regarded as their destiny; the Papal State remained under the Holy See's secular jurisdiction—an aspect of papal power that proved, for the most part, more consistently effective than its spiritual claims; and the northern peninsula was still divided into a sprawl of urban principalities. Of these Florence, Milan, and Venice still throve as the larger states. Genoa and Pisa were falling on rather hard times but were still highly influential. Smaller upstarts like Mantua, Verona, Siena, and Ferrara had also emerged as forceful entities. The political map, in other words, had altered somewhat in terms of the relative strengths and weaknesses of the states, but statecraft itself had not changed significantly from what it had been in the fourteenth or even the thirteenth century. Even one of Renaissance politics' most distinctive features—diplomacy as an ongoing, permanent enterprise, with resident professional ambassadors and networks of intelligence gathering and private negotiations—had been a staple of Mediterranean life at least since the 1290s, and possibly earlier.

ECONOMIES NEW AND OLD CIRCA 1400

The state of the European economy at the end of the fourteenth century is difficult to gauge. War and plague had caused, or had at least catalyzed, so much retrenchment and reorganization that historians see profoundly different pictures depending on which sectors of the economy they are examining. Some emphasize the bustling sprawl of commercial Venice, which seemed oblivious to economic worry. According to one contemporary, Marino Sanudo Torselli,

> In this city located in an area where nothing at all grows one can find an abundance of everything. Every commodity you can imagine—but especially food—is brought here from every country on earth that has anything worth sending; and here there are plenty of buyers, for everyone here has money. The Rialto looks like a garden, since there are so many local herbs, vegetables, and

fruits of every variety—and all of them so inexpensive!—on display. It truly is marvelous to behold.

Keeping up with all this trade required Venice to construct the largest shipworks in the then-known world, the Arsenal, which at its height employed nearly three thousand laborers. Other scholars have studied the rental incomes of baronial landholders in England and found that they maintained a consistent standard of living, and many even improved their standards, after surviving the initial shock waves of the Black Death. Manufacturers shared in the profits. By around 1400, several sites in England (most importantly Coventry, Norwich, Salisbury, and York) had become centers of actual wool-cloth production; no longer was England kept in the economically servile status of producing the raw material that others refined and reaped the principal profits of. Manufacturers and financiers in the Rhine river valley did well by establishing further trade links throughout the Baltic and North seas, while merchants further east, along the Danube, erected new houses, guildhalls, and the occasional small palace with the profits of their trade with eastern Europe and Russia.

But other historians regard these examples as mere islands of prosperity in a sea of European poverty. They can point to other contemporary witnesses who are just as wide-eyed in horror gazing upon the common suffering as Marino Sanudo Torselli was wide-eyed gushing forth about all there was to buy in Venice. Thus Jean de Montreuil, writing in 1395:

> If I were to describe all the evils that have resulted from the war that still rages [i.e., the Hundred Years War], I would be compelled to quote Virgil: "What words shall I use to begin?" . . .
>
> Who could possibly describe the slaughter of so many nobles of high rank, and even of kings? of the robbery and arson of holy places? the sacrileges, rape, violence, oppression, extortion, plundering, pillaging, banditry, and rioting? Who could describe (to sum up a multitude of crimes in only two words) the *inhuman savagery* of this cruel, horrible war? . . .
>
> And who, except one whose heart was made of lead, could keep from tears when describing the cries of so many babies who are fainting and starving and freezing to death even while at their mothers' breasts. . . . [Famine is so wide-spread] that some infants who are born prematurely are even eaten by their own mothers—horrific, cattle-like behavior! Truly, it is the madness of starvation and want that drives people to such desperation. . . .

One eminent historian, Robert Lopez, went so far as to argue that the Renaissance was actually a period of full-fledged economic depression. He certainly seems to have been right for the period up to 1400.

Beyond that, it may be more accurate to say that the European economy was characterized by severe inequities in the distribution of capital. The power of the guilds and aristocratic voices in royal government ensured that rents and wages worked to the merchants' and landlords' advantage rather than to the farmers' and laborers'. Capital and political power remained concentrated in the hands of a finite

sector of society, although that sector, since it now included merchants, manufacturers, and financiers, was considerably larger than just the aristocracy. A gradual
economic recovery began in northern Italy in the early fifteenth century but did not
characterize the rest of the continent until the early sixteenth century; even then, renewed prosperity was centered in the industrial and commercial towns. The Renaissance was a poor time to be a common farmer—which is precisely what most
people were. Ironically, the very success of the medieval world at developing parliamentary institutions of government ensured that wealth remained concentrated
in a mercantile and aristocratic oligarchy: Since those were the sectors of society
that comprised the civic representatives, they unsurprisingly tended to pursue public policies that favored their own positions.

Plague continued to make the world a parlous place. Full-scale outbreaks of the
Black Death occurred on average once every generation until well into the sixteenth
century, and the periods in between were punctuated with smaller, localized epidemics. These, combined with occasional bad harvests and local wars, meant that
the European population was subject to sudden drastic declines, sometimes as often as every five to six years.[2] In such circumstances inflationary spirals became
commonplace: A failed harvest sent food prices skyrocketing, and the death of so
many workers sent labor costs in the same direction. In general only those merchants and landowners who had enough capital at hand to allow them to ride out
the turbulent years survived; in the relatively calmer years in between, they vied
with one another for monopolies to shore up their positions. Thus wealth continued
to concentrate in the hands of a smaller and smaller clique of extremely wealthy
elites; in Italy, the names of some of the wealthiest of these elites have become familiar: the Visconti, the della Scala, the Sforza, and the Medici families.

Those with capital to spend gave themselves over to luxuriant living and con-
spicuous consumption on a fantastic scale. Eastern silks and spices, high-quality
wines (winemaking had progressed to such an extent by this time that some vint-
ners had begun to establish vintages), sugar and saffron, were all in high demand.
So too were works of art and scholarship, which were aimed to promote an aura of
patronage and public mindedness. In short, the economy of the early Renaissance
resulted in the re-creation of an urban class of elites with much the same social position as the old Roman *curiales,* a class that was in fact consciously emulating that
group through its promotion of the individual and civic ethic called *humanism.*

THE MEANING OF HUMANISM

Humanism was an outlook on life new to the Renaissance. It was hardly an entire
philosophy or an organized body of thought, although that codification would follow in later generations. More than anything else, the term described an inchoate

---

2. Between 1350 and 1450, the city of Florence was hit by a series of plagues, wars, and famines that resulted in a population loss of 75 percent.

generational mood, much like the Romanticism of the early nineteenth century. Humanism began as an attitude of youthful rebellion (can anyone name a first-generation humanist, around the mid-fourteenth century, over the age of forty?) against the worst excesses of medieval synthesism, and an insistence on the intrinsic value of the specific, the individual, the solitary and unique. In this regard humanism had much in common with late medieval Franciscanism. Individual things, persons, or ideas can have autonomous value, independent of their positions in a grander scheme, the humanists believed, and they ought to be valued accordingly.

Humanism in the early Renaissance also implied a special dedication to the liberal arts—the study of grammar, history, literature, philology, and rhetoric (that is, the *studia humanitatis*)—for these were the tools that best suited the appreciation of unique human experience. They were also the subjects that predominated the curricula of classical Rome, especially in the Republican period, and of Athenian Greece; the Renaissance humanists placed a high value on classical mores and sentiments, believing that the ancients had most nearly perfected the philosophy of loving life for its own sake and appreciating human nature as it truly was rather than for what it should or could be. Certainly the Greek scholars who achieved prominence in Italy in the fourteenth and fifteenth centuries—figures like Manuel Chrysoloras, who became the principal tutor in Greek in Florence around 1400—encouraged this idea. One of the hallmarks of early humanism was the extent to which its followers embraced the study of classical literature and philosophy. Their accomplishments were considerable: They recovered large bodies of near-lost classical writing, in both Latin and Greek, and wrote extensive and sensitive commentaries on what they found. But there were other aspects to their passions as well. For example, in their zeal to emulate the ancients, many humanist enthusiasts evinced a desire to "purify" the Latin language, which scholars and churchmen had been speaking and writing for a thousand years, of its medieval "barbarisms" and neologisms. The most extreme demanded that anyone who wanted to write in a pure Latin style could use no word or grammatical construction that had not been used by Cicero. The effect of an artificial reform like this was to kill Latin as a living language.[3]

But these are easy targets. Humanism on the whole was a profoundly moving phenomenon, as one can see by glancing briefly at the works of Francesco Petrarca (1304–1374), who is usually considered humanism's founder. He was born in Arezzo, near Florence, and grew up in Avignon near the papal palace. While in grammar school he read and fell in love with Cicero's writings. He studied law at the University of Montpellier and spent a few years, unhappily, in that profession. But when his parents died and left him a comfortable legacy, he gave himself over to

---

3. Imagine what would happen to the English language if it was decreed that henceforth no one could use any word or grammatical construction that does not appear in the *Complete Works of William Shakespeare*. How on earth, for example, would one talk about computers?

poetry and literary study. He spent the rest of his life gathering, editing, publishing, and writing commentaries on classical Latin literature, and writing his own poetry. It is in his poetry, especially, that one can see the difference between his mode of thinking and that of a poet like Dante. Petrarca too dedicated his artistic life to the praise of a woman—in his case, a woman named Laura—but his poetry, while it still engages in a share of idealism, mitigates the ideal by celebrating the actual woman, her genuine beauty, the specific graceful movement of her unique body, the gentleness and loving sentiment generated in the poet by her real physical presence. The point here is not that Dante could not write Petrarca's type of poetry, nor Petrarca write Dante's type, but that neither of them *wanted* to write the other's type of poetry. Their aims were different; and that difference we call humanism. Giovanni Boccaccio (1313–1375) was a disciple of Petrarca's. He too began his career as a classical scholar (he claimed to have been the first person to reintroduce Greek poetry to Italy) but soon moved on to creating his own imaginative literature. His masterpiece—one he repudiated in later life because of its supposed immorality— was the story collection known as *The Decameron*.

Perhaps the most moving feature of early humanism was the circumstance in which it was born. Amid all the calamities of the fourteenth century—famine, plague, economic depression, war, social upheaval, and ecclesiastical division—the younger generation of writers emphasized a worldview that focused on the immediate and the particular. The world may have no longer made sense, and the larger Truths that had been the focus of medieval life may have been drawn into question, but that did not mean that one had to give in to despair. One still had one's life, one's friends, one's beloved, one's books. One could still delight in the sight of a flowing river at dawn, in the taste of a grilled steak, the sound of a pleasant melody, or the thrill of a lover's kiss. Life may be a meaningless broken jumble, but genuine beauty resides in those shards about one's feet, so why not celebrate them? As Petrarca put it in one of his more famous sonnets to Laura: "Blessed is the year, the month, the week, the day,/the hour, the minute, the moment, in which I first saw *you*." Beatrice, to Dante, was a cosmological miracle; Laura, to Petrarca, was simply Laura—but that was miracle enough. The humanism of the early Renaissance clung to and celebrated such simple glories.

THE CANONIZATION OF CLASSICAL CULTURE

Why classical literature? The passion for it was hardly new. Latin literature had been the bedrock of western education since the sixth century; virtually every educated person in the Middle Ages cut his or her teeth, intellectually speaking, on Cicero, Tacitus, Sallust, Virgil, and Ovid. The trivium and quadrivium were based on the study of the ancients, and from the twelfth century on ancient Greeks were the intellectual masters of Europe. Medieval science, mathematics, and philosophy were dominated by Plato, Aristotle, Galen, Ptolemy, Euclid, and Hippocrates. To this extent, the Renaissance passion for classical writing is obviously just a continuation of the medieval norm. What was different about the early Renaissance atti-

Giotto's "The Marriage at Cana." Arena Chapel, Padua. Giotto di Bondone of Florence was the greatest painter of the medieval era, and the Arena Chapel in Padua, on which he began to work in 1303, was his first masterpiece. His innovations in perspective, foreshortening, and portraiture set a new standard in the visual arts, especially in fresco painting. Source: Cameraphoto/Art Resource, NY

tude was its *sense* of the valuation (not the *degree* of it) this literature deserved. For most medievals, classical literature was valuable in so far as it helped to make one a better Christian; the way in which studying Plato served the purpose of helping one understand Christian mysteries, for example, determined Plato's usefulness. But for the early humanists, the classical writers were, like Petrarca's Laura, to be valued in and of themselves, for themselves, and without reference to a larger purpose. Those larger purposes, after all, were precisely what the traumas of the fourteenth century had most drawn into question.

*Giotto's "Joachim and the Shepherds." Arena Chapel, Padua. The naturalism of
Giotto's figures and the hanging of their robes shows clearly in this scene of Joachim
(the father of the Virgin Mary) visiting a group of shepherds. Source:
Cameraphoto/Art Resource, NY*

The achievement of the Renaissance in recovering and reviving the study of the
ancients is considerable—especially of the Latin authors in the early Renaissance. A
largely self-taught judge and notary named Albertanus of Brescia (d. 1270) had
reintroduced the Roman Stoic philosopher and playwright Seneca to Italy in the
thirteenth century, and in the process gave rise to a literary cult; Seneca proved to be
second only to Cicero in significance for the first two generations of Renaissance
humanists. Knowledge of Greek still had not advanced far enough to spark a meaningful revival of Greek literature until the latter half of the fifteenth century; nevertheless, enough people before that faked a sufficient knowledge of Greek to make
Greek things fashionable in Italy from the middle of the fourteenth century.

Leonardo Bruni (1370–1444) was the first and greatest Greek scholar of the early Renaissance; he translated numerous philosophical works of Aristotle and Plato, and historical works by Plutarch and Xenophon, while also writing a famous treatise on the education of girls and a Latin history of his native city of Florence. Many new texts were discovered in monastic libraries across Europe, also superior texts of older known works. Petrarca himself discovered many of these, most famously a copy of Cicero's *Letters to Atticus* in a monastic library in Verona. Scribes and scholars diligently circulated these new and improved works.

Apart from the texts' intrinsic value as literature or philosophy, the people of the early Renaissance valued them as practical guides to living. After all, if something is true it is worthy not only of study but of practical application. This attitude, too, was not entirely new. When medieval scholars rediscovered the *Corpus iuris civilis*, they were not slow in recognizing that it could be put to actual use in administering twelfth-century life. Similarly with the new texts rediscovered in the fourteenth and fifteenth centuries. Since the bulk of them had been written in and for small urban republics, and since they were found by figures in and of the same sort of societies, why not encourage their direct application? Hence Cicero's notions of the role of the citizen in the republican state, of the power and limits of the law, and of the sense of civic responsibility all struck a chord that people increasingly strove to follow. Poems like Virgil's *Eclogues*, with their rhapsodic praises of the glories of rural landscapes and rustic pleasures, helped to encourage artists to paint stirring images, increasingly realistic or representational, of the beauties of nature. Roman interest in biography, in the portrayal of the life histories of individuals, inspired a revival of that genre.[4] Petrarca famously described the difference between medieval scholasticism and Renaissance humanism precisely in terms of potency. Scholastic philosophy, he argued, could define a virtue like goodness but was incapable of inspiring anyone to become good, whereas the greatness of humanistic study was its capacity to inflame the heart, to make us crave virtue. It is more important to want to pursue truth than it is to define truth—in other words, to be an impassioned traveler than to be a sedentary possessor of a brilliant map.

By the end of the sixteenth century, the west had recovered virtually the entire classical literary canon as we know it. It was a remarkable achievement. Armed with critical skills to match their convictions, Renaissance scholars had scoured Europe's libraries, sifted through thousands of manuscripts, rescued scores of unknown works from oblivion, and produced dramatically improved texts of the ancient world's greatest authors. (One fellow, Giovanni Aurispa [d. 1459], traveled east to Constantinople in the years prior to the Turkish siege and came back with nearly 250 manuscripts that might otherwise have gone up in flames.) Moreover, scholars made these works available to other scholars on an unprecedented scale:

---

4 Not to mention that of autobiography: The autobiography of a Renaissance adventurer like Benvenuto Cellini is not to be missed.

Hundreds of copyists were employed to get the texts in circulation; the city of Florence in the early fifteenth century established the first lending library; and of course the invention of the printing press allowed books to pour over Europe like a tide. The most celebrated of humanist publishers was Aldus Manutius (d. 1515), who set up his printing shop in Venice in 1493 and managed to produce editions of well over a hundred separate classical texts before his death.

Renaissance classicism is perhaps the least innovative aspect of humanist life, the aspect most directly linkable to its medieval past. But its accomplishments were considerable, not only in expanding the literary canon but in expanding the western heart and urging it on to new challenges. The passion with which scholars pursued their classical quest had its negative consequences, most notably in the artificial manipulations of a still-living Latinity, but on the whole the extraordinary expansion of classical learning was one of the Renaissance world's (and the medieval world's) greatest legacies.

THE REJECTION OF THE MIDDLE AGES

While the early Renaissance had much in common with the medieval period, it also loudly rejected it. Perhaps the very loudness of that rejection should make us wary of its genuineness, for people are seldom so absolutely insistent that they have nothing at all to do with a given thing as when they in fact do. Nevertheless, as early as Petrarca, the leading figures in the new humanist movement were openly declaring their total opposition to all things medieval. The medieval Church was, it went almost without saying, a horror show of corrupt politics and dry-as-dust scholastic hairsplitting. Medieval Latin was a brutish, adulterated language twisted and mangled beyond recognition from the pure elegance of writers like Cicero and Tacitus; medieval architecture (by which the humanists meant chiefly Gothic architecture) was a nightmare of spires, pointy arches, sculptural excess, and tacky coloration; medieval philosophy was a charade of mind-numbing abstraction and foolhardy systematization; medieval politics (by which they meant feudal monarchy, for the most part) was mere barbarism by another name, savage tribalism dressed up in robes and crowns. The grand role assumed by the humanists was to configure a new path. The fifteenth-century philosopher Marsilio Ficino (d. 1499) expressed admiration for his aggressively non-medieval age: "This century has been a Golden Age, one that has restored to light all the liberal arts—grammar, poetry, rhetoric, painting, sculpture, architecture, and music—arts that were virtually extinct."

Of course, the arts were hardly extinct in the Middle Ages, but they were certainly devoted to somewhat different aims. Consider architecture, for example. Ever since the rise of the great castles and cathedrals of the late twelfth and thirteenth centuries, architecture had been one of the dominant arts in Europe. In the Middle Ages it was also an overwhelmingly public art form: A cathedral represented far more than a single building or plan designed by a single architect; it was a public statement of faith, a commitment of hundreds of thousands of labor hours and the equivalent of hundreds of millions of dollars over several generations (and sometimes over as many as two centuries) in pursuit of a spiritual vision. It was an exaltation in stone. The first direct and overt challenge to Gothic architectural style came with Filippo Brunelleschi (1377–1446), who completed the cathedral of Florence around 1420. He did away with Gothic towers and pointed arches, stripped away unnecessary statuary, and based his overall design on simple geometrical shapes (circular windows set within square panels that are themselves part of a clearly delineated rectangular wall plane, for example). The overall effect is of a simpler and more harmonious gracefulness than a Gothic cathedral, and its use of domes and columns consciously evokes the architectural styles of the Roman world. From Brunelleschi's revolt on, Renaissance architects never looked back. Anything that was not, for a time, in conscious revolt against the High Gothic style and the world that had created it was deemed artistically and intellectually backward. *Medieval* had become a dirty word.

For all its positive qualities, early humanism had its problems. One was its obvious elitism. The humanists did not want to speak like common people, think like common people, or believe what common people believed. Petrarca went so far as to criticize his beloved Cicero for having ventured into the messy world of politics instead of staying at home to breathe the cleaner air of philosophy in his private study, far from the sullying crowd; he also heaped scorn on the intrigues in the papal court at Avignon, but the mess never bothered him enough to make him leave or renounce his annuities. Giovanni Boccaccio magnificently sang the praises of the everyday in his *Decameron*, but he wrote his stories while living in the comfortable quarters of the Neapolitan royal palace surrounded by aristocratic admirers and aesthetic neophytes. Not until the end of the fourteenth century, with figures like Coluccio Salutati (1331–1406) in Florence, did leading humanists become directly involved in administering the day-to-day life of their communities.[5] The humanists, in other words, were guilty of celebrating humanism more than humans.

By 1400, then, Europe was still recognizably medieval in its main outlines, even though there was a powerful and fascinating new set of ideas and values in the air. The Church, bedraggled though it was, was still the dominant institution in European life. The political makeup of the continent was still mostly what it had been in the thirteenth century. Philosophical and scientific thinking were still shaped by the knowledge of the ancients. But important, even transformative, shifts were also underway. A profound sense of skepticism and of the world's jumbled nature was widespread; the economic center of European life had begun to shift to the Atlantic

5. Salutati wrote, "The people of Florence are the defenders of the liberty of all people everywhere," but he never blinked an eye when Florence seized an advantage and subjugated any of her neighbors. By Salutati's death, Florence had even brought Pisa to heel and had become the third major power in northern Italy.

seaboard, although it would take another hundred years for that shift to become fully tangible; an acceptance of the idea that one could approach God and know Him other than through the Church and its sacraments was rapidly gaining ground. The Renaissance that began in the midst of the dramas of the fourteenth century was an inspired and inspiring response to great troubles and doubts, one that quickly developed into something quite different and wonderful. For all its innovative glory, though, the Renaissance owed much to the medieval world from which it sprang.

SUGGESTED READING

Texts

Cellini, Benvenuto. *Autobiography*.

Petrarca, Francesco. *Lyrics*.

Salutati, Coluccio. *Autobiography*.

Source Anthologies

Cohen, Timothy V., and Elizabeth S. Cohen. *Words and Deeds in Renaissance Rome: Trials before the Papal Magistrates* (1993).

The Portable Renaissance Reader.

Studies

Bolzoni, Lina. *The Gallery of Memory: Literary and Iconographic Models in the Age of the Printing Press* (2001).

Grendler, Paul F. *Schooling in Renaissance Italy: Literacy and Learning, 1300–1600* (1991).

Haas, Louis. *The Renaissance Man and His Children: Childbirth and Early Childhood in Florence, 1300–1600* (1998).

Hamilton, Alastair. *Heresy and Mysticism in Sixteenth-Century Spain: The Alumbrados* (1992).

Hollingsworth, Mary. *Patronage in Renaissance Italy: From 1400 to the Sixteenth Century* (1996).

King, Margaret L. *Women of the Renaissance* (1991).

———. *Venetian Humanism in an Age of Patrician Dominance* (1986).

Martines, Lauro. *Strong Words: Writing and Social Strain in the Italian Renaissance* (2001).

Mazzotta, Giuseppe. *Cosmopoeiesis: The Renaissance Experiment* (2001).

Ozment, Steven. *The Age of Reform, 1250–1550* (1980).

Rabil, Albert. *Renaissance Humanism: Foundations, Forms, and Legacy* (1988).

Shuger, Deborah Kuller. *Habits of Thought in the English Renaissance: Religion, Politics, and the Dominant Culture* (1997).

Stinger, Charles. *The Renaissance in Rome* (1998).

Wilkins, Ernest Hatch. *Life of Petrarch* (1961).

Appendixes

Appendix A. The Medieval Popes

The table below lists the popes in chronological order, gives the dates of their pontificates, indicates their lay names and ethnicity, and records the ecclesiastical position held by each individual prior to assuming the Holy See. The dates of pontificates are subject to much scholarly revision; I have adhered to the dates published by the Vatican's own *Anuario pontificio*.

Pope	Papacy	Birth Name	Nationality	Previous Ecclesiastical Rank
St. Peter	d. 64	Simon	Galilean	fisherman
St. Linus	67–76		Tuscan	
St. Anacletus	76–88		Greek	
St. Clement I	88–97		Roman	
St. Evaristus	97–105		Greek	
St. Alexander I	105–115		Roman	
St. Sixtus	115–125		prob. Roman	
St. Telesphorus	125–136		Greek	
St. Hyginus	136–140		Greek	
St. Pius I	140–155		Friulian	
St. Anicetus	155–166		Syrian	
St. Soter	166–175		Latin	
St. Eleutherius	175–189		Greek	deacon
St. Victor I	189–198		North African	
St. Zephrynus	199–217		Roman	
St. Calixtus I	217–222			archdeacon
St. Urban I	222–230		Roman	
St. Pontian	230–235		Roman	
St. Anterus	235–236		Greek	
St. Fabian	236–250		Roman	
St. Cornelius	251–253			
St. Lucius I	253–254		Roman	
St. Stephen I	254–257		Roman	
St. Sixtus II	257–258		Greek	
St. Dionysius	260–268		Roman	priest
St. Felix I	269–274		Roman	
St. Eutychian	275–283			
St. Gaius	283–296			
St. Marcellinus	296–304			
St. Marcellus I	308–309			
St. Eusebius	309–310		Greek	
St. Melchiades	311–314		North African	
St. Sylvester I	314–335			

(continued)

Pope	Papacy	Birth Name	Nationality	Previous Ecclesiastical Rank
St. Mark	336		Roman	
St. Julius I	337–352		Roman	
Liberius[a]	352–366			
St. Damasus	366–384		Portuguese	deacon
St. Siricius[b]	384–399			
St. Anastasius	399–401		Roman	
St. Innocent I	401–417		Roman	
St. Zosimus	417–418		Greek	priest
St. Boniface I	418–422		Roman	priest
St. Celestine I	422–432		Roman	archdeacon
St. Sixtus III	432–440			
St. Leo I the Great	440–461		Roman	deacon
St. Hilarius	461–468			archdeacon
St. Simplicius	468–483		Latin	
St. Felix III (II)	483–492		Roman	
St. Gelasian	492–496		African	
Anastasius II	496–498		Roman	
St. Symmachus	498–514		Sardinian	deacon
St. Hormisdas	514–523		Latin	
St. John I	523–526		Tuscan	
St. Felix IV (III)	526–530		Roman	card.-priest
Boniface II	530–532		Ostrogoth	archdeacon
John II[c]	533–535	Mercurius	Roman	priest
St. Agapitus I	535–536			deacon
St. Silverius	536–537			subdeacon
Vigilius	537–555		Roman	deacon
Pelagius I	556–561		Roman	deacon
John III	561–574	Catalinus		deacon
Benedict I	575–579		Roman	deacon
Pelagius II	579–590		German	deacon
St. Gregory I "the Great"[d]	590–604		Roman	monk (O.S.B.)
Sabinian	604–606		Latin	deacon
Boniface III	607		Roman	deacon
St. Boniface IV	608–615		Roman	monk (O.S.B.)
St. Adeodatus I	615–618			priest
Boniface V	619–625		Neapolitan	priest
Honorius I	625–638			
Severinus	640		Roman	
John IV	640–642		Croatian	
Theodore I	642–649		Greek	
St. Martin I	649–655			
St. Eugenius I	654–657		Roman	priest
St. Vitalian	657–672			
Adeodatus II	672–676			monk (O.S.B.)
Donus	676–678		Roman	
St. Agatho	678–681		Greek-Sicilian	monk
St. Leo II	682–683		Sicilian	
St. Benedict II	684–685		Roman	
John V	685–686		Syrian	archdeacon

Pope	Papacy	Birth Name	Nationality	Previous Ecclesiastical Rank
Conon	686–687		Thracian	priest
St. Sergius I	687–701		Syrian-Sicilian	
John VI	701–705		Greek	
John VII	705–707		Greek	
Sisinnius	708		Syrian	
Constantine	708–715		Syrian	
St. Gregory II	715–731		Roman	deacon
St. Gregory III	731–741		Syrian	
St. Zacharias	741–752		Greek	
Stephen II (III)ᵉ	752–757		Roman	priest
St. Paul I	757–767		Roman	deacon
Stephen III (IV)	768–772		Sicilian	
Hadrian I	772–795		Roman	deacon
St. Leo III	795–816			
Stephen IV (V)	816–817			
St. Paschal	817–824		Roman	abbot of St. Stephen's (O.S.B.)
Eugenius II	824–827		Roman	archpriest
Valentine	827		Roman	
Gregory IV	827–844		Roman	card.-priest
Sergius II	844–847		Roman	card.-priest
St. Leo IV	847–855		Roman	monk (O.S.B)
Benedict III	855–858		Roman	card.-priest
St. Nicholas I	858–867			deacon
Hadrian II	867–872		Roman	card.-priest
John VIII	872–882		Roman	archdeacon
Marinus Iᶠ	882–884		Roman	card.-bishop of Cerveteri
St. Hadrian III	884–885		Roman	
Stephen V (VI)	885–891		Roman	card.-priest
Formosus	891–896		Roman	card.-bishop of Porto
Boniface VI	896		Roman	priest
Stephen VI (VII)	896–897		Roman	card.-bishop of Anagni
Romanus	897		Roman	
Theodore II	897		Roman	
John IX	898–900		Roman	abbot (O.S.B)
Benedict IV	900–903		Roman	
Leo V	903		Latin	priest
Sergius III	904–911		Roman	deacon
Anastasius III	911–913		Roman	
Landus	913–914		Latin	
John X	914–928			archbishop of Ravenna
Leo VI	928			priest
Stephen VII (VIII)	928–931			
John XI	931–935		Roman	
Leo VII	936–939			monk (O.S.B)
Stephen VIII (IX)	939–942			
Marinus II	942–946			
Agapitus II	946–955		Roman	
John XIIᵍ	955–964	Octavianus	Roman	layman

Period of papal history often referred to as the "Pornocracy"

(continued)

Pope	Papacy	Birth Name	Nationality	Previous Ecclesiastical Rank
Leo VIII	963–965		Roman	layman
Benedict V	964		Roman	card.-deacon
John XIII	965–972		Umbrian	bishop of Narnia
Benedict VI	973–974		Roman	card.-priest
Benedict VII	974–983		Roman	bishop of Sutri
John XIV	983–984	Pietro Campanova	Lombard	bishop of Pavia
John XV	985–996		Roman	card.-priest
Gregory V	996–999	Bruno of Carinthia	German	priest
Sylvester II	999–1003	Gerbert d'Aurillac	French	archbishop of Ravenna
John XVII	1003	Giovanni Siccone	Roman	layman
John XVIII	1004–1009	Giovanni Fasano	Roman	card.-priest
Sergius IV	1009–1012	Pietro Boccapecora	Roman	bishop of Albano
Benedict VIII	1012–1024	Theophylact	Roman	layman
John XIX	1024–1032	Romanus	Roman	layman
Benedict IX[h]	1032–1048	Theophylact	Roman	layman
Sylvester III	1045	Giovanni Crescenzi	Roman	bishop of Sabina
Gregory VI	1045–1046	Giovanni Graziano	Roman	archpriest
Clement II	1046–1047	Suitger von Morsleben	German	bishop of Bamberg
Damasus II	1048	Poppo	Bavarian	bishop of Brixen
St. Leo IX	1049–1054	Bruno von Egisheim	Alsatian	bishop of Toul
Victor II	1055–1057	Gebhart	Swabian	bishop of Eichstätt
Stephen IX (X)	1057–1058	Frédéric de Lorraine	French	abbot of Monte Cassino (O.S.B.)
Nicholas II	1059–1061	Gérard de Bourgogne	French	bishop of Florence
Alexander II	1061–1073	Anselmo da Baggio	Milanese	bishop of Lucca
St. Gregory VII	1073–1085	Hildebrand di Soana	Tuscan	card.-archdeacon
Bl. Victor III	1086–1087	Dauferio [Desiderius]	Beneventan	abbot of Monte Cassino (O.S.B.)
Bl. Urban II	1088–1099	Eude de Châtillon	French	card.-bishop of Ostia (O.S.B.)
Paschal II	1099–1118	Raniero	Romagnan	abbot of S. Paolo (O.S.B.)
Gelasius II	1118–1119	Giovanni Coniulo	Amalfitan	archdeacon (O.S.B.)
Calixtus III	1119–1124	Guy de Bourgogne	Burgundian	archbishop of Vienne
Honorius II	1124–1130	Lamberto Scannabecchi	Romagnan	card.-bishop of Ostia

Pope	Papacy	Birth Name	Nationality	Previous Ecclesiastical Rank
Innocent II	1130–1143	Gregorio Papareschi	Roman	card.-deacon
Celestine II	1143–1144	Guido del Castello	Tuscan	card.-priest
Lucius II	1144–1145	Gerardo Caccianemici	Bolognese	card.-priest
Bl. Eugenius III	1145–1153	Bernardo Pignatelli	Pisan	abbot (O.Cist.)
Anastasius IV	1153–1154	Corrado Suburra	Roman	card.-bishop of S. Sabina
Hadrian IV	1154–1159	Nicholas Breakspear	English	card.-bishop of Albano (O.S.A)
Alexander III	1159–1181	Orlando Bandinelli	Sienese	card.-priest
Lucius III	1181–1185	Umbaldo Allucingoli	Tuscan	card.-bishop of Ostia
Urban III	1185–1187	Umberto Crivelli	Milanese	archbishop of Milan
Gregory VIII	1187	Alberto Morra	Beneventan	card.-deacon
Clement III	1187–1191	Paolo Scolari	Roman	card.-bishop of Palestrina
Celestine III	1191–1198	Giacinto Bobone	Roman	card.-deacon
Innocent III	1198–1216	Lotario dei Segni	Roman	card.-deacon
Honorius III	1216–1227	Cencio Savelli	Roman	card.-priest
Gregory IX	1227–1241	Ugolino dei Segni	Roman	card.-bishop of Ostia
Celestine IV	1241	Goffredo Castiglione	Milanese	card.-bishop of Sabina (O.S.B)
Innocent IV	1243–1254	Sinibaldo Fieschi	Genoese	card.-priest
Alexander IV	1254–1261	Rinaldo Conti	Roman	card.-bishop of Ostia
Urban IV	1261–1264	Jacques Pantaléon	French	patriarch of Jerusalem
Clement IV	1265–1268	Gui Faucoi	French	archbishop of Narbonne
Bl. Gregory X[i]	1271–1276	Teobaldo Visconti	Milanese	card.-archdeacon (O.Cist.)
Bl. Innocent V	1276	Pierre Tarantaise	French	card.-bishop of Ostia (O.P.)
Hadrian V	1276	Ottobuono Fieschi	Genoese	card.-deacon
John XXI	1276–1277	Pedro Julião	Portuguese	card.-bishop of Tusculum
Nicholas III	1277–1280	Giovanni Orsini	Roman	archpriest (O.S.B.)
Martin IV	1281–1285	Simon de Brie	French	card.-priest
Honorius IV	1285–1287	Giacomo Savelli	Roman	card.-deacon

(continued)

Pope	Papacy	Birth Name	Nationality	Previous Ecclesiastical Rank
Nicholas IV	1288–1292	Girolamo Maschi	Abruzzese	card.-bishop of Palestrina (O.F.M.)
St. Celestine V[j]	1294	Pietro Murrone	Neapolitan	hermit monk
Boniface VIII	1295–1303	Benedetto Gaetani	Tusculan	card.-priest
Bl. Benedict XI[k]	1303–1304	Niccolò Boccasini	Venetano	card.-bishop of Ostia-Gaetani (O.P.)
Clement V[l]	1305–1314	Bertrand de Got	Gascon	archbishop of Bordeaux
John XXII[l]	1316–1334	Jacques Duèse de Cahors	French	card.-bishop of Porto
Benedict XII	1335–1342	Jacques Fournier	French	card.-bishop of Mirepoix (O.Cist.)
Clement VI	1342–1352	Pierre Roger	French	archbishop of Rouen
Innocent VI	1352–1362	Etienne Aubert	French	card.-bishop of Ostia
Bl. Urban V	1362–1370	Guillaume Grimard	French	abbot of S. Victoire (Marseilles) (O.S.B)
Gregory XI	1370–1378	Pierre Roger de Beaufort	French	card.-deacon
Urban VI	1378–1389	Bartolomeo Prignano	Apulian	archbishop of Bari
Boniface IX	1389–1404	Pietro Tornacelli	Neapolitan	card.-priest
Innocent VII	1404–1406	Cosimo dei Migliorati	Abruzzese	archbishop of Bologna
Gregory XII	1406–1415	Angelo Correro	Venetian	card.-priest
Martin V[m]	1417–1431	Odo Colonna	Roman	card.-deacon
Eugenius IV	1431–1447	Gabriele Condulmaro	Venetian	card.-priest (O.S.A)
Nicholas V	1447–1455	Tommaso Parentucelli	Bolognese	archbishop of Bolognaa (O.P.)

(Clement V through Gregory XI bracketed as: the "Avignon Popes")

[a] Liberius is the first pope not to be canonized.

[b] Siricius is the first pope to use the title *papa* ("pope").

[c] John II (533–535) was the first pope to take a new name upon election to the Holy See. He did so presumably because of the pagan connotations of his birth name. The taking of a new pontifical name did not become the norm until the turn of the first millennium A.D. Prior to the year 1000, only four popes (John II, John III, John XII, and John XIV) did so.

[d] Gregory I (590–604) was the first monk to become pope. Innocent V (1276) was the first Dominican pope, and Nicholas IV (1288–1292) was the first Franciscan.

[e] On 23 March 752 a man named Stephen was elected pope, which would have made him Stephen II. But he died only three days later, and is sometimes omitted from papal lists. On 26 March 752 another Stephen was elected; he is usually considered Stephen II (as here)—but in some lists he is referred to as Stephen III.

[f] Marinus I (882–884) was the first bishop to become pope. Canon XV of the Council of Nicaea (325) forbade the translation of bishops from one see to another, and since the office of the papacy was inextricably linked with the episcopacy of Rome, no bishop of another city could be considered a candidate. A handful of exceptions were made in the difficult post-Carolingian period (of which Marinus was the first); but the Nicaean ban was gradually set aside during the Gregorian Reform, paving the way for the virtual monopoly on the papacy held by bishops since the eleventh century.

[g]John XII (955–964) was the first layman elected to the papacy.

[h]Benedict IX was pope three separate times: 1032–1044, April-May 1045, and 1047–1048.

[i]The papacy was vacant from 29 November 1268 (Clement IV's death) to 1 September 1271 (Gregory X's election).

[j]The papacy was vacant from 4 April 1292 to 5 July 1294.

[k]Prior to his pontificate, Benedict XI was the Minister-General of his Dominican order.

[l]The papacy was vacant from 20 April 1314 to 7 August 1316.

[m]The papacy was vacant from 4 July 1415 to 11 November 1417.

APPENDIX B: The Carolingians

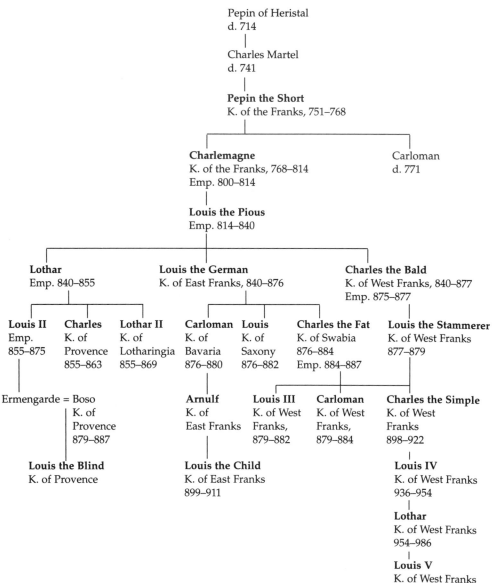

Pepin of Heristal
d. 714

Charles Martel
d. 741

Pepin the Short
K. of the Franks, 751–768

Charlemagne
K. of the Franks, 768–814
Emp. 800–814

Carloman
d. 771

Louis the Pious
Emp. 814–840

Lothar
Emp. 840–855

Louis the German
K. of East Franks, 840–876

Charles the Bald
K. of West Franks, 840–877
Emp. 875–877

Louis II
Emp.
855–875

Charles
K. of
Provence
855–863

Lothar II
K. of
Lotharingia
855–869

Carloman
K. of
Bavaria
876–880

Louis
K. of
Saxony
876–882

Charles the Fat
K. of Swabia
876–884
Emp. 884–887

Louis the Stammerer
K. of West Franks
877–879

Ermengarde = Boso
K. of
Provence
879–887

Arnulf
K. of
East Franks

Louis III
K. of West
Franks,
879–882

Carloman
K. of West
Franks,
879–884

Charles the Simple
K. of West
Franks
898–922

Louis the Blind
K. of Provence

Louis the Child
K. of East Franks
899–911

Louis IV
K. of West Franks
936–954

Lothar
K. of West Franks
954–986

Louis V
K. of West Franks
986–987

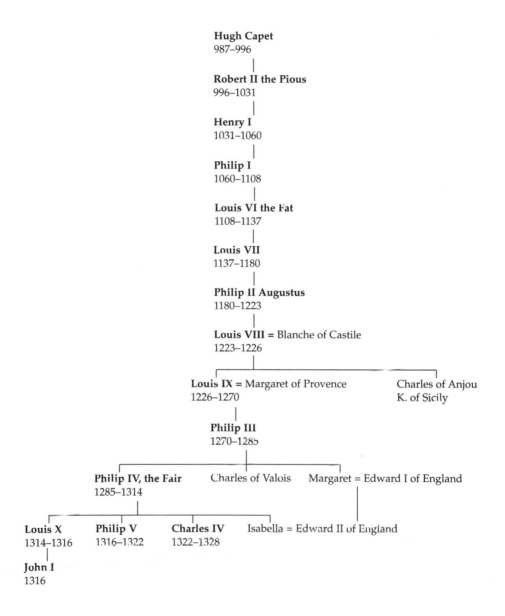

Hugh Capet
987–996

Robert II the Pious
996–1031

Henry I
1031–1060

Philip I
1060–1108

Louis VI the Fat
1108–1137

Louis VII
1137–1180

Philip II Augustus
1180–1223

Louis VIII = Blanche of Castile
1223–1226

Louis IX = Margaret of Provence   Charles of Anjou
1226–1270   K. of Sicily

Philip III
1270–1285

Philip IV, the Fair   Charles of Valois   Margaret = Edward I of England
1285–1314

Louis X   **Philip V**   **Charles IV**   Isabella = Edward II of England
1314–1316   1316–1322   1322–1328

John I
1316

APPENDIX D: France: The Valois

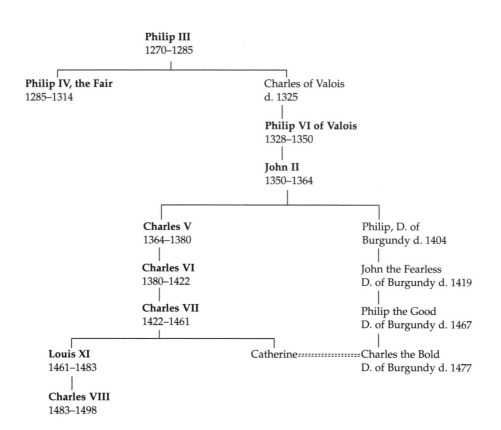

Philip III
1270–1285

Philip IV, the Fair
1285–1314

Charles of Valois
d. 1325

Philip VI of Valois
1328–1350

John II
1350–1364

Charles V
1364–1380

Philip, D. of
Burgundy d. 1404

Charles VI
1380–1422

John the Fearless
D. of Burgundy d. 1419

Charles VII
1422–1461

Philip the Good
D. of Burgundy d. 1467

Louis XI
1461–1483

Catherine⋯⋯⋯⋯⋯⋯Charles the Bold
D. of Burgundy d. 1477

Charles VIII
1483–1498

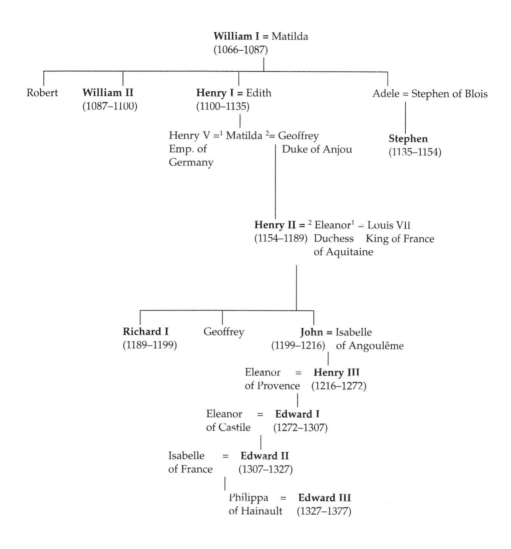

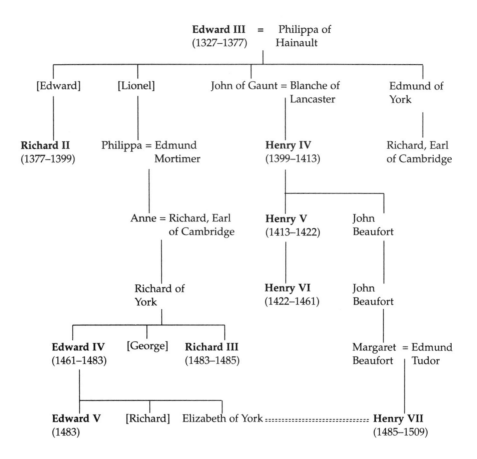

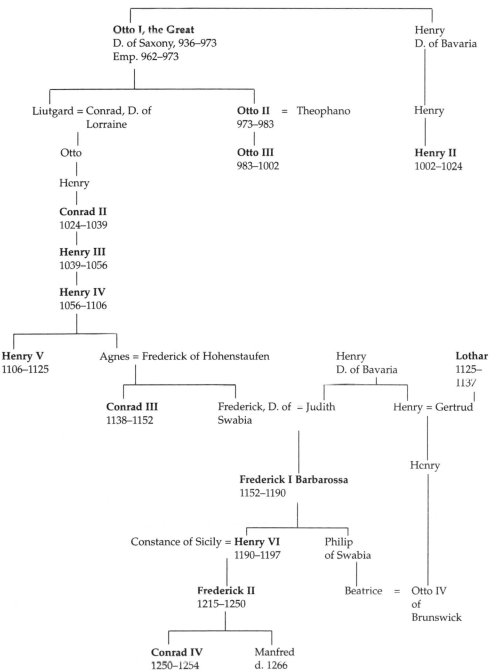

Otto I, the Great
D. of Saxony, 936–973
Emp. 962–973

Henry
D. of Bavaria

Liutgard = Conrad, D. of
Lorraine

Otto

Henry

Conrad II
1024–1039

Henry III
1039–1056

Henry IV
1056–1106

Otto II = Theophano
973–983

Otto III
983–1002

Henry

Henry II
1002–1024

Henry V
1106–1125

Agnes = Frederick of Hohenstaufen

Henry
D. of Bavaria

Lothar
1125–
1137

Conrad III
1138–1152

Frederick, D. of = Judith
Swabia

Henry = Gertrud

Henry

Frederick I Barbarossa
1152–1190

Constance of Sicily = Henry VI
1190–1197

Philip
of Swabia

Frederick II
1215–1250

Beatrice = Otto IV
of
Brunswick

Conrad IV
1250–1254

Manfred
d. 1266

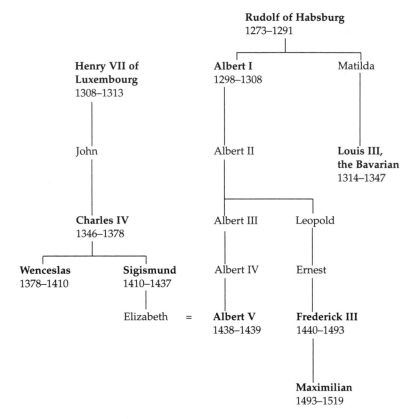

Rudolf of Habsburg
1273–1291

Henry VII of Luxembourg 1308–1313   Albert I 1298–1308   Matilda

John   Albert II   Louis III, the Bavarian 1314–1347

Charles IV 1346–1378   Albert III   Leopold

Wenceslas 1378–1410   Sigismund 1410–1437   Albert IV   Ernest

Elizabeth   =   Albert V 1438–1439   Frederick III 1440–1493

Maximilian 1493–1519

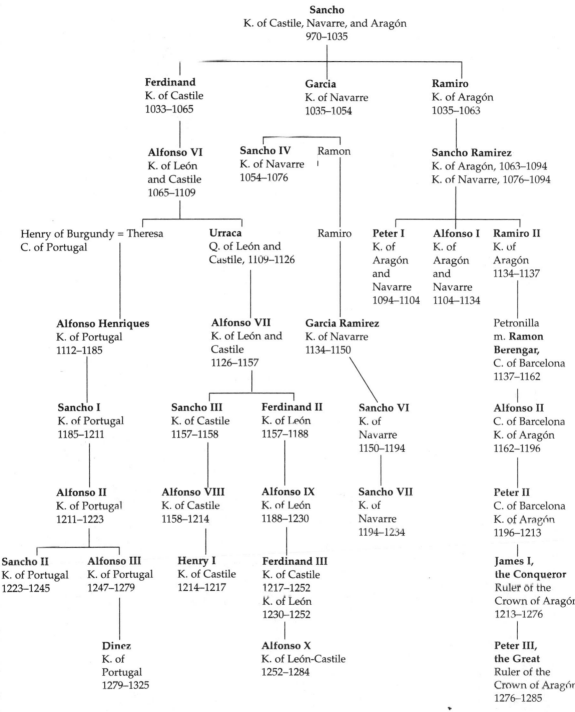

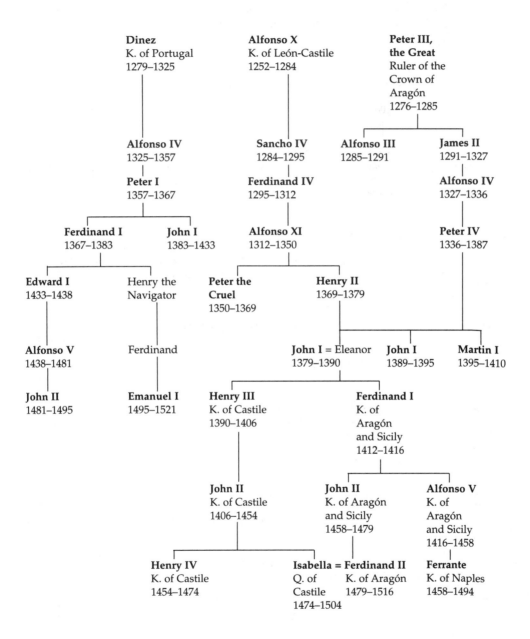

Dinez
K. of Portugal
1279–1325

Alfonso X
K. of León-Castile
1252–1284

**Peter III,
the Great**
Ruler of the
Crown of
Aragón
1276–1285

Alfonso IV
1325–1357

Sancho IV
1284–1295

Alfonso III
1285–1291

James II
1291–1327

Peter I
1357–1367

Ferdinand IV
1295–1312

Alfonso IV
1327–1336

Ferdinand I
1367–1383

John I
1383–1433

Alfonso XI
1312–1350

Peter IV
1336–1387

Edward I
1433–1438

Henry the
Navigator

**Peter the
Cruel**
1350–1369

Henry II
1369–1379

Alfonso V
1438–1481

Ferdinand

John I = Eleanor
1379–1390

John I
1389–1395

Martin I
1395–1410

John II
1481–1495

Emanuel I
1495–1521

Henry III
K. of Castile
1390–1406

Ferdinand I
K. of
Aragón
and Sicily
1412–1416

John II
K. of Castile
1406–1454

John II
K. of Aragón
and Sicily
1458–1479

Alfonso V
K. of
Aragón
and Sicily
1416–1458

Henry IV
K. of Castile
1454–1474

Isabella = **Ferdinand II**
Q. of   K. of Aragón
Castile   1479–1516
1474–1504

Ferrante
K. of Naples
1458–1494

Appendix K: The Emperors in Constantinople
(Latin rulers after the Fourth Crusade are listed in italics)

Ruler	Reign	Ruler	Reign
Constantine I the Great	324–337	Leo VI the Wise	886–912
Constantius II	337–361	Alexander	912–913
Julian the Apostate	361–363	—Regency for Constantine VII—	913–945
Jovian	363–364	Constantine VII Porphyrogenitus	945–959
Valens	364–378	Romanus II	959–963
Theodosius I	379–395	Basil II the Bulgar-Slayer	963–1025
Arcadius	395–408	Constantine VIII	1025–1028
Theodosius II	408–450	Romanus III Argyrus	1028–1034
Marcian	450–457	Michael IV the Paphlagonian	1034–1041
Leo I	457–474	Michael V the Caulker	1041–1042
Leo II	474	Zoë	1042
Zeno	474–491	Constantine IX Monomachus	1042–1055
Anastasius I	491–518	Theodora	1055–1056
Justin I	518–527	Michael VI	1056–1057
Justinian I	527–565	Isaac I Comnenus	1057–1059
Justin II	565–578	Constantine X Ducas	1059–1067
Tiberius II	578–582	Michael VII Ducas	1067–1078
Maurice	582–602	Nicephorus III Botaniates	1078–1081
Phocas the Tyrant	602–610	Alexius I Comnenus	1081–1118
Heraclius	610–641	John II Comnenus	1118–1143
Constantine III	641	Manuel I Comnenus	1143–1180
Heraclonas	641	Alexius I Comnenus	1180–1183
Constans II the Bearded	641–668	Andronicus I Comnenus	1183–1185
Constantine IV	668–685	Isaac II Angelus	1185–1195
Justinian II the Slit-Nosed	685–695	Alexius III Angelus	1195–1203
Leontius	695–698	Isaac II Angelus (again)	1203–1204
Tiberius III	698–705	Alexius V Ducas	1204
Justinian II the Slit-Nosed (again)	705–711	*Baldwin I of Flanders*	1204–1205
Philippicus Bardanes	711–713	*Henry of Flanders*	1206–1216
Anastasius II	713–715	*Peter of Courtenay*	1217
Theodosius III	715–717	*Yolanda*	1217–1219
Leo III the Isaurian	717–741	*Robert of Courtenay*	1221–1228
Constantine V the Shit-head	741–775	*John of Brienne*	1228–1237
Leo IV the Khazar	775–780	*Baldwin II of Courtenay*	1237–1261

(continued)

Ruler	Ruler	Reign	Reign
Constantine VI the Blinded	780–797	Michael VIII Palaeologus	1261–1282
Irene	797–802	Andronicus II Palaeologus	1282–1328
Nicephorus I	802–811	Andronicus III Palaeologus	1328–1341
Stauracius	811	John V Palaeologus	1341–1376
Michael I	811–813	Andronicus IV Palaeologus	1376–1379
Leo V the Armenian	813–820	John V Palaeologus (again)	1379–1391
Michael II	820–829	Manuel II Palaeologus	1391–1425
Theophilus	829–842	John VIII Palaeologus	1425–1448
Michael III the Drunkard	842–867	Constantine XI Palaeologus	1449–1453
Basil I the Macedonian	867–886		

GLOSSARY

(A = Arabic. AS = Anglo-Saxon. F = French. G = German. Gr = Greek. L = Latin. S = Spanish)

Albigensian—adjective derived from the southern French town of Albi, a famed Cathar stronghold. Hence Catharism is sometimes referred to as Albigensianism; the crusade against the Cathars is always named the Albigensian Crusade.

allod—a free landholding, the opposite of a fief.

apanage—a land grant to a lesser member of the royal family, as compensation for not inheriting the crown. Recipients of an apanage did not have any feudal obligations of service for it.

Arianism—The most widespread Christian heresy of the early Middle Ages. Arianism derives its name from Arius, a fourth-century bishop who denied the idea of a co-eternal and co-equal Trinity.

assize—In Carolingian times, an assize was a public hearing convened by the *missi dominici*; later, assizes were the judicial inquests performed by the itinerant justices in England and Wales.

bailiff—In England, the chief manager of a medieval manor. In France, a royal officer who collected revenues due to the king in territories outside the royal demesne.

banalities—Both the rights of serfs to use their manor's utilities (mills, ovens, presses), and the rights of the lords to collect fees from the serfs using them.

basileus (Gr)—"King," literally. The chief title designating the Byzantine emperor.

basilica—A type of ancient Roman building used for the earliest Christian churches. An open rectangular structure, with a wide atrium at one end, and a sloping wooden roof.

Beguine—A member of a religious sorority. Beguines dedicated themselves to poverty and service, lived in cities, and held communal worship services, but they stopped short of the type of vows that designated one as a nun. These sororities lived in houses known as *beguinages*.

bull—an official document from the pope, rendering an authoritative judgment on an particular issue.

caliph **(A)**—"Successor." The title originally was held by the Sunni rulers who were regarded as the sole legitimate successors to Muhammad's authority, in the Umayyad and Abbasid dynasties. With the breakup of the empire and the establishment of Shi'ism, the title was more generally used by rulers who aspired to higher standing than their contemporaries—most notably the caliphs of Cordoba and of Fatimid Egypt.

canon law—the laws by which the institution of the Church operates. These laws accumulated haphazardly over the centuries; the first efforts to systematize them began in the ninth century. The most well-known and influential of the canon law codes was the *Decretum* of Gratian, which appeared in the twelfth century.

Catharism—The most widespread Christian heresy of the second half of the Middle Ages. Centered in southern France, the Cathars were a dualist sect who rejected the material world as the creation of the Evil God while embracing the spiritual world created by the Good God. Catharism was formally condemned as heresy in 1207 and was suppressed by the Albigensian Crusade (1209–1229).

chancery—a bureaucratic department responsible for drafting all official documents. The official in charge of a chancery is called a *chancellor*.

chansons de geste **(F)**—A popular literary genre in the aristocratic courts of Capetian France. The term translates as "songs of [noble] deeds." The best-known of the *chansons* was (and still is) the *Song of Roland*.

coloni **(L)**—Tenant farmers in late Roman and Carolingian times. They were not slaves, but their freedoms were limited.

comitatus **(L)**—A warrior band among the early Germanic peoples. The members of a *comitatus* swore loyalty to their chieftain; a fanciful description of the bands appears in Tacitus' *Germania*.

curia—The term of a royal or papal court.

curiales **(L)**—The class of municipal officers in Roman cities.

Danelaw—Region of England seized from the Anglo-Saxons by the Danes and formally recognized as autonomous in the ninth century; comprised chiefly of the old kingdoms of East Anglia and Mercia.

deacon—Clerical ranking just below that of priests. While they possessed some sacramental authority (baptizing), the position of a deacon was essentially that of an administrative manager, directing the mundane affairs of a parish. Women served as deaconesses until the ninth century (several are mentioned as being in the court of Pope Leo III); an Anglo-Saxon missal from the eleventh century includes a prayer for deaconesses.

demesne—The portion of a manor that was cultivated expressly for the benefit of the lord (the remaining parts being for the support of the peasants). In England, France, and Germany the royal demesne consisted of all the territories controlled directly by the monarch.

Diet—In a general sense, an assembly of nobles or of ecclesiastical leaders. More narrowly, the name of the German assembly that met usually for the election and acclamation of a new emperor.

dynatoi **(Gr)**—The "powerful ones," descriptive term for the local military figures and political bosses who operated more or less independently of the Byzantine emperor in the tenth and eleventh centuries.

emir **(A)**—"Commander," literally, but sometimes translated as "prince." Used to describe high military officers, provincial governors, or rulers of small independent states during the Abbasid period.

Estates General—The French representative assembly, first convened by Philip IV.

Exchequer—The chief financial office of a kingdom in general, and of England in particular, responsible for collecting taxes and auditing the accounts of regional officials.

fabliaux **(F)**—Popular vernacular tales, frequently bawdy, filled with broad comedy.

fealty—One of the oaths sworn to create a bond of vassalage (the other being homage); fealty was a vow to perform loyal service to a lord at all times.

feudal aids—Payments due to a lord from his vassals, to offset specified expenses—the most representative being the knighting of the lord's son, the marriage of the lord's daughter, or the ransoming of the lord himself if taken in battle.

fief—A gift to a vassal in return for his service to his lord. Most commonly, the fief was land and the service was military.

fiqh **(A)**—"Understanding," or "comprehension." *Fiqh* denotes the discipline of legal philosophy or jurisprudence, one of the means by which new Islamic law can be crafted. It does not denote Islamic law itself—which is *shari'ah*.

flying buttress—A part of the exoskeleton of a Gothic cathedral; a buttress that is connected to the main support-walls of a nave, allowing the elevation of the roof to unprecedented levels.

fyrd **(AS)**—The militia of the Anglo-Saxon kingdoms.

glebe—The part of a manor dedicated to the support of the local church.

gloss—The systematic marginal commentary on a text, characteristic of the teaching methods of scholasticism.

Goliards—Popular itinerant entertainers, usually university students or low clerics, who wrote and performed satirical verse and songs; their targets were frequently ecclesiastical. Much of their work was extemporaneous, and was usually performed in taverns.

Gothic—The architectural style that began in the twelfth century and flourished well into the fourteenth, used most famously for the great cathedrals of that period. The style was complex, but its most characteristic features were the pointed arch, ribbed vaults, flying buttresses, and elaborate stained-glass windows.

guilds—Urban manufacturing- and trade-cartels that determined the standards of quality, price, and manufacture of individual goods in a medieval town. Guilds also supervised the training of artisans and merchants through the apprenticeship system, and engaged in widespread social work.

hagiography—A modern terms for the medieval literary genre of *vitae sanctorum* ("Lives of the saints"). These lives were not biographies but were rather portraits (often quite fanciful) of the spiritual heroes of the age, filled with tales of miracles, heroic defenses against temptation, and glorious death.

Hajj (**A**)—The pilgrimage to Mecca required of all Muslims at least once in their life.

Hijrah (**A**)—The "journey" (or even "exodus") of Muhammad and his initial corps of believers from Mecca to Medinah in 622, and the symbolic starting-point of the Islamic Empire. Denotes the start of the Islamic calendar (Year 1, A.H.)

homage—The part of the ceremony of vassalage in which a vassal recognizes the authority of his new lord to command him.

iconoclasm—The dispute, in both the Greek and Latin Churches, over whether or not icons of the saints could be used in worship.

imam (**A**)—In Sunni Islam, a leader of the religious community, one who recites passages from the Qur'an and leads the group in prayer. In Shi'ite Islam, the *imams* were exalted and charismatic leaders, the heirs of Ali, with unquestioned authority; depending on the specific branch of Shi'ite Islam, there have been a different number of authentic *imams*. All Shi'a await the return of the "hidden *imam*" (*mahdi*) who will return to earth and inaugurate the Day of Judgment.

inquisitio (**L**)—Originally, a process in Roman law, it provided the model for the Church's program for the detection and correction of heretics. The *inquisitio* is based on the idea that certain crimes represent so grave a danger that the Church and State have a moral obligation to investigate them preemptively— that is, to investigate a crime even before it is committed, if there is credible evidence that such a crime is about to be committed. This "teaching mission" of the Church, under the direction chiefly of the Dominican order, devolved into the heavy-handed and punitive "Inquisition."

interdict—An absolute ban on the performance of sacraments within any given area. Any bishop has the authority to impose an interdict (upon his own diocese or archdiocese); only the pope can impose one on an entire kingdom or country.

jihad **(A)**—The spiritual struggle to obey Allah and practice Islam unwaveringly; this includes, but is not limited to, the notion of waging war against the perceived enemies of the faith.

jongleurs **(F)**—Itinerant court-performers (clowns, singers, dancers, jugglers, animal trainers, etc.) popular in aristocratic circles in the twelfth through fourteenth centuries.

Ka'ba—The sacred shrine in Mecca that houses the "Black Stone" (*al-hajar al-aswad*) which Islamic tradition identifies as a large white stone given to Adam after his expulsion from paradise (it has supposedly blackened from the millions of kisses bestowed upon it over the centuries). Tradition maintains that Adam built a shrine on the site; Abraham later erected another. During the pre-Islamic period it was the chief shrine of Arab paganism. Muhammad's return to Mecca and his purging of the Ka'ba made it the holiest site on earth to all Muslims, who face in its direction during all their daily prayers.

lay investiture—Secular control of ecclesiastical appointments, originally; but after the Concordat of Worms, the practice of a lay ruler (usually a king) investing a bishop or abbot with the symbols of their office.

liege lord—A lord who had primary claim to a vassal's service, in the event of plural lordship.

magnate—A feudal lord who, on account of his wealth or unique social prominence, had direct access to, and significant influence upon, the king.

Manicheanism—An ancient Persian religion, originating in the third century B.C., based on a dualist cosmogony. The much-later Christian heresy of Catharism shared many traits of Manichean belief.

mendicant—From the Latin verb *mendicare*, meaning "to beg"; a mendicant was in the broadest sense any cleric who lived entirely on alms. In common usage, though, the term designates the new religious orders of the thirteenth century (Dominicans and Franciscans, primarily) that came into being to assist the clergy in bringing Christian teachings to the masses.

metropolitan—A bishop or archbishop who had precedence in honor over the other bishops or archbishops of a province, and who oversaw their activities.

mihrab **(A)**—A special niche built into the wall of a mosque, to indicate the direction of Mecca—toward which the faithful must face when performing their daily prayers.

ministeriales **(L)**—Lesser knights and prominent burghers who were appointed to administrative positions within the Holy Roman Empire, to offset the influence of the great magnates. Their appearance (eleventh century) marks the origin of a professionalized government in Germany.

missi dominici **(L)**—The "traveling lords" of the Carolingian empire, specially trained representatives of Charlemagne who traveled in circuit through the realm, checking on the activities of the local counts.

Neoplatonism—A revived and revised version of Plato's philosophy, significant for its influence on early Christian thought. It posited the existence of a transcendent and unknowable (by reason) Being—called God, the Good, or the One—to whom humans could attain by spiritual elevation or mystical experience.

oblation—The act, discouraged by the Church but common in the pre-Reform era, whereby parents would hand over a child to a monastery or convent, so they would be raised to be monks or nuns.

ordeal—A custom derived from early Germanic practice, whereby a charged criminal's guilt or innocence was left to be determined by divine intervention.

Orthodox—From a Greek term meaning "right thinking" (*orthodóxos*), the capitalized version of the word denotes the eastern Churches led by their various patriarchs.

Patarines—A popular movement for social and religious reform in eleventh-century Milan, and the precursor of the communal movement in northern Italy.

Pax romana **(L)**—The "Roman Peace," the name sometimes given to the era of internal prosperity and social order in the first two centuries A.D. in the Mediterranean world.

Peace of God—The popular protests of the mid-tenth to eleventh centuries that triggered the Church Reform. Specifically, the term refers to the prohibitions of violence against clerics, women, and pilgrims bestowed by the bishops who took over leadership of the reform movement.

plenary indulgence—The total remission of the temporal punishment due to sin. It does not forgive the sinner of the guilt of his sin. The plenary indulgence was awarded to all sworn crusaders who died in a state of grace while on the crusade.

plenitudo potestatis **(L)**—The "plenitude of power" claimed by the papacy in the thirteenth century as the legitimating force for the Church's involvement in all matters of human life that contain a significant moral element. It is not a claim of supreme power, but rather a declaration that the Church has a compelling right to voice an opinion and to be heard.

primogeniture—The inheritance practice whereby a man's estate passes to his first-born son.

quadrivium **(L)**—The second phase of the monastic (and later, liberal arts) educational curriculum, consisting of arithmetic, geometry, astronomy, and music.

quodlibet **(L)**—Literally, "whatever." A quodlibet was a very popular aspect of university life in from the twelfth through fourteenth centuries. It usually consisted of a challenge to a speaker's opinion or interpretation of any given issue; the speaker and the challenger then made their cases before an audience, and the audience declared a victor. Primarily an oral phenomenon, the "winning" quodlibets were often written down and published as free-standing works.

Qur'an—The holy book of Islam. Sometimes transliterated as Koran.

Ramadan—The holiest month if the Islamic year, commemorating Muhammad's reception of the Qur'an and his practice of fasting from dawn to dusk throughout the month.

relic—A physical object associated with a particular saint (a lock of hair, a bone, a cloak, etc.) and venerated.

riddah **(A)**—Apostasy from Islam, punishable by death.

romance—One of the most literary genres of the Twelfth-Century Renaissance, frequently set in historical or legendary time periods (as with the King Arthur romances), and usually involving the tension between the demands of knightly valor and the claims of courtly love.

Romanesque—The dominant architectural style of the eleventh and early twelfth centuries, characterized by rounded arches, barrel vaults, and thick walls that allowed for few windows.

Scholasticism—Generally, the pedagogical method used in the medieval universities; more specifically, the philosophical system that culminated in St. Thomas Aquinas, based on the conviction that all truths are rationally based and therefore comprehensible to humans, and that all truths are harmonious with one another.

scriptorium—The room in a monastic library where monk-scribes copied and illuminated books.

scutage—A payment that could be given to one's lord in lieu of providing the military service one owed to him.

serf—A manorial peasant who worked on the lord's land and lived under his jurisdiction, not slaves but not free.

shariah **(A)**—Islamic religious law, consisting of the teachings of the Qur'an, the *hadith* of Muhammad, and the legal judgments of the *ummah* ("community of believers").

Shi'a—The branch of Islam that holds that leadership of the Islamic world rests with those who are physical descendants of Muhammad via the line of Fatimah (his daughter) and her husband Ali.

simony—The purchase and/or sale of ecclesiastical office; one of the most widespread abuses in the corrupted Church of the post-Carolingian era.

studium generale **(L)**—A special title granted to universities of particular prominence and reputation. The German emperors and the papacy contended with one another over who had the right to grant this honorific. By 1300 eight universities held the title: those at Bologna, Cambridge, Montpellier, Oxford, Palencia, Paris, Reggio Emilia, and Vicenza. It is possible that Salerno held it as well. The status entitled the faculty of these universities to teach at any university in Latin Europe *(ius ubique docendi)*. (This is the origin, within academic culture, of the notion of "superstar professors.")

summa **(L)**—A "summary," literally. The supreme genre of the Scholastic writers, in which they would attempt a comprehensive presentation of all knowledge on a topic.

Sunni—The largest branch of Islam, originating in the notion that leadership of the Islamic community comes about through the consensus of the community.

surah **(A)**—A "chapter" in the Qur'an.

synod—An ecclesiastical assembly. Synods differ from councils in that they consist only of clerical leaders from one particular area.

tertiary orders—groups of laymen and laywomen affiliated with the Dominican and Franciscan orders; they participated in worship with the friars but were not full members, and they continued to have family and business lives.

thegn **(AS)**—Term for a warrior in Anglo-Saxon England.

theme **(Gr)**—A form of military land-tenure devised by the Byzantine state in the time of Heraclius; this system militarized Byzantine society to an unprecedented extent. Instead of receiving pay from the imperial officials, soldiers instead received plots of land and some limited jurisdictional rights over it. Groups of soldiers in a given area were organized into a fighting unit under a regional officer known as a *strategos*.

trivium **(L)**—The first portion of monastic (and later, liberal arts) educational curriculum, comprised of grammar, rhetoric, and logic.

troubadour **(F)**—A poet-musician from southern France, who worked in the local aristocratic courts, composing songs to fit special occasions.

Truce of God—A ban on warfare at particular times (such as major feast days) and in particular places.

ulama **(A)**—The community of Islamic clergy and religious scholars.

ummah **(A)**—The entire community of Muslim believers.

usury—Charging interest for a loan, a practice initially banned by the Church. The Church eventually moderated its stance and defined usury as the charging of excessive interest.

vassal—A knight who owed service to his lord, after having sworn homage and fealty to him—in return for which the lord gave the vassal a fief.

villein—A free-born peasant who owed a degree of service to a manorial lord, but who possessed greater rights than a bound peasant.

Vulgate—The Latin Bible prepared by St. Jerome in the early fifth century. The standard Bible throughout the Middle Ages.

wergeld **(G)**—Fee paid to a victim (or his family) as compensation for physical harm, a common practice among the early Germanic peoples.

witan **(AS)**—Anglo-Saxon noble council.

INDEX